THE PHILOSOP

INTERNATIONAL LAW

THE PHILOSOPHY OF

INTERNATIONAL
LAW

Edited by

SAMANTHA BESSON AND JOHN TASIOULAS

OXFORD
UNIVERSITY PRESS

OXFORD

UNIVERSITY PRESS

Great Clarendon Street, Oxford OX2 6DP

Oxford University Press is a department of the University of Oxford.
It furthers the University's objective of excellence in research, scholarship,
and education by publishing worldwide in

Oxford New York

Auckland Cape Town Dar es Salaam Hong Kong Karachi
Kuala Lumpur Madrid Melbourne Mexico City Nairobi
New Delhi Shanghai Taipei Toronto

With offices in

Argentina Austria Brazil Chile Czech Republic France Greece
Guatemala Hungary Italy Japan Poland Portugal Singapore
South Korea Switzerland Thailand Turkey Ukraine Vietnam

Oxford is a registered trade mark of Oxford University Press
in the UK and in certain other countries

Published in the United States
by Oxford University Press Inc., New York

© the several contributors, 2010

The moral rights of the authors have been asserted
Database right Oxford University Press (maker)

First published 2010

British Library Cataloguing in Publication Data

Data available

Library of Congress Cataloging in Publication Data

Library of Congress Control Number 2009943758

Typeset by Laserwords Private Limited, Chennai, India
Printed in Great Britain
on acid-free paper by
CPI Antony Rowe, Chippenham, Wiltshire

ISBN 978–0–19–920858–6 (hbk.)
978–0–19–920857–9 (pbk.)

Contents

SECTION VII INTERNATIONAL RESPONSIBILITY

PART II SPECIFIC ISSUES IN THE PHILOSOPHY OF INTERNATIONAL LAW

SECTION VIII HUMAN RIGHTS

SECTION IX SELF-DETERMINATION AND MINORITY RIGHTS

SECTION X INTERNATIONAL ECONOMIC LAW

Contributors

Samantha Besson is Professor of Public International Law and European Law, University of Fribourg, Switzerland.

Allen Buchanan is James B. Duke Professor of Philosophy, Duke University, United States.

Thomas Christiano is Professor of Philosophy and Law, University of Arizona, United States.

Jean L. Cohen is Professor of Political Science, Columbia University, United States.

James Crawford is Whewell Professor of International Law, University of Cambridge, United Kingdom.

Roger Crisp is Uehiro Fellow and Tutor in Philosophy, St Anne's College, University of Oxford, and Professor of Moral Philosophy, University of Oxford, United Kingdom.

Antony Duff is Professor of Philosophy, University of Stirling, United Kingdom.

Timothy Endicott is Fellow in Law, Balliol College, University of Oxford and Dean of the Faculty of Law, University of Oxford, United Kingdom.

Thomas M. Franck was Murry and Ida Becker Professor of Law Emeritus, New York University, United States. He died in May 2009.

James Griffin is Emeritus White's Professor of Moral Philosophy, Oxford University, United Kingdom.

Robert Howse is Lloyd C. Nelson Professor of International Law, New York University, United States.

Benedict Kingsbury is Murry and Ida Becker Professor of Law, New York University, United States.

Will Kymlicka is Canada Research Chair in Political Philosophy, Queen's University, Canada.

David Lefkowitz is Associate Professor of Philosophy, University of Richmond, United States.

David Luban is University Professor and Professor of Law and Philosophy, Georgetown University, United States.

Daniel Magraw is President and Chief Executive Officer of the Center for International Environmental Law, United States and Switzerland.

Jeff McMahan is Professor of Philosophy, Rutgers University, United States.

Liam Murphy is Vice Dean and Herbert Peterfreund Professor of Law and Professor of Philosophy, New York University, United States.

James Nickel is Professor of Philosophy and Law, University of Miami, United States.

Andreas Paulus is Professor of Public and International Law, Georg-August-University, Göttingen, Germany.

Amanda Perreau-Saussine is Fellow and Lecturer in Law at Queens' College, University of Cambridge, and University Lecturer in Law, University of Cambridge, United Kingdom.

Philip Pettit is Laurance S. Rockefeller University Professor of Politics and Human Values, Princeton University, United States.

Thomas Pogge is Professor of Philosophy and International Affairs, Yale University, United States.

Joseph Raz is Thomas M. Macioce Professor of Law, Columbia University Law School, New York, United States.

Donald H. Regan is William W. Bishop Jr. Collegiate Professor of Law and Professor of Philosophy, University of Michigan, United States.

Henry Shue is Senior Research Fellow Emeritus, Merton College and Professor Emeritus of International Relations, University of Oxford, United Kingdom.

John Skorupski is Professor of Moral Philosophy, University of St Andrews, United Kingdom.

Benjamin Straumann is Visiting Assistant Professor in the History Department, New York University and Alberico Gentili Fellow at the School of Law, New York University, United States.

John Tasioulas is Fellow and Tutor in Philosophy, Corpus Christi College, Oxford, and Reader in Moral and Legal Philosophy, University of Oxford, United Kingdom.

Ruti Teitel is Ernst C. Stiefel Professor of Comparative Law, New York Law School, United States.

Jeremy Waldron is University Professor in Law, New York University, United States.

Jeremy Watkins is Lecturer in Philosophy, Queen's University, United Kingdom.

Danilo Zolo is Professor of the Philosophy of Law, University of Florence, Italy.

Acknowledgements

The editors and publisher gratefully acknowledge the following for permission to reproduce the copyright material in this book:

Chapter 14: Cambridge University Press for Thomas Pogge, 'Recognized and Violated by International Law: The Human Rights of the Global Poor,' in *Leiden Journal of International Law*, 18 (2005), 717–45.

The publisher apologizes for any errors or omissions in the above list and would be grateful if notified of any corrections that should be incorporated in future reprints or editions of this book.

Preface

International law has recently emerged as a thriving field of philosophical inquiry. This volume contains twenty-nine cutting-edge essays by thirty-three leading philosophers and international lawyers. An introduction co-authored by the two editors sets the scene by identifying the value of developing the philosophy of international law, addressing some of the main challenges it confronts, and presenting the aims of the volume together with a brief summary of the essays included in it. The ultimate goal is to help shape an agenda for future research in a burgeoning field.

The contributions to this volume, published here in English for the first time, address central philosophical questions about international law. The volume's overarching theme concerns the articulation and defence of the moral and political values that should guide the assessment and development of international law and institutions. Some of the essays tackle general topics within international law, such as the sources and legitimacy of international law, the nature of international legal adjudication, whether international law can or should aspire to be 'democratic', the significance of state sovereignty and the contours of international responsibility. The other contributions address problems arising in specific domains of international law, such as human rights law, international economic law, international criminal law, international environmental law, and the laws of war. Of course, the volume is not exhaustive and many more issues could have been addressed in an even longer book.

This volume is distinguished by its 'dialogical' methodology: there are two essays (and, in the case of human rights, three essays) on each topic, with the second author responding in some measure to the arguments of the first. At the same time, each chapter may be read independently from the others, as a self-standing contribution to the topic. Cross-fertilization and coherence among the different themes and trends in the book were created thanks to the excellent and intensive discussions that took place in the two workshops that were organized in February and September 2007, respectively in Fribourg and in Oxford.

We wish to thank Mrs Joanna Bourke-Martignoni, research assistant at the University of Fribourg from 2006 to 2008, for her editorial assistance, Mr Keith Bustos, research assistant at the University of Fribourg from 2007 to 2008, for his help at early stages of the editorial process, and Mr Thierry Leibzig, research assistant at the University of Fribourg, for his meticulous work on this volume's index. We are grateful to Mr Peter Momtchiloff at OUP for his unfailing support and kind forbearance during the long, and sometimes challenging, process of putting this book together. We should also like to thank the Swiss National Science Foundation and the British Academy for providing vital financial support for the conferences in Fribourg and Oxford. Last but not least, our special thanks are owed to all of our contributors for making this ambitious inter-disciplinary project such a stimulating and worthwhile experience.

Samantha Besson and John Tasioulas
Fribourg and Oxford, 20 April 2009

INTRODUCTION

SAMANTHA BESSON AND JOHN TASIOULAS

I. THE EMERGENCE OF THE PHILOSOPHY OF INTERNATIONAL LAW

Since the publication in 1961 of H. L. A. Hart's *The Concept of Law*, power-fully augmented a decade later with the appearance of John Rawls's *A Theory of Justice*, the philosophy of law in the English-speaking world has enjoyed a renais-sance. Legal philosophers during this half-century have engaged extensively with what might loosely be called conceptual questions about the nature of law, legal reasoning, and notions integral to an understanding of law, such as authority, obligation, and coercion. They have also addressed normative questions about the values that the institution of law ought to serve and in light of which it should be assessed and reformed—values such as justice, liberty, equality, tol-eration, and integrity. And, of course, they have reflected on the enterprises of conceptual and normative philosophical inquiry into law, sometimes calling into question the coherence or utility of any such distinction. The result has been an outpouring of theories about the nature and value of law, many of them developed in considerable detail and with remarkable ingenuity, often as a result of sus-tained dialectical exchange among their various proponents. These developments have taken place both in General Jurisprudence, which addresses conceptual and normative questions about law in general,[1] and in Special Jurisprudence, with important contributions being made to the philosophical investigation of discrete

---

[1] What follows is a highly selective list: Hart, H. L. A., *The Concept of Law* (1961; rev. edn., Oxford: Clarendon, 1994); Fuller, L. L., *The Morality of Law* (New Haven: Yale University Press, 1964); Raz, J., *The Concept of a Legal System* (Oxford: Clarendon, 1970); Dworkin, R. M., *Taking Rights Seriously* (Cambridge, Mass.: Harvard University Press, 1978); MacCormick, N., *Legal Reasoning and Legal Theory* (Oxford: Clarendon, 1978); Raz, J., *The Authority of Law* (Oxford, Clarendon, 1979); Finnis, J. M., *Natural Law and Natural Rights* (Oxford: Clarendon, 1980); Dworkin, R. M., *Law's Empire* (Cambridge, Mass.: Harvard University Press, 1986); Raz, J.,

provinces of law such as criminal law, contract law, and the law of torts, or specific types of law, such as municipal state law, judge-made law, and customary law.[2]

The philosophy of international law can be readily envisaged as a branch of Special Jurisprudence, one that encompasses both conceptual and normative questions about international law. The conceptual questions include those of whether international law is genuinely law (as distinct from a form of social morality or convention); how the existence and content of its norms is to be ascertained; what relationship obtains between the international legal system, if one exists, and the legal systems of individual states, among many others. The normative questions include those of whether state consent, democracy, or some other standard is the touchstone of international law's legitimacy; whether human rights and distributive justice, in addition to peace and co-operation, figure among the values international law should realize; what conditions must be satisfied to justify the creation of international criminal law and the infliction of punishment on those who violate it; whether international environmental law should be ultimately responsive only to the interests of (existing) human beings, among many others.

Now, it is certainly true that philosophers from Grotius to Kelsen have grappled with both conceptual and normative questions about international law. Yet it is also the case that, until comparatively recently, the post-1960 revival of legal philosophy has tended to neglect international law. As a result, the philosophy of international law is significantly less developed than, say, the philosophy of criminal law. This 'poor relation' status is probably attributable to a variety of causes. In part, it may reflect a commendable intellectual prudence. For one might reasonably suppose that many of the questions of legal philosophy are best approached in the first instance via their application to municipal state legal systems, which are both more familiar and more highly developed, before advancing to their international counterparts. Of course, one should guard against this prudential policy hardening into the dogma that the philosophical study of international law can shed no independent light on philosophical questions either about law in general or its municipal instantiations. However, there are probably less obviously benign causes as well. These include the relative insularity of international law as a field within

---

Ethics in the Public Domain (Oxford: Clarendon, 1994); and Coleman, J., *The Practice of Principle: In Defence of a Pragmatist Approach to Legal Theory* (Oxford: Clarendon, 2001).

[2] A merely indicative list includes the following: Hart, H. L. A., *Punishment and Responsibility* (Oxford: Clarendon, 1968); Fried, C., *Contract as Promise* (Cambridge, Mass.: Harvard University Press, 1981); Feinberg, J., *The Moral Limits of the Criminal Law*, vols. 1–4 (Oxford: Clarendon, 1984–8); Munzer, S. R., *A Theory of Property* (Cambridge: Cambridge University Press, 1990); Coleman, J., *Risks and Wrongs* (Cambridge: Cambridge University Press, 1992); Weinrib, E. J., *The Idea of Private Law* (Cambridge, Mass.: Harvard University Press, 1995); Dworkin, R. M. *Freedom's Law: The Moral Reading of the American Constitution* (Cambridge, Mass.: Harvard University Press, 1996); Duff, R. A., *Answering for Crime: Responsibility and Liability in the Criminal Law* (Oxford: Hart Publishing, 2007).

legal studies, widespread scepticism about whether international law is really law, as well as the nagging suspicion that, with its cumbersome and obscure methods of norm-creation and its frail enforcement mechanisms, international law does not yet constitute a worthwhile subject for normative inquiry. Another likely cause is the corrosive influence of the general 'realist' thesis that political morality does not reach beyond the boundaries of the state, or that only a very minimalist morality does, or more charitably still, that although a richer political morality might eventually come to apply globally, to elaborate on it in the current state of the world is to engage in a wistfully utopian endeavour. Finally, there is a comparative dearth of empirical, as opposed to doctrinal, investigation of international law, which in itself poses a problem for any philosophical theorizing about international law that 'pretends to be grounded in reality and to have practical import'.[3]

To the extent that international law has been the object of theoretical attention in recent decades, much of it has come from writers drawing on either international relations theory or various approaches inspired by post-modernism. Whatever one's view of the respective merits of these two schools of thought, their prevalence has had the consequence of sidelining the discussion of philosophical questions, particularly those of a normative character. Adherents of both schools tend to be sceptical about the coherence, tractability, interest, or utility of the conceptual questions addressed by philosophers. More importantly, the purportedly scientific, 'value-neutral' method favoured by the great majority of international relations theorists, especially adherents to the dominant 'realist' tradition, and the scepticism about reason endorsed by post-modernists, seem to allow little scope for an intellectually respectable form of normative inquiry. So, from the perspective of contemporary legal philosophy, the similarities between these two camps are perhaps at least as important as their differences. But this common ground is hardly surprising given their shared historical lineage; in particular, it is worth noting that a theorist who has exerted a remarkable degree of influence on both the realist and post-modern traditions of thought about international law, in the former case indirectly through his follower Hans Morgenthau, is the controversial German jurist Carl Schmitt. From Schmitt they inherit—philosophically—both a grim view of human nature as driven by a quest for power and a general scepticism about the possibility of reasoned normative argument and—politically—a hostility to a broadly 'liberal' agenda aimed at the global spread of principles of human dignity and human rights.[4]

---

[3] This last theme is well developed in Buchanan, A., 'International Law, Philosophy of', in Craig, E. (ed.), *Routledge Encyclopedia of Philosophy* (London: Routledge; retrieved 18 July 2008, from <http://www.rep.routledge.com/article/T070SECT4>).

[4] For a general discussion of Schmitt's life and ideas, including his role as Hitler's 'crown jurist', see Lilla, M., *The Reckless Mind: Intellectuals in Politics* (New York: New York Review of Books, 2001), ch. 2. For a critical appraisal of his ideas on international law, see Koskenniemi, M., *The Gentle Civilizer of Nations: The Rise and Fall of International Law 1870–1960* (Cambridge: Cambridge University Press, 2004), ch. 6.

The marginalization of normative inquiry into international law is especially regrettable, since the most pressing questions that arise concerning international law today are arguably primarily normative in character. On the one hand, the ambit of the authority claimed by international law has grown exponentially in recent years, with the proliferation of international legal institutions and norms entailing that many more aspects of life on our planet are now governed by international law than ever before in human history. For example, post-war institutions such as the United Nations, and its judicial arm, the International Court of Justice, have been joined in recent years by new institutions, such as the World Trade Organization (WTO), the International Criminal Court (ICC), a plethora of human rights treaty bodies, regional organizations and courts, and so on. On the other hand, the emergence and intensification of various problems with a strong global dimension—widespread violations of human rights, the proliferation of weapons of mass destruction, the rise of global terror networks and the 'war on terror' launched by some states in reaction to them, the mutual interdependence and vulnerability wrought by economic globalization, the environmental crisis, the threat posed by pandemics, illegal movements of people across state boundaries, and so on—appears to outrun the problem-solving capacity of any individual state or group of states to deal with adequately, and seems to necessitate the development of appropriate international legal frameworks.

One manifestation of the pressing nature of these normative questions is that even those international relations and post-modern theorists who purport to desist from any form of ethical advocacy often seem, at least to their opponents, to be operating with a normative agenda. But surely it is preferable to be explicit about one's normative commitments? And this self-consciousness is in turn a necessary preliminary to defending, or else revising or abandoning, that agenda in light of the criticisms it attracts as well as the results of trying to implement it in practice. Now, of course, it is possible to adopt a self-critical normative approach to international law without drawing on anything recognizable as a tradition of *philosophical* thought. The writings of the New Haven School, and especially those of its most influential contemporary representative, Richard Falk, offer ample testimony of the potential value of such an approach.[5] So too do some critical writings on international law that draw their inspiration from the feminist, environmental, and anti-globalization movements. It would be a mistake to suppose that the normative questions thrown up by international law can *only* be fruitfully clarified and addressed by recognizably *philosophical* modes of inquiry. Nonetheless, this book has its origins in the conviction that the philosophical tradition in which both Hart and Rawls are central figures has an important contribution to make to both of these tasks.

---

[5] From among his many publications on international law over many years, see Falk, R. A., *Law in an Emerging Global Village: A Post-Westphalian Perspective* (Ardsley, NY: Transnational Publishers, 1998). The work of the Cambridge international lawyer Philip Allott, although in some ways more philosophical in orientation than that of Richard Falk, deliberately distances itself from Anglo-American philosophy of the last hundred years or so. See Allott, P., *Eunomia: New Order for a New World* (Oxford: Clarendon, 1990).

Indeed, in many ways this volume owes its existence to the fact that philosophers have already started tackling such questions over the last few decades. Comparatively early landmark works on international themes in normative political philosophy, such as Michael Walzer's *Just and Unjust Wars*,[6] Charles Beitz's *Political Theory and International Relations*,[7] and Henry Shue's *Basic Rights: Subsistence, Affluence, and U.S. Foreign Policy*[8] have more recently been joined by the influential writings of philosophers and lawyers such as James Nickel, Onora O'Neill, Thomas Pogge, Fernando Teson, Martha Nussbaum, Larry May, Mortimer Sellers, James Griffin, and William Twining.[9] Special mention should be made of three important monographs. The first is Thomas Franck's treatise *Fairness in International Law and Institutions* published in 1995, a pioneering effort by a distinguished international lawyer to apply Rawls's theory of justice to large tracts of international law, one that outdoes Rawls himself in its ambitions for international justice.[10] Especially important, given his dominant influence on Anglo-American political philosophy, has been the publication in 1999 of John Rawls's final work, *The Law of Peoples*, which has already sparked a voluminous secondary literature.[11] Finally, Allen Buchanan's *Justice, Legitimacy, and Self-Determination: Moral Foundations for International Law*, which appeared in 2004, is arguably the most systematic and comprehensive discussion of the morality of international law by a contemporary philosopher.[12] The rapid growth of the philosophy of international law as a field of inquiry is

---

[6] Walzer, J. *Just and Unjust Wars: A Moral Argument with Historical Illustrations* (1977; rev. edn., New York: Basic Books, 2006).

[7] Beitz, C., *Political Theory and International Relations* (Princeton: Princeton University Press, 1979).

[8] Shue, H., *Basic Rights: Subsistence, Affluence, and US Foreign Policy* (1980; 2nd edn., Princeton: Princeton University Press, 1996).

[9] Nickel, J., *Making Sense of Human Rights: Philosophical Reflections on the Universal Declaration of Human Rights* (Berkeley and Los Angeles: University of California Press, 1987; 2nd edn., Oxford: Blackwell, 2007); Teubner, G., *Global Law Without a State* (Aldershot: Dartmouth, 1997); Twining, W., *Globalisation and Legal Theory* (Evanston, Ill.: Northwestern University Press, 2000); O'Neill, O., *Bounds of Justice* (Cambridge: Cambridge University Press, 2000); Pogge, T. W., *World Poverty and Human Rights: Cosmopolitan Responsibilities and Reforms* (Oxford: Polity Press, 2002; 2nd edn., Oxford: Polity Press, 2008); Teson, F., *A Philosophy of International Law* (Boulder, Colo.: Westview Press, 1998); Nussbaum, M. C., *Women and Human Development: The Capabilities Approach* (Cambridge: Cambridge University Press, 2000); Buchanan, A., *Justice, Legitimacy, and Self-Determination: Moral Foundations for International Law* (Oxford: Oxford University Press, 2004); May, L., *Crimes Against Humanity: A Normative Account* (Cambridge: Cambridge University Press, 2004); Sellers, M. N. S., *Republican Principles in International Law: The Fundamental Requirements of a Just World Order* (New York: Palgrave Macmillan, 2006); May, L., *War Crimes and Just War* (Cambridge: Cambridge University Press, 2007); May, L., *Aggression and Crimes Against Peace* (Cambridge: Cambridge University Press, 2008); Griffin, J., *On Human Rights* (Oxford: Oxford University Press, 2008); and Twining, W., *General Jurisprudence: Understanding Law from a Global Perspective* (Cambridge: Cambridge University Press, 2009).

[10] Franck, T. M., *Fairness in International Law and Institutions* (New York: Oxford University Press, 1995). Issue 13 of *European Journal of International Law* (2002), 901–1030 contains a review essay symposium on this book.

[11] Rawls, J., *The Law of Peoples with 'The Idea of Public Reason Revisted'* (Cambridge, Mass.: Harvard University Press, 1999). For a useful collection of critical essays, see Martin, R., and Reidy, D. (eds.), *Rawls's Law of Peoples: A Realistic Utopia?* (Oxford: Blackwell Publishing, 2006).

[12] Buchanan, A., *Justice, Legitimacy, and Self-Determination* (above, n. 9).

underlined by the fact that eight years after the publication of its first, print edition, the online version of the *Routledge Encyclopedia of Philosophy* has since 2006 included a lengthy entry on 'International law, philosophy of'. Nearly three-quarters of the items listed in its extensive bibliography were published from 2000 onwards.[13]

This volume aims to build on these recent developments that have led to the emergence of a tradition of philosophical inquiry into international law, partly by spurring philosophical reflection specifically on international *law* rather than just on the more general topic of international *political morality*. What constitutes such a tradition and how are its boundaries demarcated? Perhaps the most useful answer is one along the lines given by Rawls in response to a similar question about moral philosophy:

> Here I think of the tradition of moral philosophy as itself a family of traditions, such as the traditions of the natural law and of the moral sense schools, and of the traditions of rational intuitionism and of utilitarianism. What makes all these traditions part of one inclusive tradition is that they use a commonly understood vocabulary and terminology. Moreover, they reply and adjust to one another's views and arguments so that exchanges between them are, in part, a reasoned discussion that leads to further development.[14]

Among the merits of this characterization is its emphasis on the open-endedness of a living tradition: participation in it is not defined by subscription to a fixed doctrine or adherence to a well-defined and highly constraining methodology, but by entry into an ongoing dialogue on an evolving range of questions that draws on a shared fund of concepts, themselves liable to revision and refinement as the dialogue proceeds. All living traditions, so understood, are a work in progress: 'a reasoned discussion that', one hopes, 'leads to further development'.

The next two sections address in a preliminary way two sources of deep scepticism—themselves ultimately philosophical in character—about the prospects for a philosophy of international law as roughly sketched here. The first questions whether international law is really law; the other is doubtful about the possibility of subjecting international law to robust ethical standards of appraisal even if it does qualify as law.

II. What is International Law? A Response to Conceptual Scepticism about International Law

Two major conceptual questions in the philosophy of international law are (i) whether what we call international law is really law and, if so, what it is that makes

13 Buchanan, A., 'International law, Philosophy of' (above, n. 3).
14 Rawls, J., *Lectures on the History of Moral Philosophy* (Cambridge, Mass.: Harvard University Press, 2000), 8–11.

a norm a norm of international law (as distinct from, say, a political or social norm) and (ii) how we identify a norm as an international legal norm. Those two conceptual questions about the identity and the identification of international law are at the core of one type of deep scepticism about a philosophy of international law. If so-called international law is not law but an ensemble of moral, political, or social norms, there can be no such thing as a philosophy of international law. So-called philosophy of international law would merge into political, social, or moral philosophy as applied to international relations.

Conceptual questions of this kind were addressed in the middle of the last century by general theorists of law such as Kelsen and Hart.[15] According to Hart, the legality of international law is problematic because it 'resembles, [. . .] in form though not at all in content, a simple regime of primary or customary law'.[16] International law is clearly more than a set of social or moral norms, but at the same time it does not fit (entirely) the concept of law developed for domestic law. The emergence of more normative discussions since the 1970s has tended to sideline the question of the legality of international law. Whether or not those norms and institutions are legal, their impact on individuals justifies subjecting them to moral scrutiny. But conceptual and normative questions about an institution, such as law, that purports to impose binding standards of conduct on its subjects, cannot be entirely separated from each other. A complete understanding of the normative questions raised by international law requires a clear understanding of the legality of international law—and vice versa.

The reasons for the meagre interest in those conceptual issues, despite the persistence and even strengthening of scepticism about the legality of international law,[17] are multiple. Partly this is a result of the more general lack of interest in the philosophy of international law until recent times, as discussed in the previous section. This is especially true when those conceptual questions are contrasted with more concrete substantive discussions of contemporary questions arising daily in international affairs. More generally, legal philosophers have tended since the 1970s to shift their interests towards Special Jurisprudence, and, as a result, away from the core legal theoretical endeavours of the 1950s.

A more problematic reason is the challenge posed by international law to General Jurisprudence. The sceptical challenge to the legality of international law is usually understood as a one-way street: if key features of a domestic legal system are missing

---

[15] e.g. Hart, H. L. A., *The Concept of Law* (above, n. 1), ch. 10, p. 214. See also Kelsen, H., *Principles of International Law* (New York: Reinhart, 1952).

[16] Hart, H. L. A., *The Concept of Law* (above, n. 1), 232.

[17] See e.g. the challenges raised in Goldsmith, J. and Posner, E., *The Limits of International Law* (Oxford: Oxford University Press, 2005) and the discussion their book has triggered since (see e.g. excellent critiques by Franck., T. M., 'The Power of Legitimacy and the Legitimacy of Power: International Law in an Age of Power Disequilibrium', *American Journal of International Law*, 100/1 (2006), 88–106; and Buchanan, A., 'Democracy and the Commitment to International Law', *Georgia Journal of International and Comparative Law*, 34 (2006), 305).

at the international level, so-called international law is not really law[18]. While there may have been a reason historically to use domestic law as a paradigm of law in general, this is no longer the case. Although there are pre-established features of a legal system in legal theory that ought to be exhibited at the international level for there to be international law, those state-centred features are not immune to theoretical challenge. As a result, if international law does not fit the criteria of the concept of law used at the domestic level, it may not (only) be a problem for the legality of international law, but (also) for those criteria themselves and hence for a given legal theory.[19] In any case, the domestic legal order is no longer self-contained and separate from the international one, so that legal theory has to account for this complex new legal reality in a holistic and integrated way.

Of the two questions distinguished at the outset of this section, only the first shall be addressed here. Once the legal nature of international law has been clarified, ways of identifying valid international legal norms and their content are a matter for the sources of international law. Two of the early chapters in the book address the sources of international law in depth.[20] Among the key features of law that are allegedly missing at the international level, three will be discussed here: a complete system of abstract and general norms stemming from an official and centralized legislature; a monopoly on the use of coercion to enforce legal norms, through centrally organized sanctions or at least a courts system with universal and compulsory jurisdiction; and, finally, the absence of effective compliance with those legal norms in practice.[21] One may also mention the alleged absence of states' moral obligations under international law (and the related complexity about a self-binding sovereign),[22] but that critique is addressed in the third section of this introduction and in four chapters in the book.[23]

Replies to these sceptical critiques may be of two kinds: theoretical answers that deny that the supposed essential feature of law really counts as such and, second, replies of a more factual kind that refer to developments in international law. Clearly, answers to those three questions have varied with the rapid developments of international law and in particular the significant changes in its subjects, objects, and normativity in the past thirty years or so. Those developments have gradually made it either more integrated within domestic legal orders and hence an integral part of their legality in this sense, or more state-like in its own spheres of competence. By reference to what was said before about the need to adapt legal theory to the new

---

[18] Hart, H. L. A., *The Concept of Law* (above, n. 1), 214–15.

[19] See Twining, W., *Globalisation and Legal Theory* (above, n. 9), 50–90.

[20] Besson, S., Ch. 7 in this volume; Lefkowitz, D., Ch. 8 in this volume.

[21] On those (multifarious) doubts and critiques, see e.g. Hart, H. L. A., *The Concept of Law* (above, n. 1), 214; Buchanan, A., *Justice, Legitimacy, and Self-Determination* (above, n. 9), 45–53; Goldsmith, J. and Posner, E. *The Limits of International Law* (above, n. 17).

[22] Hart, H. L. A., *The Concept of Law* (above, n. 1), 216–32.

[23] In this volume see Buchanan, A., Ch. 3; Tasioulas, J., Ch. 4; Endicott, T., Ch. 11; Cohen, J., Ch. 12. See also Besson, S., 'The Authority of International Law: Lifting the State Veil', *Sydney Law Review*, 31/3 (2009, 343).

circumstances of domestic law in an international setting, and not only to make sure international law fits the criteria for the concept of law derived from domestic jurisprudence, it is essential not to fall into the trap of minimizing differences between domestic and international law and hence of lapsing into a statist bias.[24] As a result, and although a straightforward response to the sceptics would simply be to show that international law is evolving into a proper legal system, it is primarily from a theoretical perspective and not one of facts only that a convincing rebuttal of the sceptics' critique needs to be launched.

The first, and most problematic doubt expressed by sceptics pertains to the making of international law, its norms and their articulation. Three sub-critiques need to be unpacked here. First of all, the absence of a centralized and official law-maker, and especially of a vertical relationship between that law-maker and its legal subjects is the most striking difference between a domestic legal system and international law. Law-makers and legal subjects are usually one and the same international subjects: states. Besides, there are many processes of law-making that coexist without being either centralized or standing in a hierarchical relationship to each other. Critics also invoke, second, the nature of the norms that are referred to as international law, and more particularly the absence of general and abstract rules in international law. International norms are often thought to stem exclusively from bilateral agreements between states and to create relative and concrete obligations. Finally, doubts about the legality of international law are often based on the alleged absence of secondary rules (rules of change and adjudication) or even of a rule of recognition which, as Hart showed, lies at the foundation of a fully-fledged and autonomous legal system.

With respect to the first sub-critique, it is true that the official or public nature of law may bear on its legality, since law is the product of a collective enterprise. The legality of customary law shows, however, that a formal legislature is not always required in a municipal legal system.[25] In practice, moreover, much of international law nowadays stems from multilateral processes that are increasingly distinct from treaty-making, but also, as a consequence, from what may be thought of as a private exchange of promises or horizontal contract-making. It suffices here to mention legislative treaties, multilateral codifications of customary law, but also, conversely, the creation of customary law through those multilateral conventional codifications of existing practices.[26] In a similar way, official international law-making has become distinct from the transnational albeit private production of standards (e.g. global administrative law). With respect to the centralization and hierarchy requirement, one should say that legal hierarchies can be of many kinds (sources, regimes, norms, etc.) and all of them are not necessarily present

---

[24] Hart, H. L. A., *The Concept of Law* (above, n. 1), 232.

[25] See Buchanan, A., *Justice, Legitimacy, and Self-Determination* (above, n. 9), 47.

[26] See e.g. Boyle, A. and Chinkin, C., *The Making of International Law* (Oxford: Oxford University Press, 2007), 98 ff. and 163 ff.

in all domestic legal orders.[27] Further, even if international law remains largely decentralized and non-hierarchical, there is a fixed set of sources. Moreover, relationships between norms and regimes are coordinated in many other ways than through a hierarchy of sources. Hierarchies of norms (e.g. *jus cogens* or imperative norms) are developing and certain regimes are increasingly deemed superior to others (e.g. general international law).

As to the second sub-critique, it is indeed essential to prove that international law norms are legal rules and that they are both general and abstract. From a practical point of view, however, the critique does not cut much ice. It gives a skewed view of the state of international law. International legal norms are distinct from moral norms: they are often quite indifferent morally and may be changed by a decision of international law-makers.[28] And they are general and abstract. General international law has developed extensively in the past twenty years or so, and norms that apply to all subjects of international law are numerous—and the same may be said about *erga omnes* norms, i.e. norms enforceable by all states. Also, international law has become more abstract as its norms potentially apply to many different situations and no longer only concern concrete situations. Prosper Weil's prognosis of the emerging 'relative normativity' of international law has now been confirmed in practice:[29] some international legal norms bind subjects who have not agreed to them (e.g. third-party effect of treaties) or who have expressly objected to them (e.g. limitations on persistent objections to customary law); they bind them even if they have made reservations when agreeing to them (e.g. objective norms such as human rights); and, finally, they sometimes bind them in an imperative fashion (e.g. *jus cogens* norms).

Regarding the third sub-critique, a set of primary legal rules may be regarded as law even in the absence of secondary rules, being deemed, in Hart's phrase, a 'primitive legal order'. This is the case if international law lacks a rule of recognition that can establish the validity of individual primary rules by reference to some ultimate rule of the system. This was Hart's view of international law given his rejection of the Kelsenian *a priori* assumption of an international *Grundnorm*.[30] While such a reductive view of international law may have been factually correct in 1961, it no longer is. General international law has internal rules that determine its own validity and may therefore be deemed an autonomous legal order, and this is true of international conventional law as much as of customary law. In the context of the discussion of the processes of international law-making and hence of the sources or identification of its norms, the question of the kind of norms created

---

[27] See Hart, H. L. A., *Essays in Jurisprudence and Philosophy* (Oxford: Oxford University Press, 1983), ch. 15.
[28] Hart, H. L. A., *The Concept of Law* (above, n. 1), 228–30.
[29] See Weil, P., 'Towards Relative Normativity in International Law' *American Journal of International Law*, 77 (1983), 413. See for a discussion, Tasioulas, J., 'In Defence of Relative Normativity: Communitarian Values and the Nicaragua Case', *Oxford Journal of Legal Studies*, 16 (1996), 85.
[30] Hart, H. L. A., *The Concept of Law* (above, n. 1), 234.

by international law will be discussed extensively, and in particular the distinction between primary and secondary rules (e.g. in the field of treaty law with the so-called law of treaties, but also of customary law with conditions of customary law-making) and the existence of a rule of recognition (by reference to the customary nature of Article 38 of the ICJ Statute, e.g.).[31]

The second main critique of the legality of international law concerns the absence of a centralized enforcement system, and in particular of a sanctions system or at least a courts system with universal and compulsory jurisdiction. The violation of certain norms of international law can trigger official coercion and (military and non-military) sanctions, but those sanctions are rare, diverse in character, and often non-systematically applied (for lack of political will or knowledge). Further, enforcement of international law is largely left to the different subjects of international law and to states in particular (e.g. self-defence, counter-measures) and this makes it akin to a primitive system of private sanction. International jurisdiction remains the exception and, when it exists, it is mostly non-universal and non-compulsory. In response, it is important to stress that very few conceptions of law nowadays make the existence of sanctions or threats a necessary condition of legality. This Austinian, and respectively Kelsenian, legacy was already discredited by Hart in 1961, both with respect to domestic and international law.[32] Its predictive component, which may be granted, ought not be conflated with a conceptual requirement. In any case, modern domestic legal systems show that not all disputes may be resolved by a supreme law enforcer; examples may be given from constitutional law or from the less formal area of customary law.[33]

Even if one concedes that in domestic law certain provisions prohibiting the use of force are necessary, together with making the official use of force a sanction for the violation of prohibitions of the use of force among individuals, international circumstances are different. The private use of force in international relations cannot remain private for long, and this fact helps prevent the spiral of violence one would fear in similar circumstances among individuals. Further, centralizing the use of force in the hands of a few states backing compliance with international law could become a source of unacceptable inequalities and also potentially of fearful risks. Natural deterrents have secured long periods of peace. Pressure for conformity with international law need not be channelled exclusively through formal sanctions, as is shown by the increasing role of civil society. In any case, international law is constantly evolving and sanctions are one of the fields in which it is becoming increasingly state-like. The law of individual and collective sanctions, especially economic ones, and of counter-measures has developed intensely

[31] See in this volume Besson, S., Ch. 7; Lefkowitz, D., Ch. 8.
[32] Hart, H. L. A., *The Concept of Law* (above, n. 1), 217–20. See also recently O'Connell, M. E., *The Power and Purpose of International Law* (Oxford: Oxford University Press, 2008), 62–8.
[33] See Buchanan, A., *Justice, Legitimacy, and Self-Determination* (above, n. 9), 47 for a discussion.

through the UN organs' practice and the ICJ's case-law. New peace-keeping and peace-making mechanisms have developed over the years. And regional agreements and organizations have been constantly strengthened to provide a more effective enforcement of international law norms at the local level. The same may be said about rules of adjudication. International dispute settlements, and compulsory judicial mechanisms in particular, have proliferated since the 1990s. True, they apply mostly at the regional level and often in certain specific international legal regimes only. However, their constant development and the expanding use of third-party and formalized settlement mechanisms are signs of the development of secondary rules of adjudication in international law.[34]

Finally, the international legal order is said to lack a third important legal feature and that is the absence of effective compliance with international law in practice.[35] Independently of the existence of enforcement mechanisms, legal norms in a legal order need to be complied with, at least in part. Compliance is a necessary albeit insufficient condition of legality.[36] A set of rules that is never complied with can hardly be regarded as valid law. It is clear, however, that what matters for the law's legality is enhanced conformity with its rules than would otherwise be the case, and not perfect conformity. After all, most municipal legal orders have serious difficulties with non-compliance. Moreover, the notion of effectivity is itself vague; it suffices to mention human rights to see that compliance with human rights can take many different forms and degrees.[37] But, in any case, international law is in large part complied with in practice.[38] True, this varies depending on the areas of law in question and on the existence of formal or informal pressures for conformity.[39] The reasons for compliance can be very different; compliance may be a reaction to the exercise of power or to the existence of sanctions, but may also result from many other (instrumental and non-instrumental) reasons, e.g. consent to legal rules, strategic reasons for respect, moral reasons to comply with a legal order that is minimally just, etc. Notwithstanding, effective compliance is easily demonstrated by reference to the ways in which powerful states seek justifications for their breaches of international law; one may mention the invocation of self-defence or of a state

[34] See e.g. Brown, C., *A Common Law of International Adjudication* (Cambridge: Cambridge University Press, 2007).

[35] See e.g. Goldsmith, J. and Posner, E., *The Limits of International Law* (above, n. 17), 165, 185 ff. for a recent version of this sceptical argument. For a discussion, see O'Connell, M. E., *The Power and Purpose of International Law* (above, n. 32), 99–149.

[36] On compliance and the sources thesis, see Raz, J., *The Morality of Freedom* (Oxford: Oxford University Press, 1986), 65, 75–6; and Raz, J., 'The Problem of Authority: Revisiting the Service Conception' *Minnesota Law Review* 90 (2006), 1003, 1005–6.

[37] Buchanan, A., *Justice, Legitimacy, and Self-Determination* (above, n. 9), 51–2.

[38] See Besson, S., 'The Authority of International Law' (above, n. 23).

[39] See Henkin, L., *How Nations Behave* (2nd edn., New York: Columbia University Press, 1979) for the first shift of focus away from enforcement (and sanctions) to compliance and the argument that international law enjoys the minimum amount of compliance needed to be regarded as law. For a discussion, see O'Connell, M. E., *The Power and Purpose of International Law* (above, n. 32), 1–16 and 57–98.

of necessity, or at least the reference to the conditions for counter-measures (which are legalized under existing international law).

In sum, there are provisionally good answers to sceptical doubts about the legality of international law. International law has specificities of its own, both in terms of form and of content, but those specificities can be accommodated in the concept of law. Theoretical arguments can be advanced for that contention, but it is also supported by factual considerations. International law is no longer the inter-state law of the 1950s; it has evolved to become more like municipal legal systems. But nor is domestic law what it used to be. International law has become more integrated within municipal legal systems than it was in the past. This has to do with developments in its material and personal scope that make it an integral part of the law applying to individuals subjects in domestic legal orders. Law itself has changed as a result of globalization and so should legal theory.

III. Does Morality extend to Public International Law? A Response to Normative Scepticism about a Morality of International Law

A key aim of this book is to contribute to the formulation of moral standards for the evaluation of public international law, both in general and with respect to its main parts. Such standards, the thought naturally goes, should play a vital role in guiding the reform of international law and institutions and in determining the basis and proper extent of our allegiance to them. What is meant by calling them 'moral' or 'ethical' standards (we use these two adjectives interchangeably)? This is a far from uncomplicated question, but the simple answer that must suffice for our purposes is that moral standards are concerned with what human beings, as individuals or groups, owe to other human beings, and perhaps also other beings (such as flaura and fauna), in light of the status and interests of the latter, where the breach of the relevant standards typically validates certain characteristic responses: blame, guilt, resentment, punishment, and so on. More concretely, we can refer to a rich and diverse repertoire of concepts through which the notion of moral concern has historically been elaborated: obligation, justice, rights, equality, among many others. Morality, therefore, consists in a set of standards which, among other things, place restrictions on our—often self-interested—conduct in order to pay proper tribute to the standing and interests of others.

Given its nature, it might be reasonably supposed that there are potentially two kinds of moral standards that have special relevance for international law.[40] On the one hand, transnational moral principles, which apply within all political communities. On the other hand, international moral principles, which govern relations among agents that are not members of the same political community (or, perhaps, that are not members of any political community or that do not stand in the relationship of governed to government within a political community). Some moral standards, of course, might be of both sorts. For example, human rights norms are typically conceived as applying within all political communities, but their (threatened) breach is also often taken to justify (at least *pro tanto*) some form of preventive or remedial response by outside political communities or international agents. The task of a normative theory of international law is to elaborate the content and draw out the practical implications of such moral principles for international law.

This enterprise, however, has provoked considerable scepticism. Sometimes this takes the form of denying the very possibility of a normative theory of international law: doubt is cast on the existence of justifiable transnational and international moral standards that might appropriately be reflected in international law. More often, however, it is scepticism about their scope and content: even if it is conceded that some moral standards obtain in the case of international law, they are thought to be severely limited in their coverage and very minimal in their demands. Let us call these two brands of scepticism, respectively, radical and moderate.

On what grounds is scepticism about a normative approach to international law advanced? One basis for radical scepticism, in particular, consists in scepticism about the objectivity of morality itself. Consider, for example, a representative statement by a leading member of the 'realist' school of international relations, in an influential work originally published in 1930:

In the last fifty years, thanks mainly though not wholly to the influence of Marx, the principles of the historical school have been applied to the analysis of thought . . . The realist has thus been enabled to demonstrate that the intellectual theories and ethical standards of utopianism, far from being the expression of absolute and *a priori* principles, are historically conditioned, being both products of circumstances and interests and weapons framed for the furtherance of interests. 'Ethical notions', as Mr. Bertrand Russell has remarked, 'are very seldom a cause, but almost always an effect, a means of claiming universal legislative authority for our own preference, not, as we fondly imagine, the actual ground of those preferences.' This is by far the most formidable attack which utopianism has to face; for here the very foundations of its belief are undermined by the realist critique.[41]

---

[40] The distinction that follows is adapted from the discussion of Buchanan, A., *Justice, Legitimacy and Self-Determination* (above, n. 9), 190–1.

[41] Carr, E. H., *The Twenty Years' Crisis 1919–1939: An Introduction to the Study of International Relations* (1930; London: Palgrave Macmillan, 2001), 65.

The thought here is that morality (pejoratively described as 'utopianism') presents itself as a set of constraints, discoverable by reason, on the pursuit of self-interest by individuals and states; in fact, 'realist critique' reveals all moral principles to be themselves 'products of circumstances and interests and weapons framed for the furtherance of interests'.

The first thing to say is that, even if correct, the corrosive implications of scepticism about moral objectivity extend not just to the normative theory of international law, but to any form of thought involving moral judgment. This is not necessarily an argument against it, but it does show that it is not a problem uniquely afflicting normative theorizing about international matters. Moreover, it places its advocates under special pressure to avoid self-refutation, since they typically do wish to assert the appropriateness of moral judgments in some non-international contexts. The second observation worth making is that it is far from obvious that either the Marxist or any other brand of 'realist' critique has securely established the advertised conclusion that morality is merely the product of, and perhaps also ideological window-dressing for, underlying interests (or preferences, desires, and so on). Moral scepticism of this sort is highly controversial in philosophical circles today, whatever may have been the situation when Carr was writing in the 1920s. How easy is it to dispute, after all, that the proposition 'Slavery is unjust' is plainly true, even as '$2 + 1 = 3$' is plainly true? And why must the best explanation of anyone's belief in the former proposition, unlike their belief in the latter, necessarily exclude appeal to the fact that the proposition in question is true?[42] All this is compatible with one needing some element of good fortune in one's historical and personal circumstances to be in a position to grasp the truth of the first proposition, but this is also true of the second.

Perhaps the more constructive observation that needs to be made is that there are many ways in which morality can be admitted to be 'subjective' without thereby failing to be 'objective' in some significant sense that allows for moral propositions to be straightforwardly true or justified, for belief in true moral propositions to consist in knowledge, and for changes in moral belief over time to represent genuine cognitive progress or regress.[43] In particular, the objectivist need not embrace the metaphysical claim that moral values, such as justice, are radically mind-independent, like the famed Platonic forms, existing in splendid isolation from human modes of consciousness and concern. In Ronald Dworkin's amusing formulation, the moral objectivist is not committed to the existence of 'some special particles—morons—whose energy and momentum establish fields that at once constitute the morality or immorality, or virtue or vice, of particular human acts and institutions and also interact in some way with human nervous systems so

---

[42] See Nagel, T., *The Last Word* (Oxford: Clarendon, 1997), ch. 6 and Wiggins, D., *Ethics: Twelve Lectures on the Philosophy of Morality* (London: Penguin, 2006), pt. III.

[43] For a development of the thought that morality can be coherently conceived as both 'objective' and 'subjective', see Wiggins, D., *Ethics* (above, n. 42), ch. 12.

as to make people aware of the morality or immorality or the virtue or vice'.[44] So, a nuanced appreciation of the kind of 'objectivity' requisite to the meaningful pursuit of a normative approach to international law may serve to quell sceptical concerns of the first sort about the prospects for developing a normative theory of international law. And this is just as well, since many of those who press such concerns seem themselves to subscribe to numerous moral propositions.

Other forms of scepticism about the enterprise of a normative theory of international law concentrate not so much on the nature of morality, but on the putative subject-matter—in particular, relations among states—regarding which such theories seek to make moral judgments. Even if moral reasoning is in principle capable of attaining a respectable degree of objectivity, the thought goes, its remit either does not extend to the case of international law, or else does so only in a highly attenuated form.

One line of argument of this kind turns on regarding the sphere of international law's application, at least in the present and the foreseeable future, as a *state of nature*. This is because it is a domain in which the key agents, territorial states, exhibit three important features (i) they are ultimately motivated by the fundamental aim of ensuring their own survival, (ii) they are approximately equal in power, in the sense that no one state (or stable grouping of states) can permanently dominate all the others, and (iii) they are not subject to a sovereign capable of securing peaceful co-operation among states by authoritatively arbitrating conflicts among them. In such circumstances, it is contended, it would be deeply irrational for a state to conform its conduct to moral demands; hence, morality is inapplicable to the sphere that international law purports to govern.[45] As Allen Buchanan has emphasized, the supposed 'inapplicability' of morality in the international domain is open to at least three interpretations. First, that there are no true or justified statements about what anyone morally ought to do in that sphere. Second, that no one in fact acts on the basis of moral considerations in international relations either now or in the foreseeable future. Third, that moral behaviour in international relations is fundamentally irrational and, in consequence, very infrequent.[46] There are interesting relations among these claims, but we can take the first one to represent an attempt to motivate radical scepticism. An alternative deployment of the state of nature analogy defends a moderate, rather than a radical, form of scepticism about the applicability of moral standards in the internationalist sphere. Perhaps the most minimalist version of this line of thought contends that, in light

---

[44] Dworkin, R. M., 'Objectivity and Truth: You'd Better Believe It', *Philosophy and Public Affairs*, 25 (1996), 87, 104.

[45] We follow here the version of the state of nature thesis about international relations outlined in Buchanan, A., *Justice, Legitimacy, and Self-Determination* (above, n. 9), 29–30, and which he attributes to 'realist' scholars in international law such as George F. Kennan and Kenneth Waltz.

[46] Ibid. 31. For persuasive critiques of the state of nature argument, which we have drawn on in our discussion below, see Beitz, C., *Political Theory and International Relations* (above, n. 7), pt. i and pp. 185–91 and Buchanan, A., *Justice, Legitimacy, and Self-Determination* (above, n. 9), 29–37.

of the character of international relations as a Hobbesian state of nature, the only moral imperative operative in the international domain is one that requires state officials to ensure the survival of their respective states.[47]

As formulated above, we have already found good cause to resist this sort of sceptical argument. If the international sphere were a state of nature, it is very doubtful that it could sustain any institution meriting the name of 'law'. Yet, as we saw in the previous section, it makes good sense to speak of international law governing the relations between sovereign states through norms and institutions enabling co-operation in matters such as financial regulation, trade agreements, scientific and technological advances, environmental protection, telecommunications, economic development, disaster relief, and the international propagation and protection of human rights, even in the absence of a global sovereign. More generally, recent work in international relations theory undermines the dogma that the ultimate or predominant determinant of a state's behaviour is the desire to ensure its survival (or, in another version, to maximize its power). In any case, it is obviously not the case that compliance with moral standards inevitably imperils a state's chances of survival. Finally, 'liberal' approaches to international relations have emphasized the responsiveness of a state's preferences to the internal character of the state (e.g. whether its constitution is democratic) and of its society (e.g. the extent to which it is pluralistic and accommodating of internal differences). Moreover, the activities of these groups within the state are powerfully shaped by transnational and international governmental and non-governmental networks to which they belong. In response, an advocate of the state of nature analogy might be tempted to stretch the notion of a state preference for survival, or power, so that it encompasses more than one might have originally imagined. But this strategy has its limits. In particular, there is the worry that, in seeking to accommodate all of the seemingly countervailing evidence for the irreducible diversity of states' interests, it leads to the trivialization of the state of nature argument, rendering it unfalsifiable by any empirical evidence.[48]

Nothing in the foregoing observations is inconsistent with acknowledging a core of authentic insight in the state of nature argument. One way of spelling it out is in terms of the feasibility constraints on an acceptable normative theory of international law (whether an ideal theory or a non-ideal theory concerned with problems arising from non-compliance with ideal standards and, in particular, effecting a transition to a state of full compliance). These are different from, and in all probability far more limiting than, those that apply in the domestic case.[49] What

---

[47] This is referred to as fiduciary realism in Buchanan, A., *Justice, Legitimacy, and Self-Determination* (above, n. 9), 35–7.

[48] The points in this paragraph, among others, are developed with due reference to the relevant literature in international relations, in Buchanan, A., *Justice, Legitimacy, and Self-Determination* (above, n. 9), 31–7.

[49] See, in this context, Charles Beitz's illuminating discussion of 'heuristic realism', which is a 'cautionary view about the role that normative considerations should be allowed to play in practical reasoning about international

we may rightly take issue with is the sweepingly negative conclusion that sceptics who appeal to the state of nature analogy seek to wring from this insight.

There are more plausible ways of motivating moderate scepticism regarding the prospects for a normative theory of international law than by invoking a state of nature analogy. One general line of thought appeals to the ethical-political significance of an important feature of the international domain: the great diversity that exists in ethical and political concepts among different cultures, and also the considerable divergence in judgments among those who deploy the same concepts. One way of elaborating this line of thought is by means of the notion of ethical pluralism. The latter doctrine is wholly compatible with the objectivity of ethics, and so is not to be confused with ethical relativism. But, given the profusion of objective ethical values, and the diverse number of ways in which their content may be acceptably elaborated and relations between them ordered, proponents of this view are doubtful that a 'global ethic' applicable to all states, and suitable for embodiment in international law and institutions, will be other than minimalist in content. Instead, it will predominantly consist in a limited set of universal norms prohibiting certain specific evils. As David Wiggins has recently put it: 'With declarations against torture, genocide, imprisonment without charge, slavery, forced labour, etc., we are in the home territory of the international spirit at its finest and least controversial, the universally valid proscription of specific evil. It is a tragic mistake to suppose that these can be a paradigm for the positive and general prescriptions of "global ethics".'[50]

A second line of thought purports to stand aloof from all philosophical controversies, such as that concerning ethical objectivism, and focuses instead on the conditions of a legitimate international law, one that can credibly claim to be binding on all its subjects. Thus, John Rawls has argued that it is necessary for the principles underlying law, in both the domestic and the international cases, to be justifiable to all those subject to them. In both cases, the operative form of justification must be in terms of a form of *public reason*—rather than ordinary, truth-oriented moral reasoning—that is responsive to the fact of reasonable pluralism. In the case of a liberal society this is a pluralism in conceptions of the good held by individual citizens, who are nonetheless reasonable in that they accept the criterion of reciprocity (they are prepared to co-operate with others on fair terms as free and equal citizens) and the burdens of judgment. In the international case, however, the justification is directed at political communities, rather than the individuals who compose them,

---

affairs, particularly that of individuals charged with making decisions about national foreign policy. It warns of the predictable kinds of errors that can occur when moral considerations are applied naively or in the wrong way', in Beitz, C., *Political Theory and International Relations* (above, n. 7), 187 (Beitz's discussion at 187–91 is generally relevant).

[50] Wiggins, D., *Ethics* (above, n. 42), 355–6. Arguing along rather different lines, Michael Walzer has challenged the applicability of norms of distributive justice to the international realm in its current form, see Walzer, M., *Spheres of Justice: A Defense of Pluralism and Equality* (Oxford: Blackwell, 1993), 28–30.

and reasonable pluralism extends to conceptions of justice, not simply conceptions of the good.[51] This means that, for Rawls, decent but non-liberal societies may be counted members in good standing of the Society of Peoples, i.e. they have good standing even in the terms of an ideal theory of international justice. This is despite the fact that such societies are not democratic and may engage in various illiberal practices such as discriminating against some of their members on the grounds of sex, ethnicity, sexual orientation, or religion. Rawls's approach also leads to a notoriously truncated list of human rights, certainly as compared with the Universal Declaration of Human Rights, and to the inapplicability of principles of distributive justice (including Rawls's famous 'difference principle') to the global sphere: neither the difference principle nor any other principle of distributive justice bears on relations *between* societies, nor is respect for it mandated *within* each society in order to ensure its good standing under the Rawlsian Law of Peoples.

Now, of course, there is a great deal that needs to be said in assessing the pros and cons of moderate scepticism of the last two varieties. Some of it is said by contributors to this volume. But the key point is that moderate scepticism of this stamp is not really all that sceptical; on the contrary, it presents itself as a self-consciously moral position *within* the enterprise of articulating a normative theory of international law. And this is just what we should expect. It would be a grave error to assume that a commitment to a normative theory of international law necessarily carries with it some specific ethical-political commitment, such as a liberal cosmopolitanism that insists on the appropriateness of implementing an essentially liberal-democratic political vision through the medium of international law. On the contrary, the appropriateness of doing so is a central question for debate once we have accepted that normative international legal theory is a viable and worthwhile enterprise.

IV. Preview of the Chapters

The volume is distinguished by its 'dialogical' methodology, modelled on the format of the annual supplementary volume of the *Proceedings of the Aristotelian Society*. There are two essays on each topic, with the second author spending some time responding to the arguments of the first as well as developing their own take on the topic (in the case of the topic of human rights, given its centrality in the normative theory of international law, we have enlisted three authors).

One reason for adopting the dialogical approach is to underscore, especially for students new to philosophy, that there is a diversity of views that might be defended on a given topic, as opposed to some canonical 'philosophical' view.

---

[51] Rawls, J., *The Law of Peoples* (above, n. 11), 11, 19 (the international case) and 136–7 (the domestic case).

However, we have not gone further and made a point of choosing in each case pairs of authors with radically contrasting views.[52] Quite apart from anything else, this would have conveyed a seriously distorted impression of the nature of philosophical disputation. Sometimes, the most interesting and instructive disagreements are between philosophers who share a lot by way of agreement on fundamentals. More importantly, we have opted for a dialogical methodology in recognition of the fact that philosophy develops through a process of genuine dialectical engagement with the views of others. Others' views are not simply fodder for literature surveys or scholarly footnotes; instead, they are to be carefully articulated and subjected to critical scrutiny in light of the best arguments that can be formulated in their support. This intellectual virtue is one that analytical legal philosophy is especially well placed to foster in contemporary theorizing about international law.

The book is divided in two main parts: General Issues in the Philosophy of International Law and Specific Issues in the Philosophy of International Law. Chapters in the first group tackle general topics such as the history of the philosophy of international law, the legitimacy of international law and in particular its democratic legitimacy, the sources of international law, the nature of international legal adjudication, the significance of state sovereignty, and the contours of international responsibility. The second group of contributions addresses problems arising in specific domains of international law, such as human rights law, international economic law, international criminal law, international environmental law, and the laws of war. In the case of each chapter, authors were invited to be selective and to concentrate on elaborating upon and responding to some questions that seemed especially pressing or interesting to them. No attempt was made by any author, or combination of authors, to offer a comprehensive discussion of the legal or philosophical questions arising within their topic. Instead, each author has had to limit their chapter's scope of coverage in order to enhance its depth.

1. General Issues

The first pair of chapters offer necessarily highly selective perspectives on themes within the vast terrain of the history of the philosophy of international law. The two chapters are ordered chronologically, around a divide in the history of international ideas: Benedict Kingsbury and Benjamin Straumann discuss the international political and legal thought of Grotius, Hobbes, and Pufendorf, while Amanda Perreau-Saussine addresses that of Kant and some of his followers. According to Kingsbury and Straumann, Grotius, Hobbes, and Pufendorf differed in their views

---

[52] Nor did we adopt the policy of ensuring that at least one of the authors on any given topic is a professional international lawyer. This is because this book is, first and foremost, a contribution to the *philosophy* of international law, and philosophy is a discipline with its own distinctive questions, approaches, and traditions of thought.

of obligation in the state of nature (where *ex hypothesi* there is no state), on the extent to which they regarded sovereign states as analogous to individuals in the state of nature, and in the effects they attributed to commerce as a driver of sociability and of norm-structured interactions not dependent on an overarching state. In her chapter, Perreau-Saussine highlights the limits of reading Kant's philosophy of international law as independent of his moral philosophy, arguing that in Kant juridical or external freedom and moral freedom (autonomy) are mutually dependent ideals. She goes on to trace the relationship between Kant's plan for peaceful international federation and his account of the moral obligations to institute systems of coercive, republican domestic law and to become members of an ever-expanding, enlightened ethical community, a 'universal republic based on the laws of virtue'.

Allen Buchanan's chapter on the legitimacy of international law characterizes legitimacy as the right to rule. It includes two main elements: the legitimate institution must be morally justified in attempting to govern (must have the moral liberty-right or permission to try to govern) in the sense of issuing rules (that prescribe duties for various actors) and attempting to secure compliance with them by imposing costs for non-compliance and/or benefits for compliance; and those toward whom the rules are directed (chiefly, though not exclusively states) have substantial, content-independent moral reasons for compliance and others (including citizens of states) have substantial content-independent moral reasons for supporting the institution's efforts to secure compliance with its directives or at least have substantial, content-independent moral reasons not to interfere with those efforts. Buchanan then identifies six key questions pertaining to the legitimacy of international law and discusses potential answers. John Tasioulas also adopts a conception of legitimate authority as the 'right to rule' but argues, in contrast to Buchanan, that the Razian normal justification condition is the appropriate standard for determining the legitimacy of international law. He outlines and assesses four broad challenges to the legitimacy of international law: the exceptionalist claim that some states are not bound by (certain) features of the international legal order which nonetheless bind other states; the claim that international law lacks legitimacy in virtue of the parochial values (or orderings thereof) that it embodies, distinguishing between sceptical and pluralist versions of this objection; the freedom-based contention that the legitimacy of international law is severely diminished in light of a due regard for state sovereignty; and formal and procedural constraints on the legitimacy of international law.

The third pair of chapters pertains to international democracy. Both authors agree in their assessment of the democratic illegitimacy of current global institutions, but disagree as to how their democratic credentials can be redeemed and also, therefore, about the needed institutional reforms. Thomas Christiano sketches an account of the moral basis of inherent legitimacy grounded in a fundamental principle of justice entitled the principle of public equality and concludes that the current international legal system is not legitimate on this criterion. He then defends what he calls the system of Fair Democratic Association. He argues that even as an ideal, the case cannot be made for global democracy. Christiano argues tentatively that the system of fair democratic association is superior to international democracy under current and reasonably foreseeable conditions. Philip Pettit outlines a neo-republican response to the same problem. He focuses on two distinctive issues. One is the membership problem regarding which entities are to play the role, in the international context, corresponding to the role played by non-dominated citizens in the domestic context. His answer is that it is legitimate domestic states or states that can be made legitimate. The other is the imbalance problem, which concerns how such states can be equally empowered in fashioning the international order. Pettit argues that there is no easy answer, but that there are no grounds for despair.

Samantha Besson and David Lefkowitz, in their chapters on the sources of international law, criticize the allegation that international law in general, and customary international law in particular, constitutes not a legal system but a primitive legal order. They both adopt a positivist approach to international law and explore difficult questions regarding the identification of international law on that basis, disagreeing about the exact relationship between international law and morality and between international legality and legitimacy. Samantha Besson develops a normative positivist argument about the legality of international law and its sources that corresponds to a democratic (coordination-based) account of the legitimacy of international law-making processes. Against that background, she discusses the existence and contours of secondary rules in international law and of a rule of recognition, in a way that illuminates the differences and the relations between domestic, regional, and international law (internal and external legal pluralism). In his contribution, David Lefkowitz discusses three rival accounts of the relationship between morality and the validity of international law, with a focus on international human rights. He then turns to the relationship between the sources of international law and its legitimacy and proposes a consent-based account of legitimacy and modifications of the current international law-making processes to make it fit that account. Finally, Lefkowitz discusses the legality of customary law and the existence of secondary rules of customary law-making.

In his chapter on international adjudication, Andreas Paulus observes that third party adjudication continues to be the exception to the rule of 'auto-interpretation' of international law by its subjects. He argues that international adjudication needs to remain within the bounds of its jurisdiction as determined by states, but should within this framework consciously embrace a larger role for consensus on values emerging in the international legal community. Donald H. Regan's chapter replies to Paulus on three main points. He begins by arguing that if our goal is to understand the activity of judging, the most important distinctive feature of international adjudication is not the absence of compulsory jurisdiction and generally reliable enforcement, but rather the difficulty of identifying sources of law such as custom and general principles. He then argues that the multiplicity of treaty regimes is not currently a major problem and criticizes the International Law Commission's expansive reading of Article 31.3(c) of the Vienna Convention on the Law of Treaties. Finally, Regan discusses the WTO's treatment of so-called 'extra-regime values' and claims that authors usually misapprehend how the WTO actually deals with conflicts between trade and other values.

Both chapters on sovereignty start from the paradox of the bound sovereign and agree that sovereignty is not only compatible with moral and international legal constraints but also that it has moral value. Timothy Endicott contends that a state is sovereign if it has complete power within a political community and complete independence. It may seem that the idea of sovereignty is objectionable because of two moral principles, or incoherent because of a paradox. The paradox is that a sovereign state must be capable of binding itself and must also be unable to bind itself. The moral principles are that no state can justly exercise complete power internally or complete independence (since complete independence would imply freedom from norms of *jus cogens*, and from interference even when it perpetrates mass atrocities). An analogy with human autonomy allows Endicott to show that the paradox is only apparent, and that the moral principles are compatible with state sovereignty. Sovereignty is to be understood as internal power and external freedom that are complete for the purposes of a good state. In her contribution, Jean Cohen argues that there are good empirical, normative, and political reasons to affirm the compatibility between state sovereignty and supranational law. She argues for a dualistic world system in which sovereign states and globalizing transnational and supranational institutions, based in part on cosmopolitan principles, can and should continue to coexist. She develops a theoretical framework for 'squaring the circle', utilizing the key concepts of changing sovereignty regimes and constitutional pluralism.

Both chapters on international responsibility contend that one cannot evaluate the current system of international responsibility without comparing the rights and obligations assumed to attach to states with those assumed to attach to governments, nations, collectives, nongovernmental institutions, and individuals. In their jointly authored chapter, James Crawford and Jeremy Watkins discuss the system of international legal responsibility to which states are subject when they violate their international obligations. They address the question of whether it is fair to impose civil liability on states when this has the effect of making whole populations pay the price for the misdeeds of their leaders and officials. An argument is then presented which is designed to show that the current law not only avoids the ethical objections which are sometimes directed against it, but also conforms to a positive standard of fairness which can be articulated in terms of hypothetical consent. Liam Murphy turns to the broader topic of international responsibility and takes it beyond the state. A foundational issue for Murphy is the moral status of states. The chapter explores the merits of an instrumental account. Such an account defuses the objection that state responsibility in international law imposes an illegitimate kind of collective responsibility, but at the same time explains why the moral justification of the state system remains an open question.

2. Specific Issues

The chapters on human rights begin with Joseph Raz's provocative critique of traditional philosophical theories of human rights, exemplified by the work of Alan Gewirth and James Griffin, which conceive of human rights in purely moral terms, as essentially moral rights possessed by all human beings simply in virtue of their humanity. Raz contends that such theories tend to overlook the distinction between values and rights and, in any case, lead to a conception of human rights that risks irrelevance because it does not adequately engage with contemporary human rights practice. In place of the traditionalist conception, Raz builds on the Rawlsian insight that human rights are the sub-set of moral rights that sets limits to state sovereignty: their violation provides a defeasible reason for intervention by external agents. However, he departs from Rawls in not conceiving of human rights as essentially triggers for *coercive* external intervention and resisting the latter's conflation of state sovereignty with legitimate authority. In his response, James Griffin restates his particular version of a traditionalist conception of human rights—the personhood theory, according to which human rights are protections of universal human interests in autonomy, liberty, and minimum provision—and responds to Raz's criticism that the theory cannot identify a plausible threshold at which a human right comes into existence. Griffin also makes independent objections to the 'political' interpretations of human rights advanced by Rawls and Raz. He concludes by offering some tentative suggestions on the unduly neglected question of the conditions under which human rights vindicated within moral philosophy should form part of international law. In his contribution John Skorupski shows greater sympathy for the sort of 'political' interpretation of human rights offered by Raz. Although the question of what rights exist is not treated by him as a political one, the utility of introducing a special sub-category of human rights in international law is. Beginning first with an account of the nature of rights in general, Skorupski contends that declarations of human rights should be understood as levers that help to eliminate serious violations of moral rights in all states. Among the criteria he identifies and elaborates for determining which rights should be declared to be human rights are universality, cross-state demandability, and efficacy.

The section on self-determination and minority rights begins with Will Kymlicka's comparison of the development of the idea of minority rights since 1989 in international law and in political philosophy. On the one hand, various attempts have been made to codify international standards relating to the treatment of ethno-cultural minorities, both at the global and regional levels. On the other hand, philosophers have sought to develop liberal theories of multiculturalism and of minority rights. Kymlicka focuses on how 'minorities' are defined and characterized in these respective traditions, and which minorities, if any, are regarded as possessing rights to self-government or self-determination. Jeremy Waldron's contribution relates specifically to the right to self-determination. He contends that it may be interpreted either (1) as a principle entitling the inhabitants of each distinct and politically viable territory to govern themselves in that territory, or (2) as a principle entitling the members of an ethnic or cultural community to govern themselves in a single territory. Waldron argues that interpretation (2) relies on conceptions of cultural distinctiveness that are outdated in the modern world, and that it yields a dangerous and misguided principle, even in more moderate versions. Interpretation (1), by contrast, is premised on the assumption that the point of political community is not to affirm cultural identity but to provide a framework for settling disputes, providing public goods, and facilitating interactions among strangers. Waldron outlines the Kantian basis of interpretation (1), which he regards as far more attractive than (2), showing how it embodies the notion of respect for individuals.

Both papers in Section X use the phenomenon of global poverty as a perspective from which to engage with the evaluation of international economic law. Thomas Pogge contends that while international human rights law enshrines certain pro-tections against specific severe harms, it also establishes and maintains structures that greatly contribute to human rights violations. Fundamental components of international law, as well as key international organizations such as the World Trade Organization, the International Monetary Fund, and the World Bank, systematically obstruct the aspirations of poor populations for democratic self-government, civil rights, and minimal economic sufficiency. In response, Pogge advocates the aboli-tion of such human rights deficits through the eradication of structural injustices in the existing global institutional architecture. In their chapter, Robert Howse and Ruti Teitel offer a sustained critique of Pogge's argument. They question whether the failure to adopt an international economic order of the sort Pogge advocates constitutes a violation of a duty of justice, on the grounds that it is very uncertain that Pogge's proposed alternative order is either feasible or would foreseeably make a significant contribution to the reduction or non-maintenance of extreme poverty. Although they find merit in some of Pogge's proposals, they would rather place emphasis on building a future international economic order that promotes human security and fulfils social and economic rights, rather than on a backward-looking argument that seeks to apportion responsibility for the failure to realize such an order hitherto.

James Nickel and Daniel Magraw's chapter on international environmental law covers three main topics. First, they defend as intelligible and workable the demand of international environmental law that the world's governments seriously take into account the interests of future generations in deciding issues involving resources and pollution. The second concerns philosophical issues about value raised by the requirements of international environmental law that species and ecosystems be protected. Here they express doubts about whether plausible accounts of the intrinsic value of nature can generate high-priority environmental rights and duties. The third topic is international environmental law's attempt to promote measures that mitigate and adapt to climate change, regarding which they defend a polluter pays approach to dealing with the costs of dealing with climate change. In his contribution, Roger Crisp contends that obligations should be attributed only to persons and that we should not understand obligations to future generations as a duty of fairness. He criticizes Nickel and Magraw's critique of the claim that nature has inherent intrinsic value, and proposes the following alternatives to their general approach: (1) environmental virtue ethics; and (2) a dualistic view combining a form of consequentialism with a self-regarding principle. Crisp argues that justice between generations requires at most giving priority to the worse-off who do or will exist, regardless of our choices. The 'repugnant conclusion' for well-being-maximizing principles when applied to issues of population is discussed. Crisp closes with some reflections on the implications of deep disagreement for ethical theory and for the making of international environmental law.

After presenting a brief history of the evolution of ideas about both the morality of war and the laws of war, Jeff McMahan contends that although the laws of war are neutral as between those who fight in just wars and those who fight in wars that are unjust because they lack a just cause, morality in fact imposes far greater restrictions on the latter than on the former. Whilst McMahan acknowledges pragmatic reasons why the law must at present diverge from morality in this way, he insists that our aim should be to design institutions that can gradually secure increasing convergence between the law and morality in this area. Henry Shue, in his companion paper, argues that McMahan's proposal mistakenly over-moralizes war. In particular, his attempt to formulate rules of war permitting attacks only against those who are morally liable to attack would require assessments of individuals that are impossible to make during combat. Instead, Shue suggests shoring up the prohibition on attacking non-combatants against its current erosion by the bombing practices of the most advanced air forces, and urgently resisting the progressively more permissive reading of the legally crucial category of 'military objective'.

Existing international law prohibits humanitarian intervention except with the prior authorization of the Security Council. Thomas Franck's chapter considers whether the law should be reformed to confer a 'right' to humanitarian intervention. Noting problems revealed by history with establishing such a right, Franck proposes instead a 'second-order' response that clarifies the terms of the putative right and establishes reliable institutional mechanisms for determining when the conditions for exercising it have been satisfied. More specifically, he argues that in the case of a 'technical' failure to authorize intervention under existing law (one due to the opposition of one or two veto states), the case for strict compliance is weakened, potentially constituting mitigation that approximates exculpation. Repeated Security Council failure may eventually lead from a practice of selective mitigation to a change in the relevant norm, but this has not yet occurred and is unlikely to be successful in the absence of reliable procedures for verifying humanitarian crises and assessing the motives and means of the would-be interveners. Danilo Zolo's contribution questions whether Franck has formulated adequate criteria for distinguishing between genuine and insincere or opportunistic humanitarian interventions. In particular, Franck's claim that humanitarian intervention 'is justifiable if, demonstrably, it saves substantially more lives than it sacrifices' is argued to be an untenable, *ex post*, criterion. Zolo stresses that any war declared unilaterally is a war of aggression under international law and that military operations inevitably cause civilian casualties which impair their legitimacy. Most importantly, the fundamental human right to life cannot be evaluated in the aggregate, therefore no political authority is entitled to destroy the lives of innocent people in order to save the lives of others.

David Luban's chapter examines the legitimacy of international criminal trials and defends them against objections grounded in the principle of legality. It advances four principal theses. First, the centre of gravity in international criminal tribunals lies in the trials themselves more than the punishments inflicted. Second, the aim is norm projection. International trials are meant to project the message that mass atrocities are heinous crimes, not political deeds that exist 'beyond good and evil'. Third, the legitimacy of the tribunals derives from the fairness of their procedures and punishments, not their political pedigree. Fourth, that the two motivating arguments behind the principle of legality—concern about fair notice, and concern about despotic abuse of the power to punish—are less compelling in international criminal law than they are in domestic law. Antony Duff's chapter focuses on the question of what can give international criminal tribunals moral legitimacy and authority. It begins with a critique of Luban's attempt to ground their legitimacy in their procedural fairness, and bases an alternative account on a conception of the criminal trial as a process through which alleged wrongdoers are called to account. This conception highlights a crucial jurisdictional issue: who has the standing to call alleged wrongdoers to account—to whom are they answerable? A plausible answer in the context of domestic law is that they are called to account by their fellow citizens, as fellow members of the political community. Duff then explores whether it can be argued in the context of international law that for some crimes the wrongdoer should be answerable to humanity, in whose name international courts should act.

PART I

GENERAL ISSUES IN THE PHILOSOPHY OF INTERNATIONAL LAW

SECTION I

HISTORY OF THE PHILOSOPHY OF INTERNATIONAL LAW

STATE OF NATURE VERSUS COMMERCIAL SOCIABILITY AS THE BASIS OF INTERNATIONAL LAW:

Reflections on the Roman Foundations and Current Interpretations of the International Political and Legal Thought of Grotius, Hobbes, and Pufendorf

BENEDICT KINGSBURY AND BENJAMIN STRAUMANN[*]

I. INTRODUCTION

Three foundational approaches to international order and law beyond the state were framed in early to mid-seventeenth-century Europe, by Hugo Grotius (1583–1645),

* We would like to thank OUP's anonymous reader for the excellent comments.

Thomas Hobbes (1588–1679), and Samuel Pufendorf (1632–94), at the same time as the recognizable modern idea of the state was itself being framed. Grotius, Hobbes, and Pufendorf each took distinctive approaches to the problems of whether and how there could be any legal or moral norms between these states in their emerging forms. They differed in their views of obligation in the state of nature (where *ex hypothesi* there was no state), in the extent to which they regarded these sovereign states as analogous to individuals in the state of nature, and in the effects they attributed to commerce as a driver of sociability and of norm-structured interactions not dependent on an overarching state. The core argument of this chapter, presented in section II, is that the differences between them on these issues are of enduring importance. To situate them in what we regard as a key element of their intellectual context, that is the Greco–Roman lineage of ideas on law and on order and justice beyond the state, we outline in section I the Carneadean debate and argue for the importance of Roman law and of Greco–Roman political ideas in sixteenth-century writings of Vitoria, Vazquez, Soto, Gentili, and others whose works influenced the seventeenth-century writers. Section II builds on this view of the importance of Roman influences, in engaging with several current historiographical debates about interpretations of Grotius, Hobbes, and Pufendorf. Section III comments very briefly on the adaptation of, or responses to, some of these seventeenth-century ideas in certain strands of eighteenth- and early nineteenth-century thought, concerning what by the end of that period had become a recognizably modern idea of international law; the particular focus is on lines of development from David Hume and Adam Smith to Jeremy Bentham and Georg Friedrich von Martens.

Any inquiry of the sort we undertake here entails some confrontation with a fundamental question: Should contemporary thought on international politics and international law be shaped by understandings of its history? Many scholars now engaged in rich debates in the historiography of political thought concerning issues beyond the polity, especially the historiography of early modern European thought on these issues, bring to these debates a set of interests and questions that are tied to the world in which we live now. At the same time, several of the leading historians of political thought (particularly those associated with the Cambridge School) who have helped develop fresh and influential interpretations of early modern writers concerned with normative international thought, place great emphasis on studying these early writers strictly in their own context, and are rightly wary of anachronism in trying to make them speak to us today.[1] In our view, several of the most significant recent interpretations of early modern international political and legal thought, some of them adumbrated by historians linked to the Cambridge School, have much to offer those interested in current problems of international law. In this chapter we will try to demonstrate this. We will refer in particular to

---

[1] See the useful discussion of Quentin Skinner's methodological precepts by Boucher, D., 'New Histories of Political Thought for Old?', *Political Studies*, 31 (1983), 112.

debates related to the work of Richard Tuck on self-preservation as the foundation of Grotius's natural law, to interpretations Noel Malcolm advances of Hobbes's views of the state of nature, and to Istvan Hont's arguments about the development of ideas of commercial sociability from Pufendorf to Adam Smith. In engaging with current debates among historians of political thought about the orientations and commitments of these thinkers, we endeavour also to transpose these debates to questions about international law with which these modern historians are not necessarily so centrally concerned. To foreshadow three basic questions we will address in this way:

1. Did Grotius construct a natural law based on self-preservation, as a means to meet the sceptical objections of Montaigne and Charron (as Tuck argues)?; or should Grotius be read as building natural law in a Ciceronian tradition?
2. What is the significance of Hobbes's view of the relation between individual and state, and of his essentially prudential rather than moral account of natural law beyond the state? Or, to put it another way: Are the political realists right about Hobbes, or can he plausibly be read (as Malcolm does) as a philosopher of international peace?
3. What has been the importance of the understanding, which Istvan Hont presents as extending from Pufendorf to Adam Smith and beyond, of commerce as a driver of social and moral order beyond the state?

We will argue in this chapter that the differences between views held by (and taken of) Grotius, Hobbes, and Pufendorf on core issues concerning the sources and nature of law and morality on matters reaching beyond a single polity will continue to be important in the future philosophy of international law. In some basic commitments, however, Grotius, Hobbes, and Pufendorf were all part of one enterprise, and must be read together. Each was acutely interested, for biographical as well as intellectual reasons, in the emergence of modern states as means to overcome civil war and religious strife. We believe it is fair to see some commonality in the engagement of each author, albeit in different ways, with the *salus populi* and reason of state. Grotius, Hobbes, and Pufendorf (as later Hume, Smith, and Bentham) all rejected the Machiavellian *ragione di stato* tradition of republicanism requiring expansionism. But all of them can be read as engaging in some way with the need to commit the sovereign to the *salus populi* while ensuring the sovereign could act to advance the *salus populi* for reasons of state. Grotius's emphasis on individual and collective self-preservation through the right of war can be read as a juridification of reason of state,[2] although his was less a political theory in the narrow sense than a theory of the norms that apply in a state of nature, understood not as a hypothetical order preceding a hypothetical social contract, but rather

---

[2] This is how Grotius is read by Hont, I., *Jealousy of Trade: International Competition and the Nation-State in Historical Perspective* (Cambridge, Mass.: Harvard University Press, 2005), 15.

as the actual natural state existing in the areas of the high seas leading to the East Indies, and in international relations more generally. To the extent that this natural law system had political implications, Grotius's accommodation of systems of divided sovereignty and constitutional limits on powers of specific rulers under agreements with their peoples gave a deeper and more context-specific meaning to the ruler's duties to uphold the *salus populi*. Hobbes sought to get away from ideas of divided sovereignty, multiplicity of representation, and popular sovereignty, instead treating the people simply as a multitude until unified by the creation of the state as the representative legal person. The sovereign upheld the *salus populi* by resolving internal conflict and assuring external defence. Pufendorf treated the *salus populi* (the security and the welfare of the people) as the supreme law (divine law excepted), thus imposing duties and constraints on the sovereign, but also freeing and indeed requiring the sovereign to act outside the positive law where reason of state required. Each was interested in the practice of politics, but in different ways. It must also be kept in mind that, while each of them wrote in juridical terms about practical politics, none had the kind of view of the relations of theory and practice that in the eighteenth century began to characterize what was becoming a field of international law, a view articulated to some extent in Vattel's *Law of Nations* (1758) and brought to one methodological culmination in the compendious collections of materials on practice by Georg Friedrich von Martens (from the 1780s to the 1820s).

II. Greco–Roman and Sixteenth-Century Foundations for Law Beyond the State

All of the seventeenth-century European thinkers we will refer to in this chapter drew heavily on the Greco–Roman classical tradition, in which ideas about empire and about the applicability of law beyond the territorial state and its citizenry had become a significant issue not later than the fifth century BC once the city-state of Athens had assembled an empire. We regard this tradition as essential to understanding the thought of these seventeenth-century writers with regard to law beyond the state, and will seek in this section to identify some ways in which this is so.

Probably the most significant Greco–Roman philosophical assessment of the moral implications of imperialism was that put forward in the mid-first century BC by the Roman orator and statesman Marcus Tullius Cicero.[3] Cicero's *Republic* has as its object the ideal constitution and government which Cicero identified with the constitution and government of the early and middle Roman Republic. This was the period that had seen the development of Rome from being one among many cities

---

[3] Another is the Melian dialogue in Thucydides, *History of the Peloponnesian War*, bk. v, 85–113.

constituting the Latin League to being the dominant power in the Mediterranean and beyond, exerting both direct rule over six provinces and controlling adjacent territories indirectly through diplomatic activity.

After discussing constitutional theory merely in terms of prudential criteria such as stability, effective rule, and longevity, Cicero in book three of the dialogue moves towards a *moral* consideration of the Roman commonwealth, framing it as an exchange of arguments modelled on a pair of famous speeches given by the Academic sceptic Carneades in Rome in 155 BC, speeches in which Carneades had argued, first for the importance of justice for a polity, and then, in the second speech, against its importance. Two things are particularly significant about Cicero's reframing of Carneades' speeches. First, Cicero turned the sequence of the speeches on its head, thus beginning with the sceptical challenge to justice and assigning the defence of justice the last word; and second, when adapting what he knew about Carneades' arguments for his own dialogue, Cicero applied the controversial discussion of the importance of justice for politics to the *international realm*, thus extending political theory beyond the *polis* and rendering Rome's acquisition of an empire a subject fit for normative, moral consideration.[4]

It is thus fair to say that book three of Cicero's *Republic* has been among the most important of the early Western philosophical treatments of imperial justice, bringing moral philosophy to bear on Rome's rule, beyond the borders of a given polity. To justify the applicability of any particular norms to trans-border issues, it could not possibly be sufficient merely to say that they were the norms of a favoured city-state. These norms would have to be justified by criteria of utility and self-interest (as Philus, the alias for Carneades, is made to argue in the *Republic*), or by criteria of justice, largely framed in Stoic natural law[5] and Roman just war terms (as Laelius, delivering the pro-justice speech in the *Republic*, maintains). Natural law provides the yardstick for gauging the justice of imperial rule and conquest, and its provisions as presented by Cicero are of a moral kind derived from Stoic ethics, not, as Carneades would have it, merely prescriptions for self-preservation appealing to our self-interest. The Roman legal provisions concerning the waging of a just war embody (in Laelius' and Cicero's view) rules of natural law.

In the sixteenth-century controversy over the justice of the Spanish conquests and the overseas empire, the Carneadean debate loomed large. Both proponents and adversaries of the Spanish conquest and rule used the Roman Empire and its forcible expansion as a prime analogy, with Augustine's ambiguous account of the justice of the Roman Empire in *City of God* serving as the main text for both sides.[6] Critics of

---

[4] For the relation between Cicero and the original Carneadean debate, see Zetzel, J. E. G., 'Natural Law and Poetic Justice: A Carneadean Debate in Cicero and Virgil', *Classical Philology*, 91/1 (1996), 297.

[5] For Stoic political theory, see Schofield, M., *The Stoic Idea of the City* (Chicago: University of Chicago Press, 1999).

[6] See Lupher, D., *Romans in a New World: Classical Models in Sixteenth-Century Spanish America* (Ann Arbor: University of Michigan Press, 2003).

Roman and Spanish imperial rule, notably the Dominican theologian Domingo de Soto, argued that the Romans' right to the territories they conquered was 'in force of arms alone', the Romans having 'subjugated many unwilling nations through no other title than that they were more powerful'.[7] Defenders of imperialism such as Juan Ginés de Sepúlveda also drew heavily on Augustine's and Lactantius's renderings of the Carneadean debate in Cicero's *Republic*. Importance continued to be given in the seventeenth century to the Carneadean debate, and to Roman political and legal theory more broadly. This orientation helps explain why natural law and the law of nations was so attractive to early modern writers who were defending imperial expansion on grounds of just war waged according to the rules of the *ius naturale* and *gentium*. Writers such as the Spanish jurist and official Ayala perceived Carneades as an orator challenging the justice of Roman imperialism and just war, rather than as an Academic philosopher expressing moral scepticism,[8] and they often countered this challenge with the arguments adumbrated in Laelius' speech in the *Republic*. Protestant lawyers such as Gentili and Grotius, who were steeped in this Roman background, built on it in their normative thinking about law and politics beyond the polity.[9] The fundamental question, which had by then arisen prominently as a consequence of the European colonial expansion, endures in international thought today: are there norms outside, and applicable to, the state? If any such norms exist, are they merely of a prudential nature, or do they rise to the level of moral or legal norms?

For Alberico Gentili, a civilian jurist, it was possible to apply rules taken from the Roman law of the *Institutes* and the *Digest* to the relations between different European polities and to some relations beyond Europe. The Spanish scholastics from Soto and Francisco de Vitoria onwards had already done this (to the extent they were sufficiently versed in Justinian's law code), drawing on the Roman law concepts of natural law and the law of nations (*jus gentium*) in order to apply them to the behaviour of Spain overseas, thus effectively using the universality of these legal ideas against the jurisdictional claims of the old universalist powers, the pope and the emperor. Gentili explicitly put forward the claim that the Roman law was valid in the extra-European domain and between sovereign polities and empires, on the ground that Justinian's rules, or at least some of them, were declaratory of the *jus naturale* and *gentium*:

[T]he law which is written in those books of Justinian is not merely that of the state, but also that of the nations and of nature; and with this last it is all so in accord, that if the empire were destroyed, the law itself, although long buried, would yet rise again and diffuse itself

---

    [7] de Soto, D., *Relección 'De Dominio'*, in Brufau Prats, J. (ed. and trans.) (Granada: Universidad de Granada, 1964), 150.

    [8] See Tuck, R., *The Rights of War and Peace: Political Thought and International Order from Grotius to Kant* (Oxford: Clarendon Press, 1999), 5; Tuck, R., 'Grotius, Carneades and Hobbes', *Grotiana New Series*, 4 (1983), 43.

    [9] For Grotius and his use of the classics, see Straumann, B., *Hugo Grotius und die Antike* (Baden-Baden: Nomos, 2007).

among all the nations of mankind. This law therefore holds for sovereigns also, although it was established by Justinian for private individuals[10]

This Roman law heritage is one of the keys to understanding important fissures in how a pivotal early modern concept of political thought—the state of nature—was elaborated and understood. Part of what distinguished the various early modern writers from each other with regard to their respective theories of international norms was differences in the views they held of rights and obligations in the realm external to established polities.

Before turning to make this argument, we note one implication of it, namely that the distinction frequently drawn between the traditions of scholasticism and humanism is not, in our view, central in distinguishing the views the seventeenth-century writers held of international relations, transnational normativity, and the state of nature. Modern studies of the international political thought of the early modern epoch often associate 'humanist' accounts of international relations with vigorous strategies of self-preservation and imperialist aggrandizement, and 'scholastic' accounts with a richer *corpus* of moral and legal constraints that reach beyond the established polities.[11] In evolutionary terms, Aristotelian and Thomist conceptions of justice underpin the scholastic tradition from Aquinas to the Spanish scholastics of Salamanca, and then the humanists, breaking with the scholastics, are said to combine a fresh account of natural rights with a Roman tradition of reason of state, drawing on Cicero and Tacitus and acknowledging to a large degree the force of sceptical anti-realist and subjectivist arguments in the domain of morals. Richard Tuck presents this humanist tradition as leading from Gentili and especially Grotius up to its most radical representative, Thomas Hobbes. Clearly the humanist and scholastic traditions are each important for the content of various doctrines. Our argument, however, is that the traditions these writers were drawing upon did not determine the content of their views on such key issues as self-interest and imperial expansion. For example, the humanist jurist Vázquez de Menchaca, in his *Controversiae illustres* (1564), quoting extensively from Roman literature and Roman law, was among the most ardent critics of the Spanish imperial endeavour, more critical in fact than any of the Spanish theologians. Affirming a strong belief in the natural liberty of all human beings,[12] Vázquez rejected any arguments designed to bestow title to overseas territories based on religious[13] or civilizational superiority.[14]

---

[10] Gentili, A., 'De iure belli libri tres', trans. Rolfe, J. C. in *The Classics of International Law*, no. 16, vol. ii (Oxford: Clarendon Press, 1933), 17.

[11] See, e.g., Tuck, R., *The Rights of War and Peace* (above, n. 8); Piirimäe, P., 'Just War in Theory and Practice: The Legitimation of Swedish Intervention in the Thirty Years War', *Historical Journal*, 45/3 (2002), 499.

[12] Vázquez de Menchaca, F., '*Controversiae illustres*', in Rodriguez Alcalde, F. (ed.), *Controversiarum illustrium aliarumque usu frequentium libri tres*, vol. ii (Valladolid: Talleres tipográficos 'Cuesta', 1931), 1. 10. 4–5. (A belief taken from Roman law; see *Institutes*, 1. 3.)

[13] Ibid. 2. 24. 1–5.

[14] Ibid. 1. 10. 9–12; 2. 20. 10; 2. 20. 27. On Vázquez's political and legal thought see Brett, A., *Liberty, Right and Nature. Individual Rights in Later Scholastic Thought* (Cambridge: Cambridge University Press, 1997),

Such arguments had on the other hand been supported both by humanists such as Sepúlveda and theologians in the medieval tradition, such as Suárez. Gentili, while in some sense a humanist and influenced by Machiavelli's account of statecraft,[15] in *De Jure Belli* (1598) eschews the humanist practice of justifying wars by reference to 'imperial power and glory'.[16] Gentili's doctrine of just war instead relies on more or less orthodox criteria for just war supplemented with reasoning from Roman law.[17] In his *De armis Romanis* (1599), a work in two books putting forward, in a Carneadean vein, first an accusation of the Roman Empire and then a defence, Gentili defends the justice of the Roman Empire and its imperial wars on grounds of natural law,[18] precisely as Cicero had made Laelius do in the *Republic*.

We contest Richard Tuck's claim that the 'new' humanist natural rights tradition established its doctrine of natural law as a defence against moral scepticism by 'building' the sceptical assumption of self-preservation 'into its theories',[19] yielding only a morally shallow set of rights and duties. The humanist Grotius, writing in support of the United Provinces' imperial expansion, set out to refute Carneades' claims as presented in Cicero's *Republic*, it is true—but it had been Carneades (or rather Philus) who had conjured up a natural order consisting purely of self-interest, while Grotius would draw upon the rich combination of Stoic natural law and Roman legal concepts that had already underpinned Laelius's response to Carneades in the *Republic* and which refused to acknowledge self-interest as the only basis of political life, evoking a Roman theory of international justice instead.[20] Thomism and canon law were undoubtedly important for the development of early modern international thought. The traditions Tuck discusses certainly provided part of the reason why authors such as Grotius removed Roman law concepts from their jurisdictional origins and couched them in a language of natural law. But in Grotius's elaborate system of natural law and natural rights, the influence of ancient political and legal thought, particularly the influence of Roman law, is of central importance.

165–204; for his stance on empire and the law of nations, see Pagden, A., *Lords of all the World: Ideologies of Empire in Spain, Britain and France, c. 1500–c. 1800* (New Haven/London: Yale University Press, 1995), 56–62.

[15] Although Gentili certainly did not start out as a *legal* humanist, but as a rather explicit follower of the *mos Italicus* and Bartolus.

[16] Tuck, R., *The Rights of War and Peace* (above, n. 8), 23.

[17] See Haggenmacher, P., 'Grotius and Gentili: A Reassessment of Thomas E. Holland's Inaugural Lecture', in Bull, H., Kingsbury, B., Roberts, A. (eds.), *Hugo Grotius and International Relations* (Oxford: Clarendon Press, 1990), 133–76.

[18] Gentili, A., *De armis Romanis* (Hanoviae, 1599), 2. 2. 112 ff; 2. 7. 168.

[19] Tuck, R., *The Rights of War and Peace* (above, n. 8), 6.

[20] For Grotius's use of the Stoic idea of *oikeiosis*, see Straumann, B., '*Appetitus societatis* and *oikeiosis*: Hugo Grotius' Ciceronian Argument for Natural Law and Just War', *Grotiana New Series*, 24/25 (2003/2004), 41.

III. SEVENTEENTH-CENTURY VIEWS OF THE STATE OF NATURE: GROTIUS, HOBBES, AND PUFENDORF

Differences about the state of nature, and about the possibilities and basis of obligation in it, are at the core of the distinctions we draw between the approaches of Grotius, Hobbes, and Pufendorf to international law.

For Grotius in his *De Jure Belli ac Pacis* (1625), moral or legal norms can apply outside the polity, and not simply for reasons of expediency: 'great states', although seemingly containing 'in themselves all things required for the adequate protection of life', are still susceptible to the claims of the 'virtue which looks towards the outside, and is called justice',[21] making the standard of justice applicable to sovereign polities or their rulers. But where were these norms that should govern the natural state to be found? And were they legal or rather moral in character? Richard Tuck has argued strongly that Grotius's natural law is based ultimately on the universal human urge for self-preservation and consists only in 'an extremely narrow set of rights and duties'.[22] We understand Grotius's approach to norms in the state of nature as broader both in their content and in their basis. Like Gentili before him, Grotius thought that norms of private Roman law were applicable to subjects beyond the polity, both to private individuals and to sovereign polities. Like Gentili, he thought that certain Roman law norms were declaratory of natural law; but for these norms to be valid for sovereigns as well this was not sufficient—an analogy between polities and private individuals had first to be established. Well aware of the importance of this move, Grotius explicitly addressed the extension of private Roman law to the relations between polities and, after applying a discussion of servitudes by the Roman jurist Ulpian to the high seas, justified it thus: 'It is true that Ulpian was referring [. . .] to private law; but the same principle is equally applicable to the present discussion concerning the territories and laws of peoples, since peoples in relation to the whole of mankind occupy the position of private individuals'.[23]

This allowed Grotius to attribute natural rights and duties not only to sovereigns in the East Indies who were trading partners of his own country, the expansionist Dutch Republic, but also to private entities such as the Dutch East India Company,

---

[21] Grotius, H., *De Jure Belli ac Pacis* (1625), prol. 21.
[22] Tuck, R., *The Rights of War and Peace* (above, n. 8), 6.
[23] Grotius, H., *De iure praedae*, 12, fo. 105 (*Mare liberum* 5. 36).

and thus made for a rich account of the state of nature.[24] Grotius applied to places that had remained in a natural state, such as the high seas, and to the relations between and across sovereign polities, a doctrine of natural rights modelled on certain remedies from Roman law. Rights to self-defence, and certain property rights and contractual rights (all capable of being vested in individuals, sovereign states, and other entities), were embedded in Grotius's natural law and applicable beyond any given polity.[25] These subjective rights, best described as claim-rights in the Hohfeldian sense, were derived from a natural law system based on Aristotle's expletive justice. Both the natural law and the subjective natural rights flowing from it were held to be of a dual nature, moral as well as legal. This meant that the rules and rights of Grotius's state of nature were not only requirements of justice, but also of *law*, in a narrow sense—that is to say, natural law, which is what Grotius termed law (*jus*) 'in the proper sense'.[26] Defining law in terms of justice by stipulating that everything that was not unjust was lawful, Grotius's theory of natural legal norms responded exclusively to the demands of justice, yielding effectively a theory of practical ethics couched in legal terms. This offered one solution to what remains a pressing problem in international legal theory—namely the source of validity for international obligations.[27] Grotius's criteria for validity of law in *De Jure Belli ac Pacis* thus blend source criteria with content criteria in a way apt to address jurisprudential problems concerning the nature of international law that remain fundamental in modern times, when a perceived lack of settled formal criteria for sources has led some scholars to assume that international law, not amounting to a legal system, is but a set of separate rules.[28] The sources are natural law, divine volitional law, and human volitional law—the human volitional law encompasses sub-municipal orders (such as *paterfamilias* over wife/children, and master over slave), municipal laws (*jus civile*, and incidental agreement among municipal laws, which is not *jus gentium*), and *jus gentium* (true law, and that which produces merely external effects).[29] Another source criterion lies in the requirement that a rule, in order to be of the *jus gentium*, must conform with the understandings and practices of all nations or all of the better nations. Additional content criteria are introduced because Grotius requires, for proof of natural law, that it conform with right reason and hence not be unjust. A rule might well be part of the *jus gentium* without being part of natural law. For example, *De Jure Belli ac Pacis* treats the

---

[24] A term (*status naturae*) used by Grotius even before Hobbes; see Grotius, H., *De Jure Belli ac Pacis* (above, n. 21), 2. 5. 15. 2; 3. 7. 1. 1. For a more detailed account of Grotius's notion of the state of nature, see Straumann, B., ' "Ancient Caesarian Lawyers" in a State of Nature', *Political Theory*, 34/3 (2006), 328.

[25] This suggests that the subjects of private Roman law served as models for the emerging early modern states rather than the other way round, see Tuck, R., *The Rights of War and Peace* (above, n. 8), 8 ff. For this argument, see Straumann, B., *Hugo Grotius und die Antike* (above, n. 9), 32 ff.

[26] Grotius, H., *De Jure Belli ac Pacis* (above, n. 21), prol. 8.

[27] See Hart, H. L. A., *The Concept of Law* (2nd edn., Oxford: Oxford University Press, 1994), 213–37, esp. 224 f.

[28] See ibid. 232–7; for criteria for a legal system and the idea of a basic rule of recognition, see ibid. 79–99.

[29] Grotius, H., *De Jure Belli ac Pacis* (above, n. 21), 1. 1. 13–14.

slavery that results from capture in war as a legal structure of the *jus gentium*, not of natural law.[30] These multiple legal orders are not necessarily in strictly hierarchical relationship one with the other, nor need they be strictly horizontal, but they all derive their validity ultimately from the natural law.

Grotius's theory of natural justice and his inclusion of diverse actors as subjects of natural law has important further implications: individuals or groups maintain certain natural rights even within a polity, so that states are parts of a larger legal order, susceptible to demands of justice even across borders. This leads Grotius to a permissive attitude to what is now called humanitarian intervention.[31] Any violation of the natural law and the rights it gives rise to triggers the right to punish,[32] a right parasitic upon the existence of a strong normative framework. For Grotius, the parallel between individuals and states is complete: polities have the same set of rights and duties in the state of nature as individuals, including the natural right to punish violators of the law of nature. While Gentili had already acknowledged a private victim's natural right to punish,[33] Grotius went further by asserting, against both theologians like Vitoria and humanists such as Vázquez and later Hobbes, a *general* right to punish.[34] The revolutionary potential of this doctrine was to become obvious in John Locke,[35] who enunciated the chief normative consequence of Grotius's teachings in his 'Second Treatise of Government':

And that all Men may be restrained from invading others Rights [. . .] the *Execution* of the Law of Nature is in that State, put into every Mans hands, whereby every one has a right to punish the transgressors of that Law to such a Degree, as may hinder its Violation. For the *Law of Nature* would, as all other Laws that concern Men in this World, be in vain, if there were no body that in the State of Nature, had a *Power to Execute* that Law.[36]

This was not only of deep importance to constitutional theory, but it also weakened both in Grotius and Locke the moral status of state sovereignty and could support, as already hinted at in Grotius's case, arguments in favour of intervention in another state's affairs by third parties.

---

[30]   Ibid. 2. 7 and 3. 14. Grotius did not accept that anyone was a slave by nature, but he accepted slavery by consent, by punishment of a delict, by capture, and in certain circumstances by birth to a mother who is a slave. Cf. Justinian's *Institutes*, 1. 3. 2: 'Slavery is an institution of the *jus gentium* by which one person is subjected to the ownership of another contrary to nature'. See Cairns, J., 'Stoicism, Slavery, and Law', *Grotiana New Series*, 22/23 (2001/2002), 197.

[31]   Grotius, H., *De Jure Belli ac Pacis* (above, n. 21), 2. 25. 6.

[32]   For Grotius's influential doctrine of a natural right to punish, see Straumann, B., 'The Right to Punish as a Just Cause of War in Hugo Grotius' Natural Law', *Studies in the History of Ethics*, 2 (2006), 1, available at <http://www.historyofethics.org/022006/022006Straumann.shtml>.

[33]   Gentili, A., *De iure belli*, 1. 18, pp. 136–7.

[34]   Grotius, H., *De Jure Belli ac Pacis* (above, n. 21), 2. 20. 40. 1. This general right was modelled upon a class of Roman penal actions, the *actiones populares*, which were open to any citizen in virtue of the public interest and not just to the injured party; see *Digest*, 47. 12. 3 pr.

[35]   See Tuck, R., 'The Rights of War and Peace' (above, n. 8), 82.

[36]   Locke, J., *Two Treatises of Government*, ed. Laslett (Cambridge: Cambridge University Press, 1967), 'Second Treatise', § 7, 271–2 (italics in the original).

In stark contrast to Grotius's notion of the state of nature is the view of the state of nature ordinarily attributed to Hobbes. Although Hobbes does refer to certain norms in the state of nature, they seem to us to be legal only in a metaphorical sense and moral only by name. It is characteristic that Hobbes does not acknowledge a natural right to punish: 'A Punishment, is an Evill inflicted by publique Authority', because the 'Right which the Common-wealth [. . .] hath to Punish, is not grounded on any concession, or gift of the Subjects'. This follows from Hobbes's conception of the state of nature, where 'every man had a right to every thing',[37] that is to say people in the natural state did not have, on Hobbes's account, claim-rights of any sort, but rather Hohfeldian privileges,[38] which cannot give rise to any duties on anybody's part. Consequently, there is nothing, no possible violation that could trigger a right to punish. In Hobbes's state of nature, rights and duties can thus be described as legal only in a very attenuated sense. Nor can they be described as moral if by 'moral' is meant anything going beyond self-interest.[39] There are no legal ones because according to Hobbes's legal theory, natural laws are called 'by the name of Lawes, but improperly: for they are but Conclusions',[40] mere principles, to which the basic obligation of the subjects in the state of nature, to preserve themselves, is owed. And there are moral ones only if one is willing to buy into Hobbes's exercise in renaming purely prudential grounds of obligation as moral ones. Opposing Hobbes's view to approaches prevalent in classical ethics, it could be said that in classical ethics there was a prevailing attempt to identify prudential with moral reasons for action by showing that to act morally is in one's own self-interest, that is to say by changing the meaning of and effectively re-defining 'self-interest' such that other-regarding, moral reasons become a requirement for acting in one's 'self-interest'. Hobbes, on the other hand, engaged in a re-definition of 'moral', so that self-interested action becomes a requirement of Hobbes's changed meaning of 'moral'. As in classical ethics, self-interest and morality in Hobbes thus do not seem to be in conflict—yet once Hobbes's exercise in renaming is understood, it becomes clear that Hobbes's state of nature is indeed conventionally 'Hobbesian' in that prudential self-interest rather than an independent sense of obligation to

---

[37] Hobbes, T., *Leviathan*, ed. Tuck, R. (Cambridge: Cambridge University Press, 1996), ch. 28, p. 214.

[38] See Hohfeld, W. N., *Fundamental Legal Conceptions As Applied In Judicial Reasoning* (New Haven: Yale University Press, 1964), 36. For an application of Hohfeld's analysis to Hobbes see Malcolm, N., *Aspects of Hobbes* (Oxford: Oxford University Press, 2002), 445.

[39] The following is based on Thomas Nagel's very persuasive interpretation of Hobbes's concept of obligation; Nagel, T., 'Hobbes's Concept of Obligation', *Philosophical Review*, 68/1 (1959), 68, 74: 'Hobbes's feeling that no man can ever act voluntarily without having as an object his own personal good is the ruin of any attempt to put a truly moral construction on Hobbes's concept of obligation. It in a way excludes the meaningfulness of any talk about moral obligation. [. . .] Nothing could be called a moral obligation which in principle never conflicted with self-interest'. The reason why there are no moral duties in the state of nature is thus that for Hobbes there are no such duties *tout court*.

[40] Hobbes, T., *Leviathan* (above, n. 37), ch. 15, p. 111. The laws of nature are not only obligatory as the commands of God, it is rather that obligations to the authority of God are derived from the laws of nature, to which the basic obligations are owed: Nagel, T., 'Hobbes's Concept' (above, n. 39), 75–8.

moral or legal norms drives behaviour in the state of nature.[41] There is no clash in Hobbes between personal aims and impartial morality, because Hobbes's redefined morality, starting from the single normative principle of rational self-interest, is not based on impartiality.

Noel Malcolm has made a stimulating case that Hobbes's state of nature is, with regard to international relations, much more substantively regulated than we have suggested above and than most interpreters of Hobbes have thought, with the dictates of natural law being applicable at the international level.[42] While Richard Tuck has interpreted Grotius and Gentili to be much more akin to Hobbes as traditionally understood, Malcolm presents a Hobbesian view of international relations much closer to Grotius, as traditionally understood. Malcolm maintains that Hobbes, in terms of what behaviour his take on international relations prescribed, was guarding against imperialism and therefore far from being a Machiavellian realist.[43] In terms of the jurisprudential justification of his normative outlook, Hobbes was, as Malcolm puts it using the idiom of modern jurisprudential disputes, a 'naturalist', and his state of nature 'not a realm of sheer amorality'.[44] Malcolm is undoubtedly correct in attaching weight to Hobbes's strong reservations against imperialism—but these reservations seem to us to be based on prudence, not on anything resembling a substantive notion of legal, let alone moral obligation.[45] Similarly, the breakdown of the analogy between states and individuals in Hobbes, the fact that the parallel between the interpersonal and international state of nature is not a complete one, might diminish the 'moral' duty of self-preservation as far as polities are concerned;[46] but, again, this diminution seems to occur for prudential reasons. If individuals were less secure in commonwealths than they contingently happen to be, commonwealths would not exist in the first place. It is thus not surprising that Hobbes's state of nature, lacking very substantive moral and legal norms, provides a continuing inspiration for so-called realist views, i.e. scepticism regarding international law and the applicability of moral standards to international affairs.[47]

The difference between Grotius and Hobbes with regard to their respective conceptions of the state of nature can be explained, at least in part, by the diverging purposes that the doctrines were at first supposed to serve. Whereas Grotius had developed his doctrine of a state of nature and the natural right to punish against

---

[41] In classical ethics, the relation between morality and self-interest is characterized by the identification of the *utile* with the *honestum* and *iustum*, and a certain redefinition of the *utile* takes place; not, however, without the attempt to show how that redefinition at a deeper level is in accord with the conventional understanding of expediency.

[42] Malcolm, N., *Aspects of Hobbes* (above, n. 38).   [43] Ibid. 441.

[44] Ibid. 439–40.

[45] See Hobbes, T., *De cive, the Latin Version*, ed. Warrender, H. (Oxford: Clarendon Press, 1983), ch. 13, para. 14, p. 202.

[46] Malcolm, N., *Aspects of Hobbes* (above, n. 38), 448.

[47] For the latter, see the criticism of Hobbes's position in Beitz, C., *Political Theory and International Relations* (Princeton: Princeton University Press, 1979), 11–66.

the backdrop of the need to show that the Dutch East India Company, even if acting on its own behalf as a private actor, had the right to wage a war of punishment against the Portuguese fleet in Southeast Asia, Hobbes's theory was a political one in a much narrower sense. Hobbes thus sought to theorize a strong form of political authority, whereas Grotius wanted to theorize an environment in which a strong overarching authority was *ex hypothesi* lacking. Thus the body of law Grotius presents in *De Jure Belli ac Pacis* is potentially applicable to many orderings (for example, a transnational commercial order) that are neither inter-state nor simply a single civil state.

Samuel Pufendorf's *De Jure Naturae et Gentium* (1672), the essentials of which were made highly accessible in his popular *De Officio Hominis* (1673), had a considerable influence on the reception and to some extent the integration of Grotian and Hobbesian international thought. But Pufendorf can also be read as having framed a distinctive approach: in the following paragraphs we will address one such reading put forward by Istvan Hont. Pufendorf distinguished between government established by (or at least understood by) Hobbesian contract (Hobbes's political union), and the non-contractual constitution of commercial society (the concord or consensus that Hobbes sought decisively to reject, but that Pufendorf was able to reframe not in a republican-political way but through a more modest conception of society). Pufendorf agreed with Hobbes that the reasons for instituting government are best understood by positing the idea of a contract, that law is the command of a superior, and that law depends for its validity not on its content but on the authority of whoever promulgates it, a view much different from Grotius's grounding of validity in natural law. Because of this, Pufendorf's ideas of government, of human law, and of non-deistic authority were treated by later thinkers as disjoint from Pufendorf's important argument that commercial sociability could create society without state or government, and that in such a society plain obligations could exist, and indeed reason and laws of nature derived from the command of God.

At the center of Istvan Hont's interpretation is the following claim:

Post-Hobbesian political theory can be said to have started with Pufendorf's reinstatement of utility as a force of social integration. Contemporaries recognized this. In the eighteenth century Pufendorf's adaptation of Hobbes's state of nature to the explanation of society came to be seen as the beginning of a distinct and separate school in natural jurisprudence. Pufendorf himself was credited with making 'society' a foundational category of modern political thought. [. . .] Although Pufendorf accepted that society was secondary in impor-tance to the [Hobbesian] political state, nonetheless he saw it as important enough to be theorized in its own right.[48]

---

[48]   Hont, I., *Jealousy of Trade* (above, n. 2), 45.

As Hont has pointed out, Pufendorf did not think collective sociability was natural quite in the same way as the drive to individual self-preservation is, but driven by the human need to cooperate stemming from incapacity and ever-growing wants. He contrasted the natural state of humans marked by *imbecillitas* (weakness) and *indigentia* (neediness), with the state of life produced by human industry, *cultura*. Society is formed as the means to overcome neediness. Commerce, and the *cultura* that is intertwined with commerce, thus corresponds with the formation and flourishing of society. This commercial society was not necessarily preceded by, and did not lead inexorably to, the contractual formation of the *civitas* (the state). In Hont's crisp assessment of Pufendorf's view: 'Hobbes was wrong in thinking that social diversity and the difficulty of survival required the creation of the *civitas*'.[49] Pufendorf illustrated the possibilities by reference to the society existing among neighbouring families in an agricultural community, and by the cross-border relations of international trade. The creation of a *civitas* depended on constitution of a state by a specific act of will—the adoption of a contract by which the participants surrender their natural liberty. Hont suggests that for Pufendorf this contract was the means to achieve not only security, but also the 'Prospect of living in a better Fashion and greater Plenty', especially in the burgeoning cities.[50]

Rulers should in ordinary times adhere both to the positive law of the state and to the natural law of relations beyond the polity—interest, sociality, reason, and commerce would normally require adherence to these. But the existence of legal norms did not mean that rulers of states must always be tightly constrained by them, nor that the juridical would necessarily dominate the political. As Horst Dreitzel observes, Pufendorf, while avoiding the language of reason of state, 'did not shirk from advocating the disarmament of citizens, the disempowerment of *potentes*, forbidding the formation of parties, and proscribing any innovation, using trade policy to disadvantage other states and cancelling treaties according to changes in the political situation'.[51] The question of when a breach of the applicable positive law was the right policy for the *salus populi* was one requiring the highest expertise in statecraft and in policy—it was not a question for ordinary judges, but nor was it a matter for capricious will or irresponsible decision.

---

[49] Hont, I., 'The Languages of Sociability and Commerce: Samuel Pufendorf and the Foundations of Smith's "Four Stages" Theory', in Pagden, A. (ed.), *Languages of Political Theory in Early Modern Europe* (Cambridge: Cambridge University Press, 1987), 271–316.

[50] Ibid. 275. See also LeGoff, J., 'The Town as an Agent of Civilization', in Cipolla, C. M. (ed.), *The Middle Ages* (London: Fontana, 1976).

[51] Dreitzel, H., 'Reason of State and the Crisis of Political Aristotelianism: An Essay on the Development of 17th Century Political Philosophy', *History of European Ideas*, 28 (2002), 163, 171. We draw here also on ongoing work by Martti Koskenniemi.

IV. From Commercial Sociability to Positive International Law in the Eighteenth Century: Hume, Smith, Vattel, Bentham, and Martens

Hobbes's political thought, which steadfastly denied any relevance to modern politics of what Hobbes believed were the dubious if ancient assertions that humans are naturally social or naturally political, generally had no great use for political economy, let alone for inter-state political economy, as a shaping force in politics.[52] It was Adam Smith who was able to construct a powerful and persuasive alternative to Hobbesian theory. Humans are born needy and must thus seek society, but Smith (like Pufendorf, Locke, and Hume) thought that the pursuit of material economic needs and desires was a substantial reason for sociability and for particular forms of social organization. Smith rejected Hobbes's 'state of nature' terminology, focusing instead on the developmental stage of economic organization in any particular society, from hunter-gatherers through pastoralists and settled agriculturalist to commercial society with a highly specialized division of labour and monetized exchange. Smith's brief histories included a place for reversal and decay, as with the destruction of Roman commercial society with its contracted-out military by pastoralist-warriors in the first cycle, then the destruction of the European feudal order under the economic burden of obsessive demand of the dominant classes for luxury goods to prove their status. But the culmination of Smith's account was a showing that post-feudal modern European liberty was integrally connected with modern commercial society. John Locke had sketched the rudiments of an evolutionary account correlating the development of political organization and structures of government with changing economic patterns, but these rudiments did not lead convincingly to Locke's own account (which purported to be empirical as well as normative) of modern English politics in which executive corruption had increased with economic affluence and was eventually overturned by revolutions which installed modern legislative supremacy based on popular consent. Smith agreed with his friend David Hume's powerful refutation of the Lockean claim that consent was the real basis of governmental authority. Smith instead proposed that authority depended in great measure on wealth, because the human tendency to sympathize much more with the rich in their success than with the poor in their misery aligns with such dependence of the poor on the rich as endures in modern commercial society. Authority in large societies typically depends much more on

---

[52] Hont, I., *Jealousy of Trade* (above, n. 2), 18–21.

the state of mind of the dependent, than it does on actual coercion or incentives deployed by the wielders of authority and their agents. The authority of the modern political state, which protects the anxious rich in their accumulations but also protects all or most of the citizenry in their basic liberty, was itself an outcome of the commercial society which made these accumulations and their distribution possible.

David Hume had defined a basic orientation to the law of nations: nations are like individuals in requiring mutual assistance, while being selfish and ambitious, yet are very different in other respects, so regulate themselves by a law of nations, which is superadded to the laws of nature but does not abolish them. Hume's three fundamental rules of justice apply to nations: the stability of possession (without which there is perpetual war), its transference by consent (upon the capacity for which, commerce depends), and the performance of promises. But while the mutual intercourse of nations on this basis is often advantageous or necessary, thus giving rise to natural obligations of interest and corresponding morality, 'the natural obligation to justice, among different states, is not so strong as among individuals, the moral obligation, which arises from it, must partake of its weakness'.[53]

Adam Smith shared this basic orientation, and did not himself develop much more explicitly the implications for international law and politics of his account of commercial society and of the twin roles of utility and authority. His persuasive rejection of mercantilism, and his insistence that closing the lines of commerce at national borders was usually (not always) a costly mistake, involved influential commitments in political philosophy as well as having immense practical importance. Among these commitments was a basic acceptance that vast economic inequality could be tolerated in states which embraced basic premises of political and juridical equality. This idea, that 'legal and political equality could coexist with economic inequality without causing endemic instability in modern Western States', was at the heart of what came in the early nineteenth century to be called liberalism, and it was not of course Smith's creation.[54] His importance was in showing how it might actually be achieved in parts of Europe, through private property, free markets without price controls in labour and essential goods such as foods, judicious intervention where necessity required it, and a suitable political order based on respect for law and legislative supremacy. The international legal order of Europe should thus be aimed at actuating and supporting these commitments. The grounds for such an international political and legal order were tied to the historical evolution of European commercial society (itself somewhat anomalous in Smith's view) rather than universals of nature; and they were secular rather than theological. Smith thus helped pave the way for the growing historicization, secularization, and European focus of international law. He was not himself insensible to global

---

[53] Hume, D., *A Treatise of Human Nature*, III. ii. 11.   [54] Hont, I., *Jealousy of Trade* (above, n. 2), 92 ff.

problems. He denounced the grotesque injustices of colonial treatment of Indians in the Americas. He struggled to see ways in which his particular idea of sympathy as a driver of society and authority could extend to relations between British commercial society and those immiserated Bengalis who increasingly supplied its wants. But his system of politics was not one in which redistributive justice was required, nor did imperfect rights and obligations carry much weight beyond sheer charity.

Although Smith lectured on jurisprudence, and paid considerable attention to law and legal institutions, his was not a jurisprudential theory in the way the theories of Gentili, Grotius, and Pufendorf had been. The jurisprudential implications of many of the commitments Smith had embraced were perhaps worked out most fully, at least in British thought, by Jeremy Bentham. Bentham differed from Smith in many respects, not least over the value of great reform projects. But Bentham's effort to base law on utility rather than on claims of natural rights, his enthusiasm for positive law and particularly for legislation over natural law, his commitment to demystification (including his showing that legal custom tended not to be utilitarian local practice but merely the customs among the judges), his condemnation of colonialism and imperial expansion on grounds of cost, all drew Smithian themes into what Bentham chose to name, apparently for the first time in English or the Romance languages, international law.

This line of development from Smith to Bentham was paralleled over the same period by German public law scholarship. In 1750, Gottfried Achenwall and Johann Stephan Pütter produced the first edition of what became Achenwall's *Elementa juris naturae*, a vast systematic effort to deduce natural law norms for real societies, based on a social view of the state of nature and on Christian Wolff's Leibniz-inspired ideas of self-perfectioning, and to integrate these with statistics and other positive empirical material on societies and government; this work was read carefully by Kant. Their short discussion of principles of the law between nations was soon echoed in much more expansive form by Vattel. Their method was refined by Martens (1756–1821), who assembled monumental compilations of treaties and other documents of official interaction between sovereigns (for the most part European sovereigns), to ground what he regarded as a public law of Europe. In Martens's thinking, speculations about the state of nature and right reason no longer played any external part—the positive legal materials he compiled were both the direct evidence of what was natural law, and the practical adaptation of natural law to the complexities of modern states and their interactions,[55] a tendency which helped to strengthen the primacy of state sovereignty, with a strong principle of non-intervention and autonomy.

---

[55] Koskenniemi, M., 'G. F. von Martens (1756–1821) and the Origins of Modern International Law', *NYU Institute for International Law and Justice Working Paper* (2006–1), <www.iilj.org>.

V. Conclusion

In this chapter we have sought to show the importance of current historiographical debates on different ideas about order and law beyond the state that were framed in Europe in the seventeenth century, presenting the ideas of Grotius, Hobbes, and Pufendorf as fundamentally distinct. Understandings of the ideas of, and especially the relations between the ideas of, Grotius, Hobbes, and Pufendorf, varied considerably in the seventeenth century and have varied in different ways ever since. Istvan Hont's interpretation of Pufendorf as having made 'society' into 'a foundational category of modern political thought' has a significant pedigree, but whether it will endure and become a dominant understanding will depend on further historiographical debates.[56] Noel Malcolm's interpretation of Hobbes's international thought also builds on some prior approaches, but seems destined to remain a minority position. Richard Tuck's interpretation of Grotius, although much contested, has by no means been decisively displaced. What is the importance of our present-day interpretation of the early theorists for today's international legal thought? On a genealogical level concerned with causes, the historical account can show us which tradition we are in fact part of, and may help identify some of the contingent features of that tradition—a vital prerequisite for any subsequent normative assessment of the tradition. Secondly, on an epistemic level concerned with reasons, we hope that historical accounts such as the one given here will contribute to a better understanding of the presuppositions of current international thought and thus enrich today's debates. This would seem to require a historiography of political thought that does not on *a priori* grounds preclude the possibility of certain questions that, remaining in important ways the same (enduring questions), have met with long-standing interest in the history of political thought, nor would this historiography of political thought seek to describe every work of political thought mainly in momentary terms as a political performance. Whether a work of political thought responds to enduring questions rather than to individual historical circumstances and whether it puts forward a proposition or argument that speaks to our concerns are empirical matters for historical investigation and theoretical matters for sustained reflection. The contemporary philosophy of international law must rest on both.

---

[56] Hont's approach has been contested, in different ways, by Palladini, F., *Samuel Pufendorf discepolo di Hobbes* (Bologna: Il Mulino, 1990) and several other works; by Saastamoinen, K., *The Morality of Fallen Man: Samuel Pufendorf on Natural Law* (Helsinki: Suomen Historiallinen Seura, 1995); and by Tully, J., *On the Duty of Man and Citizen According to Natural Law* (Cambridge: Cambridge University Press, 1991).

CHAPTER 2

IMMANUEL KANT ON INTERNATIONAL LAW

AMANDA PERREAU-SAUSSINE*

I. INTRODUCTION

In 1754, Jean Jacques Rousseau arranged with the Saint-Pierre family to edit the Abbé de Saint Pierre's works, focusing on his proposal for the creation of a Europe-wide federal government designed to respect both sovereignty and individuals' basic rights.[1] Rousseau did indeed publish extracts from Saint-Pierre's works, including the details of this scheme for a perpetual European alliance in which states would make financial contributions to a congress for the resolution of disputes, a

* The standard critical edition of Kant's works, to be completed in 2010, is *Kant's gesammelte Schriften* (Berlin: Georg Reimer, subsequently Walter de Gruyter, 1900–) edited by what is now the Berlin-Brandenburg *Akademie der Wissenschaften*. Quotations cited, indicated by the *Akademie* volume and pagination, are from the English translations by Mary Gregor of 'An Answer to the Question: What is Enlightenment?' (1784), 8. 33–42; 'Groundwork of the Metaphysics of Morals' (1785), 4. 385–463; *Critique of Practical Reason* (1788), 5. 1–271; 'On the Common Saying: That may be correct in theory, but it is of no use in practice' (1793), 8. 273–313; 'Toward Perpetual Peace' (1795), 8. 341–86; 'Metaphysics of Morals' (1797), 6. 203–493, all in *The Cambridge Edition of the works of Immanuel Kant: Practical Philosophy* (Cambridge: Cambridge University Press, 1996); by George di Giovanni of *Religion within the Boundaries of Mere Reason* (1793), 6. 1–202; and by Mary Gregor and Robert Anchor of *The Conflict of the Faculties* (1798), 7. 5–116 in *The Cambridge Edition: Religion and Rational Theology* (Cambridge: Cambridge University Press, 1996). Emphases are in the original. I am indebted to Nicholas McBride, Patrick Capps, Alix Cohen, Katrin Flikschuh, James Murphy, Onora O'Neill, Arthur Ripstein, Veronica Rodriguez-Blanco, members of University College London's 'Political theory' seminar group, the editors of this volume and OUP's reader for discussion and criticism of earlier drafts. Oxford's HLA Hart Fellowship scheme and the British Academy generously supported the research leave that allowed me to write this paper.

[1] Sully had published a similar proposal (as a 'Grand Design' of Henri IV) in his *Mémoires ou Œconomies Royales* (1638). William Penn's 'Essay towards the present and future peace of Europe' (1693) also outlined a design for an international arbitral tribunal.

congress with a president, legislative powers, a 'coercive force' to compel obedience to the federation's laws, and a prohibition on any state's withdrawal from the federation.[2]

Key to his proposal, Saint-Pierre argued, was a hard-headed understanding of human nature. He assumed human beings to be 'as they are, unjust, grasping and setting their own interest above all things': if the project remained unrealized, 'that is not because it is utopian; it is because men are crazy, and because to be sane in a world of madmen is in itself a kind of madness'.[3] But Rousseau concluded that Saint-Pierre underestimated the insanity of the world. For the scheme to be put into action:

> it would be essential that all the private interests concerned, taken together, should not be stronger than the general interest, and that everyone should believe himself to see in the good of all the highest good to which he can aspire for himself. But this requires a concurrence of wisdom in so many heads, a fortuitous concourse of so many interests, such as chance can hardly be expected ever to bring about. But, in default of such spontaneous agreement, the one thing left is force; and then the question is no longer to persuade but to compel, not to write books but to raise armies.[4]

Faced with the barbarities of warfare, optimistic writings of philosophers came to seem themselves obscene in their detachment from reality: 'Barbarous philosopher! Come and read us your book on the field of battle!'[5]

Immanuel Kant's 'Toward Perpetual Peace', structured like Saint-Pierre's essay as if itself a peace treaty, aims to show how writing books really *could* challenge a prince's confidence in his own wisdom, and as such help to transform a perpetual state of war into one of perpetual peace.[6] Following both Rousseau and Saint-Pierre, Kant treats international insecurity and competition as the self-perpetuating results of bad counsel, the advice of 'political moralists' or 'moralising politicians' who pretend that 'human nature is not capable of good' and whose advice can lead ultimately only to annihilation, the peace of the graveyard.[7]

For Kant, the understanding of human nature that any good counsellor ('moral politician') requires must be based on an understanding of what human beings can become; this in turn requires knowledge of what humans ought to do—a 'metaphysics of morals'. Students of human nature (whom Kant calls moral anthropologists) require universal, *a priori* moral principles to serve as 'guides to judgment' and 'for the discipline of the mind in its obedience to duty, whose precept must absolutely be given only a priori by pure reason'. In denying to reason a guiding role prior to observation of the bleak side of human nature, realists make

---

2 Rousseau J. J., 'Abstract and Judgment of Saint Pierre's Project for Perpetual Peace', in Hoffman, S. and Fidler, D. (eds.), in *Rousseau on International Relations* (Oxford: Clarendon, 1991), 69–71 (my emphasis). On Saint Pierre's five articles of federation, see Hoffmann's introduction at pp. xv–xxvi. The *Extrait* was published in Rousseau's lifetime (1761); the rest, including Rousseau's *Jugement*, was published posthumously in 1782.

3 Rousseau, J. J. 'Abstract and Judgment', in Hoffmann, S. and Fidler, D. (eds.), 87–8.   4 Ibid. 93–4.

5 Rousseau, J. J. 'The State of War', in Hoffman, S. and Fidler, D. (eds.), *Rousseau on International Relations* (above, n. 2), 33.

6 Kant, I., 'Toward Perpetual Peace', 8: 378.   7 Ibid. 8: 373, 357.

'improvement *impossible* and perpetuate, as far as they can, violations of right'.[8] Worse still, they risk engendering the truth of their own position:

a pernicious theory of this kind may perhaps even bring about the evil that it prophesies. For, in accordance with such reasoning, man is thrown into a class with all other living machines which only require the consciousness that they are not free creatures to make them in their own judgment the most miserable of all beings.[9]

Kant argues that a correct understanding of human nature requires a metaphysics of morals, a reflective, reasoned understanding of moral judgment and the moral principles on which such judgment is based. And at the core of this metaphysics of morals lies a recognition of human freedom: freedom must be presupposed or 'postulated' by practical reason.[10]

Kant's argument raises two fundamental sets of questions. The first set of questions, the focus of this essay, concerns Kant's claims for the practical relevance of his metaphysics of morals. Section II of this essay outlines the role Kant defends for international law and his treatment of concrete rules of international law; Section III second half suggests that at the core of Kant's philosophy of international law lies a notion of an ever-expanding ethical community.

John Rawls and Jürgen Habermas, celebrated contemporary Kantians, substitute political institutions for this ethical community. When investigating this substitution, and more generally the relation between what Kant calls outer or juridical freedom and inner, moral freedom (autonomy), a student of Kant's philosophy of international law will ultimately confront a second, metaphysical set of questions concerning the nature of Kant's account of human freedom.

II. Kant on the Role of International Law in Securing Freedom

For Kant, the closer a state approaches perpetual peace with its potential enemies, the more secure citizens' juridical freedom will be. There is 'only one way' for states to approach this peace and that is to 'give up their savage (lawless) freedom, accommodate themselves to public coercive laws, and so form an (always growing) *state of nations* (*civitas gentium*) that would finally encompass all the nations of the earth'.[11] Yet perpetual peace is 'unachievable': there are risks of tyranny and homogenization in creating a world government and problems for such a government in attempting to govern effectively; states' attachment to

---

[8] Ibid. 8: 373. Kant also argues that such thinkers operate in bad faith and rely on an unattainable empirical knowledge of the future: the only correct prudential maxims must be those that promote rational ideals, ibid. 370.

[9] Ibid. 8: 378.   [10] Kant, I., *Critique of Practical Reason* (above, n. 6), 5: 132.

[11] Kant, I., 'Toward Perpetual Peace' (above, n. 6), 8: 357.

sovereignty and the right of nations will anyway prevent the establishment of a world government; and in the absence of a world state, defensive wars *will* sometimes be necessary.[12] Given this, only 'the *negative* surrogate of a *league* that averts war, endures, and always expands can hold back the stream of hostile inclination that shies away from right, though with constant danger of its breaking out'.[13]

Many commentators have been puzzled by Kant's apparent and uncharacteristic reliance on arguments from experience in dismissing the notion of a global state.[14] Some scholars argue that the logic of Kant's own position *should* have led him to advocate as a practical ideal—as well as an aim in theory—the establishment of a federative union of states or world state with coercive powers to ensure compliance with its system of world law. Thomas Pogge, for example, treats Kant's account as 'extremely unsettled' because Kant tried to evade calling for a world state.[15] Pauline Kleingeld interprets Kant as advocating the establishment of a non-coercive league of states without any highest or legislative authority 'because he regards it as the only possible road to the ultimate ideal, a state of states'.[16]

But in 'Perpetual Peace' Kant also offers a principled distinction between the relationship among states (and the role of international law) and that among individuals in a state of nature (and the role of domestic law): 'what holds in accordance with natural right for human beings in a lawless condition, "they ought to leave this condition", cannot hold for states in accordance with the right of nations'.[17] To understand this distinction, it is necessary to understand why Kant argues that human beings *are* under a duty to institute a system of just public laws, to constitute a juridical community.

1. Kant on Anarchy, Freedom, and the Duty to Form a 'Coercive' Juridical Community

For Kant, morality concerns the motivation for a particular individual's choice to perform a permissible action: the virtuous person acts only on reasons (maxims)

---

[12] Kant, I., 'Metaphysics of Morals' (above, n. 6), 6: 350.

[13] Kant, I., 'Toward Perpetual Peace' (above, n. 6), 8: 357.

[14] Kant argues that any attempt to derive moral principles from experience runs 'the risk of the grossest and most pernicious errors'. Kant, I., 'Metaphysics of Morals', 6: 217.

[15] Pogge, T., 'Kant's Theory of Justice', *Kant-Studien*, 79 (1988), 427–33. See also Habermas, Section II. 4 below, 72–3; Wood, A., 'Kant's Project for Perpetual Peace', in Robinson, H. (ed.), I.1 *Proceedings of the Eighth Kant Congress* (Milwaukee: Marquette University Press, 1995), 3–18 at 11; Cavallar, G., *Kant and the Theory and Practice of International Right* (Cardiff: University of Wales Press, 1999), 123; Höffe, O., 'Some Kantian Reflections on a World Republic', *Kantian Review*, 2 (1998), 51–71.

[16] Kleingeld, P., 'Kant's Theory of Peace', in Guyer, P. (ed.), *The Cambridge Companion to Kant and Modern Philosophy* (Cambridge: Cambridge University Press, 2006), 477–504 at 483, 485.

[17] Kant, I., 'Toward Perpetual peace' (above, n. 6), 8: 355. In 'Idea toward a universal history' (1784: 8: 24–5), Kant had treated relations between states as directly analogous to that between individuals in the state of nature.

that can be formulated as laws capable of receiving universal consent. When she does so act, she is internally free, autonomous: an action will be free if and only if done for the sake of this rational moral law rather than at the promptings of 'sensible nature'. Kant argues that if I deny that my will is free, I must deny that I can conceive the possibility of my willing autonomously: to obey the moral law, I must will autonomously and so I must accept my inner freedom as a practical postulate.[18] Action in accord with moral law is motivated by reason: as such, reason 'is not simply a means for *reconciling* oneself to reality, but provides man with the destination of *transforming* reality itself, desiring and striving for the attainment of a rational ideal in his own person and in the world as a whole'.[19]

Relying on this connection between inner freedom, self-legislation, and moral virtue, Kant argues that juridical laws are incapable of promoting virtue. Human beings can be physically coerced, but another person cannot make me act for the sake of a moral obligation: 'I can never be constrained by others to *have an end*'.[20] Juridical law cannot dictate the motives for one's actions: all it can do is create the conditions for moral, autonomous action. Justice or Right is inherently relational, governing the permissibility of 'outer' or 'external' actions by human beings whose actions inevitably limit those of others. Just law requires one 'to obey no other external laws than those to which I could have given my consent';[21] it permits any action that 'can coexist with everyone's freedom in accordance with a universal law, or if on its maxim the freedom of choice of each can coexist with everyone's freedom in accordance with a universal law'.[22]

Kant argues that individual judgments of justice *cannot* always be made in a political state of nature: in disputes relating to property, judgments remain at best 'provisionally' just in the absence of an agreed system of juridical rules on acquisition and transfer.[23] The laws required in fleshing out this system of juridical rules are in content arbitrary, needed simply because authoritative rules are required. By Kant's definition this juridical law is necessarily 'coercive', not because of the physical sanctions that may follow disobedience but because it obliges individuals to subject their will to that of the law-giver: 'any limitation of freedom through another's choice is called coercion'.[24]

Since just actions require juridical law, its institution is 'the unconditional and first duty in any external relation of people in general, who cannot help mutually affecting one another'.[25] Even a society of devils could be persuaded to comply with the rule of law as the freedom it assures them can be exploited to pursue

[18] Kant, I., 'Metaphysics of Morals' (above, n. 6), 6: 214, 6: 221.
[19] Wood, A., *Kant's Moral Religion* (Ithaca, NY: Cornell University Press, 1970), 34–7, 186.
[20] Kant, I., 'Metaphysics of Morals' (above, n. 6), 6: 381.
[21] Kant, I., 'Toward Perpetual Peace' (above, n. 6), 8: 350.
[22] Kant, I., 'Metaphysics of Morals' (above, n. 6), 6: 230.   [23] Ibid. 6: 257.
[24] Kant, I., 'On the common saying: That may be correct in theory, but it is of no use in practice' (above, n. 6), 8: 290.
[25] Ibid. 8: 289.

their own 'internal' evil ends: it is possible to comply with just law with selfish or wicked motives. But without a legal system, even the most moral human beings will find themselves either under the whimsical dictates of an absolute sovereign or in an anarchy where there is no clear source of definitive legal judgment to resolve disputes and where property rights remain indeterminate. They lack the '*public coercive laws*, by which what belongs to each can be determined for him and secured against encroachment by any other'.[26]

In providing citizens with this juridical freedom, Kant argues that domestic law, international law, and cosmopolitan law are mutually dependent.[27] They operate not as parallel legal systems but as complements to one another: juridical freedom cannot be protected by domestic law alone, given the perpetual threat posed by international war to individual's external freedom (including their property) and the need for cosmopolitan law if individuals are to be free to relate to and trade with foreigners. If domestic law, international law, or cosmopolitan law is unjust, 'the framework of all the others is unavoidably undermined and must finally collapse'.[28]

2. Kant on the Nature of International Law

According to Kant, the moral right and duty of individuals to create a system of 'coercive public laws' does not apply to relations between states: 'they already have a lawful internal constitution and hence have outgrown the constraint of others to bring them under a more extended, law-governed constitution in accordance with their concepts of right'.[29]

Kant's position here might appear close to that of Hobbes, who argues that the need for positive law is satisfied with the establishment of the state. Hobbes treats moral rights and duties as existing in the state of nature; those rights conflict and the Leviathan is needed to create harmony. Hobbes's often-misunderstood acknowledgement of violence and deceit as 'the two cardinal virtues' in war is part of an argument that war is the worst possible state for mankind.[30] Hobbes aims to convince rulers that wars of aggression are usually undesirable, presenting 'alliances and confederacies' as important deterrents in the brutal international state of nature. 'Leagues between Commonwealths', Hobbes suggests, are 'profitable for

---

[26] Kant, I., 'On the common saying: That may be correct in theory, but it is of no use in practice' (above, n. 6), 8: 289.

[27] Kant, I., 'Metaphysics of Morals' (above, n. 6), 6: 311. In earlier works, Kant claims that a perfect state constitution is not possible until rightful relations have been established between states ('Idea toward a Universal History', above, n. 6, 8. 24) and that international peace will not be achieved until states have become republics ('On the Common Saying: That may be correct in theory, but it is of no use in practice', above, n. 6, 8: 24 8: 311).

[28] Kant, I., 'Metaphysics of Morals' (above, n. 6), 6: 311.

[29] Kant, I., 'Toward Perpetual Peace' (above, n. 6), 8: 355–6.

[30] Hobbes, T., *Leviathan*, XIII. 63 (Cambridge: Cambridge University Press, 90). See Malcolm, N., 'Hobbes' Theory of International Relations', in *Aspects of Hobbes* (Oxford: Clarendon, 2002), 433–56 in contrast with Kingsbury, B., and Straumann, B., chapter 1 in this volume at 45, 51 (following Nagel in imposing on Hobbes an alien distinction opposition between the prudential and the moral).

the time they last': the most that can be hoped for is a shifting, unstable set of leagues or federations.[31]

Is Kant best read as a Hobbesian, treating international law as an articulation of unstable and conflicting moral rules rather than law properly so called? After all Kant finds it 'astonishing that the word "right" has not yet been entirely banished from the politics of war as pedantic':

[F]or Hugo Grotius, Puffendorf, Vattel and the like (only sorry comforters)—although their code, couched philosophically or diplomatically, has not the slightest *lawful* force and cannot even have such force (since states are not subject to a common external constraint)—are always duly cited in *justification* of an offensive war, though there is no instance of a state ever having been moved to desist from its plan by arguments armed with the testimony of such great men.[32]

If Kant's position really is distinct from Hobbes's, must he be committed to the need for the 'external constraint' of a global state and global law—despite his own argument that the moral obligation to institute a juridical state does not apply to the relations between states? If not, are Kant's provisional rules of international law the same as Hobbes's shifting moral rules?

The argument about Job's 'sorry comforters' introduces Kant's response to pessimistic assessments of peace plans. In the Book of Job, Eliphaz, Bildad, and Zophar all err in counselling Job that God never allows the innocent to suffer and so that his current dreadful sufferings must be punishment to encourage repentance for some personal sin, after which all will be well. As a man of integrity, Job refuses to repent because he knows himself to be innocent. Grotius, Pufendorf, and Vattel, Kant argues, gloss the undisguised 'depravity of human nature' manifest in international relations as punishment warranted by an evident and just international legal code. But just as Job's comforters had a childish notion of the justice of God's ways, so the lip-service of bellicose states to the law of nations and the writings of jurists on the law of nations pay homage to a slumbering idea of juridical right. Widespread consent to rules of the law of nations reflects an unarticulated international social contract: the very concept of the law of nations is 'necessarily connected' with the idea of a 'free federation' of republican states.[33]

In 'Perpetual Peace', Kant proposes three key terms for peaceful federation. The first 'definitive article of perpetual peace between states' requires that the civil

[31] Hobbes, T., 'Leviathan', xv. 73, xiii. 60, xxii. 122 (above, n. 31, 102, 87, 163). Compare Kant, I., 'Metaphysics of Morals' (above, n. 6), 6. 350.

[32] Kant, I., 'Toward Perpetual Peace' (above, n. 6), 8: 355.

[33] Ibid. 8: 356. In arguing that Kant's 'ingenious idea was that the textbooks of natural jurisprudence could be seen [. . .] as the lawbooks of an international Leviathan', Richard Tuck rightly highlights the positive role played by Kant's 'sorry comforters' but misrepresents Kant's position as a defence of an 'international Leviathan'. Tuck, R., *The Rights of War and Peace: Political Thought and International Order from Grotius to Kant* (Oxford: Oxford University Press, 1999), 219–20. Kant's ideal of a global state is much closer to the 'fiction' of a 'natural' global state or 'great society of societies' introduced by Christian Wolff in the Prolegomena to his *Jus gentium methodo scientifica pertractatum* (1750), (Oxford: Clarendon Press, 1934), trans. J. Drake. paras. 7, 9, 15.

constitution of every state member of the federation be republican: political power must be dispersed between a separate legislature, executive, and judiciary and the sovereign (whether a monarch, an aristocracy, or a democratic government) must enact laws in line with the principle of right, laws that are capable of receiving universal consent. The second article requires the creation of this peaceful federation, already incipient in states' recognition of rules of the law of nations.

The third article requires as a 'supplement' (to republican domestic law and the law of nations), recognition of 'the rights of men, as citizens of the world' to 'the conditions of universal hospitality'.[34] The rights 'of visitation' permit 'an attempt at intercourse with the original inhabitants'. Thanks to these, the peaceful federation will gradually extend: 'distant parts of the world can enter peaceably into relations with one another, which can eventually become publicly lawful and so finally bring the human race ever closer to a cosmopolitan constitution'.[35]

Kant insists that the league of peace (*foedus pacificum*) 'does not look to acquiring any power of a state but only to preserving and securing the *freedom* of a state itself and of other states in league with it, but without there being any need for them to subject themselves to public laws and coercion under them (as people in a state of nature must do)'.[36] Although there *is* a moral obligation on neighbouring states to form a peaceful league, that league must 'involve no sovereign authority (as in a civil constitution), but only an *association* (federation); it must be an alliance that can be renounced at any time and so must be renewed from time to time'.[37] Kant's point is that 'the individual *Rechtstaat* considered on its own cannot fully solve the problem of Right *even at the domestic level*': Kant's account of the law of nations is an acknowledgement of states' 'need for (non-coercive) containment of their own coercive powers'.[38]

The international law recognized by this league is a matter of 'right' yet, as self-imposed, it is not coercive in Kant's sense. Perhaps Kant's approach to rules of international law is best understood as akin to his approach to rules of equity in domestic law, which he treats as rules of 'equivocal right'. Equity, Kant argues, is a 'right in a *wider* sense (*ius latium*), in which there is no law by which an authorization to use coercion can be determined': it 'admits a right without coercion'. Claims of equity, according to Kant, do concern claims of right, not 'merely calling upon another to fulfil an ethical duty (to be benevolent and kind)'.[39]

Equitable claims cannot usually be resolved by a judge as their 'conditions' are 'indefinite': the motto of equity is 'the strictest right is the greatest wrong', which means that 'this ill cannot be remedied by way of what is laid down as right, even though it concerns a claim to a right'. As such, equitable claims usually belong

---

[34] Kant, I., 'Toward Perpetual Peace' (above, n. 6), 8: 360.   [35] Ibid. 8: 358.
[36] Ibid. 8: 356.   [37] Kant, I., 'Metaphysics of Morals' (above, n. 6), 6: 344.
[38] Flikschuh, K., 'Justice without Coercion? Kant's Problem of "International Right"' (manuscript on file with the author), text preceding n. 30.
[39] Kant, I., 'Metaphysics of Morals' (above, n. 6), 6: 234.

'only to the *court of conscience* (*forum poli*) whereas every question of what is laid down as right must be brought before *civil right* (*forum soli*)'.[40] But Kant does argue that a judge in a civil court may and should rely on rules of equity 'where the judge's own rights are concerned, and he can dispose of the case for his own person', as when a sovereign indemnifies his servants for damages incurred in his service even though that sovereign 'could reject their claim by strict right on the pretext that they undertook this service at their own risk'.[41]

Analogously, Kant is clear that no state is entitled to impose international obligations on another. This seems to render Kant's rules of international law rules of 'equivocal right' binding in conscience, with the sovereign or the people in the place of the judge in Kant's example, above. In the absence of world law, some of the rules of international law (particularly those relating to territory) remain 'provisional' (like property rights in the state of nature) and some disputes will continue to be settled by war. But extant international law can gradually achieve its role in promoting and spreading peace, Kant seems to believe, so long as one crucial change is introduced: a ban on espionage.

3. Kant on the Legal Prerequisites for Peaceful Federation

Kant argues that six 'preliminary articles', negative rules of international law, are a prerequisite for the firm establishment of a peaceful federation of states. Three of these six rules (the first, fifth, and sixth) are 'of the *strict* kind (*leges strictae*), holding without regard for differing circumstances' and 'insist on [the ruler's] putting a stop to an abuse *at once*'.[42] With one significant modification, they articulate identical versions of rules found in the writings of 'sorry comforters' like Vattel. They declare peace treaties invalid if drafted to reserve justifications for future hostilities; that no state may use force to interfere with the constitution or administration of another state except where anarchy prevails; and a ban on all 'such modes of hostility as would make mutual confidence impossible in a subsequent state of peace'.[43]

In accord with Vattel, Kant includes in this last rule a ban on the use of assassins. But unlike the use of poisoning and assassination, for Vattel seducing a subject of the enemy to turn spy or betray his country does not 'strike at the foundation of the common safety and welfare of mankind': it is 'practised in all wars' and not 'contrary to the external law of nations', although if at all excusable, 'only in a very just war, and when the immediate object is to save our country, when threatened with ruin by a lawless conqueror' since he who 'tramples upon justice and probity, deserves in his turn to feel the effects of wickedness and perfidy'.[44]

---

[40] Ibid. 6: 235.   [41] Ibid. 6: 234–5
[42] Kant, I., 'Toward Perpetual Peace' (above, n. 6), 8: 357.   [43] Ibid. 8: 346.
[44] De Vattel, E., *Le droit des gens* (1758), bk. III, ch. x, s 180.

By contrast, Kant argues emphatically that the use of spies is as dangerous as that of assassins: it encourages vices of dishonesty which 'would also be carried over into a condition of peace, so that its purpose would be altogether destroyed'.[45] Just as the concept of the law of nations is senseless if not potentially the fruit of a federation of states with republican constitutions, so a law of nations that countenances fundamental deceit falls into the deathly error of the moralizing politicians who make improvement impossible.

Kant's three remaining preliminary articles he characterizes as *leges latae*: premature insistence on these rules of international law would be counter-productive. The second preliminary article allows that, provisionally, the 'inheritance, exchange, purchase or donation' of territory remains licit as it might prevent war: these modes of acquisition are to be abolished in the future as incompatible with the right of a people to rule and dispose of itself, but delay implementing this prohibition is permitted so that restitution should not be made precipitately. Under the third preliminary article, standing armies are to be abolished in the course of time; under the fourth, states will no longer be permitted to contract national debts to finance war. But the ruler may '*postpone* putting these laws into effect, without however losing sight of the end'.[46]

In the *Rechtslehre*, Kant reiterates that the attempt to expand the peaceable federation of republics should not be made by way of revolution, by a leap, that is, by violent overthrow of an already existing defective constitution (for there would then be an intervening moment in which any rightful condition would be annihilated). But if it is attempted and carried out by gradual reform in accordance with firm principles, it can lead to continual approximation to the highest political good, perpetual peace.[47]

4. Injustice and Reform of the Law of Nations: The Public Role of the Philosopher

It is to a group of 'part-time men of learning'[48] that Kant entrusts oversight of this ultimate political end. For Kant, enlightened legal refinements, reorganizations, and reforms are defined against a standard of 'publicity'—by which Kant means not confused public discourse but 'the use which someone makes of it *as a scholar* before the entire public of the *world of readers*'. The 'extra-vocational' use of reason, for Kant, is *public*; the 'vocational' use of reason is *private*, the use which one 'may make of it in a particular *civil* post or office [with] which he is entrusted', a use where it is

---

45 Kant, I., 'Toward Perpetual Peace' (above, n. 6), 8: 347.   46 Ibid.
47 Kant, I., 'Metaphysics of Morals' (above, n. 6), 6: 355.
48 Laursen, J. C., 'The Subversive Kant: The Vocabulary of "public" and "publicity" ', in Schmidt, J. (ed.) *What is Enlightenment?: Eighteenth Century Answers and Twentieth Century Questions* (Berkeley and Los Angeles: University of California Press, 1996), 253–69, 259.

'impermissible to argue' and one behaves 'passively', as 'part of a machine', bound by an 'artificial accord' to promote certain 'public ends'.[49]

The bulk of Kant's public were the military officers and clergymen as well as the professors, all of whom, as civil servants, had their salaries paid by the state—along with a small supplement of independent writers who made their living by their pens.[50] Officials obey, but off-duty they also argue for reform of the laws which they obey. So a 'private' army officer must follow orders, but he must be allowed the freedom to publish his criticisms of 'the errors in the military service'; a private citizen must pay his taxes, but he must also be free to publish 'his thoughts about the inappropriateness or even injustice' of fiscal measures.[51] Public (published) debate among scholars 'on the inadequacies of current institutions' Kant envisages as spreading 'public insight into the nature of these things', culminating in a petition to the crown for reform.[52] Publicity, freedom of the quill, informs the prince of law reforms he would have introduced himself if only he had thought of them.[53]

After bitter experiences under Frederick William II, Kant narrows the privilege he claims for free debate, limiting it to the 'learned community' of professors. Scholars in the traditionally designated 'higher' faculties (theologians, lawyers, and medics) have to teach what they are told, although they may debate freely among themselves. For the scholars in the 'lower' philosophy faculty, however, Kant claims full freedom as 'without a faculty of this kind, the truth would not come to light (and this would be to the government's own detriment)'.[54] The philosophers' reading 'public' remains that of the members of government and the higher faculties, whose arguments must be assessed and if necessary counteracted by philosophers lest the lawyers, medics, and theologians set themselves up as 'miracle workers' offering false remedies to the wider public or even encouraging insurrection.[55]

Philosophers' role in advising government is the focus of Kant's ironically titled 'secret' supplementary article in 'Perpetual Peace': Kant argues not 'that a state must give principles of philosophers precedence over the findings of lawyers (representatives of the power of the state), but only that they be given a *hearing*'.[56] Practising what he preaches, in the second Appendix Kant explains that 'the formal attribute' of justice can be articulated in terms of a test of public admissibility or 'publicity'.[57] Negatively, 'actions relating to the rights of others are wrong if their maxim is incompatible with publicity';[58] affirmatively, 'maxims which *need* publicity

---

[49] Kant, I., 'An Answer to the Question: What is Enlightenment?' (above, n. 6), 8: 37.

[50] Laursen, J. C., 'The Subversive Kant: The Vocabulary of "public" and "publicity" ', (above, n. 48), 257.

[51] Kant, I., 'An Answer to the Question: What is Enlightenment?', (above, n. 6), 8: 37–8.

[52] Ibid. 8: 39.

[53] Kant, I., 'On the Common Saying: That may be correct in theory, but it is of no use in practice' (above, n. 6), 8: 304.

[54] Kant, I., *The Conflict of the Faculties* (above, n. 6), 7: 20. 'Perpetual Peace' appeared in 1795, after the bulk of pt 1 of the *Conflict* had been written but before its publication.

[55] Kant, I., *The Conflict of the Faculties* (above, n. 6), 7: 31.

[56] Kant, I., 'Toward Perpetual Peace' (above, n. 6), 8: 369.   [57] Ibid. 8: 381.   [58] Ibid.

(in order not to fail in their end) harmonize with right and politics combined'.[59] The 'transcendental principle of publicity' can be used to give a principled account of the law of nations, dispensing with the 'prolixity' and 'subtle reasoning' of jurists who want to settle questions of international law 'by a dogmatic deduction of grounds of right'.[60]

Kant offers four examples. First, maxims proposing the legality of insurrection or tyrannicide could not be acknowledged openly without conceding lawful authority to the people rather than the sovereign. The 'wrongfulness of rebellion is therefore clear'.[61] A free press is the only lawful outlet for protest against tyranny—although *if* a (necessarily unconstitutional) revolution takes place, the head of state 'would return to the status of a subject and must not start a rebellion for his restoration'.[62]

After this rejection of a limit on a sovereign's power, Kant addresses a sovereign's own limiting of his responsibility by classifying a treaty as personal (rather than real) and so not binding on the state. He targets the claim to 'double personality' by the prince as both head of state and highest official accountable to the state: 'what it has bound itself to do in the first capacity it is released from in the second'.[63] The principle of publicity shows that with his signature a sovereign always binds his country: 'if a State (or its head) divulged this maxim of his, then every other would naturally either shun him or unite with others in order to oppose his pretensions'.[64]

Kant then considers the use of force against a neighbouring sovereign. Grotius and Pufendorf had denied any collective right to use force pre-emptively against a neighbouring state growing in strength, but Vattel granted one. Kant argues that this 'maxim of political expediency', if publicly acknowledged, will 'thwart its own purpose' since 'the greater power would anticipate the smaller ones, and as for their uniting, that is only a feeble reed against someone who knows how to make use of *divide et impera*'. And, he concludes swiftly, it 'is therefore unjust'.[65]

But while small states have no right to use force collectively against a neighbour growing in strength, neither has a 'great' state a right to annex a smaller state that 'breaks up' its territory: the larger state 'must not divulge such a maxim in advance; for either smaller states would unite in good time or other powerful ones would do so in order to contest this booty, so that this maxim makes itself impracticable by its very openness'.[66]

The first of these two bans on the use of force Kant lifts in his later *Rechts-lehre*, permitting as 'legitimate' the pre-emptive use of force against a 'menacing' enemy—and also allowing the use of force without prior peaceful negotiation in retaliation for 'an offence' or against an 'unjust enemy', one opposed to a peaceful league whose words or deeds reveal 'a maxim by which, if it were made a universal rule, any condition of peace among nations would be impossible and, instead, a state of nature would be perpetuated'.[67]

---

[59] Kant, I., 'Toward Perpetual Peace' (above, n. 6), 8: 386.   [60] Ibid. 8: 382.   [61] Ibid.
[62] Ibid. 383.   [63] Ibid.   [64] Ibid. 8: 384.   [65] Ibid.
[66] Ibid.   [67] Kant, I., 'Metaphysics of Morals' (above, n. 6), 6: 346–9.

Despite the narrowing of his 'public' and the eroding of his bans on the use of force, Kant's hope remains: that of progress, through reasoning able to bear the light of publicity, towards a spreading system of republican government and an ever-expanding peaceful federation of republican states. With this will come 'an increase of the products of *legality* in dutiful actions whatever their motives':

Gradually violence on the part of the powers will diminish and obedience to the laws will increase. There will arise in the body politic perhaps more charity and less strife in lawsuits, more reliability in keeping one's word, etc., partly out of love of honor, partly out of well-understood self-interest. And eventually this will also extend to nations in their external relations toward one another up to the realization of the cosmopolitan society, without the moral foundation in humanity having to be enlarged in the least; for that, a kind of new creation (supernatural influence) would be necessary. For we must also not hope for too much from human beings in their progress toward the better lest we fall prey with good reason to the mockery of the politician who would willingly take the hope of the human being as the dreaming of an overstressed mind.[68]

III. Beyond Peaceable Federation: Cosmopolitan Ethical Community or Cosmopolitan International Institutions?

The nature of Kant's hope for international law is widely disputed: is it that the peaceable federation of individual republics will one day be *superseded* by a cosmopolitan world state governed by a system of world law, or that the peaceable federation of individual republics will be *complemented* by an ethical cosmopolis which will expand thanks to recognition of 'equivocal' principles of international and cosmopolitan right?

1. Juridical and Internal Freedom as Mutually Dependent Ideals

Some contemporary scholars focus on Kant's suggestion in the passage above that an increase in legality—up to and including the 'realization of the cosmopolitan society'—does not require the 'enlarging' of 'the moral foundation in humanity'. On this account (which I will contest), 'Kant wants his argument for *Recht*, and

---

[68] Kant, I., *The Conflict of the Faculties* (above, n. 6), 7: 92–3.

for a republican instantiation thereof, to be independent from his morality'.[69] Kant presents humanity with a choice between a prudential or 'self-interested' focus on the building of institutions (to offer the peace and freedom moral people need) and a focus on converting every devil into a virtuous man, only then building together political institutions. The first alternative is then presented as the only one possible, given Kant's bleak vision of humans' capacity for evil combined with his understanding of moral virtue as a self-mastery to be achieved only for and by oneself. So Kant's justifications for legal authority, such scholars conclude, can and indeed must stand without his moral philosophy.[70]

Kant's moral philosophy does entail his doctrine of Right, since morally autonomous individuals need the freedom, absence of violence, and determinacy with which Kant's principle of Right is concerned and which is ensured by a state that respects the rule of law. But selfish, self-interested, and vicious people also need this same 'external' freedom. Kant famously argues that intelligence, fortune, courage, and happiness have no intrinsic moral value as they can lead to pride and arrogance,[71] yet these are crucial elements of the 'unsocial sociability' that leads people to subsume themselves in a social order. He treats war as an empirical force of progress, encouraging heads of state to show respect for humanity, spreading populations over the earth, and compelling people to enter into 'more or less lawful relations'.[72] At the international level, suffering and the commercial costs of war are to lead free civil institutions to force their governments into an international federation of nation states.[73] None of these empirical causes of progress have intrinsic moral value—and neither does juridical freedom. Kant's account of Justice or the principle of Right, as a set of legal constraints protecting zones of freedom from the interference of others, can be 'embedded' within either a Kantian morality or a Hobbesian one—as evidenced by Kant's argument that even a group of intelligent devils would set up a state.[74]

A central problem with such interpretations is that they assume that for Kant there *could* be a world in which justice or *Recht* prevailed only because every citizen was selfishly motivated (rather than acting from duty, for the sake of moral principles): this conflicts with Kant's insistence that 'if justice goes, there is no longer any value

[69] Pogge, T., 'Is Kant's *Rechtslehre* a "Comprehensive Liberalism"?', in Timmons, M. (ed.), *Kant's Metaphysics of Morals: Interpretive Essays* (Oxford: Oxford University Press, 2002), 150.

[70] Wood, A., 'The Final Form of Kant's Practical Philosophy', in Timmons, M. (ed.), *Essays on Kant's Moral Philosophy*, (New York: Cambridge University Press, 2000), 8, and Wood, A., *Kant* (Oxford: Wiley-Blackwell, 2004), 172; Pogge, T., 'Is Kant's *Rechtslehere* a "Comprehensive Liberalism"?' (above, n. 69), 133–58; Tuck, R., 'Rights of War and Peace', (above, n. 33), 208; Murphy, J., 'Practical Reason and Moral Psychology in Aristotle and Kant', in Frankel Paul E. (ed.), *Moral Knowledge* (Cambridge: Cambridge University Press, 2001).

[71] Kant, I., 'Groundwork of the Metaphysics of Morals' (above, n. 6), 4: 393.

[72] Kant, I., 'Idea for a history with a cosmopolitan purpose', 8: 121, Toward Perpetual Peace, 8: 363, 365.

[73] Toward Perpetual Peace, 8: 350.

[74] Pogge, T., 'Is Kant's *Rechtslehere* a "Comprehensive Liberalism"?' (above, n. 69), 148, 149, contesting John Rawls's categorization of Kant's liberalism as 'comprehensive' (Rawls, J., *Political Liberalism* (New York: Columbia University Press, 1993), pp. xv–xvi).

in human beings living on the earth'.[75] The interpretation defended here is that in Kant juridical or external freedom and moral freedom (autonomy) are *mutually dependent* ideals.[76]

This rival interpretation of Kant's account of the relationship between law and morality focuses on the links that Kant makes between subjection to just juridical law and the possibility of a growth in charity, reliability, and 'progress towards the better'. For Kant, the enactment of juridical law is a necessary step for moral progress, although far from sufficient for moral 'rebirth'. The civilization or law-abidingness assured by juridical legal institutions not only gives the state;

a moral veneer (*causae non causae*), but also, by its checking the outbreak of unlawful inclinations, the development of the moral predisposition to immediate respect for right is actually greatly facililitated . . . ; thereby a great step is taken *toward* morality (though it is not yet a moral step), toward being attached to this concept of duty even for its own sake, without regard for any return.[77]

So while law-abidingness will often lead to legalism, only in a juridical society can man win for himself culture, civilization. In Kant's famous extended simile, it is with men as with trees in a forest: 'just because each one strives to deprive the other of air and sun, they compel each other to seek both above, and thus they grow beautiful and straight. Whereas those that, in freedom and isolation from one another, shoot out their branches at will, grown stunted and crooked and awry'.[78] All civilized or 'social' virtues, including those inculcated by juridical law, are 'small change': 'it is a child who takes it for real gold'. But this is *not* an argument for dismissing social conventions and habits as valueless:

it is still better to have small change in circulation than no funds at all, and eventually they can be converted into genuine gold, though at considerable loss. It is committing high treason against humanity to pass them off as *mere tokens* that have no worth at all [. . .]. Even the illusion of good in others must have worth for us, for out of this play with pretenses, which acquires respect without perhaps earning it, something quite serious can finally develop.[79]

Following Rousseau closely, Kant also associates the evils or passions 'which wreak such devastation' on a human being's 'originally good predisposition' with this same entry into stable juridical community: envy, addiction to power, avarice, 'and the malignant inclinations associated with these' arise 'as soon as he is among human beings'. Any group of human beings 'will mutually corrupt each other's

---

[75] Kant, I., 'Metaphysics of Morals' (above, n. 6), 6: 332.

[76] George Kelly summarizes Kant's position well in Kelly, G., *Idealism, Politics and History* (Cambridge: Cambridge University Press, 1969), 166. See similarly Louden, R. B., *Kant's Impure Ethics: From Rational Beings to Human Beings* (New York: Oxford University Press, 2000), 145–51; Kleingeld, P., 'Kant's Theory of Peace', in Guyer, P. (ed.), *The Cambridge Companion to Kant and Modern Philosophy* (Cambridge: Cambridge University Press, 2006), 477–503.

[77] Kant, I., 'Toward Perpetual Peace', (above, n. 6), 8: 375–6.

[78] Kant, I., 'Idea for a Universal History' (1784), 8: 22 (Fifth proposition).

[79] Kant, I., Anthropology from a Pragmatic Point of View, 7: 152–3 (trans. Louden, R. B. (Cambridge: Cambridge University Press, 2006).

moral disposition and make one another evil'.[80] The question of *quis custodiet*, of who guards the guards, haunts Kant's political essays:

Man is an animal which, if it lives among others of its kind, requires a master [. . .] who will break his will and force him to obey a will that is universally valid, under which each can be free. But whence does he get this master? Only from the human race. But then the master is himself an animal, and needs a master [. . .] The highest master should be just in himself, and yet a man.[81]

2. Guarding the Guards: The Ethical Community and the Political Community

Kant's famous argument about the rule of law for a nation of rational devils is part of a response to 'Princes' who reject republican constitutions as fit only for a people of angels: the problem of government is solvable 'even *for* (not *by*) a people of (rational) devils, because it depends only on a right 'ordering' of society'.[82] But what ensures that solvers of this problem, the enlightened, scholarly community of public guardians, will give good, disinterested advice? Kant after all recognizes that in the quarrel between politics and morals, 'true courage' lies not so much in braving external trouble and sacrifice 'but in looking straight in the face what is far more dangerous, the deceitful and treacherous yet subtly reasoning principle in ourselves which pretends that the weakness of human nature justifies any transgression'.[83]

Kant's ultimate answer involves a combination of rational theology and practical anthropology. There are, he claims, no truly diabolical human actions (principled decisions to do evil): evil actions are inherently *un*principled.[84] Moral 'rebirth' or conversion brings one to see principled, legislative form as the moral filter for one's personal reasons and the test to be articulated and applied to ensure the justice of juridical law. While the 'small change' of law-abidingness nurtured by juridical law is far from sufficient to cause this conversion, it is nonetheless a prerequisite. It is ultimately because even oppressive legal regimes nurture this small virtue of law-abidingness that Kant rejects forceful rebellion or revolution as a means to enlightened domestic or international law.[85] But once they have complied with their moral duty to enter into a juridical community, given the risks of mutual corruption human beings will need the support of an *ethical* community

---

[80]   Kant, I., *Religion within the Boundaries of Mere Reason* (above, n. 6), 6: 93–4.

[81]   Kant, I., 'Idea for a Universal History' (1784), 8: 23 (Sixth proposition).

[82]   Ludwig, B., 'Whence Public Right?', in Timmons, M. (ed.), *Kant's Metaphysics of Morals: Interpretive Essays* (Oxford: Oxford University Press, 2002), n. 4, 162.

[83]   Kant, I., 'Toward Perpetual Peace' (above, n. 6), 8: 379.

[84]   Kant, I., *Religion within the Boundaries of Mere Reason* (above, n. 6), 6: 37. Also Kant, I., *Anthropology from a Pragmatic Point of View* (above, n. 79), 7: 293.

[85]   Kant, I., 'Toward Perpetual Peace' (above, n. 6), 8: 378.

'solely designed for the preservation of morality by counteracting evil with united forces'.[86]

Not only will individuals need the support of an ethical community, they are, Kant argues, under a moral obligation to become members of this 'universal republic based on the laws of virtue'. This duty to try to leave the *ethical* state of nature (which Kant distinguishes sharply from a juridical state of nature) is a unique duty 'not of human beings toward human beings but of the human race toward itself'. This duty presupposes 'another idea, namely, of a higher moral being through whose universal organization the forces of single individuals, insufficient on their own, are united for a common effect'.[87] This divine co-ordinator is a lawgiver who is 'purely internal' and 'who knows the heart, in order to penetrate to the most intimate parts of the dispositions of each and everyone'.[88]

Some argue that as a matter of philosophical consistency, Kant's references to a cosmopolitan constitution to be a *juridical*, the constitution of a coercive world state. On the rival reading proposed here, the juridical law to be nurtured in distant territories will be republican domestic law supplemented by 'equivocal' rules of international right (preserving peace) and 'equivocal' rules of cosmopolitan right (allowing a limited 'right to visit'[89]). In creating 'external freedom' and nurturing law-abidingness, this juridical law allows for (although certainly does not necessitate) international publicity for enlightened thought and the emergence of an ever growing *ethical* cosmopolitan community.

It is far from the spirit of Kant's writing on law to argue that he 'fails' to propose a world state or greater powers for an international federation out of cowardice, because he 'thought unhistorically' or was an insufficiently 'passionate' reformer and republican.[90] Kant's point is more revolutionary: that our ultimate allegiance belongs to *no* mere form of government, no temporal power, but instead to the moral laws elaborated autonomously within an ever-expanding ethical community.[91] For Kant, the revolution must come within men's hearts, and spread via their heads both to their 'characters' and to their juridical laws; that revolution is to be led by philosophers. Kant's famous use of Horace's phrase, *Sapere Aude!*, as the 'motto of enlightenment' indicates how for Kant enlightenment is *both* a process in which men

---

[86] Kant, I., *Religion within the Boundaries of Mere Reason* (above, n. 6), 6: 94. Louden, R. B., *Kant's Impure Ethics: From Rational Beings to Human Beings* (above, n. 76), 160, rightly treats the idea of an ethical commonwealth as 'the most important single legacy of Kant's ethics; indeed of Enlightenment thought generally'.

[87] Kant, I., *Religion within the Boundaries of Mere Reason* (above, n. 6), 6: 97–8.   [88] Ibid. 6: 100, 99.

[89] Kant, I., 'Toward Perpetual Peace', 8: 358.

[90] Habermas, J., 'Kant's Idea of Perpetual Peace, with the Benefit of Two Hundred Years' Hindsight', in Bohman, J. and Lutz-Bachmann, M. (eds.), *Perpetual Peace: Essays on Kant's Cosmopolitan Ideal* (Cambridge, Mass.: MIT Press, 1997), 132; Williams, H., *Kant's Political Philosophy* (New York: St Martin's Press, 1983), 246–7.

[91] See Nussbaum, M., 'Kant and Cosmopolitanism', in Bohman and Lutz-Bachmann (eds.), *Perpetual Peace* (above, n. 89), 25–58, 31. On Kant's rejection of Stoicism (for rooting evil in natural desires rather than in the will), see Beiser, F., 'Moral Faith and the Highest Good' in Guyer, P. (ed.), *The Cambridge Companion to Kant and Modern Philosophy* (Cambridge: Cambridge University Press, 2006), 588–629.

participate collectively *and* an act of courage to be accomplished personally. It is through that very process of enlightenment, at once collective and personal, that law will be improved, that the binding but non-coercive force of international law will be recognized, and that the ethical cosmopolis will expand. And increasingly just law can nurture the discipline or 'law-abidingness' without which that enlightenment cannot begin.[92]

3. Rawls's Rewriting: A 'Realistic Utopia'

In the work of both Jürgen Habermas and John Rawls, two of the most influential twentieth-century political philosophers whose work builds on themes from Kant, faith is staked firmly on the effects of correctly designed international institutions instead of on a link between the transformative capacities of reason and the growth of a 'public' ethical community.

Like Kant, Rawls aims to justify practical principles by appealing to a conception of practical reasoning. But unlike Kant, Rawls does not aspire to construct an account of principles that render practical reasoning possible (and so 'publicizable'): Rawls argues that 'not everything can be constructed and every construction has a basis, certain materials, as it were, from which it begins'.[93] Rawls's principles of justice are designed to cohere with 'our moral experience'.[94] He aims to construct not a full moral philosophy of ethical community but only principles of justice that fit with the 'experience', 'convictions', or 'intuitions' of those living in a liberal democratic polity: in his later work, drawn together in his *Political Liberalism*, his principles are explicitly defended on the basis not of their rationality but of their political acceptability as political standards of 'public reason'.[95]

Rawls offers a social contract model to illustrate his procedure: his story of 'the original position' is presented as 'a natural guide to intuition'. The imaginary individuals in the original position are veiled in ignorance of their vision of the good life, their aspirations and natural endowments, and their social position: the placing of this veil is designed to reveal shared intuitions about the irrelevance of such knowledge to a theory of justice. Those in this original position will agree on a first

---

[92] See also Kleingeld, P., 'Kant's Theory of Peace,' (above, n. 16), 493–4 on the 'self-reinforcing process' which 'gradually makes the legal peace ever more secure because peace becomes less a matter of mere self-interest and more a matter of moral disposition'.

[93] Rawls, J., 'Themes in Kant's Moral Philosophy', in Forster, E. (ed.), *Kant's Transcendental Deductions* (Paolo Alto: Stanford University Press, 1989), 514. See O'Neill, O., 'Constructivism in Rawls and Kant', in Freeman, S. (ed.), *The Cambridge Companion to Rawls* (Cambridge, Cambridge University Press, 2003), 347–67.

[94] Rawls reads Kant's own conception of autonomous freedom as 'elicited from our experience'. Rawls, J., 'Themes in Kant's Moral Philosophy' (above, n. 93), 514.

[95] As such, his project is fundamentally *un*Kantian: see O'Neill, O., 'Constructivism in Rawls and Kant' (above, n. 93), 359; Flickshuh, K., *Kant and Modern Moral Philosophy* (Cambridge: Cambridge University Press, 2000). See also Scanlon, T. M., 'Rawls on Justification', in Freeman, S. (ed.), *The Cambridge Companion to Rawls* (Cambridge, Cambridge University Press, 2003), 139–67.

principle of justice that 'Each person is to have an equal right to the most extensive total system of equal basic liberties compatible with a similar system of liberty for all'. This principle of equal basic liberties is combined with a second principle of justice, a principle of 'fraternity', requiring social and economic inequalities to be arranged to the greatest benefit of the least advantaged, consistent with a just savings principle (the difference principle), and attached to offices and positions open to all (fair opportunity).[96] Although accepted for reasons of political pragmatism, these principles of justice will transform a polity from a society held together by a *modus vivendi* into one that affirms the principles of justice on varied moral grounds. As such, the principles of justice articulate a thin conception of ethical community. Rawls offers limited explanation let alone justification for why or how at the domestic level the juridical institutionalisation of 'public reasons' will be morally transformative.[97]

Rawls distinguishes his original account of justice, which applies to representative people within a state, from an account of the just laws that are to apply to a society of states or 'peoples'.[98] Explicitly following Kant, Rawls assumes that a world government 'would either be a global despotism or else would rule over a fragile empire torn by frequent civil strife as various regions and peoples tried to gain their political freedom and autonomy'.[99] He introduces a 'double contract', a second 'original position' to illustrate how liberal societies can play a leading role in developing a 'law of peoples'. In this second 'original position', the 'people's representatives' will agree on a 'Law of Peoples' which will offer fair terms of cooperation to illiberal, hierarchical societies (including Kant's ban on forceful interference in other states' affairs) and protect minimal rights of asylum for individuals (expanding on Kant's minimal cosmopolitan 'right to visit'). This 'reasonable Law of Peoples' aims to reflect extant international law limitations on the use of force and contemporary accounts of international human rights law.[100]

Rawls does not include Kant's ban on espionage and, in direct conflict with Kant's position, Rawls accepts what he calls a 'Supreme Emergency Exemption', countenancing attacks on non-combatant civilians.[101] He alludes to Kant's empirical

---

[96] Rawls, J., *A Theory of Justice* (Cambridge, Mass.: Harvard University Press, 1971), 302–3.

[97] Ibid., chs. 8 and 9. Rawls relies on an 'Aristotelian principle' that it is intrinsic to people's good to realize their nature as free, equal, and rational beings, and as such to act with justice; he recasts his argument in Rawls, J., *Political Liberalism* (New York: Columbia University Press, 1993), 147–8, but limited justification is offered for the move beyond an instrumentalist *modus vivendi*. See generally Freeman, S., 'Congruence and the Good of Justice', in Freeman, S. (ed.), *The Cambridge Companion to Rawls* (Cambridge: Cambridge University Press, 2003).

[98] See Mertens, T., 'From Perpetual Peace to the Law of Peoples: Kant, Habermas and Rawls on International Relations', *Kantian Review*, 6 (2002), 60–84. Contemporary 'cosmopolitans' derive principles of global justice without this 'double contract', taking individuals rather than states as the primary focus of international justice. Rawls objects to this not for Kantian reasons (as ignoring the moral worth of the state and extant juridical law) but for ignoring the fact of 'reasonable pluralism'.

[99] Rawls, J., *The Law of Peoples* (Cambridge, Mass.: Harvard University Press, 1999), 36.

[100] Ibid. 26–7.   [101] Ibid. 98; compare Kant, I., 'Toward Perpetual Peace' (above, n. 6), 8: 347.

suggestions that republics are inherently peaceful and have no cause to go to war against each other; that international commerce is capable of replacing war; and that philosophers' public articulation of the real interests of their society will help politicians act as true statesmen.[102] But Rawls's aim is not perpetual peace.[103] Although Rawls's account of international law strips away Kant's most fundamental principles, his general ambitions for juridical institutions go far beyond Kant's.

The great evils of human history, Rawls insists, follow not—as Kant ultimately argued—from personal moral failings, but from *political* injustice.[104]

[T]wo ideas motivate the Law of Peoples. The first is that the great evils of human history—unjust war, oppression, religious persecution, slavery, and the rest—result from political injustice, with its cruelties and callousness. The second is that once political injustice has been eliminated by following just (or at least decent) social policies and establishing just (or at least decent) basic institutions, these great evils will eventually disappear.[105]

This 'just or at least decent world' Rawls calls 'a realistic utopia', one that he believes is 'in the tradition of the late writings of Kant' because the 'very possibility of such a social order . . . suffices to banish the dangers of resignation and cynicism . . . and gives meaning to what we can do today'.[106]

Although Rawls's 'representatives' in the second original position bring to the second original position only their 'political conception of justice' and no 'conception of the good', in agreeing on a law of peoples they must decide 'what moral climate' they wish to see.[107] No account is offered of how this moral judgment is to be made nor of how 'institutions' constructed in line with 'the Law of Peoples' can and will eliminate the great evils of human history.[108]

4. Habermas's Rewriting: Democratic World Government

In his work in the 1990s, Habermas focuses on Kant's emphasis on the moral role and potential of juridical law, but Habermas's faith in institutions exceeds even Rawls's, conferring on juridical law the role played by Kant's ethical community.[109] While Rawls aims to articulate a liberal account of justice based on contemporary western intuitions, Habermas sets up a 'moral point of view' immanent within our use of language and which he argues cannot be attained by any one philosopher

---

[102] Rawls, J., *The Law of Peoples* (above, n. 99), 8, 37, 47, 106, 117, 97.

[103] Mertens, T., 'From Perpetual Peace to the Law of Peoples: Kant, Habermas and Rawls on International Relations', (above, n. 98), 77–8.

[104] Rawls, J., *The Law of Peoples* (above, n. 99), 7.   [105] Ibid. 126.

[106] Ibid.   [107] Ibid. 40, 42.

[108] Raymond Geuss rightly objects that the 'most basic deficiency' of Rawls's approach is its discouragement of theoretical self-consciousness. Geuss, R., *Outside Ethics* (Princeton: Princeton University Press, 2005), 36.

[109] On the contrast between Habermas's and Rawls's positions, see Müller, J.-W., 'Rawls in Germany', *European Journal of Political Theory*, 1 (2002), 163–79.

'expert on justice': 'what is needed is a "real" process of argumentation in which the individuals concerned cooperate'.[110]

Rejecting Kant's notion of international law as a complement to constitutional and cosmopolitan law, Habermas argues that international law must be transformed into a global or cosmopolitan 'law of individuals': treating Kant's objections to a global state as focused exclusively on preserving diverse national cultures, Habermas argues that Kant's position was 'colour blind', 'provincial', and ignored the point that ' "peoples" of independent states who restrict their sovereignty for the sake of a federal government need not sacrifice their distinct cultural identities'.[111] Habermas's global Leviathan, 'a juridification of the state of nature among states', can be realized only through the democratic discourse enabled by democratic institutions: this will result in 'the democratic transformation of morality into a positive system of law with legal procedures of application and implementation'.[112] 'Democratically generated' law is inherently rational and legitimate: democratic legislation is a 'legitimacy generating procedure'.[113] Invoking 'the moral universalism that guided Kant's proposals', Habermas endorses proposals to transform the United Nations into a 'cosmopolitan democracy', concentrating on 'establishing a world parliament [of elected representatives of the totality of world citizens], developing a more complete world court system, and beginning the long overdue reorganization of the Security Council'.[114]

Habermas's response to the question of how these vast institutional reforms address the problem of *quis custodiet* is to return to the publicizing of democratic debate: publicity alone is enough to hold institutions accountable, without reference to the rational moral principles it is hoped such public debate will articulate, let alone to the moral faith that this hope requires.[115]

IV. Conclusion

Some conclude that Kant's own hopes for publicity and the class of philosophers were misplaced: publicity has shown itself to be 'a very important weapon to gain

---

[110]   Habermas, J., *Moral Consciousness and Communicative Action*, trans. Lenhardt, C. and Weber Nicholson, S. (Cambridge: Polity Press, 1990), 67.

[111]   Habermas, J., 'Does the Constitutionalization of International Law still have a Chance?', in Cronin, C. (ed. and trans.), *The Divided West* (Cambridge: Polity Press, 2006), 128.

[112]   Habermas, J., *Moral Consciousness and Communicative Action* (above, n. 110), 140, 149 and Habermas, J., 'Does the Constitutionalization of International Law still have a Chance?' (above, n. 111), 124.

[113]   Habermas, J., 'Does the Constitutionalization of International Law still have a Chance?' (above, n. 111), 131 and 149.

[114]   Habermas, J., *Moral Consciousness and Communicative Action* (above, n. 110), 134; Habermas, J., 'Does the Constitutionalization of International Law still have a Chance?' (above, n. 111), 173–5.

[115]   Cf. Herbert Marcuse on 'the systematic moronization of children and adults alike by publicity and propaganda' in US democratic politics. Marcuse, H., 'Repressive Tolerance', in Wolff, R. P., Moore, B., and Marcuse, H. (eds.), *A Critique of Pure Tolerance* (Boston: Beacon Press, 1965), 83.

support for concealed private interests', while 'large numbers of well educated intellectuals have engaged in the gravest betrayals of reason and supported policies that could by no means meet Kant's idea of morality'.[116]

But Kant's hope is founded *not* on an account of the empirical actions of others but on a moral faith in future possibilities: he does not rely on an illusory wisdom that imagines it 'can see further and more clearly with its dim moles' eyes fixed on experience than with the eyes belonging to a being that was made to stand erect and look at the heavens'.[117] Kant is revisionary: he thinks that we can transform the 'is' of human nature in the light of the 'right', an ambitious enterprise that can only be achieved with the help of moral faith. This moral faith requires a 'rebirth', a vow to make 'truthfulness his supreme maxim, in the heart of his confessions to himself as well as in his behaviour toward everyone else'.[118]

The highest good of a just world, the realization of an 'ethical community', cannot be achieved solely through the cooperation of individuals of righteous will allied to the principle that injustice is inherently 'a threat to everyone'.[119] It also requires the cooperation of nature or fortune. In one powerful contemporary account, O'Neill argues that to adopt Kant's position we need only assume 'that there is no evidence that progress is impossible': by adopting and acting on an assumption that rational, enlightened progress towards the growth of an enlightened ethical community is possible, we create that very possibility.[120] But such austere, non-metaphysical reconstructions require an unreasoned faith in the possibility of personal and cultural progress—with the faint encouragement of a few inspiring, empirical 'signs'.[121]

One of Kant's worries is that people will lack motivation to act unless they have assurance that their efforts will have an effect in the world: they want assurance, that, unlike Sisyphus, they will not witness the boulder they pushed uphill rolling straight back down. A righteous man must be persuaded to accept a limited metaphysics, including the practical postulates of God and immortality: a righteous atheist like Spinoza who sees nothing but futility and 'aimless chaos' around him, will be unable to maintain the right 'moral sentiment'.[122]

---

[116] Mertens, T., 'From Perpetual Peace to the Law of Peoples: Kant, Habermas and Rawls on International Relations', (above, n. 98), 67.

[117] Kant, I., 'On the Common Saying: That may be correct in theory, but it is of no use in practice' (above, n. 6), 8: 227.

[118] Kant, I., *Anthropology from a Pragmatic Point of View* (above, n. 79), 7: 294–5.

[119] Kant, I., 'Toward Perpetual Peace' (above, n. 6), 8: 381.

[120] O'Neill, O., 'Historical Trends and Human Futures', *Studies in History and Philosophy of Science*, 39 (2008), 529–34, 533.

[121] Cf. Geuss, R., *Outside Ethics* (above, n. 108), 36. Geuss describes contemporary Kantians as representing 'an understandable but defeatist position. They encourage us to give up the search for a philosophically enlightened substantial discussion of "the good life" and to limit our philosophical ambitions to describing—or perhaps also: claiming to "ground"—the minimal conditions of smooth human cooperation'.

[122] Kant, I., *Critique of Practical Reason* (above, n. 6), 5: 122; Kant, I., *Critique of judgement*, 5. 452–3. See also Beiser, F., 'Moral Faith and the Highest Good' (above, n. 91), 616–17.

Kant believed that it was necessary to offer not evidence but rational grounds for his hope, for his moral faith in historical progress. Key elements of that moral faith (beliefs in freedom, the immortality of the soul, and the existence of God) had to be defended as practical postulates, 'not as such demonstrable' but corollaries of freedom and its *a priori* unconditionally valid practical laws.[123] Without a moral 'conversion', on Kant's account moral action is impossible. Without Kant's practical postulates, a hope in the endurance of moral conversion and in the spread of the ethical community is rationally unwarranted. And without Kant's moral anthropology, in particular the role he gives to his 'ethical community' (a church whose texts are public and whose priests are scholars), Kant's account of the worth of juridical law and of justice is unintelligible, and, according to Kant himself, the fight against 'radical evil' hopeless.

The absence of proof of the *impossibility* of progress is not enough to persuade a moral politician that her duty is to adopt a progressive, reforming attitude. With Moses Mendelssohn, she could adopt a cyclical understanding of history and a piecemeal approach to international law, an approach defended by some classical realists.[124] Or with gloomier conservatives like Christian Garve she might focus on international law's role in damage limitation.[125] From such perspectives, a moral politician would be particularly wary of the risks of unaccountability and tyranny in international institutions.

For Kant, the priority of a metaphysics of morals is both unavoidable and inherently morally transformative. If we were to adopt Mendelssohn's theory that 'humanity constantly vacillates between fixed limits', we could only understand life as a farce—and one of which any reasonable spectator would rapidly tire.[126] A metaphysics of morals is needed to convince us that every one of us must act 'as if everything depended on him'.[127]

---

[123] Kant, I., *Critique of Practical Reason* (above, n. 6), 5: 122. It inverts Kant's argument to suggest that his moral faith is a *result* of pessimism about the success of humanly willed action (Williams, H., *Kant's Political Philosophy* (above, n. 90), 244, 253). Neither is it correct that conclusions based 'on rational faith in providence [. . .] had a much lower epistemological status for Kant than those based on practical (ethical) necessity' (Ellis, E., *Kant's Politics: Provisional Theory for an Uncertain World* (New Haven: Yale University Press, 2005), n. 88, 220). For Kant it is not possible to *conceive* of practical necessity without his three practical postulates of God, immortality, and freedom.

[124] See Ned Lebow's defence of the 'hybrid orders that attempt to blend the best of the old and the new' envisaged by Thucydides, Clausewitz, and Morgenthau. Lebow, N., *The Tragic Vision of Politics: Ethics, Interests and Orders* (Cambridge: Cambridge University Press, 2003), 32–3.

[125] See Geuss, R., *Outside Ethics* (Princeton: Princeton University Press, 2005), 12: 'in an uncertain, dangerous and unpredictable world there are good general reasons not to embark on radical changes in one's social formation unless one is forced to it by demonstrable overwhelming necessity'.

[126] Kant, I., 'On the Common Saying: That may be correct in theory, but it is of no use in practice' (above, n. 6), 8: 308.

[127] Kant, I., *Religion within the Boundaries of Mere Reason* (above, n. 6), 6. 101.

LEGITIMACY OF INTERNATIONAL LAW

CHAPTER 3

THE LEGITIMACY OF INTERNATIONAL LAW

ALLEN BUCHANAN[*]

I. The Concept of Legitimacy as Applied to International Law and Institutions

1. The Primacy of Institutional Legitimacy

Although writers on international law and international relations frequently fail to make the distinction, 'legitimate' has both a sociological and a normative meaning.[1] An institution that attempts to rule (govern) is legitimate in the normative sense if and only if it has *the right to rule*. Rival theories of legitimacy differ on what the right to rule is and on what conditions must be satisfied for an institution to have the right to rule. Calling an institution legitimate in the sociological sense is a misleading way of saying that it is widely *believed to have the right to rule*. Here I will focus on the normative sense of 'legitimacy'.

Both laws and legal institutions are said to be legitimate or illegitimate, but institutional legitimacy is primary in so far as the legitimacy of particular laws or of a corpus of law depends on the legitimacy of the institutions that make, interpret, and

[*] I am grateful to Haim Ganz, Stephen Ratner, Lukas Meyer, Samantha Besson, and John Tasioulas for their comments on earlier versions of this paper.

[1] Fernando Tesón has focused squarely on the normative sense of legitimacy and is among the first (if not the first) contemporary international legal scholars writing in English to advance the idea that the legitimacy of states depends upon their satisfying at least minimal standards with respect to the protection of human rights. Tesón, F., *Humanitarian Intervention, An Inquiry Into Law and Morality* (3rd edn., New York: Transnational Publishers, 2005) and *A Philosophy of International Law* (Boulder, Colo.: Westview Press, 1998).

apply the laws (although legitimate institutions may sometimes produce illegitimate laws). Accordingly, international laws are legitimate only if the institutions that make them are legitimate. Let us call international law-making institutions (ILIs). By an institution here is meant (roughly) a persisting pattern of organized, rule-governed, coordinated behavior. Using this broad sense of 'institution', we can say there are three types of ILIs: the institution of treaty-making, the institution of customary international law, and global governance institutions, which includes a diversity of entities such as the World Trade Organization (WTO), the United Nations (UN) Security Council, environmental regimes such as that established by the Kyoto Accords, and various judicial and regulatory 'government networks' composed of officials from several states. Global governance institutions, though created and sustained through treaties made by states, are increasingly taking on law-making functions.

At present, there is nothing approaching an adequate theory of legitimacy for international law. Before much headway can be made on this task, several questions must be answered. (1) What is the distinctive character and point of legitimacy judgments and how do they differ from other evaluations of institutions? (2) What concept or conceptions of legitimacy are relevant to international law and what standards of legitimacy ought ILIs meet, assuming that a particular concept of legitimacy is relevant? (Is there one concept of legitimacy and one set of standards for legitimacy that applies to all ILIs?). (3) What are the chief challenges to the legitimacy of international law? (What features of ILIs call their legitimacy into question?). (4) What is at stake in assessments of the legitimacy of international law—more specifically, why does the legitimacy of ILIs matter and to whom? (5) What conditions should a theory of legitimacy for international law satisfy? (6) What are the main rival approaches to theorizing the legitimacy of international law and which seem most promising, given an account of the conditions such theories should satisfy? The aim of this chapter is to answer these six questions.

2. The Nature of Legitimacy Assessments

Assertions about the legitimacy or illegitimacy of institutions (as opposed to reports about people's beliefs about their legitimacy) are moral evaluations, not statements of legal fact. The issue is whether ILIs have the *moral* right to rule and what does the right to rule entail.[2]

Just as legitimacy judgments cannot be reduced to statements of legal fact, they are also not reducible to statements to the effect that non-compliance with the institution's rules will elicit coercion or that compliance with the rules is

---

[2] The rest of this section draws on Buchanan, A. and Keohane, R. O., 'The Legitimacy of Global Governance Institutions', *Ethics & International Affairs*, 20/4 (2006), 405.

advantageous. An institution can be effective in coercively enforcing rules and yet not be legitimate; indeed, in the case of the state it has been precisely its success in coercing that has most urgently raised the question of its legitimacy. Similarly, an institution might be advantageous—even advantageous to all whom it attempts to govern—and yet it might still be illegitimate, for example, if it came about through usurpation.

The moral evaluation that institutional legitimacy judgments express is also different from that of justice. Although extreme and persisting injustices can render an institution illegitimate, legitimacy is a less-demanding standard than justice in the sense that an institution can be legitimate though not fully just.[3] Different parties' legitimacy assessments of a particular institution can agree, even if they have serious disagreements about what justice requires. Thus, legitimacy judgments can facilitate morally based coordinated support—or criticism—of institutions even where consensus on justice is lacking. The current concern about the legitimacy of international law may be due in part to the widespread belief that present disagreements about justice—especially global distributive justice—are not likely soon to be resolved.

Achieving morally based coordination can be of great practical importance when two conditions are satisfied. The first, which I have already suggested, is that there is serious disagreement about justice but considerable consensus that institutions ought to satisfy some moral requirements—a widespread belief that merely being able to enforce their rules and being advantageous relative to the non-institutional alternative are not sufficient. The second is that the distinctive benefits that an institution creates are most reliably secured if, in addition to the fear of coercion and the expectation of advantage relative to the non-institutional alternative, there are moral reasons to support the functioning of the institution. Moral reason-based support can enable an institution to function successfully when there are lapses in its ability to coerce and during periods when there is reason for some to doubt that it is indeed advantageous for all relative to the non-institutional alternative. Moral reason-based support can reduce the costs of achieving compliance, which might be prohibitively high if the threat of coercion were the only reason for compliance.

3. Stronger and Weaker Senses of 'the Right to Rule'

There are stronger and weaker senses of 'the right to rule', although prominent accounts of legitimacy often assume that only one of these senses is of central importance for political philosophy. What might be called the dominant philosophical

---

[3] However, an institution might be operating in a perfectly just way yet be illegitimate, if it came about through serious injustice, for example, by usurping the functions of a pre-existing legitimate institution.

view (DPV) of *state* legitimacy employs a very strong understanding of the right to rule, as including six elements: (a) the institution's agents are morally justified in engaging in governance functions, including issuing rules and attaching costs and benefits to various agents to facilitate compliance with them (the justified governance condition); (b) the institution's agents are morally justified in using coercion to secure compliance with the institution's rules (the justified coercion condition); (c) only the institution's agents are morally justified in engaging in governance functions in the domain of action in question (the exclusive justification condition); (d) the institution's agents are morally justified in using coercion to prevent others from attempting to engage in governance activities in its domain (the coercive exclusion condition); and (e) those whom the institution attempts to govern have a content-independent moral obligation to comply with (all) the rules the institution imposes (the content-independent moral obligation condition).[4] A content-independent obligation to comply with a rule is an obligation that exists independently of any assessment of the rule itself. In all legal systems, those to whom the rules are addressed typically have content-*dependent* moral obligations to comply with some of the rules: for example, if the law prohibits murder, one has a moral obligation to comply with this law because it is simply the legal expression of a valid moral rule. Since (e) presumably implies (f), a similar obligation *not to interfere* with the institution's efforts to secure compliance with its rules, there are in fact six elements of legitimacy on this account. Because the DPV was developed with the case of the state in mind, it emphasizes the right to coerce.

The DPV's conception of the right to rule is extraordinarily strong, both with regard to what counts as *ruling* (that is, governance) and with regard to what counts as having a *right* to rule. It assumes that legitimacy not only involves justified governance (ruling) of some sort (element (a)), but *also* justified coercive governance (element (b)), *and* the exclusive right to use coercion to secure compliance with rules (element (c)), *and* the right to use coercion to exclude others from engaging in governance activities in its domain (element (d)). However, there is no reason to assume that only institutions that govern (rule) in this very strong sense can be said to be legitimate or illegitimate, that is, can have the right to rule or lack it. Indeed, there are many institutions, including all existing international institutions, which do not rule in this robust way and do not even claim to do so. It is *more* plausible

---

⁴ By the dominant philosophical view I mean that view of the legitimacy of the state that is generally assumed in the extensive contemporary analytic philosophical literature on the question of whether there is 'a duty to obey the law'. For what may be the most developed and carefully reasoned contribution to this literature, see Simmons, J. A., *Justification and Legitimacy, Essays on Rights and Obligations* (Cambridge: Cambridge University Press, 2001). Item (d) above may not be explicit in Simmons's own understanding of legitimacy, but it is included in the Weberian conception of the state as an entity that claims a monopoly on the use of force within a territory, and it seems clear that Simmons and others in the mainstream debate about the obligation to obey the law assume the Weberian conception. However, nothing in my central argument in this paper depends on the claim that the dominant philosophical view includes (d).

to say that the very strong notion of governance encompassed by the dominant philosophical conception of legitimacy is pertinent if we are focusing only on the legitimacy of one peculiar kind of institution, namely, the state.[5]

A better way of understanding 'being morally justified in governing' element of legitimacy is as follows: being morally justified in issuing rules and seeking to secure compliance with them through attaching costs to non-compliance and/or benefits to compliance. This characterization covers coercion but is not limited to it and can therefore serve as an element in a concept of legitimacy that is applicable to institutions that do not rule coercively, including most ILIs.

The DPV rightly emphasizes that legitimacy, as the term is often used, includes more than being justified in governing if this means merely having the liberty-right to govern.[6] A can have the liberty-right to do X and it can nonetheless be true that no one has any duty or even any reason not to interfere with A doing X. Merely being justified in governing in this sense is arguably insufficient for what might be called the focal sense of 'legitimacy' because it fails to encompass the distinctive *relational* aspect of legitimacy.[7] More specifically, the mere liberty-right to govern omits the crucial idea that the rules of a legitimate institution *have a privileged status vis à vis our reasons for acting and that their having this privileged status is not dependent on their content*. At least in what might be called the focal sense of the term, legitimacy involves not only the liberty-right to govern but also *a content-independent requirement of practical support for (or at least non-interference with) the institution's efforts to govern*.[8]

---

[5] It is not even clear, however, that the dominant philosophical conception of legitimacy applies to states as they actually are at present, as opposed to how they have been conceived in recent analytic political philosophy. The dominant philosophical conception appears to assume a unitary and unqualified sovereignty that no longer exists, if it ever did. Sovereignty is now increasingly 'unbundled' and distributed, in two ways. First, there is increasing political differentiation within states, with various forms of federalism (symmetrical and asymmetrical) and other kinds of intrastate autonomy regimes, as well as a separation of powers at both the state and Federal levels. Under these conditions of complex political differentiation, there may be no definitive answer to the question 'who has exclusive authority over domain D?'—or at least no answer prior to the actual resolution of some particular conflict over authority, which may or may not occur. Yet it still makes sense to ask whether the state is legitimate. Second, there are substantial external limitations on sovereignty, including the increasingly effective institutionalization of international criminal law and international (and, in the case of the EU, regional) human rights law. These external limitations on sovereignty diminish the authority of the state even within its own territory. Given the internal dispersal of sovereignty and the external limits on it, the dominant philosophical conception of legitimacy appears to be too strong for application to the contemporary state.

[6] 'Justified' in the phrase 'being justified in governing' is itself ambiguous between (a) having a liberty-right to govern, that is, it being morally permissible to govern; and (b) there being good moral reasons in favour of (the institution's) governing. I will operate with the former, weaker notion, but nothing in my argument hinges on this.

[7] Simmons, J. A., *Justification and Legitimacy* (above, n. 4), 128.

[8] There are different possible interpretations of the idea that these content-independent obligations are 'weighty'. In particular, it could be argued that the right to rule implies not only that there are content-independent reasons for compliance with the institution's rules but also that these content-independent reasons are peremptory in the sense that they rule out certain kinds of reasons for not complying *ab initio*, rather than

The DPV's very robust requirement of a content-independent *moral obligation* to comply with rules is not needed to capture the idea of a requirement of content-independent practical support and hence is not necessary for legitimacy in the focal, relational sense. The weaker combination of a content-independent moral obligation or substantial content-independent reason not to interfere, along with substantial content-independent *moral reasons* to comply—where these reasons may fall short of grounding an obligation—does the job. Therefore, it is not the case that a proper recognition of the distinction between merely being justified in governing and being legitimate requires anything as strong as the DPV's conception of legitimacy.[9] One can acknowledge that legitimacy as the right to rule involves more than being justified in ruling without assuming that it entails something as strong as a content-independent moral obligation to comply.

The DPV's understanding of what counts as *rule* (that is, governance) is as unduly strong as its understanding of the right to rule. Many international legal institutions do not claim an *exclusive* right to rule, yet it makes perfectly good sense to ask whether they are legitimate (in a relational sense). For example, the World Trade Organization (WTO) does not claim that it alone is justified in engaging in multilateral efforts to promote the liberalization of trade; it recognizes the legitimacy of regional trade regimes that promote liberalization. Similarly, the International Criminal Court (ICC) does not claim to be the only tribunal that may justifiably prosecute the international crimes specified in its statute; it allows for both prosecution of individuals by their own states and the exercise of 'universal jurisdiction' by states over foreign individuals. Second, even when international legal institutions claim the exclusive right to govern in a certain domain, they do not always, or even typically, also claim the right to use coercion to exclude others from attempting to engage in governance functions. Third, 'rule' in the DPV's understanding of the right to rule means governance in the peculiarly strong sense in which *states* (sometimes) govern: seeking to ensure compliance with rules through *coercion*, understood as a credible threat of the use of physical force against non-compliers. Although most international legal institutions do not govern, or attempt to govern, or even claim the right to govern, in this very strong sense, it nevertheless makes sense to ask whether these institutions are legitimate, where legitimacy is understood as relational, as implying more than being morally justified in governing.

merely being weighty relative to them. On this view, if an institution that addresses a rule to one is legitimate, then the mere fact that not complying with its rule would be to one's advantage does not count as a reason that could be weighed against one's reason for compliance. The points I wish to make about the legitimacy of ILIs in this paper do not depend upon resolving the issue of whether the content-independent reasons for compliance are peremptory, but my assumption is that they are and this is one of the reasons for the qualifier 'substantial' in the phrase 'substantial content-independent reasons'.

9 This is true even if 'being justified' is understood more robustly than 'having a mere liberty-right', for example, if it is taken to signify that there are strong reasons in favour of having the institution in question (for example, for prudential reasons).

My proposal, then, is to proceed on the assumption that for ILIs, legitimacy as the right to rule includes two main elements: (1) the institution must be morally justified in attempting to govern (must have the moral liberty-right or permission to try to govern) in the sense of issuing rules (that prescribe duties for various actors) and attempting to secure compliance with them by imposing costs for non-compliance and/or benefits for compliance and (2) those toward whom the rules are directed (chiefly, though not exclusively states) have substantial, content-independent moral reasons for compliance and others (including citizens of states) have substantial content-independent moral reasons for supporting the institution's efforts to secure compliance with its directives or at least have substantial, content-independent moral reasons not to interfere with those efforts.

This formulation has several advantages. First, it acknowledges the fact that most ILIs, like international institutions generally, do not employ coercion to secure compliance with their rules, and do not claim the right to do so. Thus it avoids the error of simply applying to ILIs the very strong conception of legitimacy that may be appropriate for the state. Second, it allows for the fact that there is variation among ILIs as to whether they attempt to achieve or claim exclusive authority over the domain in which they operate. Third, the second conjunct of (2), it recognizes that the legitimacy of ILIs can reasonably be of concern to actors other than states, some of whom may not be subjects of duties the institution attempts to impose.

This understanding of legitimacy seems superior to the Razian conception of authority that John Tasioulas advances, according to which A has the right to rule over B if and only if B's complying with A's rules enables B to do better than B would do were she to act directly on reasons that independently apply to her. The difficulty with the Razian notion is that the mere fact that others would do better were they to obey one does not justify one's attempting to rule over them. So an entity could have authority in the Razian sense but not be justified in attempting to secure compliance with the norms it promulgates. Yet, whatever else having the right to rule entails, it surely includes being justified in attempting to rule.

4. The Chief Challenges to the Legitimacy of International Law

Challenges fall mainly under the following five headings. First, there is a challenge from the perspective of states: it is frequently said that particular ILIs, like the UN Security Council or the WTO, or even the entire international legal order, are unfairly controlled by a handful of powerful states, thereby unfairly disadvantaging weaker ones. Whether it is supposed to be a claim about injustice or about legitimacy is often unclear. It could be both, of course—the idea being that from the perspective fairness to states, this or that ILI or the current international legal order as a whole, is so unjust as to be illegitimate. Some who advance this charge assume that the remedy is state-majoritarian democracy: ILIs should operate according to procedures that assure an equal voice for all states.

A second, quite different challenge to the legitimacy of ILIs is that they are unfair to individuals and/or non-state groups, such as indigenous peoples or that they fail to take the legitimate interests of non-state individuals or groups seriously enough and often operate so as to threaten their welfare. On this view, the unfairness of ILIs regarding states is of concern only so far as it results in unfairness to non-state individuals or groups or threats to their welfare. Some versions of this challenge assume that some kind of global democracy is required if ILIs are to be legitimate.[10]

The third legitimacy-challenge focuses on whether ILIs credibly do the jobs they are supposed to do or act in accordance with the goals and procedures to which they publicly commit. For example, some have argued that the failure of the Security Council to authorize armed intervention to stop genocides or other forms of mass murder have been so egregious as to undermine the legitimacy of the Council. An institution may also be deemed illegitimate if it is deeply and persistently corrupt. Some have concluded that the massive corruption of the Iraq 'Oil For Food' programme, when considered in the light of a long history of corruption or at least poor management in many other cases, impugns the legitimacy of the UN Secretariat, which was in charge of the programme.

The fourth challenge to the legitimacy of ILIs alleges that all or some of them usurp the proper authority of states or, on one variant of the view, of democracies. There are two different ways of understanding this challenge. On the first, less radical variant, the charge is that *as a matter of fact* some ILIs have so seriously encroached on the proper domain of authority of the state (or democratic states) as to render themselves illegitimate, but there is no claim that international law and sovereignty or the sovereignty of democracies are *in principle* incompatible. On the second, more radical variant, the charge is that the supremacy of international law is incompatible in principle with sovereignty or with democratic constitutional sovereignty. According to the second interpretation, ILIs, so far as they claim supremacy for their norms, are *necessarily* illegitimate, at least *vis à vis* constitutional democracies, because by definition the supreme law in a constitutional democracy is determined by its own constitution.

It appears, however, that there is no problem of incompatibility in principle. If democracies can subject themselves to international laws by following processes

---

[10] These first two challenges to the legitimacy of ILIs are all seriously incomplete. Each merely cites an unfairness or injustice of ILIs, but then slides immediately to the conclusion that the institution is illegitimate. Something more must be said, because, as I have already noted, injustice does not entail illegitimacy. The gap here is symptomatic of a more general problem: the characteristics that appear to be relevant to legitimacy (fairness, avoidance of discrepancies between institutional goals and actual behaviour, accountability, transparency, etc.) are all scalar (they admit of degree), yet at least in some context, the legitimacy must be regarded as a threshold concept (an institution either has it or doesn't), if legitimacy assessments are to play their practical role of distinguishing institutions that have the right to rule from those that don't. Having the right to rule, on the face of it, is not a matter of degree.

that accord with their own constitutional principles, there is no bar to saying both that they are bound by those laws and that the constitution is the supreme law of the land. One way of accomplishing this is to create a new constitution or amend an old one so that it recognizes the supremacy of international law, or of some types of international law, such as human rights law. Moreover, if a democratic state ratifies a treaty and incorporates the relevant laws into its domestic legal system through a process that satisfies constitutional requirements, then presumably it will be true to say that the state has a substantial content-independent moral reason to comply and that the citizens of the democracy have a substantial content-independent reason to support their state's compliance—namely, because the law in question became the law of the land through a constitutionally-sanctioned process. If the worry is only that international law is being incorporated in ways that violate the democracy's constitution and proper constitutional processes for incorporation are available, then the objection is not that constitutional democracy and the supremacy of international law are *in principle* incompatible.

The fifth and final challenge to the legitimacy of international law is that ILIs are not themselves democratic. *If* 'democracy' here means what it does in the case of the state, namely, that those who make the law must be accountable, through periodic electoral processes in which individuals have an equal vote, most theorists agree that democracy (in this 'individual-majoritarian' sense) at the global level is not presently feasible or likely to become so in the foreseeable future. Instead of concluding from this that ILIs cannot be legitimate, some argue that they can be, so long as they exemplify the same basic *democratic values* (or principles) that mandate individual-majoritarian democracy in the case of the state. Whether the current democracy deficit is sufficiently serious to deprive the existing international order of legitimacy is a further question, and one which in my judgment has not been adequately addressed.

5. Why and to Whom the Legitimacy of International Law-making Institutions Matters

It is misleading to say that international law is created by states, through treaty and custom, both because this formulation overlooks the growing contribution of global governance institutions to international law-making and because various non-state actors increasingly play a role in international law-making. The legitimacy of international law is not just a concern of states, but also of non-state groups and individual citizens, who sometimes may reasonably question the legitimacy of international institutions even though they know that their own states have consented to them. As I noted earlier, individuals and groups may still question the legitimacy of ILIs even though their state has voluntarily consented to them, not because they believe that these institutions treat weaker *states* unfairly, but rather because they believe that these institutions act unfairly toward *them* or threaten *their* welfare. To a large extent, this concern on the part of citizens reflects the growing penetration of international law into life within states. The further we depart from the picture of international laws as being created solely by states and as dealing solely with the relations of states to one another—and the more seriously we take the idea that human beings, not states, are the ultimate objects of moral concern—the clearer it becomes that a satisfactory account of the legitimacy of international law must include more than an explanation of why *states* ought to regard the international institutions through which law is made as having the right to rule. More precisely, appreciating the new face of international law shows just how inadequate the traditional framing of the question of the legitimacy of international law is. The question is much broader than 'why should states consider international law binding?'

6. A Deeper Sense of the Question 'Is International Law Legitimate?'

There is a still more basic issue about the legitimacy of international law. This is the question of whether or to what extent democratic state leaders and the citizens of democratic states ought to be morally committed to the project of international law—to the endeavour to build and sustain an international legal order. The query here is not whether this or that international law or this or that type of ILI (for example, treaty-law or customary law) is legitimate; rather, it concerns the moral status of the goal of developing the rule of law at the global level. This is an important question, even if one concludes that international law as it now exists has a serious legitimacy deficit. Even if no existing international institutions were legitimate, we could still sensibly ask whether the project of international law makes moral sense.

Recently some American legal theorists, like some American political leaders, have answered this question in the negative, advocating what I have elsewhere called a purely instrumental stance toward international law.[11] On this view, the citizens of democratic states should direct their state leaders to support international legal institutions only when it is in the national interest to do so or when those citizens happen to have moral 'preferences' (such as the 'preference' that human rights not be violated) that are best promoted by doing so. There is no non-instrumental reason for entering into any particular international agreement or for keeping agreements already entered into, nor for contributing to the work of building and improving the international legal order.

---

[11] See e.g. Goldsmith, J., and Posner, E. *The Limits of International Law* (Oxford: Oxford University Press, 2005).

7. The Ideal of the Rule of Law

The most obvious reply to the purely instrumentalist view is that there are substantial moral reasons to promote *the rule of law* at the international level. Although there is much controversy as to just what the ideal of the rule of law consists of, there is considerable consensus that the principles that constitute it include the following: the law should be general (and when there are departures from generality they should be controlled by processes that are informed by general principles); the law should be understandable and publicly proclaimed; there is a presumption against retroactive law, especially retroactive criminal law; and the administration of the law should be impartial. In a wider sense, the commitment to the rule of law is the commitment to resolving or managing conflicts by effectively institutionalizing the impartial application of publicly known general rules that are based on the assumption that there is to be an accommodation of interests. The commitment to the rule of law in this wider sense goes beyond the assertion that *if* there is to be international law it should conform to the principles that constitute the ideal of the rule of law; it is the commitment to subjecting international relations to law, in conformity to this ideal.

The traditional answer to the question 'why should we try to subject international relations to the rule of law?' was that doing so is necessary to achieve peace among states. This answer is compatible with the purely instrumental view, but it is also compatible with its rejection, if the commitment to peace is understood to be a moral duty, not merely a matter of rational prudence. Increasingly, the contemporary answer to the question is that subjecting international relations to the rule of law is necessary not only for the sake of peace among states but also for justice, where justice is understood, first and foremost, though not exclusively, as the realization of human rights.

Those who hold the purely instrumental view of international law may do so because they subscribe to a Realist theory of international relations: Realists deny that there is a non-instrumental moral obligation to promote the rule of international law because they believe that, given the nature of international relations as they understand it, international law will never be capable of making a significant contribution to justice. (In addition, they may in fact hold that the concept of justice has no application to international affairs.) Given the weaknesses of Realism, which have been increasingly exposed in recent years, this reason for denying that there is a non-instrumental moral obligation to support the project of international law is hardly conclusive.

Resolving the dispute between the purely instrumentalist view and the view that there is a moral obligation to promote the rule of international law is clearly beyond the scope of the present investigation. My purpose is only to distinguish different senses of the question 'is international law legitimate?' and to indicate that the deepest of these goes to the heart of our understanding of the relationship between law and justice and our predictions about the human capacity for creating lawful relationships among different societies.

8. Conditions an Adequate Theory of the Legitimacy of International Law Should Satisfy

The preceding analysis yields criteria of adequacy for a theory of the legitimacy of international law. Such a theory must encompass all three types of ILIs—it must provide an account of the legitimacy (or otherwise) of customary law, treaty law, and law produced by global governance institutions. It must also acknowledge that it is no longer true that states alone make international law, accommodating the fact that global governance institutions engage in rule-making that is not accurately described as the creation of law through state consent and that non-state actors, including agents of transnational, non-governmental organizations, now sometimes contribute to the making of international law.

II. Standards for the Legitimacy of International Law

1. The Simple state Consent View

Proceeding on the assumption that institutions are the primary subject of legitimacy assessments and that the legitimacy of laws depends on the legitimacy of institutions that make them, it may be initially tempting to say that the question of the legitimacy of international law can be answered in a rather simple and straightforward way: rules are legitimate international laws if and only if they are produced through *the institution of state consent*, that is, if they are created in accordance with the procedures that states have consented to for the making of international laws, which include the requirement that states must consent to laws. The state consent view of legitimacy has been by far the dominant view among international legal theorists. Let us consider the first half of the biconditional: is state consent sufficient for legitimacy?

   On the simplest interpretation of the view that state consent is sufficient, the legitimacy of treaty law is assured by the explicit consent of states, the legitimacy of customary international law is assured by a kind of implicit consent inferred from the behaviour of states, and the legitimacy of law generated by global governance institutions is assured by their being created and sustained by state consent. The attraction of this view lies in an analogy with individual consent: if you and I consent to a certain arrangement as to how we shall treat each other, then surely that arrangement is legitimate. Similarly, it is said, if States consent to a certain arrangement for how their interactions are to be regulated, then it is legitimate.

The analysis of Section I indicates that there are several reasons for rejecting the view that *under current and foreseeable conditions* state consent is sufficient for the legitimacy of international laws. The consent of weaker states may be less than substantially voluntary, because stronger states can make the costs of their not consenting prohibitive. Further, in many cases, states do not represent all of or even most of their people; they are not sufficiently democratic to make it reasonable to say that state consent by itself legitimizes what states consent to.

In addition, even if we focused only on treaty law—setting aside the dubious assumption that customary law can reasonably be understood as enjoying state consent—and even if all states represented all their people, it would still not follow that state consent suffices for legitimacy, for two distinct reasons. First, the problem of questionable voluntariness would still remain: the fact that a weak state is democratic does not change the fact that it is weak and therefore may face pressures that undermine the voluntariness of its consent. Second, as I have already noted, international law increasingly is not limited to rules to which States can be said to consent in a normatively substantial sense; instead, some important international law is created by global governance institutions of various sorts. Even though these institutions are created by state consent and cannot function without state support, they engage in *ongoing* governance activities, including the generation of laws and/or law-like rules, that are not controlled by the 'specific consent' of states. Hence, the problem of 'bureaucratic distance' looms large, even if the states that create these institutions are democratic; the links between the popular will in democratic states that consent to the creation of global governance institutions and the governing functions these institutions perform seem too anaemic to confer legitimacy. Given the reality of bureaucratic distance, the mere fact that democratic states consented to the creation of a global governance institutions and have not withdrawn their consent does not seem sufficient to make such institutions legitimate. Finally, to the extent that non-state actors play a role in the creation of international law, state consent seems insufficient for legitimacy, unless it can be shown that the legitimacy of the contribution these non-state actors make to the creation of international law is somehow assured by state consent.

So far I have argued that, under current conditions in which (1) there is great disparity of power among states, in which (2) many states do not represent all of their people, and in which (3) there is a serious problem of 'bureaucratic distance', state consent is not sufficient for the legitimacy of international institutions nor, therefore, for the legitimacy of the laws they make (given that the legitimacy of the latter derives from the legitimacy of the former). At this point one might argue that *in different circumstances*—where conditions (1), (2), and (3) do not obtain—state consent would be sufficient for legitimacy. In other words, we might view the claim that state consent is sufficient for legitimacy as a claim in the ideal theory of international legal order, not as a claim about what suffices for the legitimacy of international law as it is or is likely to be in the foreseeable future. Whether state consent would be a sufficient condition for legitimacy in ideal theory cannot be determined, however, until the ideal theory is laid out.

More troubling still, we cannot begin to evaluate claims about ideal theory until we specify just what an ideal theory is a theory of. The answer to the question 'would state consent be sufficient for the legitimacy of international law-making institutions in ideal theory?' may differ depending upon whether or not we assume that ideal theory is a theory for a world in which only states (as opposed to other political entities, regional or sub-state) are the primary agents for the establishment of justice.

2. Is State Consent Necessary for Legitimacy?

So far I have argued that, under current conditions, state consent is not sufficient for legitimacy. This leaves open the question of whether it is necessary. If we assume that state consent is a necessary condition for legitimacy under current conditions, then it appears that we must conclude that much of existing international law, perhaps especially customary international law (CIL), is illegitimate. The view that states tacitly or implicitly consent to CIL does not stand up to scrutiny. CIL norms apply to states that did not exist at the time of their emergence, even if they object to them, yet surely their objecting to them is pretty good evidence that they are not now consenting to them. To say that such states have consented to the *process* by which CIL norms emerge is equally unconvincing, given the inability of weaker states to opt out of the process or to do so without excessive costs. To summarize: if state consent is a necessary condition for legitimacy under current conditions, then a substantial portion of existing international law appears to be illegitimate.

Whether state consent is a plausible necessary condition for the legitimacy of international law in ideal theory cannot be determined unless we first have a specification of the background conditions for ideal theory, including the role of states in the overall system the ideal theory prescribes. In contrast, there is a straightforward non-ideal theory argument for a norm according to which state consent is a necessary condition for the legitimacy of international law under current conditions: adherence to this norm would reduce the ability of strong states to hijack the project of international law. In other words, the best reason for saying that state consent is a necessary condition for the legitimacy of international law may be that, under current and foreseeable conditions, it provides an important safeguard against the rule of the strong. Whether strict adherence to the requirement of state consent is the only feasible and adequately effective safeguard is a complex issue that cannot be pursued here. It is worth pointing out, however, that strict adherence to the requirement of state consent is a costly way of protecting against predation: it gives every state, including the most oppressive ones, a veto over any progressive change in international law.

3. The Demand for Democratic Legitimacy

A growing awareness of the insufficiency of state consent for legitimacy under current and foreseeable conditions, along with the widespread belief that democracy is a necessary condition for the legitimacy of the state, may explain why the debate about the legitimacy of the international legal order has shifted from a preoccupation with state consent to a debate about the possibilities of 'global democracy'. A major focus of this discussion has been global governance institutions, in large part because they appear to be inadequately controlled by state consent or at least by the will of democratic publics and yet seem to be growing more consequential, not just for state sovereignty, but also for the well-being of individuals. Let us call the Global Democracy View the claim that at least one important type of ILI, global governance institutions, cannot be legitimate unless they are democratic in the individual-majoritarian sense. The Global Democracy View is often criticized for being utopian. The idea is that the conditions for global democracy (in the individual-majoritarian sense)—do not exist and are not likely to exist in the foreseeable future. This seems to me to be right, if, as the Global Democracy View holds, the requirement for legitimacy is that ILIs must be democratic in what I referred to earlier as the individual-electoral sense. Here one might either conclude that the standard of democracy now increasingly applied to states is too demanding to be applied to ILIs or one might conclude that no ILIs are legitimate, because they fail to satisfy that standard. Robert O. Keohane and I opt for the former conclusion. We argue that once the distinctive practical function of legitimacy assessments in achieving moral reason-based coordination is understood, it becomes clear that a requirement of global democracy in the individual-majoritarian sense is an unreasonably strong necessary condition in the case of global governance institutions for the foreseeable future.[12] In a nutshell, we argue that the demand for global democracy in this sense is unreasonably strong given two conditions: first, the benefits that global governance institutions provide are quite valuable and not likely to be reliably provided without them; second, the key values that underlie the demand for global democracy can be reasonably approximated if these institutions satisfy other more feasible conditions, including what we call Broad Accountability. By the latter we mean that these institutions must cooperate with external epistemic actors—individuals and groups outside the institution,

---

[12] Buchanan, A. and Keohane, R. O., 'The Legitimacy of Global Governance Institutions' (above, n. 2).

in particular transnational civil society organizations—to create conditions under which the goals and processes of the institution as well as the current terms of institutional accountability, can be contested and critically revised over time, and in a manner that helps to ensure an increasingly inclusive consideration of legitimate interests, through largely transparent deliberative processes. Broad Accountability, we argue, would provide a reasonable second-best for global democracy in the individual-majoritarian sense, under current, highly non-ideal conditions. Although Broad Accountability may not qualify as democracy on some accounts, it does realize some important democratic values.

Rather than recapitulate that argument in detail here, I simply want to note that even if one could argue, contrary to what Keohane and I contend, that global democracy in the individual-electoral sense is a necessary condition for the legitimacy of ILIs, *it would not be sufficient*. Even the most enthusiastic advocates of democracy at the domestic level ought to admit that the legitimacy of *any* majoritarian electoral process can be undercut if it results in serious and persistent violations of basic human rights, for example, the rights of a minority ethnic or national group. The same would be true at the global level. So, whether or not democracy (in the individual-electoral sense) is a necessary condition for the legitimacy of global governance institutions, it is not sufficient. Nor would global democracy understood as an arrangement that achieves equal political power for all states (rather than all individuals)—what I referred to in section I as the state-majoritarian view—be sufficient for legitimacy, because that too is compatible with serious violations of human rights. In sum, it is difficult to imagine that any institution of governance, democratic or otherwise, at the global or the domestic level, could be legitimate if it persistently engaged in serious violations of basic human rights norms. Of course, on some understandings of democracy (whether global or domestic) respect for basic human rights is already included, but this conflation is unhelpful. A political order could be democratic, even in the very strong sense that each individual has an 'equal say' in law-making, and yet the laws could provide insufficient protection for human rights or even violate them. So, assuming that the protection of human rights is generally a necessary condition for the legitimacy of a political order, it appears that state consent, even under much more ideal conditions than those in which it now operates, is not sufficient for legitimacy.

III. Human Rights and International Legitimacy

It is something of a commonplace that the international legal order is becoming less exclusively state-centered and more concerned with human rights. The Security

Council has authorized military interventions to stop large-scale human rights violations in Bosnia and Somalia. *Ad hoc* tribunals and a permanent international criminal court have been created to prosecute war crimes, genocide, and crimes against humanity. The idea that state sovereignty itself is conditional on the protection of human rights seems to be taking hold.

These changes are rightly viewed as moral progress; yet they raise a fundamental issue of legitimacy that those who greet them with enthusiasm have not squarely faced. In order to be legitimate, an international legal order that takes the protection of human rights to be a fundamental goal must address a familiar challenge to the very idea of human rights: what I have elsewhere labeled *the parochialism objection*, according to which what are called *human* rights are not really universal but instead are simply reflections of one particular cultural point of view (variously said to be 'Western' or 'liberal' or 'liberal individualist').

To meet this objection, it is not enough to point out that most states have ratified the major human rights conventions. The question is not whether states have agreed to treat human rights norms *as if they were* universally valid but rather whether they *are* universally valid. To elide the latter distinction is to assume that state consent, under current conditions, is sufficient for legitimacy. But that claim, I have argued, is indefensible. Nor will it do to say that the international legal system includes institutions that articulate legal international human rights norms (call them IHRIs) and ensure that these norms conform to the criteria for legality in the international legal system. By itself, the legality of a putative human rights norm does nothing to establish that a human right exists. Further, nothing in the texts of human rights conventions seems to provide an adequate response to the fundamental issue of justification that the parochialism objection raises. Indeed, aside from some vague gestures toward human dignity in the Preambles, the texts scrupulously avoid the task of justification.

One might argue that the parochialism objection is hardly credible when applied to *basic* human rights norms such as the rights against enslavement, the right to physical security, the right against religious persecution, and the right to subsistence. And, indeed, it does seem implausible to say that these rights are of value only to 'Westerners' or 'liberal individualists'. The parochialism objection arises anew, however, once we realize that there can be serious disagreements, in some cases apparently rooted in different cultural, religious, or philosophical views, about the specific content of these rights and about how they ought to be balanced against one another in cases of conflict. For example, there may be near universal agreement that there is a human right not to be subjected to torture or to cruel and inhumane punishment, but cultural variation as to what counts as torture or cruel and inhumane punishment. In brief, even the most basic human rights norms are not self-specifying and specifications may be reasonably questioned as to whether they are parochial or not. The more fully an intuitively plausible, highly abstract human rights norm becomes legalized—that is, expressed as an international legal human right—the more vulnerable it can become to the charge of parochialism, because legalization involves, *inter alia*, greater specificity.

It is often said that the Universal Declaration of Human Rights and the various human rights treaties that followed it wisely avoided attempting a justification for the norms they asserted. To paraphrase the philosopher Jacques Maritain, it was possible to agree on a list of human rights only on the condition that almost nothing was said about how they are grounded. As an explanation of the absence of a public moral grounding for international human rights law, Maritain's remark is cogent. It does nothing to rebut the parochialism objection, however. Therefore, it also does nothing to allay the worry that an international legal order that increasingly relies on the idea of human rights in its conception of its own legitimacy, in the legitimacy assessments it makes, and in its efforts to enforce the conditions of legitimacy on other institutions, is of questionable legitimacy if it persists in doing so without being able to provide a credible public justification for the claim that it has properly identified and specified a set of genuinely universal rights.

In the end, whether such a justification becomes available will depend not only upon the further development of the moral foundations of the idea of human rights—a task which until recently most contemporary moral and political philosophers, like most international legal theorists, have avoided—but also upon improvements in the global public deliberative processes that occur within the complex array of institutions within which human rights norms are articulated, contested, and revised over time.[13] What I am suggesting is that grappling with this fundamental legitimacy problem requires an investigation of the moral-epistemic functions of these institutions. This means viewing them, not merely as venues in which antecedently justified moral norms are given legal form, but as institutions for global public deliberation that can contribute to the moral justification of human rights norms and thereby to their own legitimacy and to the legitimacy of the international legal order as a whole, so far as that order takes human rights seriously.

---

[13] I develop this idea of a complementary relationship between philosophical argumentation about the justification of human rights and global public deliberative processes occurring through international legal institutions in 'Human Rights and the Legitimacy of the International Legal Order' *Legal Theory*, 14 (2008), 39–70.

CHAPTER 4

....

THE LEGITIMACY OF INTERNATIONAL LAW

....

JOHN TASIOULAS*

I. LEGITIMACY AS 'THE RIGHT TO RULE'

....

For many years the pitifully meagre interest shown by philosophers in public international law (PIL) centred on the 'ontological' question whether it really is law, the discouraging implication being that there are respectable grounds for a negative verdict. Its lack of various supposed hallmarks of legality—reliable enforceability, an unfettered and habitually obeyed sovereign, a rule of recognition, and so on—seemed to render PIL either not genuinely law or at best a borderline instance. But this sceptical threat has now receded markedly, partly because the theories of law on which it drew have come to seem less compelling. Hence the timeliness of Thomas Franck's call for a 'post-ontological' phase in the theory of PIL that addresses the *normative* question: given that PIL is law, which standards should guide its evaluation and development?[1]

Alongside peace, justice, prosperity, and the preservation of nature, legitimacy figures prominently among these standards. If PIL is law, then it necessarily claims legitimate authority over its subjects.[2] Legitimate authority—in the normative, rather than sociological, sense—is the 'right to rule', the exercise of which 'binds'

* My thanks are owed to Allen Buchanan, Thomas Franck, Samantha Besson, Tim Sellers, Jean Porter, Robert McCorquodale, and William Twining for helpful written comments on a draft of this paper.

[1] Franck, T. M., *Fairness in International Law and Institutions* (Oxford: Oxford University Press, 1995), 6.

[2] See Raz, J., 'Authority, Law and Morality', in *Ethics in the Public Domain* (Oxford: Oxford University Press, 1994).

its subjects by imposing duties of obedience.[3] The fact that PIL inherently lays claim to legitimacy does not entail that it actually has it; that it has it to the full extent of its claim; or that it is capable of possessing it under realistically attainable conditions. Nor, conversely, would its lack of legitimacy necessarily deprive it of its status as law. Instead, whether PIL is, or can be, legitimate depends on (a) what the 'right to rule' amounts to, (b) the standard that must be met for that right to obtain, and (c) the extent to which PIL, as it is or might be, satisfies that standard. Call these, respectively, the conceptual, justificatory, and verdictive questions.

A familiar answer to the conceptual question is this: A has legitimate authority over B when A's directives are content-independent and exclusionary reasons for action for B. In other words, the directives are reasons in virtue of the fact that A issued them and not because of the content of any particular directive, and these reasons are not simply to be weighed along with other reasons that apply to B but, instead, have the normative effect of excluding at least some countervailing reasons.[4] Against this monistic account, on which 'legitimacy' bears a unitary meaning, Buchanan's contribution to this volume might be taken to suggest a dualist view.[5] According to dualism, the meaning of legitimacy as claimed by sovereign states is given by the DPV (the dominant philosophical view), a compound of six elements: justified governance, justified coercion, exclusive justified governance, coercive exclusion, content-independent moral obligation, and obligation of non-interference.[6] However, in relation to PIL, a weaker, double-barrelled conception of legitimacy operates (WCL): (1) a moral justification for governing, and (2) content-independent moral reasons for compliance and for non-interference with efforts to secure compliance.[7]

But given that there is a plausible univocal account of the focal meaning of legitimacy, an especially persuasive case must be made for rejecting it in favour of dualism. This is all the more so given the threat dualism poses to PIL's status as fully-fledged law. If it belongs to the essence of law to claim authority, and if the authority claimed by PIL is a diluted version of that claimed by domestic law, PIL's status as the poor relation of domestic law is confirmed.

Rather than embrace dualism, we should distinguish the variable *content* of laws from the invariant normative *status* which laws assert in virtue of their inherent claim to legitimacy. The content of laws includes such matters as whether they assert exclusive jurisdiction or an entitlement to use coercion, while the normative status they necessarily claim is that of content-independent and exclusionary reasons. In

---

[3] In Chapter 3 this volume, 84, Allen Buchanan suggests that legitimacy may also be interpreted in terms of reasons to obey, or even reasons not to interfere with the attempt to govern. Even so, the claim to impose duties belongs to the core or focal sense of legitimacy; indeed, so much is implied by speaking of a 'right' to rule, since rights ground duties.

[4] See Raz, J., *The Morality of Freedom* (Oxford: Oxford University Press, 1986), ch. 2 and Raz, J., 'The Problem of Authority: Revisiting the Service Conception', *Minnesota Law Review*, 90 (2006), 1003.

[5] Contrary to his own intentions, it turns out (personal communication).

[6] Buchanan, A., this volume, 82.   [7] Ibid. 84.

this way, we can allow that the content of PIL typically differs in the ways noted by Buchanan from that of domestic law, while preserving both a univocal concept of legitimacy and, to that extent, the fully legal character of PIL. This distinction also accommodates another phenomenon stressed by Buchanan, viz., that domestic law itself now often falls short of asserting the DPV due to the internal dispersal of, and external limitations on, the authority of the state (as illustrated, respectively, by federalist states, such as the US, and schemes of 'pooled sovereignty', such as the EU). Moreover, PIL increasingly includes elements, such as exclusive jurisdiction and coercive measures that go beyond the WCL; for example, the UN Charter confers exclusive jurisdiction on the Security Council to respond to threats to international security by coercive measures. A dualist, by contrast, must somewhat artificially interpret these developments as involving a switch from one sense of legitimacy to another.

This leaves us with the choice between the concept of authority I have described and the WCL. Arguably, the latter only differs from the former in adding the apparently superfluous requirement of a moral justification for governing, since it is not obvious what justified *governing* could be other than the issuing of directives that are genuinely content-independent reasons for action. Buchanan's response is that 'being justified in governing' imports a liberty-right to govern and, contrary to the Razian view of authority I have endorsed, 'the mere fact that others would do better were they to obey one does not justify one's attempt to rule over them'.[8] Now, Buchanan offers no argument for this assertion, which in any case seems misdirected, being addressed to the standard, and not the concept, of legitimate authority (see section II, below). But this reply is not entirely satisfactory, since there is pressure to make reference to the standard of legitimate authority in the analysis of its concept.[9] Another reply is that Buchanan's objection trades on a misreading of the Razian standard, one according to which a putative subject's 'do[ing] better' is not determined by reference to *all* the reasons that apply to that subject, but only a sub-set of them. For Buchanan's objection to be decisive, he must show that there is a systematic discrepancy between our considered judgments about legitimate authority and the Razian standard properly interpreted. This he does not attempt to do.

Does it matter whether PIL is legitimate? After all, legitimacy is only one standard of assessment among others, and PIL could possess considerable value even if it lacked legitimacy. PIL norms may be *instrumentally* valuable despite not binding those they purport to bind, for example, by attaching reputational and other costs to undesirable behaviour. Alternatively, PIL might acquire value by giving forceful *expression* to correct ethical standards irrespective of its instrumental

---

[8] Ibid. 85.
[9] In order, for example, to distinguish content-independent and exclusionary reasons that have their source in, e.g. promises, from those that have their source in legitimate authority.

efficacy in securing compliance with them. Still, the existence of a valuable but non-legitimate legal order is not an ideal scenario, because a claim to authority is integral to PIL's identity as a legal order: the law's distinctive contribution to a community's realization of valuable goals consists precisely in successfully laying down authoritative standards of conduct.

II. THE STANDARD OF LEGITIMACY

What standard must be satisfied for the claim to legitimate authority to be justified? Buchanan does not venture a complete answer to this justificatory question, arguing only that both consent and global democracy are insufficient, and compliance with human rights is necessary, for the legitimacy of international legal institutions. I believe a bolder approach is warranted. Just as PIL does not need a bespoke concept of legitimacy nor, I shall assume, does it need a bespoke standard of legitimacy. Following Joseph Raz, the leading contemporary exponent of a classical tradition of thought about authority, the Normal Justification Condition (NJC) is typically a sufficient condition for legitimate authority both domestically and internationally:

NJC: A has legitimate authority over B if the latter would better conform with reasons that apply to him if he intends to be guided by A's directives than if he does not.[10]

So, an authority is legitimate when its putative subjects would likely better conform with the reasons that apply to them by treating the putative authority's directives as content-independent and exclusionary reasons for action than if they adopted some other guide. This is aptly dubbed a 'service conception' of legitimate authority, but the adjective should not mislead us into supposing that what confers legitimacy on an authority is its role in enabling its subjects to fulfil their subjectively given preferences or goals. Instead, the reasons in question are ultimately objective: they concern what the subjects' goals should in fact be, not what they are (see section IV). Moreover, they are highly diverse, embracing not only reasons of self-interest but crucially also moral reasons. The latter include the human rights-based reasons stressed by Buchanan, but also go beyond them to include sources of moral reasons that do not belong to the province of justice, such as the humanitarian concern to alleviate suffering, as well as those not exclusively centred on human interests, for example the preservation of nature.

On this view, neither the consent of the governed nor democratic rule are *fundamental* criteria of legitimacy; instead, they can only have a derivative bearing

---

[10] Raz, J., 'The Problem of Authority' (above, n. 4), 1014. See also Raz, J., *The Morality of Freedom* (above, n. 4), pp. 53–69 and ch. 4.

on legitimacy, by affecting (whether instrumentally or constitutively) the fulfiment of the NJC. What significance they have, if any, is to be determined case-by-case. So far as the NJC is concerned, it is possible for A to have legitimate authority over B even if A's rule is neither consented to nor democratic; conversely, it is possible for B to consent A's rule, or for A to rule democratically over B, without A's rule being legitimate. This is welcome news for PIL's prospects for legitimacy, since PIL does not now enjoy, and is unlikely to achieve in the foreseeable future, a significant grounding either in the consent of its subjects or in democratic law-making processes.[11]

Capitalizing on this promising start, a defender of PIL's legitimacy may go on to enumerate some of the ways it might plausibly be taken to fulfil the NJC.[12] First, PIL and its institutions might enjoy *cognitive* advantages over their subjects in determining what the latter have reason to do. It is a familiar claim, for example, that customary international law is a distillation of the time-tested collective wisdom of states, fruitfully drawing on their divergent cultural perspectives and historical experience in the resolution of common problems, thereby making it a more reliable guide to right reason than any other alternative. Similar claims are made for multilateral treaty regimes, for example, that the inclusive process of negotiation through which they emerge helps ensure that they are not skewed in favour of sectional interests.

Second, PIL's legitimacy might stem from curing *volitional* defects. Even when states are able in principle to discern reason's demands, they may be deflected from acting accordingly by cultural prejudices, economic and political self-interest, external or internal pressure, etc. Subjection to PIL may act as a bulwark against these influences. Consider, for example, the claims of genocide in Kosovo and weapons of mass destruction in Iraq, made by the British and US governments when justifying military interventions in violation of the UN Charter, claims which were subsequently revealed to be false or grossly exaggerated. These errors might be partly explicable in terms of purely cognitive deficiencies, but arguably volitional defects also played a significant role in shaping British and US policy. In such cases, the reasons all states have to foster peace and promote human rights would be better served by taking the UN Charter regime for threats to international security as authoritative.

---

[11] For more on consent and democracy under the service conception, see Raz, J., *The Morality of Freedom* (above, n. 4), 80–94 and Raz, J., 'The Problem of Authority' (above, n. 4), 1031 n. 20 and 1037–40. For compelling arguments to the effect that consent is neither a necessary nor a sufficient general condition for the legitimacy of international law, see Buchanan, A., *Justice, Legitimacy and Self-Determination* (Oxford: Oxford University Press, 2004) and this volume, 90–4.

[12] For a general discussion see Raz, J., *The Morality of Freedom* (above, n. 4), 75. States, of course, are not the only subjects of PIL, but they are for good reasons its primary subjects, and at the risk of some distortion, in this chapter I focus on states rather than those other subjects, e.g. international organizations, peoples, multinational corporations, NGOs, individuals, etc.

Third, PIL can enjoy legitimacy by virtue of the *decision-procedural* benefits it confers on its subjects. Sometimes a state's attempt to identify and act on the balance of reasons can be self-defeating. For example, all states have reasons to promote peace, but efforts to do so directly, for example, by a super-power that pursues a policy of coercive pro-democratic regime change, risk being counter-productive, creating a backlash among 'rogue states', with a consequent escalation in nuclear proliferation and the threat of war. Instead, reason may be best served if even the super-power follows an indirect strategy in its pursuit of peace, one that subjects it to a PIL regime which prohibits unilateral military action aimed at countering threats to international security.

Fourth, the fulfilment of the NJC may arise from PIL's *executive* advantages, that is, its power to effect certain outcomes. Classically, a powerful agent can resolve problems of co-operation and co-ordination by laying down standards that its putative subjects have reason to comply with because, *inter alia*, it is likely to be generally obeyed. All states face problems—epidemics, economic instability, environmental degradation, the proliferation of weapons of mass destruction, refugee movements, etc.—that cannot be adequately addressed by individual states acting alone but only through a framework for co-operation and co-ordination. PIL can provide such a framework, largely in virtue of the propensity of states to obey it. In order to maintain this source of legitimacy, of course, PIL must not stray too far from implementing values that resonate widely with its would-be subjects. Of course, PIL conspicuously lacks generally effective enforcement mechanisms in dealing with recalcitrant states. Although formal mechanisms exist—ranging from military enforcement measures under chapter VII of the UN Charter to the power of the UN High Commissioner for Human Rights to criticize states for serious human rights violations—they often lie dormant due to lack of political will, or else are deployed ineffectively or selectively. But what matters for legitimacy is enhanced conformity with reason than would otherwise be the case, not perfect conformity. Moreover, the pressure to conform need not be channelled exclusively through formal sanctions, as is shown by the way respected NGOs such as Amnesty International invoke PIL to influence state behaviour, often by shaping public opinion.

Of course, sceptics about the legitimacy of PIL will dispute many of the preceding claims. Arguably, however, the question of real interest is not whether PIL possesses *any* authority, even in such workaday domains as international telecommunications or postal services, but the *extent* of its authority. On the service conception, the scope of legitimacy is prone to 'domain fragmentation', so that a legal system's claims of legitimacy are justified in some domains but not in others. This permits us to judge that some PIL regimes, such as the UN Charter and corresponding customary norms governing the use of force, are legitimate even if other branches of PIL, such as the doctrines and institutions animated by a Procrustean free market ideology or by hopelessly vague and endlessly proliferating claims about 'human rights', are not.[13] Making such judgments is no easy task, with the result that we may often be uncertain whether a given segment of PIL satisfies the NJC; by contrast, consent-based or democratic standards of legitimacy seem to promise greater certainty. Rather than take this as an objection to the service conception, however, one might regard it as faithfully reflecting our complicated epistemic situation.

III. Exceptionalism

But now the prospect of another kind of fragmentation looms. Certain PIL norms might enjoy legitimacy with respect to *some*, but by no means *all*, of its putative subjects. The service conception admits this possibility, since whether the NJC is fulfilled is a relational matter that can vary from one subject to another.[14] In allowing this possibility, it diverges from theories of legitimate authority according to which the very existence of a legal order (or of a legal order minimally compliant with the rule of law) *ipso facto* imposes a general obligation of obedience on its putative subjects. The possibility of 'subject fragmentation' might be exploited in support of the doctrine of 'American exceptionalism'. Of course, a variety of policies are subsumable under that label, the least defensible being that the US arrogates to itself the prerogative of acting in its perceived self-interest irrespective of the costs to the rest of the world. But a not obviously indefensible interpretation of exceptionalism goes as follows: although PIL may possess legitimate authority over all other states, it does not have authority, or does not have it to anything like the same extent, over the US, because for a significant number of PIL norms the NJC is not fulfilled with respect to that state. On this view, the US acts perfectly justifiably and unhypocritically in assuming a leading role in creating PIL norms intended to bind other states, and perhaps also in enforcing them against states that act illegally, while regularly exempting itself from their scope. This is because, uniquely among states, it is more likely to conform with the reasons that apply to it, including moral reasons to uphold the human rights of people throughout the globe, if it is unconstrained by those norms.

Subject fragmentation is most plausible when defended in tandem with a claim of domain fragmentation: *this* putative subject is not bound by *this* domain of PIL. Such an argument might be advanced in connection with the current UN

---

[13] The domain fragmentation of the legitimacy of PIL is one reason for resisting Buchanan's suggestion in this volume (p. 79–81) that we should focus legitimacy assessments on *institutions*, e.g. such as treaty-making and customary international law. Even if we began by doing that, it seems to me that such an inquiry would likely be upstaged eventually by one into whether certain domains of PIL have legitimacy (domains that are constituted by norms generated by a variety of institutions).

[14] See Raz, J., *The Morality of Freedom* (above, n. 4), 73–4.

Charter's use of force regime which outlaws unilateral military action on the basis of preventative self-defence and coercive pro-democratic regime change. Call it the 'neo-conservative argument', which could be encapsulated as follows: 'Our world is disfigured by the presence of various failed, oppressive and aggressive states. Apart from often posing a severe threat to the human rights of their own populations, they also pose dire threats to people elsewhere, either because they intend to acquire and use weapons of mass destruction or else because they give succour to international terrorist organizations that seek access to such weapons. The existing PIL regime, with the pivotal role it assigns to the UN Security Council, has repeatedly shown itself impotent in the face of these threats. Only the US, the sole remaining super-power with its unequalled military, economic and political capabilities and its powerful liberal democratic tradition, is able to deal with these problems effectively through preventative military action geared to pro-democratic regime change. It therefore would not best conform with the reasons that apply to it if it were fettered by PIL on the use of force and intervention'.

The neo-conservative argument prompts many questions. Can we readily accept that the US is as well intentioned as the argument supposes? And, even if it is well intentioned at present, would it long remain so when exposed to the profoundly corrupting temptations associated with the role of global hegemon? Moreover, doesn't the US itself bear significant responsibility for the humanitarian and other crises that the UN Security Council has failed to avert, such as in Rwanda? And when the US has previously used unilateral force in violation of Charter norms, haven't the subsequent outcomes generally confirmed the superiority of the UN regime? If the US bears a duty to foster the international rule of law, then will not the adoption of a policy of exceptionalism contravene that duty, given the likelihood that states who see themselves as prime targets of unilateral coercion will be motivated to engage in illegal behaviour, for example, violating norms against the non-proliferation of weapons of mass destruction? And doesn't the argument rather overlook the benefits, both instrumental and intrinsic, of societies finding their own way to democracy?

Finally, any case for American exceptionalism regarding PIL on the use of force must reckon with the following alternative. It begins by observing that the duty to obey a legitimate authority is not absolute but can on occasion be defeated, such as in cases of dire emergency. So, rather than being exempted from PIL in any given area, the US may be bound by it, with its duty to obey being defeasible. The opposition to exceptionalism, therefore, is not a rigid legal absolutism that denies it is ever all-things-considered permissible to violate PIL. Is this alternative merely cosmetic? No, as the difference it makes to the normative situation shows. First, the starting-point for determining the correctness of US policy is a duty to obey PIL on the use of force, one that must be defeated if deviation from PIL is to be justified. In practical terms, this means the US will typically have to exhaust all feasible legal means before a compelling moral case exists for law-breaking. Nor is this first point rendered nugatory by the duty's defeasibility, leaving the US free rein to 'decide the exception'. No moral reason is self-executing, but it hardly follows that we cannot distinguish valid from specious claims to be acting for such a reason or an exception to it. Second, even when the US has justifiably breached the duty of obedience, various consequential duties may arise—duties to apologize, make reparation, undergo punishment, etc.—since a defeated duty is not necessarily extinguished in virtue of being overriden.

The neo-conservative argument, I conclude, faces an uphill battle. But perhaps a stronger case for US exceptionalism can be mounted in other domains, such as human rights law, at least in its domestic application. Nor should we think of exceptionalism as the exclusive preserve of rich and powerful states; on the contrary, it may well be that the most plausible case for exceptionalism is one that applies to severely impoverished states—exempting them, for example, from key elements of the international economic legal order.

IV. Parochialism

A recurrent challenge to the legitimacy of PIL is that it foists 'parochial' values on people and societies who do not share them. In this vein, many critics see PIL as a manifestation of Western cultural 'imperialism'; for feminists, it embodies partriarchal values; neo-conservatives decry the influence on PIL of bureaucratic and pacifist European traditions of governance; while for critics of globalization, it is an instrument of the capitalist market's quest for world-wide dominance. All these claims can be explicated under the aegis of the service conception. According to the NJC, legitimacy is secured by enhancing conformity with *objective* reasons—reasons that obtain independently of individual or societal preferences and beliefs. In their different ways, the complaints about parochialism deny that PIL facilitates conformity with such reasons, as opposed to the counterfeit 'reasons' asserted by certain dominant groups, no doubt in furtherance of their own agendas. Contrast exceptionalism, according to which the reasons underlying PIL *may* apply to the putative subject, but even if they do the latter does not best conform with them by obeying PIL. Henceforth, I shall refer to the first version of the objection, and to human rights morality and law as its target.

The initial response to the challenge of parochialism must be to undertake the taxing work of deliberating about whether or not, in any given domain, objective reasons are best fulfilled through obedience to PIL. In conducting such an inquiry, we need to avoid two crude errors. The first is the genetic fallacy that the localized historical origin of ethical notions by itself precludes their objective standing; conversely, we should not imagine that world-wide adherence to certain values would of itself show that they are objectively correct. Even granting the contestable claim that the idea of human rights has an exclusively Western pedigree, this is not incompatible with its containing objective truths that bear on all human beings, any more than the European origin of the theory of relativity renders non-Europeans rationally impervious to its claim to truth. Of course, we should guard against the danger that these ideas might embody an etiolated view of the layout of reason, especially given the ignorance, arrogance, and downright malevolence that Westerners have historically displayed towards other cultures. But its tainted historical origins cannot pre-empt the answer to the question whether PIL informed by human rights morality here and now satisfies the NJC.

The other error is that objective reasons dictate uniform outcomes because, in virtue of their objectivity, they are insensitive to variation in circumstances. But objectivity does not entail prescriptive invariance: contingent, non-normative circumstances may objectively alter cases, so that what counts as fidelity to the same values, reasons, and norms is a dynamic matter, varying from case to case. Hence, the practical import of the reasons we have to respect human rights will vary according to such contingent facts as a society's level of economic development, technological capacities, and even its climate. One implication of this environmental relativity for human rights law is that the reasons to respect and promote human rights do not necessarily single out one specific institutional arrangement for doing so, such as democratic elections, free markets, or American-style judicial review, as required in all societies. Another is that, once appropriate institutions are established, they need leeway to interpret and implement human rights in light of the relevant societal context (something reflected in the legal doctrine of 'margin of appreciation').

The anticipated reply—that we have grossly underestimated the force of the parochialism objection—will come in at least two significantly different versions.

(a) Scepticism. The sceptical version involves an outright rejection of ethical objectivity: the NJC cannot be satisfied, because there are no objective (ethical) reasons for action. Value scepticism is a deeply entrenched, yet seldom defended, dogma in contemporary PIL theory. It is a supposed platitude that unites not only writers as otherwise apparently diverse as realists in international relations, post-modern feminists, 'critical theorists', and liberal cosmopolitans but even authors of sober black-letter texts. The suggestion that the threat of parochialism can be addressed by engaging in piecemeal deliberation is dismissed by them as a pious hope, since any instance of deliberation inevitably operates within some arbitrarily privileged viewpoint.[15] Now, it is not easy to exonerate these sceptics of the charge of self-contradiction, since the evident moral animus conveyed by denunciations of 'Western imperialism' seems to assume the objective superiority

---

[15] For an unusually lucid statement of the view, see Zolo, D., *Cosmopolis: Prospects for World Government* (Cambridge: Polity Press, 1997), 118–19.

of certain non-Western ethical traditions.[16] But even if they could be exonerated, their rejection of ethical objectivity remains deeply problematic because it forecloses on the possibility of radical, non-question-begging criticism of social practices, no matter how seemingly wicked. This is a consequence that has not exercised many self-styled 'critical theorists' nearly as much as it should.

It is a testimony to the powerful grip of this largely unreflective sceptical orthodoxy that a number of prominent writers try to evade the apparently corrosive implications of scepticism for PIL's legitimacy without impugning the former's truth. One such attempt is the argument from modernity, which proceeds roughly as follows: (i) commitment to the values that underlie human rights, for example individual autonomy, is ultimately the product not of any specific cultural ethos, but of the 'independent variables' that define the conditions of modernity—industrialization, urbanization, growth in scientific and technological understanding, etc., (ii) these conditions are pervasive and inescapable features of the modern world, exerting a steady liberalizing influence on both Western and non-Western societies, therefore (iii) those societies that do not currently display a notable allegiance to human rights will eventually come to do so.[17] This argument has the merit of reminding us that cultures are not static and self-enclosed, but constantly evolving, partly as a result of interactions with other cultures. But it fails to neutralize the sceptical challenge. First, its empirical premises are highly contestable: why should we subscribe to the vulgar Marxist thesis, seemingly implicit in (i), that value commitments are merely by-products of underlying socio-economic forces? And, even if we grant it, it is hardly obvious that the 'inexorable forces of economics, technology and communications'[18] reliably work in favour of belief in personal freedom and human rights, as per (ii). Consider the plausible rival hypothesis that by fraying traditional identities and communal bonds modernity provokes an illiberal backlash in the form of authoritarian government and religious fundamentalism. Even bracketing these empirical reservations, the argument fails because its conclusion shows only that history is 'on the side' of human rights, not that there is any compelling reason to endorse their victory, inexorable or not. But it is the absence of any such reason that animates the sceptic about human rights.

An alternative evasive strategy, famously employed by John Rawls, avoids this defect by appealing not simply to conditions of modernity, but to the *values* implicit in a liberal democratic culture. Yet it aims to defuse the charge of Western parochialism

---

[16] There is another paradox in this vicinity: the boundaries of states on behalf of which the parochialism complaint is made are often themselves products of Western colonialism.

[17] See Franck, T. M., 'Is Personal Freedom a Western Value?', *American Journal of International Law*, 91 (1997), 593. Cf. also Habermas, J., 'Remarks on Legitimation through Human Rights', *The Postnational Constellation: Political Essays* (Cambridge: Polity Press, 2001), 121. For a more detailed critique of the argument from modernity, see Tasioulas, J., 'International Law and the Limits of Fairness', *European Journal of International Law*, 13 (2002), 1000–4.

[18] Franck, T. M., 'Is Personal Freedom a Western Value?' (above, n. 17), 624.

while strenuously prescinding from any commitment to the 'objectivity' of those values, in any sense of that term debated by philosophers. How does Rawls square this circle? Although his Law of Peoples is an 'extension' of a liberal conception of justice to the regulation of a Society of Peoples, it is 'not necessarily . . . ethnocentric or merely western'—in Rawls's cautious formulation—since its *content* can be affirmed for their own moral reasons by non-liberal societies.[19] This is because the Law of Peoples does not simply reproduce, at the global level, the requirements of justice applicable within a liberal state. For example, its schedule of human rights is only a sub-set of the full array of liberal constitutional rights, omitting rights to free speech, equal religious liberty, an adequate standard of living, among others.[20]

But this argument manifestly fails to address the parochialism objection in just the situation in which an answer is most needed: when the objection is advanced by non-liberal and non-decent states that, as a result of persistent and grave violations of the human rights of their own members, are rendered vulnerable by the Law of Peoples to military intervention by well-ordered societies.[21] And even decent peoples, the sole category of non-liberal society that can accept the Law of Peoples for moral reasons, might understandably baulk at being designated objects of 'toleration' under its principles, to be protected from forcible intervention only because they are 'not fully unreasonable',[22] when the operative criterion of reasonableness ultimately derives, by way of little more than stipulation, from a liberal democratic outlook they do not share. And this is not yet to raise the question whether liberal societies can accept, and act on, the Law of Peoples in the absence of a justified belief that the aspects of liberal democratic culture from which it derives can be given an objective vindication. In short, Rawls's strategy smacks more of a capitulation to parochialism than its successful avoidance.

Richard Rorty has suggested Rawlsians should respond to such difficulties by biting the bullet. They should frankly embrace a 'liberal ethnocentrism' by maintaining their commitment to the global spread of Enlightenment *values* while jettisoning the Enlightenment *philosophical* aspiration of giving those values an objective grounding.[23] Yet this beguiling manoeuvre fails to grasp that the claim to objectivity is internal to ethical thought, not a dispensable or outmoded philosophical add-on, partly because Rorty presupposes an outlandish interpretation of what objectivity is.[24] On the view I find most defensible, it comes to nothing more, or less, than

---

[19] Rawls, J., *The Law of Peoples* (Cambridge, Mass.: Harvard University Press, 1999), 121.

[20] Ibid. 68, 78–9.   [21] Ibid. 90.   [22] Ibid. 74.

[23] Rorty, R., 'Justice as a Larger Loyalty', in Cheah, P. and Robbins, B. (eds.), *Cosmopolitics: Thinking and Feeling Beyond the Nation* (Minneapolis: University of Minnesota Press, 1998), 56.

[24] See Tasioulas, J., 'The Legal Relevance of Ethical Objectivity', *American Journal of Jurisprudence*, 47 (2002), 211–54.

the fact that questions posed within a certain subject-matter admit of answers that are, in an ordinary sense, true. One mark of the availability of such answers is the possibility of convergence on certain ethical propositions (e.g. that torture is a human rights violation) where the best explanation of such convergence commits us to the truth of the proposition converged upon.[25] Contrary to Rorty, this is not tantamount to the historicist dogma that truth is a force that is destined, or even likely, to triumph in shaping belief and action.[26] Historicism is no more implied by the thesis of ethical objectivity than it is, *contra* the argument from modernity, capable of putting it in abeyance. The objectivist affirms only the *possibility* of such vindicatory explanations, and he would be wise to pair this metaphysical claim with advocacy of inter-cultural dialogue, conducted in an inclusive and fallibilist spirit, as a vital conduit to the truth. As Buchanan observes, a key function of human rights institutions is to foster such dialogue, thereby enhancing the prospects of legitimacy of the legal norms they generate.[27]

(b) Pluralism. The most formidable version of the parochialism complaint, although one seldom articulated as such in the voluminous literature on the parochialism of PIL, springs from value pluralism. Pluralism has no truck with ethical scepticism; instead, it is itself an ethical doctrine, one that purports to be objectively correct. It holds that: (i) there are many irreducibly distinct values, (ii) these values can come into conflict in particular situations, (iii) some of these conflicts are incommensurable in that responses to them are not subject to a complete ranking, i.e. they cannot all be ranked as better or worse than each other, nor yet as equally good, and (iv) at the level of individual and collective forms of life, there are many different and conflicting ways of responding to these values, which also are not subject to a complete ranking. An implication of (iv) is that the idea of the single best way of individual or collective life, even given 'ideal' conditions, is a chimera.

If pluralism is correct, the question arises whether particular PIL norms, even if they exemplify an in-principle eligible ordering of the relevant values, represent only one such ordering among others. If this possibility is realized, then societies subject to PIL norms that reflect orderings they do not share might properly complain that those norms unjustifiably impose an alien, 'Western' perspective on them at the expense of no less valuable forms of life sustained by their own cultures. They need not deny that, abstractly considered, there are objective and undefeated reasons

---

[25] For a compelling defence of ethical objectivity so understood, see Wiggins, D., *Ethics: Twelve Lectures on the Philosophy of Morality* (London: Penguin, 2006), 359 ff.

[26] See Rorty, R., 'Human Rights, Rationality, and Sentimentality', in Shute, S. and Hurley, S. L. (eds.), *On Human Rights* (New York: Basic Books, 1993).

[27] Buchanan, A., this volume, 95–6.

for adopting the Western outlook. All they need to establish is that the situation is symmetrical with respect to their own outlook and that, since this outlook is already theirs, they have a conclusive (or at least an undefeated) reason to adhere to their own ethical tradition without being subject to countervailing PIL norms.

To the extent that the PIL of human rights (to keep with our original focus) purports to reflect background moral norms of human rights, the worry is that the latter lack the requisite universality needed to confer legitimacy on the former. If so, human rights law is a mechanism through which non-Western societies are illegitimately pressured into refashioning themselves along Western lines. But can anyone credibly deny that a right to be free from torture is possessed by all humans and should be respected by all societies? Of course not, but other putative norms of human rights morality might be less easily defended against the pluralist assault. It is in relation to this pluralist concern, and not simply that of environmental relativity, that we may interpret David Wiggins's suggestive distinction between 'true internationalism' and the ambitious 'global ethic' that inspires much of the contemporary human rights culture.[28] The latter seeks to lay down a mass of highly general principles, such as those contained in the UN Millennium Development Goals, that aim to generate solutions to the major problems confronting all societies. The former, in a pluralistic spirit, seeks to arrive at international norms by starting out from the identification and critical elaboration of ideas that members of different societies find they can really share—the qualification 'really', presumably, underscores an objectivist constraint. In so far as this process has a legal-political upshot, Wiggins believes it is best exemplified by instruments that express the 'universally valid proscription of specific evil'—torture, genocide, imprisonment without charge, forced labour, etc. Like Rawls's argument, this suggests a briefer list of human rights as compared with that which currently finds favour in PIL, yet without sidelining the aspiration to objectivity.

Now, of course, one might dispute Wiggins's minimalist conclusion even within a pluralist framework. For example, it is not obvious why the eradication of extreme poverty, and a human right to be free from it, does not count as a universally valid proscription of specific evil to which all societies have decisive reason to adhere. Certainly, such a right is vulnerable to disastrously Procrustean or self-serving forms of interpretation and implementation on the part of powerful states, NGOs, and multinational corporations, but the same is true of the universally valid prohibitions endorsed by Wiggins. Still, the key point for present purposes is not where precisely to draw the line between universal norms and objective norms with a narrower scope of application, but that pluralism indicates that this line will need to be drawn somewhere. Thus, a pluralist who is sanguine about basic socio-economic human rights might wonder whether supposed human rights

---

[28] Wiggins, D., *Ethics: Twelve Lectures on the Philosophy of Morality* (above, n. 25), 355–6.

to equal religious liberty or non-discrimination on the grounds of sex or sexual orientation do not presuppose orderings of values that although in principle eligible are certainly not demanded of all societies. Indeed, with respect to some of these rights, it is not even clear whether Western societies have unequivocally committed themselves to the requisite orderings of values, as is suggested by the interminable and divisive character of disputes about gender equality and gay rights in those societies.

The implications of pluralism for the PIL of human rights are not confined to the question of which supposed human rights genuinely count as such in morality. Although no one is likely to deny the existence of a human right against torture, pluralism allows for the existence of a diversity of acceptable ways of justifying such a right. If this possibility is realized, we should not automatically lock the official justification of the legal human rights against torture into the ordering of values represented by just one justification.[29] This lets us put a benign gloss on Jacques Maritain's notorious quip that the drafters of the Universal Declaration of Human Rights proceeded on the basis that they 'agree[d] about the rights, but on condition no one asks us why'. If there are incommensurable pathways to the same schedule of human rights, then it is not the case that one of them is superior to all the others. There is no compulsion, therefore, to disagree at the level of underlying justifications. Here pluralism rides to the assistance of PIL's legitimacy, since it liberates us from the constraining assumption, which has dominated the philosophical discourse of human rights, that there is a single correct grounding of those rights. Notice, however, that the pluralist point seems available only to an interpretation of human rights that regards them not as underived moral norms that occupy a foundational role in morality, but as grounded in (a multiplicity of) other, non-rights-based considerations, such as universal human interests.

Having recognized a plurality of justificatory routes to the same human right, we should also acknowledge that there may be diverse ways of specifying the content of that right, and of trading it off against countervailing considerations in cases of conflict, that are also not subject to a complete ranking. Again, PIL will be impaired in its legitimacy to the extent that it does not appropriately reflect such diversity. None of this is to suggest, however, that accommodating pluralism to the fullest extent is everywhere a necessary condition of PIL's legitimacy. Often there are reasons that tell against such an approach, for example, the desirability of co-ordination on the basis of highly determinate legal norms in certain areas may make it all-things-considered acceptable to privilege one ordering of values in interpreting those norms over alternative eligible orderings favoured by other societies. My contention is only

---

[29] For an instructive comparison of Western/liberal and Buddhist justifications of that right, appealing respectively to autonomy and the non-infliction of suffering, see Taylor, C., 'Conditions for an Unforced Consensus on Human Rights', in Bauer, J. R. and Bell, D. A. (eds.), *The East Asian Challenge for Human Rights* (Cambridge: Cambridge University Press, 1999).

that value pluralism has a significant, but insufficiently appreciated, bearing on the satisfaction of the NJC.

V. FREEDOM

Among the reasons that apply to the various agents subject to PIL are some grounded in the value of freedom. By freedom, I mean both autonomy (having and exercising the capacity to choose from a range of plausibly valued options) and liberty (having and exercising the capacity to pursue, without interference, the options one has chosen).[30] We have reasons to make and pursue our own choices, and to respect and protect the similar freedom of others. Some of these reasons are instrumental: if we choose and act freely, we may be more likely to conform to other reasons that apply to us. Others are intrinsic, grounded in the value of free choice and action as such, independent of its causal consequences. In what follows, I focus on the intrinsic value of freedom.

As a source of practical reasons, freedom bears on the fulfilment of the NJC. Regarding some matters, it is more important that I reach and act on my own decision, rather than take a putative authority's directives as binding, even if doing the latter would result in decisions that, in all other respects, better conform to reason.[31] Thus, even if citizens would make better major life decisions—selection of a life-partner, a career, a religion, and so on—by following the directives of government experts on well-being, rather than by acting on the basis of their own assessment of the balance of reasons, this would not confer legitimate authority on the experts in relation to those matters. Within broad limits, individuals have greater reason to make certain decisions themselves, thereby giving expression to their nature as rational agents, than to do what is best in all other respects. Notice that, in the strongest such cases, what respect for freedom rules out is legitimate authority itself, and not simply some mode or other (e.g. coercive) of enforcing legitimate directives.

Now, one prominent challenge to the legitimacy of PIL is that it fails to respect the freedom of states, intruding upon domains in which they should be free to make their own decisions. This presupposes that the intrinsic value of freedom extends to the choices and actions of states. It seems plausible that it does, given the value of shared membership in a national political community and, in consequence,

---

[30] I take this distinction from Griffin, J., *On Human Rights* (Oxford: Oxford University Press, 2008).

[31] Joseph Raz expresses the point thus: 'the matters regarding which the [NJC] is met are such that with respect to them it is better to conform to reason than to decide for oneself, unaided by authority', in Raz, J., 'The Problem of Authority' (above, n. 4), 1014. This is a somewhat unhappy formulation, since the contrast is not between conformity to reason and deciding for oneself: in the excluded cases one best conforms to reason precisely by deciding for oneself.

of the collective self-determination of such communities. This does not imply that states have an ultimate value comparable to that of the individual human beings who are their members; on the contrary, collective self-determination has value only in so far as it serves the interests of those individuals. Moreover, I leave aside the thorny question of whether such collective self-determination is only intrinsically valuable in the case of democratic states. However, it seems to me that Rawls rightly considers that some non-democratic states—such as decent hierarchical societies—are capable of realizing this value to an extent that merits protection through PIL. And even if the value of collective self-determination is largely confined to broadly democratic societies, it may be appropriate for PIL to extend the protection it justifies to all societies except in certain extreme cases, on the grounds that the primary responsibility for bringing about the democratic reforms necessary for that value to be realized falls on the members of the society in question and that, in any case, intervention by external bodies is likely to be counter-productive.

The supposed incompatibility between PIL and the self-determination of states might be either contingent or necessary.[32] Necessary incompatibility is hard to credit. One reason is that PIL norms of state sovereignty—such as prohibitions on the use of force and intervention—are designed, in significant part, to protect the self-determination of states with respect to certain external and domestic matters. The protection thus afforded is not limited to the freedom to make and pursue objectively sound choices, which is why the value of freedom has a significance that transcends the need to accommodate environmental relativity and value pluralism. What may obscure this, especially for very powerful states, is the assumption that they do not need the protection of PIL to safeguard their own freedom. But, even in the unlikely event that this belief does not embody a fantasy of self-sufficiency, the reasons states have include reasons to respect and promote the collective self-determination of people belonging to *other* states. It is difficult to see how the latter can be fulfilled without a network of international legal norms that is universally binding.

As for contingent conflicts between freedom and PIL, they have to be identified as such, and their significance assessed, on a case-by-case basis. Under this heading the proliferation of legal human rights norms acquires a new significance. Even if certain PIL human rights norms reflect reasons that are both objective and suitably universal in light of a due regard for value pluralism, they may lack legitimacy because they purport to bind states regarding matters that should be left to their own free choice. In other words, even if rights not to be subjected to capital punishment or discrimination on grounds of sexual orientation really are universal rights as a matter of morality—let alone more disputable cases, such as an entitlements to annual paid leave or to the highest attainable standard of

---

[32] Buchanan, A., this volume, 86.

health—they may nevertheless fall within a domain wherein different societies should be free to make their own, albeit potentially inferior, decisions without being bound by norms of PIL or subject to intervention as a result of their breach.

Of course, this understanding of human rights deviates from that endorsed by Rawls and Raz, according to which human rights are *essentially* limitations on state (or political) sovereignty, such that their (sufficiently grave) violation justifies intervention by outside bodies. But it is none the worse for that. For it seems to me that the 'interventionist' account of human rights erroneously links the very idea of such rights to the concept of sovereignty, thereby rendering it a more superstructural ethical notion than is plausible. After all, it seems perfectly intelligible for cosmopolitans to advocate, on the grounds of securing human rights more effectively, a geopolitical order that does away with sovereign states (or 'peoples', their Rawlsian counterparts) in favour of a unitary world government. This analysis still leaves us with the difficult question of deciding which human rights may be embodied in PIL norms intended to impose limits on state sovereignty. But this question has to be confronted anyway, even if the answer to it only yields, contra Rawls and Raz, a subset of human rights proper.

Obviously, much more needs to be said on this topic—in particular, about the mechanisms through which a legitimate PIL might accommodate claims of state sovereignty short of refraining from establishing any legal norms on a given topic. These include reliance on state consent or democratic procedures (although it is a real question to what extent proper respect for their own freedom prevents states from binding themselves to some PIL norms through such means); allowing states priority or discretion in deciding how best to implement PIL norms (for example, regarding how to deal with political leaders who are responsible for gross human rights abuses); and, adjusting the content of the relevant PIL norms, e.g. by not imposing sanctions (of certain kinds) on states that fail to comply with them or by not encompassing all the normative implications generated by a given human right. These are complex matters for judgment; we can hardly expect their resolution to be pre-empted by any simple formula derived from philosophical reflection.

The foregoing suggests that there is a justification, contrary to what liberal cosmopolitans are apt to suppose, for conferring on states a limited power to make reservations even to multilateral human rights conventions or to escape being bound by customary norms of human rights (those that are not properly accorded *jus cogens* status) by persistently objecting to them. Of course, states often exercise these powers misguidedly or disingenuously, thereby failing to stake out a domain that properly falls within their freedom of choice and action. But one can uphold these incidents of state sovereignty without denying that the norms in question are genuine human rights as a matter of morality or that it would be preferable if the states in question did not exempt themselves from them in a given case.

VI. FORMAL AND PROCEDURAL STANDARDS

There is a broad category of reasons bearing on the NJC that are formal or procedural in nature, many of which are captured by the familiar requirements of the Rule of Law: laws must be clear, publicly accessible, stable, non-retrospective in content and application, and official behaviour must be congruent with pre-existing legal norms. All these requirements reflect the idea that those subject to the law should be able to identify the law and conform with it. Other procedural norms include requirements of transparency, responsiveness, and even democratic accountability in law-making. The value of freedom also plays a significant role in justifying many of these norms; but whereas in the previous section we considered freedom as a constraint on the content of legitimate PIL, here it operates as a source of formal and procedural requirements.

These requirements have figured prominently in discussions of the legitimacy of PIL; indeed, some writers treat legitimacy as deriving exclusively or predominantly from the fulfilment of certain formal and procedural standards. This is an understandably strong incentive to fall back on such standards in the hope of bypassing divisive substantive divergence among cultures in ethical, religious and political beliefs and practices. On the line of argument we have pursued, however, this is a gross overreaction. Nevertheless, these standards are certainly relevant to the fulfilment of the NJC, and in the space that remains I briefly set out one challenge they pose to the legitimacy of customary international law (CIL) as traditionally conceived, i.e. as an amalgam of *opinio juris* and general state practice.

The challenge can be formulated as a Catch-22 quandary. In order to secure the legitimacy of CIL in many domains, it is necessary to reform its content. However, the very process of reforming existing CIL involves a violation of the rule of law. This is because the process of reform will depend on the accumulation of sufficient state practice that breaks existing law; hence, states, which are not only the subjects but also the officials of PIL, will be acting in violation of its standards. Now, law-reform through law-violation has been advocated (subject to certain constraints) by various philosophers as a means of improving PIL.[33] But they have often shown scant appreciation of the legitimacy cost this procedure incurs, especially in such

---

[33] See Buchanan, A., 'From Nuremberg to Kosovo: The Morality of Illegal International Legal Reform', *Ethics* 111 (2001), 673; Goodin, R. E., 'Toward an International Rule of Law: Distinguishing International Law-Breakers from Would-Be Law-Makers', *Journal of Ethics*, 9 (2005), 225; and Altman, A., and Wellman, C. H., 'A Defense of International Criminal Law', *Ethics*, 15 (2004), 35.

areas as international criminal law and the law on the use of force, in which the predictability and constraint on arbitrary power imported by the rule of law carries great weight. This is not to deny that incurring this cost may sometimes be justified or that doing so may even be compatible with the legitimacy of the newly emergent CIL norms. Perhaps the gain in retributive justice, for example, warrants instituting international criminal trials that violate the principle *nulla poena sine lege* (partly in the hope that, after a sufficient number of such unlawful trials, the requisite laws will eventually come into existence). But we should not excuse ourselves from the burden of finding an interpretation of the role of state practice in the formation of CIL that does not deal this self-inflicted wound to the latter's legitimacy.[34]

VII. Conclusion

In this chapter I have sketched a framework for thinking about the legitimacy of PIL, highlighted some challenges to its legitimacy, and suggested a few lines of response. No general answer to the verdictive question has emerged, but none should have been expected: as with any legal system, the issue of legitimacy must be pursued in relation not only to the specific putative subjects of law, but also the different domains over which it claims authority.

---

34 Elsewhere, I have offered a solution to this problem by elaborating an interpretative account of the formation of CIL, see Tasioulas, J., 'Customary International Law and the Quest for Global Justice', in Perreau-Saussine, A. and Murphy, J. B. (eds.), *The Nature of Customary Law* (Cambridge: Cambridge University Press, 2007).

SECTION III

INTERNATIONAL DEMOCRACY

CHAPTER 5

DEMOCRATIC LEGITIMACY AND INTERNATIONAL INSTITUTIONS

THOMAS CHRISTIANO*

I. INTRODUCTION

In assessing proposals for international democracy we will need to make a distinction between democracy in the sense of a set of political institutions and processes and democratic values in the sense of those values that underpin democratic institutions and processes. With the help of the underlying values, I argue, we can arrive at an assessment of the worth of democratic institutions at the global level. I will discuss two kinds of institutional system that might be thought to have democratic legitimacy: one based on the idea of a fair voluntary association of democratic states and the other based on global democratic institutions in a unified form as in proposals for a global democratic assembly. I will assess these institutions on the basis of the values I take to underpin voluntary association and democracy in the domestic setting.

I start with some brief remarks about legitimacy and the basis of what I call inherent legitimacy followed by an idealized version of the system of international institutions we already have. I examine some of the principal objections to such a system framing them within my conception of public equality. I defend what

* I would like to thank Samantha Besson, Allen Buchanan, John Dryzek, Gerald Gaus, James Nickel, Thomas Pogge, and David Schmidtz for their helpful comments on previous drafts of this paper.

I call the system of Fair Democratic Association. I then discuss whether or not a case can be made for global democracy. I argue that even as an ideal, the case cannot be made. I argue tentatively that the system of democratic association is superior to international democracy. I conclude with some remarks on whether or not legitimacy can be attributed to current international institutions, at least from a broadly democratic standpoint.

The results of this study are inevitably quite messy since we are dealing with the fast-changing and polymorphous arrangements of the global order and there is so much disagreement about how it works. This is an attempt to impose some order on our understanding of international institutions while at the same time respecting the complexity of the system.

II. THE CONCEPT OF LEGITIMACY

The principles that underpin democracy are primarily concerned with the grounding of inherently legitimate political institutions. In the case of the nation-state, the theory of democracy is normally meant to give us an account of legitimate political institutions. The role of considerations of inherent political legitimacy is to define a fair system of collective decision-making when there is disagreement on the substance of the decisions and fundamental interests are at stake. It answers the question: by what right has this decision been made and imposed on all? It determines who has the right to make certain decisions. If a system of decision-making is legitimate then the decisions become legitimate as well (within some clearly defined limits). Members then have content-independent reasons to go along with decisions even if they think them unjust. These reasons are grounded in the right of the legitimate decision-maker.

Instrumental legitimacy grounds content-independent reasons in the fact that one is likely to do better by the reasons that apply to one independent of the decision-maker by following the directives of the decision-maker.[1] This kind of legitimacy is weaker because it tends to be piecemeal and its hold varies from person to person.

A conception of legitimacy only lays down some constraints on how one may pursue justice in the international realm but it does not define justice or morality in its entirety for that realm.

---

[1] See Raz, J., *The Morality of Freedom* (Oxford: Oxford University Press, 1986) for this conception of legitimate authority and its justification.

III. A Provisional Account of the Basis of Political Legitimacy

The basic idea behind the democratic conception of legitimacy is that legitimacy is a property of institutions publicly committed to the equal advancement of the interests of the persons who are affected by those institutions. This idea is based on two notions: the principle of equal advancement of interests, which is a morally cosmopolitan principle; and the requirement of publicity, which attaches to the principle once it is implemented in actual political and economic institutions. The principle of equal advancement of interests has two aspects worth bringing out: it directs us to advance the good of all persons and it constrains the pursuit of the common good by equality.[2] Public equality implies that people can see that they are being treated as equals in the operation of the institutions even if they do not always accept the outcomes of the decision-making process. The public realization of equality is required when we try to establish justice among persons in a system of rules and institutions.

In the modern state, democratic institutions are legitimate to the extent that and because they publicly realize the equal advancement of the interests of the members of the society. Democracy is a way of publicly realizing equality when persons who have diverse interests and backgrounds need to establish rules and institutions for the common world in which they live. There is substantial disagreement on how the common world should be shaped. The diverse interests and backgrounds make persons cognitively biased towards their interests and backgrounds in the judgments they form about how to accommodate the interests of all others in a common system of institutions. And persons have interests in living in a world that makes sense to them. Consequently, persons have fundamental interests in participating in shaping the world they live in. Democracy is a way to advance the fundamental interests of all persons in a publicly equal way. In the context of biased disagreement the only way to treat persons as equals so that all can see that they are treated as equals is to give each an equal say in the shaping of the shared institutions they live under. To the extent that democracy realizes public equality, a democratic assembly has a right to rule in the sense that persons have strong reasons to go along with the decision

---

[2] I defend this principle in 'A Foundation for Egalitarianism', in Holtug, N. and Lippert-Rasmussen, K. (eds.), *Egalitarianism: New Essays on the Nature and Value of Equality* (Oxford: Oxford University Press, 2007), 41. Equality of advancement of interests is not as demanding as one might at first think. The institutionalist idea that the domestic institutions of a society matter a great deal to the advancement of the interests of the members combined with the idea that outsiders can do little to reform one's institutions, suggest that equality implies mostly that one must help others escape severe poverty and disease.

just because it was democratically made and despite the fact that they might disagree with the content of the decision. The reasons to comply are grounded in the pooled rights of all persons to have a say in shaping the common world they live in.[3]

This idea of legitimacy as public equality is a defensible way to think about struggles over the legitimacy of international institutions and law. The principal type of criticism of institutional legitimacy in the international realm is that the institution unfairly favours the interests of certain individuals or groups over others. In particular, the interests of the members of the wealthy and powerful states prevail over the interests of individuals in the rest of the world. They publicly treat the interests of the members of the developing world as having less importance than the interests of the members of the developed world.

Because democracy is the best realization of public equality in the domestic context it is natural to think that democracy is the best way to realize public equality in the international context. The application of the idea of legitimacy to international institutions and law is difficult and uncertain. There are two basic models of the legitimacy of institutions in modern democratic societies: one is the democratic model; the other is the model of institutions as voluntary associations. I want to explore both of these and mixtures of these as possible models of legitimate international institutions. I will start with the voluntary association model.

IV. The Voluntary Association Model of International Institutions

A plausible interpretation of the principles that underpin the current system is a modified version of the traditional state consent model. Call it the *voluntary association model* of the international system. It says that the legitimacy of international institutions and law derives from the fact that the system of international law and institutions is a system of voluntary association among states.

The idea that international society is a voluntary association of states seems to animate the traditional view that state consent is the main source of international law; but it permits that some propositions of international law are valid even though not consented to because they support a system of free association among states.

1. Some laws and institutions may be structural—or causal—prerequisites to making the system one of voluntary association. The principle that agreements must be performed, the norm against aggressive war, and the concern for preserving international borders are prerequisites of this nature.

---

[3] See Christiano, T., 'The Authority of Democracy', *Journal of Political Philosophy* (Sept. 2004); and Christiano, T., *The Constitution of Equality: Democratic Authority and its Limits* (Oxford: Oxford University Press, 2008).

2. Some laws are necessary for the stability of such a system. That peace treaties imposed on defeated aggressors are valid can be seen to be a necessary component of a peaceful international order that respects voluntary association.
3. Some laws may specify internally grounded limits to voluntary association. The *jus cogens* norms against slavery, genocide, and aggressive war are connected with voluntary association because they are grounded in the values that underpin voluntary association.

Even customary international law can be seen as respecting a kind of tacit consent. It is a generally understood principle that a state will not be bound by a proposition of customary international law if it has made persistent and clear objections to it when it arose and that it will be bound if it has made no such objections.[4] The tacit consent principle in the international context does not presuppose the authority of the candidate proposition of law over the entity whose consent is asked for, unlike the case of tacit consent to the authority of the state.[5]

Finally, it is important to note that the voluntary association model is compatible with the fact that some international organizations enjoy some independence from the states that create them. The capacities of some organizations to adjudicate disputes among states, and to make the rules created by states more precise in the process, are certainly compatible with claiming that the capabilities of some organizations exist at the pleasure of the states. The capacities of organizations to make soft law and to propose hard law are also compatible with this claim. Indeed, the very limited capacities of organizations to make hard law are compatible with this model as long as states have a right to exit. In general though, even the most advanced international organizations do not allow very much in the way of making hard law without the participation of all the states that are subject to it. And in the exceptional cases where only a qualified majority is required, the most powerful states have real veto power.

V. Some Grounds and Limits to the Voluntary Association of States as a Basis of Legitimacy of International Law

States should have the principal say in the making of international law. If states do not have a say and they do not want to do something, the rules of the international

---

[4] See Simmons, A. J., *Moral Principles and Political Obligations* (Princeton: Princeton University Press, 1979) for a statement of this requirement of tacit consent.

[5] See Brilmayer, L., *Justifying International Acts* (Princeton: Princeton University Press, 1980) for this critique of tacit consent as a basis of the authority of the state.

system simply won't be observed except by accident since the international system relies on their cooperation. This reason is grounded in a concern for the stability of the system of international law and organization since states are by far the most powerful players in the international system.

The moral foundation of the voluntary association model of legitimate international institutions and law consists in the importance of states to the advancement of the interests of persons. The state and, more particularly, the modern democratic state is an extremely sophisticated system for the identification and advancement of the interests of a very broad proportion of its population. It is important to understand that this is a comparative claim; the modern democratic state is far from what we want it to be. In comparison with other institutions, it is relatively successful.

The voluntary association model also suggests a very weak kind of equality among persons in the advancement of the interests of persons. Because states have equal rights of exit and entry there is a sense in which the interests of persons are being given a kind of equal weight by the system in a way that is publicly clear to the persons in the system. This will give rise to many objections but it is important to see that the equality of states could be thought to provide some kind of weakly egalitarian protection for the interests of all persons.

Now we can see why the *jus cogens* norms against genocide, slavery, torture, and some forms of radical discrimination make sense within the voluntary association conception of the international system. States that engage in these practices cannot be said to be representing the interests of their members, and so the point of voluntary association seems to be clearly defeated in the cases of states violating these *jus cogens* norms.

VI. THE REPRESENTATIVENESS PROBLEM

There is a natural objection to the voluntary association model of international legitimacy: the consent and lack of consent of some states does not reflect the interests of most people in those states. As a consequence, numerous individuals' interests are not being considered in the making of international law and institutions. The *representativeness problem* comes in three variants: the authoritarian variant, the minority variant, and the secrecy variant.

The first is that many states are not democratic, or not very democratic, and so they do not even represent their majority populations very well. Generally, democratic states are likely to represent their populations reasonably well and so the states' interests are going to be closely connected with the interests of a substantial proportion of their populations. When a democratic state agrees to undertake a duty or burden, it is doing so with the agreement of a significant proportion of the people on whom the burden is ultimately imposed. The question is: if a state is non-democratic, do its decisions adequately reflect the significance of the duties to and burdens imposed on its population? The answer is not a simple one. Clearly non-democratic states have to be responsive to the interests of some of their populations. But in general there is reason to think that they will be much less responsive to their populations than are democratic states.[6]

The second representativeness problem is that even democratic states do not always represent their minorities very well, in particular indigenous peoples and insular minorities. And this could amount to a significant proportion of the world's population.

The third source of under-representation is the fact that states have traditionally invested foreign-policy making powers in their executive branches.[7] Traditionally, the branch of government most responsible for relations with other states has been the executive branch. And the exercise of its foreign-policy functions has been relatively non-democratic. Such functions often occur in secret and it is often the case that citizens in democratic societies have paid less attention to foreign affairs than to domestic affairs. But now international law is expanding into the areas of trade, the environment, and human rights. And international law demands more and more reform of the internal institutions of societies. The consequence of this is that if the voluntary association model is to have any chance at being a reasonable source of legitimacy, the foreign policies of states must become more democratic.

VII. Hard Bargaining

The most serious problem of the voluntary association model is that it seems to allow for all forms of hard bargaining, which may not be coercive in a strict sense but allows for a great deal of unfairness. The basic idea of hard bargaining is that two states may arrive at an agreement whose benefits are highly asymmetric between those states because one state is credibly able to threaten withdrawal from the arrangement while the other is not. The development of trade law provides an instructive example. Regarding many goods, the US is capable of dictating terms of trade that are highly favourable to itself or at least to its domestic industries and exporting industries because the relative market share of the US economy is so great and the market share of many developing countries so small. It can lay down terms

---

[6] There is a very large literature defending this proposition, see esp. Przeworski. A., et al., *Democracy and Development* (Cambridge: Cambridge University Press, 2000).

[7] See Siedentop, L., *Democracy in Europe* (New York: Columbia University Press, 2001) for a discussion of this problem in the case of the EU. See also Stein, E., 'International Integration and Democracy: No Love at First Sight', *American Journal of International Law*, 95 (July 2001).

and say to the developing country 'take it or leave it'. And this also holds true for the European Union and some other economies.[8]

To secure terms of trade that are highly asymmetrically in one's favour through the more credible threat of withdrawal, particularly against a society in dire need, seems to be a fundamental violation of norms of fair exchange. Though the agreement is voluntary there is something highly problematic about it morally.

And this impression is borne out when we think in terms of the underlying principles of the voluntary association model. It seems clear that the asymmetric outcomes, due to hard bargaining, violate an intuitive sense that the interests of all are being advanced equally. The interests of those in the developing country seem to be relatively neglected for the benefit of those of the developed country. Let us call this the *problem of asymmetrical bargaining*. Asymmetrical bargaining has been by far the most serious objection to the claim of international institutions to legitimacy. Complaints about the Security Council, the International Monetary Fund (IMF), the World Bank, and the World Trade Organization (WTO) are all instances of this phenomenon.[9]

It should be noted that asymmetric bargaining need not be motivated by self-interest alone. The terms the IMF imposes on countries seeking relief may often be the result of well-meaning policies in accordance with neo-liberal political economy. But the fact that the countries seeking relief are in such dire need makes them capitulate quickly to the IMF demands without having much of a say in determining the terms of the loans. It is the position of asymmetric bargaining that enables the IMF to impose terms without taking into account the opinions of the society in need. This must be regarded by all as a violation of the principle that people should have some say in the things that deeply affect their lives.[10]

VIII. FAIR DEMOCRATIC ASSOCIATION

If we take into account the above worries about the current system of voluntary association, we can give an abstract description of what it would have to be like to be

---

[8] See Steinberg, R., 'In the Shadow of Law or Power? Consensus Based Bargaining and Outcomes at the GATT/WTO', *International Organization*, 56 (2002), 339. See also Schlesinger, S., *Act of Creation: The Founding of the United Nations* (Boulder, Colo.: Westview Press, 2003) for a lively account of the bargaining that produced the great power veto in the Security Council.

[9] Indeed, even the dispute resolution system of the WTO (which has received high marks for its adherence to the rule of law) gives ample opportunity for wealthy and powerful states to take advantage of poorer states. See Pauwelyn, J., 'Enforcement and Countermeasures in the WTO: Rules Are Rules-Toward a More Collective Approach', *American Journal of International Law*, 335 (2000), reprinted in Hathaway, O., and Hongju Koh, H. (eds.), *Foundations of International Law and Politics* (New York: Foundation Press, 2005), 282–93, esp. 283.

[10] This is one of the key complaints of dissident economists concerning the IMF. See Stiglitz, J., *Globalization and Its Discontents* (New York: Norton Publishers, 2002) as one example among many.

a minimally legitimate system of decision-making. It would have to be a *fair system of voluntary association among highly representative states*. I will call this a system of *fair democratic association*.

The representativeness problem (in all of its variations) is theoretically and partially soluble. First, one can push states to become democratic or more democratic. This has become an increasingly widespread norm in the last twenty five years.[11] Second, one can insist that the foreign-policy establishments of states become more transparent and more democratically controlled and that the negotiations among states as well as the institutions that arise from them be made more transparent.[12] Third, one can set up special consultative or representative bodies for indigenous peoples and insular minorities in the different democratic states. At least, these are all reforms with which societies have had some experience in the past.

The representativeness problem has not been solved in practice yet. Though election monitoring has become a common norm in the international arena there are serious questions as to its effectiveness in advancing genuinely democratic values.[13]

The problem of asymmetrical bargaining is much harder to get a handle on. But it should be noted first that there are some mitigating factors here. First, less powerful states can group together and attempt to bargain collectively and thereby acquire more leverage over the larger economies. This is now being tried in the case of the WTO and it will take some time before we know that the collections of smaller states can actually achieve a greater degree of symmetry in defining trade law. The question is whether or not this will lead to agreement.[14] Second, wealthy states may not be exclusively self-interested in their foreign policies. Developed countries have allowed developing countries to delay setting up policies to reduce carbon emissions in the Kyoto protocol; the WTO permits trading preferences to developing countries; and there is a large, influential body of opinion in the developed countries in favour of bringing down agricultural barriers in the developed countries that have been thought to harm developing countries.[15] These are modest achievements, but they do give some credibility to the hope that wealthy countries will not merely press for their own interests even to the detriment of developing countries. Third,

[11] See Franck, T., *Fairness in International Law and Institutions* (Oxford: Oxford University Press, 1995), ch. 4.

[12] This has been happening in part with the IMF and the World Bank. See Keohane, R. and Nye, J., 'The Club Model of Multilateral Cooperation and Problems of Democratic Legitimacy', in Keohane, R. (ed.), *Power and Governance in a Partially Globalized World* (Boulder, Colo.: Westview, 2002), 219.

[13] See Hyde, S., *Observing Norms: Explaining the Causes and Consequences of Internationally Monitored Elections*, PhD thesis (University of California, San Diego, 2006) for scepticism about the association of the recent increase in election monitoring and genuine democracy.

[14] Drahos, P., 'When the Weak Bargain with the Strong: Negotiations in the World Trade Organization', *International Negotiation*, 8 (2003), 79; and Singh, J. P., 'Coalitions, Developing Countries, and International Trade: Research Findings and Prospects', *International Negotiation*, 11 (2006), 499.

[15] See Franck, T., *Fairness in International Law and Institutions* (above, n. 11), 58–9, 426–7 for a discussion of these trading preferences.

relative market share is not the sole determinant of bargaining power even when coalitions do not form. Nationalistic sentiment sometimes increases the bargaining position of small, poor states. Fourth, a world in which there is more than one large society to negotiate with can give small and poor states alternatives that enhance their bargaining positions.[16]

Still the problem of asymmetric bargaining is a large one, and it is hard to see how this problem can be avoided. There are really two main ways in which asymmetric bargaining can be held in check. First, the playing field can be levelled by greatly diminishing the economic inequalities among the parties. Second, establishing independent standards of fairness in the process of forming agreements, which are then implemented in international agreements.

But the level playing field condition seems to require something that has eluded the international community for a long time. Not only is it not clear that the international community has succeeded in lessening inequality or even severe poverty among persons and among societies, it may have exacerbated one or both of these. When nearly 20 per cent of the world's population lives in extreme poverty and when nearly 40 per cent of the world's population lives in severe poverty and these populations are concentrated in particular political societies, it is hard to see how we are going to be able to set up a scheme of fair bargaining. These populations are extremely vulnerable to deeply unfair terms of association.[17]

On the other hand, overcoming the bargaining problem by setting outcome standards on the results of bargaining and having them implemented by international institutions would require that the results of bargaining live up to certain standards. This seems to give up on inherent legitimacy altogether. The problem here will be determining both who will set the standards and who will implement them.

Finally, we do not have a clear normative principle for the evaluation of the fairness of the system of international negotiations. A rough standard is that power in the process of negotiation should be roughly proportionate to the stake each society has in it, where the stake is a function of population size as well as the populations' relative need for agreement. But these are very rough standards that call for significant theoretical elaboration and justification.

Nevertheless, if the agreements among states come about by a process of fair association among democratic states, they can satisfy the basic constraint of public equality. All persons are publicly treated as equals by the process that generates

[16] See the essays in Zartman, I. W., and Rubin, J. Z. (eds.), *Power and Negotiation* (Ann Arbor: University of Michigan Press, 2000); and Ingebritsen, C., Neumann, I. B., Gstohl, S., and Beyer, J. (eds.), *Small States In International Relations* (Seattle, Wash.: University of Washington Press, 2006).

[17] For contrasting perspectives, see Wade, R., 'Is globalization reducing poverty and inequality?', *World Development*, 32 (2004), 567; and Chen, S., and Ravallion, M., 'How have the World's Poorest Fared Since the Early 1980's?', *World Bank Research Observer*, 19 (2004), 141.

these agreements. As a consequence, states have reasons to conform to treaties that are grounded in public equality. And since the grounding is in the process of coming to agreement, the reason generated is a content-independent one. Furthermore, citizens of those states have content-independent reasons, founded in the fact that the agreements are reached through an egalitarian process, to act in accordance with the provisions of the treaty and the institutional implications of the treaty. And since the requirement of public equality is a weighty requirement, the reasons generated are weighty reasons, normally outweighing contrary reasons.

My guess is that in the absence of much greater collective bargaining power on the part of developing countries or greater economic equality among societies, the system of voluntary association cannot be made legitimate. It simply cannot be seen as advancing the interests of the persons in the global order equally.

IX. Democracy as a Basis of Legitimacy of International Law

With these worries about the legitimacy of the current system of decision-making in mind it is time to take a look at some proposals for democratic decision-making that have been made for the international system. My focus here must be limited to the aspiration to have a global peoples' assembly or parliament with representatives of constituencies of individuals making up the parliament, which has legislative powers. This need not involve a world state and could be connected with a federal structure of institutions. Though this institution would have formal and legal status it must be contrasted with something like the General Assembly of the United Nations in which a majority of states participates (though of course they do not have legislative power).[18]

I emphasize the formal and legal character of the basis of democratic legitimacy due to the importance of publicity to legitimacy. It seems to me that people can see that they are being treated as equals by institutions only if these institutions have an egalitarian formal and legal character. Informally, democratic arrangements are likely to be far more opaque to their participants in terms of whether or not they realize equality, especially on a large scale.[19]

---

[18] See Held, D., *Democracy and the Global Order* (Stanford, Calif.: Stanford University Press, 1995); and Falk, R. and Strauss, A., 'On the Creation of a Global People's Assembly: Legitimacy and the Power of Popular Sovereignty', *Stanford Journal of International Law*, 36 (2000), 191. See also Archibugi, D., 'Cosmopolitan Democracy and its Critics: A Review', *European Journal of International Relations*, 10 (2004), 437, esp. 451, which states 'A cardinal institution of democratic *governance* is therefore a world parliament'.

[19] See, in contrast, Dryzek, J., *Deliberative Global Politics* (Cambridge: Polity Press, 2006) for a conception of democracy that de-emphasizes the formal and legal character of democracy.

X. Conditions of Intrinsic Justification of Democracy

I sketched a justification for democracy grounded in the principle of public equality in section III. But democracy can be used to realize public equality only under certain conditions. The conditions under which democracy is intrinsically justified for a community are the following;

1. A number of important issues must arise for the whole community.
2. There must be a rough equality of stakes among persons in the community concerning the whole package of issues.
3. It must not be the case that the community is divided into discrete and insular groups with distinct preferences over all the issues in the community so that one or more substantial groups always lose out in majority voting. In other words there should not be persistent minorities.
4. Democracy is justified only when it protects at least the fundamental human rights of all the persons in the community.
5. Democracy is justified when the issues with which it deals are not primarily of a purely scientific or technical character.
6. A final institutional condition for the justification of democracy is that there be a dense network of institutions of civil society that connect individuals to the activities of the democratic legislative power. A system of political parties, interest group associations, and other types of associations are necessary to give ordinary citizens an orientation among the vast array of issues that arise in a democratic polity.

XI. Interdependence and Equality of Stake

The first two conditions must be taken together. There must be an interdependence of interests among persons or groups on many issues. Since democratic decisions must be taken by majority rule, it is important that there be many issues so that those who come up losers on some issues be winners on others. This condition enables people to trade votes between issues that are of great importance to them and those that are of lesser importance to them.[20]

But this complex interdependence is not sufficient. There must be some kind of equality of stake in the interdependence, where by 'stake' I mean the susceptibility of a person's interests or well-being to be advanced or set back by realistically possible ways of organizing the interdependent group. If one group of persons has a very large stake in a community, in which there is interdependence of interests, and another has a fairly small stake, it seems unfair to give each an equal say in decision-making over this community. We can recognize this in faculty decisions. Those who are permanent members of the faculty clearly have a much greater stake in the decisions than those who are only visiting. We do not think it is fair that everyone's vote has the same weight in decision-making. And I think we recognize this idea in many different contexts of collective decision-making. Democratic decision-making over entities in which some have a much greater stake than others, treats unequally those who have a much greater stake. The equality of stake at issue need not be on every issue. Some persons or groups may have more at stake in one set of issues and another may have more at stake in another set of issues. The key is that, in general, people have something at stake in each decision, and each has roughly equal stake in the overall package of issues.

We see some such rough equality of stake in the case of the modern state. The citizens of a modern state usually have most of their fundamental interests at stake in the decisions of a modern state. And so there is a kind of rough equality of stake. To be sure, some individuals are only temporarily or rarely residents of the state in which they are citizens. Some are wealthy enough so that they are capable of avoiding the decisions of the state by some form of emigration. But on the whole, the modern state does involve a great degree of interdependence on matters concerning nearly all of the fundamental interests of the citizens. And so there is a rough equality of stake in its decisions. This is presumably an important reason why democracy has come to be seen as an important ideal for the modern state.[21]

---

[20]   For variations on the thesis that complex interdependence is sufficient see Gould, C., *Globalizing Democracy and Human Rights* (Cambridge: Cambridge University Press, 2004); and Held, D., *Democracy and the Global Order* (Stanford, Calif.: Stanford University Press, 1995); and Pogge, T., *World Poverty and Human Rights* (Cambridge: Polity Press, 2002), 168.

[21]   To be sure, equality of stake does not imply equality of outcome.

XII. Are There Equal Stakes?

Many have argued that democracy at the international level is justified because there is interdependence among persons at the global level. But this thesis is extremely vague and is rarely made more precise than this. First, how much interdependence exists at the global level? And most important, is the interdependence such that the different peoples of the world have equal stakes in it?

The problem is complicated by the fact that the answer depends on the institutional capacity of the international system. The reason why the modern state seems to be a community of roughly equal stakes is because of the immense institutional capacity of the modern state. It plays a role in nearly all the main activities that human beings engage in. The same cannot be said of the set of international laws and institutions. They play a fairly small role in the lives of people throughout the world. They do not set anything but very vague standards for education or health. They do not enter into the systems of property and exchange in domestic societies except in very abstract ways. Human rights standards are quite vague; in any case the international institutions do not have the capacities to monitor human rights very effectively and have little or no chance of getting the judgments of human rights courts implemented.[22]

The principal sources of global interdependence in the modern world are the expansion of international trade and communications, the effects of global environmental degradation and pollution, and the preservation of peace. The prevention of the spread of some diseases has also been an accomplishment in part of the international system. No countries are left untouched by the modern system of international trade. But the system of international trade does not reach nearly as deeply into people's lives as most domestic systems of trade and exchange. Furthermore, the capacity of international institutions to regulate the flow of trade is still quite small. And regarding global environmental conditions: most cross-border environmental effects are regional in importance, though there are some genuinely global concerns such as that of global warming.

We cannot at the moment give a very clear answer to the question of relative stakes, but here are some indicators that suggest inequality of stakes. States do not participate equally in the process of international trade. The ratios of export to gross domestic product of economies and the ratios of foreign investment vary quite a bit

---

[22] See Buchanan, A., *Justice, Legitimacy and Self-Determination* (Oxford: Oxford University Press, 2004) for an account that places human rights at the heart of the legitimacy of the international order. See Hathaway, O., 'Do Human Rights Treaties Make a Difference?', *Yale Law Journal*, 111 (2002) for a sceptical argument about the positive effects of human rights treaties. For some scepticism about this particular argument see Goodman, R. and Jinks, D., 'Measuring the Effects of Human Rights Treaties', *European Journal of International Law*, 14 (2003), 171.

between societies. In this respect societies, and plausibly individuals, do not have equal stakes in the international system. Environmental problems are still mostly regional in character so that the extent to which people are affected by these is still quite uneven.

But there may be a general argument for why individuals do not have equal stakes in international institutions: since international institutions still cover only a relatively thin set of issues (compared to the modern state) within the global order and since individuals' interests and circumstances are likely to be quite distinct, many individuals are not likely to have as great a stake in these issues as others. The reason for this is that in general for any particular issue, individuals' interests and circumstances are likely to be distinct and as a consequence, individuals are not likely to have as much at stake as others within that issue space. This holds in the international order—particularly if we confine the issues to what international institutions can do about the issue, which is in general quite limited.

People have very different stakes in that order and so democracy would actually be a way of treating persons unequally in that context. Hence, there is substantial reason to doubt that democracy can realize equality publicly in the international order.[23]

XIII. Persistent Minorities

Another connected worry about international democracy is the problem of persistent minorities. If the issues upon which a democratic international institution makes decisions are such that discrete and insular coalitions tend to form (with some forming a majority and some forming minority blocs), then there is a significant chance that some groups will simply be left out of the decision-making process. And this leaves open the possibility that their lives will be heavily determined by strangers.

As I argued in section III, democracy is justified to the extent that it is a collective decision-making process that publicly realizes the equal advancement of the interests of the persons involved. Normally, democratic decision-making is determined by majority rule—resulting in some groups being winners on some issues and other groups being winners on other issues. Though there is no clear system for making interpersonal comparisons, as long as there is sufficient rotation among winners and losers, the system is reasonably fair. But sometimes a discrete and insular minority rarely if ever wins on any issue. Since the successful exercise of power is normally necessary to advance fundamental interests within a diverse and contentious polity,

---

[23] My worry in this section is about whether or not global democracy can be legitimate. Despite this worry, Thomas Pogge has pointed out in discussion, it may still be better than what we have. But the worries that follow call that thesis into question as well.

if the minority never succeeds in making legislation, we have strong reason to think that the interests of the minority are not being advanced. If there is a minimum amount of rotation of majorities and minorities, we can think of the collective decision-making process as publicly realizing equality. But when one group never gets its way, then the collective decision-making process is no longer publicly advancing the interests of members equally. But if the collective decision-making process is not publicly advancing the interests equally, then it loses its legitimacy—at least in significant part.[24]

It is important to note the difference between the problem of persistent minorities and the problem of majority tyranny. Though they often go together, they need not. Indeed, it is quite possible for a dominant group to act in accordance with what it takes to be the human rights of the minority, while the minority never gets its way. This seems to me a serious problem above and beyond the violation of human rights, and may itself constitute such a violation.

The possibility of persistent minorities in the international system is very great. To the extent that this is a serious danger at the global level, it seems that there is a real risk that a global democratic institution will be illegitimate in an important way.

This conclusion must be qualified in a couple of different ways. First, we do not know that the problem of persistent minorities would occur. What could happen instead is that groups of persons around the world see common interests so that groups that are persistent minorities in individual societies could form coalitions and form majorities in some circumstances.[25] Second, the problem of persistent minorities has been handled by democratic societies, with mixed success, by means of institutions that qualify majority rule such as consociational institutions or even federalist institutions. It is not obvious to me that these solutions will arise in the case of global democracy partly because of the weakness of civil society in global democracy. The idea is that because of this weakness, states will take the primary role in mediating between persons and global assembly.

XIV. Institutional Incapacity of Civil Society

The other fundamental problem with global democracy is that we do not have institutions that can mediate well between individuals and legislative institutions. In the modern democratic state, political parties, interest groups, and diverse media

---

[24] See my 'Political Equality and the Problem of Persistent Minorities', *Philosophical Papers* (1995).

[25] See Madison, J., Hamilton, A., and Jay, J., *The Federalist Papers*, ed. Kramnick, I. (Harmondsworth, UK: Penguin, 1987), paper n. 10 for an argument to the effect that enlarging the size of a republic may diminish permanent minorities.

outlets all provide a fairly wide representation of views and provide means by which citizens can come to understand what is at stake in collective decision-making. The institutions we know are deeply imperfect and do not represent as widely as they should, but nevertheless they do provide citizens with some sense of what is going on from a wide variety of standpoints. In my view these institutions are absolutely necessary to democracy because citizens can only devote a small amount of time to political questions so there must be intermediate institutions that enable citizens to acquire a grasp of the key political issues and alternatives.[26] Without these institutions, citizens are at sea with the great number of issues and alternatives. They become prey to demagogic politicians and the system seems to be run essentially by elites.

The trouble in international politics is that the institutions of civil society, while certainly growing quite rapidly, are not anywhere near the capacity necessary to act as intermediaries between the great majority of persons in international society and international institutions. Even in the European Union, mass political parties have yet to form and these are an absolute minimum condition for successful democracy. The consequence of this situation in the international realm, were it to be democratized, would be a state of affairs in which elites rule mostly without any serious check on their power. Some groups, mostly representing selected Western interests and concerns, would have some capacity to embarrass and shame states and international institutions.[27]

XV. COMPARISONS BETWEEN GLOBAL DEMOCRACY AND THE SYSTEM OF FAIR DEMOCRATIC ASSOCIATION

Let us compare these two purported ideals. Our observations above suggest that global democracy is not currently an ideal for the global order at all. Without the condition of equal stakes in global collective decision-making, democracy cannot be intrinsically justified for the global system. But the condition of equal stakes in collective decision-making is not itself intrinsically desirable or required. Since equal stakes is not required as part of an institutional ideal, then democracy, which is justified intrinsically only if there are equal stakes, cannot be justified intrinsically under current circumstances.

[26] See Christiano, T., *The Rule of the Many* (Boulder Colo.: Westview Press, 1996), chs. 5 and 7 for a discussion of the nature and role of citizenship in an egalitarian conception of democracy and of the central role of political parties, interest groups, and other associations in mediating between state and citizen.

[27] See Dahl, R., 'Can International Organizations Be Democratic? A Skeptic's View', in Shapiro, I. and Hacker-Cordon, C. (eds.), *Democracy's Edges* (Cambridge: Cambridge University Press, 1999).

In contrast, the system of fair democratic association can be thought of as an ideal to be pursued, though its realization is at best quite far off. The point of a scheme of voluntary association in domestic society is to deal with the reality of uneven stakes. It is designed to allow individuals to choose for themselves what ventures they wish to engage in and to tailor those ventures to their particular interests. Democratic association allows states to pick and choose what terms they enter into and so allows them to determine how important issues are to their peoples and to sub-populations within their societies. It allows for the possibility of the kinds of regional and other kinds of more particular associations that have proven to be the most effective institutions beyond the state.

The system of fair democratic association also deals with the problem of permanent minorities much better than does a global democracy because states must consent to the terms they come under. This provides protection for these states by ensuring them a say in what happens to their societies. Global democracy would have to deal with this problem by significantly qualifying majority rule.

Concerning the problem of institutional incapacity, the system of democratic association makes use of the most powerful institution in the current environment, which is the state. The democratic state is a reasonably successful mechanism for accommodating and representing the interests and concerns of its members. Many democratic societies have thriving civil societies that help ensure this function of the democratic states. The absence of a dense global civil society does not undermine the capacity of democratic states to represent the interests and concerns of their citizens.

If we compare the two ideals, I tentatively conclude that the system of fair democratic association is a superior ideal to aim at and it gives us a better picture of what inherently legitimate institutions would have to look like.

XVI. Do International Institutions and Law Have Democratic Legitimacy Now?

For the moment, it seems that we should not think of the system as a whole as legitimate because of the problems of representativeness and asymmetric bargaining. This does not entail that we need to think of it as illegitimate. The basis for saying that a system of decision-making is illegitimate is that it has either produced the conditions that undermine its legitimacy or it stands in the way of improving those conditions or is failing to do what it knows it can do to ameliorate the problem. Only under these circumstances can the system be thought to be treating the worse-off as inferiors. We might think that the problems of extreme and severe poverty are problems that we currently do not have the tools to solve. There is clearly a lot of disagreement among expertly informed persons. Furthermore, there is progress in the direction of more democracy throughout the world and greater pressure in favour of representation of indigenous and insular minorities.

We must think of international institutions and law as works in progress. We must evaluate the products of this system mostly on a case-by-case basis to make sure that it is making progress towards resolving the major problems of human rights, severe poverty, environmental degradation and pollution, and that it is advancing the common good through a process of free and fair trade, investment, and finance. And finally we must evaluate it in terms of the progress it is making towards a more inherently legitimate system of decision-making.

XVII. Conclusion

If our aim is to realize the democratic values in the international order, then we should aim primarily at what I have called a system of fair democratic association among states. Global democracy is highly unlikely to succeed given the weakness of global civil society and it is highly unlikely to be legitimate given the unevenness of stakes in its decisions and given the high chance of permanent minorities. And since we are quite far away from a fair system of voluntary-association among highly representative states, we cannot think that the current system has legitimacy overall. Nevertheless, there may be some reason for hope for progress towards a more equal and representative system of association. According a greater say to developing countries in what are the most powerful institutions in the international order may help to advance a system that is more equitable and that could eventually become legitimate.

CHAPTER 6

LEGITIMATE INTERNATIONAL INSTITUTIONS: A NEO-REPUBLICAN PERSPECTIVE

PHILIP PETTIT*

I. INTRODUCTION

In Chapter 5, 'Democratic Legitimacy and International Institutions', Thomas Christiano argues that the legitimacy of the international order requires the development of a voluntary association of representative states—an association only dimly foreshadowed in current conditions—and not anything that we might describe as a global democracy. This paper supports the position defended by Christiano, arguing to a broadly similar conclusion from a starting point provided by neo-republican ideas.[1]

What follows is in three sections. Section II identifies a republican view of legitimacy as it would apply in the national and international contexts. Section III

* This is a companion paper to 'A Republican Law of Peoples', *European Journal of Political Theory*, special issue on 'Republicanism and International Relations' (forthcoming). I am grateful to the editors, Samantha Besson and John Tasioulas, for their very useful comments on an early draft of this paper.

[1] See, Pettit, P., *Republicanism: A Theory of Freedom and Government* (Oxford: Oxford University Press, 1997); Skinner, Q., *Liberty Before Liberalism* (Cambridge: Cambridge University Press, 1998); Maynor, J., *Republicanism in the Modern World* (Cambridge: Polity Press, 2003); Laborde, C. and Maynor, J. (eds.), *Republicanism and Political Theory* (Oxford: Blackwell, 2007).

looks at how legitimacy might be attained in the national context. And then Section IV outlines a picture of how it might be achieved in the international. I would have liked to concentrate more exclusively on the international context but the notion of legitimacy emerges in the first place with domestic regimes and, in any case, the legitimacy of the international order turns in good part on the domestic legitimacy of the states that constitute it.

II. Legitimacy, National and International

1. Freedom as Non-Domination

The main focus in neo-republican theory is on the value of freedom as non-domination. Take a given choice between alternatives, A, B, and C. You will be dominated in that choice, and lose your freedom, to the extent that others exercise non-deliberative control over what you choose; you will be free to the extent that you avoid such control.

Let others have a degree of control over your choice in so far as they can raise the probability that you choose an option they favour. Such control will be deliberative, and so no threat to freedom, if others exercise the control just by sincerely giving you advice, on a take-it-or-leave it basis, about reasons to act one way or another; you may seek an articulation of these reasons or accept the advice on trust. Deliberative control will not affect your freedom because it does not intentionally mislead you about your options and it leaves the choice between those options up to you; it serves the role that deliberating with yourself may serve. Thus, it does not remove any options, as in the exercise of force; it does not replace any by options that have penalties attached, as in the case of coercion; it does not undermine your capacity for choice, as in manipulation; and it does not mislead you about any of those factors.[2]

Avoiding the non-deliberative control of others in a given choice means avoiding these kinds of force or coercion or manipulation or deception. But avoiding non-deliberative control is not ensured by avoiding the interference of others in that choice: that is, avoiding their active obstruction or coercion or manipulation or deception. Others may control you non-deliberatively without active interference, since they may stand by in a monitoring or invigilating position and only interfere on a need-for-interference basis. They let you go as you will, if you are inclined to act as they want, but they are prepared to take steps to block or inhibit or redirect your choice—or at least

---

[2] Pettit, P., 'Republican Liberty: Three Axioms, Four Theorems', in Laborde, C. and Maynor, J. (eds.), *Republicanism and Political Theory* (above, n. 1).

to make you regret that type of choice and avoid it in the future—if your pattern of behaviour, or their pattern of preference, should change. Thus, interference may be absent while invigilating control remains in place. And interference may remain absent, if you become aware of the invigilation—or just think there is invigilation—and inhibit yourself so as not to activate any interference: say, by resorting to self-censorship or self-ingratiation.[3]

But not only may non-deliberative control obtain without active interference. The opposite is also true. You may undergo the active interference of others without having to endure their control. Suppose that you prefer that others exercise a certain obstruction or coercion or even manipulation in your life, say in order to cope with an addiction; you are happy to allow your spouse to lock away the whisky or the cigars for fear of your own inclination. To the extent that you can call off this interference in your life and affairs, should you change your mind, that interference will not represent a way in which you are controlled. Others figure as agents of interference in this story but they do not control you, since they operate subject to your own control; the interference they practice is non-arbitrary: it is forced to track your conscious interests, not the interests of the interferer.[4]

On this neo-republican account, the non-deliberative control that affects your freedom is identified with domination. You will be dominated by others in a given choice in the measure to which they have a power of interfering in that choice and that power is not subject to your own control: it is, in that sense, an arbitrary power in your life. The account implies that freedom in a particular choice requires the absence of an arbitrary power of interference on the part of others. But it does not require the absence of a non-arbitrary power of interference. To the extent that others interfere only non-arbitrarily, the interference practised will restrict your choice, as natural obstacles may do, but it will not make you unfree in that choice; you will be the one who is ultimately in charge.

So much for what republican freedom requires in a given choice. But people cannot be free in every possible choice, if only because some choices—say, that of exercising interference or not—may be inimical to the freedom of others. So what choices in particular should be free, on the republican approach?

The approach hails freedom as non-domination as an ideal for those choices that each can enjoy, consistently with others enjoying them equally at the same time: that is, for those choices that count as basic liberties.[5] Freedom in this sense is a property of persons; it is a status that they enjoy to the extent that they are

---

[3] This will remain true even if others become so well disposed—even if you prove to be so charming or amusing—that they allow you to act on whatever happens to be your preference. To the extent that they retain the power of interference, and are ready to interfere should their disposition change, they remain your masters. You operate only within their power and whatever you do is done *cum permissu*, in the old republican phrase: by their implicit or explicit leave.

[4] Pettit, P., *Republicanism: A Theory of Freedom and Government* (above, n. 1).

[5] Pettit, P., 'The Basic Liberties', in Kramer, M. (ed.), *Essays on H. L. A. Hart* (Oxford: Oxford University Press, 2008). The domain of choice over which the freedom is defined may not seem to be very extensive but

more or less proof against dominating control by others in basic domains of choice. Intuitively, it is the property of being able to stand equal with others in a position where all can see, and all can see that it is universally seen, that the person cannot be pushed around with impunity. Attempts to push the person around will be met with resistance or, should they succeed, the perpetrators will be subject to a sort of redress that is designed to vindicate the standing of the victim.[6]

2. Republican Justice and Republican Legitimacy

One of the features of neo-republicanism, unlike the older tradition on which it draws, is that it embraces an inclusive conception of the members of any society; they include at least all permanent residents who are adult and able-minded, not just the propertied, mainstream males on which political theory had traditionally focused. For that reason, the approach might be described as liberal republicanism.[7] What are the requirements of freedom as non-domination from the point of view of such an inclusive citizenry?

A first requirement is that citizens should each have sufficient resources not to be subject to personal domination by other agents, individual or corporate; such resources will include financial clout, social standing, and legal protection. A second is that they should have sufficient resources as a group not to be subject to collective domination by agents such as states, multinational corporations or international organizations. And a third is that the agencies whereby such a distribution of empowering resources is ensured—and, as it may be, some other collective goods are made available—should not themselves dominate those people either personally or collectively.

---

the degree of independence required in that domain ensures that freedom as non-domination makes heavy demands.

[6] Should I have said that the neo-republican maxim is equal freedom as non-domination, not just freedom as non-domination, period? If the equal-freedom formula is preferred, I am happy to go along with it. But for the record I think that freedom as non-domination is a property such that the best way to maximize it from any less than perfect position will be to take steps towards ensuring greater equality in its enjoyment. See Pettit, P., *Republicanism: A Theory of Freedom and Government* (above, n. 1); Lovett, F. N., 'Domination: A Preliminary Analysis', *Monist* (2001) 84, 98. Let the weaker be further protected and that will increase their aggregate non-domination without necessarily reducing anybody else's. Let the stronger be further protected and two features of the move are likely to make it ineffective. First, the extra protection is unlikely to increase the non-domination of the strong as much as it would have increased the non-domination of the weaker; it may just make assurance doubly assured. And second, the extra protection is likely to give them yet a further resource for imposing on the weaker and so reducing the non-domination of the weaker.

[7] Dagger, R., *Civic Virtues: Rights, Citizenship, and Republican Liberalism* (Oxford: Oxford University Press, 1997).

The first of these requirements is naturally identified as a demand of domestic justice and the second as a demand of international justice. Both prescribe that resources should be allocated according to a distributional ideal whereby individuals are given their due:[8] their due, on the neo-republican conception, as potentially free, undominated subjects. Domestic justice would ensure that the people of a country are given their due in their individual right as citizens, global justice their due in their right as a collective citizenry.

The third demand, by contrast with the first two, is one of legitimacy. It requires that the agencies whereby domestic and global justice is achieved operate on a suitable pattern in pursuit of those ends. Whatever the options taken for the distribution of resources—and however right they may seem to be—they should at least be taken on the right basis. The options will often involve interfering in the affairs of the relevant parties; this is obviously so in the case of the coercive state. The republican requirement for legitimacy is that such interference should be conducted on a non-arbitrary basis: on a basis that gives ultimate control of what happens to those on the receiving end. The interference, ideally, should resemble that whereby my partner, on my own instruction, hides the key to the whisky cabinet or the cigar box.

This demand of legitimacy divides into two, since the agency whereby justice is domestically assured is the state, and the agency whereby global justice is assured is bound to involve the actions of many states and perhaps many individuals; I describe it, for short, as the international order.

The problem of domestic legitimacy is that of ensuring that in the exercise of its public power, the domestic polity is not a dominating presence in the lives of its citizens. It is a non-dominating guardian against private domination and it is a non-dominating organizer of whatever other collective goods it seeks to advance. The problem of international legitimacy is that of ensuring that the exercises of power whereby the international regime guards against domination over national groupings, and pursues any other goods, does not itself involve the domination of any individuals or their groupings. It is a non-dominating counterpart, at the international level, of the non-dominating state.

So much for the general approach to issues of legitimacy that neo-republicanism would sponsor. In the next two sections I look at the appeal and implications of the republican criterion of legitimacy, first in the context of the domestic state, and then in the international context. I argue, though only in a sketchy manner, that the criterion makes a good deal of sense in each context and that it points us towards sensible and attractive reforms.

[8] Rawls, J., *A Theory of Justice* (Oxford: Oxford University Press, 1971).

III. Legitimacy in the National Context

1. The Republican Criterion of Domestic Legitimacy

According to neo-republicanism, the state can claim to be legitimate just to the extent that it exercises its role in a non-dominating way. It must discharge its functions under the ultimate control of the citizens. Specifically, it must give its citizens effective and equally shared control over how it performs.

That a state is legitimate does not necessarily mean that you as a citizen are morally obliged to obey its laws; other moral considerations might argue against obeying them in particular instances. The notion of legitimacy is tied, rather, to two distinct implications.[9] The first is that you have to acknowledge the right of the regime to enforce the law coercively, to charge law-breakers with offences and to punish them if they are duly convicted. And related to this, the second is that you are only entitled to challenge the law by means that are available within the system.[10]

The republican criterion of legitimacy contrasts with more standard approaches in focusing on how the state functions, not on how it is formed. There are two formational constraints that might be suggested for legitimacy. One, associated with Hobbes and Locke, is that citizens should consent to live under the state they form. This is unappealing, since consensual entry won't mean much unless there is consensual exit; and in any case it would make all states illegitimate. The other constraint is that citizens, however they enter, should have the option of leaving a state if they wish. This is normatively more attractive, since freedom of exit would mean that anyone who continues to live under a state does so voluntarily.

The republican criterion of legitimacy will require, in accordance with this exit constraint, that the state should allow its citizens to leave if they wish; if it denied citizens this right, then its status as a non-arbitrary source of interference would surely be put in question. Giving citizens the right to exit, however, doesn't mean much in the contemporary world since there is no possibility of being able to emigrate to an area where no state rules and only a limited possibility of being able to emigrate to another state; no other state may grant the right of entry. Does that mean that no state is legitimate, then? Surely not. The fact that everyone has to live under some state, and that no one can opt for a state-free existence, is the product of natural and historical necessity, not in itself the effect of dominating interference by the local state.

---

[9] Simmons, A. J., *Moral Principles and Political Obligations* (Princeton: Princeton University Press, 1979).
[10] Notice, however, that civil disobedience is an act of protest within the system, not without, since the protestors accept the right of the system to penalize their law-breaking; the idea, at least with overt disobedience, to display the intensity of the protest by the willingness to risk and accept such penalties.

In view of these considerations, republican theory focuses on a functional rather than a formational account of legitimacy; thus it is generally dismissive of the idea of a state of nature from within which people would voluntarily form a state.[11] The crucial requirement, according to almost all versions of the approach, is that the state operates on a non-arbitrary basis: that is, as I interpret the requirement that it operate under the effective equally shared control of its citizens.

2. Satisfying the Republican Criterion of Domestic Legitimacy

What might it mean in practice for a state to operate under the effective and equal control of its citizens or people? The people will control the state in this way only if two broad conditions can be fulfilled. The first is that government is exercised by agents and agencies that are subject to effective, popular influence: they are suitably susceptible to inputs originating with the people. And the second is that this influence is channelled and organized so that it forces government to operate on terms that are endorsed across the population as a whole—or at least across those who are reasonable enough not to think that they should be given special treatment. In a phrase, the government of the non-dominating, legitimate state should be constrained by the people to operate on the people's terms; it should answer to that broadly democratic ideal.

a. First Condition: The People's Influence

Government cannot be exercised by an assembly of the citizenry as a whole, if only in view of the numbers of individuals involved. It must be exercised, then, via individuals who in some sense represent the people. There are broadly two different types of representatives that we can expect to be duly sensitive to the influence of the people. I describe these, respectively, as deputies and proxies.[12]

Let us assume that the popular terms on which government should operate have already been established; we return to how this might happen in a moment. To take the first of our two kinds of representative, people might find or induce in certain agents or agencies a disposition to track, within flexible boundaries, whatever terms they specify. And they might then rely on those agents or agencies as on deputies: servants of their will. Or, to take the second possible channel, they might find

---

[11] Rousseau may seem to be the great exception, since the state of nature plays such an important role in his theory. But Rousseau is an innovative thinker who draws on many sources and he is not a typical representative of the neo-Roman republican tradition that I have in mind. See Spitz, J.–F., *La Liberté politique* (Paris: Presses Universitaires de France, 1995).

[12] Pettit, P,. 'Joining the Dots', in Smith, M. et al. (eds.), *Common Minds: Themes from the Philosophy of Philip Pettit* (Oxford: Oxford University Press, 2007).

and induce in certain agents or agencies a disposition to behave more or less inflexibly, out of a fixed motivational or institutional frame, in a way that happens to fit with the terms they endorse. And they might then rely on those agents or agencies as on proxies: independent centres whose operation in suitable positions of power answers to their standing will as to how power should be exercised there.

Deputies are most obviously recruited in the process of electoral appointment, as when public authorities are elected for a period on the basis of their electoral promises and then held to account for those promises when they seek re-election. Or at least that is how it works in the ideal. But election is not the only way of appointing deputies, and the desire for re-election is not the only basis on which deputies can become disposed—or be reinforced in an existing disposition—to track civic targets. Deputies may be recruited without election, as when those elected appoint other functionaries to office. And elected or unelected deputies may be given extra incentives to track civic targets on the basis of a desire to achieve certain rewards—perhaps just the good opinion of those they serve—or to avoid any of a range of penalties: the loss of office, a legal sanction, a public rebuke, or of course the bad opinion of others. Elected deputies will include most of the members of parliament or congress in all democracies and in presidential systems they will include a variety of other public officials as well, in particular the president or head of the executive. Unelected deputies will include the members of the executive in parliamentary democracies and, in all systems, the members of the executive staff: the functionaries whose job it is to carry out the wishes of the administration.

Where do proxies fit in the standard political picture? At a variety of points, I would say. Take the judge who is appointed for life, or not at least at the pleasure of the appointing executive. Or take the statutory officer—the head of an electoral commission, the head of the central bank—who is appointed on similar terms. Given such terms of appointment, these agents and their agencies will not constitute deputies who are triggered to respond to varying demands. But they may still serve the people well. Suppose that the popular terms on which government should operate require the fair and sensible application of the law, fair and sensible electoral districting, and fair and sensible decisions on interest rates. Suitably constrained and motivated, individuals and bodies of the sort mentioned should be capable of imposing those terms very effectively.

But the proxies in a democratic system are not confined to those with official appointments. Take the democracy in which there is such transparency of information, such freedom of speech, and such access to the courts and parliament—and to the press and the streets—that individual citizens and groups of citizens are enabled to make challenges to those in power, and to do so with some chance of success. Those who make such challenges within the system can be seen as proxies for the people as a whole, since the people license such contestation and may do so with a view to imposing suitable terms on government. The contesters may or may not mount their challenges for public-spirited reasons—they may just be acting out of a felt, personal grievance—but in any case the actions they bring against government may help to keep the authorities on their toes, exposing their decisions to public scrutiny and assessment.

b. Second Condition: The People's Terms

The people in a democracy can have a sustained influence on how they are governed to the extent that they recruit deputies and proxies into a suitable network for aggregating their efforts and can impose a suitable framework of opportunity, incentive, and constraint on what they actually do. But such an organization of deputies and proxies might give the people a lot of influence on government without giving them control. The influence might be as wayward and directionless as the influence of the weather. And if it were, then it would not deserve to be described as control; it would not serve the imposition of any particular terms on the way government is conducted. A crucial question, then, is whether we can find a basis for specifying terms that the organization of democratic deputies and proxies might be recruited to implement.

There are broadly two classes of terms that we might expect to have popular support as terms on which government should operate. One class we might describe as terms of association, the other as terms of argument. The first directs us to those terms that have to be satisfied under any arrangement in which the members of a population can claim to share equally in the control of government. The second directs us to terms, apart from the terms of association themselves, which command popular acceptance as relevant if not conclusive considerations in arguments about what should be done by government.

There are a number of ways in which government might be conducted that would breach the terms of association required for the very possibility of legitimacy. Here are some obvious possibilities.

- Government is conducted on the basis of bargaining from unequal positions of wealth and power, with resolutions depending on the compromises that parties are willing to accept, given their beliefs about what others will accept.
- Government is conducted on the basis of debate about what is acceptable—that is, what ought to be accepted—but not about what is acceptable equally to each; some parties are given a privileged position in the exercise.
- Government is conducted on the basis of what is acceptable equally to each but those who claim a privileged position are given an equal role with others in determining whether something is acceptable.
- Government is conducted via elected or appointed representatives but outsiders do not have any access to the exercise and do not have an opportunity to contest or gain a hearing for claims about equal acceptability.

- Government is conducted with a view to achieving unanimity and no policy is adopted that falls short of being endorsed as acceptable on all sides; no recourse is allowed to procedures for aggregating non-unanimous views.
- Aggregation is allowed but the procedure that is used in any instance—majority voting, the use of a lottery, referral to the expert committee—is not required to be acceptable to each as a procedure to govern such cases.

Suppose that decision-making is organized in a society so that possibilities like this are avoided and plausible terms of association are implemented. There is still an abstract possibility that in arguing about what is equally acceptable to each, citizens or their representatives will find nothing to say in favour of any proposal or any procedure other than the bare claim: this is equally acceptable to each. But if this happens, then there is going to be no way beyond assertions and counter-assertions about equal acceptability. There will be a stalemate between those on different sides.

While such a stalemate is possible in principle, however, it is not the sort of thing that materializes in practice when people manage to conduct an ongoing debate about issues of acceptability. Typically, the debate will go forward, however slowly, as the parties succeed in finding considerations—terms of argument—that pass muster on all sides as evaluations that are relevant to the issues under discussion. Those considerations may not be equally weighted on all sides. And for that reason, or because of differences in related empirical beliefs, their acknowledgement may not lead to any consensus about the policy or procedure under discussion. But the dissensus that appears will be built up on the basis of an agreement, perhaps even an accumulating body of agreement, in normative presuppositions. Those presuppositions will provide emerging terms of argument in the polity. They will identify values that everyone is prepared to acknowledge as *pro tanto* grounds for explaining why a policy or procedure ought to be equally accepted by each.

I assume that the people and the representatives in any potentially legitimate state will routinely participate in deliberation and discussion about what the government should be doing and that they will frame this on the basis of considerations relevant to what each ought to accept. They will conduct a debate that radiates throughout the society, engaging citizens in their neighbourhood and workplace, in their churches and associations. They will conduct the debate, not on a sectarian or in-group basis, but on a basis that is common to more centralized, diverse forums: for example, forums like the media, the hustings, the parliament or congress. And they will give the debate particular importance in contexts, formal or informal, where it is used as a basis for publicly justifying or contesting what government has actually done or is proposing to do.

If public debate has this prominence in a society, and does not run straight into stalemate, it is bound to give rise to the sorts of common, normative presuppositions

I have in mind.[13] When we find an argument relevant in any discussion then we must give some credence to the connection it posits or presupposes between the premises and the conclusion. We may not find the argument compelling, because of rejecting a premise or because the support the premises offer for the conclusion is outweighed by other considerations. But even if we reject an argument, marking out a point of explicit disagreement with our interlocutor, the fact of accepting its relevance means that we will have acknowledged an implicit point of agreement. The intended effect of the response may have been to focus on a difference but the unintended side-effect will be to mark out a common presupposition.[14]

Let one person argue from the value of fairness to the need for a universal health service, for example, and another argue from the value of quality in health provision to the need for keeping a private component in the system. In so far as they do not reject one another's arguments as irrelevant, they will display a common presupposition to the effect that both fairness of distribution and quality of service are relevant values. They will divide on the case for a universal health service only because of weighting those values differently or differing on some related matter of fact: they may differ, for example, on whether universal health provision would reduce the quality of service. But from our viewpoint, the important thing to notice is how much they agree on. They presuppose in common that the fairness of medical treatment and the quality of health provision both matter in the society.

3. Building on These Conditions

Let us suppose that government is organized on a representative basis—a framework and network of deputies and proxies—that allows for popular influence. And let us suppose that there are terms of association and argument available that have popular endorsement in the society. If those conditions are fulfilled, then there is room for

---

[13] See Rawls, J., *The Law of Peoples* (Cambridge, Mass.: Harvard University Press, 1999). Rawls may often have such normative presuppositions in mind when he speaks of public reasons and my ideas have clearly been influenced by his discussion. I prefer to speak of common presuppositions, emphasizing points that are not made in Rawls and might even be rejected by him: first, that they are generated as a byproduct of ongoing debate; second, that they are relevant to such debate, no matter at what site it occurs, private or public, informal or formal; and third that the presuppositions that operate in a society, or even in the international public world, may include some that carry no independent moral force: we may think that it is a mistake that the relevant parties endorse them. The language of common presuppositions, as used here, may be more in the spirit of Habermas (see Habermas, J., *A Theory of Communicative Action*, vols. 1 and 2 (Cambridge: Polity Press, 1984, 1989) than Rawls (Moon, J. D., 'Rawls and Habermas on Public Reason', *Annual Review of Political Science*, 6 (2003), 257). I am grateful to Tim Scanlon for a discussion on this point.

[14] Can't we put everything up front in the premises of an argument and not allow presuppositions to sneak in and establish areas of agreement behind our backs? No, we can't. Every set of premises supports a conclusion on the basis of a principle of inference that is not itself quoted as a premise. See Carroll, L., 'What the Tortoise said to Achilles', *Mind*, 4 (1895), 278.

organizing the state so that it is more or less effectively and equally controlled by the citizens: so that, in the etymological sense, it is a democracy, a regime that is subject to the power of the people. This goal will be achieved to the extent that the organization of representatives ensures that government is conducted under the discipline of those popular terms of reference.[15]

A suitable organization of deputies and proxies will have two aspects. Any policies that are inconsistent with the terms of reference will tend, for that very reason, to be taken off the agenda of government; they will become unthinkable options. And where a number of policies are consistent with those considerations, as many will certainly be, then the decision between those tied candidates will be made via a procedure whose use in the case at hand is supported by those considerations. The procedure may be a vote in parliament, a referral to a community or expert committee, a lottery device of some kind, or a society-wide referendum. Or it may involve a mix of such processes: think, for example, of the gamut of tests that a bill must pass under many democratic constitutions before it can become law.

I shall assume that a well-designed frameworking and networking of deputies and proxies can enable a people to regulate government for its conformity to local terms of association and argument; it can provide a constitution under which those values are reliably satisfied. The constitution, plausibly, would distribute opportunities, incentives, and constraints among officials so as to maximize the chance that they honour those values; it would require officials to justify their initiatives on the basis of such considerations; and it would enable a variety of individuals and bodies to challenge such initiatives for their conformity with the considerations.

Would this sort of organization serve to vindicate the legitimacy of the governing regime? It would control government by considerations that equally reflect the concerns of each. But would it give them effective control? I think so. The sort of control that people would have over democratic decision-making in the scenario envisaged can be compared with the control that individual agents enjoy when their values are duly empowered in their decisions. If I am to be a self-controlled agent, not just an arena where attitudes and actions form, then I must impose my values on how those states evolve, not micro-manage them; I must ensure that I judge according to the evidence or form desires that cohere with my values, not that I judge that p or desire that q.[16] What the people controls for is conformity to the public values of democratic exchange, in more or less exact parallel, not for the detailed direction of policy. If the control in self-controlled agents is significant, then so is this form of democratic control.

15 Pettit, P., 'The Power of a Democratic Public', in Gotoh, R. (ed.), *Against Injustice* (Cambridge: Cambridge University Press, 2008).

16 Pettit, P., and Smith, M., 'Freedom in Belief and Desire', *Journal of Philosophy*, 93 (1996), 429. Reprinted in Jackson, F., Pettit, P., and Smith, M. (eds.), *Mind, Morality and Explanation* (Oxford: Oxford University Press, 2004).

IV. Legitimacy in the International Context

1. Approaching the International Context

Under the republican conception of legitimacy an agency that interferes in the lives of a community will be legitimate to the extent that it is subject to the effective, equally shared control of the members—to the extent that it is a non-arbitrary power that is forced to track the interests they are disposed to avow. The legitimacy of the agency means, not necessarily that members are obliged to obey its dictates, but that they are required to acknowledge its right to issue those dictates and their own obligation, if they do not approve, to oppose them within given systemic guidelines.

We have now seen how this conception of legitimacy applies in the national or domestic context, requiring a legitimate government to be constrained by the people—say, by the frameworking and networking imposed on representatives—to operate on the people's terms. The discussion of national legitimacy provides a model for the discussion of international legitimacy and, as we shall see, it identifies an ideal—that of the legitimate state—that plays an important role in the specification of what international legitimacy requires.

The issue of international legitimacy is raised by the various agencies that are established by states—ultimately for the certainty and order that they confer[17]—in the international forum. These are organized on the basis of a more or less shared understanding of international law and its jurisdiction; they develop around a framework of international and regional agreements and treaties; and they constitute a network in which each body operates in a relatively distinct sphere but seeks more or less successfully to coordinate its actions with those of other such entities. They include military as well as more political bodies, and bodies of a regional as well as a global character. But the agencies of most pressing concern are those of a global, regulatory character.

Kingsbury, Krisch, and Stewart identify a variety of players in global regulation: formal treaty-based international organizations (such as the World Trade Organization, the Security Council, the World Bank, the Climate Change regime, etc.); informal intergovernmental networks of domestic regulatory officials (such as the Basel Committee of national bank regulators); domestic authorities implementing global regulatory law; and hybrid public-private as well as purely private

---

[17] Keohane, R. O., *After Hegemony: Cooperation and Discord in the World Political Economy* (Princeton: Princeton University Press, 1984).

transnational regulatory regimes.[18] These implement a regime of global regulation over commercial and other activities.[19] They establish international networks of agencies and officials that have been said to constitute a 'new world order'.[20]

Legitimacy in the international context raises two particularly sharp problems that do not have domestic analogues. I describe one of these as the membership problem, the other as the imbalance problem. In what follows I first sketch the membership problem and how to resolve it; then I introduce the line on international legitimacy that a republican approach would support; and after that I discuss the imbalance problem and the difficulty that it raises for republican theory.

2. The Membership Problem

By analogy with domestic legitimacy, the legitimacy of the international order is going to depend on the extent to which that order is subject to the effective, equally shared control of the members of the order. But in the domestic case there is little or no question as to who should be the relevant members. Membership is individual and inclusive; it extends at least to all adult, able-minded, and more or less permanent residents of the state's territory. In the international context, however, the analogous question of membership is naturally subject to dispute. Should the parties who are to exercise effective, equally shared control be all individuals on earth, or all the states under which such individuals live, or perhaps all 'peoples', in John Rawls's preferred term?

There are difficulties with taking all actual individuals to be the relevant parties to international legitimacy. One problem with the proposal is that there is no such thing as an international discourse, analogous to the discourse in a deliberative democracy, which would identify considerations that all individuals understand, regard as relevant, and would want to be empowered. Christiano emphasizes perhaps the most important aspect of this problem when he says that international civil society—the society of vigilant citizens and civic movements—is not nearly as dense as the civil society that keeps domestic governments on their toes.[21]

A further problem with the idea that individuals should be taken as the parties to international legitimacy is that if people form domestic states, and if those states are legitimate in the sense explained, then it is hard to see why they would want the international order to be controlled by them in an individual capacity rather than via the states that they form. 'The democratic state is a reasonably successful

---

[18] Kingsbury, B., Krisch, N., and Stewart, R., 'The Emergence of Global Administrative Law', *Law and Contemporary Problems*, 68 (2005), 15.

[19] Braithwaite, J., and Drahos, P., *Global Business Regulation* (Cambridge: Cambridge University Press, 2000).

[20] Slaughter, A.-M., 'The Real New World Order' *Foreign Affairs*, 76 (1997), 183; Slaughter, A.-M., *A New World Order* (Princeton: Princeton University Press, 2004).

[21] Christiano, T., in this volume, 134–5.

mechanism', as Tom Christiano says, 'for accommodating and representing the interests and concerns of its members'.[22] And that being the case, it is hard to see why the members of such a state should not prefer to rely on the states to police the international order.

So should we say that an international order will be legitimate to the extent that it is effectively and equally controlled by all states? That doesn't appeal as a way to go either, since there is no persuasive ground for wanting states to exercise such control over the international order, if those states include some that are undemocratic and domestically illegitimate; if they include some that oppress their peoples or some that do not have the capacity to serve them appropriately. We have to condemn the exercise of dominating control over legitimate states that speak and act for their peoples; dominating those states means dominating the individuals who form them. But we may applaud certain exercises of dominating control over illegitimate states: those that fail to serve the interests of the individuals who live within their boundaries. Certainly we will take this line if we are normative individualists: that is, if we hold, plausibly, that a treatment given to an institutional entity like a state counts as good or bad just in so far as the effects are good or bad for individuals.[23]

Christiano effectively raises the same problem when he says that while democratic states might do very well at policing the international order on behalf of their members, this is not so with what he describes as non-representative states. These include states that act primarily for an elite or a preferred majority, or that do their business in such secrecy that there is no possibility of holding officials to popular account.

Might we avoid these problems by claiming that the international order will be legitimate in so far as it is effectively and equally controlled by legitimate, democratic states? The difficulty with that approach is that it gives no role, as intuitively it should do, to those individuals who live under illegitimate states: that is, under oppressive, ill-ordered states that only serve a minority or under poor, disordered states that serve few if anyone. There would be no problem if all states on earth were more or less legitimate, for giving such states equal and effective control over the international order would be consistent with normative individualism. But the difficulty is that not all states are of that kind.

These observations irresistibly push towards the conclusion that a legitimate international order must, ideally, discharge two separate tasks: first, establish conditions under which all populations can form legitimate states to speak and act for them as peoples; and second, set up a suitable international order that is effectively and equally controlled by such states. That conclusion takes us into ideal-world theory, of course, but it gives guidance on what should be attempted

---

[22] Ibid. 136.

[23] Kukathas, C. and Pettit, P., *Rawls: A Theory of Justice and its Critics* (Cambridge and Stanford, Calif.: Polity Press and Stanford University Press, 1990).

by the international order in the real, deeply imperfect world. It suggests that while the international order should be maintained by states that are more or less legitimate—and maintained on terms that those states accept—it should be committed as a first priority to trying to establish legitimate states for peoples who are denied them.

This policy would argue for international steps to help relieve suffering and deprivation in disordered states and to take suitable, if proportional measures to replace or reform oppressive regimes. The international order would be primarily an arrangement among domestically legitimate states—in effect, well-ordered democracies—but it would be committed to enabling more and more states to become legitimate in that sense.

If we adopt this approach to international legitimacy, then we effectively take sides with John Rawls when he argues for an international order of peoples rather than states. A people exists and operates, on his view, just in so far as its government is a 'representative and effective agent',[24] so that the state counts as 'the political organization of the people'.[25] A people exists and operates when the state it forms is a liberal one, in Rawls's terminology: in effect, a state that conforms to our requirements for domestic legitimacy. To take the line suggested here, then, is precisely to give priority to peoples in Rawls's sense.

Rawls's insistence that a people properly exists and functions only in the presence of a fully liberal state represents his ideal-world theory. Famously, however, he allows that in the real, imperfect world peoples may also be taken to form and act—and should gain recognition in the international order—under what he calls 'decent' regimes. In these regimes, everyone will have a say but some may have a less direct say than others. As the members of a religious or other minority, for example, they may have the collective voice provided by a minority spokesperson: they may not have a vote in their own right or they may not be able to contest government decisions in their own right.

Rawls's line is attractive to the extent that it guards against the danger that only a relatively small, culturally homogeneous group of states might count as the primary units in the international order. But it lowers the standards for when a state is legitimate or representative, and it may make the line taken here seem to be less normatively commanding. What should we say on the issue?

I think that the line taken by Rawls is quite reasonable but for reasons other than any that he canvases. There are grounds for thinking that treating less than properly legitimate and representative states as if they commanded such a status, giving them full membership in the international order, will sometimes be the best way of achieving the first priority mentioned above: that of enabling a maximum number of peoples to live under legitimate states. This is because the best way to

---

[24] Rawls, J., *The Law of Peoples* (above, n. 13), 38.   [25] Ibid. 24.

push a state towards greater legitimacy may be by treating it as if it were legitimate, incorporating it fully into the international order.

Treating immature or irresponsible individuals as responsible may 'responsibilize' them, as David Garland argues.[26] This is because it may offer those individuals an extra incentive to prove worthy of being held to the relevant standards and it may thereby help to give them the capacity to live up to the standards; it may make them fit to be held responsible.[27] Something similar is true, I suspect, of state legitimacy.

Few states are likely to be fully or unfailingly legitimate, in the terms of our earlier discussion, and incorporation into an international order may actually serve to increase or sustain domestic legitimacy. It can do this in two ways. First, indirectly, by pressing states to recognize in their domestic practice principles that they are led to endorse within international covenants and organizations. And second, directly, by enabling individuals to launch an appeal against their own states to international bodies that states are diplomatically or formally committed to respecting.[28] This thought is worthy of further exploration but cannot be pursued further here. It suggests that the international order should be seen as having a partly developmental rationale. Not only can it establish a mode of relationship between states that facilitates the achievement of shared, global goals. It can also help to promote and sustain the attainment of domestic legitimacy in those states that are incorporated as full members.

3. The Republican Line

Suppose we adopt the view, then, that the international order will be legitimate in so far as two conditions are fulfilled: it is designed at any time to maximize the number of peoples who live under domestically legitimate governments; and it conducts the business of protecting legitimate states against domination, and securing other collective benefits, in a manner that gives legitimate states equal and effective control over how it operates. The central question bears, then, on how the condition of equal, effective control can be fulfilled. What form should the international order take, if it is to be subject to such control? And what means are available whereby it can be suitably controlled?

Taking the issue of form first, should the international order function like a state: say, a federal state under which existing states are incorporated irrevocably? Or should it assume a less demanding shape: one, in particular, that allows states to secede from any arrangements that it puts in place?

[26] I have benefited from discussion with the authors of R. E. Keohane, S. Macedo, and A. Moravcsik 'Democracy-enhancing Multilateralism', International Organization vol. 63, 2009, 1–31.

[27] Pettit, P., *A Theory of Freedom: From the Psychology to the Politics of Agency* (Cambridge and New York: Polity and Oxford Press, 2001).

[28] I have benefited from a number of discussions with Bob Keohane, and Steve Macedo on how international institutions can bolster and improve the domestic democracies of those states that are party to them.

Considerations of feasibility alone would argue against seeking a federal, world state: it is very hard to see how existing states and peoples might be persuaded to give up their sovereignty irrevocably to a distinct entity. But those considerations are supported in any case by a distinct, normative argument. It is not clear how a state could be legitimately denied the right of exit, as federation would strictly require, in the event of its members deciding against continuing membership. There is no room here for the argument that we used at the domestic level to the effect that there is nowhere that an exiting member may be able to go.

On the question of the form to be taken by the international order, these considerations argue that international agencies should have the backing provided by a voluntary association of states, not the backing that a world federation—in effect, a world state—would provide. What should we say, then, on the second question? How is the order that is constituted by international agencies to be controlled by member states?

It might be thought that the right of exit will be enough on its own to give legitimate states all the control they might want and to establish thereby the legitimacy of the international order. The exit constraint means that states will be free to leave the international organizations whose legitimacy is in question. If states do not vote with their feet by leaving such agencies, as a right of exit would enable them to do, that may in itself seem to provide a guarantee that the agencies are operating in a pattern that member states approve. Christiano seems to go broadly along with this thought, when he says that voluntary association 'allows states to pick and choose what terms they enter into'.[29] Freedom of exit would seem to ensure the ultimate form of control over an organization and thereby guarantee its legitimacy. It would give each member state a conditional veto on how the organization behaves: a veto on how the organization operates, if it is to retain that state as a member.

Things, unfortunately, are not as straightforward as that. Any individual state that signs up to a trading agreement, or to any organization in which its interests overlap with those of other members, is going to find it very hard to exercise the right of exit. The other members will generally be disposed to penalize any defector and the penalties in prospect may act as a powerful deterrent against secession. Given this pressure to stay within an international organization, then, any state may find itself under the thumb of that agency. For when the agency imposes its rules on a member state—when the WTO finds, for example, against one or another member of the organization—then that state will be effectively coerced into compliance. The existence of a formal right of exit may guard in principle against domination by such an agency. But in practice it will not do so. States lock themselves into potentially dominating sources of influence and control when they sign up to different international arrangements. They may have a fully effective

---

[29] Christiano, T., this volume, 136.

freedom of entry—though even this is not certain, in view of the pressures to join that other states may impose—but they will not have a fully effective freedom of exit. And freedom of entry does not do much for securing legitimacy in the absence of a corresponding freedom of exit; it may be just the freedom to suffer for a past mistake.

How can states impose an equal, effective control on international bodies, then, thereby establishing the republican legitimacy of the order that those bodies constitute? I see only one plausible path: by frameworking and networking those organizations so that they are more or less forced in their decisions to honour terms of association and argument that command allegiance on all sides.

If this is right, then there has to be an international discourse among states that parallels the discourse of a domestic democracy. That discourse has to give rise to a currency of considerations that are recognized as relevant considerations that any state may reasonably invoke in assessing one or another international initiative.[30] And those considerations have to be empowered by the ways in which international agencies and their officials are frameworked and networked with each other. Plausibly, the agencies will be subject to conditions that favour acting on such considerations; they will have to justify their decisions on the basis of the considerations; and those justifications will be exposed to public, potentially effective challenges from non-states as well as states: say, from the non-governmental organizations that operate in a global context.

Is it plausible to expect relatively egalitarian terms of association to be established amongst states in the international arena and more or less universally endorsed terms of argument to get endorsed there? Many will say that what we should expect to find, rather, is a pure power play in which states bargain with one another, each seeking to make only the minimal concession required to elicit the cooperation of others. Given the power differentials between states, it may be said, nothing else would be compatible with the self-seeking incentives of states and their representatives.

Incentive-compatibility is not the only constraint, however, on what may emerge in the dealings of states or indeed any agents with one another. Equally important, or important in only a slightly reduced degree, is something that we might describe as constraints of discourse-compatibility.[31] A proposal or ideal will fail to be discourse-compatible to the extent that it is not one that can be supported in a deliberative forum by reasons that are accepted on all sides as relevant to the issue. The most egregious examples would present one side in the deliberations as unequal in some significant manner to the other. Consider in this connection the memo by Lawrence Summers, then chief economist to the World Bank, which was leaked in 1991.

---

[30] For an extension of the Rawlsian idea of public reasons to the international forum see Cohen, J., 'Minimalism about Human rights: The Most We Can Hope For', *Journal of Political Philosophy*, 12 (2004), 190.

[31] Pettit, P., *Rules, Reasons, and Norms: Selected Essays* (Oxford: Oxford University Press, 2002), 276.

This made a case for exporting heavy polluting industries to the third world on the ground, roughly, that the anti-pollution preferences of poorer, shorter-lived individuals would not be as strong as those of the richer and longer-lived. The memo caused indignation world-wide, precisely because the proposal was incompatible with the assumptions of equality that underpin deliberation. A Brazilian official wrote in understandable incredulity that the lesser reasoning was 'perfectly logical and totally insane'.[32]

If discourse-compatibility plays an important role in the relations between states, it need not be excessively optimistic to expect that relatively egalitarian terms of association will be recognized in international forums and that universally endorsed terms of argument will tend to get established there. But is it plausible to think that international agencies might be capable of being forced to implement such terms of reference, thereby allowing legitimating control of their operations to member states? At this point we confront what I called the problem of imbalance. This is closely related to the problem that Christiano describes as one of 'asymmetrical bargaining'.[33]

4. The Imbalance Problem

We confront a striking dilemma when we think about how to appoint to international bodies and how to police those appointed authorities—those deputies or proxies—so that they reliably act on suitable terms of association and argument. Either the distribution of appointments and the organization of offices will reflect the greater power of some countries, where that power may depend on population, territory, resources, or wealth. Or it will not reflect such inequalities of power but be devised on an egalitarian basis. But in the first event, won't the arrangements tend to favour the fewer, more powerful countries; and in the second, the more numerous and less powerful? And isn't any such favouritism inconsistent with legitimacy?

The first point to make in response is that there are some ways in which it is reasonable that the stronger or the weaker be favoured, on plausible terms of reference, and that these should be distinguished from modes of favouritism that are indefensible. It is hard to imagine an international forum of discussion in which there was no agreement that those with larger populations should get greater access to some common benefit—say, a vaccine that is distributed by international agencies—and that those with more natural resources should be enabled to use them to their commercial advantage. And, equally, it is hard to imagine that there might not be agreement that those with lesser wealth should not have to pay the

---

[32] For the content of the memo and criticism of it, including mention of this response, see <http://www.counterpunch.org/summers.html>.

[33] Christiano, T., this volume, 126.

same as those with greater wealth into international agencies and that those with smaller populations should not be subject to unconstrained, majority control in international bodies.

Let such positions on differential treatment be accepted in international discourse, and they may have an impact, not just on how argument is conducted in international agencies and bodies, but on the appointments that different countries are allowed to control and on the modes in which appointees operate. They will support certain allowable asymmetries within those agencies and bodies. But won't any asymmetries tend to facilitate unwarranted favouritism, whether towards the more powerful or towards the less powerful? Not necessarily, I think. The second point to make in response to the general problem of imbalance is that this is not an inevitable effect, however difficult it may be to avoid it.

Many international authorities and agencies will be proxies who are subjected to incentives, opportunities, and constraints that support decision-making according to accepted terms of reference; the very reputation of the individuals and bodies involved may depend on the display of such impartiality.[34] And while there will certainly be many decisions that are up for negotiation between countries of different levels of power, the asymmetry can be muted by the capacity of weaker countries to make common cause with one another.

Stronger countries may always seek advantages that would be hard to support in multilateral, egalitarian discussion of what ought to be accepted by each. This appears, for example, in their tendency to shift to another forum of debate when one forum proves disadvantageous, and in their attempts to opt out of multilateral discussions altogether in favour of bilateral, one-by-one arrangements with other states.[35] But it is by no means assured, and by no means evident, that they can always get away with these initiatives. Coalitions among weaker countries, if they can only hold together, may often be able to drag them back to the table and exploit constraints of discourse-compatibility in their own favour.

But is it possible, in that case, that the coalitions of weaker countries will be able to implement a regime that is unduly favourable to them? I do not think so, for two reasons. First of all, the constraints of discourse-compatibility will militate against such favouritism on the same grounds that they militate against favouritism towards the strong. And secondly, stronger countries will inevitably be able to exit from international arrangements at a lesser cost than others; thus they will be able to bail out of any organizations in which the balance of power has shifted uncomfortably towards coalitions of the weaker.

International forums are always in danger of becoming sites for the exercise of brute power, of course, but there is no necessity attaching to that result. If the power

---

[34] Brennan, G. and Pettit, P., *The Economy of Esteem: An Essay on Civil and Political Society* (Oxford: Oxford University Press, 2004).

[35] Braithwaite, J. and Drahos, P., *Global Business Regulation* (above, n. 19).

on different sides looks to be even roughly balanced, then that may create a space where the international order can interfere in the affairs of different states under the equal and effective control of terms that are accepted on all sides. It may constitute a regime of global regulation that has a good claim to legitimacy. We may be very far from that ideal, as things currently stand, but there are no blocks in evidence that good institutional design might not prove capable of removing.

SECTION IV

SOURCES OF INTERNATIONAL LAW

CHAPTER 7

THEORIZING THE SOURCES OF INTERNATIONAL LAW

SAMANTHA BESSON*

I. INTRODUCTION

Although, and probably because, it is one of the most central questions in international law, the identification of the sources of international law, that is, its law-making processes, remains one of the most difficult. Not only is it important in practice to identify valid international legal norms and the duties that stem from international law. It also implies understanding the nature of international law itself, i.e. the *legality* of international law.[1] Furthermore, determining the sources of international law also means (briefly) explaining some of the origins of its *normativity* and claim to authority, but more importantly of its *legitimacy* and justification in imposing exclusionary reasons to obey on its subjects.

* Many thanks to John Tasioulas, Anthony D'Amato, David Lefkowitz, and Allen Buchanan for helpful feedback and comments.

[1] Hart, H. L. A., *The Concept of Law* (rev. edn., Oxford: Clarendon, 1994), 213–16; D'Amato, A., 'Is International Law Really "Law"?', *Northwestern Law Review*, 79 (1985), 1293; Higgins, R., *Problems & Process, International Law and How We Use it* (Oxford: Oxford University Press, 1994), 17–18.

1. Legal Accounts of the Sources of International Law

Interestingly, the question of sources is often met with placative confidence among international legal scholars. It is usually solved by reference to the formal sources of international law, and in particular to the now largely obsolete but still venerated triad of sources one finds in Article 38 of the 1945 International Court of Justice (ICJ) Statute: treaty law, customary law, and general principles, complemented by other sources usually deemed as 'ancillary' or 'auxiliary', that is, the case law and the writings of eminent specialists.

The first drawback of those legal accounts is to unduly corset international legal sources in state-like categories despite important differences in practice. First of all, international *law-makers* are of a collective nature, i.e. mostly states and international organizations (IOs), and only sometimes individuals, whereas law-makers in the national legal order are individuals. There, individuals are the primary law-makers, albeit not in their private capacity: either directly *qua* citizens or indirectly *qua* officials. In international law, by contrast, there is a plurality of different law-makers and they usually take part in international law-making processes individually rather than officially in the name of an international political community. Traditionally, states have been the prevalent international law-makers and have produced alone laws that apply not only to them, but also to other international subjects such as IOs and, more and more, to individuals. As a consequence, there is a widespread lack of congruence between international law-makers and legal subjects, whereas that congruence is the main claim of democratic constitutional municipal orders.

Second, the *law-making process* is mostly legislative in national legal orders, with other sources retaining a minor role, whereas there is currently no single world legislator in the international legal order and hence a plurality of equivalent sources of international law. As a result, those sources have always been and are increasingly intermingled in their respective processes and they influence each other mutually. Of course, treaty-making has been prevalent and increasingly so, but customary law traditionally constitutes the backbone of general international law and has been strengthened in recent years by the development of multilateral treaty-making and codification processes. Finally, the national *legal order* is usually centralized and unitary with a hierarchy among sources and even among various areas of national law, whereas the international legal order is vertically pluralistic in the absence of a hierarchy among legal sources, on the one hand, and horizontally pluralistic or fragmented in many parallel legal regimes on different matters but also in different regions, on the other.

A second difficulty with current legal accounts of the sources of international law is their relative blindness to the important changes that have occurred in international law-making in recent years. Through the so-called legalization of international law, its density has increased with more legal norms being adopted over more issues previously left to national law-making processes and by many law-makers at the same time.[2] First of all, international *legal subjects* have multiplied and with them the potential scope of law-makers, thus threatening the legal monopoly of states *qua* law-makers in favour of international organizations and, to a lesser degree, individuals.[3] Second, with the emergence of new law-makers, international *law-making processes* have become institutionalized and evolved towards similar multilateral and quasi-legislative processes. Finally, and as a result, international law's *normativity* has also evolved drastically: from being subjective international law has become more objective, from relative it has turned more universal and, in terms of degree of normativity, it now ranges from low-intensity or soft law to imperative law.

2. Philosophical Accounts of the Sources of International Law

Traditional philosophical accounts of the sources of international law also offer a skewed view of international law-making. Theories of international law are often starkly contrasted, with legal positivism, on the one end of the spectrum, and natural law theory, on the other. This contrast leads to a Manichean opposition of treaty-law *qua* posited law, on the one side, to customary law and general principles *qua* natural law, on the other.

An important reason for this opposition lies in the central feature of the modern international legal order, that is, the equal sovereignty of states. This principle has implications for international law's authority: *pacta sunt servanda*, i.e. the principle according to which states are only bound by the laws they have consented to. Consensualism can mean three things in terms of international law's authority: international law can only be subjective in content, i.e. limited to what those states have consented to; it can only be relative in (personal) scope, i.e. limited to those states which have consented; and it can only be of one single degree, i.e. the one set by the consent of each and every state. No wonder therefore that this binary opposition was translated in terms of a stark opposition between legal positivism

---

[2] See the discussion in Cassese, A. and Weiler, J. (eds.), *Change and Stability in International Law-Making* (Berlin, New York: De Gruyter, 1988); Lowe, V., 'The Politics of Law-Making: Are the Method and Character of Norm Creation Changing?' in Byers, M. (ed.), *The Role of Law in International Politics* (Oxford: Oxford University Press, 2000), 207.

[3] See e.g. Alvarez, J., *International Organizations as Law-Makers* (Oxford: Oxford University Press, 2006); McCorquodale, R., 'An Inclusive International Legal System', *Leiden Journal of International Law*, 17 (2004), 477.

and natural law theory. In terms of legal validity, indeed, consensualism implies legal positivism, i.e. the account of law which links its validity to its being posited, as opposed to natural law theory, which links the validity of law back to its moral content.

The difficulty with this approach to legal validity and to legal sources is double, however. First of all, consensualism is primarily an approach to normativity and to legitimacy and not—at least immediately—to legality. Moreover, as we will see, state consent can no longer be deemed as the most important source of normativity and legitimacy in international law. It is important therefore that the theory of sources of international law be clearly separated from the latter. The problem, however, is that legal positivism is often coined as necessarily consensualist in international law, and the reverse is also true: a non-consensualist approach to international law and legitimacy is only deemed as plausible in a natural law framework. The second difficulty, therefore, is that legal positivism does not necessarily imply consensualism and its opposition to natural law theory has been seriously exaggerated. There is nothing about legal positivism that is incompatible with objective, universal, and imperative international law. Nor, more importantly, does legal positivism contradict majoritarianism. As a result, the opposition between legal positivist and natural law accounts of international law is far less diametrical than it is alleged to be.

The aim of the present chapter is to develop a theory of the sources of international law that takes up those different challenges. Its purpose is not, therefore, to provide a detailed discussion of all sources of international law.[4] Theorizing international law does not amount to descriptive sociology, but sets standards for a coherent and legitimate international legal practice. As a result, it is as normative as the processes it purports to explain. There are, it shall be argued, normative grounds for positing international law and adopting a positivist approach to the sources of international law, and these are in particular grounds of global justice and peaceful cooperation among equal international subjects whose conceptions of justice diverge. The proposed account of international law relies on a democratic theory of sources, according to which the democratic nature of the international law-making process makes for the conditions of equal respect and inclusion of all those affected, necessary for legal coordination among different subjects of international law in conditions of pervasive and persistent moral and social pluralism.

---

[4] See e.g. Boyle, A. and Chinkin, C., *The Making of International Law* (Oxford: Oxford University Press, 2007); Degan, V. D., *Sources of International Law* (The Hague: Kluwer Law International, 1997); Danilenko, G., *Law-Making in the International Community* (The Hague: Nijhoff, 1993); Van Hoof, G. J. H., *Rethinking the Sources of International Law* (Deventer: Kluwer, 1983).

II. Public International Law and Its Sources

1. Public International Law

a. Notion

In a nutshell, one may say that public international law is a set of legal norms pertaining to the international community and to the cooperation between international legal subjects, whether states, international organizations, or, less frequently, individuals.

First of all, the *international* dimension of international law should be understood as broader than *interstate* or *intergovernmental* law, since its subjects, object, and law-making processes now implicate individuals and IOs as much as states. In fact, international law also differs from other forms of law generated beyond the municipal level such as *supranational* law. The difference between international and supranational law has been said to revolve around the decision-making procedure (unanimity versus majority-rule), the personal scope of the law produced (relative versus universal), and the origin of its normativity (subjective versus objective). Nowadays, however, the development of multilateral and majority-based international law-making provides a good example of the increasing overlap between those categories.

What is strictly speaking international as opposed to *national* about international law no longer lies in its subjects nor in its objects; certain international legal norms now apply directly to individuals in national territories (even without national transposition or specification in national law) and overlap with other national and regional norms over the same territory and the same legal subjects, since they address at least in part the same objects. Nor can the difference be traced back to the law-makers since individuals have become law-makers in certain regional and international law-making processes as in the European Union (EU). The difference must therefore lie in the law-making processes themselves or, in other words, in the sources of international law: international law-making processes take place above the national state or sometimes inside it, but by implicating other subjects than the national law-makers only. It is important, in other words, to distinguish carefully the *sources of national, regional, or international law* from the *national, regional, or international sources of the law* applicable at each and every layer of the complex global legal order.

Second, international law is sometimes referred to as *public* international law. For a long time, international law was the product of a law-making process between states only and its object was inter-state relations only, thus making it public both in respect of its subjects and objects. Nowadays, however, there is no longer much that is only public about international law whether in its legal subjects and its law-makers (which also include individuals) or in its objects (which also include private relationships). As a result, it is the public or, more exactly, the official nature of the international law-making process itself, by contrast to mere inter-state contracts or transnational forms of private regulation,[5] that makes international law public. In this context, the international law-making role of individuals should be thought of as official, taking part in processes where states participate *qua* officials and where individuals participate *qua* post-national citizens or accountable representatives as in the EU and not only *qua* bankers, NGO lobbyists, or natural resource dealers.[6] Whereas private norms are a common feature of autonomous regulatory mechanisms in certain areas of national law as well, they are not usually regarded as sources of law, but merely as legal acts empowered by law to give rise to legal obligations in specific cases.[7]

b. Distinctions

International law is often divided between *general* international law and international law *tout court*. In principle, law is by definition general in its personal scope as opposed to a relative source of mutual obligations. The distinction can therefore only be one among legal obligations as opposed to sources. The personal scope of a specific obligation, as when it is *erga omnes* or *omnium* for instance, is not necessarily a function of its sources. As a result, the universality of international law should not be confused with its generality that is a quality of its being law; international law applies *per se* to an indefinite number of subjects provided they qualify with the conditions set by each legal norm (generality) and it is then up to each legal norm to define its personal scope more or less universally. The distinction is made difficult in international law, however, because, contrary to national law, certain sources of general law, like treaty-law, usually give rise to non-general legal norms.[8]

What the distinction means therefore is, first of all, that general international law is the kind of international law that applies to all international legal subjects, like customary law or general principles, while international law *tout court* applies only

[5] See e.g. Krisch, N. and Kingsbury, B., 'Introduction: Global Governance and Global Administrative Law in the International Legal Order', *European Journal of International Law*, 17/1 (2006), 1.

[6] Besson, S., '*Ubi Ius, Ibi Civitas:* A Republican Approach to the International Community', in Besson, S., and Martí, J. L. (eds.), *Legal Republicanism and Republican Law* (Oxford: Oxford University Press, 2009), 204.

[7] On legal acts in international law, see section II.2.b.

[8] Higgins, R., *Problems & Process: International Law and How We Use It* (above, n. 1), 33.

to those subjects which are its law-makers as with most kinds of treaties. Of course, this does not exclude all treaties from the scope of general international law;[9] many of them regulate all legal subjects and, even when they regulate the case of certain states only, as with treaties applying to states with a seashore, they are general in their specific personal scope. In fact, the distinction between general and non-general treaty-law is becoming increasingly moot, as demonstrated by the third-party effect of certain multilateral treaties, the development of so-called world-order treaties and, more generally, what one may refer to as the 'customization' of given parts of multilateral treaties.[10]

International law can also be deemed as *general* in a second sense. It is opposed to the specific international law stemming from so-called special regimes.[11] The difference here is not (only) one of personal scope, but one of material scope and more precisely of specificity of the legal norms at stake. Special regimes regulate a functional area of law, as with World Trade Organization law, or a specific territory, as with EU law. The distinction has been heavily contested of late given the progressive consolidation of a background general regime common to all international regimes; this is the case of the international responsibility regime or treaty-making procedures.[12] In fact, one may argue that special regimes are not so different from specific material regimes in national law. As we will see, they are not autonomous legal orders—with the exception of EU law which is not only a special regime, but arguably also a self-contained and independent legal order—but merely groups of specific legal norms with territorial or material specificity in application.

2. Sources of Public International Law

a. Notion

The sources of law are all the facts or events that provide the ways for the creation, modification, and annulment of valid legal norms.[13] Sources of international

---

⁹ D'Amato, A., *The Concept of Custom in International Law* (Ithaca: Cornell University Press, 1971), 105–7.

¹⁰ See Simma, B., 'From Bilateralism to Community Interest in International Law', *Recueil des cours*, 250 (1994), 217; Pauwelyn, J., *Conflict of Norms in Public International Law* (Cambridge: Cambridge University Press, 2003), 155–7.

¹¹ See on those and other international legal regimes, Simma, B., 'Self-Contained Regimes', *Netherlands Yearbook of International Law*, 16 (1985), 111; Simma, B., and Pulkowski, D., 'Of Planets and the Universe: Self-Contained Regimes in International Law', *European Journal of International Law*, 17/3 (2006), 483.

¹² See International Law Commission, *Report on Fragmentation of international law: difficulties arising from the diversification and expansion of international law*, 13 Apr. 2006, UN/DOC/A/CN.4/L.682.

¹³ See Marmor, A., 'The Nature of Law', in Zalta, E. N. (ed.), *Stanford Encyclopedia of Philosophy* (Stanford: Stanford University, Winter 2007 edn.), <http://plato.stanford.edu>; Green, L., 'Legal Positivism', in Zalta, E. N. (ed.), *Stanford Encyclopedia of Philosophy* (Stanford: Stanford University, Winter 2003 edn.), <http://plato.stanford.edu>.

law refer to *processes* by which international legal norms are created, modified, and annulled, but also to the *places* where their normative outcomes, i.e. valid international legal norms, may be found.

A first distinction ought to be drawn between *formal* and *material* sources of international law; the latter refer to all the moral or social processes by which the content of international law is developed (e.g. power play, cultural conflicts, ideological tensions), as opposed to the formal processes by which that content is then identified and usually modified to become law (e.g. legislative enactment). Second, formal sources of international law *stricto sensu* should be kept distinct from so-called *probationary* sources, i.e. places where one finds evidence of the outcome of the law-making process. It is important in this respect to distinguish the documents issued by the law-making process from the outcome of that process; not all international law-making processes result in a document evidencing their outcome. Often, of course, distinguishing material and probationary sources from formal sources of international law becomes rather artificial. For instance, in the case of a custom *qua* formal source of customary law, the latter is difficult to distinguish from the material source of those customary norms, that is, the practice or *consuetudo*, and from its probationary source, for example, a United Nations (UN) General Assembly Resolution which attests of an *opinio juris* or of an existing and widespread practice.[14]

International law-making processes can give rise to complete legal norms (*lex lata*), but also to intermediary results such as legal projects (*lex ferenda*);[15] both types of outcomes may have the same sources and are part of the same law-making processes. Intermediary legal products, although they are not yet valid legal norms, may be vested with a certain evidentiary value in the next stages of the law-making process. Thus, non-binding UN resolutions may provide evidence of both state practice and *opinio juris* which might then support the final development of a customary norm. This is what is often meant by the distinction between hard and soft law,[16] although soft law is also sometimes used to refer to *lex lata* and hence to valid legal norms whose degree of normativity is very low.[17] Given the plurality of international law-making processes, it should come as no surprise that such intermediary or incremental legal products may be important both in quantity and quality. While many regret the lack of a clear passage from non-law to law in the international legal practice, soft law provides a useful source of coordinative

---

[14] ICJ, Advisory opinion, *Legality of the Threat or Use of Nuclear Weapons* (ICJ Reports 1996), 226, 254–5.

[15] Brownlie, I., 'To what extent are the traditional categories of lex lata and lex ferenda still viable?', in Cassese, A., and Weiler, J. (eds.), *Change and Stability in International Law-Making* (Leyden: De Gruyter, 1988), 66, 81.

[16] See e.g. Abi-Saab, G., 'Eloge du 'droit assourdi': Quelques réflexions sur le rôle de la soft law en droit international contemporain', in Abi-Saab, G. (ed.), *Nouveaux itinéraires en droit: Hommage à François Rigaux* (Brussels: Bruylant, 1993), 59.

[17] See the discussion in Cassese, A. and Weiler, J. (eds.), *International Law-Making* (above, n. 2), 66 ff.; Boyle, A. and Chinkin, C., *The Making of International Law* (above, n. 4), 211–29.

norms. This is even more important as soft law-making processes are usually more multilateral and inclusive than others, and implicate more IOs and individuals.

b. Distinctions

International law-making processes should be distinguished from their outcome: the great variety of *international legal norms*. Certain international legal norms may be found in different sources, of which only the first one created the norm and the latter amended or re-edicted it to give it another personal or material scope. As a result, sources of international law should also be distinguished from their outcome's personal scope or degree of normativity. Thus, contrary to what one often reads, soft law is not a source of international law; it is a kind of intermediary international legal outcome whose legality might be questioned and hence whose normativity *qua* law is almost inexistent. Soft law may stem from many sources of international law and not only from unilateral acts. Nor is *jus cogens* a source of international law; it is a kind of international legal norm whose degree of normativity is the highest, but which may be found in various sources of international law.

Second, if international legal norms ought to be distinguished from their sources, legal obligations ought to be distinguished from legal norms. International legal norms create *legal obligations* which are general and abstract, but not all international legal obligations arise out of legal norms. For instance, certain relative obligations may arise out of specific international agreements without corresponding to general obligations. Whereas in principle all sources of international law including treaties, like any source of national law, should give rise to legal norms and hence to general obligations, this is not true of all treaties. Legislation-like treaties give rise to general obligations, while contract-like treaties only provide relative and reciprocal obligations.[18]

Finally, one sometimes finds mention of an intermediary layer between the international legal norm and its source: that of the *legal act* by which legal obligations are created. The difficulty with this intermediary step is double: first, it only exists in the case of voluntary or subjective sources of international law, as with the exchange of consent in the treaty-making process, and, second, it begs the pre-existing question of the source itself.[19] Indeed, if the exchange of consent is able to create general legal obligations, it is because treaty-making is in itself a source of general international law. The problem is that, contrary to contracts in national law, certain treaties are sources of international law *stricto sensu*, while others are legal acts and cannot produce general legal obligations.

---

[18] D'Amato, A., *The Concept of Custom in International Law* (above, n. 9), 161.
[19] Abi-Saab, G., 'Les sources du droit international: Un essai de déconstruction', in Boutros-Ghali, B. (ed.), *Liber Amicorum E. Jimenez de Aréchaga* (Montevideo: Fundaciòn de Cultura Universitaria, 1994), 29, 40–1.

III. Sources and the Legality, Normativity, and Legitimacy of International Law

1. The Sources of International Law and its Legality

a. Legality and International Law

Legality is the normative quality of legal norms as opposed to other social norms and hence the quality of a legal order in general as opposed to other kinds of social orders.

In a stronger and more substantive sense adopted here, legality is also often associated with the political ideal of the *Rule of Law*. To identify a society as having a system of law, as opposed to some other sort of order, is to identify it as satisfying some or all of the requirements associated with the Rule of Law.[20] The Rule of Law celebrates features of a well-functioning system of government such as among others publicity and transparency in public administration, the generality and prospectivity of the norms that are enforced in society, the predictability of the social environment that these norms help to shape, the procedural fairness involved in their administration, the independence and incorruptibility of the judiciary, and so on. More precisely, it identifies a society where those in power exercise it within a constraining framework of public rules rather than on the basis of their own preferences, their own ideology, or their own individual sense of right and wrong.

As a result, legality is also a matter of the quality of the law's sources. The law-making processes by which we identify valid legal norms should themselves be such as to satisfy the requirements associated with the Rule of Law. The same should be said about the legality of international law. International law-making processes should therefore be such as to satisfy some of the requirements associated with the *Rule of International Law* and in particular the requirements of clarity, publicity, certainty, equality, transparency, and fairness.[21]

b. International Legality and the Sources of International Law

The contours of the Rule of International Law are less well defined than at the national level and primarily so because the main international legal subjects are

---

[20] Simmonds, N. E., 'Law as a Moral Ideal', *University of Toronto Law Journal*, 55 (2005), 61; Waldron, J., 'The Concept and Rule of Law', *Georgia Law Review*, 43:1 (2008), 1.

[21] See e.g. Watts, A., 'The International Rule of Law', *German Yearbook of International Law*, 36 (1993), 15; Teitel, R., 'Humanity's Law: Rule of Law for the New Global Politics', *Cornell International Law Journal*, 35 (2002), 355.

states. The indeterminate nature of the ideal at the international level should not, however, hide the fact that the ultimate legal subjects of those laws are individuals, whether indirectly or, and increasingly so, directly and that when states act as law-makers, they act not only as subjects of international law, but also as officials.[22] As a consequence, there is no reason not to vindicate that ideal in international law as well.[23]

The connexion between the Rule of International Law and the quality of the sources of international law explains why the idea of illegal international law propounded by some authors[24] does not pay sufficient heed to the value in the legality of international law and hence to the normative requirements this value imposes on its law-making processes. These normative requirements inherent in the very legality of international law—together or possibly by contrast to those relative to its procedural or substantive legitimacy—make it counterproductive to hope for the illegal making of international law whatever the urgency of the matter.[25] In the long run, and despite the occurrence of such forms of illegal law-making in the current circumstances of international law, international law's legality will only be able to consolidate itself if its law-making processes are organized so as to reflect the very values inherent in the Rule of International Law.

2. The Sources of International Law and Its Normativity

a. International Legality and Normativity

Legal normativity corresponds to the law's claim to authority, that is, its claim to provide its legal subjects with exclusionary albeit *prima facie* reasons for action through binding legal norms or in other words its claim to create obligations to obey the law that in principle preclude some countervailing reasons for action.[26] By contrast to the plain normativity of social rules in general, legal rules are characterized by their claim to exclusionary normativity.

---

[22] On states (and groups of states) *and* individuals (and groups of individuals) *qua* members of the international community and on the decoupling of national from popular sovereignty in certain cases, see Besson, S., '*Ubi Ius, Ibi Civitas*' (above, n. 6).

[23] See Waldron, J., 'The Rule of International Law', *Harvard Journal of Law and Public Policy*, 30/1 (2006), 15, 24–6.

[24] See e.g. Buchanan, A., 'From Nuremberg to Kosovo: The Morality of Illegal International Law', *Ethics*, 111/4 (2001), 673, 680; Goodin, R., 'Toward an International Rule of Law: Distinguishing International Law-Breakers from Would-Be Law-Makers', *Journal of Ethics*, 9 (2005), 225.

[25] This does not exclude the possibility of civil disobedience to international law, which can sometimes be justified *qua ultima ratio* on grounds of justice (i) and provided the legal and democratic channels of deliberation have been exhausted (ii): see Besson, S., *The Morality of Conflict* (Oxford: Hart Publishing, 2005), ch. 14.

[26] See Raz, J., *The Authority of Law* (Oxford: Oxford University Press, 1979), 19, 223–4; Raz, J., *Practical Reason and Norms* (2nd edn., Oxford: Oxford University Press, 1999), 178 ff.; Raz, J., 'The Problem of Authority: Revisiting the Service Conception', *Minnesota Law Review*, 90 (2006), 1003.

The same may be said of the normativity of international law. International law claims to give its subjects, whether states, international organizations or individuals, exclusionary albeit *prima facie* reasons for action. Of course, these differ depending on the subjects; individual and collective agents cannot necessarily abide by the same reasons, or at least not in the same ways. They also differ depending on the law-makers. When states are only binding themselves through treaty obligations, the reasons they need to provide are different from those they have to provide when they also aim at binding other states non-parties and other subjects of international law.

b. *International Normativity and the Sources of International Law*

The normativity of a legal rule may vary in degree, in personal scope, and in sources, depending on the values underlying a legal norm. International legal norms as well may have different degrees of normativity: their normativity can range from being low (or soft)[27] as with legal norms in the making to being imperative as with norms of *jus cogens*. International legal norms may also have different personal scopes: some may have a general *erga omnes* scope, while others may be relative to a few subjects (even though the obligations are general). Finally, the quality of the normativity of international legal norms may vary: some international norms may have only a subjective authority due to their consensual origin, while others may, on the contrary, draw their normativity from their objective nature.

As a matter of fact, international law's normativity has increased and diversified over the years, and with it have emerged difficult questions pertaining to international legal norms' universality, objectivity, and hierarchy. Prosper Weil's fears about what he called the 'relative normativity' of international law have now been confirmed in practice:[28] some international legal norms bind subjects who have not agreed to them (e.g. third-party effect of treaties) or who have expressly objected to them (e.g. limitations on persistent objections to customary law), be they states or individuals; they bind them even if they have made reservations when agreeing to them; and, finally, they sometimes bind them in an imperative fashion.

This does not yet mean, however, that all questions pertaining to the normativity of legal rules are specific to their legal sources. On the contrary, there are good reasons for keeping legal sources apart from the question of international law's normativity. While normativity is linked to legality, its degree and personal scope do

---

[27] See the discussion in section II.2.a.
[28] See Weil, P., 'Towards Relative Normativity in International Law', *American Journal of International Law*, 77 (1983), 413. See for a discussion, Tasioulas, J., 'In Defence of Relative Normativity: Communitarian Values and the Nicaragua Case', *Oxford Journal of Legal Studies*, 16 (1996), 85.

not directly depend on the sources of international law, but on each international legal norm. The same sources may give rise to soft and imperative norms and to general or relative norms. For instance, a treaty may entail *erga omnes* and relative norms, while UN resolutions may contain *jus cogens* norms as much as so-called soft law. Moreover, certain treaty-based norms such as human rights have become objective law, while others still accommodate consent-based inroads such as reservations. Finally, while a *jus cogens* norm is usually *erga omnes*, there are *erga omnes* rules which are not imperative.

As a consequence, the recent evolution in the normativity of international law does not *per se* threaten the equivalence of sources of international law or the generality of international law; if the latter are threatened, it is for reasons broader than changes in the sources of international law. It is merely the effect of the coming of age of the international legal order. Progressively, indeed, the international community is emerging through legalization and constituting itself through the recognition of certain values recognized at law, values whose degree and personal scope may vary.[29]

3. The Sources of International Law and Its Legitimacy

a. *International Legality, Normativity, and Legitimacy*

The legitimacy of law refers to the justification of the law's claim to authority and of its normativity. Reasons traditionally brought forward for the legitimacy of law are multifarious and range, very schematically, from consent to justice.

The same diversity may be found relative to international law's legitimacy. As we saw in the introduction, the traditional ground put forward for international law's legitimacy is *state consent*. This explanation fails to convince entirely, however, both *per se* for well-known reasons and, in international law, for reasons related to the emergence of new subjects of international law and the development of its law-making processes.[30] Without going all the way to the other end of the spectrum, and arguing that international law's legitimacy stems from natural duties of *justice*, with the well-known epistemological difficulties and other complexities linked to moral and social pluralism this approach implies, one may suggest a middle path explanation of the legitimacy of international law. The proposed account explains both the duty to constitute an international legal order and the duty to obey some of its legal norms.

---

[29] See e.g. Besson, S., '*Ubi Ius, Ibi Civitas*' (above, n. 6).

[30] See Buchanan, A., *Justice, Legitimacy and Self-Determination. Moral Foundations for International Law* (Oxford: Oxford University Press, 2004), 301–14 and Chapter 3 in this volume.

To start with, one may argue for the duty to create a positive international legal order to secure peaceful cooperation over matters of global justice.[31] The legitimacy of international law might be better explained therefore by reference to the duty to coordinate on issues of justice, and in particular the duty of peaceful cooperation among equal international subjects whose perspectives about issues of global justice and governance are bound to diverge. In those circumstances, international law is the most adequate means of signalling the intention to coordinate and of securing clear and efficient coordination among different international legal subjects.

With respect to the duty to obey international legal norms themselves, second, one should start by emphasizing that there is no general *prima facie* obligation to obey the law *qua* law. Legality alone is not a sufficient ground for legitimacy. At the same time, the authority of a given legal norm should not be conflated with that stemming from the correct moral content of the legal norm; the reasons it gives are content-independent and are specific to its legal nature. As a result, following Raz's normal justification thesis, a given legal norm can be said to have legitimate authority when it matches pre-existing moral reasons, but in such a way that the person is in a better position to comply with the latter if it complies with the former.

Although legality in itself is not sufficient for legitimacy, it is an important part of it; the law binds differently from a moral norm of the same content because it is law and this is due to the ways in which the law can signal participants' intention to coordinate and abide by a certain rule by reference to social facts.[32] Of course, signalling and coordinating is not enough; there must be something about the way the law signals that calls for obedience in each case. If this is so, legitimacy is an essential part of legality, in the sense that the law should be made in such a way that it *can claim* to be legitimate and hence to bind those to whom it applies. This in turn means that the sources of law, i.e. the law-making processes, should be organized so as to vest the law with a claim to authority. In circumstances of pervasive and persistent disagreement about substantive moral issues and justice, the *democratic* nature of the law-making process is often regarded as the best justification for that claim.[33] It allows for a decision to be made by coordination, while also respecting the equality of all participants and their own individual reasons—at least by taking turns in getting the final word on controversial issues.

---

[31] See e.g. Waldron, J., 'Special Ties and Natural Duties', *Philosophy and Public Affairs*, 22 (1993), 3, 22 ff.; Besson, S., *The Morality of Conflict* (above, n. 25), 465–77.

[32] See e.g. Besson, S., *The Morality of Conflict* (above, n. 25), 459 ff.

[33] See on this democratic account of the normal justification thesis, ibid. 490–9, 505–6; Besson, S., 'Review Article: Democracy, Law and Authority', *Journal of Moral Philosophy*, 2/1 (2005), 89; Waldron, J., 'Authority for Officials', in Meyer, L. H., Paulson, S. L., and Pogge, T. W. (eds), *Rights, Culture, and the Law: Themes from the Legal and Political Philosophy of Joseph Raz* (Oxford: Oxford University Press, 2003), 45.

b. International Democratic Legitimacy and the Sources of International Law

Because legality alone is not enough for the legitimacy of international law,[34] international law should be made so that it can claim legitimacy.[35] It follows from what was said of democracy *qua* most respectful source of legitimacy in pluralist societies that international law should be produced according to democratic procedures that vest its norms with legitimacy. This coordination-based approach to legal legitimacy is suited to international law as the latter applies to very different subjects and in very different places in the pluralistic international community.[36]

This is not the place to give a full account of what the democratization of international law-making could amount to. In a nutshell, global democracy groups all democratic processes that occur within and beyond the national state and whose outcomes affect individuals within that state, but in ways that link national democracy to other transnational, international, or supranational democratic processes. As I have argued elsewhere, the best account of international legitimacy is a *demoi-cratic* account, that is, an account based on the functional and territorial inclusion (pluralistic) in national, regional, and international law-making processes, and at different levels in those processes (multilevel), of all states (and groups of states) *and* individuals (and groups of individuals) *qua* pluralistic subjects of the international political community (multilateral), whose fundamental interests are significantly and equally affected by the decisions made in those processes.[37]

Of course, democratic international law will not always be *substantively* legitimate in practice, but in conditions of moral disagreement it is sufficient that it can justifiably claim to be such. This is the case if it is *procedurally* legitimate and respects the political equality of all participants. This does not, however, preclude the coexistence of other sources or enhancers of legitimacy of international law, such as justice or state consent in certain more limited cases. Nor does it imply that all sources of international law should become democratic to be vested with legitimacy; some simply cannot for reasons pertaining to their law-making process[38] and draw their

---

[34] *Contra* Kumm, M., 'The Legitimacy of International Law: A Constitutionalist Framework of Analysis', *European Journal of International Law*, 15/5 (2004), 907, 918.

[35] See Franck, T., *Fairness in International Law and Institutions* (Oxford: Clarendon Press, 1995), 7–8, 22–4, 26.

[36] See Buchanan, A. and Keohane, O., 'The Legitimacy of Global Governance Institutions', *Ethics and International Affairs*, 20/4 (2006), 405. See also Besson, S., 'The Authority of International Law—Lifting the State Veil', *Sydney Law Review*, 31/3 (2009), 343.

[37] See Besson, S., 'Deliberative *Demoi*-cracy in the European Union: Towards the Deterritorialization of Democracy', in Besson, S. and Marti, J. L. (eds.), *Deliberative Democracy and its Discontents* (Aldershot: Ashgate, 2006), 181; Besson, S., 'Institutionalizing Global *Demoi*-cracy', in Meyer, L. (ed.), *Justice, Legitimacy and Public International Law* (Cambridge: Cambridge University Press, 2009), 58.

[38] See Weiler, J., 'The Geology of International Law—Governance, Democracy and Legitimacy', *Zeitschrift für ausländisches öffentliches Recht und Völkerrecht*, 64 (2004), 547.

legitimacy from other justifications and may call for respect on grounds of state consent. However, even in the latter cases, one may identify democratic probationary processes to attest of the existence of norms of non-democratic sources. Finally, democracy requires minimal guarantees of human rights to function properly and these should therefore be part of the legitimating processes of international law besides democracy.[39]

IV. A DEMOCRATIC ACCOUNT OF THE INTERNATIONAL LEGAL SYSTEM

1. International Secondary Rules

If international law is to be considered as a system of law and not only a set of rules, sources of international law should be organized according to *secondary rules*; these rules identify in advance the ways in which primary rules of international law may be validly created, modified, and annulled, that is, the processes of international law-making. This requirement follows from the argument made before about the *International Rule of Law*, but also about the circumstances of *international democratic legitimacy*.

Of course, some may claim, following Hart,[40] that international law is not yet sufficiently developed to be regarded as a legal system. On such an account, international subjects would know how international legal rules are created, amended, or annulled simply by observing or not observing them at each moment in time. This critique is largely obsolete, however, and shows too little respect for the *facts of international law*. Numerous secondary rules may be retrieved in international law nowadays. They can be of various legal origins: some are treaty-based like the Vienna Conventions on the law of treaties, while others are customary like the secondary rules pertaining to the creation of customary law. Of course, secondary rules are less determinate in international law than they are at national level. This is due to the scope and density of the international law-making process, but also to the extreme variety between its different sources and their respective processes, on the one hand, and to their complementarity and overlap in practice, on the other.

A common critique at this stage is that there can be no secondary rules about international *customary law-making*. The importance of the practice of coordination in the creation of the norm seems indeed to imply that creating a new norm always paradoxically implies breaking the previous one.[41] The greater weight recognized in

---

[39] See Besson, S., *The Morality of Conflict* (above, n. 25), 319–23.
[40] Hart, H. L. A., *The Concept of Law* (above, n. 1), ch. x.
[41] See D'Amato, A., *The Concept of Custom in International Law* (above, n. 9).

practice[42] to the *opinio juris* proves, however, that state practice is often elusive,[43] or at least that, when a new customary norm is about to arise, it is unlikely that the previous norms will be respected extensively in practice and this without, however, threatening the existence of the norm. A customary norm, once created and confirmed by state practice, can subsist without being respected actively and even despite being violated by some. Holding the contrary would mean conflating the creation and content of a legal norm with the practice of those respecting it.

In this context, Tasioulas distinguishes between the *opinio juris* that is necessary to create a customary norm and the *opinio juris* that one needs to maintain it in force. While the former seems paradoxical (it requires mistakenly believing that something which is about to become law through being practised as such is already law), the latter is perfectly understandable once the customary norm has been created.[44] The paradox can be lifted away even further by considering the first *opinio juris* as the expression of the belief that others will keep their coordination commitment and that one should therefore abide by the outcome of coordination. Since this first *opinio juris* is actually the belief that all participants in the coordinative practice need to have to then be able to coordinate and hence create this legal norm, one may expect it to differ in its expression from the further *opinio juris* relative to the persistence of an existing customary norm. Thus, the difference between a mere breach of customary law and a legal change of customary law must lie in the way in which the coordination around the new customary norm is signalled and hence in the way the new practice that will give rise to the new norm is organized.

This is actually confirmed by the ways in which customary law-making procedures are developing, making increasing use of multilateral law-making arenas to ascertain the existence of an *opinio juris*. One of the advantages of these mechanisms lies precisely in the fact that they match the requirements of the international Rule of Law, such as transparency and inclusion, and those of international democracy through their quasi-legislative iterative and deliberative qualities. Of course, one may claim that these mechanisms are evidentiary at the most, rather than law-making processes *per se*. Even so, however, they constitute a signal that is respectful of all international subjects' equality and necessary to coordinate legitimately on customary norms. This suffices to draw a line between secondary rules about customary law-making and customary law-making itself.

---

[42] ICJ, *Nicaragua v. United States of America* (ICJ Reports 1984), 392, 418.

[43] See Tasioulas, J., 'In Defence of Relative Normativity' (above, n. 28), 96–100.

[44] See Tasioulas, J., 'Customary International Law and the Quest for Global Justice', in Perreau-Saussine, A. and Murphy, J. (eds.), *The Nature of Customary Law: Legal, Historical and Philosophical Perspectives* (Cambridge: Cambridge University Press, 2006), 307, 320–4; and before him, D'Amato, A., *The Concept of Custom in International Law* (above, n. 9).

2. The International Rule of Recognition

a. The Single and Finite Rule of Recognition

For the rules regulating the international law-making processes to be respected as secondary rules, the international system needs a rule of recognition, that is, a rule which identifies the secondary rules and hence the sources of valid international law. It is the rule by reference to which the validity of the other rules in the system is assessed, and in virtue of which the rules constitute a single system.[45] As a matter of fact, having a rule of recognition constitutes one of the normative requirements of the International Rule of Law and of democratic legitimacy in the international legal order. The identification of an international rule of recognition is not a 'luxury', contrary to what Hart would say,[46] but a requirement in a democratic international community in which participants should be able to constitute themselves as such in advance and determine together the legal processes by which they will bind themselves in the future.

First of all, having a rule of recognition implies identifying a *finite number of sources* or else the canonical and signalling function of legal norms as opposed to other social norms would not arise. *Prima facie*, of course, the list of sources of international law seems to be less determinate and hence finite than in national law.

Even if recent years have seen an important development in international law-making procedures, not all of the new law-making mechanisms constitute new sources of international law, however. Thus, the extensive development of soft law as opposed to hard law is a sign *a contrario* of the existence of a finite and precise list of formal sources of international law. Moreover, these new instruments serve a finite list of law-making processes; thus, multilateral conferences and instruments are used to produce customary law, treaty law, or general principles. What they show is an increasing convergence in terms of law-making procedures and law-makers among the different sources of international law. While those sources and their processes can still apply in many cases as they always did,[47] their outcomes are increasingly reached following the same multilateral, inclusive, and quasi-legislative procedures. This qualitatively important, albeit quantitatively limited, convergence may be taken as a sign of democratization of international law-making processes.

Secondly, the international rule of recognition should in principle be *single*. If sources of law help us identify signals for coordination from others, it is important that the list of sources is unique to avoid conflicting signals. In terms of origins,

---

[45] See Hart, H. L. A., *The Concept of Law* (above, n. 1), 233.   [46] Ibid. 235–6.

[47] See e.g. Charney, J., 'Universal International Law', *American Journal of International Law*, 87 (1993), 529, 543–50.

the source of sources of international law cannot itself be legal, at least in a common sense of stemming from the very sources it identifies. This is why rules of recognition are usually constitutional in a constitutive sense, although they need not be written.

At this stage, there is no international constitution in a formal (and entrenched) sense that might entail such a list of sources.[48] There clearly seems, however, to be coordination over the three formal sources of international law mentioned before and, increasingly, over the extension of the triad of sources to two further sources: unilateral law issued by states but most importantly by IOs, on the one hand, and non-conventional concerted acts issued by states, on the other.[49] Confirmation of this coordinative practice on sources may be found in various lists of sources available in positive international law and in particular in arbitration conventions' lists of applicable law.[50] The most universal list to date is, of course, the list of the law applicable by the ICJ in Article 38 ICJ Statute. True, the latter only applies to the International Court of Justice and dates back to 1945. But many of the lists of sources in municipal law are equally limited and dated.

b. The Rule of Recognition and the Plurality of Sources

The existence of a single international rule of recognition does not equate with the existence of a *hierarchy of sources of international law*. There is none to date since there is no general priority of the norms issued by one source of international law over the other and this even in the context of general international law. This is confirmed by the evidence one gets from existing lists of sources such as Article 38 ICJ Statute, despite its numbering and the reference to subsidiary means for the determination of rules of law. This is also what one may coin *(internal) international vertical pluralism*.

In fact, there is nothing about the existence of a rule of recognition, however, that requires a hierarchy among the sources recognized by the rule of recognition. It is not because rules of recognition are usually entrenched in formal constitutions at national level, that they require priorities among other sources of national law. All that is required is that the rule of recognition itself is protected through entrenchment from secondary rules of change, i.e. from the sources of primary law in a given legal order. This implies, in other words, a *superior rank in the legal order* and, as a consequence, autonomous secondary rules of change. This clearly seems to be the case of the current list of sources of general international law and of

---

[48] See Besson, S., 'Whose Constitution(s)? International Law, Democracy and Constitutionalism', in Dunoff, J. and Trachtman, J. (eds.), *Ruling the World: Constitutionalism, International Law and Global Governance* (Cambridge: Cambridge University Press, 2009), 343.

[49] See Boyle, A. and Chinkin, C., *The Making of International Law* (above, n. 4), 262.

[50] See e.g. Permanent Court of Arbitration, 'Optional rules for Arbitrating Disputes between Two States', *International Legal Materials*, 32 (1993), 572.

Article 38 ICJ Statute in particular. Historically, the quasi-universal compromise on Article 38 was difficult to attain. Nowadays, it could not realistically be discarded without quasi-universal state assent.[51]

More positively, there are democratic reasons for the absence of hierarchy of other sources in general international law, with respect to both process and content.

One of the first reasons to recognize a hierarchy of sources is to acknowledge the superiority of certain law-making processes over others in terms of their legitimacy and in particular of the *democratic quality of the processes*. In national law, the superiority of the legislative process over customary law lies in its democratic inclusion and majority-based functioning. Given the embryonic democratic dimension of international law-making processes and the lack of perfect overlap between the different international law-makers, it does not come as a surprise that sources of international law are still deemed as equivalent in rank.

Another reason for the absence of hierarchy of sources of international law might be related to the *content of the norms* issued according to certain sources. Thus, in the national legal order, fundamental rights are usually protected by constitutional law and their ultimate value explains the need to make their source hierarchically ultimate. Constitutional entrenchment provides a first barrier of agreement against pervasive disagreement, but also an agreement to disagree further about the detail of the values entrenched and their respective normative strengths.[52] Here again, the fact that international legal norms protecting important values are scattered across different legal sources does not favour the formal prioritization of some of them over others according to their source. In fact, the diversity of law-makers and the moral and cultural pluralism that prevails at the international level might explain the fear of quasi-constitutional entrenchment of certain international legal sources over others. Thus, although *jus cogens* norms are imperative and cannot be infringed, their revision process corresponds to the processes of revision applicable to their sources in each case, whether treaty-based or customary; there are no mechanisms of entrenchment barring change in their content other than that of the degree of normativity of the norm replacing them in the eye of the international community (see e.g. Article 53 Vienna Convention on the Law of Treaties). Similarly, even though international secondary rules about law-making processes are usually normatively weightier, as in the case of the equal sovereignty of states or *pacta sunt servanda*, their sources can be treaty-based or customary and usually both, without a higher ranking of their sources over those of primary norms of international law.

---

[51] See Tomuschat, C., 'Obligations Arising for States Without or Against Their Will', *Recueil des cours*, 241 (1993), 191, 239–40.

[52] See Besson, S., *The Morality of Conflict* (above, n. 25), 287.

Of course, the absence of a hierarchy of sources of international law does not affect the numerous *hierarchies of international legal norms*.[53] Sometimes, the priority of norms stems from the degree of their normativity as in the case of the priority of *jus cogens* norms over other international norms. This is also what one calls *material* hierarchies of norms. As a result, if one may argue that certain international legal norms have a constitutional status, it is in terms of normative weight and by reference to their content rather than to their formal source. The material nature of international constitutionalism confirms that the decentralization, and what some have called the fragmentation, of international law, are not something to be feared, but on the contrary a constitutive and democratic feature of international law. Of course, the more democratic the international law-making procedures, the more hierarchical the sources of international law might become.

c. The Rule of Recognition and the Plurality of Legal Regimes

The existence of a rule of recognition in general international law does not equate with the existence of a *hierarchy of regimes in international law* either. There is no such hierarchy to date given the fragmentation of the international legal order between different legal matters and regions, and what one may refer to as *(internal) horizontal legal pluralism.*

Of course, the progressive consolidation of a background regime of general international law common to all special international regimes is now accepted. As a result, the rule of recognition and secondary rules of general international law are also common to other regimes of international law, as far as sources of general international law are concerned. The sources of law in those special regimes are determined within those regimes, only provided they differ from those of general international law; if they do, however—which does not seem to be the case at the moment, except in EU law which has become a self-contained regime—those regimes have actually become separate legal systems or at least separate sets of rules.

The existence of a rule of recognition of international law (with its minimal entrenched content) common to all regimes of international law does not provide a rule of conflict when norms from the general regime conflict with those of special ones. All we have, besides normative hierarchies based on the content of the norms in conflict, are special rules of conflict within specific regimes (so-called *formal* hierarchies of norms), such as Article 103 UN Charter applicable to UN Member States. One should also mention the *lex specialis* or *lex posterior* principles which also find application in international law. Finally, it is important to mention other

---

[53] See e.g. Shelton, D., 'Normative Hierarchy in International Law', *American Journal of International Law*, 100/2 (2006), 291.

coordination principles such as the principle of compliant interpretation or the principle of coherence that help prevent and possibly solve conflicts of international norms, without prioritizing one over the other.

As a matter of fact, the multilateral and pluralistic nature of global democracy alluded to previously, together with the interlocking political communities constituting the international community, explain why the fragmentation of international law between different regimes is a constitutive feature of international law. Those communities do not perfectly overlap in all areas of international law and this is what forbids clear hierarchies among the law they produce. Of course, the more inclusive and egalitarian international law-making processes will become, the clearer priorities will become in terms of *democratic credentials*, with certain processes being more inclusive of all those with equal stakes than others.

d. The Rule of Recognition and the Plurality of Legal Orders

Last but not least, the rule of recognition of general international law can coexist with national and regional rules of recognition, without threatening the autonomy of the respective legal orders. And this despite the fact that the international rule of recognition identifies some of the (international) law applicable within regional and national legal orders and hence legal norms that can be immediately valid and applicable to the same set of people.

When conflicts between legal orders occur, the solution lies in the principles governing the relations between legal orders. In a nutshell, these could be organized according to the principle of monism (one single legal order grouping all others under one single rule of recognition with a priority given either to the national or the international legal order), dualism (separate legal orders with no interferences apart from those decided by each order's rule of recognition), or pluralism (separate legal orders with separate rules of recognition but mutual validity). Because neither monism nor dualism can fully account for both the increasing intermingling between the national and international legal orders and the fact that neither of them gets primacy in deciding about mutual validity in all cases,[54] the model of pluralism between legal orders is usually favoured. In fact, *external legal pluralism* is actually called for by the pluralistic model of global democracy promoted in this chapter. Political self-constitution and hence democratic legitimacy lie behind the autonomy of legal orders. Because the political communities constituted in those different legal orders overlap but only partly so, neither monism nor dualism can perfectly account for their relationships and their mutual validity.

What remains to be seen, once pluralism among legal orders has been ascertained, is how conflicts between national, European and international legal norms ought

---

[54] See Gaja, G., 'Dualism—A Review', in Nollkaemper, A. and Nijman, J. (eds.), *New Perspectives on the Divide between International Law and National Law* (Oxford: Oxford University Press, 2007), 52.

to be resolved. This can first be done by reference to *democratic credentials*, and in particular to the principle of inclusion of all those equally affected by a decision—which amounts to a democratic conception of the principle of subsidiarity albeit one that can privilege either the local or the international level. Conflict resolution can also depend on the *content* of each norm. When the international legal norms in question are imperative, the conflict is resolved by reference to the hierarchy of norms. This normative hierarchy cuts across legal orders, however, and may result in giving priority to the most imperative norm whether international, as in most cases, or, more rarely, regional or national. Finally, one should also mention preventive duties of (normative) coherence that apply to the different legal orders binding the same people. [55]

V. CONCLUSION

Sources of international law condition its legality, normativity, and legitimacy. They are best organized, this chapter has argued, by following a normative positivist model of international law that grounds the latter's legality in the respect for the International Rule of Law, its normativity in the duty to coordinate over issues of global justice, and its legitimacy in multilevel and pluralist democratic processes of international law-making. International legal subjects have multiplied and are often described as members of a pluralist international community. This community's main bond is international law and the values it decides to express through its laws. As a result, sources of international law are the processes of self-constitution and constant reshaping of that community. Developing international law in due respect of the equality of all those affected in that community is what international constitutionalism is about. Nothing more but nothing less.

[55] See e.g. Besson, S., 'From European Integration to European Integrity. Should European Law Speak with Just one Voice?', *European Law Journal*, 10/3 (2004), 257.

CHAPTER 8

THE SOURCES OF INTERNATIONAL LAW: SOME PHILOSOPHICAL REFLECTIONS

DAVID LEFKOWITZ*

I. INTRODUCTION

It seems only natural to begin the study of international law with a description of its sources. After all, whether as practitioner or scholar a person cannot begin to ask or answer questions about international law until he or she has some sense of what the law is. This requires in turn a basic grasp of the processes whereby international legal norms and regimes come to exist. Thus students of international law must engage immediately with some of the most basic questions in the philosophy of law: what is law, and what is a legal order or system.[1]

* I wish to thank Joshua Kassner, Terry McConnell, and the editors of this volume for their comments on an earlier version of this paper.

[1] Perhaps the second most common approach to the study of international law begins with the concept of obligation; see e.g. Bederman, D. J., *The Spirit of International Law* (Athens, Ga.: University of Georgia Press, 2002). However, this approach also leads quickly to the question 'what is law?' since a primary reason for adopting it is to address immediately scepticism regarding international law's status as genuine law, which frequently has its roots in a (perhaps implicitly held) command theory of law.

These questions frame much of Professor Besson's excellent discussion of the sources of international law.[2] In this essay I seek to build upon a number of Besson's arguments regarding the nature of law and legal order, and her use of those arguments to describe and evaluate both existing and possible though currently non-existent sources of international law. Occasionally I argue at length in support of a particular conclusion, but more often I aim simply to indicate avenues for future research and debate. As will become clear, many theoretical questions regarding the sources of international law remain in need of further exploration.

II. The Nature of Law and the Sources of International Law

1. Conditions for International Legal Validity: Social Facts and Morality

Most contemporary philosophers of law agree that the normativity characteristic of law and legal order is that of practical authority: law necessarily claims a right to rule its subjects, to which correlates a duty on their part to obey the law. They disagree, however, about the implications this analysis of law's normativity has for the sources of law, and in particular, whether it entails that correctness as a moral principle, or at least consistency with certain moral principles, can or must serve as a condition for legal validity.

Joseph Raz argues that law can function as a practical authority only if those it addresses are able to identify the existence and content of legal norms solely by appeal to social facts, such as the signature and ratification of a treaty. This is so, Raz maintains, because law's claim to legitimate authority rests on its ability to mediate between its subjects and the reasons that apply to them. Law enjoys legitimacy only when it serves those it addresses by improving their conformity to right reason. Yet law cannot possibly serve this function if in order to determine its existence and content, law's subjects must first exercise the very moral judgment for which legitimate law is meant to substitute. Thus Raz concludes that it follows from the very nature of law that morality cannot serve as a condition for legal validity.[3]

Similarly, Scott Shapiro argues that rules, including legal rules, can make a practical difference to an agent's deliberation only if his conduct might diverge from that required by the rule in counterfactual circumstances in which the agent does

---

[2] Besson, S., 'Theorizing the Sources of International Law', Chapter 7 in this volume.
[3] See Raz, J., *The Morality of Freedom* (Oxford: Clarendon Press, 1986) and Raz, J., 'The Problem of Authority: Revisiting the Service Conception', *Minnesota Law Review*, 90 (2006), 1003.

not seek to guide his conduct by following it.[4] Assume for the sake of argument that all agents have a moral obligation to take no more than their fair share of the oceans' fish. With respect to an agent's deliberation, the addition of a legal obligation to do so adds nothing to the existing moral obligation. Obedience to this law will not make an agent any more likely to act as he has most reason to act, namely by taking no more than his fair share of the oceans' fish. Nor is there any situation in which the agent's attempt to act on his own judgment rather than the law's will lead him to act differently than if he sought to obey the law.

Contemporary legal philosophers refer to the view that the existence and content of law must be identifiable without recourse to moral argumentation as Exclusive Legal Positivism. If true, it implies that where international law references morality (as, at least apparently, do many of the norms that constitute International Human Rights and International Humanitarian Law), and where there are few or no social facts that stipulate how those moral norms are to be understood in the law (such as verdicts in previous cases or widely endorsed memoranda of understanding), legal officials will frequently create law when they act on these norms. For example, given the paucity of social facts pertaining to the content of human rights norms, at least at the international level, courts and tribunals called upon to decide cases under such norms are almost certainly engaged in an activity that is far more legislative than it is adjudicative. Thus Exclusive Legal Positivism provides a theoretical argument, grounded in an analysis of the very nature of law, for the conclusion that international courts and tribunals are a source of international law.

The claim that morality can provide neither a necessary nor a sufficient condition for legal validity has not gone unchallenged even among legal positivists. Inclusive Legal Positivists argue that consistency with, or correctness as, a moral principle is a possible but not a necessary condition for legal validity.[5] Whether it actually plays this role in a given legal order depends on the specifics of the rule of recognition to which officials of that order adhere.[6] Elsewhere I suggest that a case for the legal validity of (certain) human rights norms can be made by reconceiving in Inclusive Legal Positivist terms Simma and Alston's well-known attempt to ground the legality of such norms in general principles of law.[7] Arguably, the claim that correctness as a moral principle currently provides a sufficient condition for the legal validity of certain human rights norms better accounts for claims made in a number of opinions issued by the ICJ—such as its appeal to elementary considerations of

---

[4] Shapiro, S. J., 'On Hart's Way Out', *Legal Theory*, 4/4 (1998), 469–507.

[5] Waluchow, W. J., *Inclusive Legal Positivism* (Oxford: Clarendon Press, 1994); Coleman, J., *The Practice of Principle* (Oxford: Clarendon Press, 2001). H. L. A. Hart also endorsed Inclusive Legal Positivism; see the postscript to Hart, H. L. A., *The Concept of Law* (2nd edn., Oxford: Clarendon Press, 1994).

[6] See section III below for a detailed discussion of the idea of a rule of recognition.

[7] Lefkowitz, D., and Kassner, J., 'Inclusive Legal Positivism, International Law, and Human Rights', manuscript on file with authors; Simma, B. and Alston, P., 'The Sources of Human Rights Law: Custom, Jus Cogens, and General Principles', *Australian Year Book of International Law*, 12 (1992), 82.

humanity in *Corfu Channel* and to the principles and rules concerning the basic rights of the human person in *Barcelona Traction*—than do alternative explanations drawing on custom or general principles of law. Yet such an approach remains committed to the view (emphasized by Simma and Alston) that international legal validity rests ultimately on a consensus regarding what counts as a source of law, and so what counts as law. Moreover, because it maintains that morality is a possible but not a necessary condition for legality, this approach is consistent with the fact that international legal officials have treated correctness as a moral principle as a sufficient condition for legality during certain historical periods but not others.

Of course, there is a long tradition in both legal philosophy and practice of arguing that agreement with (certain) dictates of morality necessarily provides a condition for the validity of any legal norm, including international ones. For example, Mortimer Sellers, a leading proponent of Republican Legal Theory, argues that 'moral justification is an inescapable element of legal validity in any conscientious, justified, or legitimate system of law', and that international lawyers 'seeking objective standards [for what the law is] must look first to popular sovereignty [i.e. democratically enacted law] . . . [and second] to fundamental principles: does the law serve justice, the common welfare, and basic human rights?'[8] Similarly, John Tasioulas employs a Dworkinian interpretive approach, with its roots in the Common Law tradition, to defend an account of customary international law according to which the best interpretation of state practice and *opinio juris* is partly a matter of which interpretation has the 'greatest ethical appeal . . . determined by reference to the ethical values it [international law] is intended to secure . . . [which] include peaceful co-existence, human rights, [and] environmental values, among others'.[9] In contrast to Exclusive Legal Positivism (and possibly, though not necessarily, Inclusive Legal Positivism), these approaches to adjudication imply that when judges or arbitrators rely upon moral arguments to reach their decisions they do not create new law, but merely apply or interpret legal norms that are valid (partly) in virtue of their agreement with true moral principles. The Common Law tradition also provides the background against which David Dyzenhaus critically evaluates the sources of international law, as he appeals to that tradition's substantive (i.e. morally laden) conception of the rule of law to challenge the legal validity of certain putative exercises of international legal authority by the UN Security Council (as well as the positivist account of the nature of law according to which the products of such acts are legally valid, though perhaps illegitimate).[10]

---

[8] Sellers, M. N. S., *Republican Legal Theory* (New York: Palgrave-Macmillan, 2003), 135; Sellers, M. N. S., *Republican Principles in International Law* (New York: Palgrave-Mcmillan, 2006), 25.

[9] Tasioulas, J., 'Customary International Law and the Quest for Global Justice', in Perreau-Saussine, A. and Murphy, J. B. (eds.), *The Nature of Customary Law* (Cambridge: Cambridge University Press, 2007), 307.

[10] Dyzenhaus, D., 'The Rule of (Administrative) Law in International Law', *Law and Contemporary Problems*, 68 (2005), 129–30.

Interestingly, the conceptions of law that during the past several decades have figured most prominently in (Anglo-American) analytical legal philosophers' debates over the nature of law have barely made an appearance (at least explicitly) in discussions regarding the nature and sources of international law. As the foregoing discussion illustrates, however, that is beginning to change, and it is likely that Exclusive Legal Positivism, Dworkinian Interpretivism, and the rest will soon join other modern theories of the nature and sources of international law, such as Feminist Jurisprudence and Critical Legal Studies, alongside the more traditional Hobbesian, Groatian, and Kantian accounts.

2. Legitimacy and the Sources of International Law

a. The Instrumental Justification for International Law's Legitimacy

Though the law necessarily claims authority over its subjects, it may not always enjoy it. Rather, law succeeds in providing its subjects with authoritative reasons for action only when its claim to authority is morally justifiable, or legitimate. Thus an analysis of law's legitimacy requires an account of the conditions under which some or all of those the law addresses have a duty to obey it, as well as an explanation of why it is they have such a duty when those conditions obtain.

Raz argues that the law's claim to practical authority over its subjects is justified if and only if the following two conditions are met. First, they are more likely to act on the balance of undefeated reasons that apply to them if they intend to obey the law than by pursuing any other strategy, such as attempting to determine for themselves what they have most reason to do, or obeying a different putative authority. Second, the domain of conduct the authority addresses is not one where it is more important that agents act on their own judgment than that they act as they have most reason to act.[11] Raz's justification for obedience to law is instrumental; under the conditions it describes law serves as a means to the end of rational action. The service conception of practical authority, as Raz calls it, provides an account of the rationality of obedience to law; however, it entails a *moral* duty to obey the law in those cases where the reasons an agent will do better at acting on by obeying the law are moral ones. In these cases, the 'ought' in the claim 'she ought to obey the law' is a moral one because the underlying reasons are moral.

From the standpoint of demonstrating the legitimacy of at least some existing international legal norms, several features of Raz's instrumental justification for law's claim to authority make it especially attractive.[12] First, it does not require

---

[11]   Raz, J., *The Morality of Freedom* (above, n. 3); Raz, J., 'Problem of Authority' (above, n. 3).

[12]   Note that while its attractiveness from this standpoint may make a small contribution to its persuasiveness, the core argument for the service conception of practical authority rests on its place in the broader theory of reasons, value, and autonomy that Raz defends.

that those the law addresses consent to its authority. Thus it explains why an international actor (henceforth, IA) may have a duty to obey certain international legal norms even if they predate the IA's existence, or even if the IA's agreement to be bound by those norms did not meet the conditions for genuine consent. Second, the service conception of law's authority does not require that the procedure whereby international law is created be fair and/or impartial. It is at least possible that an unfair procedure—for example, one in which a few powerful IAs do most of the work crafting new laws, while weaker IAs are left to take it or leave it—results in legal norms that meet Raz's conditions for legitimacy. In practice, the development of new international legal norms is often unfair in just this way, even though in principle all states, at least, are sovereign equals.[13] Third, the normal justification thesis allows for the partial or piecemeal legitimacy of international law. Whether obedience to law makes it more likely that an agent will act as right reason dictates likely varies from case to case, both with respect to the agent and to the type of conduct at issue. Given the degree to which military, political, and economic power have shaped the development and content of international law, many people will likely welcome the possibility of defending something less than a general and universal duty to obey international law.

All three of the aforementioned implications for the legitimacy of international law have important consequences for an analysis of the sources of international law. If genuine consent or procedural fairness were a necessary condition for international law's legitimacy, then the current practices of international law creation would almost surely need to undergo significant modification in order to give rise to legitimate law—and there is little reason to think that the necessary changes would occur any time soon. Of course, Besson may be right to suggest that international law will enjoy its greatest claim to legitimacy (sufficient, perhaps, to generate a general duty to obey the law) if it is created democratically. Indeed, there may even be a moral duty to create democratic processes charged with creating, modifying, and annulling international law, and in some cases that duty may defeat a duty of obedience to law. Nevertheless, in so far as the current sources of international law do not qualify as democratic, those concerned to defend the legitimacy of at least some of its current norms may welcome the fact that Raz's instrumental justification enables them to do so.

b. Consent as a Basis for International Law's Legitimacy

Raz's scepticism with respect to the role consent plays in justifying law's claim to authority goes deeper than the above remarks suggest, as he maintains that neither instrumental nor non-instrumental justifications for treating putative acts

---

[13] See Kingsbury, B., 'The International Legal Order', in Cane, P. and Tushnet, M. (eds.), *Oxford Handbook of Legal Studies* (Oxford: Oxford University Press, 2003), 293.

of consent as genuinely normative (i.e. ones that genuinely alter an agent's normative situation) suffice to justify a moral duty to obey the law.[14] It may be possible to challenge this conclusion, however, if it can be shown that at least some (actual or possible) states have a right to self-determination, in light of which they can come to be morally bound by certain international legal norms only if they consent to them.[15] For example, if it is more important that such a state choose which economic policies to adopt than that it choose the best ones (however exactly that is understood), then it follows that those laws that pertain to international trade will morally bind this state only if it consents to be bound by them. Obviously these claims stand in need of a careful defence. However, I shall assume their truth here in order to engage with a different (and more frequently made) objection to grounding international law's legitimacy in state consent, namely that consent can give rise to genuine moral obligations only if it is free and informed, and that most acts of putative consent to be bound by international legal norms fail to meet at least one, if not both, of these conditions.[16] This is true, yet those who criticize consent on this basis may draw an overly broad conclusion, and be too quick to dismiss the importance of consent for legitimate international law.

It is at least possible and, I suggest, maybe even likely that certain states' agreement to be bound by particular treaties were made voluntarily; that is, in the absence of duress and with an adequate understanding of the legal obligations they were thereby acquiring. If they meet the two additional requirements described below, then these states do have a consent-based obligation to uphold the legal obligations created by these treaties, and this is so even if some of the other signatories to the same treaties did not accede to them voluntarily. It may be that those states that are able to genuinely consent to be bound by a particular body of international law do so only because they believe that the other signatories (and perhaps non-signatories as well) will abide by the terms of the treaty. Yet the necessary assurance may have its origins in the very same fact that renders those other states' consent merely putative (i.e. not genuinely obligating), namely the economic and military power of the genuinely consenting states and their willingness to use it to enforce the terms of the treaty against the merely putatively consenting states.

Moreover, some international legal norms may serve interests that are believed to be common to all those international actors subject to them, and to do so in a manner that is universally viewed as acceptable even among IAs with different understandings of what would be ideal. If such laws exist, then consent to be bound by them is morally binding. This is so, I suggest, even if unbeknownst to them

---

[14] Raz, J., *The Morality of Freedom* (above, n. 3), 80–94; Raz, J., 'Problem of Authority' (above, n. 3), 1037–41.

[15] Or, perhaps, if they willingly and knowingly accept the benefits provided them by others' obedience to the legal norms in question. See Lefkowitz, D., 'The Principle of Fairness and States' Duty to Obey International Law', under review.

[16] See e.g. Allen Buchanan, Chapter 3 in this volume.

the less powerful states would have been coerced into complying with these laws if they had not already endorsed them. Genuine consent—for international actors as for all other agents—does not require that agents could have voluntarily done otherwise. Rather, it requires only that the reasons that explain (i.e. motivate) an agent's consent not include fear of morally unjustifiable coercion by another agent, or non-culpable ignorance or mistaken belief.

If they are to create moral obligations, then in addition to being free and informed putative acts of consent must not conflict with certain other moral duties. For example, given a duty not to facilitate murder, a voluntary agreement to lend a criminal assassin the use of your gun is void *ab initio*, and so creates no duty to lend the gun or to compensate the assassin for failing to do so. In so far as certain international legal norms necessarily require immoral conduct, even free and informed consent to obey them will not make those laws legitimate. For example, suppose that by barring states from enacting trade regulations aimed at ensuring the morally proper treatment of non-human animals and the natural environment, the World Trade Organization (WTO) necessarily renders its signatories complicit in immoral conduct.[17] It follows that even a state's free and informed consent to abide by the rules incumbent upon members of the WTO will not give rise to a moral duty to obey those rules.

Finally, consent generates a moral duty to obey the law only for those officials and citizens of states with a legitimate claim to domestic authority. Officials of illegitimate states lack the standing to morally bind members of the political community they rule or, in many cases, the moral power to give effect to the international legal obligations they acquire (e.g. by enacting domestic laws or administrative rules that their subjects have a moral duty to obey).

Recognition that consent can—and perhaps in a limited number of cases, does—justify international law's claim to legitimate authority has important implications for the sources of international law. For example, a focus on the conditions in which consent actually generates an obligation can lead to changes in the processes whereby international legal norms are created, modified, or annulled that aim specifically at clarifying when an IA has genuinely consented to be subject to (some part of) international law, and increasing opportunities for them to do so. This may add further impetus to the project of codifying customary international law, as it can contribute to states' knowledge of those norms (especially their content) and present opportunities for states to freely agree to be bound by them.[18]

---

[17] For an argument that, in practice, this is what the WTO does, see Singer, P., *One World* (2nd edn., New Haven: Yale University Press, 2004), 51–70.

[18] To clarify, states and other IAs can be legally bound by customary international law without consenting to it, and perhaps even despite their explicit objection to being bound by certain customary legal norms. In both cases, the states in question have a *legal* obligation to act as the law demands, but they do not have a *moral* duty to fulfil their legal obligation based in consent.

3. Legality and the Sources of International Law

Just as legal philosophers disagree over whether the legal validity of a norm is necessarily conditional upon its moral correctness, or at least its consistency with certain moral principles, so too they disagree over the relationship between morality and legality, or the rule of law. On the formal conception of legality, which will be the focus of my remarks here, the rule of law amounts to the rule of rules; that is, formal legality sets out those conditions that must be met (to some degree) for a rule-guided social order to exist.[19] Law's essential function (or at least one of its primary functions) is to guide its subjects' conduct. Whether, or how well, law does this depends on its subjects' ability to identify what the law requires of them, which means that the law must be publicly promulgated and prospective, clearly formulated and without contradiction or demands for the impossible, applied to particular cases in a manner consistent with a reasonable understanding of its demands, and so on. To these properties of formal legality many also add certain institutional mechanisms that seem practically necessary for their realization, such as an independent judiciary and procedural fairness in the administration of the law. The virtue of the rule of law (understood formally) lies in the contribution it makes to agents' ability to plan their lives, and to follow through on those plans. It does so by reducing uncertainty about what they should do, not only by clarifying what sorts of conduct they may engage in without risking sanctions from those who rule (through law), but also by solving coordination problems, providing the assurance necessary to overcome prisoner's dilemmas, and in other ways as well. Whether it is a morally good thing that a given society realizes formal legality largely depends on the ends and the means to them that society's law permits, requires, or forbids officials and other members to pursue.

Clearly formal legality can be realized to varying degrees, both with respect to individual legal norms and entire legal orders, and this has important implications for law's legitimacy. There can be no duty to obey secret laws or laws that demand the impossible (including, but not limited to, laws that apply retroactively). But do agents have a duty to obey laws that are less than perfectly clear yet also far from opaque? What about laws that are occasionally applied unequally (i.e. where all are not equal before the law), particularly where the law's subjects can predict with a fair degree of accuracy when this will occur? What are agents with a duty to obey the law to do when confronted with conflicting legal obligations, particularly in the absence of well-functioning institutional mechanisms for resolving such conflicts?

---

[19] The formal understanding of the rule of law includes no moral constraints on law; rather, all of the constraints follow purely from what is necessary for the existence of a rule-guided social order. For substantive conceptions of legality, in contrast, those properties constitutive of the rule of law follow from a moral ideal, such as reciprocity between ruler and ruled.

As Brian Tamanaha points out, all of these questions arise for subjects of international law. For example, inequalities of power, together with features of the current international legal order such as the absence in most cases of a legal duty to submit to adjudication by a court or tribunal, significantly weaken the equal application of the law.[20] Also, 'the proliferation of uncoordinated tribunals and the disaggregation of international law along subject-specific lines . . . generate problems with consistency and coherence . . . [particularly] in overlapping areas between separate treaty regimes, as when environmental issues have implications for trade'.[21] The different approaches among municipal legal systems to the interpretation and incorporation of international law only add to these problems of consistency and clarity. Besson rightly emphasizes the need to craft institutions for the creation, modification, and annulment of international legal norms, as well their application to particular cases, that more fully realize formal legality. Nevertheless, given international law's sometimes tenuous hold over the conduct of actors influenced as well by considerations of political, economic, and military power, occasional deviation from the demands of formal legality may be a positive feature of the current international legal order.

III. The Nature of a Legal Order and the Sources of International Law

Having identified some of the implications that certain analyses of the nature of law, legitimacy, and legality have for the sources of international law, I concentrate in the remainder of this paper on the nature of a legal order or system, again with an eye on the consequences for a proper understanding of international law's sources.

1. Is International Law Primitive?

Among the most influential of H. L. A. Hart's insights is his analysis of a legal system as a union of primary and secondary rules.[22] Primary rules govern actions by spelling out particular obligations (or their absence); secondary rules, in contrast, are rules that govern primary rules. Hart argues for this analysis of a legal system by considering three shortcomings or defects endemic to what he labels a primitive legal

---

[20] Tamanaha, B., *On Rule of Law* (New York: Cambridge University Press, 2004), 132.

[21] Ibid. See also Boyle, A. and Chinkin, C., *The Making of International Law* (Oxford: Oxford University Press, 2007); Kingsbury, B., 'International Legal Order' (above, n. 13), 280–1. But see Donald Regan, Chapter 10 in this volume.

[22] Hart, H. L. A., *The Concept of Law* (Oxford: Clarendon Press, 1961).

order. First, participants in such an order labour under a great deal of uncertainty because they lack an authoritative practice for settling disagreements over what the law is, including whether a given rule is law, what the content of that law is, and how to resolve conflicts between different laws. Second, a primitive legal order has a static character, since it lacks any authoritative procedures for changing primary rules and the obligations they create. Third, it suffers from inefficiency (and likely ineffectiveness as well) since all members of the community share equally in the authority to determine when violations of the law have occurred and how to respond to them, and bear equally the duty to exercise this authority.

Different types of secondary rules address each of these three shortcomings. The solution to the last of them lies in the development of rules of adjudication, which authorize and obligate only certain actors to apply and enforce the law. Rules of change address the second of the aforementioned defects, as they specify the means by which agents may change general rules as well as particular obligations. As for the uncertainty common to practically any primitive legal order, Hart contends that it is overcome through legal officials' adherence to a rule of recognition: a rule 'by reference to which the validity of the other rules of the system is assessed, and in virtue of which the rules constitute a single system'.[23]

Legal orders can suffer to varying degrees from the shortcomings of uncertainty, inefficiency, and a static character. Therefore, rather than asking whether international law is primitive, as if that is an all-or-nothing feature of legal orders, we should instead examine in what respect and to what degree it manifests those qualities that when fully realized characterize a primitive legal order. For example, with respect to its adjudicatory practices, the current international legal order occupies an intermediate place between a primitive and an advanced legal order, since in some cases the authority to apply and enforce certain laws lies only with designated officials, while in others the law may or must be applied and enforced by any and all members of the international community.

Adopting this nuanced approach helps clarify Hart's own remarks on the primitiveness of international law. Though he briefly criticizes several arguments intended to demonstrate that international law contains rules of adjudication, his case for the international legal order's primitiveness rests primarily on the argument that 'that there is no basic rule providing general criteria of validity for the rules of international law, and that the rules which are in fact operative constitute not a system but a set of rules'.[24] In other words, Hart maintains that international law lacks a foundational rule of recognition. A legal order rests on such a rule, Hart claims, only when there are criteria for settling what the law is other than the current beliefs of those subject to it. In so far as the existence and scope of international legal norms is simply and entirely a matter of consensus amongst IAs, as positivists in the international law sense maintain, it follows that the international

---

[23] Ibid. 228.   [24] Ibid. 231.

legal order lacks a rule of recognition at its base, and so does not constitute a legal system.[25]

No international legal scholar will dispute the claim that international law currently lacks a single basic rule that serves both of the functions that Hart assigns to a rule of recognition: validating norms as law and systematizing them, in particular by establishing relations of superiority and subordination between laws of various types. The defect of uncertainty, recall, attends not only the absence of an authoritative process for identifying norms as legally valid, but also the absence of such a process for establishing the precise scope of particular legal norms. Unlike a domestic legal order that treats common law as subordinate to statutes, for example, international law currently lacks a hierarchy of sources of international law. Besson suggests that 'there is nothing about the existence of a rule of recognition . . . that requires a hierarchy among the sources recognized by the rule of recognition'.[26] Hart's view of the matter is somewhat ambiguous; on the one hand, he suggests that merely being validated by a single rule of recognition provides a kind of minimal unity to a set of rules, while on the other he emphasizes in several places the importance of the rule of recognition's systematizing function.[27] Regardless, the absence of any hierarchy of sources clearly entails that members of the international political community will experience greater uncertainty with respect to their legal obligations, and so in that sense be subject to a legal order that is more primitive, than is true for officials and subjects of a domestic legal system like the one mentioned above. Moreover, the uncertainty caused by the absence of a ranking of international legal norms in virtue of their source may be further exacerbated by the lack of any systematic ordering of different international legal regimes.

Despite the resulting uncertainty, however, the primitiveness of the international legal order can be viewed in a positive light. For example, as was previously suggested in the discussion of the rule of international law, it may be that the existing international legal order can better accommodate the realities of power in current international relations than would a less primitive legal order. In particular, the larger space left by a primitive legal order for politics and power may make it more conducive to the achievement of peace than would be the case were international law to strive to place greater limits on these modes of interaction—limits that might encourage some states to ignore the demands of international law, or worse yet, to challenge the international legal order's legitimacy. Conversely, however, international law's current primitiveness may make it a less effective vehicle for the achievement of justice than it would be were it less primitive in various respects; for instance, were the ICJ to enjoy compulsory jurisdiction.

[25] Positivism (in the international law sense) was the most influential paradigm of international legal relations during the time Hart was writing *The Concept of Law*, so it would have been natural for him to conceive of international law in positivist (or consensualist) terms, and given such a conception, to conclude that international law lacks a basic rule of recognition.

[26] Besson, S., this volume, 181.   [27] Hart, H. L. A., *The Concept of Law* (above, n. 22), 92–3; 97–8.

2. Does Customary International Law Rest on a Rule of Recognition?

Suppose international law were to rest on a rule of recognition with something like the following content:[28] X is a legally valid norm if and only if it originates in a treaty or customary practice.[29] Each of the disjuncts can serve as a criterion for legal validity only if it makes a norm's status as law turn on some feature of the world other than the belief by those subject to it that it counts as law. This condition appears to be met for treaty law, which is clearly akin to the 'authoritative list or text of the rules' that Hart offers as an illustration of a relatively simple rule of recognition.[30] But what about customary international law (henceforth CIL)? Hart rejects as both normatively and epistemically redundant the rule that states should behave as they customarily behave.[31] As he puts it, such a rule 'is an empty repetition of the mere fact that the society concerned (whether of individuals or states) observes certain standards of conduct as obligatory rules', which is just to say that the (positive) obligations, and the primary rules that create them, exist only because those subject to these rules believe themselves to be bound by them.[32] Moreover, it is at least arguable that no authoritative procedure exists for settling disputes over the existence, content, and scope of customary international legal norms. When called upon to apply CIL to particular cases, the International Court of Justice and other tribunals claim that their decisions rest on judgments regarding the existence of a consensus among states (i.e. practice plus *opinio juris*). It seems that just as 'in the simpler [i.e. primitive] form of society we must wait and see whether a rule gets accepted or not', so too disputes over customary international legal norms end only once states reach a consensus.[33] Is Hart right, then, to conclude (contra Besson) that there is no rule of recognition for CIL?[34]

Ideally, a rule of recognition serves two functions. The first, ontological, function makes possible the kind of justification and criticism constitutive of a rule-governed practice for identifying norms as legally valid. The second, authoritative resolution, function makes possible the settling of disputes over the content and scope of

[28] The following discussion draws partly on Lefkowitz, D., '(Dis)solving the Chronological Paradox in Customary International Law: A Hartian Approach', *Canadian Journal of Law and Jurisprudence*, 21/1 (2008), which also contains a more detailed discussion of Hart's analysis of international law and responses to it by a number of prominent international legal theorists.

[29] Until recently, such a rule (perhaps also including general principles of law) was likely the least controversial candidate for a basic international rule of recognition. It is probably more accurate today to include the ICJ and certain other international tribunals, as well as global governance institutions such as the WTO, among the sources of international law.

[30] Hart, H. L. A., *The Concept of Law* (above, n. 22), 92.

[31] The rule cited in the text is the one Kelsen proposes as the *Grundnorm* for international law. I consider it here only as a rule of recognition, and only for customary international law.

[32] Hart, H. L. A., *The Concept of Law* (above, n. 22), 230.   [33] Ibid. 229.

[34] Besson, S., this volume, 180–1.

particular legal norms. I maintain that CIL rests on a rule of recognition that performs only the first of these two functions, one with the following content: N is a customary legal norm if most states regard it as a customary legal norm from what Hart calls the internal point of view, and what makes it a customary legal norm is that most states regard it as such. Agents adopt the internal point of view with regard to some rule when they believe that they (and the others the rule addresses) ought to conform to it, such that an appeal to the rule provides a sufficient justification for behavior that conforms to it, as well as for criticism of behaviour that deviates from it.[35]

The second phrase in the proposed rule of recognition for CIL plays a crucial role because it distinguishes a legal order in which there is a mere convergence of beliefs that N is a legally valid norm from one in which belief in the legal validity of N is rule-guided. In a legal order of the first type, the relevant agents might have different reasons for accepting norms N1, N2, etc. as legally valid; one might do so because he thinks those norms substantively just, another because a third agent has pronounced them legal, and so on. Regardless of their reasons for believing that N is a legal norm, however, these actors will agree that an agent that violates it acts illegally. In a legal order of the second type, agreement that acts contrary to N count as illegal follows from a shared understanding of what makes a customary norm legally valid, one they manifest in practice through adherence to the aforementioned rule. The existence of such a rule warrants a kind of normative claim unavailable to participants in the first type of legal order, namely the justification of a judgment regarding the legality of a particular act in terms of fidelity to the rule or criticism of such a judgment as a deviation from it. I contend that customary international law, as it currently exists, is an example of this second type of legal order; that is, it rests on a rule of recognition, albeit one that serves only the ontological function.

The above characterization of the rule of recognition for CIL may seem to conflict with the traditional and still widely shared view that CIL rests on *usus*, or practice, as well as *opinio juris*, but this is not so. The existence in society S of a customary rule C governing acts of type T depends on a shared belief in such a rule among (most) members of S. Shared beliefs differ from those that are merely had in common in that they involve a mutual awareness among those that share the belief. The proper characterization of that mutual awareness is a matter of some debate: individualists describe it in terms of members of S knowing that other members of S believe that customary rule C governs acts of type T, and that other members of S know that (most) other members of S know this, while collectivists characterize it holistically as either a plural intention, a group belief, or a joint commitment to accept as a

---

[35] Hart, H. L. A., *The Concept of Law* (above, n. 22), 56–7, 101–3. See also Coleman, J., *The Practice of Principle* (above, n. 5); Shapiro, S. J., 'What is the Internal Point of View?', *Fordham Law Review*, 75/3 (2006), 1157–70.

body that members of S should perform acts of type T (or should perform acts of type T only under certain specific conditions, or should not perform acts of type T, etc.).[36] Regardless, achieving the necessary mutual awareness requires that members of S communicate with one another (though the content of the beliefs they must communicate varies depending on the proper analysis of a shared belief). This communication can take the form (at least in part) of the commission of acts of type T, but it need not do so; there is no conceptual barrier to the successful development of a new rule of CIL solely through so-called verbal acts, such as statements in international organizations, policy or white papers, and instructions to armed forces, even if this is highly unlikely to occur in practice. The crucial point is that on the proposed account the necessity of practice for the creation of a new customary norm, and so a new norm of CIL, follows from the very nature of customary rules as shared beliefs.

Of course, state practice (and, perhaps, the practice of other types of IAs) frequently contributes to the development of new norms of CIL in ways other than the one just mentioned. For example, state practice often provides the raw material of 'facts on the ground' that over time both shape and become the subject of rule-guided behaviour. Additionally, state practice can provide evidence of the existence and content of a customary norm, not only in cases of conformity to it but also where the rule is honoured in the breach; that is, where states make significant efforts to cover up or deny violations of the rule. This epistemic role provides adjudicative bodies such as the ICJ with a good reason to emphasize state practice in reaching their decisions.[37] Nevertheless, the epistemic value of state practice for the process of customary law formation (as opposed to the identification of existing norms of CIL) follows from the contribution it makes to the communication necessary to create a shared belief that acts of type T are subject to customary norm C, and that norm C counts as law.

3. (Dis)solving the Chronological Paradox in Customary International Law Formation

The foregoing defence of a rule of recognition for customary international law plays a crucial role in resolving an alleged paradox in the formation of new rules of CIL,

---

[36] Hart was most likely an individualist; the three collectivist accounts gestured at in the text are those of Michael Bratman, Raimo Tuomela, and Margaret Gilbert respectively.

[37] International Law Association, London Conference, *Final Report of the Committee on Formation of Customary (General) International Law* (2000), <http://www.ila-hq.org/en/committees/index.cfm/cid/30>, 40; The report notes that with some exceptions, 'if there is a good deal of State practice, the need (if such there be) also to demonstrate the presence of the subjective element is likely to be dispensed with'. The fact that the ICJ does not always require parties to *demonstrate* the existence of a belief that conduct of a certain sort is subject to CIL does not entail that such norms can *exist* in the absence of that belief, a point the Court emphasizes in its own repeated insistence that CIL rests on both *usus* and *opino juris*.

namely that their creation requires that states act from the belief that the law already requires the conduct specified in the rule. This so-called chronological paradox rests on two confusions, the first regarding the process whereby a customary rule comes to exist, and the second regarding the process whereby that customary rule becomes law.

Briefly, a customary rule exists amongst a group of actors if and only if most of them, most of the time, believe that such a rule exists and applies to them, where that belief manifests itself in both the actors' conduct and their justification and/or criticism of their own and others' conduct.[38] Such a state of affairs may arise in myriad ways.[39] For instance, at some initial point in time a few members of the group may believe falsely in the existence of a certain customary rule, but if they persist in this belief enough other members of the group may come to share it so that at some later point in time the customary norm truly does exist and apply to members of this group.[40] Alternatively, a few members of the group may believe that all should be bound by some rule, and that the best way to bring about a state of affairs in which they are is to act *as if* the rule already exists and applies to members of the group.[41] Or perhaps the rule is imminent in the practices of members of the group, and all come to believe in its existence at the same time. The crucial point these examples illustrate is that the evolution of a new customary rule does not require that agents believe truly that they are subject to the rule prior to their actually being bound by it.

As adherence to the rule exempting diplomatic vehicles from minor parking prohibitions illustrates, the belief by most states that they are subject to a customary rule does not suffice to make that rule legally valid. Rather, it must also be the case that officials of the international legal order adhere to a rule of recognition that directs them to treat customary rules in that domain of conduct as legally valid—that is, as a source of law. Distinguishing (at least conceptually) between the processes of custom formation and the legal validation of customary norms dissolves the chronological paradox: the rule-guided judgment regarding the legal validity of a customary norm is conceptually distinct from the process whereby

---

[38] In other words, a customary rule governs the conduct of members of a particular group when they adopt the internal point of view with respect to that rule. As the rule of recognition for CIL described previously illustrates, a rule of recognition is nothing more than the customary rule to which officials adhere when determining the legal validity of various norms, and in some cases, their systematic relation to one another.

[39] Many scholars err (or so I contend) when they identify as a necessary condition for the creation of a new customary norm what is only one possible means by which such a norm may come to exist.

[40] Geny, F., *Méthode d'interpretation et sources en droit privé positif* (2nd edn., Paris: F. Pichon et Durand-Auzias, 1919), 367–71.

[41] Kontou, N., *The Termination and Revision of Treaties in the Light of New Customary International Law* (New York: Oxford University Press, 1994). This procedure for the creation of new customary international law fits the image of claim and response some international lawyers use to describe certain examples of customary law creation, such as the so-called Truman Proclamation. See Walden, R. M., 'Customary International Law: A Jurisprudential Analysis', *Israel Law Review*, 13 (1978), 97.

that customary norm comes to exist.[42] The failure to distinguish between these conceptually distinct aspects of CIL formation may be a consequence in part of the fact that states have historically comprised both the actors whose conduct and beliefs give rise to the existence of a customary rule, and the vast majority of the officials in the international legal system whose adherence to the rule of recognition leads them to deem some of those rules legally valid.

Given the rapidity with which international law has recently been evolving, and the exponential growth in its reach and sophistication, philosophers of law have good reason to pay greater attention to it than many currently do. This is so not only for the contributions that legal philosophers can make to a proper understanding and evaluation of international law, but also because reflection on it may lead to refinements or even wholesale modifications to our understanding of the nature of law and a legal order.

---

[42] The point may be made more vivid by considering that as a conceptual matter, the agents whose beliefs in the existence of a customary rule are necessary for the existence of that rule need not overlap at all with the agents whose beliefs in the existence of a rule of recognition that treats custom as a source of law are necessary for the legal validity of that customary rule.

SECTION V

INTERNATIONAL ADJUDICATION

CHAPTER 9

INTERNATIONAL ADJUDICATION

ANDREAS PAULUS

I. Introduction: Adjudication and International Law

Oliver Wendell Holmes famously described law as 'what the courts will do'.[1] In international law, however, the formal adjudication of a legal dispute by a court or tribunal constitutes the exception to the rule of 'auto-interpretation' of international law by states, which are free to choose a mechanism for the settlement of disputes.[2] Formal adjudication is only one—and usually the last—method of dispute settlement resorted to by states. Nevertheless, dispute resolution has never been so popular. A document by the Project on International Courts and Tribunals lists no less than 125 operative international dispute settlement bodies, twelve of which are judicial bodies in the narrow sense.[3] Fears in relation to the 'fragmentation' of international law abound.[4]

---

[1] Holmes, O. W., 'The Path of the Law', *Harvard Law Review*, 10 (1897).

[2] Collier, J., and Lowe, V., *The Settlement of Disputes in International Law* (Oxford: Oxford University Press, 1999), 3.

[3] The Project on International Courts and Tribunals, International Judiciary in Context, synoptic chart, Nov. 2004, available at <http://www.pict-pcti.org/publications/synoptic_chart.html>. All websites most recently checked in Dec. 2007.

[4] See Koskenniemi, M. and Leino, P., 'Fragmentation of International Law. Postmodern Anxieties?', *Leiden Journal of International Law*, 15 (2002), 553; Report of the Study Group of the International Law Commission, finalized by Koskenniemi, M., 'Fragmentation of International Law: Difficulties Arising from the Diversification and Expansion of International Law' (International Law Commission, 2007), UN Doc. A/CN.4/L.682.

In this environment, it appears less and less possible to achieve a coherent international jurisprudence. International courts and tribunals have to undertake an ever-more difficult balancing act between different legal and moral value systems.

The fact that recourse to adjudication in international law is optional changes its character compared to the domestic context: Both parties need to agree, in one way or another, before a case can be brought before an international tribunal. Certainly, such agreement can be general and in advance, but it must always be there. The same is true with respect to enforcement: Although domestic judgments will not always be enforced, any party can rely on a third party, namely the state, to enforce them. In international law, enforcement and legal settlement are often distinct, and, in spite of the competences of the Security Council under article 94 of the UN Charter, a third party rarely, if ever, enforces international judgments.

The present contribution is an exercise in 'non-ideal' theory,[5] which begins with an observation of the current practice and then asks whether and how this practice reflects the expectations and criticisms voiced in international legal theory. In light of the increasing diversity of adjudicatory bodies that deal with matters of international law, the following contribution must limit itself to inter-state adjudication, in particular before the International Court of Justice. But many of the problems of inter-state adjudication reappear, in one way or the other, in human rights and criminal law litigation between a state or international organization, on the one hand, and individuals, on the other. For domestic courts, the pluralism of the international legal order poses the additional problem of the limits domestic law sets for the reception of international decisions within the domestic legal order.[6] In each case, however, the basic challenge remains the same: the interpretation and application of international law in spite of the legal and social fragmentation of the contemporary international order.

Various approaches exist to deal with this functional, but also ethical and religious pluralism. One approach consists in embracing the fragmentation of international law, because an increase in the number of specialized systems, such as trade law or international criminal law, enables the establishment of stronger mechanisms of adjudication. Minimalism advocates the finding of a political consensus that is compatible with several moral and religious doctrines. Another escape route consists in a regionalization of adjudicatory mechanisms because regional courts benefit

---

[5] For the distinction between 'ideal' and 'non-ideal' theory, see Rawls, J., *The Law of Peoples* (Cambridge, Mass., and London: Harvard University Press, 1999), 59.

[6] See the contributions to Nollkaemper, A. and Nijman, J. E. (eds.), *New Perspectives on the Divide between National and International Law* (Oxford: Oxford University Press, 2007). For recent examples of national courts embracing or distancing themselves from international decisions in various degrees, see e.g. *Sanchez-Llamas v Oregon*, 126 SCt 2669 (US 2006); Bundesverfassungsgericht (BVerfG, German Constitutional Court), Chamber decision, 2 BvR 2115/01, 19 Sept. 2006, available at <http://www.bverfg.de>; *Mara'abe v. Prime Minister of Israel*, HCJ 7957/04 (Supr. Ct. Isr. 2005).

from a denser set of common values and principles among their members. Some liberal approaches advocate a shift from a state-centric to a human rights-centric interpretation of international law and emphasize the role of the implementation by domestic courts. A 'critical', or postmodernist, view would further encourage international courts and tribunals to embrace the political nature of judicial choices.

This contribution intends to demonstrate that none of these approaches alone properly describes the role of international adjudication. Minimalism identifies the problem, but fails to account for the aspirational aspects of international legal principles. While informative for the ethical evaluation and critique of the law, radical liberalism lacks cross-cultural acceptance. Fragmentation can moderate, but not solve the value clashes between different issue areas. Regionalization reflects international pluralism, but cannot maintain universality. Postmodernism opens the perspective to the diversity of actors and stakeholders in contemporary international law, but all too often attacks a consensus that remains to be established.

A reference to background principles of the international community may help to bridge gaps in international law. But different from the picture Ronald Dworkin has drawn for domestic society,[7] the international community is deeply divided on the principles on which the international legal order should be based. At times, the debates between state rights and human rights, democracy and effectiveness cannot be solved on the basis of existing law.[8]

While the success of postmodernists in international legal theory may be explicable by the diversity of the international community, international adjudication does not need to end up in mere politics or in an arbitrary choice between incompatible 'background norms'. Rather, it describes a process by which international adjudication can arrive at decisions both respecting the legal foundation of international law in state consent or acquiescence and providing the reasons for a decision where the result is not 'fixed' by international legal sources. When faced with conflicting principles or gaps in the law, the adjudicator may find a solution in the particular rationality of a sub-order, from trade law to human rights law. In other cases, balancing of principles from different sub-systems will provide for a solution. Where this proves impossible, a reasonable decision needs to be found that helps the parties resolve their dispute and furthers the development of the rule of law in international relations. This contribution argues that international adjudication can maintain integrity if and to the extent that the choice between different—and at times conflicting—rationales is made in a conscious and transparent manner.

---

[7] Dworkin, R., *Law's Empire* (Cambridge, Mass.: Belknap Press, 1986), 239.

[8] Fastenrath, U., 'Relative Normativity in International Law', *European Journal of International Law*, 4 (1993), 333.

II. The Core Purpose of International Adjudication

Classical international dispute settlement consists in the resolution of a dispute between two or more parties by a neutral third party, ideally a court or an arbitral tribunal, in an adversarial procedure on the basis of international law. The Hague Peace Conferences of 1899 and 1907 established the first universal mechanism for the resolution of disputes.[9] Adjudication was acceptable to states not only due to the fairness of the procedural law embodied in the statute and rules of the court or tribunal in question, but also because the point of reference for the adjudicatory bodies was relatively clear and undisputed: providing for minimum order in the relations between states, in particular when the sovereignty of several states intersects, and supervising the interpretation and application of international law on the basis of treaties, customary law, and general principles of law.[10] Before a permanent court, states are free to give or withhold their consent to jurisdiction, but they cannot select the judges or the applicable law beyond the confines of the Statute.[11]

The strictly consensual view of the role of international tribunals informs the way judges have historically interpreted international law. Traditional international adjudication was thus based on the sovereignty of the state, and this approach also determined the interpretation of international legal sources according to state will. In the words of the Permanent Court of International Justice (PCIJ) in the *Lotus* case (1927), 'restrictions on the independence of States cannot . . . be presumed'.[12] Traditional means of interpretation are tailored to this view.[13] Such narrowness also solves the problem of legitimacy. When a state approved a clause allowing for arbitration or adjudication, it had an idea of what the approval was about. In other words, the relative determinacy and narrowness of the rules administered by international courts and arbitral tribunals provided them with a legitimacy derived from the domestic legal sphere.

Contemporary international law, however, is supposed to regulate and advance interests going beyond the maintenance of inter-state peace, from human rights to the protection of the environment. But the individual interests of states—and their

---

[9] See Hague Convention for the Pacific Settlement of Disputes, 54 LNTS 435 (18 Oct. 1907).

[10] Spiermann, O., *International Legal Argument in the Permanent Court of International Justice* (Cambridge: Cambridge University Press, 2005), 106.

[11] See the distinction between adjudication and arbitration by the Advisory Committee of Jurists, Documents Presented to the Committee Relating to Existing Plans for the Establishment of a Permanent Court of International Justice (1920), 113.

[12] PCIJ, *S.S. 'Lotus'*, Series A, No. 10 (1927), 18.

[13] See PCIJ, *Mossul (Interpretation of Article 3, Paragraph 2, of the Treaty of Lausanne)*, Adv Op, PCIJ, Series B, No. 12 (1925), 25: '[I]f the wording of a treaty provision is not clear, in choosing between several admissible interpretations, the one which involves the minimum of obligations for the Parties should be adopted'.

mutual rights and obligations—do not simply submerge into these 'community interests'.[14] To the contrary, community interests need to be integrated into the classical bilateral structure of reciprocal obligations between states.[15] States remain the main subjects of international law, the law-givers as well as the law-appliers and the law-breakers.

Even if the ultimate justification for 'state values' is grounded in 'human values' such as rights, diversity, or efficiency, international legal sources continue to be based on the aggregation of human interests in and by states, whose perceived self-interest may clash with rights accorded to individuals. Recent attempts to limit state interests to their immediate goal of winning a certain case in a concrete litigation, and to discard their interest in a stable and functioning international legal and judicial order,[16] draw a far too narrow picture of state interests. In a liberal conception of the state, the realization of 'community interests' is also a state objective, from sustainable development to human rights. That is the reason for the codification of these principles in a great number of international treaties and conventions. 'Community interests' are common interests of states relating to public goods, whereas individual interests are those essentially selfish interests in which one state can realize its objectives only at the detriment of another, for instance in boundary disputes.

The increasing crystallization and codification of international human rights, humanitarian and criminal law, but also trade law, development law, and environmental law, is not limited to the regulation of inter-state relations in the narrow sense of the term, but goes beyond the 'mediatization' of the human being by states. Two areas of international law that are gaining importance, namely international criminal law and international trade law, have created dispute settlement mechanisms of a judicial or quasi-judicial character. They exemplify the need for special regimes—but not self-contained regimes[17]—for dealing with issues going beyond inter-state relations. Regional courts such as the European Court of Justice are also playing an increasingly important role. In addition, domestic courts adjudicate much of international law—in particular those rules of international law that are of a self-executing character within the internal legal order.

---

[14] See Simma, B., 'From Bilateralism to Community Interest in International Law', *Recueil des Cours*, 250 (1994 VI), 217; Tomuschat, C., 'International Law: Ensuring the Survival of Mankind on the Eve of a New Century', *Recueil des Cours*, 281 (1999), 9, 78–9, para. 33; Henkin, L., *International Law: Politics and Values* (The Hague: Kluwer Law International, 1995), 97; Paulus, A. L., *Die Internationale Gemeinschaft Im Völkerrecht* (Munich: C.H. Beck, 2001), 250.

[15] See Simma, B., 'From Bilateralism to Community Interest' (above, n. 14), 248.

[16] Goldsmith, J. L. and Posner, E. A., *The Limits of International Law* (Oxford: Oxford University Press, 2005), 7; Posner, E. A. and Yoo, J. C., 'Judicial Independence in International Tribunals', *California Law Review*, 93 (2005), 14; But see Helfer, L. R. and Slaughter, A.-M., 'Why States Create International Tribunals: A Response to Professors Posner and Yoo', *California Law Review*, 93 (2005), 905.

[17] See Simma, B., 'Self-Contained Regimes', *Netherlands Yearbook of International Law*, 16 (1985), 111; Simma, B. and Pulkowski, D., 'Of Planets and the Universe: Self-Contained Regimes in International Law', *European Journal of International Law*, 17 (2006).

Nevertheless, it is not by accident that the International Court of Justice (ICJ) continues to show a certain reticence in adjudicating rights and obligations for individuals. International courts are not tamed by mechanisms of democratic control and are thus perceived as lacking democratic legitimacy, in particular when intervening in domestic law.[18] In the probably most characteristic example, the Court did not decide, in its Advisory Opinion on the *Threat or Use of Nuclear Weapons*, on the question of whether the state interest of survival or humanitarian principles prevail when in conflict with each other. To modify the *Lotus* presumption of state sovereignty, then-ICJ President Bedjaoui created the category of 'neither allowed nor forbidden' for a clash between state and individual values.[19]

Some judges regarded Bedjaoui's position as an inadmissible abdication of the proper role of the Court. In the words of one of his successors, Rosalyn Higgins, 'the judge's role is precisely to decide which of two or more competing norms is applicable in the particular circumstances'.[20] A *non liquet*—for example, the impropriety or impossibility for a court or tribunal to hand down a judgment or opinion—indeed reflects the inability of a court or tribunal to decide a value conflict by judicial means. Classical international law of the *Lotus* variety could not come into such a situation—in the absence of a legal rule, a state was free to act however it pleased, even if it intersected with the sovereignty of another state. Yet, the contrary view—namely that a *non liquet* should be avoided not by the application of a formal default rule as in the *Lotus* case, but by reference to the values of the international community[21]—appears utopian.

President Higgins rightly emphasizes the resolution of disputes for the mainte-nance of peace and security as the central purpose of international adjudication, which serves not only state, but also human interests. However, since the prohi-bition on the use of force generally prevents states from using force against each other—the Iraq wars being the exception rather than the rule—international law has broadened towards including the whole range of state interaction. Thereby, the regulation of community interests also comes under the jurisdiction of international courts, both advisory[22] and contentious. This multi-purposive task of international law creates problems for its coherent application.

---

[18] For such criticism, see, e.g. Goldsmith, J. L. and Posner, E. A., *Limits of International Law* (above, n. 16), 205 ff.; Posner, E. A. and Yoo, J. C., 'Judicial Independence' (above, n. 16), 27.

[19] ICJ, *Legality of the Threat or Use of Nuclear Weapons*, ICJ Rep. 1996, 226; Decl. Bedjaoui, ICJ Rep. 1996, 271, para. 14.

[20] ICJ, *Legality of the Threat or Use of Nuclear Weapons*, Diss. Op. Higgins, ICJ Rep. 1996, 592, para. 40.

[21] Lauterpacht, H., *The Function of Law in the International Community* (Oxford: Clarendon Press, 1933), 123.

[22] See e.g. the ICJ *Nuclear Weapons* opinion (above, n. 19).

III. The Role of Adjudication in the Contemporary International Community

Whereas even the pluralist Western democracies share a minimum set of common values, the 'international community' is, in spite of an increasing number of treaties regulating everything from the use of force to human rights and economic affairs, marked by deeply entrenched moral, ethical, religious, and economic divisions that render accommodation difficult, if not, at times, impossible. International courts and tribunals have thus to undertake an ever-more difficult balancing act between different legal and moral value systems.

At the same time, the increasing diversity of international adjudication in the broadest sense of the term, ranging from classical inter-state disputes under a *compromis* before an arbitral tribunal or the ICJ via advisory opinions of the ICJ onto quasi-courts such as the World Trade Organization (WTO) Dispute Settlement Body and criminal tribunals dealing with individual crimes rather than state behaviour, are difficult to bring under one single umbrella. In this section, we will identify some of these approaches and ask ourselves how they cope with the pluralism of subjects, issues, and institutions.

1. Fragmentation and Functionalism

In view of the diversity in contemporary adjudication, 'fragmentation' has become one of the key terms used to describe the contemporary international community. Whereas some lament—or try to re-establish[23]—the lost unity, others embrace the shift, in Niklas Luhmann's terms, 'from territoriality to functionality',[24] from a world of sovereign territorial states to a world of functional institutions. More radical representatives of this view claim that the different systems lack minimal commonality to maintain any coherent overarching system of general international law.[25]

[23] Dupuy, P. M., 'L'Unité de l'ordre juridique international', *Recueil des Cours*, 297 (2002).

[24] Luhmann, N., *Das Recht Der Gesellschaft* (stw edn.; Frankfurt/Main: Suhrkamp, 1995), 571 ff.; Luhmann, N., *Die Gesellschaft Der Gesellschaft* (Frankfurt/Main: Suhrkamp, 1997), 158–60; see also Paulus, A. L., 'From Territoriality to Functionality? Towards a Legal Methodology of Globalization', in Dekker, I. F. and Werner, W. G. (eds.), *Governance and International Legal Theory* (Leiden, Boston: Martinus Nijhoff, 2004), 59.

[25] Fischer-Lescano, A. and Teubner, G., 'Regime-Collisions: The Vain Search for Legal Unity in the Fragmentation of Global Law', *Michigan Journal of International Law*, 25 (2004), 1004.

The fragmentation of international law is accompanied by a fragmentation of adjudicatory bodies. Most of these bodies, such as the International Criminal Court (ICC), the WTO Dispute Settlement Body, or the regional human rights courts, belong to one single 'issue area'. Thus, they appear incapable of solving disagreements or value conflicts between different issue areas, such as trade and human rights.[26] In such an environment, international adjudication is not limited to the minimal accommodation of different state interests along the lines of state consent or acquiescence. Rather, the task of adjudicatory mechanisms is to implement the logic of the relevant sub-system. *Lacunae* in the law are not to be filled by the residual norm of state sovereignty and autonomy, as in the *Lotus* world of the past, or international 'community interests' as in the cosmopolitan world of tomorrow, but by the optimization of the rationality of the system in question. For example, in spite of attempts at the accommodation of other values, the WTO Dispute Settlement Body is called upon to further facilitate trade liberalization rather than to foster human rights, preserve world cultural heritage, or protect the environment. Nevertheless, the doctrine of *effet utile* used by the European Court of Justice for promoting European integration at times of political reluctance and incapacitation, is a case in point for the potential of adjudication to transform an international organization and its members by enhancing the functionality of a specialized international legal system.[27]

While the existence of a multiplicity of international adjudicatory bodies in specialized systems is certainly to be regarded as an advance towards a more 'legalized' or rather judicialized international system, it may become problematic when dealing with issues beyond the purview of the individual sub-system for which it was originally designed. The difficulty of the WTO Dispute Settlement Body with animal protection in the *Shrimp/Turtle*-saga is a case in point.[28] The unequal institutionalization of the different functional sub-systems gives the stronger system an advantage over the weaker system.[29] Thus, trade stands a better chance than labour rights before the WTO panels, and the International Criminal Tribunal for the Former Yugoslavia (ICTY) will tend to prefer the interests of the prosecution over the right of the accused to a fair trial.

While this effect may be mitigated by the judges taking account of other values than those of their own sub-system, such moderation cannot solve the structural problem, namely the need for a neutral arbiter. In the absence of obligatory jurisdiction over other international tribunals, the ICJ can seldom take over a moderating role,

---

[26] See Leebron, D. W., 'Linkages', *American Journal of International Law*, 96 (2002).

[27] See Weiler, J. H. H., *The Constitution of Europe* (Cambridge: Cambridge University Press, 1999), 22–3; See also ICJ, *Reparation for Injuries Suffered in the Service of the United Nations*, ICJ Rep. 1949, 182.

[28] WTO, *United States—Import Prohibition of Certain Shrimp and Shrimp Products*, 38 International Legal Materials (1999), 118.

[29] Howse, R., 'Human Rights in the WTO: Whose Rights, What Humanity? Comment on Petersmann', *European Journal of International Law*, 13 (2002), 651, 658; Paulus, A. L., 'From Territoriality to Functionality?' (above, n. 24), 88.

and it may well suffer from its own biases. For example, in *Arrest Warrant*,[30] the Court avoided making a decision on the value conflict between traditional state immunity and the universality principle for the prosecution of international criminal law violations through a minimalist opinion that nevertheless showed a preference for the former. In the *Application of the Genocide Convention* case, in a hardly veiled defence of its prerogative of the interpretation of international law, the Court lectured the ICTY for its broad theory of attribution of the acts of guerrilla groups to the state supporting them,[31] thus protecting states from responsibility for non-state terrorist groups in spite of their considerable role in their establishment and operation.

Of course, this does not imply that judges and arbiters in 'functional' courts and tribunals are inherently biased and necessarily oblivious of other systems. In *Shrimp/Turtle*, for example, the WTO Appellate Body accepted animal protection when applied in a fair manner; in *Al-Adsani*, the European Court of Human Rights narrowly favoured state immunity over individual claims against human rights offending states.[32] Whatever one may think of the two decisions, it can hardly be maintained that the judges of the trade body were unaware of international environmental law or that the judges of the human rights court were oblivious of state immunity. However, such individual virtue can only be a second-best option for institutional fairness—which would require representation of all the interests and rights involved before the adjudicatory body.

Thus, functionalism cannot, by itself, legitimize international adjudication beyond the will of states. However, it may provide a *ratio* for the filling of *lacunae* in the law by such a tribunal. Nevertheless, in order to decide value conflicts between different issue areas, international tribunals need to go beyond the narrow confines of their own system to include general international law and to accommodate the concerns of other sub-systems. Special regimes do not exist in a vacuum, but in a more complex world of global inter-state and inter-human relations.[33] In this environment, courts and tribunals need to strike a balance not only between potentially conflicting rules within a system, but also with the rules of other systems and the body of general international law. Functionalism cannot account for this role of international adjudication, a role that is becoming ever more important in the increasingly fragmented system of contemporary international law.

---

[30] ICJ, *Arrest Warrant of 11 April 2000 (DR Congo v Belgium)*, (2002) ICJ Rep. 3.

[31] ICJ, *Application of the Convention on the Prevention and Punishment of the Crime of Genocide (Bosnia and Herzegovina v Serbia and Montenegro)*, Judgment of 27 Feb 2007, available at <http://www.icj-cij.org>, paras 403–7.

[32] European Court of Human Rights, *Al-Adsani v UK*, (2002) 34 EHRR, 11.

[33] See the very first WTO Appellate Body Report, *US—Standards for Reformulated and Conventional Gasoline*, 35 International Legal Materials (1996), 621: The GATT 'is not to be read in clinical isolation from public international law'. See also Article 3 (2) of the WTO Dispute Settlement Understanding.

2. Liberalism and International Adjudication

The inter-state model of international community, in which individual human beings acquire rights and duties only via their national states, appears to be in trouble when not only goods and services, but also individuals are increasingly moving internationally, and where their ideas cross borders via the Internet. While states remain the only law-givers in international law, this law is increasingly being shaped by non-state actors—whether in the area of law-making, by participating in law-making conferences, or in the area of implementation, when human rights organizations such as Amnesty International or Human Rights Watch 'name and shame' states in breach of human rights obligations. Mass protest may be more effective than diplomatic interventions by state agents. Jürgen Habermas and Jacques Derrida have celebrated the protests against the most recent war against Iraq as the birth of a common European (if not world-wide) public opinion.[34]

A liberal concept of international community draws the consequences of these developments by focusing on individual rights and duties. Liberals and neo-liberals demand a reconstruction of international law on an inter-individual basis. In the liberal perspective, individuals, not states, are the ultimate stakeholders in international law.[35] States draw their legitimacy from their representation of human beings. State rights must be justified before international courts and tribunals not as aims in themselves, but in their service of individuals. Whereas more moderate representatives of liberal ethics, such as John Rawls,[36] view the peoples as the basic units of the international legal order, more radical liberals demand the establishment of a 'world social order' on cosmopolitan foundations.[37]

In their attitude towards international adjudication, liberals display a certain disregard for 'collective' legitimacy in favour of a more pragmatic concept of international tribunals as service providers to individuals. Thus, individualist liberalism will be oriented to individual outcomes, not collective state interest. Liberals will emphasize cooperation between international and national courts and thus opt for a more general perspective, leaving a narrow inter-state view of international law. This does not imply, however, a loss of importance for international adjudication. Anne-Marie Slaughter has concluded that 'transjudicial

---

[34] Habermas, J., *Der Gespaltene Westen* (Kleine Politische Schriften X; Frankfurt am Main: Suhrkamp, 2004), 44.

[35] Buchanan, A. E., *Justice, Legitimacy, and Self-Determination: Moral Foundations for International Law* (Oxford and New York: Oxford University Press, 2004); Buchanan, A. and Keohane, R. O., 'The Legitimacy of Global Governance Institutions', *Ethics and International Affairs*, 20 (2006), 406, 417.

[36] Rawls, J., *A Theory of Justice* (Cambridge, Mass.: Harvard University Press, 1971), 377 ff.; Rawls, J., *Law of Peoples* (above, n. 5), 37.

[37] See Beitz, C. R., *Political Theory and International Relations* (Princeton: Princeton University Press, 1979), 8–9, 128; Pogge, T. W., *Realizing Rawls* (Ithaca, NY and London: Cornell University Press, 1989), 244 ff.; But see Rawls, *Theory of Justice* (above, n. 36), 457.

networks' of judges and lawyers play an increasing role in the professional self-awareness of courts and tribunals, resulting in the establishment of a 'community of courts' beyond state borders.[38] Judges from liberal states are considered to have as much, if not more, in common with each other than with their domestic counterparts in the other branches of government.

For anti-institutionalist neo-liberals, a liberal and democratic sovereign state does not need to accept international precedents that do not meet the most basic criteria of democratic legitimacy and human rights protection.[39] For others, international adjudication will be persuasive, but only as long as it conforms to substantive liberal and democratic values. It is thus telling that many liberals emphasize (democratic) legitimacy over international legality.[40] Networks of domestic institutions are preferable to global courts and tribunals with the authority to issue decisions binding for both liberal and non-liberal states. At the same time, making individual rights the main criteria for international adjudication may de-legitimize traditional inter-state adjudication for the sake of criminal and human rights tribunals dealing with individual rights and duties of persons.

While liberalism may suit states with 'liberal' values, it tends to underestimate the lasting relevance of differing value concepts not only between 'liberal' and authoritarian states.[41] Filling *lacunae* of existing law with liberal values opens international courts to the charge of political bias. International adjudication aims not only at the realization of 'liberal values' such as human rights, but also—and maybe primarily—at the peaceful coexistence and cooperation of different value and belief systems. The differentiation of rights and duties between 'liberal' and other states or peoples may thus endanger the peace-making role of international adjudication.

3. The Postmodern Critique of International Adjudication

Postmodernists are deeply critical regarding the claim that international adjudication—or adjudication in general—can apply 'objective' law to reality. The belief of a clear direction of history towards the realization of liberal values, the idea of progress itself, is discarded; diversity and subjectivity are celebrated.[42]

---

[38] Slaughter, A. M., 'A Global Community of Courts', *Harvard International Law Journal*, 44 (2003); Slaughter, A. M., *A New World Order* (Princeton and Oxford: Princeton University Press, 2004), 68; Keohane, R. O., Moravcsik, A., and Slaughter, A. M., 'Legalized Dispute Resolution: Interstate and Transnational', *International Organization*, 54 (2000).

[39] Goldsmith, J. L. and Posner, E. A., *Limits of International Law* (above, n. 16), 205 ff.

[40] See e.g. Buchanan, A. and Keohane, R. O., 'Legitimacy of Global Governance Institutions' (above, n. 35), 406.

[41] But see Rawls, J., *Law of Peoples* (above, n. 5), 5 *et passim* (arguing for an international law applicable to liberal and 'decent' human rights abiding states only).

[42] Bauman, Z., *Intimations of Postmodernity* (London and New York: Routledge, 1992), 189–196; Lyotard, J. F., *La Condition postmoderne: Rapport sur le savoir* (Paris: Éditions de Minuit, 1979), 8–9.

According to an 'internal' critique, the indeterminacy of rules and principles precludes a definite outcome for legal analysis. International law navigates between an apology for narrow-minded state interests or power and a utopian search for a global community of values.[43] At the same time, indeterminacy enables the (ab)use of international law for political purposes hidden under the alleged objectivity of legal analysis, a process termed 'reification'.[44] Whereas, in the internal critique, international law is presented as lacking determinate content, the external critique regards international law as a powerful tool for the attainment of political objectives. Although there is an obvious tension between these two critiques, they are not necessarily contradictory: The law can be abused because its authority does not conform to its lack of substance.

Both the external and the internal critique seem to render futile any attempt, judicial or otherwise, at deriving determinate results from legal analysis independent of the ideological position of the judge. It appears useless to strive to find an overlapping consensus by applying formal sources to new cases, when the absence of consensus was at the source of the conflict. Devoid of either substance or formal procedure, international law falls prey to political abuse.

The refutation of the objectivity of law leads postmodern authors to the person of the lawyer and her social role.[45] In Martti Koskenniemi's early view, the task of the lawyer is to contribute to acceptable solutions to social problems even in the absence of legal guidance.[46] In his more recent work, he proposes to regard the practice of judges and lawyers as a 'culture of formalism' that mitigates power by listening to the voices of 'the other'.[47] In this perspective, international adjudication should broaden its constituency to individuals, and, in particular, the excluded. It would not speak the language of the powerful, but give voice to the oppressed. However, the turn to the lawyer—and by extension the judge—raises even more questions. What is the lawyer without the application of 'the law'? Where does her authority come from, if not from legal rules and principles emanating from law-making procedures accepted by society?

---

[43] Koskenniemi, M., *From Apology to Utopia: The Structure of International Legal Argument* (Helsinki: Lakimiesliiton Kustannus, 1989), 48.

[44] Carty, A., 'Critical International Law: Recent Trends in the Theory of International Law', *European Journal of International Law*, 2 (1991), 66, 67 n. 1.

[45] Koskenniemi, M., *From Apology to Utopia* (above, n. 43), 490; Korhonen, O., 'New International Law: Silence, Defence or Deliverance', *European Journal of International Law*, 7 (1996), 1.

[46] Koskenniemi, M., *From Apology to Utopia* (above, n. 43), 486. See also Kennedy, D., 'The Disciplines of International Law and Policy', *Leiden Journal of International Law*, 12 (1999), 9, 83 (international law as 'group of professional disciplines in which people pursue projects' within different institutional settings).

[47] Koskenniemi, M., *The Gentle Civilizer of Nations: The Rise and Fall of International Law, 1870–1960* (Cambridge: Cambridge University Press, 2002), 502.

IV. Towards a Methodology of International Adjudication

As it turns out, none of these approaches alone properly describes the role of international adjudication. While instructive for the ethical evaluation and critique of the law, radical liberalism lacks the cross-cultural acceptance that would be necessary to achieve universality. Without universality, however, international adjudication remains unable to deal with disputes between actors of different philosophical and ethical traditions. If the goal of international adjudication remains the peaceful settlement of disputes, abandoning universality of reach would be too big a price to pay for ideological cohesion.

While it may be correct to criticize a formalist conception of law as a mechanical application of rules in the tradition of Montesquieu, a return to a purely political conception of the task of the lawyer fails to grasp the point of adjudication: judicial pronouncements do not constitute *ad hoc*-compromises, but they attempt to solve disputes by the application of general and abstract standards previously agreed or acquiesced to by the members of society. It is in this detachment from the political environment, and not in the involvement in it, that the authority of rules and principles lies. An unprincipled 'adhocery' would lead to a loss of faith in international adjudication—and ultimately to the withdrawal of consent to jurisdiction.[48] Thus, international adjudication cannot, and should not, disregard the legal sources from which it derives its authority. For example, the International Court of Justice must respect the limits of its jurisdiction and cannot rule over war crimes or crimes against humanity when its jurisdiction is limited to genocide.[49] Embracing politics would lead to the loss of judicial authority. This does not imply a denial that adjudication plays a political as well as a legal role. But it is by its judicial, not by its political, authority that adjudication does so.

One way of dealing with the pluralism of international value system may lie in the application of the Rawlsian concept of an 'overlapping consensus' that accepts the lack of agreement on the philosophical and religious foundations by finding a 'political' compromise that does not affect the different concepts of legitimacy, but

---

[48] Fastenrath, U., 'Relative Normativity' (above, n. 8), 336. This may be even more so in adjudicative mechanisms in special fields such as international trade law, see Abi-Saab, G., 'The Appellate Body and Treaty Interpretation', in Sacerdoti, G., Yanovich, A., and Bohanes, J. (eds.), *The WTO at Ten: The Contribution of the Dispute Settlement System* (Cambridge: Cambridge University Press, 2006), 461.

[49] See ICJ, *Application of the Genocide Convention* (above, n. 31), paras. 147–8.

allows both sides to integrate a decision in their own value and belief system.[50] In the case of the International Court of Justice, such inclusiveness can be reached by fuller reasoning contained in separate and dissenting opinions.[51] Whereas the decision itself represents the compromise among the different legal views within the international legal community, individual opinions provide a comprehensive reasoning based on the diverse judicial and ethical views of the individual judges.

Of course, the difference between openly liberal concepts of adjudication and a consensual model may well be over-stated. One needs to emphasize that Rawls anchors his notion of an overlapping consensus in 'reasonableness', that is the resonance of these principles with the idea of public reason implicit in the traditions of a liberal democratic society.[52] For the 'law of peoples', Rawls includes the 'reasonable justness' of societies of 'decent' but non-liberal peoples, but categorically excludes authoritarian regimes as 'outlaw states'.[53] While the Rawlsian vision may thus be compatible with different religions and belief systems, it excludes any fundamentalism demanding a common religious (or ideological) basis for the establishment of political community. To a certain extent, consensualism thus requires the previous acceptance of a liberal idea of political community—the very consensus lacking in the international sphere.

What international adjudication is thus called upon to achieve may result in an even more Herculean task than Ronald Dworkin's concept of 'law as integrity' demands in a domestic legal order.[54] Dworkin 'asks judges to assume, so far as this is possible, that the law is structured by a coherent set of principles about justice and fairness and procedural due process'.[55] He has maintained that his critics[56] are short of examples to show that there are either *lacunae* in the law or that an application of his theory leads to insoluble contradictions to be filled by the political or psychological preferences of the judge rather than by legal principles.[57]

---

[50] Rawls, J., *Political Liberalism* (paperback edn.; New York: Columbia University Press, 1996), 133, esp. 147. For the application of the overlapping consensus to the global realm see e.g., Franck, T., *Fairness in International Law and Institutions* (Oxford: Clarendon, 1995), 14; Pogge, T., *Realizing Rawls* (above, n. 37), 277; Roth, B. R., *Governmental Illegitimacy in International Law* (Oxford: Clarendon Press, 1999), 6.

[51] See ICJ Statute, article 57; See also Hofmann, R. and Laubner, T., 'Article 57', in Zimmermann, A., Tomuschat, C., and Oellers-Frahm, K. (eds.), *The Statute of the International Court of Justice—a Commentary* (Oxford: Oxford University Press, 2006). For a conspicuous recent example, see ICJ, *Oil Platforms (Iran v US)*, Sep. Op. Simma, ICJ Rep. 2003, 161, 324–5; See also Jouannet, E., 'Le Juge international face aux problèmes d'incohérence et d'instabilité du droit international', *Revue générale de droit international public* (2004), 929.

[52] Rawls, J., *Political Liberalism* (above, n. 50), 36–7; Rawls, J., *Law of Peoples* (above, n. 5), 172–3. Rationality is also a precondition for the ordering of international society, *Law of Peoples*, 32.

[53] Rawls, J., *Law of Peoples* (above, n. 5), 5, 17, 62–3.

[54] See Dworkin, R., *Law's Empire* (above, n. 7), 239–40.   [55] Ibid. 243.

[56] Altman, A., 'Legal Realism, Critical Legal Studies, and Dworkin', *Philosophy and Public Affairs*, 15 (1986); Waldron, J., 'Did Dworkin Ever Answer the Crits?' in Hershovitz, S. (ed.), *Exploring Law's Empire: The Jurisprudence of Ronald Dworkin* (Oxford: Oxford University Press, 2006), 155.

[57] Dworkin, R., *Justice in Robes* (Cambridge, Mass. and London: Belknap Press, 2006), 105; Dworkin, R., 'Response', in Hershovitz, S. (ed.), *Exploring Law's Empire* (above, n. 56), 299 ff.

Within contemporary international law, however, there seems to be no shortage of examples of contradiction. Its basic principles appear to be divided between the maintenance of state sovereignty and human rights, between apology for state behaviour and the utopia of a just international order.[58] For clashes between state survival and human rights or humanitarian considerations, the International Court of Justice has occasionally been unable to find a broadly acceptable solution.[59] Another example is the clash between the duty of states to prosecute offenders for core crimes against international criminal law, on the one hand, and state or personal immunity, on the other.[60] A Dworkinian concept of international law as integrity may respond that state and individual rights can be applied in a way that avoids a clash.[61] 'Soft law' or, rather, a differentiation between different grades of authority, may help in filling *lacunae* in the 'hard' law of the sources triad of article 38 ICJ Statute.[62] Nevertheless, it appears almost impossible to place both state and individual existence at the top of the scale of international legal principles.

In the absence of a global liberal and democratic society—or a free global association of liberal and democratic societies—international adjudication may thus not always be able to maintain the coherence of international law. When the balancing and accommodation of state and individual rights fails, this may require a taking of sides between state and individual rights, community and state interests. However, when done openly and transparently, international adjudication will still be able to remain faithful to the idea of the integrity of international law. In this event, judges should openly admit to the indeterminacy of the sources and the clash of the underlying principles and clearly distinguish between the constraints of the law and the reasons for their adoption of a particular solution and their preference for one principle over another.

Thus, the judge must decide within the confines of the law. But her responsibility also extends to the maintenance of the integrity of the international legal system—in other words, international judges must uphold the broader idea of an international rule of law. This may cut both ways: in some cases, it may require the Court to follow a literal interpretation of the wording of a treaty where its meaning is clear. In others, gaps in the law may allow the judge to further develop the law to meet the needs of its constituents, which includes both states and humanity at large, with the goal to establish a new legal precedent.[63] This was the original purpose behind the inclusion of 'general principles of law' in article 38 of the ICJ Statute.[64] In conflicts

---

[58] See Koskenniemi, M., *From Apology to Utopia* (above, n. 43), 8–50.

[59] ICJ, *Legality of the Threat or Use of Nuclear Weapons*, Adv Op, ICJ Rep. 1996, 266.

[60] ICJ, *Arrest Warrant* (above, n. 30); European Court of Human Rights, *Al-Adsani v. UK*, (above, n. 32); and UK, *R v Bow Street Metropolitan Stipendiary Magistrate ex parte Pinochet (No. 3)*, [2000] AC, 151.

[61] Dworkin, R., *Justice in Robes* (above, n. 57), 112, 116.

[62] Fastenrath, U., 'Relative Normativity' (above, n. 8), 339–40.

[63] Similarly, Lowe, V., 'The Politics of Law-Making: Are the Method and Character of Norm Creation Changing?' in Byers, M., (ed.), *The Role of Law in International Politics* (Oxford: Oxford University Press, 2000), 207–26, 215.

[64] See Pellet, A., 'Article 38', in *The Statute of the International Court of Justice* (above, n. 51).

between different sub-systems of international law, the competent court or tribunal must strive to draw a full picture of the relevant legal rules to avoid realizing one legal goal at the expense of another.[65] Article 31 (1) (c) of the Vienna Convention on the Law of Treaties also gives a hint in this direction in its stipulation that the interpretation of a treaty must take into account 'any relevant rule of international law applicable in the relations between the parties'.[66] The court or tribunal must also look to the broader systemic implications of its interpretation for the whole of the international community.[67] However, there may not always be a clear and unequivocal solution to dilemmas in the law. Legal principles may help to fill the gaps, but also add to the contradictions.

Faced with this problem, the task of the lawyer is not fulfilled through a simple restatement or formulation of an existing consensus. Rather, the judge may be called upon to play a role in maintaining, and at times even establishing, the integrity of the system.[68] Jürgen Habermas once suggested that the conflict between human rights and the prohibition on the use of force should be evaluated not on the basis of contemporary law, but with regard to an international legal system to come.[69] Further, the Swiss Civil Code authorizes the domestic judge to decide pursuant to the law she herself would put forward to avoid a *non liquet*.[70] Referring to Kant and Dworkin, Martti Koskenniemi has suggested an application of 'constitutionalism as a mindset' to find a solution as inclusive of the rights and interests at stake as possible.[71] The authority states have delegated to the Court must be deemed to include the necessary filling of the gaps in resolve their dispute. It is, therefore, not appropriate for a court to send a case back to states instead of filling the gaps in the law for the sake of the solution of the dispute.[72]

However, the 'filling' of the gaps of the law is heavily constrained by the willingness of states and other international legal subjects to implement the conclusions of the Court. States remain free to modify the rule put forward by the Court.[73] It

---

[65] This was recognized by the WTO Appellate Body in its first report, see *US—Gasoline*, WT/DS2/AB/R, III.B, 17; see also Pauwelyn, J., 'The Role of Public International Law in the WTO: How Far Can We Go?' *American Journal of International Law*, 95 (2001), with ample references.

[66] Vienna Convention on the Law of Treaties, 23 May 1969, 1155 UNTS 331; on the relevance of this provision for the WTO DSB and the ICJ, respectively, see Abi-Saab, G., 'The Appellate Body and Treaty Interpretation' (above, n. 48), 462–4; Guillaume, G., 'Methods and Practice of Treaty Interpretation by the International Court of Justice', in *The WTO at Ten* (above, n. 48), 470–1.

[67] Fastenrath, U., 'Relative Normativity' (above, n. 8), 337.

[68] For a similar conclusion see Jouannet, E., *Le Juge international* (above, n. 51), 943–4.

[69] Habermas, J., 'Bestialität Und Humanität. Ein Krieg an Der Grenze Zwischen Recht und Moral', in Merkel, R., (ed.), *Der Kosovo-Krieg und Das Völkerrecht* (Frankfurt: Suhrkamp, 2000), 51.

[70] Swiss Civil Code, § 1 (2): 'If the law does not contain a rule, the court shall decide according to customary law and, where such law is lacking, according to the rule that he would establish as legislator' (our translation).

[71] Koskenniemi, M., 'Constitutionalism as Mindset: Reflections on Kantian Themes about International Law and Globalization', *Theoretical Inquiries in Law*, 8 (2007), 32.

[72] But see ICJ, *Gabíkovo-Nagymaros Project (Hungary v Slovakia)*, ICJ Rep. 1997, 83 (referring the case back to the parties). The matter remains undecided until this day.

[73] See the introduction of the Exclusive Economic Zone by the UN Convention on the Law of the Sea, 1833 United Nations Treaty Series 397, art. 55 ff., after the contrary holding in the *Fisheries Jurisdiction* cases, ICJ,

appears thus as misleading to speak of 'law-making' in the true sense of the term, because it is the law that constrains the international judge, and not *vice versa*.[74] This argument does not deny, however, the factual influence the judgment of an authoritative international court will have on the parties and on international law in general—not least because the winning side will have little incentive to change a rule enunciated by an international court.

Thus, the legal methodology of international adjudication requires a process of three steps: a 'positivist' regard for the confines of the judicial task of interpreting existing legal rules; a Dworkinian examination of the foundational principles of an international legal order allowing for legal decisions standing on principle; and a postmodern view of the element of choice involved in any legal interpretation that enables the judge to consciously and transparently apply her own reasoned judgment, subject to the constraints of the law in force.

V. CONCLUSION

Contemporary international adjudication has gone well beyond the limits of a traditional, quasi-arbitral system in which international judges could not exercise an independent role. But the loss of a clear point of reference has left uncertainty as to how to cope with this newly won independence without losing the indispensable support of the state constituency. At times, courts and tribunals have confined themselves to a narrow, purely functional role, without regard to more general norms and principles. In most cases, however, they have understood their role in a broader fashion as a contribution to the rule of law in international affairs administered by courts and tribunals as third parties.

This contribution does not claim to present an additional 'superior' version of adjudication. Neither does it advocate a return to a judicial minimalism that fails to account for the aspirational aspects of international adjudication, namely the establishment of an international rule of law. Proper international adjudication will have to acquire the characteristics of each of the different strands: it will fill the gaps in international law by invoking the goals of the concrete legal institution(s) and the states it serves, while remaining mindful of the broader implications; it will take account of the move towards individual rights and duties in the international sphere, but will not forget that Western individualism cannot be imposed upon

---

United Kingdom v. Iceland and Germany v. Iceland, ICJ Rep. 1974, 3, 175. The Court confirmed this development in *Continental Shelf (Libyan Arab Jamahiriya/Malta)*, ICJ Rep. 1985, 33, para. 34; on the episode see Schulte, C., *Compliance with Decisions of the International Court of Justice* (Oxford: Oxford University Press, 2004) 154–5.

74 But see Ginsburg, T., 'Bounded Discretion in International Judicial Lawmaking', *Virginia Journal of International Law*, 45 (2005), 635–7, referring to Shapiro, M., 'Judges as Liars', *Harvard Journal of Law and Public Policy*, 17 (1994) (courts are 'liars' when they present their conclusions as required by existing law).

others; it will need to be conscious of the relevance of political circumstances when it applies legal prescriptions, but know that adjudication derives its authority from the relevant legal sources emanating, for better or for worse, from states.

Legal answers are supposed to refer to standards, rules, and principles established by some kind of generally recognized formal procedure. A failure by judges to use these standards would result in arbitrariness and thereby in a dereliction of duty. But that leaves a lot of space to the imagination and creativity of the individual judge as to how to best apply these standards, rules, and principles to the diversity and richness of life. In legal analysis self-conscious of its limits, these individual value judgments are not exercised in the closet but in the open.[75] That includes an effort to break out of the traditional bounds of international law as applying only within the public sphere and moving towards an inclusion of private actors such as non-governmental organizations, and towards an acceptance and encouragement of cultural diversity.

International courts must find a consensus within their constituency, and can hardly step out of this role to become law-makers rather than law-appliers. Global adjudication cannot escape the need to strike a balance between state and community interests, to find a common ground between different cultures and religions, or even between professional sensitivities in different issue areas, by pointing to commonly agreed standards that go beyond the self-interest of the parties and the particularities of the functional sub-system in which the judge operates. Such value judgments might allow for the very international public discourse that can build and elaborate areas of international consensus, beyond doctrinal formalism and postmodern particularism. In this way, international law is not (only) what international courts will do. What international courts are doing will not only shape the role of international law within the international community, but will itself become part of community-building.

---

[75] For a critique of some of the practices of the WTO Dispute Settlement Body see Abi-Saab, G., 'The Appellate Body and Treaty Interpretation' (above, n. 48), 461–2.

CHAPTER 10

INTERNATIONAL ADJUDICATION: A RESPONSE TO PAULUS—COURTS, CUSTOM, TREATIES, REGIMES, AND THE WTO

DONALD H. REGAN[*]

I. INTRODUCTION

I am pleased to have the opportunity to respond to Andreas Paulus's very interesting contribution, and to elaborate on some of the matters he raises. As will be all too obvious, I am not an expert on general public international law. I undertook this assignment in the hope that I would learn something (as I have), and that I would eventually think of something useful to say (less clear). Happily, the one area of international law where I do have some expertise is the law of the World Trade Organization (WTO). The WTO is often used as an example in discussions of the 'fragmentation' of international law, which is one of the problems Paulus discusses, so I hope some remarks at the end about how the WTO and its Appellate Body

* For helpful discussion of this chapter I thank Samantha Besson, Andreas Paulus, Bruno Simma, and John Tasioulas. All views expressed are my own.

handle problems of conflicting values may be useful. But I shall begin with more general issues.

II. COURTS AND CUSTOM

What are judges doing when they adjudicate cases involving international law? The first way we might hope to answer this question is by denying that there is any special problem about *international* adjudication. Judges deciding international law cases are doing the same thing judges do when they decide cases under domestic law, except that the substantive law is different, and from different sources. Of course, even if we could say this, it would not solve our problem. There is no agreement about just what judges are doing in domestic adjudication. To remind the reader of the obvious, we have never found an uncontroversial solution to two related puzzles or problems about (domestic) adjudication: (1) However much we may have imbibed the lessons of legal realism and its philosophical descendants, we still want it to be the case that there is some sort of law/politics divide. Crudely, we want to believe that legislatures make the law and judges apply it. But of course, the law is often not clear. So the question is, what is the judge doing in the area of opacity? If we want particular cases to be decided by general rules knowable in advance, how can a judge produce a legitimate decision in a particular case where the rules have (or appear to have) run out? (2) Another puzzle, related but distinct, is that we want the law to be both knowable and ideally moral or just (for the circumstances). In practice, these two desiderata are likely to be in tension in many instances. So, assimilating international adjudication to domestic adjudication would not remotely solve the problem of understanding international adjudication. But it would at least mean that we did not have a new problem, and it would give us a large literature ready-made.

Unfortunately for this 'assimilationist' approach, international law and adjudication are different from domestic law and adjudication in significant ways, some of which seem important when we are thinking about the role of the judge. For a start, it is not clear that there is even a single type of 'international adjudication'. We now have a vast range of international tribunals, with remarkably different tasks. For example, a large part of the business of the International Court of Justice (ICJ) consists of identifying and applying general principles of law and customary international law. The Appellate Body of the WTO, in contrast, is mainly concerned to interpret and apply one large and complex treaty. The International Criminal Court (ICC) and the special international criminal tribunals, even though they must inevitably decide some questions of general international law, are primarily concerned with fact-finding.

Paulus notes briefly that international courts differ from domestic courts in having no fully compulsory jurisdiction and no reliable coercive enforcement mechanism, and he suggests that this 'changes the character' of international adjudication.[1] But the reality is complex, and I am not sure in any event that the differences here between domestic and international adjudication change the task of the judge. The international criminal tribunals (including the ICC) have fully compulsory jurisdiction over the defendants brought before them, although of course they are dependent on other agencies to produce those defendants. The Appellate Body of the WTO has compulsory jurisdiction over all WTO Members; the only way to avoid the jurisdiction is to withdraw from the treaty. Even the ICJ has what is often referred to as 'compulsory' jurisdiction, a general jurisdiction granted conditionally by states in advance of particular disputes under the ICJ Statute article 36.2, although of course no state is required to grant such jurisdiction, and a disgruntled state can always withdraw it prospectively. With regard to enforcement, the criminal tribunals again can expect their judgments to be coercively enforced. That is not true of either the WTO Appellate Body or the ICJ, but compliance with judgments of these bodies has been reasonably high nonetheless,[2] presumably because of a combination of reputational pressure and the losing party's commitment to the existence and efficacy of the relevant international system.

Still, it is true that most international courts differ to some degree from domestic courts with regard to the compulsoriness of their jurisdiction and the enforceability of their judgments (or the expectation of compliance). The question is, does this make any difference to what the court is doing when it decides an individual case? So far as I can see, it does not. The central role of a court is to answer questions that are brought to it about the state of the law.[3] A court with no compulsory jurisdiction will be asked fewer questions; and a court whose judgments are unenforceable may expect its judgments to have somewhat less effect on the world; but still, there is no obvious reason why the court's approach to deciding what the law says should be affected. The absence of courts with fully compulsory jurisdiction and fully enforceable judgments may or may not be a problem for the international *system*; but I do not see that the lack of compulsory jurisdiction or enforcement is a problem for the court itself.

A much more important difference between international courts and domestic courts is the 'sources of law' that they rely on. For domestic courts, the sources of law are constitutions, statutes or codes, administrative regulations, and in some systems, judicial precedent (and also in some systems international law, but this

---

[1] Paulus, A., 'International Adjudication', Chapter 9 in this volume, 208.

[2] With regard to the ICJ, see generally Schulte, C., *Compliance with Decisions of the International Court of Justice* (Oxford: Oxford University Press, 2004).

[3] I ignore the fact-finding role, not because it is unimportant, but because it is *relatively* unproblematic philosophically.

will be relevant to at most a small number of domestic cases). These domestic sources of law are for the most part easily identified. Of course these sources still require interpretation, and there is room for enormous controversy about interpretation, both at the level of hermeneutics and of exegesis. But still, it is usually reasonably clear what the texts are that need to be interpreted and applied. That is not true in general for international adjudication. The Statute of the ICJ lists as sources of law: international conventions (general or particular), 'international custom, as evidence of a general practice accepted as law', and 'the general principles of law recognized by civilised nations'.[4] International conventions, including treaties, are easily identifiable. (Treaties raise other problems, which I shall discuss in section III.) But the other sources are not easily identified; identifying the source may be the hardest part of the adjudicative project.

Taken at face value, the definition of what is known as 'customary international law' seems to require a broad empirical investigation into the behaviour of nations and the attitudes behind that behaviour. The ICJ is widely thought to have revised the conception of custom in the *Nicaragua* case, so that even a putative norm that is frequently violated may count as 'custom' if violators consistently offer some justification for their violation.[5] This reduces the importance of uniform practice and elevates the importance of *opinio juris*, but it does not eliminate the need for extensive empirical investigation. Nor does it eliminate the possibility for spirited disagreement about whether some supposed custom exists. Some scholars want to move beyond *Nicaragua* and base customary law on the pronouncements of international assemblies, and congresses, and the like—significantly de-emphasizing questions about the practice or rhetorical behaviour of individual states.[6] On this view, it is the role of the court (assisted, of course, by scholars) to say when a norm that is announced or adumbrated in a variety of often largely hortatory documents has crystallized into international law. At this point, the courts are being asked to play a role that hardly seems like 'adjudication' at all. But if the demand on judges at this extreme end of the spectrum of views about custom seems clearly unacceptable (at least to me), the same *sort* of demand is already being made even at the other end of the spectrum, under the most traditional view of custom. Even here, the judge plays a role in identifying the law to be applied that is quite different from the judge's usual role in domestic systems. Familiarity with this scheme has bred acceptance—familiarity and necessity. In the international system, where there is no general legislature, we must recognize customary law if there is to be any

---

[4] Statute of the ICJ, article 38. Also, as 'subsidiary means', non-binding precedent and 'the teachings of the most highly qualified publicists'. For a much fuller discussion of the sources of international law, see Samantha Besson, 'Theorizing the Sources of International Law', Chapter 7 in this volume, 163.

[5] ICJ, *Military and Paramilitary Activities in and against Nicaragua (Nicaragua v. United States of America)* (ICJ Reports 1986), 14 (see esp. paras. 186, 202).

[6] e.g. Charney, J., 'Universal International Law', *American Journal of International Law*, 87 (1993), 529, 543–50.

universally applicable (i.e., non-treaty-based) positive law at all. But familiar or not, the role of the international court in identifying and applying customary law in a controversial case is very different from the role of a domestic court.

In the central section of his paper, Paulus discusses three approaches to international adjudication; the 'functionalist' approach, the 'liberal' approach, and the 'post-modern' approach. The discussion of the functionalist approach focuses on the problem of 'fragmentation' of international law; this problem arises largely from the multiplication of treaties, and we will take it up in section III. But in the discussions of both the 'post-modern' approach and the 'liberal' approach, Paulus is grappling with the same problems that bedevil our understanding of domestic adjudication, except that in the international sphere the problems are magnified by the absence of a legislature or a true world community. The post-modern view of international adjudication is a response to the puzzle about what judges are doing, or should do, when they decide a case where the *lex lata* is unclear, a puzzle that we have encountered in the domestic sphere. But as we have seen, in the international sphere the absence of a legislature means the judge must first identify the law before applying it. Hence a 'political' contribution by the judge seems even more inevitable in the international sphere, and the magnitude of the political contribution greater. Similarly, calls for 'liberal' international law, coupled with Paulus's warning that international law must not simply exclude non-liberal regimes lest it 'endanger the peace-making role of international adjudication',[7] reflect the tension between wanting the law to be ideally moral or just, on the one hand, and wanting it to be knowable and effective on the other—again, a problem we have encountered in the domestic sphere. This problem is magnified in the international context because there is no international polity with common values except in the thinnest sense. To be sure, even in the national context, any appeal to community values inevitably overrides some conflicting views on the disputed question, but even so, most functioning states represent societies with a much greater commonality of fundamental values than we can find over the world as a whole.

With regard to both the post-modern and liberal views, Paulus's conclusion seems to be that there is some truth in them, but we cannot take either approach to the extreme.

Proper international adjudication . . . will take account of the move towards individual rights and duties in the international sphere, but will not forget that Western individualism cannot be imposed on others; [also] it will be mindful of the relevance of political circumstances when it applies legal prescriptions, but knows that it derives its authority from the relevant legal sources emanating, for better or worse, from states.[8]

In sum, judges should just muddle through. They should also do it transparently. In appropriate cases, 'judges should openly admit to the indeterminacy of the sources and the clash of the underlying principles and clearly distinguish between the

---

[7] Paulus, A., this volume, 217.   [8] Ibid. 223–4.

constraints of law and the reasons for their adoption of a particular solution and their preference for one principle over another.[9] The hope is that if judges are open in this way about when they are going beyond the *lex lata* and about their reasons for the choices they make when they do, then they can facilitate 'the very international public discourse that can build and elaborate areas of international consensus, beyond doctrinal formalism and postmodern particularism' and can 'not only shape the role of international law within the international community, but will itself become part of the community building'.[10]

Taken as advice to judges, this is rather amorphous. (And the judges may not feel in need of advice.) Perhaps the real usefulness of Paulus's prescriptions is as a reminder to us observers to be tolerant of judicial pronouncements that may not meet our standards for scholarly argument. But amorphous or not, if I thought I could do better than Paulus has done at describing what judges should be doing with these two problems, I would be writing a different paper. There is just one respect in which Paulus's prescriptions may be unrealistic, and may actually be in tension with one of his most interesting points elsewhere in the chapter. Paulus calls for judges to be clear about when they are going beyond the *lex lata*, but judges may not always know just when they are going beyond the *lex lata* (unless we think the *lex lata* ends where even the slightest possibility for controversy begins, a definition which is surely too strict). Paulus suggests (and I agree) that a virtue of having multiple opinions supporting a judgment of the ICJ on different grounds is that this multiplicity can reveal an 'overlapping consensus', in which different legal views with different value premises converge on a common result.[11] But in at least some such cases of overlapping consensus, each concurring judge will think she is simply announcing the *lex lata*, whereas the whole constellation of opinions may persuade the observer that about that, they are all wrong.

III. TREATIES AND REGIMES

The third approach Paulus discusses is 'functionalism', which he describes as 'em-brac[ing] the fragmentation of international law, because more specialized systems, such as trade law or international criminal law, can establish stronger mechanisms of adjudication'. Surely the advantage is not just stronger adjudication, but more precise and specialized rules—which is what makes the stronger adjudication ac-ceptable. But whatever the advantages of specialized regimes, Paulus discusses two possible disadvantages. He worries that specialized regimes may be committed to the promotion of a single regime value (trade, the environment, punishment for war criminals, protection of human rights, whatever) to the exclusion of other values;

---

[9] Paulus, A., this volume, 221.   [10] Ibid. 224.   [11] Ibid. 219–20.

and he worries that even if the regime recognizes the need to reconcile the principal regime value with other values, the regime's courts will be biased in favour of the regime value (for example, construing narrowly exceptions in favour of the other values).[12] Paulus focuses on regimes that are created by states through the treaty mechanism, so issues about fragmentation are closely bound up with issues about treaty interpretation, which brings us back to the other main source of international law.

I am not persuaded that the problems Paulus discusses give much cause for concern at present. Paulus himself mentions more examples where regime courts have acknowledged and accommodated values other than the putative regime value than examples where they have not. The International Law Commission (ILC) Report on Fragmentation also concludes that 'the emergence of special treaty-regimes . . . has not seriously undermined legal security, predictability or the equality of legal subjects'.[13] Although the authors of the Report say 'the emergence of conflicting rules and overlapping legal regimes will undoubtedly create problems of coordination at the international level', and 'no homogeneous, hierarchical meta-system is realistically available to do away with such problems', they seem to be distinctly not alarmed. Specifically, they think techniques for reasoning about treaty conflicts that are already embodied in the Vienna Convention on the Law of Treaties go a long way towards dealing with inter-regime conflict. Although I agree with the ILC in not being alarmed, I shall explain why I reject some of their arguments about just how conflict of regime values is to be dealt with.

The first of Paulus's worries is that a specialized regime may commit itself to the promotion of a single value and ignore all others. As a matter of fact, I am unaware of any regime that operates this way; and so long as we focus on regimes created by states, there is every reason to expect regimes *not* to operate this way, since states, after all, have multiple interests and values. For example, the WTO explicitly recognizes the importance of the environment and various other non-trade values in the 'General Exceptions' articles of the General Agreement on Tariffs and Trade (GATT) and the General Agreement on Trade in Services (GATS), and elsewhere. (More on this in section IV.) Similarly, no international criminal court could rationally pursue conviction of criminals to the total exclusion of defendants' rights, since a major reason for having a court, as opposed to summary punishment, is to protect those rights. And so on.

Many authors, not satisfied with the empirical fact that extant regimes are not focused on a single value and are not likely to be, want to argue that as a conceptual

---

[12] There are other possible problems that have been discussed under the rubric of 'fragmentation', e.g. conflicting judgments by different international courts on what seems to be the identical legal point, or the possibility that a state will find itself subject to conflicting obligations under different regimes; but I shall limit myself to the issues about value conflict treated in the text.

[13] ILC, *Fragmentation of International Law: Difficulties Arising from the Diversification and Expansion of International Law* (Report of the Study Group of the International Law Commission), UN General Assembly A/CN.4/L.682, 13 Apr. 2006, paras. 492–3.

matter regimes *cannot* be focused on a single value, because they must be open to values embodied in general international law. The ILC Report, for example, argues that a regime based on an agreement between states gets its legitimacy from international law, and so it must acknowledge (and in particular, its dispute-settlement organs must acknowledge) whatever values international law says it must acknowledge.[14] But this does not seem to me right. To be sure, we normally think of the validity of agreements between states as grounded in international law. But the question is whether the regime *must* be viewed as grounded in this way. So far as I can see, the answer is no. Suppose we ask how international law itself is grounded—what is the source of its validity? There are two basic possibilities: (1) that international law is somehow self-subsistent, grounded in nothing more than its own constitutive set of practices and attitudes; or (2) that it is grounded in morality, or natural law, as that operates between states. But if either of these forms of grounding is available for international law as a general system, I see no reason why it should not be available for a narrower, specific regime as well. The regime might be self-subsistent, grounded simply in its own constitutive set of practices and attitudes; or it might be based directly on the inter-state morality of inter-state agreements, without the mediation of international law. If this is right, then there is no reason why a regime could not coherently and legitimately instruct its courts to consider only values recognized by the positive law of the regime itself (and perhaps also values whose consideration is required by international *morality*, which may or may not include even all of what is referred to as *jus cogens*), to the exclusion of other extra-regime values of international law.

A regime that instructs its courts to ignore extra-regime values is 'self-contained' in a certain sense, but why should we be troubled by the possibility of a regime that is self-contained in this sense?[15] We are focusing for the moment on state-created regimes, so if the regime is self-contained, it will be because the states that created it (who are the only states bound by its decisions) chose to create it that way. Why not assume they knew what they were doing? The one reason for doubt might be a suspicion that the states' right hands may not know what their left hands are doing. That is, there may be a trade treaty negotiated by trade ministers, and an environmental treaty negotiated by interior ministries or foreign ministries, and so on, with no real coordination between these governmental departments in any of the states. But even if this happens, the problem is a political failure within each state; it hardly seems that an international court, regime-based or otherwise, is the right place to look for a policy-based solution.

---

[14] e.g. ILC, *Fragmentation of International Law*, (above, n. 13) paras. 177, 193.
[15] I say 'self-contained in a certain sense' because there are various things we might mean by 'self-contained', some of which are acceptable even to the people who deny the possibility of self-containment in the present sense, and some of which even I would concede are conceptually impossible. My concern here is *only* with the sense of 'self-contained' I define in the text.

The ILC Report advances another argument to show that regime courts are required, in many instances, to take account of extra-regime values. This argument appeals to article 31.3 (c) of the Vienna Convention on the Law of Treaties (VCLT), which says that in interpreting a treaty, 'there shall be taken into account . . . any relevant rules of international law applicable in the relations between the parties'. Now, this does unquestionably require that non-regime values be taken into account in some cases (at least, if the regime follows the VCLT in interpreting the regime treaty). But just how broad the requirement is depends on a much-debated question about the meaning of the phrase 'the parties' in article 31.3 (c). Does this phrase refer to all parties to the treaty under interpretation, or does it refer only to the parties to the particular dispute in which the question of treaty interpretation has arisen? I shall refer to these two possibilities as the 'all parties' reading and the 'dispute parties' reading. The question which of these readings is correct may seem too recondite to discuss in the present context, but I want to pause over it, because doing so will reveal that there are a variety of ways in which 'other treaties' may be relevant to the interpretation of the primary treaty under interpretation. This is a point it is essential to keep in mind in a discussion of fragmentation.

Now, it seems to me that if we interpret the VCLT by VCLT principles, the 'ordinary meaning in context' of the phrase 'the parties' can only be 'the parties to the treaty', which is to say, all the parties. The use of the definite article 'the' implies that the relevant set of parties has already been identified, explicitly or implicitly, earlier in the text. No set of parties has been identified explicitly for purposes of article 31.3 (c), and the only set that can possibly have been identified implicitly is the set of all parties to the treaty. The set of parties cannot be the parties to 'the dispute', because there has been no reference to a dispute. Nor does article 31 presuppose the existence of a dispute. Article 31 is of course *relevant* to disputes, but what it is about in the first instance is how treaties shall be interpreted by states for purposes of self-application. If textual evidence for that claim is needed (aside from the absence of any reference to a dispute), consider the reference to 'good faith' in article 31.1, which would surely be superfluous if the primary addressees were courts.

Nonetheless, the ILC Report opts for the 'dispute parties' reading of article 31.3 (c), mainly because this reading will require other treaties to be considered more often than will the 'all parties' reading.[16] The ILC Report complains that if we adopt the 'all parties' reading, then 'the more the membership of a multilateral treaty such as the WTO covered agreements expanded, the more those treaties would be cut off from the rest of international law'.[17] But 'cut off' is much too strong. Even if article 31.3 (c) does not *require* a treaty to which only some members of the WTO are party to be taken into account in interpreting the WTO agreements, that does not mean that the treaty can have no possible relevance. Consider, for

---

[16] ILC, *Fragmentation of International Law* (above, n. 13), para. 472.   [17] Ibid., para. 471.

example, *US—Shrimp*.[18] In that case, the WTO Appellate Body referred to various environmental treaties in support of its finding that sea turtles were an 'exhaustible natural resource' under GATT article XX (g). The Appellate Body was not referring to those environmental treaties because of article 31.3 (c). It did not mention 31.3 (c) in this part of its opinion; and it plainly could not rely on 31.3 (c), even on the 'dispute parties' reading, because not even all parties to the *dispute* were parties to all the environmental treaties. Rather, the Appellate Body could only have been appealing to those environmental treaties as evidence concerning the understanding of the phrase 'natural resources' (and what it is for a resource to be 'exhaustible') that was 'in the air' when the WTO was being negotiated. This seems perfectly appropriate in the circumstances, even without complete identity of the parties. The environmental treaties are facts in the world, and they are being used just as factual evidence on the empirical question of the likely reference of a phrase in ordinary language. (As I shall explain in a moment, this is quite different from the role the environmental treaties would play if they came within article 31.3 (c).)

There are other ways as well that an extra-regime treaty might be relevant as evidence on an empirical question, even though it would not come within article 31.3 (c) on the 'all parties' reading or even the 'dispute parties' reading. For example (and still in the WTO context), it might be an issue whether a respondent Member really cares about turtles or is merely using an asserted concern for turtles as a cover for protectionism. In such a case, it would be relevant, although not dispositive, to learn from other treaties that many other states had manifested a concern for preserving turtles, regardless of the precise identity of the parties to those treaties. Or similarly, the existence of other treaties favouring or disfavouring particular shrimp-fishing techniques because of their effects on turtles might be significant evidence on the question whether some measure was 'relating to' turtle conservation, or whether it was 'necessary' to protect turtles. This is by no means an exhaustive list. Even for the WTO context, it is illustrative only. The general point, to repeat, is that even the 'all parties' reading of article 31.3 (c) will not cut off the courts interpreting the regime treaty from all consideration of other treaties.[19]

The reader may wonder why I want to insist on the 'all parties' reading of article 31.3 (c), since I am willing to admit the possible relevance of treaties that do not come within the article on this (or any) interpretation. The reason is that extra-regime treaties may be relevant in different ways, and we should be attentive to the question of what use may properly be made of those treaties in

---

[18] WTO, *United States—Import Prohibition of Certain Shrimp and Shrimp Products*, WT/DS58/AB/R (adopted 6 Nov. 1998).

[19] ILC, *Fragmentation of International Law* (above, n. 13). The ILC Report refers to the sort of arguments I have just suggested for the relevance of extra-regime treaties as 'contrived' (para. 450). I see nothing contrived about them. Of course, they would be contrived if they were offered in support of the wholesale relevance of extra-regime treaties that the ILC seems to favour. But as I explain in the continuation in the text, my point is precisely that extra-regime treaties may be relevant for different purposes in different circumstances. Such a view hardly seems to be a 'contrivance'.

various circumstances. As already noted, the uses of extra-regime treaties that I suggested above all involve considering the treaties as evidence on some *empirical* question—the meaning of some phrase in general contemporary usage, or the likely purposes of governments, or the usefulness or necessity of some particular measure to a putative goal. The extra-regime treaties are facts in the world, after all; and where they are relevant, just as such facts, as evidence on a disputed empirical question, it seems obviously proper for a regime court to consider them, regardless of identity of parties. Of course, the broader the membership of the extra-regime treaties, and the greater the overlap with the regime membership, the weightier evidence the extra-regime treaties will be on the sort of question I have mentioned. But identity of parties is not necessary for the treaties to be useful as *empirical* evidence.

In contrast, other uses of extra-regime treaties accord them *normative* significance. Even here, there are at least two cases to be distinguished: (1) If an extra-regime treaty is relevant to a dispute between two regime parties because of article 30 on successive treaties (which will be the case whenever the disputing regime parties are both party to the extra-regime treaty), then whether we are technically under article 30.3 or 30.4 (a), to the extent the treaties are incompatible, the later in time will control the dispute.[20] But article 30 is about the *application* of treaties, as its title makes clear. It presupposes that we have already determined, in accordance with the principles of article 31, what each treaty means; and then the question is whether there is a conflict between the requirements of the treaties, and if so, which should prevail. So, article 30 gives directions for dealing with a normative conflict between treaties, but it takes the normative requirements of each treaty individually as given. In contrast, (2) if we are in a situation where article 31.3 (c), under whatever reading we favour, requires some 'other treaty' to be taken into account in the interpretation of the primary treaty, then that other treaty exercises a sort of 'normative gravitational force' on the *meaning* of the primary treaty being interpreted. We should try to interpret the primary treaty so that it forms part of a coherent overall normative structure with the other treaty. This 'normative gravitational force' gives the other treaty a much stronger role in determining the meaning of the primary treaty than it has *either* when it is appealed to as evidence on some empirical issue *or* when we interpret the treaties separately and then apply the 'later in time' rule of article 30.[21]

---

[20] It may seem that this explicit endorsement of *lex posterior* when both treaties are relevant pays too little attention to arguments about *lex specialis* and *lex superior*, but we can build such considerations into the analysis of 'compatibility'.

[21] I have distinguished between cases where the issue is interpretation and cases where the issue is application. The ILC Report suggests that issues of interpretation and conflicts cannot be separated (para. 412). This is true, if the claim is that there are *some* cases where these issues cannot be separated, namely, cases where one treaty is subject to a 'normative drag' on its interpretation from another treaty coming under 31.3 (c). But still, the VCLT itself has distinct provisions on interpretation and application; it seems to presuppose, what also seems

Space limitations prevent me from giving an extended example to illustrate concretely the three ways we have now distinguished in which 'other treaties' may be relevant to the interpretation or application of a primary treaty. But to summarize: (1) The 'other treaty' may be appealed to purely as empirical evidence on some question relevant to the interpretation or application of the primary treaty. This use may well be appropriate even when some parties to the *dispute* are not parties to the 'other treaty'. (2) The 'other treaty' may be appealed to prevent the application of the primary treaty, if all parties to the dispute are also parties to the other treaty and the other treaty is incompatible with, and later in time than, the primary treaty. This is a normative use of the other treaty, and so it depends on the parties to the *dispute* being parties to the other treaty, but it does not require that all parties to the primary *treaty* be parties to the other treaty. The treaties should still be interpreted independently (unless all parties to the primary treaty are also parties to the other treaty). The reason for preferring the later treaty is not that the treaties are presumed to form a coherent whole, but is rather a version of estoppel (or a finding of bad faith, or *abus de droit*) against the party who tries to rely on the earlier treaty after signing the incompatible later one. Finally, (3) the 'other treaty' may be appealed to for its 'normative gravitational force' on the meaning of the primary treaty, which requires that the primary treaty be interpreted (if possible) so as to form a coherent normative whole with the other treaty. This is appropriate only where the parties to the primary treaty are all parties to the other treaty.

Whether or not the reader accepts all my claims about when various uses of the 'other treaty' are appropriate, I hope she will at least recognize that there are different uses, and that we need to attend to the question of what the right circumstances are for each use, instead of just discussing whether regime courts can/should/must look to extra-regime sources without distinguishing between possible uses.

IV. Fragmentation and the WTO: Example or Counter-Example?

In this last section, I want to consider briefly four suggestions that one encounters in discussions of fragmentation: (1) that specialized regimes recognize only one 'regime' value; (2) that even if a regime court considers other values than its own regime value, it will inevitably be biased in favour of the regime value (for example, by construing narrowly treaty exceptions in favour of non-regime values); (3) that what is needed is greater sensitivity on the part of regime courts to values from elsewhere in international law; and (4) that if such extra-regime values are

obviously true, that there are cases where the interpretation of each of two treaties can be settled before issues of conflict or application arise.

recognized, the court will be required to 'balance' the regime value(s) and the extra-regime values. I shall not attempt a general discussion, but since the WTO is often pressed into service as an example for these various claims—both as illustrating a problem under (1) and (2) and sometimes as illustrating a possible solution under (3) and (4)—I want to consider briefly what the WTO experience really indicates. Incidentally, although Paulus refers to the WTO more than once, and my comments are partly stimulated by his references, my comments should not be taken as directed at Paulus's claims specifically, since I do not want to discuss just how far he is committed to each of the four propositions. Now, as to the propositions and the WTO:

(1) It is not true that the WTO recognizes only the value of promoting trade. As the Appellate Body reminds us in *Shrimp*, the Preamble to the WTO Agreement makes specific reference to the value of the environment, via the phrase 'sustainable development'. In addition, GATT article XX and GATS article XIV (both entitled 'General Exceptions') recognize a number of non-trade values that can justify national measures that would otherwise violate the GATT or GATS—including 'public morals' (which the Appellate Body has signalled it will interpret very generously),[22] 'human, animal or plant life or health', 'protection of national treasures of artistic, historic, or archaeological value' (in GATT), and 'privacy' (in GATS).[23] Similarly, there are references to the environment and other non-trade values in the Technical Barriers to Trade Agreement, the Sanitary and Phytosanitary Measures Agreement (SPS), the Agriculture Agreement, and so on. There is a sense in which the core purpose of the GATT was, and the core purpose of the WTO is, to promote trade. But we must be careful how we understand this claim. There is nothing in the texts to suggest that trade is valued in such a way that more trade is always better. The focus of the system is not on increasing trade by forbidding or even disfavouring all national measures that reduce trade. Rather, the focus is on restraining or eliminating *certain sorts* of national measures that *distort* trade. Some of the measures that are forbidden are in fact trade-*promoting*, as in the case of export subsidies. There is much controversy, to be sure, about what amounts to a 'distortion', and trade experts sometimes speak as if any reduction of trade is a distortion. But wiser heads have always rejected such a view. And to repeat, there is nothing to suggest such a 'trade above all' view in the WTO texts.

(2) The WTO is also a counter-example to the claim of inevitable bias on the part of regime courts in favour of the 'regime value'. It is true that many GATT Panels

---

[22] See WTO, *United States—Measures Affecting the Cross-Border Supply of Gambling and Betting Services*, WT/DS285/AB/R (adopted 20 Apr. 2005).

[23] In my own view (admittedly not uncontroversial), a proper interpretation of the basic prohibitory provisions of the GATT and GATS imposes essentially no limit on the purposes that can be pursued by Member States, even at the cost of a reduction in trade, provided the measures are facially neutral and not adopted with a protectionist purpose (and in the case of GATS, do not involve quotas).

(from the days before the formation of the WTO) seemed to be biased in favour of trade. The worst examples are the two *Tuna-Dolphin* cases, which unfortunately are all that many people know about the WTO (even to the exclusion of the Appellate Body's very different treatment of the same basic problem in *Shrimp*). The *Tuna-Dolphin* reports were indefensible, but they were not adopted by the Contracting Parties to the GATT and never became part of the GATT *acquis*. Even under the GATT, some Panels were considerably more sensitive to non-trade values, although I would not contest the claim that overall, GATT Panels showed an unfortunate pro-trade bias. But with the advent of the WTO and the Appellate Body, things have changed dramatically.

The Appellate Body cannot plausibly be accused of trade bias. Of course there are particular decisions of the Appellate Body that environmentalists and other sections of the global audience loudly disapprove of—most salient is *EC-Hormones*.[24] But on the whole (and even in *Hormones*) the Appellate Body has done a remarkably fair-minded job of interpreting and applying the WTO treaties, which as I have explained are *not* essentially biased in favour of trade. There is a great deal in *Hormones* that is very regulator-friendly: for example, the Appellate Body holds that a Member need not do required risk assessments itself, but can rely on risk assessments carried out by others; it says that the risk assessment can be in qualitative terms rather than quantitative; it says a goal of zero-risk is acceptable (provided the risk in question is not purely 'theoretical'); it says a Member can rely on respectable *minority* scientific opinion; and more. The problem in *Hormones* was that for some aspects of the EC regulations, there simply were no supporting risk assessments at all as required by the SPS. The EC tried unsuccessfully to excuse this lack by appeal to the 'precautionary principle'; but in a peculiar argumentative move, the EC refused to rely on the particular provision of the SPS that explicitly embodies a version of the precautionary principle. Even *Hormones* is no real evidence of trade bias in the Appellate Body.

I cannot discuss here all the Appellate Body's decisions that touch on the environment or other values. But let me point out that two important recent cases are counter-examples to the specific claim that exceptions in favour of non-trade values will be construed narrowly. In *US—Shrimp* the Appellate Body was interpreting the 'General Exceptions' article of the GATT when it eventually upheld the United States' revised import ban on shrimp harvested with turtle-endangering methods;[25] and in *US—Gambling*, the Appellate Body treated as matters of 'public morals' under the 'General Exceptions' article of the GATS: preventing under-age gambling, preventing compulsive gambling, preventing fraud, and preventing

---

[24] WTO, *EC—Measures Concerning Meat and Meat Products (Hormones)*, WT/DS26&48/AB/R (adopted 13 Feb. 1998).
[25] WTO, *United States—Import Prohibition of Certain Shrimp and Shrimp Products (Recourse to Article 21.5)*, WT/DS58/AB/RW (adopted 21 Nov. 2001).

money-laundering. Indeed, the Appellate Body has explicitly rejected the idea that exceptions are to be read narrowly. It has said, quite correctly, that exceptions are as essential to the structure of the treaty as any other provisions, and they are to be read in the same way as other provisions.[26] It is striking that the greater legalization of the dispute-settlement process that was part of the establishment of the WTO in 1995 has led to *reduced* trade bias in decisions made under a treaty that is portrayed as being all about promoting trade. But to my mind this makes perfect sense. Much more than under GATT, dispute settlement is now about serious interpretation of the treaty by traditional means. What is being revealed is that the treaty was never the pure pro-trade instrument of the trade-sceptic's horror story.[27]

(3) Is the sensitivity of the Appellate Body to non-trade values the result of their taking into account the normative demands of extra-regime treaties, either in interpretation or application of the WTO agreements? So far as I can see, the answer is no. I have already argued that in *Shrimp*, when the Appellate Body refers to other treaties in connection with the interpretation of the phrase 'exhaustible natural resources', it is using those treaties only as evidence on an empirical question. That is, it is treating them as facts in the world, not as sources of relevant norms. It is also often suggested that in a different part of the *Shrimp* opinion, the Appellate Body relies on normative support from other environmental treaties to find a duty to negotiate. Just what the Appellate Body says about negotiation is far from clear, and this is not the place for an extended discussion. My own view is that they do not find a duty to negotiate at all, but only a duty not to *discriminate* by negotiating with some affected countries and not others. (They may also have in mind a slightly different non-discrimination duty, as explained in the next footnote.) The central point in favour of this reading is that the bit of article XX that the Appellate Body finds the United States has run afoul of is about 'unjustifiable discrimination'. This treaty language simply would not support a finding of an unconditional duty to negotiate. And if the Appellate Body did not find a duty to negotiate, they can hardly have relied on other treaties in finding such a duty.[28]

---

[26] WTO, *EC—Measures Affecting Asbestos and Asbestos-Containing Products*, WT/DS135/AB/R (adopted 5 Apr. 2001).

[27] Arguably, one of the reasons for the decline in trade bias was that the early Appellate Body members were not all trade lawyers, but included general international lawyers and an EU lawyer. But to my mind, the reason this was important is not the greater sensitivity of these members to extra-regime values as such, but rather their greater attention to what the WTO agreements themselves actually said about non-trade values.

[28] This does leave the question of why the Appellate mentions the other treaties at all—and frankly I am not certain there is an explanation that makes the reference to the other treaties anything more than window-dressing. The best explanation I can think of is that the other treaties confirmed the empirical usefulness of talking to other countries about what techniques of turtle protection were needed in different shrimping grounds. This is relevant because the Appellate Body opinion suggests that perhaps the failure to negotiate with Malaysia was not just illegal because of the more favourable negotiation treatment of the Caribbean countries, but also because the failure to 'negotiate' at least to the extent of exchanging technical information exacerbated the distinct discrimination (according to the Appellate Body) involved in requiring Malaysia to use a turtle-protection

(4) Finally, does the Appellate Body in *Shrimp* balance the value of the environment against the value of trade? No, it does not. It does not even claim to.[29] If the Appellate Body is balancing any value against the value of trade, it is not the value of the environment, but rather the value of national regulatory autonomy—which the United States is using in this case to protect the environment, but which is hardly the same thing. But I would say they are not balancing at all; they are simply interpreting the limits on national regulatory autonomy in the treaty. To see that the Appellate Body does not balance the environment and trade, observe that they do not impose any conclusion of their own about the proper 'balance' on any Member. Rather, they leave it up to each member to balance for itself in respect of its own production and its imports. On the one hand, the Appellate Body eventually upholds the United States' revised turtle-protective import regulations; but on the other hand, it does *not* require Malaysia to adopt turtle-protective shrimping techniques, nor could it conceivably do so under the agreements. Indeed, by apparently requiring the United States to offer shipment-by-shipment certification for shrimp from non-certified countries, the Appellate Body carefully guarantees that Malaysia can *both* sell turtle-friendly shrimp into the United States market (if it so chooses) *and* continue to harvest shrimp by turtle-hostile techniques for its own or third country markets. So, the Appellate Body never chooses for itself between trade and the environment. It finds (correctly) that the treaty leaves the choice up to each Member in its treaty-defined sphere.

Paulus suggests that in cases of value conflict, we cannot fully trust regime courts. Even if they appear to take account of extra-regime values, he still wants them to be supervised by extra-regime international courts as 'neutral arbiters' between the competing values and the associated interests.[30] In other words, faced with a conflict between trade and the environment, for example, Paulus wants to move 'upwards' from the WTO to a systematic international law. In fact, as we see in *Shrimp*, we move 'downwards' from the WTO back to the several Member states (whose choices remain subject, of course, to the WTO's various non-discrimination principles and the like).

In the WTO context, this 'downwards move' is the right move, even though it would not be in many other contexts. The WTO is a very distinctive regime, not

---

technique that was actually unnecessary in the waters their shrimpers frequented. Still, there is no evidence at all that the Appellate Body found a duty to negotiate in other treaties and imported it into the WTO, or even that they gave any *normative* weight to the other treaties.

[29] The Appellate Body does talk about balancing, but what it claims to balance is the complaining member's 'rights' against the respondent member's duties. (para. 156 ff.) Even this talk of balancing is logically inappropriate, since the only rights created by the WTO agreements are the Hohfeldian correlates of the duties the agreements impose on other member countries, and such correlates obviously cannot be 'balanced' against each other. (The agreements may create some non-correlative rights like the right to invoke the dispute-settlement process, but that is clearly a different sort of issue.)

[30] Paulus, A., this volume, 214.

so much because it is devoted to the value of trade, which we have seen is true in only a limited sense, but because the only national laws it purports to constrain are laws that directly affect trade. Its specific concern is with those laws' trade effects, which consist of allowing or prohibiting market transactions. This is quite unlike international environmental law, say, which concerns itself with physical cross-border effects that are not market-mediated. Such physical effects may result from behavior undertaken for commercial purposes, but the effects themselves move independently of any market transactions. Effluents dumped into a river by an upstream country affect the downstream country even if the countries have no trading relationship. It is the WTO's focus on market-mediated effects that makes the 'downwards move' apt, although I have no space for a full explanation here.[31] That also means, of course, that the downwards move is not a solution for the problems of many other international regimes.

So, I am not holding up the WTO as a model of how all regimes should operate. But since the WTO often appears in discussions of fragmentation, it seems desirable to understand how it actually operates. Also, the Appellate Body's 'judicial restraint' with regard to balancing competing values may be suggestive for other areas. Many writers move too easily from the premise that we need a lot more effective international law than we currently have, which is certainly true, to the problematic conclusion that since no other institution is currently able to give it to us, judges should step in to supply our need.

---

[31] See Regan, D., 'What Are Trade Agreements For?—Two Conflicting Stories Told by Economists, With a Lesson for Lawyers', *Journal of International Economic Law*, 9/4 (2006), 951.

SECTION VI

SOVEREIGNTY

CHAPTER 11

THE LOGIC OF
FREEDOM AND POWER

TIMOTHY ENDICOTT[*]

I. INTRODUCTION

State sovereignty may seem to be necessarily unjust, or to be incompatible with the existence of international law, or to be incoherent. Sovereignty, it seems, is:

- absolute power within a community, and
- absolute independence externally, and
- full power as a legal person in international law.

The first two of those traits seem necessarily unjust, as they imply a power to abuse people with impunity. Norms of *ius cogens*[1] seem to be incompatible with state sovereignty, and therefore international law seems to be incompatible with state sovereignty.

And absolute independence seems to be an incoherent idea. Can the state bind itself? If the state has absolute independence, then the answer must be 'no'. But if the state has the capacity to act as a legal person in international law, it seems that the answer must be 'yes' (or it would be incapable of entering into treaties). So,

---

[*] I am grateful for comments from the editors, from participants in this volume, and from Anne Peters.

[1] A norm of *ius cogens* or a 'peremptory norm' is 'a norm accepted and recognized by the international community of states as a whole as a norm from which no derogation is permitted and which can be modified only by a subsequent norm of general international law having the same character'. Vienna Convention on the Law of Treaties (1969), art. 53 (providing that a treaty is void if it conflicts with such a norm when concluded). The rule against wars of aggression is an example.

state sovereignty seems both to demand the power to enter into treaties, and to rule out the binding force of treaties.

These paradoxes may seem to make international law impossible, if states are to be sovereign—or to make sovereignty impossible, if there is to be any international law.[2] And the problem of injustice may seem to imply that international law ought to oppose the sovereignty of states. I will argue that state sovereignty is coherent in conception, that it is compatible with international law, and that it is a valuable feature of states in the international order.

II. The Paradox of Freedom

To be free is not to be bound. In a sense, then, a state is not free if it is bound by treaties. Yet a state would be constrained by a severe disability if it lacked the capacity to pursue its purposes by entering into treaties. It would lack a power that makes states what they are—a power that is linked to its power within the community itself, and that is one of the chief incidents of personality in international law.

So, can a *sovereign* state bind itself? Yes!—so it seems—or it suffers a disability that is incompatible with the sovereign power of a state in the international order. But no!—so it seems—because being bound means that it is not independent, and therefore that it is not sovereign.

To clear up this puzzle as to whether sovereignty demands that a state be bound by treaties or that it not be bound by treaties, consider the difficulties that philosophers have had in working out whether human freedom demands or forbids the power to bind oneself.[3] The logical structure of the paradox of freedom is the same in the

---

[2] Scholars of international law have often addressed this problem and related problems in understanding sovereignty, and have concluded that the idea has to be abandoned as a myth or confusion. For a review, see the discussion of the 'sovereignty dilemma' in Klabbers, J., 'Clinching the Concept of Sovereignty: Wimbledon Redux', *Austrian Review of International and European Law*, 3 (1999), 345–67. The 'dilemma' is this: 'can the existence of rules binding upon states be reconciled with the very notion of sovereignty?', 348. Some have tried to resolve the dilemma by treating the sovereign state as the source of international law, preceding the law and capable of suspending it (see e.g. Paul Kahn's discussion of Carl Schmitt's views in Kahn, P. W., 'The Question of Sovereignty', *Stanford Journal of International Law*, 40 (2004), 259, 263). That resolution fails for reasons that H. L. A. Hart gave in *The Concept of Law* (Oxford: Clarendon, 1962) in the course of debunking John Austin's idea that the domestic law of a state is a set of commands of a legally absolute and unlimited sovereign. On Hart's views concerning sovereignty in international law, see n. 20 below.

[3] For another argument that 'sovereignty (conceptually) must be limited', see Shue, H., 'Limiting Sovereignty', in Welsh, J. M. (ed.), *Humanitarian Intervention and International Relations* (Oxford: Oxford University Press, 2004), 16. Shue's convincing argument is based on two related insights: (i) that the nature of sovereignty as a right of states implies correlative (and otherwise related) duties of states, so that sovereignty would be incoherent if it were conceptualized as freedom from duty (13–15), and (ii) that the principle of non-intervention both protects state sovereignty and also limits state sovereignty (14). So he concludes that 'attempts to state a doctrine of sovereignty without limits turn out to be quite literally incoherent' (13).

case of persons as in the case of states. The solutions to the paradoxes differ in the two cases, as radically as persons differ from states. But the analogy can help us to see how to resolve the paradox in the case of states.

The solutions in the two cases demand an understanding of what it takes for a person to lead a good life, and for a state to be a good state. A person is autonomous (sovereign—in a sense—over his own life) if his freedom is complete for the purposes of leading a good life. A state is sovereign if it has power over the community, and power and independence in external affairs that are complete for the purposes of a good state.

III. MILL ON CONTRACTS OF SLAVERY

Concerning human freedom, John Stuart Mill proposed an absolute principle:

That the only purpose for which power can be rightfully exercised over any member of a civilized community, against his will, is to prevent harm to others. His own good, either physical or moral, is not a sufficient warrant.[4]

The legal enforcement of a contract entails an exercise of power over members of the community against their will, to require them to perform certain agreements (or to compensate other parties for breach). Mill favoured the enforceability of contracts.[5] We can reconcile it with his harm principle, if the breach of a contract harms the other party. But why call it a harm, rather than a failure to confer a benefit?[6] Suppose that we agree that I will sell you my car. I refuse to deliver it when I realize that I could have got a better price, but I return the purchase monies you paid me. What harm have I done you? Mill did not explain. He pointed out that the liberty of the individual 'implies a corresponding liberty in any number of individuals to regulate by mutual agreement such things as regard them jointly', and he suggested that contract law is a necessity, because the will of the parties to such agreements 'may change'. But if a party's will changes between the time when the agreement is made and the time for performance, what justifies an interference with their liberty at the time for performance?

Now suppose that there is a good answer to that question. What of slavery agreements?[7] Mill favoured the English legal doctrine (but of course, it is not

---

[4] Mill, J. S., *On Liberty* (1869), ch. 1, <http://www.bartleby.com/130/1.html>. All websites most recently checked in Nov. 2009.

[5] Ibid., ch. 5, 'it is fit, as a general rule, that those engagements should be kept'.

[6] To be more precise, I am asking why contract remedies are designed to put the innocent party in the same position as if the contract had been performed, rather than merely to give restitution of benefits received for which consideration was not actually given, or to compensate for detrimental reliance on a promise.

[7] Assume genuine, informed agreement, without an inequality of bargaining power that would make it unconscionable for a party to seek to enforce the agreement (if these assumptions are untenable—because,

distinctively English), that they are unenforceable.[8] But if it is compatible with liberty to enforce my agreements, then it seems that entering into an agreement is an exercise of my liberty. And then, isn't my liberty curtailed if the law will not enforce my agreement to serve as a slave? Mill rationalized the law in a paradoxical fashion:

The reason for not interfering, unless for the sake of others, with a person's voluntary acts, is consideration for his liberty. His voluntary choice is evidence that what he so chooses is desirable, or at the least endurable, to him, and his good is on the whole best provided for by allowing him to take his own means of pursuing it. But by selling himself for a slave, he abdicates his liberty; he foregoes any future use of it beyond that single act. He therefore defeats, in his own case, the very purpose which is the justification of allowing him to dispose of himself. . . . The principle of freedom cannot require that he should be free not to be free. It is not freedom, to be allowed to alienate his freedom.[9]

But I am allowed to alienate my freedom to use my car. If we do have liberty to regulate our affairs by mutual agreement, and the regulation is to be enforceable against my will, why are we not to have the liberty to regulate our affairs by agreeing that I will be your slave? If it is freedom to be able to *bind* myself to deliver my car to the purchaser (with the resultant loss of freedom after I agree), why is it not freedom to be allowed to bind myself to be a slave (with the resultant loss of freedom after I agree)?

Mill deprives himself of any answer to these questions. Should we say that the slavery contract is different from the car sale contract because it would deprive me of *too much* freedom? Yes, of course. But the application of Mill's 'absolute' liberty principle cannot turn on the question of *how much* freedom a contract would take away. And if we say that slavery deprives me of too much freedom (whereas selling my car only deprives me of a little freedom), we have given no good explanation of the difference. Being bound by my agreement is not like a minor dose of slavery. If you kidnap me for an hour, I lose a little freedom and my autonomy is diminished a little. Being bound by my agreement to sell my car is different: it is an aspect of a normative ordering of our lives that *enhances* my autonomy. My life is more my own to live, because of my ability to bind myself to perform agreements.[10]

We might be tempted to conclude that the idea of human freedom is incoherent, because it demands freedom to enter into binding agreements, and it also demands

e.g., no one would actually agree without such an inequality unless affected by some condition that diminishes responsibility—that will not affect the argument, but will only mean that there are additional reasons for slavery agreements to be unenforceable).

[8] See the uncontested remarks of counsel in *Somerset v. Stewart* (1772), Lofft 1, 3.

[9] Mill, J. S., *On Liberty* (above, n. 4).

[10] So minors suffer a disability, in virtue of their incapacity to enter into agreements that are binding *per se* in English law. The disability is correlative to the lack of autonomy that the law ascribes to them.

that no one should be a slave, so that if a person agrees to slavery, freedom both demands that the agreement be enforced, and demands that it not be enforced. To be free to enter into a slavery contract (or a contract to sell a car) is freedom in a sense, and to be free not to serve as a slave (or to deliver the car), even after having agreed to do so, is freedom in a sense.

Achieving a coherent understanding of human freedom requires us to choose between such contradictory freedoms. We need to do what Mill thought that we should not do: ask which freedoms would be good for a person's life. It would be incoherent to set out to attain freedom as such: that would require us to seek freedom to enter into contracts and freedom not to perform a contract, both. Freedom is not, in itself, an unequivocal good. Lawmakers need to judge which forms of freedom are conducive to a good life.

IV. WHICH FREEDOMS ARE FOR THE GOOD OF PERSONS?

This complex, difficult question is, in some particular respects, straightforward. We only need to consider what freedoms you and I need for living a good life. It is right, as Mill suggests, for the law to enforce a contract to sell a car (even if the vendor has made a bad deal), and not to enforce contracts of slavery. I do not simply lose *more freedom* if I sell myself into slavery, than if I sell my car. In order to lead a decent life, I need a continuing freedom to choose a calling in life, and freedom to integrate my work life with the rest of my life, and to develop relationships that may be incompatible with slavery. I may have many other needs that are incompatible with slavery, and needs that are incompatible with carrying the *label* of 'slave'. I need to be able to engage in relationships with other human beings without a form of domination that is degrading in its abolition of time that is my own. The choice to enslave myself by agreement does not call for state enforcement, because state enforcement of such an agreement would not help me to exercise my autonomy for my good.[11]

By contrast, the law can facilitate my ability to lead my own life, by treating me as capable of binding myself to deliver my car to you. That capacity enables

---

[11] I am ignoring various complex further aspects of good legal policy in contract law doctrine. There can be other reasons for refusing to enforce contracts of slavery, such as a precautionary approach to a danger of undue influence that the law cannot control, and the same sort of welfare concerns that motivate regulation of working time, and a concern to abolish traditional abusive status roles of groups in a society. But the concern not to lend coercive state enforcement to a degrading and potentially destructive relation of dominance is always enough to justify unenforceability.

people to enter into transactions not merely relying on recouping an investment, but also counting on a profit on an investment—so that we can use the system for speculation in a way that improves commerce for my good and for yours,[12] and it enables us to plan cooperative enterprises with an expectation of performance.

The essential task for the law is to discern the difference between choices that must not be treated as binding if I am to lead a good life, and choices that I ought to be held to when I agree to them. That judgment is to be made by the lawmaker, and it cannot be made by leaving it to the subject of the law to decide his or her own good. A satisfactory explanation of human freedom must pass judgment on the various ostensible goods that a person may desire. Enforcing agreements for the sale of goods is sound legal policy, because freedom to enter into such contracts (entailing the obligation to perform) is valuable to the subjects of the law.[13] Refusing to enforce slavery contracts is good legal policy because of the would-be slave's own good, which according to Mill 'is not sufficient warrant for interfering with him'.

The most poignant support for this approach to the paradox of freedom lies in the implications of Mill's formulation that 'The principle of freedom cannot require that he should be free not to be free'.[14] That cannot be a general maxim. Any account of the liberty that persons ought to have must make room for freedom to sacrifice one's freedom. Such decisions are never, of course, made in complete freedom, because they arise as a response to dangers or catastrophes or dire needs from which the willing agent might well wish that he or she were free. But the choice to pursue a course that will deprive me of all freedom—leaving me a hostage, a prisoner for life, a slave, or dead—can be a true expression of my own independence and autonomy as a person. The freedom to make such a choice may be crucial to my responsibility for my own life. Then, it would be vicious to interfere with my freedom to sacrifice my freedom. Not that all forms of self-sacrifice deserve respect from lawmakers, or assistance from the law. The rule against enforcing voluntary slavery agreements is legitimate if (as I think) it is right for a state to deny you and me that particular avenue for self-sacrifice.

It is not freedom in itself but autonomy—the capacity[15] for leading one's own life—that is valuable. As Joseph Raz put it, 'Autonomous persons are those who

---

[12] Improving commerce helps the people of a community in a fragmentary fashion; I won't deal here with the problems of social justice that (1) are not solved and may be worsened by thriving commerce, and (2) may have crucial implications for the content of a just scheme of contract law.

[13] The reasons are actually more complex, although the value mentioned here is essential to any sound explanation of the legitimacy of contract law.

[14] Mill, J. S., *On Liberty* (above, n. 4).

[15] Autonomy is in one sense a capacity; the exercise of the capacity, too, is itself autonomy in another sense.

can shape their life and determine its course'.[16] There are various incompatible freedoms, and a coherent political theory needs to choose among them; it should promote those freedoms that are conducive to autonomy and to other human goods. And although personal autonomy implies freedom to make bad choices, autonomy 'is valuable only if exercised in pursuit of the good'.[17]

Personal autonomy is compatible with subjection to law. It is compatible with the obligation not to murder, and with the enforcement of laws against murder. And it is compatible both with the enforceability of sales of goods in contract law, and the unenforceability of slavery contracts. These very ordinary insights have no basis without an assessment of which freedoms are necessary for a good life.

Since authority is not necessarily incompatible with autonomy, it may seem tempting to think that authority only becomes incompatible with autonomy when it is illegitimate in scope, or is abused in practice, and that an authority has legitimate jurisdiction only to impose norms that are compatible with their subjects' autonomy. But that is not right: a child's lack of autonomy is strictly correlative to her parents' legitimate authority over her.[18] For the present purpose only the following programmatic maxims are necessary or defensible: authority and autonomy are not incompatible; illegitimate claims of authority and the abuse of authority are inimical to autonomy; a lack of autonomy may reflect a need for the service that an authority can provide, in offering direction that a more fully autonomous person would not need; human autonomy requires the capacity for forms of self-direction that are essential for a person to lead a good life for himself or herself.

The goods that autonomy may justifiably be used to pursue are plural and incommensurable. Potential forms of freedom are diverse and uncountable. For these reasons, the content of human autonomy is *various*. That is, it can come in various forms that are neither more nor less complete than each other. We could say that there is no such thing as complete human autonomy,[19] or that complete human freedom is compatible with a vast diversity of forms of constraint. If any form of human autonomy deserves to be called complete, there is a vast diversity of such forms. Human autonomy is, in particular, compatible with a vast diversity of legal regimes. And human autonomy is *vague*: there is no precise answer to the question of how autonomous a person is, or to the question of which forms of freedom, in which amounts, are necessary for autonomy.

[16] Raz, J., *The Morality of Freedom* (Oxford: Oxford University Press, 1986), 154.

[17] Ibid. 381.

[18] See Endicott, T., 'Interpretation, Jurisdiction, and Authority', *American Philosophical Association Newsletter*, 6 (2007), 14.

[19] As Joseph Raz does: 'Autonomy is possible only within a framework of constraints. The completely autonomous person is an impossibility'. Raz, J., *The Morality of Freedom* (above, n. 16), 155.

V. The Content of State Sovereignty

The analogy with personal autonomy shows how to resolve the paradox of freedom in the case of states. It would be incoherent to say that sovereignty demands absolute independence. It would be true to say that sovereignty is lost if the state is subject to *too much* regulation by international law and to too much external constraint. But that would offer no explanation of what it takes for a state to be sovereign.

H. L. A. Hart very effectively opposed 'the *a priori* argument which attempts to deduce the general character of international law from an absolute sovereignty, which is assumed, without reference to international law, to belong to states'.[20] He opposed 'the theory that states are subject only to rules which they have . . . imposed on themselves', and he argued that international law consists entirely of customary rules treated as binding in the international community, and rules validated by such rules. The binding force of treaties depends on '*rules* . . . providing that a state is bound to do whatever it undertakes'[21] in a treaty. He insisted, with his generous share of common sense, that if a state's sovereignty is *limited* by rules of international law, it can still be sovereign.[22] The result is that in his view, a state is a form of ordering according to law of a population inhabiting a territory, with 'a vaguely defined degree of independence'.[23]

This is all good sense, and it is consistent with a resolution of the paradox of freedom. But while it is an important truth that the degree of independence needed for sovereignty is only vaguely defined, I think that we can say more than that. We can say what defines it.

State sovereignty is a complex of various forms of power and independence that is complete for the purposes of states. In the case of states, the resolution of the paradox of freedom lies in an identification of those powers and forms of independence. The purposes of states are identical with the purposes that a good state actually pursues. So the content of sovereignty is determined by the powers and the forms of independence that a state needs *in order to be a good state*. It won't quite be possible to explain what counts as a good state in the following, but we can start.

VI. The Concept of the State

The state (in the relevant sense of the word) is that which issues passports. An explanation of the nature of a passport would convey much of what it takes to

---

[20] Hart, H. L. A., *The Concept of Law* (2nd edn., Oxford: Oxford University Press, 1994), 223.
[21] Ibid. 224.   [22] Ibid. 223.   [23] Ibid. 221.

understand the nature of states. Not that there is any conceptual necessity to the existence of passports; like states, they are a social arrangement that people happen to have adopted to accomplish purposes that might reasonably have been pursued in other ways (and other purposes might reasonably have been pursued). The purposes of states in issuing passports have sometimes been perverse, but they are capable of being just.

The issuance of a passport is an act by which a state implicates itself in a network of relationships that makes the state what it is. As the entity that issues the passport, the state relates itself to:

- persons eligible for passports
- the person who holds a particular passport
- persons who have no passport
- the territory of which the passport holder is a national
- states to which the passport holder may travel.

The state is the organization capable of (and responsible for) carrying on relations, in respect of a territory, with the people (or peoples) of that territory (including the relations that entitle those people to enter the territory as nationals). It carries on relations in respect of a territory (relations that include exclusion and admission of visitors, and immigration control) with people from other territories. And finally, it is capable of (and responsible for) carrying on relations with states. Passports function in a community of states, and it is an essential feature of a state that it is able to relate to other states, and to do so in respect of a territory and its people. Each of these relations reflects an essential feature of the state. It is the political organization in a territory that can exercise responsibility toward and for the people of the territory in respect of their relations with other territories and their peoples. That capacity implies internal power, for the responsibility for relations with other states cannot be well discharged by a political entity that has no responsibility for or capacity to control the internal affairs of a polity.

State sovereignty is not an incoherent pseudo-complex of paradoxically unlimited freedoms and powers. It is the complex of powers and independence that is involved in issuing passports. Needless to say, there is more to the good state than the issuing of passports. But the connection between passports and states indicates what states ought to do well. A good state does not only treat the people of the territory justly. It acts justly in identifying membership in the community, it exercises responsibility for the community in a territory, and it acts justly on behalf of the community toward other states in international relations, and toward individuals with no passport.

VII. What Powers and Freedoms Does a State Need in Order to be a Good State?

A political community is a form of relationship among the people of a territory. The state has responsibility for a community (that is, responsibility for a relationship among the people of its territory), and for peace, order, and good government within the community. And the state has responsibility to act as a member of the international community. A good state is one that carries out these responsibilities well. To carry out its responsibility to act as a member of the international community, the state needs full personality in international law. That is, it needs to be able to participate in international affairs in a way that is determined by and regulated by international law for its purpose of promoting the common good in international relations—a purpose that requires norms of international law that accomplish justice (at least, justice in those limited aspects that can be accomplished by law) and support order and peace, and enable coordination among states for shared good purposes. The resulting form of personhood in international law includes the capacity to enter into treaties, though it need not include the capacity to be bound by, for example, a treaty of subjugation—or by any treaty that need not be regarded as valid in order for international affairs to be subject to the rule of law.

So in order to be sovereign, a state needs:

1. power to regulate the life of the community
2. the freedom from external interference that is necessary for (1)
3. full personhood in international law.

The idea of sovereignty is coherent because these needs are compatible with each other, and capable of being met (and it happens to be the case that they are met—variably but substantially—by very many states today, and even by states subject to unjust regimes). Treaties could violate sovereignty, and so could rules that are treated by the international community as *ius cogens*, but neither sort of rules does so just in virtue of imposing obligations.

Suppose that the people of Iceland woke up one day and found that the rest of the world was covered by ocean, apart from their island. All their treaties would be frustrated, and they would be freed from all obligations under international law. They would gain freedoms they do not have today. But their nation's sovereignty would not be enhanced; it would become meaningless.

Sovereignty is potentially valuable, because it can serve the good of persons (within the state and outside the state): it can protect a community from aggression, and enable its people to act justly and effectively in international trade, and sovereignty itself can have good symbolic effects, such as to indicate the capacity of a people or of a nation to act as a responsible community. And so on. But of course, a state may not actually act for those various goods; sovereignty only gives a state freedom and power. Many states neglect to use their freedom and their power for good purposes, and many states abuse their power. So why conclude that sovereignty *is* valuable?

VIII. The Value of Sovereignty

State sovereignty is valuable in international law and international relations for (at least) three interrelated reasons. First, it is part of a just answer to the question of personhood in international law (because it offers a technique for the people of any territory to participate in international relations in a way that is regulated and facilitated by international law[24]). Secondly, state sovereignty is valuable in so far as there is value in national self-determination (the capacity of a nation[25] to make decisions—good or bad—(within limits) for itself). Thirdly, the very substantial independence involved in state sovereignty is valuable because:

1. Other states and non-state organizations tend to be less good than the state at judging the purposes the state ought to pursue.
2. Other states and non-state organizations are not generally good at interfering with the state.

These virtues of state sovereignty can be compared to the virtues of relative independence of local and regional governments within a state. Subsidiarity is the principle that informs them. But subsidiarity has a more radically important value in international law, than in domestic law.

The role of Parliament in Westminster is subsidiary to the institutions of the town of Bicester, and the lawmaking institutions of the European Union are subsidiary to both; decisions about the opening hours of the public library in Bicester should not be taken over by Parliament or the EU, if they can be made more effectively in light of all the relevant considerations by the Bicester town council (which itself should leave them to the library board unless it can do better).

Why is subsidiarity a more radically important value in international law? Sovereignty is valuable to the British State, whereas it would not be valuable to the town of Bicester. The role of international organizations is more radically subsidiary

---

[24] I mean to imply nothing about the legal personality of organizations other than states in international law; there may be good reason for such personality in a variety of forms.

[25] But we might include the potential value in self-determination of forms of community other than nations; this is not the place for any attempt to work out the nature of nations (or to specify what other forms of community might justly form the substratum of a state). I am grateful to John Tasioulas for pointing out that state sovereignty may have a value in giving effect to self-determination that is distinct from (though related to) the values, discussed in the text below, that are based on subsidiarity and comity.

to the role of the British State than the role of Parliament in Westminster is to the town of Bicester, because the capacity of such organizations to help the people of the United Kingdom to lead a good life (today, the way things are in global international relations) is radically more tenuous and remote than the capacity of the British government to help the people of Bicester. The British government cannot justly and effectively step in to run the library in Bicester. But it can justly regulate the framework for those decisions. And it acts directly (i.e. *as* their government) *for* the people of Bicester in respect of what concerns them as part of the United Kingdom. International organizations are radically subsidiary, because unlike the British government, they do not have a general claim to act directly *for* the people of Bicester in respect of any of their concerns (with the remarkable exception of the European Union). Subsidiarity is an essential element in the nature of state sovereignty, because it is a principle that identifies purposes that a state must be able to pursue, in order to serve its community *as* a state. It must be independent of action by international organizations that disregards the radical implications of the principle of subsidiarity as it applies to the compound relation between those organizations, and the people of a community, and their state.

The good state needs substantial independence not only because of the subsidiarity of international organizations to the role of the state, but also because of the related principle of comity among nations. Comity requires states to respect each other's acts regardless of some injustices, and not to interfere with each other, even to right some injustices. Yet, just as obligations under international law can be compatible with sovereignty, interference by one state with the internal affairs of another can be compatible with sovereignty. The requirements of comity are not set by the rightness or wrongness of state action,[26] but by the capacity of one state to act justly and constructively in interfering with another state. So, military action to defend an ally against a war of aggression is compatible with comity toward the aggressor state.[27] A respect for comity is compatible with humanitarian intervention, but on what principle?

Henry Shue proposes that 'if the primary duty regarding the vital interest at the core of a basic right is not performed, a secondary, or default, duty must immediately take hold'.[28] That view supports his argument that states can have a moral duty (called a 'default' duty, because it arises only when another actor fails in a primary duty) to interfere to prevent genocide. The conclusion is true, although I think it should be emphasized that the violation of basic rights by a state is not in

---

[26] Perhaps, though, it is a condition for just interference by State B that State A refuses or fails to carry out its responsibilities.

[27] You might say the war of aggression is a reason to abandon comity, but that is only using the word 'comity' in a different sense, and I think that it is best to remember that duties of comity survive total warfare. After the Allied action against Germany in World War II, the Allies owed Germany a duty not to absorb it, but to treat it as a state wounded by its own regime and by the war, and to support the development of just and independent German self-government.

[28] Shue, H., 'Limiting Sovereignty' (above, n. 3), 17.

itself enough to justify (let alone to require) intervention by another state.[29] And there is no reason to think that any other state or any other agent of any kind necessarily acquires a default duty to interfere, when a state fails in its primary duty to respect a basic right. Suppose that the regime in a state proposes to execute a political dissident on trumped-up charges of rape or murder. There is no right more fundamental than the dissident's right to life, and there is no clearer case of a failure in the primary duty to respect that right. But we do not yet have even the beginning of a case for another state 'to step in either to prevent or to punish the duty-violating deprivation'.[30] Comity (reflected, imperfectly, in the complexities of the rule of non-intervention as it currently is in international law) stands in the way, and it does so for underlying reasons that can be unified with the reasons that underlie subsidiarity: they have to do with the relative incapacity both of other states and of international organizations to judge the purposes that the state ought to pursue and, even where the state's actual purposes can be judged to be abusive, the relative incapacity of other states or international organizations to remedy the situation in a way that achieves peace, order, and good government better than non-interference would do (see points 1 and 2, above). The best argument against a world government is that this radical instance of subsidiarity would make global institutions of government (or the institutions of, say, one powerful nation) poor judges of what aspects of life to interfere with in the communities that are now nation states. And when it makes those judgments wisely, the global government might be inept at giving them effect in a way that answers to local (which used to be national) conditions.

Genocide is no clearer a violation of a fundamental right than judicially sanctioned state murder of a lone dissident. But it may be very different in its implications for interference by another state. Interference by State B may be justified to prevent the extermination of a people in State A, for at least the following reasons. First, because of the scale of mass atrocities, it may be more feasible for State B to pass judgment on what is going on in State A. More importantly, effective interference may require action on the massively destructive, violent scale that is characteristic of even limited military action, and such action may be disproportionate in response to any abuse of rights by State A that is not on the scale of a mass atrocity. Finally, a mass atrocity connotes not just an injustice, but a large-scale breakdown in the state's responsibility for the people (or peoples) of the territory. Other states may be capable of interfering with a mass atrocity justly, where they could not justly interfere with an abuse of one person's fundamental rights. It is not enough that a crisis involves abuse of fundamental rights.

---

[29] Ibid. Shue does note that 'the nature of the secondary duty, like the nature of any primary duty, will depend on the nature of the interest to be protected, the most effective means for protecting it, and so on, and cannot be specified purely in the abstract'. But I propose that its nature depends also on considerations that the primary duty does not depend on.

[30] Ibid.

We can say generally that justifying interference by sovereign State B with the internal acts of sovereign State A may require:

- Action by A that represents not only a breach of a fundamental right, but a fundamental breakdown of state responsibility for peace, order, and good government.
- Capacity on the part of B to act responsibly in identifying the need for interference, and
- A genuine prospect that B will improve things by interfering.

For State B to have a *duty* to intervene, we need to add (as Shue suggests) the condition that it must be possible for State B to intervene without disproportionate cost. If we are in the position of State B, then aside from uncertainties as to what State A is doing or will do, and aside from the massive uncertainties that are liable to be involved in assessing the risks of intervention in another state, we may face a dilemma in any attempt to draw a true judgment of proportion among the prospect of an atrocity, the destructive consequences of interference itself for the people of State A, and the number of our young soldiers who will die if we intervene.

The duty of State B to interfere with State A therefore arises only in very restricted circumstances. It is analogous to the duty of citizens of State A to rebel against injustice. For that duty to arise, it is not enough that the state is violating fundamental rights. You or I have a *duty* to rebel only if the injustice represents a full-scale breakdown in responsible government, and if we are able to do it effectively without making things worse. The duty of other states to interfere is analogous. State B may or may not be better placed than the citizens of State A to overpower a regime in State A that is committing atrocities. But its duty to interfere can be even more restricted than the duty of citizens to rebel, in so far as other states are not liable to be in as good a position as citizens to achieve just regime change.

IX. CONCLUSION

Sovereignty (which is the autonomy of states) is at least potentially compatible with the authority of international law. What counts as sovereignty, and also whether states ought to be sovereign, depends on the nature and structure of the international order, and on the behaviour of states. Remember the complex relations between authority and personal autonomy (above). Analogously, international law may encroach on state sovereignty either legitimately (when there is good reason to treat a state as not capable of exercising sovereignty) or illegitimately. And acts of interference with sovereignty by another state may be legitimate or illegitimate, depending on whether they are compatible with respect for the value that sovereignty would have. The lack of sovereignty of a protectorate or mandated territory may legitimately reflect an incapacity of the state to act justly and effectively as a state (and indeed, there may be no state in a territory). It is not necessarily right to treat all states as sovereign, or to pretend that an anarchic territory has a state. But as with the authorities who have responsibility for children (and do not treat them as fully autonomous), the authorities with responsibility for territories that are not part of their state ought to treat the peoples of those territories with due concern for the development of their capacity for sovereignty. It is easier said than done, because it requires humility on the part of state officials.

The fact that sovereignty is valuable does not mean that it is the only just way to arrange things, or the best way. Personal autonomy is various, and so is state sovereignty. The goods that states may serve are not nearly as diverse as the goods for which persons may act, but they are still diverse. Sovereignty is various because it is compatible with a vast array of different regimes of international law, even though it is also incompatible with many conceivable doctrines. International law in various stages of development does not necessarily treat states as more truly or less truly sovereign, as potential limits on state independence are diverse. Even a substantial change in international law (such as the development of the United Nations) may not make states more truly or less truly sovereign. The rule that treaties are binding enhances sovereignty; rules of international law in general do not necessarily enhance or detract from sovereignty.

States do, however, stand to lose their sovereignty (to a greater or lesser extent) if rules of international law or treaty obligations prevent them from exercising the freedom and power that they need in order to act justly and effectively as states. That can conceivably happen through illegitimate developments in international law (or even through trade treaties that make it impossible for a state to engage in just and effective labour market regulation or environmental regulation).

Unlike a slavery contract, a treaty of confederation could be a legitimate act of sovereignty, even if it terminates a nation's sovereignty. A free state might exercise its sovereignty well for the purposes of a good state, precisely in building a new nation along with other states (or in becoming part of a larger state). This fact, incidentally, belies Mill's paradoxical notion that, in the case of a human individual, 'It is not freedom, to be allowed to alienate his freedom'.[31] Freedom in agency in general does not require that the agent not alienate its freedom; the reasons for not enforcing slavery contracts have to do with those human goods that enable us to judge one freedom to be valuable, and another to be worthless.

[31] Mill, J. S., *On Liberty* (above, n. 4).

CHAPTER 12

SOVEREIGNTY IN THE CONTEXT OF GLOBALIZATION: A CONSTITUTIONAL PLURALIST PERSPECTIVE

JEAN L. COHEN

I. INTRODUCTION

Timothy Endicott provides a well-reasoned clarification and defence of sovereignty in Chapter 11, 'The Logic of Freedom of Power'. He shows that if one understands the concept properly, there is no incompatibility of sovereignty with international law. The dilemma that a sovereign state can not be bound or bind itself yet must be able to act as a legal person in international law and hence to bind itself and be bound by that law dissolves once one abandons the absolutist conception of sovereignty that it presupposes. I support this conclusion along with Endicott's claim that sovereignty is compatible with moral principles, protects moral values, and thus has moral value. Endicott is right: the content of sovereignty is 'various' depending in part on the nature and structure of the international order and the existing sovereignty regime. Nevertheless, Endicott's paper leaves us without an alternative *conception* of sovereignty (distinct from its content or purpose), that would equip us to broach the really hard question today, namely, the compatibility of sovereignty not with international law (long resolved) but with autonomous supranational legal orders that have constitutional quality and claim supremacy and jurisdictional reach that penetrates the black box of the territorial state. How can we understand state sovereignty within the framework of a supranational polity like the EU or a globalizing political and legal order like the UN Charter System? Is the concept of state sovereignty an anachronism: useless for understanding the globalizing world order and pernicious because it blocks projects for its progressive development? Or are the principles of sovereignty and sovereign equality, along with human rights, central to such a project?

I defend the latter position. My first thesis is that it is empirically more accurate and normatively preferable to construe some of the changes in the contemporary world order in terms of the emergence of a new, dualistic sovereignty regime, not as portending the irrelevance of state sovereignty. The core of this order remains the segmentally differentiated international society of sovereign states, creating consent-based international law. This is overlain by a functionally differentiated global political system whose legal rules reference an 'international community' in which states are the key but not the only actors. A new sovereignty regime is taking shape, redefining the legal prerogatives of sovereign states thanks partly to the emergence of cosmopolitan principles and institutional elements within this dualistic system. States no longer have the monopoly of the production of international/global law, and consensus operates on key levels of this system (*jus cogens* and within the UN organs based on forms of majority voting). Nevertheless, states remain sovereign.

It is my second thesis that to understand the relation between sovereign states and the global legal/political system, one must adopt a constitutional pluralist rather than a monist theoretical approach.[1] I see the constitutional pluralist approach as the theoretical analogue of the sociological concept of a dualistic sovereignty regime. There now exists alongside the domestic constitutional law of each sovereign state an increasingly autonomous legal order coupled to the global political system. The constitutionalist character of that system, however, is rudimentary. To insist on the constitutional nature of the global legal system from a monist perspective is to risk 'symbolic constitutionalism'—the invocation of the values and legal discourse of the international community to dress up arbitrary regulations, strategic power plays, military interventions and impositions, in the universalistic garb of 'enforcement'. The concept of a dualistic sovereignty regime based on the principles of sovereign equality and human rights, and the stance of constitutional pluralism are an important barrier to this.

Yet I also argue for institutional and legal reform along the lines of the further constitutionalization of international law. Since 1945, sovereign equality and human rights have been the core legal principles of the dualistic international system, and both are needed in order to construct a more just version of that system. Given their

---

[1] Walker, N., 'The Idea of Constitutional Pluralism', *Modern Law Review*, 65/3 (2002), 317.

global governance functions, it is now necessary to bring powerful international organizations and not only sovereign states under the rule or law, through institutional and legal reform. This is part of the counter-project to empire or to new forms of condominium that use global institutions for self-interested purposes.

What follows will be in four sections. Section II reconstructs the absolutist conception of sovereignty that is presupposed by many who argue for abandoning the concept. Section III discusses the challenges to this version by theorists in the early twentieth century, focusing on Kelsen's reconceptualization of sovereignty as legal concept, instead of as a fact of power or as a set of competences. This will allow us to see that the real dilemma of sovereignty is not that it cannot be self-binding, but that it seems to entail the impossibility of two autonomous legal orders operative within the same territory or regulating the same subject matters. Kelsen believed that the existence of an autonomous international legal system would require that sovereignty be radically suppressed. Section IV addresses the revival of this idea in the current context. Section V challenges the monist theoretical basis of this assessment and defends the competing approach of constitutional pluralism.

II. Ruler Sovereignty and the Impossibility of International Law

Cosmopolitan theorists are eager to abandon the concept of sovereignty because they see it as a claim to power unrestrained by law, and a legal bulwark against international enforcement of human rights. Yet the absolutist conception of sovereignty that corresponds to this assessment has long since been abandoned.

The modern discourse of sovereignty is associated with absolute monarchy and the modern state. From both perspectives, it involves a claim to supreme authority and control within a territory signifying the coherence, unity, and independence of a territorially based political and legal community. It thus has an internal and external dimension. Internally, sovereignty involves supremacy: a claim to unified, comprehensive, supreme, exclusive, and direct authority within a territory over its inhabitants construed as members of a polity. The correlative external dimension involves a claim to autonomy from outside powers. External sovereignty entails independence and impermeability of the territorial state to jurisdictional claims or political control by foreign authorities.

On the absolutist conception, internal sovereignty had to be located in a unified organ at the head of the state. The absolutist conception also involved the command theory of law: to ensure the unity of a legal and political system all posited law had to be traced back to the will of a sovereign that is *legibus solutus*. Limited sovereignty thus seemed an oxymoron. Because it was also assumed that sovereignty entails what the Germans call *Kompetenz Kompetenz*—the unrestricted competence to decide the extent of jurisdiction and competences—sovereignty and constitutionalism were deemed incompatible. This and other prerogatives, especially the right to make law and the *jus belli*, were assumed to flow directly from the fact of sovereign power.

The external claim to autonomy was directed against the universalisms of emperor and pope. This implied the existence of a plurality of sovereign states, and an international society that attributed sovereignty to polities on a coherent basis. The same is true of a third idea constitutive of external sovereignty: the equality of sovereign states in respect of their legal status and basic rights. Equal sovereignty provided a basic rule of coexistence within the system of states; it made the practice of mutual recognition and the regulation of interactions among sovereign states possible. Accordingly, a state is sovereign if it exercises effective control over its territorial boundaries and population through a governing apparatus able to maintain law and order. In theory, recognition as a sovereign state followed from these empirical political facts.

On the Westphalian model the sole subjects and sources of international law are sovereign states, bound only by those rules to which they consent. Individuals could not be subjects of international law. Hence another meaning of impermeability: international law did not have direct effect on individuals: its norms regulated external relations between sovereign states, primarily via bilateral agreements. All this seemed to reduce international law to an instrumentally useful medium of coordination reflecting underlying power relations, without effectively constraining or transforming them. The absolutist conception of sovereignty is the one that Endicott rightly rejects.

By the second half of the nineteenth century, sovereignty appeared as a claim to power unrestrained by law within as well as outside of Europe. Once the ideas of sovereignty, the nation state, and imperialism had joined together, fierce competition among sovereign (European) states construed as self-contained self-interested entities undermined the rudimentary mechanisms enabling coexistence within European international society. Sovereignty has been associated with arbitrary and rapacious power politics ever since.[2]

III. Rule Sovereignty: The Legalist Challenge

This is the context in which attempts to reinterpret the concept of sovereignty took shape. Four assumptions of the absolutist conception were contested: That

---

[2] Fassbender, B., 'Sovereignty and Constitutionalism in International Law', in Walker, N. (ed.), *Sovereignty in Transition* (Portland: Hart, 2003), 119.

sovereignty must be apex sovereignty located in an organ of the state, that it entails a supreme will which must be *legibus solutus*, that the coherence of a legal system must be traced back to the will of such a sovereign, and that key prerogatives of the ruler derive from the essence of sovereignty, including comprehensive, exclusive jurisdiction and legislative competence within a territory and the *jus belli*. The work of jurists like Georg Jellinek, Hans Kelsen, Carre de Malberg, and later H. L. A. Hart challenged this conception.

Since my focus, like Endicott's, is on the external dimension, I only note in passing that the claim that internal sovereignty must be located in a single body (organ) whose will is *legibus solutus* has been belied ever since the first modern constitutional democracy emerged in the US in the eighteenth century based on the separation of powers, checks and balances, and the idea of popular sovereignty, not to mention the division of powers entailed by federalism. The theory and practice of modern constitutional states demonstrates that sovereignty, constitutionalism, and the rule of law are not incompatible.

The conceptual error behind these claims identified by these legal theorists is the assumption that sovereignty is a matter of fact and power which law merely registers. But sovereignty, they argue, is a juridical concept of public law. A state is sovereign when its legal order is unified, supreme, and autonomous. As a legal concept, sovereignty is not tied to a particular form of the state. The state's political structure and its ruler's prerogatives derive from the legal rules of its constitutional order rather than the reverse. While organ sovereignty is one rare form of the sovereign state, it is not the only one. It is perfectly possible to have a legal system in which legal limits on the supreme legislative authority are legal disabilities contained in the very rules that qualify the ruler to legislate, and constitute the organ as a legal power in the first place.[3]

It was Hans Kelsen who developed the strongest, most influential theory of sovereignty as a legal and normative concept.[4] Yet, Kelsen also famously argued that sovereignty should be radically suppressed. Why? For Kelsen, sovereignty is the essential characteristic of a state. The state is the supreme authority, but since authority is a normative concept, only a normative order can be sovereign. Indeed, for Kelsen the state is equivalent to its objective normative legal order whose referent is a legal community. To be a sovereign state means that the ultimate reason for the validity of the system of norms constituting the domestic legal order is traceable back to the constitutional order of that state. Only a norm can be the basis of validity of another norm. The question of why the fundamental constitutional norms are valid leads to the concept of an ultimate norm, whose validity the jurist does not question but must presuppose. This is the famous concept of the *grundnorm*—a

---

[3] Hart, H. L. A., *The Concept of Law* (Oxford: Oxford University Press, 1961), 49–76.
[4] Kelsen, H., *General Theory of Law and the State* (Cambridge, Mass.: Harvard University Press, 1945), 325–88.

transcendental postulate, not a substantive legal principle. A legal system must be characterized by strict unity and hierarchy in the structure of validity claims.

The constitutional order of a sovereign state is the highest underived legal authority above which there can be no higher authority that is its source of validity, regulating and determining its conduct. Sovereignty as supremacy is a negative legal concept. Accordingly, international law as an autonomous legal system that authorizes and obligates states must be denied on the sovereignty thesis. This is the level of the sovereignty paradox that Endicott does not address.

Kelsen famously makes two claims regarding the sovereignty thesis: first that it precludes viewing international law as a valid autonomous legal order, and second that it blocks viewing other states as equally sovereign. Ironically the principle of equal sovereignty constitutive of the Westphalian system is undermined by the concept of sovereignty that subtends it.

The sovereignty thesis means that from the perspective of a domestic legal order, international law is law only if it is consented to or 'recognized' by that state. Its principle of validity lies in the domestic constitution. The recognition theory of international law presupposes a monistic understanding of the relationship between the domestic legal order and international law: the latter is a subordinate part of the national legal order. International law is able to determine the sphere and validity of national law only if international law has validity, but it has legal validity, only on the basis of the principle of validity of the domestic constitutional order recognizing it. The recognition theory of international law thus entails the primacy of national over international law as well as the monist interpretation of the unity of these legal systems.[5]

But this also means that equal sovereignty of a plurality of states is impossible from this perspective. The sovereign state cannot, from its internal perspective, acknowledge the simultaneous autonomous validity of any other legal order. The necessary relationship of equal autonomy between sovereign states can be established only by international law and only if it is granted that international law determines the spheres of validity of the legal orders of these states. Under the monist thesis of the primacy of national law, however, the solipsistic sovereign state can recognize only its own sovereignty, which it assumes to be independent of the recognition by international law or any other state. This stance is likened by Kelsen to subjectivist philosophy that proceeds from the sovereignty of the ego, interprets the world as the will and idea of the subject, and is incapable of comprehending another subject, as an equal being.[6] As a consequence of the thesis of the primacy of national law, the recognition theory, and the monist interpretation, the sovereignty of one state excludes the sovereignty of every other. In so far as supremacy and validity are concerned, the logic of sovereignty leads to imperial sovereignty—to the construal of one state's legal order as the universal legal order.

---

[5] Kelsen, H., *General Theory of Law and the State*, 384.   [6] Ibid. 387.

The alternative hypothesis is a monist interpretation that accepts the unity of national and international law, but construes the international legal system as the autonomous and supreme legal order whose basic norm is the principle of validity for national legal orders. This would enable one to account for the autonomy of binding rules of international law and its constitutive principle: equal sovereignty. It is the essential function of the international legal order to delimit the spheres of validity and guarantee the equal sovereignty of each territorial state. International law enables states to coexist as equal legal subjects. The state as a subject of international law is a juristic person, recognized by that law according to the principle of effectiveness and as such constituted by it. The paradox that public international law is constituted by states but states are constituted by public international law is resolved by Kelsen by arguing that when states make treaties or customary law they function as 'organs' of the international legal community. On the monist interpretation of the primacy of international law, every national legal order is connected with the international legal order and through this with every other national legal order so that there is one integrated legal system. The international legal order by means of the principle of effectiveness thus not only determines the spheres of validity of the national legal orders, making possible the coexistence of a multitude of states, it also provides the reason of validity of the national legal orders. So the *grundnorms* of national legal orders are basic norms only in a 'relative sense'.

To be sure, the idea of a relative *grundnorm* is quite meaningless in Kelsen's own framework. What he is actually saying is that the equality of all states is a legal principle that can be maintained only on the basis of the primacy of public international law, monistically interpreted. This means that 'states can be considered equal only if they are not presupposed to be sovereign'.[7]

Tertium non datur. The pluralist approach which construes national and international law as two autonomous and independent legal systems is, to Kelsen, incoherent. From the internal legal perspective, it is simply not possible for there to exist two valid legal norms that are not part of the same legal system, yet which regulate the same issues or actors. Nor can two legal norms which contradict each other both be valid. To posit such a thing would, given the need to decide which order is supreme and to enforce the law, lead to irresolvable conflicts. Absent an impartial adjudicator, it would also lead to the fragmentation and loss of efficacy of the legal system.[8] Since there is no subject matter that due to its essence can only be regulated by national and not by international law, the pluralist thesis cannot make its stand on that ground.[9]

We thus face a choice between the two monistic postulates: the primacy of the domestic legal system linked to subjectivist philosophy or that of the international legal system linked to an objectivistic approach. Kelsen framed this as an ethical

---

[7] Ibid.   [8] Ibid. 374–5.   [9] Ibid. 348–9, 365.

political choice, the former having an elective affinity to nationalism and imperialism, the latter with internationalism and pacifism.[10] Clearly his preferences lay with the latter.

The premise of my argument is that this is a false choice, based on several conceptual errors. Because he insisted on a pure theory of law, Kelsen failed to see that it is the dynamics of mutual recognition and inter-subjectivity that create and subtend the relationships between two subjects and not only the theoretical stance that reasons from the 'objective' world which lets us see both *ego* and *tu* as parts of a whole. Imperialism is inherent in the logic of sovereignty only on its solipsistic, monistic, and subjectivist conception. Kelsen wrongly assumed that equality can be guaranteed only from the objectivistic stance that reasons from the primacy and autonomy of international law. He ignored the political context of law, and the inter-subjective political dynamics of recognition can subtend the mutual ascription of equal sovereignty.

This insistence on a pure theory of law independent of any considerations (or practices) of legitimacy, coupled with the sanction theory of law according to which every legal norm must have a sanction attached to it for the legal system to be efficacious, led the monist position. Kelsen had to reject constitutional pluralism as incoherent because two conflicting legal norms could not both be valid and enforced. But, as H. L. A. Hart argued, there are constitutional norms that are not attached to sanctions.[11] Moreover, from the perspective of legitimacy and the political practice of mutual recognition, the idea of constitutional tolerance between independent legal systems that compete for but do not have to resolve the question of the final locus of authority (because practitioners can take a doubly reflexive internal and external stance) is at least conceivable.[12] So is the concept of changing sovereignty regimes, an idea the monistic construction would have to reject.

IV. GLOBAL 'CONSTITUTIONAL MOMENTS': COSMOPOLITAN MONISM REVIVED

While Kelsen's political choice for the primacy of international law is understandable, given his assumptions, it made little practical sense prior to 1945. States certainly deemed themselves sovereign, in possession of the *jus belli*, and acted accordingly. However, some have interpreted changes in the international

---

[10] Kelsen, H., *General Theory of Law and the State*, 388.
[11] Hart, H. L. A., *The Concept of Law* (above, n. 3).
[12] Maduro, M. P., 'Sovereignty in Europe: The European Court of Justice and the Creation of a European Political Community', in Volcansek, M. and Stack, J. F. (eds.), *Courts Crossing Borders: Blurring the Lines of Sovereignty* (Durham, NC: Carolina Academic Press, 2005), 50–2, 55–8.

system since then as 'constitutional moments'—steps in the constitutionalization of international law, vindicating the overall thrust of Kelsen's approach.[13]

Accordingly, the erection of the UN Charter system in 1945 and its subsequent development, amounts to the construction of an autonomous, global, increasingly integrated legal order of constitutional quality claiming supremacy that has profoundly modified state sovereignty.[14] The changes in the positive rules of international law this entailed are well known: the most important being the principle of collective security eliminating the *jus belli* except for self-defence. This is now seen as an unprecedented attempt to legally regulate the use of force. The legal principles of sovereign equality, non-intervention, territorial integrity, domestic jurisdiction, and self-determination were enunciated and universalized. Since 1960, colonialism was dismantled, wars of annexation became illegal, political autonomy and territorial integrity of borders was ascribed to all states.

Moreover, human rights principles were enunciated in the Charter and codified in important subsequent international Covenants. Genocide, ethnic cleansing, and enslavement are not considered to be within the domestic jurisdiction of any state and no treaty will be deemed valid that involves an agreement to engage or tolerate such action. These *jus cogens* principles are deemed auxiliary to the UN Charter system. Since 1989, it is considered the responsibility of the sovereign state to protect its civilian population against serious rights violations and in case of default, this responsibility (responsibility to protect or R2P) devolves to the international community.[15] Some have referred to this expectation as a second 'constitutional moment' involving the emergence of a new basic norm in the international system, described as a principle of civilian inviolability.[16] Finally the elevation of human as distinct from state security to a central concern of the Security Council, its practice of transformative 'humanitarian occupation', and its recent assumption of the power to list and sanction individual terrorists and to legislate for the rest of the United Nations membership regarding transnational terrorism indicates to some that a third international constitutional moment has occurred.[17] The international

---

[13] Slaughter, A.-M. and Burke-White, W., 'An International Constitutional Moment', *Harvard International Law Journal*, 43 (2003), 1. For a critique see Andreas Fischer-Lescano, 'Redefining Sovereignty via International Constitutional Moments?' in O'Connell, M. E., Bothe, M., and Ronzitti, N. (eds.), *Redefining Sovereignty: The Use of Force after the End of the Old War: New Options, Lawful and Legitimate?* (Ardsley, NY: Transnational Publishers, 2005).

[14] Fassbender, B., 'The United Nations Charter as Constitution of the International Community', *Columbia Journal of Transnational Law*, 36 (1998), 579.

[15] International Commission on Intervention and State Sovereignty, *The Responsibility to Protect* (Ottawa: IDRC, 2001) and Report of the Secretary General's High Level Panel on Threats, Challenges and Change, *A More Secure World: Our Shared Responsibility* (New York: United Nations, 2004) available at <http://www.un.org/secureworld>.

[16] Slaughter, A.-M. and Burke-White, W., 'An International Constitutional Moment' (above, n. 13).

[17] Fox, G., *Humanitarian Occupation* (Cambridge: Cambridge University Press, 2008); Talmon, S., 'The Security Council as World Legislature', *American Journal of International Law*, 99/1 (2005), 175; and Szasz, P., 'The Security Council Starts Legislating', *American Journal of International Law*, 96/4 (2002), 901–5, both of whom are enthusiasts of this development.

order has become more legalized than ever before. The equal legal standing of states within the global legal order is backed up by an international community based on collective security, sovereign equality, and human rights.

The question is how to characterize these shifts and what kind of global political and legal order they constitute. There are two competing interpretations of what it would mean to ascribe autonomy and constitutional quality to the expanding legal order regulating the global political system: one cosmopolitan, monist, the other pluralist and based on the concept of changing sovereignty regimes.[18] These are the main alternatives to the third approach that construes these shifts as already amounting to a new form of imperial right.[19]

On the first interpretation, the principle of sovereign equality enunciated in the Charter is not a principle of sovereignty at all.[20] The changes in the positive rules of international law are indicative of a step away from sovereignty in favour of the constitutionalization of the global political system. The grammatical shift from noun to adjective in the term that appears in the Charter, 'sovereign equality', expresses this.[21] Instead of being the supreme power of a state, existing apart from and prior to international law, or as indicative of the self-referential autonomy and supremacy of that state's constitutional legal order, 'sovereignty' is now seen as a set of rights ascribed by positive public international law to states. As one commentator put it,

'in other words, sovereignty is a collective or umbrella term denoting the rights which at a given time a state is accorded by international law and the duties imposed upon it by that same law. These specific rights and duties constitute 'sovereignty'; they do not flow from it'.[22]

This accords perfectly with Endicott's position.

Moreover, the concept of equal sovereignty focused on national interest is replaced by the new principle, sovereign equality, with 'community-oriented' content: hence, the shift from the concept of international society to international community. The autonomous international legal and political community constituted by the UN Charter system, is allegedly more than a sum of its member states' interests—it is an entity committed to 'humankind', with its distinct purposes and legal personality enforceable against recalcitrant states.[23] Through the Charter, it is now equipped with its own organs and can articulate community law, adjudicate, and enforce it. Thus, there is now a hierarchy of rules of global international law: those with constitutional quality enjoy the highest rank.[24] The Charter is supreme over international treaty law as per its article 103, and it 'incorporates' prior customary

---

[18] By cosmopolitan I mean a global legal order that references individuals (human rights) and which is based on the principle of the equal worth and dignity of all human beings. See Pogge, T., 'Cosmopolitanism', in Goodin, R., Pettit, P., and Pogge, T. (eds.), *A Companion to Contemporary Political Philosophy* (2nd edn., Oxford: Blackwell, 2007), 312–31.

[19] Hardt, M. and Negri, A., *Empire* (Cambridge, Mass.: Harvard University Press, 2001).

[20] Fassbender, B., 'Sovereignty and Constitutionalism in International Law' (above, n. 2), 115–45.

[21] Ibid. 134–41.   [22] Ibid. 129.   [23] Ibid. 130.   [24] Ibid. 131

international law.[25] 'World order treaties' like the two human rights covenants and the genocide convention, are 'constitutional by-laws' of the international community, adding to and implementing the objectives and law of the Charter. In short, the monist constitutional 'view dissolves the dualism of "general international law" and the law of the Charter'.[26]

Accordingly, the UN Charter system is now an autonomous legal order referencing an autonomous legal and political community. But on the monist reading, in order for a legal order to be autonomous and of constitutional quality, it is not enough that it be supreme. The subordinate legal orders have to be construed as belonging to the same legal system: supremacy and hierarchy require unity. This entails more than the idea that states are sovereign in so far as they are subordinate 'only' to international law but not to one another. It means that they are no longer sovereign at all: their legal orders are not supreme or autonomous, their constitutions do not derive their validity from their own *grundnorm* nor can their constitutional legal orders be imputed to their own autonomous demos (the idea of popular sovereignty). Rather, states are now construed as subsidiary organs of the politically constituted world society and its globalizing legal system. This legal order grants them a wide range of political and legal autonomy although the intrusions on domestic jurisdiction are not trivial. Moreover, on this reading, their legal systems have their condition of validity not in themselves but in the higher, supreme, autonomous international legal order of the UN Charter system. Strictly speaking, the rules of this legal system do not depend on the consent of the independently sovereign states: they bind states as members of a constitutional order whose validity inheres in the Charter itself. The latter is not only supreme over other treaties, but also over the constitutional orders of the member states themselves! Autonomy in this framework does not describe the self-referential nature of the sovereign states' legal system; it now merely refers to a set of prerogatives accorded to states (equally) by the global constitutional legal order—it is a matter of degree. The supreme international constitutional order decides the competence of domestic legal orders, and this order cannot be altered by traditional treaty methods. Clearly, then, subsidiarity and multi-level governance are not equivalent to sovereignty.

The monist constitutionalist approach also leaves us facing an either/or: either there is a global legal system coupled to the global political system, based on the twin principles of sovereign equality and human rights but without the sovereign state, or there are sovereign states, and international law based on their consent but it is not an autonomous legal system. Either the UN Charter establishes a supranational political organization whose rules have acquired constitutional quality, and which, despite its origins in an international treaty now subordinate the constituent units

---

[25] United Nations Charter, article 103.
[26] Fassbender, B., 'Sovereignty and Constitutionalism in International Law' (above, n. 2), 135.

to the new creation such that its decisions apply to each of them irrespective of their continuous individual consent. Or the Charter remains a treaty, the UN, a treaty organization, with legal personality but no power to eradicate its subordination to the member states or its subjection to the classical laws governing the treaty organizations.[27] It should, however, be obvious that neither side of this either/or is compelling.

Instead this either/or reveals the inadequacy of the monist cosmopolitan approach. I thus want to argue for the cogency of the pluralist interpretation, linked to the concept of a dualistic world order and changing sovereignty regime. Despite the expanding regulatory role of supranational institutions, increased integration of the international community does not amount to the end of sovereign territorial states. Segmental pluralism still exists although it is overlaid by global functional differentiation. The global political system is dualistic, composed of sovereign states and the international law they make, alongside new legal subjects with new functions and global cosmopolitan legal elements. The sociological thesis of the disaggregation of the state is unconvincing. Certain competences once associated with the sovereign state can and have been delegated to other supranational actors. Indeed, this is a key premise of the concept of changing sovereignty regimes. But sovereignty as the autonomy and supremacy of a legal order cannot be divided, pooled, or shared.[28] Sovereignty is a legal as well as a political concept, but it is not reducible to a bundle of rights or prerogatives. Instead, sovereignty is the unifying and self-identifying claim of a polity regarding the supremacy and autonomy of its legal order, the self-determination of its political system, and its status as the ultimate authority in its respective domain of jurisdiction and as an equal under international law.

V. The Constitutional Pluralist Approach

It is certainly still the case that states are deemed by the relevant domestic actors (judges, civil servants, politicians, their publics) to be sovereign: supreme domestically and autonomous internationally.[29] The principle of 'sovereign equality' articulated in the UN Charter is a legal principle, but it is still a principle of sovereignty from the internal perspective of member states. In other words, the

---

[27] Fassbender, B., 'The United Nations Charter as Constitution of the International Community' (above, n. 14), 560.

[28] Walker, N., 'Late Sovereignty in the European Union', in Walker, N. (ed), *Sovereignty in Transition* (Hart Publishing: Oxford, 2003), 15.

[29] Ibid. 10, 17. Neil Walker rightly states that sovereignty is still a central part of the 'object language' of the domestic constitutional law of states and hence cannot be abandoned at the level of the meta-language of theorists.

legal principle of sovereign equality both registers and constitutes the autonomy and self-determination of states and it expresses this through the related Charter principles of non-intervention, domestic jurisdiction, self-determination, and the right to self-defence.

Nonetheless, my claims that we are not in a 'post-sovereignty' system and that sovereignty cannot be disaggregated, do not bring us back to a Westphalian model, nor need they entail the denial of the autonomy of the legal order of the global political system. It is as wrong to see the UN Charter system's legal order today as simply delegated authority on the treaty model as it is to see the validity of state constitutions as derivative of the *grundnorm* of the global legal system. The non-derivative character of legal supranationalism is as important to grasp as the non-derivative character of domestic constitutions. Taking sovereignty discourse seriously does not mean that one can ignore shifts in the substantive rules of sovereignty, the structural changes in the international system, or the emergence of a functionally differentiated autonomous global legal order referencing the international community, and claiming supremacy.

The only way to make sense of these claims is to adopt the stance of constitutional pluralism. Accordingly, it is perfectly conceivable that a state can give up the *jus belli*, accept that all states are bound by enforceable human rights norms, and open up its territory to jurisdiction by a functionally delimited supranational legal order, and still be sovereign. From the internal perspective, the state is sovereign so long as it is politically self-determining, so long as there is an autonomous relationship between the government and the citizenry, and so long as its legal order is supreme. The sovereign state can delegate competences, and even accept the primacy of rules made by a supranational organization in certain domains, since it is the capacity of the sovereign domestic legal order to make such delegations and to accept such decisions. From its internal perspective, the domestic legal order remains supreme and retains interpretative autonomy over jurisdiction and over issues of compatibility of external decisions with its internal constitutional legal order. Endicott is right, sovereignty also requires political self-determination in the negative sense of the non-imposition of a constitutional order or regime by foreigners, but more is involved here than the general principle of subsidiarity.

However, internal supremacy needn't be tightly coupled to exclusivity of jurisdiction. On the Westphalian model, overlapping jurisdictions within the territory of a state meant that the latter was not sovereign: a nonexclusive authority was typically a dependent one. In today's sovereignty regime, these two dimensions have been decoupled. It is possible to conceive of supremacy and without comprehensive territorial exclusivity and to imagine jurisdictional overlap without subsumption.[30] The development of functionally delimited supranational jurisdictional claims in

---

[30] Ibid. 23.

the global political system can thus supplement and overlap without abolishing the autonomy of territorial sovereign states.

Yet from *its* internal perspective, the global legal order is an autonomous one with constitutional quality. It is a functional order, not a territorial polity, although it too (especially the UN Security Council) makes the claim of supremacy and interpretive autonomy over the precise extent of the functional mandate. Functions and purposes like 'international peace and security' and 'respecting human rights' can be interpreted very broadly. Yet, no one could claim under current conditions that the global political system and its autonomous legal order is equivalent to that of a federal state. The status of supranational organizations, including the UN, remains contested in international law: its Charter is a 'constitutional treaty', and it is still left to member states to define its international legal position, even though the UN's legal order has become autonomous.[31] In other words, the UN has a dualist structure: its member states are sovereign but they are also bound by the legal system of the Charter which is now autonomous *vis à vis* their ongoing individual consent. As the constitutional treaty of the global political system, the Charter changes the status of the parties and the nature of their relationships, and is protected against unilateral interpretation and alteration, via its amendment rule.[32] Yet the efficacy of the binding obligations imposed by the Council still depends very much on its legitimacy from the perspective of sovereign states because the Charter is not self-executing. The understanding of the Charter as a constitutional treaty expresses this dualism. Indeed given the flaws in the Charter's constitutional design, the rudimentary character of the separation of powers, the absence of a Court with compulsory jurisdiction or powers of judicial review, its constitutionalist character is aspirational.

This is why constitutional monism has to be avoided on the level of meta-language. The thesis of 'constitutional pluralism' is empirically, pragmatically, and normatively far more compelling for the global political system. It is an external perspective—of the political or legal theorist—but it can, I believe, also inform that of the internal legal practitioner. The stance of constitutional pluralism is linked to the unavoidable political problematic of legitimacy and mutual recognition regarding the construction of legal orders. The basic idea is to acknowledge the existence of distinct autonomous legal orders—of sovereign states and of the global political system itself—and that the latter's claims to autonomy, supremacy, and constitutional quality, exist alongside the continuing claims of states. The

---

[31] As an autonomous legal order the UN Charter system has its own legal sources and determines the validity and rank of norms within globalizing international law. Constitutionalization entails hierarchization of international legal sources to match developing hierarchies of norms (e.g. art. 103 of the UN Charter). For a discussion, see Samantha Besson, 'How International is the European Legal Order? Retracing Tuori's steps in the exploration of European legal pluralism', *No Foundation: Journal of Extreme Legal Positivism*, 5 (2008), 54–5 available at <http://www.helsinki.fi/nofo>.

[32] On the need to reform this amendment rule see Cohen, J. L., 'Global State of Emergency or the Further Constitutionalisation of International Law', *Constellations*, 15 (2008), 465.

relation between these orders must be seen as heterarchical and horizontal, not as hierarchical. This empirical and epistemological claim is accompanied by a normative and political one: as against monist sovereigntism and monist globalism, neither of which are compelling descriptions or interpretations of the world today, constitutional pluralism involves the normative idea that what is required in acknowledging and handling competing claims to authority coming from national and supranational constitutional sites is an ethic of political responsibility premised on mutual recognition and respect.[33]

Constitutional pluralism thus involves the normative commitment of taking both sovereignty and monism in the internal perspective of an autonomous legal order and pluralism on the meta-level, seriously.[34] Autonomous legal systems, by their nature assume the role of higher law. From the internal perspective of global law as autonomous (and of its constitutionalization as an ongoing project), the Charter is primary, supreme, and higher law. From the perspective of a national constitution, global law, including Article 103 of the UN Charter, owes its supremacy to recognition by the national legal order and thus the ultimate power of legal adjudication belongs to national constitutional courts. Constitutional pluralism entails acknowledging these competitive claims to independent political and legal ultimate authority.[35] This can lead to collisions and conflict since the question of supremacy has different answers in the domestic and global context. There is no neutral higher 'third' to decide this question. But it can also lead to reflexivity and cooperation and it need not end in fragmentation of either legal system.[36] The unity of a legal system requires that each new legal decision is coherent with the previous legal decisions. But *pace* Kelsen, this doesn't require a single generalized legal theory: as Maduro rightly argues, it is possible to have a coherent legal order in a context of competing interpretations of the law (and competing claims to ultimate authority) so long as all the participants share the same commitment to a coherent global legal order and adjust their competing claims accordingly.[37] To use Rawls's phrase, there can be an 'overlapping consensus' on legal outcomes. What is required is political and juridical *phronesis*—the willingness to make the effort to avoid ultimate conflicts by anticipating them and trying to cooperatively resolve them. A non-hierarchical conception of the relationship between norms and courts and informal cooperation could and should prevail given the appropriate level of reflexivity on the part of the relevant actors. But reflexivity requires communication,

[33] Walker, N., 'Constitutional Pluralism' (above, n. 1), 337–8. He is referring to the European Union.

[34] Walker, N., 'Late Sovereignty in the European Union' (above, n. 28), 18.

[35] Maduro, M. P., 'Contra Punctual Law: Europe's Constitutional Pluralism in Action', in Walker, N. (ed.), *Sovereignty in Transition*, 501.

[36] On 'cooperative sovereignty' see Samantha Besson, 'Sovereignty in Conflict', in Warbrick, C. and Tierney, S. (eds.), *Towards an International Legal Community?: The Sovereignty of States and the Sovereignty of International Law* (London: BIICL, 2006), 168–71.

[37] Maduro, M. P., 'Contra Punctual Law: Europe's Constitutional Pluralism in Action' (above, n. 35), 525, 527–8.

the 'internal attitude' toward global as well as domestic law and willingness to justify interpretations of global law in universal rather than parochial terms.[38] Such 'constitutional tolerance' is a political normative stance, predicated on belief in the legitimacy of the supranational legal and political order of which states are members (and of the desirability of the project of a global rule of law). Given legitimacy, and assuming the relevant actors value it, devising mechanisms to facilitate adjustments to respective claims over jurisdiction and authority to avoid collision, is certainly not impossible.

Indeed, the status of claims to legal autonomy and supremacy is inseparable from the political question of legitimacy. It is not the role of the political theorist to come up with mechanisms for 'ordering pluralism' from the internal validity perspective, but to reflect on the conditions of political legitimacy that legal systems ultimately depend on.[39] The constitutional pluralist approach was developed to address the shifting nature of state sovereignty in the European Union. But it fits the global political system as well. There are several versions of this approach but they all involve taking a reflexive theoretical and normative political stance that relates the legal question of internal validity to the political question of external legitimacy. Reflexivity is crucial in such a dynamic system. The point is that disputes need not lead to disintegration so long as political legitimacy is maintained and prudence is practised by supranational institutions and by member states. Given the heterogeneity of political regimes of member states in the UN Charter system and the low degree of integration of the globalizing international legal order compared with the EU, the legitimacy of the global legal order turns on whether it respects the principles of sovereign equality and human rights. It is not appropriate at this point to make it contingent on the principle of democratic subsidiarity as some try to do generalizing from the model of the EU.[40] It is appropriate to insist on the fair inclusion of all affected states in generating global rules and global law.

Under current conditions, it is the monist cosmopolitan approach to the global legal order that would lead to irresolvable conflict, undermining the legitimacy of the entire construction. This is especially true because its 'constitutionalist' character is so underdeveloped. Legal autonomy and constitutional quality are not, after all, the same thing, and the further constitutionalization of international law must be seen as a project within the conceptual field of constitutional pluralism, not a *fait accompli*, under a monist interpretation. It must target not only states but also international organizations and their foundational charters. The absence of an international human rights court with compulsory jurisdiction, the fact that the International Court of Justice does not engage in judicial review, the lack of adequate checks and balances or a clear separation of powers, and the difficulty of

---

[38]   The concept of the internal attitude is Hart's most brilliant contribution to legal theory. See Hart, H. L. A., *The Concept of Law* (above, n. 3), 89–90 and 100–1.

[39]   Delmas-Marty, M., *Le Pluralisme ordonnée* (Paris: Éditions du Seuil, 2006).

[40]   Besson, S., 'How International is the European Legal Order?' (above, n. 31).

applying human rights norms to the UN or legal limits to the Security Council, in view of its new role in the world means that its further constitutionalization is now a pressing need. Bringing the latter under the rule of law is indispensable to claims to constitutional quality and political legitimacy. The monist model of national constitutions is inapposite here. Since the primary means of enforcement (courts and armed forces) remain in the hands of states, their cooperation and willingness to adopt the internal point of view regarding global law will depend on the perceived legitimacy of that law and of global governance institutions.

That is why it makes sense to interpret the principle of 'sovereign equality' in the framework of constitutional pluralism. The changing rules of positive international law are indeed indicative of a new political culture of sovereignty that has shifted from one of impunity to one of responsibility and accountability. From this perspective, sovereign equality and human rights are the interrelated principles of the dualistic global political system, indicative of the existence of a new sovereignty regime. The relation between these principles has changed, but sovereign equality and the correlative principles of non-intervention, domestic jurisdiction, and self-determination remain the legitimating basis and default position of the international order. It is conceptually meaningless and ideological to redefine sovereignty as a duty or function—the responsibility to protect—and to 'disaggregate' it so that other instances could take on this responsibility that should be the state default. Endicott is on the right track when he argues that one must understand state sovereignty in relational terms, and that a political community organized into a sovereign territorial state involves membership (a population, passports), territory, and a governmental apparatus that represents the citizenry in international law. When a state engages in genocide, ethnic cleansing, massive crimes against humanity it forfeits the claim to stand for and coercively rule the groups it oppresses in these radical ways. In other words, the government itself has abolished the political relationship between the rulers and the targeted group that sovereignty establishes. The issue is when the sovereignty argument should be suspended and outside intervention legally permitted, not the redefinition of sovereignty.[41]

It is also incorrect and ideological to describe the important shifts regarding sovereignty, rights, or security as 'constitutional moments'. The post-1989 discursive practices of humanitarian intervention, transformative occupations, and the post-9/11 coupling of the discourse of human security to the listing and legislative practices of the Security Council in the war on terror are political facts. They should be analysed, and when appropriate, given normative status in terms of the concept of a shifting sovereignty regime and not seen as constitutional moments that take us into a cosmopolitan world order beyond sovereignty.[42] Indeed, the UN

[41] See Raz, J., Chapter 15 in this volume and Cohen, J. L., 'Rethinking Human Rights, Democracy and Sovereignty in the Age of Globalization', *Political Theory*, 36/4 (2008), 578.
[42] The concept of informal constitutional moments is pernicious in so far as it deflects efforts to use or reform the formal amendment rule in a constitution or constitutional treaty.

reform project aimed at legally articulating and steering these shifts was a *failed constitutional moment* rather than a successful example of regulating power by law.[43] The danger is that these shifts further the de-formalization of international law and weaken limits on the use of force by the powerful, instead of being normatively desirable adjustments in the interrelation between sovereignty and human rights.

VI. CONCLUSION

Formal legal rules should be devised to regulate these new practices and understandings of competences and jurisdiction. Such rules have to be widely discussed, negotiated, and shaped in a representative political process in which all member states of the international community have a voice. Two things are at stake here: establishing thresholds and procedures for suspending the strictures against forceful intervention into a sovereign state and the application of constitutionalist principles and the rule of law to global governance institutions.

The discourse of constitutionalism involves regulating and limiting power but an autonomous global order could also centralize it and undermine the rule of law. Constitutional pluralism (acknowledging state sovereignty as well as an autonomous global legal order) serves as a bulwark against concentration and abuse of power on the global level. On the other hand, the further constitutionalization of a global legal and political system could enhance rights and justice by checking abuses in domestic legal and political orders and forcing them to take into account possible negative externalities and the external interests of the global community and of other members. For this to be a virtuous circle, legitimacy is needed on both levels of the dualistic sovereignty regime: regarding changes in what is deemed to be the domestic jurisdiction of sovereign states and regarding the new procedures and substantive rules of public international/global law. Both require institutional mechanisms providing for fair participation of political communities (states) in shaping the norms and rules (the further constitutionalism) of the global political community. Today it is increasingly the case that for states to realize their sovereignty (as international lawmakers, as exercisers of international political influence, and as having a say in decisions that affect their citizens) they need the status of member with the right to participate in the decision-making processes of the various international organizations and networks that regulate the international system, on fair terms. Unlike some, however, I

---

[43] See the Report of the Secretary General's High Level Panel on Threats, Challenges and Change, *A More Secure World: Our Shared Responsibility* (above, n. 15).

argue that this new dimension of sovereignty as status and inclusion in coercive global governance institutions supplements but does not replace sovereignty as autonomy.[44]

It also requires that global political institutions, especially the UN, are regulated by and comport with constitutionalist principles, the rule of law and human rights. This is why a UN reform project, however difficult, is so important today. Otherwise, the invocation of cosmopolitan right or global constitutional law to justify radical innovations on the part of unilateral or multilateral actors will either amount to little more than symbolic constitutionalism, playing into the hands of the imperial or great power projects, and/or culminate in the loss of legitimacy.

Finally the question arises, even if constitutional pluralism does articulate and help secure the sovereignty of states along with the autonomy and legitimacy of globalizing legal orders, why is this desirable? Why not just abandon sovereignty for a multileveled cosmopolitan world order? Apart from the obvious fact that such a system is hardly a feasible utopia at present, I agree with Endicott that sovereignty protects moral values and has normative value itself. I have argued that we should understand sovereignty not as a set of competences, but as a negative concept involving the supremacy of a domestic legal order and external autonomy in the political sense of self-determination (a non-imposition by foreigners). Accordingly, sovereignty protects the special relationship between a citizenry and its government that may involve domestic constitutionalism and democracy. Sovereignty protects the normatively special status of members and their prerogative to assess the legitimacy of their domestic system, and to struggle to make it more just, more democratic, more inclusive.[45] The principle of sovereign equality, accords this to all states. On the global level, functional equivalents for democracy are possible (accountability, avenues of influence for civil society, non-decisional parliaments, communication about best practices, subsidiarity, etc.) but they could never duplicate the kind of representative democracy and effective electoral participation possible at the level of the modern state or even a regional polity.[46] We must learn

[44] Chayes, A. and Handler Chayes, A., *The New Sovereignty: Compliance with International Regulatory Agreements*, (Cambridge, Mass.: Harvard University Press, 1998), 27. Slaughter, A.-M., 'Security, Solidarity and Sovereignty: The Grand Theme of UN Reform', *American Journal of International Law*, 99 (2005), 619, 627–30.

[45] In the process learning to compromise and engage in consensus politics that reinforces whatever degree of democracy and justice they establish. See Cohen, J. L., 'Rethinking Rights, Democracy and Sovereignty in the Age of Globalization' (above, n. 41).

[46] I agree with the thrust of the papers by Christiano (Chapter 5) and Pettit (Chapter 6) in this volume. 'Peoples' could attain representation in an inter-parliamentary body elected through domestic parliaments, alongside the General Assembly (consisting of executives and diplomats). This 'global parliament' could serve as a forum of discussion and debate. Inclusion of transnational NGOs could also be provided for, but such a parliament would not, in the foreseeable future, be a decisional body. The EU analogy is inapposite in my view given the degree of heterogeneity of political systems in the world. A global parliament could air views and exercise not (decisional) power but influence, and when appropriately attended to be an additional source of legitimation.

from the difficulties posed by the democratic deficit on the intermediary level of the EU and see that there is a strong normative argument for the constitutional pluralist position. For those embracing republican political principles and democratic aspirations, the constitutional pluralist approach is a feasible utopia and the best way to protect their normative bases.

SECTION VII

INTERNATIONAL RESPONSIBILITY

CHAPTER 13

....

INTERNATIONAL RESPONSIBILITY

....

JAMES CRAWFORD AND JEREMY WATKINS*

I. INTRODUCTION: THE DIMENSIONS OF INTERNATIONAL RESPONSIBILITY

....

One of the complications that besets any treatment of responsibility inside or outside of the law comes from the ambiguities in the term itself. 'Responsibility' has a bewildering array of meanings, each of which occupies a distinctive role in legal and moral reasoning.[1] The meaning that is most strongly suggested by etymology is what might be termed 'responsibility as answerability'.[2] To declare that a (natural or legal) person is responsible in this sense is to indicate that they can be called to account for their conduct and made to respond to any moral or legal charges that are put. Understood thus, responsibility need not necessarily imply that a wrong has been done since a person may respond to a charge by offering a valid justification for their conduct, thereby deflecting any imputation of wrongdoing. The idea of responsibility as answerability for this reason needs to be set apart from what

* We are especially grateful to the editors of this volume for their encouragement and patience and to Lukas Meyer, Liam Murphy, and audiences at the Lauterpacht Centre for International Law, the 2007 British Academy Postdoctoral Fellowship Symposium and the Fribourg Workshop on the Philosophy of International Law for their helpful questions and comments.

[1] For two excellent surveys of the various meaning of 'responsibility', see Hart, H., 'Postscript: Responsibility and Retribution', in his *Punishment and Responsibility* (Oxford: Clarendon Press, 1968), 210–37, and Kutz, C., 'Responsibility', in Coleman, J. and Shapiro, S. (eds.), *The Oxford Handbook of Jurisprudence and the Philosophy of Law* (Oxford: Oxford University Press, 2002), 548.

[2] This meaning is given prominence in e.g. Lucas, J., *Responsibility* (Oxford: Oxford University Press, 1993), 5–12, and Gardner, J., 'The Mark of Responsibility', *Oxford Journal of Legal Studies*, 23/2 (2003), 157.

might be termed 'responsibility as liability'—the idea that a person has violated their obligations and become liable to some negative response such as punishment, censure, or enforced compensation.

Both senses of responsibility are in evidence in the international legal system, albeit at somewhat different points in its operation.[3] The idea of responsibility as answerability is at work at the point in the legal process *before* it has been decided one way or another whether a breach of international law has taken place. It finds expression, for example, in the rules that determine *locus standi* and the admissibility of claims. These rules organize the lines of international legal accountability, determining who is answerable to whom, and in respect of what conduct. In recent years they have undergone a process of significant development, reflecting the changing demands that actors on the international scene can make on one another. Whereas once only states could invoke responsibility, and only then in respect of putatively unlawful conduct which was directly injurious to their interests, now states can hold one another accountable for the violations of at least certain norms regardless of whether they have been individually victims,[4] and, at least in a limited sense, individuals can both be held to account—as, for example, when they are made to stand trial in the International Criminal Court—and force others to account, as, for example, when 'just satisfaction' is sought before the European Court of Human Rights.[5]

The idea of responsibility as liability, by contrast, comes into operation *after* it has been decided that a breach of international law has occurred, in the principles that determine the legal consequences following from the violation of an international obligation. These principles shape the judicial response to international lawbreaking and the legal obligations which responsible parties thereby acquire. In their present formulation, they are complicated by the interplay of a number of variables, including the identity of the responsible agent (state, individual, international organization, etc.) and the type of legal response (enforced reparation, monitoring, punishment, etc.), with the end result that liability gets fragmented into several distinct regimes, including the regime of 'civil' liability to which states—and, by derivation, international organizations—are subject when they perform an internationally wrongful act and the regime of criminal liability to which individuals are subject when they commit an international crime.

---

[3] However, international law tends to use the word 'responsibility' as a synonym for 'liability', not least because other UN languages have equivalents for the former but not the latter. For example article 263 of the 1982 Law of the Sea Convention is entitled in English 'Responsibility and Liability'; in French and Spanish it is entitled simply '*Responsabilité/Responsibilidad*', and likewise in Chinese, Russian, and Arabic.

[4] See the ILC Articles on Responsibility of States for Internationally Wrongful Acts, annexed to UNGA Res. 56/117, 12 Dec. 2001, reprinted in Crawford, J., *The ILC's Articles on State Responsibility: Introduction, Text and Commentaries* (Cambridge: Cambridge University Press, 2002), esp. article 48 and commentary, 276–80.

[5] The sense is limited because individuals can only bring claims under special treaty arrangements (such as the European Convention on Human Rights or under bilateral or multilateral investment treaties). They do not have a general prerogative to bring claims under international law. On this see Okawa, P., 'Issues of Admissibility and the Law on International Responsibility', in Evans, M. (ed.), *International Law* (2nd edn., Oxford: Oxford University Press, 2006), 479.

Both at the level of conceptual analysis and legal practice, international responsibility is thus a large and multifaceted subject. Besides the cleavage between answerability and liability, it encompasses a number of theoretical and practical distinctions, including the distinctions between individual and corporate subjects, criminal and civil responsibility, and claims brought at domestic and international levels. In what follows, we focus specifically on the portion of this complex field that centres on the liabilities of states implemented through international bodies such as the International Court of Justice (ICJ) and inter-state tribunals. This is not to discount the philosophical interest of other dimensions of international responsibility, such as the accountability of international organizations and the criminal liabilities of individuals. But it does acknowledge the primacy of state responsibility within the international system as presently arranged. To the extent that one regime stands out in terms of its institutional refinement, it is the regime of liability that states trigger when they violate an international rule. From a philosophical as well as a legal perspective, it provides an obvious point of departure.

II. The Character of State Liability

In the event that a state breaches an international obligation and commits 'an internationally wrongful act',[6] it incurs an obligation (i) to cease that wrongful act, if it is still continuing, and (ii) to make full reparation for any material or moral damage caused. These two obligations, which have been articulated in the judgments of international tribunals and courts and which are codified in the International Law Commission's (ILC) Articles on State Responsibility,[7] make up the core content of the general international law relating to the liabilities of states. They bring out the underlying character of state responsibility as a system of civil—as opposed to criminal—liability. At present, the burdens that are imposed on delinquent states are exclusively reparative rather than penal in character. In spite of the arguments of those who have wanted to see introduced a category of state crime,[8] there has been no development of corporate criminal responsibility to parallel the introduction of individual criminal responsibility on the international plane, nor has there been any trend among arbitral tribunals to impose punitive damages on states.

---

[6] 'Internationally wrongful act' is the general term used for a breach of an international legal obligation by a state. It need not imply a *moral* transgression.

[7] (above, n. 4). The ILC Articles were adopted by the ILC itself in Aug. 2001 and are annexed to GA resolution 56/83 of 12 Dec. 2001.

[8] For such arguments, see Pellet, A., 'Can a State Commit a Crime? Definitely, Yes!', *European Journal of International Law*, 10/2 (1999), 425–34, and Jorgensen, N., *The Responsibility of States for International Crimes* (Oxford: Oxford University Press, 2000), esp. ch. 13. The ILC eventually rejected the category: see Crawford, J., *The ILC's Articles on State Responsibility* (above, n. 4), 35–8.

The twin obligations of cessation and reparation, moreover, give an important insight into the underlying character of those international legal prohibitions that are imposed on states. If we ask for a specification of the hallmarks of an internationally wrongful act, two features come to mind, corresponding to the two dimensions of state liability. First, an internationally wrongful act is one that is forbidden or disallowed by an international rule. This is fundamental. By prohibiting conduct, the international legal system provides a legal reason against performing it that would otherwise be absent. An internationally wrongful act is not a permissible act for which a price is charged or an act which a state is entitled to perform so long as it provides adequate reparation for any resulting harms; it is an act which should not be done; if done and the performance is ongoing (as when one state is unlawfully occupying the territory of another), it should cease.

Secondly, an internationally wrongful act is one whose harmful consequences should, as far as possible, be undone by the responsible state and should not be left to the injured party to suffer without remedy or compensation. By attaching an obligation of repair to acts which it prohibits, international law marks out a certain class of losses—namely, those that follow directly from unlawful conduct—as ones which should not lie where they fall. Of course, not every material harm or loss that can befall a state gives rise to a right to compensation. A state whose interests are damaged as a result of the withdrawal of economic aid, for example, has to bear the loss itself because the withdrawal of economic aid is (absent an express treaty commitment) legally permissible. But it belongs to the nature of an internationally wrongful act that any resulting injuries must not be endured by the injured party but must be transferred back to the responsible state. As the Permanent Court of International Justice (PCIJ) put it in the *Chorzów* case:

The essential principle contained in the notion of an illegal act—a principle which seems established by international practice and in particular by the decisions of arbitral tribunals—is that reparation must, so far as possible, wipe out all the consequences of the illegal act and re-establish the situation that would, in all probability, have existed if that act had not been committed.[9]

Needless to say, both of these features of the internationally wrongful act require elaboration and qualification if they are to mesh with the realities of international practice, including legal practice. The reference to undoing past injury, in particular, is complicated by the fact that states can rarely take back the consequences of their conduct and restore the *status quo ante* in any literal sense: the best that can be managed in most situations is to offer victims compensation for the financially assessable losses or—failing that—to provide an apology or expression of regret (so-called 'satisfaction'). But the twin hallmarks of the internationally wrongful act are nonetheless worth setting out in these abstract terms because they help to shed light on what is at stake in decisions to prohibit conduct under international law.

---

[9] PCIJ, *Factory at Chorzow, Jurisdiction*, PCIJ Series A, No. 9 (1927), 47.

By virtue of the reason—giving and loss-shifting dimensions of the internationally wrongful act, the imposition of a new obligation on a state has a particular evaluative complexion, serving to limit the state's freedom of action whilst at the same time enhancing the security of those to whom the obligation is owed. When the United Kingdom (UK) signed the UN Convention Against Torture, for example, it surrendered its right to extradite suspects to countries in which they would be in danger of torture whilst at the same time affording to such suspects legal protection from torture and remedial rights in the event that such protection was unforthcoming. Through its support for the Convention, the UK thus signalled (among other things) its commitment to a particular normative judgment, namely that individual protection against torture is more important than its own freedom to shape its extradition procedures. And this kind of judgment, at least in a generalized form, is at work in any decision to impose a new obligation on a state: whenever a decision is made to impose a new obligation on a state, then the assumption is present that the freedom of action of the obligated state is worth restricting for the sake of the interests of those who acquire the corresponding rights and that the range of losses which should be reassigned through enforced reparation should be expanded to include the losses resulting from the breach of the proposed obligation.[10]

This point is germane because it helps to demystify some of the general preconditions of international liability. By convention, the law on state responsibility not only spells out the legal consequences of an international breach but also defines some of the terms under which such a breach occurs. The ILC Articles, for instance, include rules on attribution and justification that are intended to interact with the definitions of particular wrongs to determine when such wrongs are committed.[11] These rules, which might otherwise seem mysterious or unmotivated, can usefully be seen as embodying higher-order decisions about the reason-giving and loss-shifting functions of international legal prohibitions. A good example is the rules on attribution of conduct to states. These determine which actions of which natural or legal persons constitute conduct of the state for the purposes of responsibility. They are indispensable to the law on state responsibility for the obvious reason that states, lacking bodies of their own, can only act through the agency of others—in the end, of natural persons. In their current formulation, they stipulate that the official and *ultra vires* conduct of any individual who is deemed a public functionary under national law counts as the conduct of the state, but that the actions of private citizens do not.[12] At the most general level of analysis, this way

---

[10] This point, which follows from the principles of international law as opposed to the psychologies of particular lawmakers, applies regardless of whether the corresponding rights-holder is a state or an individual and regardless of whether the obligation is peremptory or non-peremptory.

[11] For rules on attribution, see ILC articles 4–10; for rules on justification ('circumstances precluding wrongfulness'), see articles 20–7.

[12] To be sure, there are complications—for example, relating to the conduct of paramilitaries and para-statal entities. See esp. ILC articles 10–11.

of construing state agency registers a determinate judgment about the scope of state obligations, marking out the range of natural persons who are bound by any given norm and the spread of losses which give rise to remedial rights. In relation to the ban on states maltreating foreign aliens, for example, it implies, first, that the legal reason which speaks against maltreatment should be addressed to any state official regardless of rank or function, and, secondly, that the victim of maltreatment should be entitled to reparation so long as the injurer was a public functionary. Were it cast differently—were it, say, to limit state agency to the actions of the leaders or 'controlling minds' of the state—it would register a different judgment about the terms of international interaction, one which would be more favourable to the interests of agents in freedom of action (since fewer natural persons would be bound by state obligations) and less favourable to the interests of victims in protection from unremedied losses (since fewer cases would give rise to remedial rights).

A similar line of analysis goes for the rules on justification too. These rules spell out considerations that render legally permissible state conduct that would otherwise be unlawful. Articles 20–6 of the ILC Articles identify six considerations which 'preclude wrongfulness': consent, self-defence, lawful countermeasures, *force majeure*, distress, and necessity. Taken together, they place determinate limits on the application of state obligations, marking out circumstances in which states are exempt from their normal duties and remedial responsibilities. As such, they embody a particular decision as to when states should be bound by legal reasons and when they should be obliged to remedy losses they have caused. By including 'necessity' in their number (to fix upon one example), they imply that states shouldn't be held to the performance of their normal obligations at a time when their vital interests are at risk.[13] Were necessity not counted as a justification, then a different conception of the scope of international obligations would be in evidence, one that would be less congenial to the interests of states in freedom of action (since they would be duty-bound in a wider range of cases) whilst being more congenial to victims in protection from unremedied losses (since they would enjoy more extensive remedial rights).

Of course, none of this is meant to vindicate the *status quo*, whether in legal terms or as concerns the relation of law to practice. There is plenty of room to query the existing rules on justification and attribution and to put forward alternatives, either by arguing that state obligations need to be assigned a broader or a narrower scope. But the point that deserves to be stressed here is that such alternatives need to be assessed in light of a proper appreciation of the character of state obligations and the values which they implicate: only by first indentifying what is at stake in

---

[13] For a more exact definition of necessity, see esp. Crawford, J., *The ILC's Articles on State Responsibility* (above, n. 4), 178–86. For a critique of the freedom which necessity, along with the other justifications, appears to give to states, see Allott, P., 'State Responsibility and the Unmaking of International Law', *Harvard International Law Review*, 29 (1988), 16–24.

decisions to prohibit conduct can we hope to evaluate the merits or demerits of any proposed precondition of liability.

The reason-giving and loss-shifting dimensions of the internationally wrongful act thus set the scene for 'internal' disagreements about state liability. They also provide the context for 'external' critiques of the system as a whole. Apart from challenging specific rules on attribution and justification, the entire practice of imposing liabilities on states can be brought into question. Those who are sympathetic to an individualist paradigm of responsibility have, in particular, argued that the existing practice is both unfair to the population of the responsible state and ineffective in promoting those ends such, as peace, security, and respect for human rights, which are often assumed to be a priority concern of the international order. For the time being, we propose to focus on their arguments and to leave to one side the rules on attribution and justification. This is not because these rules are unimportant or uncontentious but because they can only earn their keep in the international system if the broader practice to which they belong can itself be justified. Only by first deflecting what might be termed the *individualist challenge* can determinate standards of state liability obtain foundational support.

III. THE INDIVIDUALIST CHALLENGE

In his textbook on international law, Antonio Cassese writes:

The international community is so primitive that the archaic concept of collective responsibility still prevails. Where States breach an international rule, the whole collectivity to which the individual State official belongs, who materially infringed that rule, bears responsibility . . . On the international plane, it is the whole State that incurs responsibility and which therefore has to take all the required remedial measures.[14]

Cassese gives the impression in this passage that whenever a state is held responsible in international law, the aggregate of persons in that state themselves incur responsibility. At one level this is misleading. A state, construed as an artificial legal person, is not the same as any 'collectivity' of natural persons, nor is the legal responsibility or liability of the state tantamount to that of any given population. But the conceptualization of state responsibility as a form of collective responsibility is nonetheless useful because it brings out an important line of complaint that can be directed at this area of international law, one that trades on the predominantly non-individualistic character of responsibility-ascriptions on the international plane.

The complaint in question concerns the effects that the imposition of liability has on the interests of the general population of the responsible state. When a state incurs liability, the resulting costs may be borne by the entire citizenry of the state

---

[14] Cassese, A., *International Law* (2nd edn., Oxford: Oxford University Press, 2005), 241.

and not its leadership or officials. In the event that a state incurs an obligation to provide compensation for the material damage it has caused, for example, the funding for the compensation payments will invariably come from general taxation rather than from the private finances of the individuals who are morally implicated in the international breach. This wouldn't be troubling if the entire population of the responsible state were, in some sense, morally blameworthy for the state's breach of international law. If, for example, the entire citizenry of a country had given its willing support to a government's decision to undertake an unlawful act of aggression, then it might be justifiable for any liabilities to be shared among the population at large. But in virtually every case of state responsibility, the population that is eventually called upon to carry the costs of responsibility includes members who are, by any standard, morally blameless. Indeed they may be a majority. So far as they are concerned, their treatment at the hands of the international system may seem as unfair and ethically backwards as the treatment meted out under primitive systems of collective responsibility in which whole tribes or nations are subject to reprisals: after all, in both set-ups innocent people are called upon to pay the price for the misdeeds and mistakes of their rulers.[15]

This sense of unfairness, moreover, can be heightened by an additional line of complaint that concerns the effectiveness of international law in promoting compliance with international values. On the face of it, state responsibility seems to be a very poor instrument for discouraging behaviour that is deemed undesirable by the international community. In terms of its deterrent possibilities, it affords to those officials on whose conduct state agency depends no motive for staying within the parameters set down by state obligations. The police officer who maltreats a foreign visitor or the military commander who violates foreign airspace, for example, will not be subject to any sanctions at the international level since liability, if it is incurred at all, will be allocated to the state as a whole and not to the officials who were personally involved in the breach. Given this fact, and given the supervenience of state agency on the agency of officials, it is, Philip Allott argues, unsurprising 'that states behave badly. The moral effect of the law is vastly reduced if the human agents involved are able to separate themselves personally both from the duties that law imposes and from the responsibility which it entails'.[16]

---

[15] The complaint has been elicited esp. by the United Nations Claims Commission, set up in the wake of the First Gulf War to facilitate claims for compensation 'resulting from Iraq's unlawful invasion and occupation of Kuwait': see e.g. Falk, R., 'Reparations, International Law, and Global Justice: A New Frontier', in De Greiff, P. (ed.), *The Oxford Handbook of Reparations* (Oxford: Oxford University Press, 2006), 486; Arnove, A. (ed.), *Iraq Under Siege: The Deadly Impact of Sanctions and War* (Cambridge, Mass.: South End Press, 2000), *passim*; and Klein, N., 'Why is War-Torn Iraq giving $190,000 to Toys R Us?', at <www.guardian.co.uk/comment/story/0,,1328664,00.html>. (All websites were most recently checked in Dec. 2007). For broader philosophical critiques of collective responsibility grounded in fairness considerations, see Lewis, H., 'Collective Responsibility', *Philosophy*, 24 (1948), 3; Sverdlik, S., 'Collective Responsibility', *Philosophical Studies*, 51 (1987), 68.

[16] Allott, P., 'State Responsibility and the Unmaking of International Law' (above, n. 13), 14.

At the most general level of analysis, both of these criticisms point in the same direction. They both imply that international law would do well to substitute or supplement state responsibility with a paradigm of responsibility which is more sensitive to considerations of individual deterrence and blameworthiness. But in spite of this common orientation, the two complaints are worth distinguishing because they threaten to discredit somewhat different aspects of the state system, thereby generating different proposals for reform.

The fairness complaint is, in essence, an objection to the loss-shifting function of state obligations. The specific feature of international law that it challenges is the imposition of obligations of repair on states. Subtract this feature from the international order and the apparent injustice done to innocent populations would disappear. By contrast, the effectiveness complaint is an objection to any feature of the state system that hinders the promotion of accepted international values. Being consequentialist in character, it is open-ended in its targets. Although it could be used to question the loss-shifting function of state obligations, it could also be used to cast doubt on their reason-giving function. A case might be made, for instance, for thinking that the motivational inefficacy of international law is due to the fact that its demands are addressed to artificial—as opposed to natural—legal persons. Perhaps the explanation given for the prevalence of international noncompliance is that international obligations speak to states as opposed to individuals, thereby allowing officials and leaders to distance themselves morally and psychologically from the wrongs in which they are implicated. The particular feature of international law that would then be impugned by the effectiveness complaint would be the imposition of legal reasons and obligations on states rather than the imposition of obligations of repair.

The charge of ineffectiveness thus has the potential to be much more radical in its implications than the fairness objection. Developed in a suitable way, it yields the recommendation that states should surrender their standing as principal duty-bearers under international law in favour of individuals. Whether this recommendation is taken seriously depends, in part, on the plausibility of the empirical assumptions on which it draws. One way of responding to the complaint is to show that it fails in its own terms. Being a consequentialist argument, it can be countered by showing that the benefits of the state system, on closer inspection, exceed the benefits of the proposed alternatives. Even if we concede that state liability has a weaker deterrent effect than individual liability, we might nonetheless think that it has other consequential benefits that tell in its favour. One such benefit, for example, might be its capacity to give proper recognition to complex corporate goals: only a state-centric system of obligations, we might argue, can give due acknowledgement to aims such as the reduction of greenhouse gas emissions or the protection of the endangered species which call for positive interaction and cooperation among a multiplicity of actors. Another benefit we might highlight relates to the longevity of states: it is not too much to define states as the principal mechanism for the transmission of the accrued rights of human communities over time. This is true not only of their boundaries and jurisdiction but also of their obligations. Governments and governmental arrangements change, leaders come and go, constitutions are overthrown, but (unless otherwise agreed or decided) the state continues. In a world in which long-term planning is important, we might argue that imposing obligations on states contributes to a sense of ongoing security and predictability which is valuable to any corresponding rights-holders, and which would be lost if obligations were allotted only to officials or leaders.

Even if these benefits don't add up to a decisive case in favour of the state system, however, there is another way to respond to the effectiveness complaint, which is to note that it falls foul of what Allen Buchanan calls the 'Vanishing Subject Matter Problem'.[17] If states were no longer assigned international obligations, then it would be questionable whether anything worthy of the name of international law—and *a fortiori* international responsibility—would be left. States would not only lack their status as duty-bearers but they would forfeit their *right* to assume duties voluntarily through treaty-making. These two adjustments would effectively strip them of international legal personality in any meaningful sense, thus subtracting from international law its defining legal entity.

Because this implication is so far removed from the current legal order and from the feasible reforms which it could undergo, we propose to leave it to one side and take for granted the existence and standing of states *qua* bearers of legal obligations and perpetrators of legal wrongs. For the rest of this chapter, we focus instead on the question whether it is unfair to impose obligations of repair on states given the impact this has on innocent populations. The charge of unfairness and ethical primitivism certainly can't be dismissed as utopian or unrealistic in its reformist agenda: it is perfectly possible to envisage a legal order in which states are subject to primary obligations without being subject to obligations to provide reparation for the wrongful damage they have caused. In fact, current legal practice approximates much more closely to such a legal order than the principles of state responsibility might seem to imply. For while it is a well-established *principle* of international law that responsible states are under an obligation to provide full reparation for the injuries they have caused, in a significant proportion of the cases which come before international arbitral tribunals, what is sought is not the payment of damages but clarification of a confused or contested legal situation. Out of the 435 inter-state arbitrations which took place in the period 1794–1972, for instance, only 261 dealt with claims for damages; the remaining 174 confined themselves to legal interpretation, of which about half concerned boundary disputes or questions of title to territory.[18] Moreover, there are branches of international law—most notably the law of the World Trade Organization (WTO)—where the basic remedy is

---

[17] Buchanan, A., *Justice, Legitimacy, and Self-Determination: Moral Foundations of International Law* (Oxford: Oxford University Press, 2003), 53.

[18] See Gray, C., *Judicial Remedies in International Law* (Oxford: Clarendon Press, 1987), 11.

cessation and damages are practically excluded. A real-world model is therefore available for a state system that does away with the feature of responsibility which causes the alleged injustice to innocent civilians. The question that needs to be addressed is whether this model should be extended more widely and be reflected in the general principles of state responsibility. Should the fairness objection motivate the abandonment of inter-state loss-shifting altogether, thus leaving the state system to focus on accountability and, as necessary, cessation?

IV. JUSTIFYING STATE RESPONSIBILITY

There is one response to the question that circumvents any need to enter into the deeper waters of political morality and normative ethics. The fairness objection is the product of two assumptions—a factual assumption to the effect that the remedial dimension of the state system imposes extra burdens on innocent populations and a moral assumption to the effect that this is unfair. Without assessing the merits of the standard of fairness on which the moral assumption calls, we might try to nullify the force of the complaint by claiming that its factual assumption is, if not quite false, seriously misleading: although states are sometimes called upon to provide reparations, the impact which this has on the private citizens is so negligible as to be barely worth mentioning.

At least three features of current legal practice, moreover, might be enlisted in order to support and develop this line of response. The first of these concerns the *transferability* of the burdens of the responsible state to innocent populations. At least some of the obligations that are imposed on responsible states don't lend themselves to a process of onwards distribution to natural persons. In the event that reparation takes the form of an apology or expression of regret, for example, then no extra burden is imposed on the general population of the responsible state at all. An official apology or expression of regret must come through a public channel and not through the words or gestures of private individuals. When France apologized for the acts of its agents in bombing the Greenpeace vessel *Rainbow Warrior* in Auckland Harbour, no individual French citizen apologized;[19] had they done so, it would have been without any relevance to the issues of state responsibility arising from the event.[20]

---

[19] See New Zealand High Court, *R v Mafart & Prieur* (1985) 74 ILR 241; UN Secretary-General's Ruling (1986), 74 ILR 256; Arbitral Tribunal, *New Zealand v France* (1990) 82 ILR 499.

[20] In this respect, international law provides a counterexample to J. Feinberg's claim that the burdens of corporate responsibility must necessarily fall on to natural persons (see Feinberg, J., 'Collective Responsibility', in May, L. and Hoffman, S. (eds.), *Collective Responsibility* (Lanham, Md.: Rowman and Littlefield, 1991), 73). Just as there are certain actions that only corporate beings can perform (e.g. signing treaties, declaring war), so there are certain burdens that only they can carry.

Secondly, some of the liabilities that are imposed on responsible states don't qualify as *burdens* in the relevant sense and *eo ipso* don't add to the burdens of innocent citizens. Especially in cases where reparation takes the form of restitution, the responsible state may be left no worse off than it would have been had there had been no unlawful conduct in the first place. A responsible state that is required to return looted property or annexed territory may be stripped of a benefit, but it is not made to suffer costs that would be absent had it stuck to its international obligations. To the extent that 'a burden' is defined relative to a counterfactual scenario of legality, it is questionable whether restitutionary liabilities are generally burdensome to responsible states or to their populations, at least in so far as they are confined to situations in which there has been no period of sustained dependence on the unlawful distribution of land or property.

Thirdly, the liabilities that are imposed on states, even if transferable and in the relevant sense burdensome, don't normally constitute especially large burdens, as these things go. In the event that a state is called upon to pay compensation for an internationally wrongful act, the resulting burdens will normally be trivial when set against the total resources of the state. To give some examples which illustrate the kind of sums at stake, in the *Corfu Channel* case, the ICJ awarded damages against Albania of £843,947;[21] in the case of *Loizidou v Turkey*, the European Court of Human Rights (ECtHR) awarded damages against Turkey of Cyp. £470,000;[22] and in the *Del Caracazo* case, the Inter-American Court of Human Rights (IACtHR) awarded total damages against Venezuela totalling US\$ 5,481,300.[23] In none of these cases were the damages awarded of an order of magnitude to have a noticeable impact on the public treasury or on the ordinary taxpayer.

An inspection of legal practice thus does much to sustain a purely empirical response to the fairness objection. Given the nature and size of awards made by international courts and tribunals, the loss-shifting dimension of the state system rarely has a large-scale impact on the population of the responsible state. However, this response, important though it is, cannot be the whole story. For one thing, the imposition of obligations of repair on states, even in those cases where the impact on blameless populations is relatively trivial, is still vulnerable to the charge that innocent people are being made to pay the price (albeit a small price) for the misdeeds of their rulers. For another thing, there have been exceptional cases in which the liabilities imposed on states have been large enough to impact significantly on the interests of private citizens. At the end of the First Gulf War, for example,

---

[21] ICJ, *Corfu Channel (UK v. Albania)*, ICJ Rep. 1949, 249 (damage and loss of life caused by mines which sank one warship and damaged another).

[22] ECtHR, *Loizidou v. Turkey* (1998) VI ECHR, 1807 (damages for wrongful exclusion from property following the Turkish invasion of Cyprus).

[23] IACtHR, *Del Caracazo v. Venezuela* (2002) 95 IACHR (ser. C). The award consisted of pecuniary damages ($1,559,800) and moral damages ($3,921,500) arising from the torture and disappearance of 37 persons and the ill-treatment of a further 3 persons.

Iraq was called upon to pay compensation totalling in excess of US$ 52 billion for its unlawful invasion and occupation of Kuwait, thus adding significantly to the burdens of a population that was also subject to a regime of stringent economic sanctions.[24]

To offer a fuller response to the fairness objection, we therefore need to engage in normative as well as descriptive reasoning. To provide a thoroughgoing response to the individualist challenge, we need to query the assumption that it is always unfair for a system of liability to impose extra burdens on innocent populations. One way in which we might do this is to show that the moral ideal that lies behind the assumption is utopian in its aspirations. Assuming for the moment that the ideal in question is that 'innocent' citizens should never suffer extra burdens as a result of matters that lie outside of their control, we might point out that this ideal is both unrealized and unrealizable both in our moral and legal practices. Not only do the domestic arrangements of states make it inevitable that citizens will sometimes be exposed to unwanted and unchosen costs (for instance, through unpopular tax programmes), but the context of international loss-shifting makes this inescapable too.[25] In cases where one of two states must bear the costs of injury, then assuming that costs are always covered through general taxation, one of two populations is bound to end up worse off than it would otherwise have been. In relation to the damage suffered by Kuwait at the end of the First Gulf War, for example, the costs of post-war reconstruction were either going to be borne by Iraq and the Iraqi people or Kuwait and the Kuwaiti people. The practical choice was not between visiting burdens on a 'guilty' population or visiting burdens on an 'innocent' population; the choice was between imposing extra burdens on one of two groups, both largely blameless for the original injuries caused but one of which suffered a great deal more.

Given this fact, it is unrealistic to insist that innocent populations should never suffer extra burdens as a result of matters that lie outside of their control. The moral ideal that apparently lies behind the fairness is impossibly demanding in its moral recommendations. However, this doesn't, by itself, show that the loss-shifting aspect of the state system is fair. There may be other interpretations of the individualist challenge that aren't so easy to meet. To provide a stronger case in favour of the practice of state reparations, we therefore need to engage in constructive moral reasoning, identifying a positive principle of fairness which is both plausible and attractive in its own right, and which the practice satisfies.

---

[24] The total amount of damages claimed was some US$350 bn. Of the US$52.5 bn awarded by the UNCC, approximately US$21 bn has been paid via the arrangements for sale of Iraqi oil. See <http://www2.unog.ch/uncc/status.htm>.

[25] For further discussion of this point, see Cane, P., *Responsibility in Law and Morality* (Oxford: Hart Publishing, 2002), ch. 3.

To this end, we might draw upon some of the intuitions that are articulated elsewhere in moral thinking, particularly those that are elicited by examples of enterprise liability and corporate responsibility. David Miller, for instance, suggests that it is fair for the partners in a business to share the costs of any resulting compensation payments regardless of the individual causal contributions which each of them made to the harms in question. His grounds for this claim are that the partners 'are beneficiaries of a common practice in which participants are treated fairly—they get the income and other benefits which go with the job . . .—and so they should also be prepared to carry their share of the costs, in this case the costs that stem from external aspects of the practice'.[26] Perhaps we could extend a rationale of this kind to the international level, exploiting the analogy between the 'innocent' partners in a trading company and 'innocent' citizens of a state. Perhaps we could claim that the practice of state responsibility is fair to its members (in spite of its 'external costs') in virtue of the profile of benefits and burdens that all-things-considered they obtain from it.

To develop this line of justification, we would need to adapt Miller's suggestion to mesh with the broader contours of the debate. It would be no good, for instance, adopting as our standard of fairness the principle that a practice is fair to a population so long as the population obtains more benefits than burdens from it overall. For one thing, this standard is too conservative to engage with some of the reform proposals of the individualist: in effect, it holds that the loss-shifting dimension of the state system is justified so long as people obtain *sufficient* benefits from it, thereby ignoring the possibility that there may be alternatives—such as a system of international civil liability in which *individual* officials or leaders are called upon to pay damages—which are even better in terms of their effects. For another thing, it relativizes fairness to specific populations, thereby yielding a series of verdicts that are unhelpful in assessing the *overall* credentials of general principles of international law.[27]

Nonetheless, it seems plausible to think that the benefit test could be refined and developed in a way that meets our dialectical needs. We could, for example, take it in a Rawlsian direction, focusing on the benefits and burdens which different schemes of liability would be assigned in a suitably defined choice-situation. Suppose, more especially, we defined a rule as fair if it would be chosen above any alternative in a position of partial ignorance, in which we were unaware of the particular state or population to which we belonged but we knew the various kinds of effects which different forms of liability had on different types of states and their populations. We would then have at our disposal a standard of fairness which, through its use of informational constraints and the consideration of alternatives,

---

[26] Miller, D. 'Holding Nations Responsible', *Ethics*, 114 (2004), 253.

[27] Unless we are willing to hold that principles of general international law should apply selectively, thereby denying the so-called 'equality of states', it is no use being told that a principle is fair to this-or-that population or this-or-that state: we need to know whether it is fair *sans phrase*.

would deliver judgements that were neither 'population-relative' nor rigged against the individualist.

This standard, moreover, could then be used to argue that the principle of state reparations is fair. We could claim that such a principle would be chosen over any feasible alternative in a fairness-conferring choice-situation. Although we would need to run through a lengthy sequence or pair-wise comparisons in order to make this argument watertight, it is not implausible to think that in the crucial choice between imposing remedial responsibilities on states or on assignable individuals (officials, leaders, etc.), we would choose the former over the latter. The grounds for this centre on the interest that we would have, from behind 'the veil of ignorance', in ensuring that we wouldn't have to bear the costs of injury in the event that we—or the state to which we belonged—were the victims of international lawbreaking. In so far as we were anxious to ensure an effective scheme of international loss-shifting, we would have at least two reasons for preferring a scheme which shifted losses onto states as opposed to individuals. First, such a scheme would give us the confidence that any large-scale damage claims could be met: in the event that we (or the state to which we belonged) were to put in a multi-million-dollar claim, for example, we could rest assured that the responsible state would have the financial resources needed to pay out in full whereas we couldn't be so certain that the same would be true of the individual officials who were personally responsible for the international breach. Secondly, it would afford us clear targets for reparations claims in cases where the alleged wrongdoing issued from organizational as opposed to individual failure: in the event that we were to bring a claim in respect of an alleged violation of our right to a fair trial or our right to marry, for example, it would be much easier for us to meet with success if we only had to identify failings 'in the system' and didn't have to identify the specific causal and moral roles of individual officials.

Whether this argument is decisive for our purposes is, of course, a matter for further speculation. A suppressed premise is that the advantages of the 'state option' in terms of enhanced remedial rights are sufficiently great to outweigh the disadvantage of having to pay the price for the misdeeds of one's officials and leaders. This seems plausible enough in the type of cases that come before international courts such as the ICJ and the ECtHR where the sums involved are unlikely to have a significant impact on the taxpayers of the responsible state. But it seems less credible in cases of war reparations where the impact could, in principle, be very serious indeed.[28] There may, in consequence, be a moral case,

---

[28] The largest damages sum in modern times was the global amount imposed on Germany pursuant to the war guilt clause of the Treaty of Versailles, 1919. Of the sum of 132 billion gold marks (approx £ 6.6 billion) Germany eventually paid around 23 billion marks (15%): see Kent, B., *The Spoils of War: The Politics, Economics and Diplomacy of Reparations 1918–1932* (Oxford: Clarendon Press, 1989), 11. The largest post-1945 agreed settlement involving damages as distinct from debt seems to have been the FRG–Israel Agreement of 10 Sept. 1952, 162 UNTS 205, involving payments of some DM 3 bn over 10 years in respect of the Holocaust.

rooted in considerations of hypothetical consent, for treating the losses which arise from illegal aggression as a special category which shouldn't come within the normal ambit of the principle of state reparations but which should be dealt with in some other way—possibly through a system of international loss-spreading which extends across the community of nations.

Nonetheless, we hope that we have said enough to show that the case in favour of divesting the state system of its loss-shifting function is open to doubt. Not only is the individualist challenge unconvincing on both empirical and moral grounds, but a positive argument, rooted in considerations of hypothetical consent, can be made for continuing to impose remedial duties on states. This argument can also be used to explain the reluctance of international law to impose criminal liability on states. Whilst international law imposes civil damages on responsible states, it doesn't impose penal damages on them. A moral justification for this asymmetry can be found in the decisions that we would make in a suitably defined choice-situation. Whilst we might acknowledge that the imposition of any kind of damages on states would have an unwelcome impact on us, we might think that penal damages are especially objectionable because they are part of a system of liability from which we don't obtain the offsetting benefits of effective remedial rights. In this respect, they would seem to have all of the disadvantages of civil liability without any of the advantages. From the relevant position of choice, we might therefore opt for a system of state responsibility very much like the one that we have at present. Delinquent states would be subject to obligations of repair but not punishments.

V. Conclusion

International law is not static. Like any legal system, it evolves with the broader moral and political climate. Over the past fifty years or so, international organizations have become increasingly important as actors on the international stage and given the development of international human rights mechanisms and international criminal law, individuals too have acquired a more prominent role. These changes have complicated the subject of international responsibility, but they have not changed its fundamentals. The regime of state 'civil' liability continues to provide the principal model of responsibility on the international plane. In this chapter, we have sought to defend it from 'external' attack and explain some of its internal architecture. Appealing to the potential benefits it brings, we have argued that it is neither a primitive form of collective responsibility nor an unfair scheme of loss-shifting. Although we don't believe it's perfect, we don't believe it's morally groundless either.

CHAPTER 14

INTERNATIONAL RESPONSIBILITY

LIAM MURPHY*

A theory of international responsibility finds its proper place in a comprehensive legal, political, and moral theory. There is no theory of international responsibility without a theory of domestic responsibility, and vice versa. Similarly, we cannot think sensibly about the domestic or international responsibilities of states without at the same time thinking about the domestic and international responsibilities of non-state actors of various kinds, including individuals.

I will try to lay out some of the structure of the relations between these issues. Like James Crawford and Jeremy Watkins, I believe that a productive place to start is with the international responsibilities of states.[1] That forces us immediately to think about the moral significance of states, which is a matter foundational for all of our connected issues. Needless to say, it is a big topic, and I will be able to do little more than indicate where my own sympathies lie.

I. Concepts

One way to begin would be to acknowledge the obvious fact that there are states and then investigate their nature to see whether it is appropriate to attribute rights and obligations to them. This would require some reflection on the very concept of the state. But that would be a false start. We may define terms however we like,

* This paper benefited greatly from discussion at the Oxford workshop and the written comments of the editors of this volume.
[1] Crawford, J. and Watkins, J., Chapter 13 in this volume, 285.

inventing whatever new entities we think are useful for our enquiries or practices; the real issue is that of the justification of attributions of responsibility to the entities thus defined. Political theory is foundational here; reflection on our concepts is not in itself going to resolve questions about rights and responsibilities.

States are not features of our natural world; when we use the concept of the state we engage in a practice of categorization that is optional. Traditionally the criteria for the identity and persistence of states over time have been controversial in international law. Crawford's celebrated treatise on the topic presumably puts an end to the idea that statehood is, all the way down, a question of fact. That could only be the case if the concept of a state were univocal within and across linguistic cultures, in a way that we could say that the concept of a table or a book is.[2] In fact, of course, law, political theory, and sociology all make use of definitions of the state that must be defended against other possible stipulations. If international law converged on an account of statehood where the only criteria were purely descriptive, the legal norm that so conceived states would itself require normative justification. Perhaps a better overall scheme of international law would employ a different understanding of its principal subjects, one that, for example, gave a role to the normative criterion of legitimacy.

So within international law the state is whatever international law says it is, and this definition requires justification along with the rest of the content of the law. For other purposes, quite different approaches to the concept of the state might be appropriate. In the philosophy of law, where the nature of domestic law remains the main focus, it is important for the English positivist tradition from Bentham through Hart that a political rather than a legal account of the state can be given and that this account be a purely descriptive one with no evaluative component.[3] Only then can we properly identify the matters of fact that, on this positivist account, provide the grounds of law. But there is no incompatibility between this position and the claim that law itself (domestic or international) either does or should employ evaluative criteria in its account of statehood.

Similarly, sociological enquiry may require a yet different account of the state. Weber's account of the state was chosen because it seemed to him that in the modern period the existence of an administrative/legal order and a claim to a monopoly on the legitimate use of force were the salient characteristics of the kind of political organization he wanted to discuss.[4] This can be defensible even if the claim to legitimacy would not be one of the criteria in the best account of the state for international law.

---

[2] Crawford, J., *The Creation of States in International Law* (2nd edn., Oxford: Clarendon Press, 2006), esp. ch. 2.

[3] Hans Kelsen, by contrast, attempted a purely legal account of the state. For discussion, with references, see Raz, J. *The Authority of Law* (Oxford: Clarendon Press, 1979), 97–102.

[4] Weber, M., 'Economy and Society', in Roth, G. and Wittich, C. (eds.), *Max Weber—Economy and Society. An Outline of Interpretive Sociology* (Berkeley and Los Angeles: University of California Press, 1978), 56.

In general, there is no reason why the account of states that best serves philosophical enquiry into their moral significance should be the same as that which best suits the purposes of legal philosophers or sociologists, or as that which would emerge as the legal definition of the state in an ideal international legal order. Nonetheless, any kind of enquiry has to start somewhere, and the obvious place to start is close by ordinary usage. If this later turns out to be distorting or otherwise hindering our understanding of the underlying issues, we can propose revisionist definitions. It seems to me that Weber's account of the state is pretty close to ordinary usage and so that is the account that I will have in mind in what follows.

II. State Responsibility and Individuals

Where talk of responsibility makes sense at all, we will need to think about people. A state or a nation may or may not be conceived as an entity 'over and above' the people who make it up, but if nations and states can act, and be held responsible, this is only because there are people involved. This is true even if legal doctrine, in treating corporate entities such as states as legal persons, averts its eyes from the relationship those entities have to people. The effect of the law on people still needs justification.[5]

This does not mean that all responsibility is, in the end, individual responsibility. It means that practices of ascribing responsibility to collectives of people or to states or to nations must make moral sense—which in turn means that the point of view of individuals cannot be ignored.

So I think that Crawford and Watkins are right to take seriously what they call 'the individualist challenge' to all ascriptions of responsibility to states, and especially to those that impose liability to make reparations. Let me pause, however, to take issue with their suggestion that in practice the attribution of responsibility to states contemplated in current international law has limited significance for natural persons—that, in particular, it would often impose no burdens on people at all. All of the obligations that might flow from attribution of state responsibility implicate the interests of people living in the jurisdiction of the state. An obligation to cease a wrongful act, if it is continuing, may be burdensome on those who benefit from the wrongful acts of their state; guarantees of non-repetition likewise. The reason why Crawford and Watkins do not see things this way becomes clear in their discussion of restitution.[6] As a baseline for the assessment of burdens on a person they have in mind a world in which the state's wrongful act never took place: Loss of what you would not have had but for the state's wrong does not count as a burden. So in the end the only losses that count as burdens are those of compensatory payments,

---

[5] As Crawford and Watkins acknowledge, this volume, 289.   [6] Ibid. 294.

since such payments may make a person worse off than she would have been if the wrong had never happened.

The use of this baseline is unjustified in the context of a discussion of the accusation that international law, by imposing liability on states, unjustifiably burdens citizens who are morally blameless. If it is the state that is to blame, not me, there can be no justification for using, as a baseline for determining whether the legal liability of the state burdens me, a world in which the state acted differently. I am happily going about my business, making ordinary economic decisions, benefiting, as it turns out, from the wrongful acts of my state. Perhaps I am a fisherman, growing rich catching more fish than I otherwise would have because the coastguard helpfully keeps foreign competitors away. If restitution requires return of those benefits, such as the fine house that I would not have been able to afford if my state had not acted wrongly, it is no comfort to me to be told that, had the state only done what was right, I wouldn't have had my fine house. I have it now, and, *ex hypothesi*, I did no wrong in getting it.

Crawford and Watkins also note that most actual damages awards in international law have been rather trivial when considered on a *per capita* basis. This fact, however, does nothing to address the issue of principle. After all, many now hope that existing principles of state responsibility will one day be applied to some of history's gravest international crimes, such as colonialism and the slave trade. In 2004 the government of Haiti demanded restitution of the current value of the reparations it had been coerced into paying France in 1825 (for having overthrown slavery and, eventually, French rule). In a recent article, anthropologist David Scott suggested that the ILC's Articles on State Responsibility mandated restitutionary payments from former slaving nations to the poor countries of the Caribbean.[7] There is, of course, no chance that either will happen, but that does not in itself show that the ILC principles do not require it. And there is no question that, at the individual level, such transfers would (rightly or wrongly) burden people who cannot be blamed for the slave trade.

Even a state apology burdens individuals, or is at least perceived to do so. The former Liberal Government in Australia resisted calls for apologies relating to the past wrongful treatment of indigenous Australians, largely on the ground that the acts in question, now acknowledged to have been wrong, were done with good intentions. This is a political position with considerable support and I imagine that one important reason for that is that so many older people, even many who had absolutely nothing to do with indigenous Australians in their youth, let alone direct responsibility for government policy, nonetheless feel that an apology would entail an unfair attribution of responsibility to them. Crawford and Watkins write that 'just as there are certain actions which only corporate beings can perform . . . , so there are certain burdens which only they can carry'.[8] I disagree. If there is a sense

---

[7] Scott, D., 'Preface: Soul Captives are Free', *Small Axe*, 23 (2007), pp. vii–viii.
[8] Crawford, J., and Watkins, J., this volume, 293, n. 20.

in which a state can be burdened that implies no burdens on people, then burdens, in that sense, are morally irrelevant and not worth talking about.

Of course Crawford and Watkins acknowledge that there is no avoiding the possibility that the costs of compensation awards imposed on states will be borne by blameless individuals and so agree that the charge of burdening the blameless still has to be answered. My digression here is just to note that we should not downplay the extent of the burdens existing principles of state responsibility could, in principle at least, impose on those who cannot be directly blamed for the wrongful act.

There's another point that is perhaps more significant in this connection. We are considering the propriety of ascriptions of state responsibility for wrongful acts. But now the same general objection applies to a state's contractual obligations, stemming from both treaties and contracts with non-state entities. The most notorious aspect of this is the fact that loans secured by corrupt or oppressive governments, loans that may have benefited only those in power at the time, must be paid back, even by the successor government. This fundamental feature of existing international legal practice is a reflection of the international legal personality of states, and raises the objection of unwarranted collective responsibility in perhaps its most urgent form.[9]

The individualist objection reminds us that the state system in international law and practice requires justification. The state system is part of our political and legal world and it is therefore something that we can change. Perhaps something like the current system is better than any radical alternatives; but even if that is so, a lot turns on why it is so. Some believe that there are intrinsic moral merits to central features of the state system, others that at best an all-things-considered instrumental defence can be given. If the latter is right, philosophers and international lawyers alike have no excuse for not thinking about ways to modify the existing system to make it better, or at least less bad.

III. INSTRUMENTALISM

As I've said, the topic of international responsibility is broader than that of the international responsibility of states even if the moral status of states is its central structural normative question. The state system is a political and legal order that attributes rights and obligations to states, seen as persisting over time, as opposed to particular governments, nations, nongovernmental organizations, or collections of individuals living at a particular place and time. We cannot evaluate or even understand this system without comparing the rights and obligations that are

---

[9] See Thomas Pogge's discussion of the 'international borrowing privilege' in *World Poverty and Human Rights* (Cambridge: Polity Press, 2002). For discussion of (arguable) limitations on the general legal principle, see Howse, R., 'The Concept of Odious Debt in Public International Law', UNCTAD Discussion Paper, No. 185 (July 2007).

assumed to attach to states with those that are assumed to attach to governments, nations, collectives, nongovernmental institutions, and individuals. That is the sense in which the state system is an aspect of an overall political and legal theory.

It is also important to remember that international responsibility can be negative as well as positive—that is, there is responsibility for not doing things as well as for doing things. Put the other way around, we have to consider not just breaches of negative duties such as a duty not to harm, but also breaches of positive obligations such as a duty to benefit others or promote justice or just institutions.

So there are a lot of moving parts in this discussion: law versus morality, positive versus negative, domestic versus international, state versus individual, and so on. The important point, however, is not that there are many distinct questions about responsibility but that each of these questions is related to each of the others. For example, to mention a perhaps surprising connection that will be important in what follows, the topic of state responsibility is tied up with the topic of global justice and the justice-related obligations of individuals.

One way into this huge subject is to consider two contrast cases, representing extremes in a continuum of views about the rights and duties of states as compared to individuals. As is often the case, utilitarianism is a helpful starting point. Utilitarianism is a simple, one-principle moral theory: Always do what will optimize aggregate welfare. In this picture, states have no moral significance in themselves, but are merely legal and social structures that should be created and sustained to the extent that their existence makes things go better. Ultimately the bearers of responsibility (which is all negative responsibility) are individuals and, as individuals, we are each responsible for the welfare of all persons wherever living. Institutions of any kind are valuable only as means to the end of welfare promotion and a division of labour among institutions that maps onto traditional geographical groupings of people—that, is, a state system—is justified only to the extent that no better global institutional arrangement is feasible.

If we assume that the state system comes out as instrumentally justified on utilitarian grounds, at least as the best feasible arrangement given the way things now are, there are nonetheless two important ways in which utilitarianism condemns the current practices of both individuals and states. Individuals pay too little attention to the welfare of others: Even if our existing institutional schemes were the best we could expect from institutional schemes, that wouldn't mean that individuals who cooperate with these schemes would have done all they can; institutions are a means to the good, but not the only one. Second, states certainly could do more for general global welfare than they currently do; to believe that states must give nearly absolute priority to the interests of their members is to mistake a *prima facie* instrumental case for a morally significant distinction.

There are of course many things wrong with the utilitarian account. There are the familiar points that utilitarianism recognizes no constraints, in the form of negative rights, on the promotion of welfare and that it ignores the distribution of welfare.

Less familiar is the point that individuals are not plausibly regarded as individually responsible for the welfare of everyone else in the world—a more plausible view is that the positive duty to make things go better for people applies to us collectively and so individuals are only required to do their share.[10]

Suppose, however, that we offer a view that responds to all these complaints while retaining the basic idea that we all (collectively) are negatively responsible for the welfare of everyone—or, more broadly, for promoting justice globally. It might look somewhat like a creative adaptation of John Rawls's theory of justice, applied to the global scene: Within the constraints of negative rights, we collectively have the responsibility to do what we can to promote social and economic justice around the world and, as it happens, the best way to achieve this aim is to promote the appropriate institutional structures. In this kind of story, which Rawls himself would have emphatically rejected, there is agreement with utilitarianism on some basic points: Justice is essentially a global concern and state boundaries are of instrumental significance only.

The central characteristic of the group of views I am discussing, obviously enough, is the instrumental attitude taken to the state system. The first thing to note about this position is that it is an entirely contingent matter whether the existing state system, with the entire set of recognized rights and responsibilities that go along with it, is justified. That depends entirely upon whether there are changes that could be made that would result in better outcomes in terms of global welfare and its distribution. This is compatible with the possibility that the state system is entirely without merit, that it is simply an artifact of history and historical injustices and the superior feasible arrangements that could be put in its place will bear no resemblance to it. To whatever extent the state system is suboptimal, it is our collective obligation to work towards putting something better in its place.

Even if radical reform is not possible or desirable, the instrumental view is radical in its implication of stringent negative responsibility, which has very demanding implications for the world's rich. Not only must our states do what they can to promote economic justice world-wide, each of us, as individuals, should at least do our fair share of what can be better done directly, without the mediation of the legal and political institutions of the state system.

To return now to the individualist objection: How does the objection that the state system lays inappropriate collective responsibility on faultless individuals fare if we take the instrumental view? If international law imposed upon states a general duty to promote economic justice or positive rights globally, there would be no objection coming from the instrumental view I have described—it would be up to the states to distribute the burdens of what are, in fact, collective obligations fairly among its people. Matters are different, however, when it comes to responsibility for violations of the negative rights of other people or other states. If a state acts

---

[10] See Murphy, L., *Moral Demands in Nonideal Theory* (New York: Oxford University Press, 2000).

wrongly by, say, annexing another state's territory, there is no direct sense in which the individual subjects of that state can be said to own that wrong act and thus bear moral responsibility for it. Moral responsibility lies with the individuals who made the decision to commit the wrong. We could say that it is up to the states to distribute the burdens of liability in accordance with moral blameworthiness, but often the people who should pay are no longer around, or cannot pay. If there is to be justification for international law's refusal to lift the state veil, then it will, again, have to be instrumental—not justifying the imposition of burdens on people because they are morally responsible, but in spite of the fact that they are not.

IV. THE POLITICAL VIEW

Before sketching the progressive possibilities of the instrumental view it is important to consider a radically different kind of view about the moral status of states. What we can call (following Joshua Cohen and Charles Sabel[11]) a 'strong statist' position can also be offered as an interpretation of Rawls, especially the Rawls of *The Law of Peoples*. I have in mind here primarily the argument by Thomas Nagel in his article 'The Problem of Global Justice'.[12] Nagel's views about the scope of justice have similarities with those of Ronald Dworkin.[13] Both put law and the idea of the state, through law, representing a political community at centre stage. Both reject the idea that the significance of the state lies in what it can get done; the true significance of the legitimate state is thought instead to lie in the particular kind of political justification it can offer for its claimed right to a monopoly on the use of coercive force. Nagel uses the label 'political' for his account of global justice. I will use the same label for the following amalgam of Nagel's and Dworkin's views of the state.

As just noted, a central concern of the political account is to provide a deontological justification for the state's use of coercion internally. Utilitarianism can offer an instrumental vindication of some states' claims to a legitimate monopoly on the use of force; the permissibility of using force and taking control over its use by private persons would follow if there was no better feasible way of arranging things. But political accounts look for something much more robust. After all, the story goes, people have a right not to be coerced without justification and instrumental calculations cannot provide the proper kind of justification for infringements of rights.

One possible justification turns on the idea that states speak and act in the name of their subjects. But, and here comes the crucial part, states can only be said to

---

[11] Cohen, J., and Sabel, C., 'Extra Rempublicam Nulla Justicia?', *Philosophy & Public Affairs*, 34 (2006), 147.

[12] Nagel, T., 'The Problem of Global Justice', *Philosophy & Public Affairs*, 33 (2005), 113; see also Blake, M., 'Distributive Justice, State Coercion, and Autonomy', *Philosophy & Public Affairs*, 30 (2001), 257.

[13] See Dworkin, R., *Law's Empire* (Cambridge, Mass.: Harvard University Press, 1986), chs. 5 and 6.

speak and act in the name of their subjects if their subjects collectively form some kind of political community—and they can only do that if they are all treated according to some appropriate conception of social and economic equality. Justice, properly understood, concerns the conditions of the creation of a genuine political community which in turn makes legitimate state governance possible. The main idea is that if I am not, in some relevant sense, an equal member of the community of subjects, the state's use of coercive force cannot be said to be done in my name and therefore remains unjustified. To make the point from a different direction, we can say that in claiming legitimate rule over us, states purport to impose obligations upon us and that this is only plausible if that rule treats us as equal members of the community.

From this point of view the poverty, even willful blindness, of the instrumental view lies in its refusal to take into account the fact that states serve as the institutional face of a political community. In fact, on this view, states, through the medium of law, can be said to constitute the political community. And just as many people believe that nations are not just arbitrary collections of people living together over time in a roughly defined geographical area, the political view has it that political communities have intrinsic moral significance.

There are different ways of filling out this deliberately vague sketch. But the main implications to note are two. First, justice concerns the criteria of equality state institutions must satisfy before there can be said to be a genuine political community and therefore legitimacy. While individuals may be said to have, in addition to their duty to not to violate negative rights, weak positive humanitarian duties, they have no duty to promote social and economic justice, either domestic or global. Second, though states must respect the negative rights of other states and foreign individuals, and though they too are subject to weak impersonal humanitarian duties, states have no duty to promote social and economic justice globally. The demand of global economic justice doesn't even arise until such time as we have a coercive world order claiming a monopoly on the legitimate use of force. If there's ever such a thing as a world state, then there will be a problem of global justice; but not before. Social and economic justice only arises as a requirement, on this view, when we have a state purporting to legitimately use coercive force and do so in the name of its subjects.

I believe that some version of this view is widely shared, especially in the New World where nationality is typically far less strong a source of identity and where membership of a certain historically continuous state is much more likely to be taken to be the test of what it is to be—say, an Argentinean.

I myself do not accept the political view but it is important to consider and not only because it claims to represent a refinement of 'common-sense' political morality. What is striking is that if the existing principles of international state responsibility are to be justified in a non-instrumental way, something like the political view will probably be required.

The political view provides a justification precisely for collective responsibility. If my state can be said to act and speak in my name, in any sense strong enough to mark the difference between the domestic case, where justice is required, and the international case, where it is not, then presumably that sense is also strong enough to make state subjects answerable and liable for what the state does or says. Dworkin explicitly makes this connection. He motivates the kind of personification of the community his theory of law and state requires by noting the intuitive plausibility of attributing collective responsibility for the acts of the Third Reich to all Germans—including those born after 1945.[14]

So this kind of view provides a very clear and focused defence against the charge of unwarranted collective responsibility. Yes, the state system implies collective responsibility, but that is entirely appropriate, because the state is properly understood as the personification of the community. As Nagel puts it, the state 'engages the will' of its subjects when it acts in their name. That is why it had better be seeking social and economic justice among those subjects. But this also allows us to make perfect sense of the idea that all members of the community are not just obligated by domestic law, but also responsible for the wrongful acts of their state.

Now it might be thought that my emphasis on the connection between state responsibility and approaches to global and domestic justice is unwarranted because the core connection I have brought out is just this: Any view that provides a deontological justification of the use of force by the state domestically will imply responsibility for wrongful acts internationally. If we thought, for example, that consent was a plausible criterion of domestic legitimacy, it would be easy to explain the responsibility of individuals for the wrongful acts of their states—individuals could be thought to have consented to the state's conduct both domestically and internationally and therefore to be bound to the domestic commands of their states and answerable for their international conduct. Similarly, the benefit or 'fair play' theory of legitimacy (according to which the burdens of being subject to state coercion are the fair price paid for its benefits) can also ground an argument justifying individuals' responsibility for states' wrongful acts.[15]

The trouble with these other deontological accounts is that they are either implausible on their own terms or if plausible do not in fact show the rule of any states over all their subjects to be legitimate (because few people actually consent, for example). As the objections to these accounts have been so thoroughly explored by others, I will not rehearse them here.[16] We can take a similarly quick line with any attempt to ground state legitimacy on nationality since, independently of its plausibility in the case of genuine nation states, it has no chance of justifying the state system overall.

---

[14] See Ibid., pp. 167–75.   [15] See Miller, D., 'Holding Nations Responsible', *Ethics*, 114 (2004), 240.
[16] See Simmons, A. J., *Moral Principles and Political Obligations* (Princeton: Princeton University Press, 1979).

So it is true that the main structural connection I have pointed to is that between deontological accounts of internal legitimacy and robust accounts of state responsibility. The reason for the focus on the political account of legitimacy is just that some form of this account seems the best hope for deontological justifications of the state system. And there is an intuitive attractiveness to it as well, coming from the role given to domestic justice: It is natural to think that any account that ties state and subject closely enough together to justify collective positive responsibility for the wrongful acts of states will at the same time justify a strong distinction between the domestic and international obligations of states as far as welfare and social and economic justice is concerned. The point may be even clearer if put the other way around: If we want to say that state boundaries are irrelevant as far as economic justice is concerned, no deontological justification for current norms of state responsibility is likely to be found.

This connection between the propriety of attributions of responsibility for wrongful acts to states rather than individuals and the scope of the demands of social and economic justice is an intriguing feature of the topic of international responsibility, broadly understood. When looked at in purely self-interested terms, a subject of a rich state would much rather shoulder the burdens of state liability for wrongful acts—even though she may be in no sense responsible for the act—than accept that either she individually or through her state has negative responsibility for the plight of the world's poor.

V. JUSTIFICATION WITHOUT RESPONSIBILITY

A fair evaluation of the political view is obviously impossible here. I will mention just briefly the objections that seem to me to undermine it. In the first place, I do not believe that requirements of social and economic justice emerge only in certain institutional contexts, specifically the context of coercive institutions that claim legitimacy. On my view, considerations of social and economic justice arise in virtue of common humanity.[17] But one needn't go that far. Perhaps, as many philosophers have believed, considerations of justice spring into being only in the context of regular interaction structured by law or other institutional arrangements.[18] What is to be resisted is that justice itself is so far a political notion that it is only in the context of actually existing coercive political structures that

---

[17] See Murphy, L., 'Institutions and the Demands of Justice', *Philosophy & Public Affairs*, 27 (1998), 251.

[18] Thomas Pogge believes that though the state system has instrumental significance only, the duties of individuals in respect of justice are never direct but always meditated through institutional structures of some kind. See *World Poverty and Human Rights* and 'On the Site of Distributive Justice: Reflections on Cohen and Murphy', *Philosophy & Public Affairs*, 29 (2000), 137.

its demands arise. Perhaps coercion without justice is illegitimate, but that does not mean that justice arises as an issue only when there is a claim to legitimate coercion.

Second, I am sceptical about the claims the political view must make about the relations between individuals, their co-nationals, and their state. My state may claim to speak in the name of all the members of a political community but I'm not sure that we are a community in any but a nominal sense and not at all convinced, in particular, that law can constitute us as one.[19] Whatever the state may claim to be doing I can doubt that it is doing it successfully, and point out that it has failed to engage my will.

Most important for current purposes, however, is that the entire story lies within the realm of ideal theory and has little to say about actual, non-ideal cases. Since few states satisfy the demands of domestic justice that any compelling version of the political view would have to propose, we must assume that the aspiration to justice is all that is required for the state's use of coercion to be legitimate, and for it to speak in the name of its subjects. But then this aspiration must presumably be genuine, and continue through time as governments come and go, and we know that this condition is not met in many cases.

So the political view does not, in the end, provide a plausible deontological justification for the state system as it currently exists. If we were to hold responsible only states that are at least trying to secure social and economic justice domestically, a reformulation of the legal definition of the state would be required that would leave many entities now counted as states out in the cold. Perhaps the legal account of statehood should be reformed to include, or understood already to include, more explicitly normative criteria.[20] But then, as Crawford and Watkins write, 'it is not too much to define states as the principal mechanism for the transmission of the accrued rights of human communities over time'.[21] Use too normatively demanding an account of the state, and too many human communities will be left out, the transmission of their accrued rights unrecognized. Some other notion would have to be employed instead—but then the old problem of holding blameless individuals responsible would re-emerge.

In the end, I doubt that there is a story we can tell that justifies the use of coercive force by (legitimate) states internally in a way that makes sense of the idea that I am, in even in a weak sense, always answerable for the content of the law that structures that coercion. The justification of internal coercion, and thus the theory of legitimacy, is likely to take an entirely instrumental form. In rejecting the political view, we deny that the state is really speaking for me, engaging my will, or realizing the principles of my political community. The other side of this, of course, is that

---

[19] For discussion see Murphy, L., 'The Political Question of the Concept of Law', 405–9, in Coleman, J. L. (ed.), *Hart's Postscript: Essays on the Postscript to 'The Concept of Law'* (Oxford: Oxford University Press, 2001).

[20] See Crawford, J., *The Creation of States in International Law* (above, n. 2).

[21] Crawford, J., and Watkins, J., this volume, 291.

there is also no theory of legitimacy that will enable us to say that, at least in the case of legitimate states, collective responsibility for the actions of states is justified.

But scepticism about the traditional problem of legitimacy actually shows the way around the individualist objection. Suppose my state enforces some law against me that requires me to do something I am not independently morally required to do and that I have no moral duty to obey. The enforcement of the law against me may nonetheless be justified. By hypothesis, I won't be deserving of the burdens of enforcement in any sense; there will be no moral responsibility on my part that in itself singles out me for the imposition of those burdens. But, so long as states can be justified at all, the imposition of this cost on me may nonetheless be justified.

The same basic story shows the way to justify the imposition of the burdens of states' legal responsibilities on blameless subjects. If we take an instrumentalist attitude to states, to the justification of their use of force internally and their status in international law, we should not be bothered by the accusation that international law burdens those who have no responsibility for the acts of the state. We would not, as instrumentalists, necessarily be looking for moral responsibility in order to justify legal liability or the imposition of burdens in the first place. That someone is morally responsible for a harm or a wrong may on its own justify the imposition of burdens, but it is not the only possibility.

Coercive enforcement of domestic law and the imposition of international legal liability on states may burden (morally blameless) people. That requires justification, just because any imposition of burdens on people requires justification. But that is different from saying that there is a need to justify holding responsible those who are in fact not. On the instrumental account, the ascription of legal obligation and legal liability do not necessarily engage the issue of moral responsibility at all.

VI. Feasible Alternatives?

But this is not the end of the matter. As I have just said, legal state responsibility that burdens (blameless) individuals still does need to be justified. Does the good done by the system of state responsibility always outweigh its burdens? More accurately, the question is whether there is a feasible alternative to the current system of state responsibility that does more good, overall.

As the form of this question makes plain, once we move to an instrumental understanding of the moral significance of states, the state system as a whole is revealed as entirely a creature of law. Like property rights, states are legal conventions and their reform is not constrained by any independent moral ideas about the rights and duties of states. Our only question is whether changing the legal convention will better or worse serve various values, such as justice, welfare, security, and so on.

One initial point is that state responsibility under law could be weakened, at least in some cases, without losing the benefits of the state system as the principal mechanism for the transmission of the accrued rights of human communities over time. It is perhaps natural to think that if states have rights, they must also have obligations. This is so in one sense—if someone has what Hohfeld called a 'claim right' someone else must have an obligation and thus the possibility of responsibility. But there is no requirement that if I have a (claim) right, I must have the obligations that are correlative to those rights when possessed by others. In contract law, for example, if you make a contract with me when I evidently lack contractual capacity—I am hopelessly drunk, for example—the result is that you are obliged to perform (if I want you to and am myself prepared to perform) but I am not. I have a right to performance, which is a genuine claim right, correlated with an obligation on your part, but I have no obligation at all associated with my right. Now of course the upshot of this is that I have a right which you lack, and this raises a *prima facie* objection: Usually, if A has a right against B, B can have exactly the same kind of right against A; that's just a fundamental assumption of moral equality. It is telling that what justifies the departure from this default position in this case is a defect in agency. An even more obvious case, of course, is that of animals: perhaps it makes sense to say they have rights, which correlate with obligations on the part of people; but nobody thinks that animals have obligations, since they are not agents in the required sense.

It is worth exploring the possibility of opening a space between obligation and rights for cases of grossly corrupt or tyrannical government. Of course there is no gain to be had from weakening general international legal obligations for those states that are governed worse. The situation where opening a gap makes sense is that of regime change; in particular the question arises of whether obligations incurred by the one regime should also bind the successor. Not all the obligations a state can have derive from positive acts of the government: Standing obligations of international law, such as the obligation not to intervene, do not. But contractual obligations, including treaty obligations, do derive from voluntary acts, and so too do remedial obligations to undo or compensate for a wrong.

To consider the contractual case first, current international legal practice already does modify the standard model of the legal personality of states for the case of non-treaty contractual obligation. Where a state is deemed to have ceased to exist, and replaced with a new state, the background legal idea is that, since there is a new legal person, obligations of the prior state do not carry over to the new state. But in the case of state to state debt, a doctrine of 'maintenance' developed, for obvious practical reasons, according to which the successor state would take over the prior state's obligation.[22] Here we see the state veil being lifted to show that the people who benefited from the loan have not changed even though the state has.

---

[22] See Howse, R., 'The Concept of Odious Debt in Public International Law' (above, n. 9).

More important from the point of view of the individualist objection, there is the possibility of releasing a state from debt obligations incurred under a former government. To the extent that there is any domestic or public international law on this matter, it goes under the label of 'odious debt'.[23] Existing notions of equity and contractual capacity provide some legal resources, but a more foundational approach is certainly worth considering—at least as a thought experiment. We could imagine a legal regime where states are defined largely descriptively[24] but the attribution of contractual capacity requires a look under the state veil at the nature of the government purporting to give its contractual assent. We could then say that states governed illegitimately (on an account of legitimacy relevant to this context) can acquire for their states only voidable contractual obligations. The desirability of this change would depend upon whether the incentive effects would be positive, compared to the status quo, both in terms of international economic justice and internal governance.

We can also open a space between attributions of primary obligation and attributions of responsibility for breach of obligation. Once we take the instrumental view, each element of the state system can be appraised more or less independently. Under a strongly personifying account of the state, by contrast, rights, primary obligations, and secondary obligations arising out of responsibility for breach would all be more closely linked just as they are for the case of individual persons. On the instrumentalist view it is entirely coherent to say that in the case of international wrongs committed by a state with an illegitimate government *ex post* responsibility lies with the government, not the state, and so does not survive the demise of the government and its replacement with a legitimate one. (It would of course also be coherent to assign the responsibility to the individuals who made up the previous government.) Once again the case for lifting the veil in this way would turn on a balance of burdens and benefits, taking into account the impact on incentives to comply with states' international obligations.

VII. INCONVENIENT IMPLICATIONS

If we take an instrumentalist view about the state system, we should always be open to possibilities for reform, since the justification for the current system is entirely contingent on international political and social conditions being a certain way and on us seeing them clearly. In my view, there is a plausible argument for driving wedges between rights and obligations and primary obligations and remedial obligations in international law. This argument, as I have said, would turn

---

[23] Ibid.
[24] Though the principle of self-determination complicates this; see Crawford, J., *The Creation of States in International Law* (above, n. 2).

on incentive effects. It is extremely difficult to know whether these possible good effects are outweighed by contrary instrumental considerations—and of course there is the entirely different issue of which reforms are politically feasible. But we should not be distracted from thinking about these possibilities for making things better by irrelevant considerations of moral responsibility or presumed conceptual constraints.

These suggestions certainly do not exhaust possible beneficial reforms. For example, the international legal personality and responsibility of non-state institutions of various kinds, ranging from the quasi-governmental to the non-governmental is, morally speaking, entirely up for grabs on the instrumental view. Everything turns on the likely effects and their contribution to the relevant values that would have to be appealed to in order to justify the current system, if that can be done.

The possibility of significantly beneficial structural reform of international law is not the only reason why the instrumental view should not induce complacency. If states have only instrumental significance, then the almost absolute priority they almost all give to domestic welfare and justice requires an instrumental justification, and it is not easy to find one that is convincing. Even more unsettling, if the instrumental view of the state is correct then it is all of us people, not states, who are responsible for justice both domestic and international. If the current institutional scheme, domestic and global, is not serving our collective moral aims well, then we all ought to be doing what we can to change it. Furthermore, in my view (though not that of everyone who takes an instrumental view of states[25]) it is not only the state system but institutional arrangements generally that should be regarded as having only instrumental significance. If that is right, we each should also be considering whether there are more effective means to our ends than agitating for institutional reform—for the world's relatively rich, the direct transfer of resources is a salient option to consider. That the direct route is more effective, at least for some individuals, is not an unlikely possibility in our actual non-ideal world since the collective will for institutional reform is weak. Institutional reform is likely to be always the right answer if our question is what it would be best for all of us to do—since as a matter of ideal theory economic and legal institutions of some design or other, with some scope or other, are clearly the best means to the ends of justice or greater welfare for the worse-off. But we are not talking about what it would be best for us all to do; nor about what the (enforced) law should be. We are talking about the implications of the instrumental view of states and institutions generally for the responsibilities of individuals, who each must decide what it would be best for them to do. As that is the question, the unpleasant answer—I should

---

[25] Such as Pogge, T., *World Poverty and Human Rights*, and 'On the Site of Distributive Justice: Reflections on Cohen and Murphy' (above, n. 18). For my argument in favour of treating institutional arrangements as having instrumental significance only, see Murphy, L., 'Institutions and the Demands of Justice' (above, n. 17).

do my own part in bringing about a more just global distribution of welfare or resources—cannot be avoided. So one main result of highlighting the connections among the domestic and international responsibilities of states and individuals is that we can see just how much is riding, for many people, on the ideology of the state system in its current form.

PART II

SPECIFIC ISSUES IN THE PHILOSOPHY OF INTERNATIONAL LAW

SECTION VIII

HUMAN RIGHTS

CHAPTER 15

HUMAN RIGHTS WITHOUT FOUNDATIONS

JOSEPH RAZ*

I. INTRODUCTION

This is a good time for human rights. Not that they are respected more than in the past. The flagrant resort to kidnapping, arbitrary arrests, and torture by the United States of America (USA), and the unprecedented restriction of individual freedom in the USA, and in Great Britain (GB), cast doubt about that. It is a good time for human rights in that claims about such rights are used more widely in the conduct of world affairs than before. There are declarations of and treaties about human rights, international courts and tribunals with jurisdiction over various human right violations. They are invoked to justify wars (for example, Haiti, Somalia, and Yugoslavia). Observance of human rights is used as a condition of participation in various international programmes, the receipt of financial aid, and so on. A number of impressive non-governmental organizations (NGOs) monitor respect for human rights. As John Tasioulas notes: 'discourse of human rights [has acquired] in recent times . . . the status of an ethical *lingua franca*'.[1]

* I am grateful to Ori Herstein for legal background research. The paper was presented at the University of Connecticut 2005, as a Minerva Lecture, Tel Aviv 2006, and at the Philosophy of International Law conference in Fribourg 2007. I am grateful for comments from many people on those occasions and in particular to J. Tasioulas, A. Buchanan, J. Griffin, J. Skorupski, S. Ratner, and S. Besson.

[1] Tasioulas, J., 'The Moral Reality of Human Rights', in Pogge, T. (ed.), *Freedom from Poverty as a Human Right: Who Owes What to the Very Poor?* (Oxford: Oxford University Press, 2007), 75.

No doubt, human rights rhetoric is rife with hollow hypocrisy; it is infected by self-serving cynicism and by self-deception, but these vices do not totally negate the value of the growing acceptance of human rights in the conduct of international relations. The hypocrite and the self-deceived themselves pay homage to the standards they distort by acknowledging through their very hypocritical and deceitful invocation that these are the appropriate standards by which to judge their conduct. However, the success of the practice of human rights, as I will refer to the range of activities I have mentioned, poses a problem for ethical reflections about them.[2]

II. The Failure of the Traditional Doctrine

Human rights practice is not only becoming better established, it is also spreading its wings. An ever-growing number of rights are claimed to be human rights, for example, the right to sexual pleasure; the right to sexual information based upon scientific inquiry; the right to comprehensive sexual education.[3] It is declared that all persons have the right to a secure, healthy, and ecologically sound environment. Future generations have rights to equitably meet their needs. All persons have the right to protection and preservation of the air, soil, water, sea-ice, flora and fauna, and the essential processes and areas necessary to maintain biological diversity and ecosystems.[4] Some academics argue that there is a human right to globalization.[5] Others—that there are rights not to be exposed to excessively and unnecessarily heavy, degrading, dirty, and boring work; to identity with one's own work product, individually or collectively; to social transparency; to coexistence with nature.[6] And of course there is a right against poverty, and a right to be loved.

The ethical doctrine of human rights should articulate standards by which the practice of human rights can be judged, standards which will indicate what human rights we have. In doing so it will elucidate what is at issue, what is the significance

---

[2] Though the inadequacy of the approach that I will criticize, while being exposed in bright light by recent human rights practice, has deeper origins. It reflects a misguided understanding of the role of rights in morality, and in the justification of political and legal institutions.

[3] World Congress of Sexology, 'Sexual Rights are Fundamental and Universal Human Rights', Hong Kong, 26 Aug. 1999, <http://www.worldsexology.org/about_sexualrights.asp> (all websites most recently checked in Nov. 2007).

[4] Draft Declaration of Human Rights and the Environment, UN Doc. E/CN.4/Sub.2/1994/9, Annex I (1994), <http://www1.umn.edu/humanrts/instree/1994-dec.htm>.

[5] Pendleton, M. D., 'A New Human Right—The Right to Globalization', *Fordham International Law Journal*, 22 (1999), 2052.

[6] Alston, P., 'Conjuring Up New Human Rights: A Proposal for Quality Control', *American Journal of International Law*, 78 (1984), 607.

of a right's being a human right. Some theories (I will say that they manifest the traditional approach) offer a way of understanding their nature which is so remote from the practice of human rights as to be irrelevant to it. They take 'human rights' to be those important rights which are grounded in our humanity. The underlying thought is that the arguments which establish that a putative right-holder has a human right rely on no *contingent* fact except laws of nature, the nature of humanity and that the right-holder is a human being.[7] And they must also be important rights—why they must be important is not clear. Neither being universal, that is rights that everyone has, nor being grounded in our humanity, guarantees that they are important. However, philosophers tend to take it for granted that human rights are important rights.[8]

In recent times, Gewirth was among the first to develop a traditionalist account:

... it is possible and indeed logically necessary to infer, from the fact that certain objects are the proximate necessary conditions of human action that all rational agents logically must hold or claim, at least implicitly, that they have rights to such objects.[9]

Gewirth argues that this 'dialectically' establishes that humans have a right, which is—by definition—a human right, to the proximate necessary conditions of human action. While his argument has long been recognized to be logically flawed, it is typical of the traditional approach, which is roughly characterized by four, logically independent, features:

First, it aims 'to derive' human rights from *basic features* of human beings which are both *valuable*, and in some way *essential to all which is valuable* in human life.

Second, human rights are basic, perhaps the most basic and the most important, *moral rights*.

Third, scant attention is paid to the difference between something being valuable, and having a right to it.

Fourth, the rights tend to be individualistic in being rights to what each person can enjoy on his or her own: such as freedom from coercive interference by others, rather than to aspects of life which are essentially social, such as being a member of a cultural group.

Traditional theories fail for several reasons. Exposing their flaws calls for a detailed examination of each of them. Here I will point to three problems. They misconceive the relations between value and rights. They overreach, trying to derive rights

---

[7] See Gewirth, A., *Human Rights: Essays on Justifications and Applications* (Chicago: Chicago University Press, 1982), 41; 'We may assume, as true by definition, that human rights are rights that all persons have simply insofar as they are human'; Jones, P., 'Human Rights', in Craig, E. (ed.), *The Routledge Encyclopaedia of Philosophy*, <www.rep.routledge.com/article/S105>; 'Human rights are rights ascribed to human beings simply as human beings'. One may allow that permanently comatose people do not have human rights. But one abandons the idea that human rights derive from our humanity once one says that babies or people with Down's syndrome do not have (certain) human rights.

[8] See Nickel, J., 'Human Rights' in Zalta, E. J. (ed.), *The Stanford Encyclopaedia of Philosophy* (Summer 2007 edn.) <http://plato.stanford.edu/entries/rights-human>.

[9] Gewirth, A., *Human Rights: Essays on Justifications and Applications* (above, n. 7), 46.

which they cannot derive. And they fail either to illuminate or to criticize the existing human rights practice.

Gewirth, for example, thinks that since we all want and value having the proximate conditions of agency we must claim a right to have them. He ignores the possibility of believing that certain conditions are essential to our life, and even of striving to secure such conditions, without either claiming or having a right to them. Thus, he misconceives the relation between value and rights. He also believes, for example, that there is a general (overridable) right to freedom because 'freedom is a necessary condition of human purposive action'[10]—a claim which is evidently false if it means that, for instance, slaves cannot act purposively. In fact there could never have been any economic interest in having slaves but for the fact that slaves can act purposively, and thus be useful to their owners.

I will turn to the third failure, the failure to exert critical pressure on the practice, later on.

First let us look at a more interesting theory which broadly shares the same faults. James Griffin asks: What is the most important feature shared by all humans?

> Human life is different from the life of other animals. We human beings have a conception of ourselves and of our past and future. We reflect and assess. . . . And we value our status as human beings especially highly, often more highly even than our happiness. This status centres on our being agents—deliberating, assessing, choosing and acting to make what we see as a good life for ourselves.[11]

Human rights can then be seen as protections of our human standing or, as I shall put it, our personhood. And one can break down the notion of personhood into clearer components by breaking down the notion of agency. To be an agent, in the fullest sense of which we are capable, one must (first) choose one's own path through life—that is, not be dominated or controlled by someone or something else (call it 'autonomy'). And (second) one's choice must be real; one must have at least a certain minimum education and information. And having chosen, one must then be able to act; that is, one must have at least the minimum provision of resources and capabilities that it takes (call all of this 'minimum provision'). And none of that is any good if someone then blocks one; so (third) others must also not forcibly stop one from pursuing what one sees as a worthwhile life (call this 'liberty'). Because we attach such high value to our individual personhood, we see its domain of exercise as privileged and protected.

Griffin too grounds all human rights in features which all human beings are supposed to share, and on the necessary conditions for their expression.[12] He too takes human rights to be general moral rights, which may or may not call for recognition or incorporation in the law.

---

[10]   Gewirth, A., *Human Rights: Essays on Justifications and Applications* (above, n. 7), 15.

[11]   Griffin, J., *On Human Rights* (Oxford: Oxford University Press, 2008), 32–3.

[12]   Griffin postulates that what he calls 'personhood' is just one of two grounds for human rights, the other being practicability. For our purposes we can ignore this second ground.

Griffin avoids one difficulty which undermines Gewirth's theory by relying not only on the fact that people value their personhood, but on its *being* valuable. But he too fails to show that that value establishes rights. He argues that personhood is not merely valuable but a ground of rights: 'autonomy and liberty are of special value to us, and thus attract the special protection of rights'.[13] By that argument if the love of my children is the most important thing to me then I have a right to it.

Griffin is aware of a simple objection: are not people whose human rights were systematically denied, like slaves, nevertheless persons? His response is:

> But that is not the picture of agency at the heart of my account . . . My somewhat ampler picture is of a self-decider (that is, someone autonomous) who, within limits, is not blocked from pursuing his or her conception of a worthwhile life (i.e. someone also at liberty). If either autonomy or liberty is missing, one's agency, on this ampler interpretation, is deficient.[14]

But this response is fatal to the whole account. The problem is that (according to him) (a) being a person endows one with human rights, and (b) these rights are to one's continued existence as a person (they are 'protections of our . . . personhood'). If personhood is understood as the capacity for intentional agency then human rights are indeed enjoyed by almost every human being, but they protect just what is essential for that capacity. They are rights against, for example, the administration of chemicals which seriously impair our ability to think, form intentions, or act. They are rights against severe dehydration, sensory deprivation, etc. But they do not include rights against slavery, arbitrary arrest, and the like as these conditions do not affect our ability to act intentionally. If, however, the rights are as ample as Griffin describes them, if personhood is the capacity to

> choose one's own path through life—that is, not be dominated or controlled by someone or something else . . . And . . . one's choice must be real; one must have at least a certain minimum education and information. And having chosen, one must then be able to act; that is, one must have at least the minimum provision of resources and capabilities that it takes.[15]

Then different problems arise. Take his first condition first: 'one must choose one's own course through life—that is, not be dominated or controlled by someone or something else'. Is it really true that someone who is dominated by his powerful mother, or controlled by his commitment to his employer (having signed a 10-year contract, on condition that the employer first pays for his education) is less of a person than someone who is not so dominated or controlled? The circumstances I mentioned may or may not be undesirable, the life of the people so controlled or dominated may be better or worse as a result, but are those people really persons only to a lesser degree? I find it difficult to avoid the suspicion that Griffin is smuggling a particular ideal of a good life into his notion of being a person to the fullest degree.

---

[13] Ibid. 46–7.   [14] Ibid. 46.   [15] Ibid. 33.

Turn now to the third condition: 'having chosen, one must then be able to act; that is, one must have at least the minimum provision of resources and capabilities that it takes'—'act' here seems to mean act with a good chance of success, of achieving one's goals. This exposes an additional problem with Griffin's rich notion of personhood. Is it not so rich as to include all the conditions of a good life which one person can secure for another? Griffin thinks that there is no problem here:

that human rights are grounded in personhood imposes an obvious constraint on their content: they are rights not to anything that promotes human good or flourishing, but merely to what is needed for human status.[16]

Finding a threshold to human rights is essential for the traditional approach. It takes human rights to mark a normatively exceptional domain. They deserve protection even if that requires exceptional measures. This task can only succeed if people do not have human rights to everything which will or may improve the quality of their life. For if people have such rights they are not exceptional, and they fail to play the role that traditional accounts assign them.

If human rights are rights of those with the capacity for intentional agency to preserve that capacity, the distinction between capacity and its exercise is relatively clear, and a case for the privileged standing of the capacity can be made, at least so long as it is not claimed that the privilege is absolute. But Griffin quite explicitly extends the grounds of human rights beyond the capacity for intentional action. He includes conditions making its successful exercise likely, conditions such as the availability of education and information, of resources and opportunities. At every point he adds 'minimal'—minimal education and information, etc. But if minimal means some information, some resources and opportunities, however little, it is a standard easy to meet, and almost impossible to violate. Just by being alive (and non-comatose) we have some knowledge, resources, and opportunities. Slaves have them. Griffin, of course, does not mean his minimal standard to be that skimpy. He suggests a generous standard. But then we lack criteria to determine what it should be. My fear is that this lacuna cannot be filled. There is no principled ground for fixing on one standard rather than another. The traditional approach offers a general theory of human rights as moral rights. There are good reasons for setting various limits to the legal implementation of those or other rights. They are mostly contingent reasons, relative to circumstances of time and place, and to the machinery of implementation there and then feasible. What Griffin does not provide are criteria for setting the minimal standards for human rights understood as universal moral rights which

---

[16] Griffin provides 'an argument' for this conclusion: 'If we had rights to all that is needed for a good or happy life, then the language of rights would become redundant. We already have a perfectly adequate way of speaking about individual well-being and any obligations there might be to promote it'. Ibid. 34. But, barring some argument that there cannot be alternative terminologies for talking about the same subject matter, this seems unconvincing.

enjoy that privileged status, and which go beyond the minimum protection of bare personhood.

These observations expose the way Griffin over-reaches. He would have liked to explain the existence of human rights as rights to protect one's personhood. Such rights may claim to be privileged, but they do not reach as far as he wants them to reach. It is crucial to his claim that 'Out of the notion of personhood we can generate most of the conventional list of human rights'.[17]

To 'generate' the conventional list he has to rely not on the protection of agency but on securing conditions which make it likely that agents will have a good life. That leaves him with no principled distinction between what human rights secure and what the conditions for having a good life secure.[18]

III. ALTERNATIVE APPROACHES

This leads me to a third worry about traditional accounts. The task of a theory of human rights is (a) to establish the essential features which contemporary human rights practice attributes to the rights it acknowledges to be human rights; and (b) to identify the moral standards which qualify anything to be so acknowledged. I will say that accounts which understand their task in that way manifest a political conception of human rights.

Theories like those of Gewirth and Griffin derive their human rights from concerns which do not relate to the practice of human rights, and they provide no argument to establish why human rights practice should be governed by them. There is nothing wrong in singling out the capacity for agency, or more broadly the capacities which constitute personhood, as of special moral significance. They are of special significance, and arguably they provide the foundation of some universal rights. Nor is Griffin wrong in thinking that not only the capacity for personhood, but also the ways it is or can be used, are ethically significant. The problem is the absence of a convincing argument as to why human rights practice should conform

---

[17] Ibid. 33.

[18] One additional point: Arguably, the capacity for intentional action is valuable for (and valued by) all human beings. Though it should not be confused with the value, if any, of longevity. It is the value of retaining the capacity for intentional action for as long as one is alive. It is valued by people who do not wish to remain alive, or who would rather end their life than betray their friend, etc. Once, however, we follow Griffin into the domain of 'rich agency' we can no longer rely on the value of bare personhood. We have to pass judgment on what makes life good and meaningful, for that judgment is needed to establish the standard which must be satisfied for rich personhood to be respected. This result is unwelcome to those who think of human rights as a basic moral domain which can command the consent of people of various religious and ethical persuasions, a domain which transcends most, if not all, ethical disputes about the good life. Protecting the minimal capacity for intentional action may command such near universal consent, though the moment we raise the question of what overrides the duty to protect that capacity, or whether one has a right to it, the consensus evaporates. Regarding rich agency it does not exist at all.

to their theories. There is no point in criticizing current human rights practice on the ground that it does not fit the traditional human rights ethical doctrine. Why should it?

Rawls's brief comments on human rights[19] constitute the best known, though extremely sketchy, political account of human rights:

Human rights are a class of rights that play a special role in a reasonable Law of Peoples: they restrict the justifying reasons for war and its conduct, and they specify limits to a regime's internal autonomy.[20]

Following Rawls I will take human rights to be rights which set limits to the sovereignty of states, in that their actual or anticipated violation is a (defeasible) reason for taking action against the violator in the international arena, even when—in cases not involving violation of either human rights or the commission of other offences—the action would not be permissible, or normatively available on the grounds that it would infringe the sovereignty of the state.[21] This is Rawls's and my answer to the first of the two questions an account of human rights faces: while human rights are invoked in various contexts, and for a variety of purposes, the dominant trend in human rights practice is to take the fact that a right is a human right as a defeasibly sufficient ground for taking action against violators in the international arena, that is to take its violation as a reason for such action.

Such measures set limits to state sovereignty for when states act within their sovereignty they can, even when acting wrongly, rebuff interference, invoking their sovereignty. Crudely speaking, they can say to outsiders: whether or not I (the state) am guilty of wrongful action is none of your business. Sovereignty does not justify state actions, but it protects states from external interference. Violation of human rights disables this response, which is available to states regarding other misdeeds.

What actions infringe state sovereignty, when not justified as reactions to violations of human rights or to other violations? International law answers this question, but our inquiry is a normative one. It assumes that, given the way things are in the world today, there is a normative, call it if you like a moral, justification to state sovereignty, that is to a limit on the permissibility of outsiders interfering in the affairs of a state, even when that state is in the wrong. The doctrine—the moral doctrine—of state sovereignty, not one whose articulation can be undertaken here, determines what forms of external interventions are rendered impermissible by the sovereignty of states.

---

[19] Rawls, J., *The Law of Peoples* (2nd edn., Cambridge, Mass.: Harvard University Press, 1999). For a powerful defence of Rawls's position see Freeman, S., 'Distributive Justice and the Law of Peoples' in Martin, R. and Reidy, D. (eds), *Rawls's Law of Peoples: A Realistic Utopia?* (Oxford: Blackwell, 2006), 243; repr. in Freeman, S., *Justice and the Social Contract: Essays on Rawlsian Political Philosophy* (Oxford: Oxford University Press, 2007), 297.

[20] Rawls, J., *The Law of Peoples* (above, n. 19), 79.

[21] Unlike Rawls who took rights to be human rights only if their serious violation could justify armed intervention, I take them to be rights whose violation can justify any international action against violators, provided that they are actions which normally would be impermissible being violations of state sovereignty.

So far, states have been the main agents in international law, and I will continue to treat human rights as being rights against states. But I do not mean that human rights are rights held only against states, or only in the international arena. Human rights can be held against international organizations, and other international agents, and almost always they will also be rights against individuals and other domestic institutions. The claim is only that being rights whose violation is a reason for action against states in the international arena is distinctive of human rights, according to human rights practice.

This being so, we have the core answer to the second question as well: human rights are those regarding which sovereignty-limiting measures are morally justified. International law is at fault when it recognizes as a human right something which, morally speaking, is not a right or not one whose violation might justify international action against a state, as well as when it fails to recognize the legitimacy of sovereignty-limiting measures when the violation of rights morally justifies them.

Rawls's own statement of the conditions which would establish a right as a human right is, however, unsatisfactory. Human rights, Rawls tells us, are: 'Necessary conditions of any system of social cooperation. When they are regularly violated, we have command by force, a slave system, and no cooperation of any kind'.[22]

This, he says 'accounts' for the features of human rights, which may imply that that is the justification for holding the rights he lists as fulfilling the role he assigns to human rights. In *The Law of Peoples* Rawls's explanation of social cooperation is very sketchy, but it implicitly refers to his earlier explanation of an ideal of social cooperation holding between 'free and equal moral persons' according to which 'social cooperation [is] not simply . . . a productive and socially coordinated activity, but . . . [one] fulfilling a notion of fair terms of cooperation and of mutual advantage'.[23] 'Social cooperation', he wrote elsewhere, 'is always for mutual benefit . . . [I]t involves . . . a shared notion of fair terms of cooperation, which each participant may reasonably be expected to accept, provided that everyone else likewise accepts them . . . all who cooperate must benefit or share in common burdens'.[24] From this he concludes that human rights include:

The right to life (to the means of subsistence and security); to liberty (to freedom from slavery, serfdom, and forced occupation, and to a sufficient measure of liberty of conscience to ensure freedom of religion and thought); to property (personal property); and to formal equality as expressed by the rules of natural justice (that is, that similar cases be treated similarly).[25]

Are human rights grounded in the conditions of social cooperation? The claim is marred by highly doubtful contentions about the conditions of social cooperation.

---

[22] Rawls, J., *The Law of Peoples* (above, n. 19), 68.
[23] Rawls, J., 'Kantian Constructivism in Moral Theory', *Journal of Philosophy*, 77 (1980), 515, reprinted in Freeman, S. (ed.), *Rawls's Collected Papers* (Cambridge, Mass.: Harvard University Press, 1980), 335.
[24] Rawls, J., *Political Liberalism* (New York: Columbia University Press, 1995), 300.
[25] Rawls, J., *The Law of Peoples* (above, n. 19), 65.

He says that societies which do not meet these, morally very demanding, conditions command by force.[26] This seems false. Furthermore, not all societies which fail to respect the human rights which Rawls lists command by force. It is implausible to suppose, for example, that communities which do not recognize personal private property (one of his human rights) must command by force. Imagine a society where everything which is not common property is owned by the clan or the larger family, in the way that some small families organize their affairs. Why should they not enjoy social cooperation? Similarly, there is no reason to think that all feudal societies, or all sexist societies, which denied women property rights, and much else, commanded by force.

My main worry, however, lies elsewhere. It is about the way Rawls connects the conditions of social cooperation with the limits of sovereignty, of the internal autonomy of a political order. The moral limits of sovereignty depend not only on the conditions within the society. They also depend on who is in a position to assert the limitations of sovereignty, and how they are likely to act as a result. It is one thing, for example, to set limits to the sovereignty of states within a well-ordered and reasonably just organization like the European Union (EU), and quite another to do so for the international arena say at the height of old-style colonialism in the nineteenth century, and still different today, the heyday of new style imperialism.

We must not confuse the limits of sovereignty with the limits of legitimate authority. The sovereignty of states sets limits to the right of others to interfere with their affairs. The notion of sovereignty is the counterpart of that of rightful international intervention. The criteria determining the limits of legitimate authority depend on the morality of the authority's actions.[27] However, not every action exceeding a state's legitimate authority can be a reason for interference by other states, whatever the circumstances, just as not every moral wrongdoing by an individual can justify intervention by others to stop or punish it.[28]

The point is controversial. One objection is that there are reasons to limit intervention in the life of individuals (respect for their autonomy and independence) which do not apply to states, since they do not have value in and of themselves. The objection is then reinforced by a distinction between principled and contingent factors which limit sovereignty. It claims that in principle actions exceeding the state's authority justify interference provided such interference is likely to succeed (in remedying the offence or preventing it) and is not counter-productive, that is that its overall benefits are not outweighed by its disadvantages.

---

[26] Rawls, J., *The Law of Peoples* (above, n. 19), 68. So far as we know all political societies command by force in some sense. This fact is often invoked as the mark of a political society. I assume that Rawls has in mind something closer to 'command by force only'.

[27] See on the conditions of legitimate authority Raz, J., *The Morality of Freedom* (Oxford: Oxford University Press, 1986), 23–109.

[28] The analogy is complicated by the fact that not all mistaken decisions and actions take states or their governments beyond the scope of their legitimate authority. So long as we bear this in mind the analogy remains useful.

While this counter-argument presents an appealing picture it is flawed both by a simplistic understanding of the moral importance of state sovereignty and by disregarding persisting features of the international situation. The moral importance of state autonomy was fully appreciated by Rawls, and is the reason for his insistence that his doctrine of the justice of the basic structure (of the state) cannot be simply extended to the international arena.[29] As I see it, the core point, which is too complex to be dwelt upon here, is that much of the content of the moral principles which govern social relations and the structure of social organization is determined by the contingent practices of different societies. Hence the principles which should govern international relations cannot just be a generalization of the principles of justice which govern any individual society. How does this bear on the issue of state sovereignty? Directly it establishes a degree of variability between standards of justice and thereby variability in the precise content and scope of rights which apply in different political societies. This speaks for caution in giving outsiders a right to intervene in the affairs of other states. It also suggests the desirability of allowing political societies freedom from too close external scrutiny, to be free to develop their own rights-affecting practices. This does not establish a precise analogy between interference with an individual and with a state, but it shows that respect for the independence and autonomy of the state is of great moral significance.

Be that as it may. The main point I wish to emphasize is that the moral principles determining the limits of sovereignty must reflect not only the limits of the authority of the state, but also the relatively fixed limitations on the possibility of justified interference by international organizations and by other states in the affairs of even an offending state. When the international situation is one in which it is clear that international measures will not be applied impartially, that they will be used to increase the domination of a super-power over its rivals, or over its client states, etc. the moral principles setting limits to sovereignty will tend to be more protective of sovereignty than in the relationship among states which exists within a union, like the European Union, which has relatively impartial judicial institutions and fairly reliable enforcement procedures.

Just as the moral limits of individual freedom *vis à vis* the state one lives in vary depending on the character of the government and the public culture of the state—whatever they are they reflect not merely the principles of individual conduct but also relatively independent constraints on the justifiability of interference by others—so in the international arena, the moral limits of state sovereignty vary with the relatively stable features of the international situation. At any given time, however, they are determined not merely by the moral limits to the authority of states but also by the possibility of morally sound interference by others.

---

[29] For his reasons see Scheffler, S., 'Egalitarian Liberalism as Moral Pluralism', *Aristotelian Society Supplementary Volume*, 79/1 (2005), 229–253 and Freeman, S., 'Distributive Justice and the Law of Peoples' (above, n. 19).

This consideration is ignored by Rawls. It exposes a lacuna in his argument. Rawls's conditions of social cooperation, whatever we think of them, are relevant to the scope of state authority. They cannot determine the limits of sovereignty in the way Rawls suggests.[30]

This criticism of Rawls's conception of human rights connects with a criticism I made against some proponents of the traditional approach: their failure to adequately examine the relations between value and rights. The same is true of Rawls. Quite rightly he did not claim that human rights set the only moral limits on the sovereignty of states, but nor did he explain what the other limits are and what distinguishes them from human rights. Some of his human rights, for example the human right against genocide, do not appear to be rights at all. To be sure committing genocide is wrong, but is it the case that I have a right against the genocide of any people? Do I have a right against the annihilation of other groups, for example, of university professors? Not all wrongs constitute violations of rights. Not all the limits of either state authority or state sovereignty are set by rights. Rawls fails to examine the distinctions involved.

On one central issue, however, Rawls's observations are consistent with the political conception of human rights: observation of human rights practice shows that they are taken to be rights which, whatever else they are, set limits to the sovereignty of states, and therefore arguments which determine what they are, are ones which, among other things, establish such limits.

IV. Following the Practice: The Ordinary Face of Human Rights

One immediate consequence of the political conception is that human rights need not be universal or foundational. Individual rights are human rights if they disable a certain argument against interference by outsiders in the affairs of a state. They disable, or deny, the legitimacy of the response: I, the state, may have acted wrongly, but you, the outsider are not entitled to interfere. I am protected by my sovereignty. Disabling the defence 'none of your business', is definitive of the political conception of human rights. They are rights which are morally valid against states in the international arena, and there is no reason to think that such rights must be universal.

Quite a few writers accept the downgrading of human rights to those individual rights which are assertible in the international arena, denying them special stringency

---

[30] Rawls's discussion of decent hierarchical societies, and of 'benevolent despotisms', can be taken to indicate that he allows for the distinction between the limits of legitimate authority and the limits of sovereignty. My criticism is that the argument for making the conditions of human cooperation the basis of human rights is radically incomplete by not taking the distinction into account.

and universality, though they are not always aware that these are the implications of their writings, most often because they are unaware of the vacuity of the assertion that human rights set 'minimal standards'.

James Nickel, for example, thinks human rights are minimal standards for governments, but neither he nor Griffin nor the others identify what is the test of the standards being minimal other than that there are or could be higher standards on the same matters. He is also one of those writers who make light of the universality of human rights. According to him

some human rights cannot be universal in the strong sense of applying to all humans at all times, because they assert that people are entitled to services tied to relatively recent social and political institutions. Due process rights, for example, presuppose modern legal systems and the institutional safeguards they can offer. Social and economic rights presuppose modern relations of production and the institutions of the redistributive state.[31]

Nickel is following Tasioulas who observes that according to some views human rights must be possessed by

all human beings throughout history—but only at the apparent cost of excluding rights that require or presuppose the existence of non-universal social practices and institutions, e.g. rights to political participation or to a fair trial. By contrast, I have suggested that human rights enjoy a temporally-constrained form of universality, so that the question concerning which human rights exist can only be determined within some specified historical context. For us, today, human rights are those possessed in virtue of being human and inhabiting a social world that is subject to the conditions of modernity. This historical constraint permits very general facts about feasible institutional design in the modern world, e.g. forms of legal regulation, political participation and economic organization, to play a role in determining which human rights we recognize.[32]

In this way, accounts of human rights become almost indistinguishable from accounts of international political morality in so far as they involve respecting some individual rights.

Charles Beitz, noting both the range of human rights, and the range of their uses, observes that:

Taken together, these rights are not best interpreted as 'minimal conditions for any kind of life at all'.[33] The rights of the Declaration [of Human Rights] and the covenants bear on nearly every dimension of a society's basic institutional structure, from protections against misuse of state power to requirements for the political process, health and welfare policy, and levels of compensation for work. In scope and detail, international human rights are not very much more minimal than those proposed in many contemporary theories of social justice.[34]

---

[31] Nickel, J., *Making Sense of Human Rights* (Cambridge: Blackwell, 2006), 25.

[32] Tasioulas, J., 'The Moral Reality of Human Rights' (above, n. 1), 76–7. He first advanced this view in 'Human Rights, Universality and the Values of Personhood: Retracing Griffin's Steps', *European Journal of Philosophy*, 10/1 (2002), 79.

[33] The reference is to Ignatieff, M., *Human Rights as Politics and Idolatry* (Princeton: Princeton University Press, 2003), 56.

[34] Beitz, C., 'What Human Rights Mean', *Daedalus*, 132 (2003), 39.

Not surprisingly Beitz, who regards human rights as the standards of international justice, also rejects their strict universality: 'International human rights are not even *prospectively* timeless. They are standards appropriate to the institutions of modern or modernising societies'.[35]

These authors do not always agree with one another, nor do they agree with my view, namely that the politics of international human rights is drifting towards becoming just the politics of international relations, in so far as they acknowledge individual rights.

While recognition of that drift is more common among those who embrace the political conception, its traces can be found among more tradition-minded writers. An example of that is Amartya Sen's recent foray into the field.[36] Sen's explanation is too narrow in limiting human rights to rights to various freedoms, which leaves the right not to be tortured (in mild ways which do not affect one's freedom), and rights to privacy which do not impede freedom, for example, beyond the range of human rights. But apart from that his analysis is simply an analysis of factors which are relevant to the morality of action. His human rights are moral rights, which may or may not call for legal recognition, may or may not be defeated by any number of conflicting considerations, and so on and so forth. He recognizes the drift in human rights practice away from taking them to have foundational standing or exceptional importance, while failing to recognize the source of that drift in the adoption of a political conception of these rights.

V. Where Do Human Rights Come From?

A few clarifications: First, I am not dealing in this article with the merits or drawbacks of the practice of human rights, or any aspects of it. My aim is to characterize in abstract terms the moral standards by which the practice is to be judged.

Second, I do not deny that there may be universal human rights which people have in virtue of their humanity alone. My criticism of that tradition is primarily that it fails to establish why all and only such rights should be recognized as setting limits to sovereignty, which is the predominant mark of human rights in human rights practice.

Third, just as rights generally while being reasons for taking some measures against their violators do not normally give reason for all measures, so human rights set some limits to sovereignty, but do not necessarily constitute reasons for all measures, however severe, against violators. Similarly, they may sanction action in some forum, but not in others.

---

[35]   Beitz, C., 'What Human Rights Mean', *Daedalus*, 132 (2003), 42–3.
[36]   Sen, A., 'Elements of a Theory of Human Rights', *Philosophy and Public Affairs*, 32 (2004), 315.

Finally, rejecting the universality of human rights is no endorsement of moral relativism. If whether someone has any of the human rights depends exclusively on contingent *non-evaluative* facts then irrational moral relativism reigns. But that is not the view defended here. Rather, it is a version of the familiar and benign social relativism: there is a moral duty to drive on the left in one country and on the right in another. Which it is depends on contingent non-evaluative facts: that everyone drives this way in one and the other way in the other country, but not on them alone. It also depends on a universal moral precept, namely that one should drive safely. But if the fact that there is a right to jury trial in one country and not in another equally depends on some more general moral right, say a right to fair trial, is not the traditional approach vindicated? All morally sound human rights, it claims, are either universal rights or applications of such universal rights to the conditions of this country or that.

This response is both right and wrong. It is right that vindicating any evaluative proposition relies, among other facts, on universal evaluative truths. But it is wrong in assuming that moral rights can be established only by reference to other moral rights. Typically rights are established by arguments about the value of having them. Their existence depends on there being interests whose existence warrants holding others subject to duties to protect and promote them.[37] Thus, the right that people who made promises to us shall keep them depends on the desirability, that is the value, of being able to create bonds of duty among people at will. That desirability—consisting in improved ability to plan for the future, to form common projects, and to forge common bonds—governs the scope of the right: only people for whom the ability is valuable have the power to make promises (and that may exclude very young children, intellectually disabled people, etc.) and only matters regarding which it is desirable to be able to form such bonds at will, can be the object of promises (and that may exclude commission of immoral acts, etc.).

So the political conception of human rights can and should accept universality of morality. Its essence as a political conception is that it regards human rights as rights which are to be given institutional recognition, rights which transcend private morality. That explains why it is not common to find the right to the performance of promises as a human right. It is pretty universal in application, as any human of mature mind has it. Yet it is not one which should be given legal or other institutional recognition. Some promises, to be sure, merit such recognition, but not all of them, and therefore there is no human right that promises made to one be kept.

Human rights are moral rights held by individuals. But individuals have them only when the conditions are appropriate for governments to have the duties to protect the interests which the rights protect. A good example is the right to education. The right lacks universality for it exists only where the social and political organization of a country makes it appropriate to hold the state to have a duty to

---

[37] Raz, J., *The Morality of Freedom* (above, n. 27).

provide education. Hence, while the right to education is an individual moral right, the considerations which establish it are complex and not all of them relate to the interest of the right-holder. The primary, though not the only, relevant interest of the right-holder is to be equipped with whatever knowledge and skills are required for him to be able to have a rewarding life in the conditions in which he is likely to find himself. Whether education, in a sense which involves formal instruction, is needed to meet that individual interest is itself a contingent matter. When it is required the question arises: what is the most appropriate way of securing it for all? Under some conditions the state should be a guarantor that education is provided, and when that is so, people have a right to education, and when it is so more or less throughout the world the last question arises: should states enjoy immunity from external interference regarding their success or failure to respect the right to education of people within their territory? If the conditions of the international community are such that they should not enjoy such immunity then the right to education is a human right.

So that is where human rights come from. They normally derive from three layers of argument: First, some individual interest often combined with showing how social conditions require its satisfaction in certain ways (for example, via various forms of instruction) establishing an individual moral right. Some writers think that some rights are as they may say rock-bottom, that is not deriving from any individual interest. Needless to say, if there are such rights they too will belong with this part of the argument. The second layer shows that under some conditions states are to be held duty bound to respect or promote the interest (or the rights) of individuals identified in the first part of the argument. With the growth of multinational corporations, and of transnational law and organizations, this second condition will be bypassed in many cases, and there will be more and more cases in which no single state will have a primary responsibility for the enforcement of human rights. Rather, the responsibility will rest directly with international bodies which mandate state actions to protect the rights. The final layer shows that they do not enjoy immunity from interference regarding these matters. If all parts of the argument succeed then we have established that a human right exists. Each layer presupposes the previous one, but to establish the conclusion of each layer requires considerations specific to it. So understood, human rights enjoy rational justification. They lack a foundation in not being grounded in a fundamental moral concern but depending on the contingencies of the current system of international relations.

VI. CONCLUSION

I have not offered an analysis of the concept of a human right. There is not enough discipline underpinning the use of the term 'human rights' to make it a useful analytical tool. The elucidation of its meaning does not illuminate significant ethical or political issues. Focusing on the use of the term in legal and political practice and advocacy, I claimed that it either relies on the legal recognition of human rights as limiting state sovereignty, or claims that they should be so recognized. Given that, I posed the question of which individual rights warrant such recognition, and what precise limits to sovereignty they should be taken to set.

One result is that a right's being a human right does not entail that it is either basic or very important. To that degree this approach deflates the rhetoric of human rights. But given the moral significance of rights which set moral limits to sovereignty, human rights are inevitably morally important. If they were not they would not warrant interference in state sovereignty. Nevertheless, the political conception does point towards a normalization of the politics of human rights. That is an inevitable consequence of the success of human rights practice. It is part of processes which saw the development of regional organizations, like the EU, of functional organizations like the World Trade Organization, and of a myriad of multinational regimes, like that regarding the utilization of deep sea resources, all of which eroded the scope of state sovereignty. It is due to the ambitions of some states to achieve singular world domination, and of others to limit that ambition. These developments enriched human rights practice, without necessarily improving conformity with human rights.

We are in the midst of fast changes in the shape of international relations. As a result, human rights practice is in flux, and the indeterminate character of my observations reflects this flux. That is inevitable, and being more precise and determinate than conditions allow is no virtue. Should we see further growth of state-transcending standards and institutions, including further international recognition and enforcement of individual rights, the rights will lose much of the aura of exceptional standing which is currently associated with 'human rights'.

CHAPTER 16

HUMAN RIGHTS AND THE AUTONOMY OF INTERNATIONAL LAW

JAMES GRIFFIN

I. A MEASURE OF AGREEMENT

There is at present sharp disagreement about the autonomy of international law. A sizeable constituency thinks that international law must rest at certain points on ethics. A sizeable constituency, in my experience even larger, denies it.

What commands widespread agreement, however, is that our concept of a 'human right' stands in need of clarification. Even here, though, there is disagreement. I think that we do not have an adequate grasp even of what one might call the 'existence conditions' of human rights—that is, what one must show in order to establish that a particular human right exists and what it is a right to. And many others would not go as far as that.

I go so far for this reason. When during the seventeenth and eighteenth centuries the theological content of the idea of a natural right was abandoned in stages, nothing was put in its place. What was abandoned was a cluster of teleological beliefs: that God has placed in us certain dispositions towards the good; that these dispositions give rise to precepts of action; that natural laws are expressions of these precepts; and that natural rights are derivable from natural laws. One would then establish a natural right, in principle, by establishing a natural law. Identifying natural laws was by no means easy, but having a source of natural rights, even though one hard to identify, was at least something, compared to our present condition. By the end of the Enlightenment, natural rights were often still thought to be derived from natural law, but natural law by then widely reduced to no more than a moral principle independent of social convention and law. This process of secularization left the term 'human right' with so few criteria for determining when it is used correctly, and when incorrectly, that today we often have only a tenuous, and sometimes a plainly inadequate, grasp on what is at issue. Its indeterminateness of sense, furthermore, is not something characteristic of ethical terms generally; it is a problem specifically, though perhaps not uniquely, with the term 'human right'. This indeterminateness is still with us, and we must reduce it.

One way of trying to reduce it seems, on the face of it, to strengthen the case for the autonomy of international law. The growth in the international law of human rights during the twentieth century has brought about changes in the extension of the term—made it broader and greatly increased its acceptance—and changes in extension and degree of acceptance can constitute changes in meaning. Has international law, then, brought about, in its own way, a satisfactory determinateness in sense?

No matter who we are we cannot establish a human right just by declaring it to be one. Not even the Universal Declaration of Human Rights by the United Nations in solemn assembly is enough. We—whoever we are—can get it wrong, and we owe attention, therefore, to the criteria for right and wrong here. For example, the Universal Declaration contains a right to periodic holidays with pay, to which the overwhelming and cheering, though not quite universal, reaction has been that, whatever kind of entitlement that might be, it is not a human right. The Universal Declaration also includes a right to democratic participation, but it is possible to argue in an intellectually responsible way whether it really is a human right. Again, we owe attention to how we would settle that argument. And there are widespread doubts about welfare rights—for instance, whether they are human or only civil rights or whether some of them have been drawn too lavishly. We quite reasonably want to know how strong the case is for their being human rights. And we need far more than just a *list* of human rights. We need to know more than just their *names*. We must also know their content. We already know the content of some human rights (for example, the right not to be tortured) but by no means all (for example, the right to welfare, to life, to liberty). In the latter cases, how do we decide it? And we need to know how to resolve conflicts involving rights. A judge on an international bench cannot resolve conflicts by *fiat*. The resolution must be reasoned. But what are to count as good reasons? Even if the list of human rights in current international law is authoritative, which I see no reason to accept, it does not give us all that we need. We also need good answers to these questions. It is a bad bargain to purchase autonomy for international law at the cost of a severe loss of explanatory power or of action-guiding weight.

II. Functional Accounts of Human Rights

Let us go back to what most of us agree on: that the term 'human right' needs clarification. How have contemporary philosophers tried to make it clearer? Very many of them have done so by focusing on the function of human rights. Take, for instance, Ronald Dworkin's view that rights are trumps over appeals to the general good. The point of rights, however, even the basic legal rights that Dworkin has primarily in mind, cannot be, as he claims, to trump the general good. The consequence of that claim would be that rights have no point in restraining most of the agents whom in the course of history they have been used, and are still used, to restrain: power-hungry popes, absolute monarchs, dictatorships of the proletariat, murderous thugs who seize political power, not all of whom (to put it no higher) had the general welfare as their goal. Nor is the claim much more plausible if we reinterpret Dworkin more sympathetically to be referring only to ideal political conditions, when the state is committed to pursuing the impartial maximization of welfare, or whatever the best conception of promoting people's good turns out to be.[1] The point of rights in those ideal conditions, we can understand Dworkin to be saying, is as trumps over the best policy of promoting the good of all. But that cannot be right either. It does nothing to lessen the implausibility of denying human rights the role they have played throughout their history. Besides, justice and fairness are also likely sometimes to trump the promotion of the good of all, and, as I have argued elsewhere, the domain of justice and the domain of human rights are only overlapping, not congruent.[2] If more than rights are trumps, one cannot use trumping to characterize rights. In any case, rights are not, strictly speaking, trumps. There is some, perhaps especially high, level of the general good at which it would override a right, as Dworkin himself accepts.[3]

At what level? To answer that, we need to know how to attach moral weight both to rights and to different levels of the general good. If the weight we attach to rights is not to be arbitrary, we must have a sufficiently rich understanding of the value that rights represent—for *human* rights that would most likely require a sufficiently

---

[1] In his reply to Herbert Hart's criticisms (Hart, H. L. A., 'Between Utility and Rights', in his *Essays in Jurisprudence and Philosophy* (Oxford: Clarendon Press, 1983), ch. 9), Dworkin acknowledges that the conception of the common good checked by rights need not be utilitarian: 'We need rights, as a distinct element in political theory, only when some decision that injures some people nevertheless finds prima-facie support in the claim that it will make the community as a whole better off on some plausible account of where the community's general welfare lies' (Dworkin, R., 'Rights as Trumps', in Waldron, J. W. (ed.), *Theories of Rights* (Oxford: Oxford University Press, 1984), 166). But this slight amendment does not make Dworkin's characterization of rights any less flawed.

[2] Griffin, J., *On Human Rights* (Oxford: Oxford University Press, 2008).

[3] Dworkin, R., 'Rights as Trumps' (above, n. 1), 191 ff.

rich understanding of the dignity, or worth, of the human person, whatever the proper understanding of that now widely used but vague phrase is.[4] A satisfactory account of *human* rights, therefore, must contain some adumbration of the term 'human dignity', again not in all of its varied uses but in its role as a ground for human rights. So the account must have more substantive evaluative elements than Dworkin supplies.[5] I say '*more* substantive evaluative elements' because no plausible account of human rights will be purely functional or purely substantive; it will be a mixture of the two. The more ethically substantive account that we need will itself have functional implications.

John Rawls rightly says that one can also make an account of human rights more substantive by spelling out the role that human rights play in a larger theory—in Rawls's case, in a theory of political justice between peoples.[6] This approach leads Rawls to a markedly shorter list of human rights than the lists common in liberal democracies.[7] Rawls's list omits such typical human rights as freedom of expression, freedom of association (except what is needed for freedom of conscience and of religious observance), the right to democratic political participation, and any economic rights that go beyond a right to mere subsistence.[8] And the role of human rights, on Rawls's conception of them, is quite restricted: it is to provide the justifying reasons for war and its conduct, and to set conditions for when one state may coercively intervene in another.[9]

However, what almost universally attract the label 'human rights' are the items on the longer list that one would get by compiling the well-established rights of the United Nations, perhaps pruned a bit here and there. Rawls's shorter list is, he says, a proper subset of this longer sort of list.[10] Why then does Rawls commandeer the label 'human rights' for his shorter list? For no sufficient reason. Even if Rawls is correct that the law of peoples needs a shortened list, which I doubt for reasons I cannot now go into,[11] that is no reason why he should consider it the canonical list of 'human' rights. He gives no reason to think that this is what human rights really are, or are now best thought of as being. He makes no effort to show that it is only the rights on his list that human beings have simply as human beings, or however else he wants to interpret 'human'. He says that his list contains 'a special class of urgent rights',[12] without telling us how they are urgent while the excluded rights on the liberal democratic lists are not. To establish that Rawls's shorter list is what human rights are best thought of as being would take a much stronger argument—say, an argument to the effect that all versions of the longer

---

[4] Widely employed because of its use by the United Nations in the Preambles to the two International Covenants of 1966.

[5] For fuller assessment of Dworkin's view of rights as trumps, see Hart, H. L. A., 'Between Utility and Rights' (above, n. 1).

[6] Rawls, J., *The Law of Peoples* (Cambridge, Mass.: Harvard University Press, 1999).

[7] Ibid. 68, 78–81.   [8] Ibid. 65 no. 2, 70, 74, 79.   [9] Ibid. 27, 79–80.   [10] Ibid. 70.

[11] But see Griffin, J., *On Human Rights* (above, n. 2).   [12] Rawls, J., *Law of Peoples* (above, n. 6), 78–9.

liberal democratic list are incorrigibly flawed. There are such arguments,[13] but none that I know of establishes anything approaching such a strong conclusion. And Rawls's characterization of the *role* of human rights—briefly, to establish rules of war and conditions for justified intervention—is similarly under-motivated. The point of human rights, on the almost universally accepted conception of them, is far wider than that. For example, they quite obviously have point intra-nationally: to justify rebellion, to establish a case for peaceful reform, to curb an autocratic ruler, to criticize a majority's treatment of racial or ethnic minorities. And they are used by the United Nations and by non-governmental organizations to issue periodic reports on the human rights record of individual countries, seen from an internal point of view. They are also used to criticize institutions within a single society. Many hospitals are still to be condemned for denying patients true informed consent. And some parents can reasonably be criticized for violating their mature children's autonomy and liberty.

Rawls's functional explanation of human rights leaves the contents of the individual rights unworkably obscure. How would he determine, for example, the minimum welfare required by human rights? If one saw human beings as deriving from the dignity of the human person, and if one added some content to the vague term 'dignity'—say, that in this context it consists of the valuable status of being a normative agent—one could fix minimum welfare as the welfare required to live as a normative agent, which is a higher standard than mere subsistence. It might look as if Rawls could, if he wanted, avail himself of an altogether different approach to fix the minimum. He could ask: at what level of welfare would its neglect start to provide *prima facie* justification for intervention by other nations? But we should not know what to answer. We should need help from some further ethical thought. It is not enough to ask: what level of welfare should another nation not tolerate? It is hard to see what resources Rawls has to provide a plausible answer.

Why have functional accounts been so attractive? My guess is that it is partly a hangover from the days of logical positivism and its immediate successors, in which value judgments were thought to be thoroughly subjective uses of language: expressions of emotion or attitude, or mere exercises in persuasion. Dworkin does not give us what we should require of an account of human rights: criteria that will tell us whether a certain right exists and, if so, what it is a right to. Rawls does not give us the latter either, though for reasons of his own.

---

[13] Examples of such arguments can be found in the works of Joseph Raz and Charles Beitz. For Joseph Raz's argument see Griffin, J. *On Human Rights* (above, n. 2) and Raz, Chapter 15 in this volume. For Charles Beitz's argument see his articles 'Human Rights and the Law of Peoples', in Chatterjee, D. (ed.), *The Ethics of Assistance: Morality and the Distant Needy* (Cambridge: Cambridge University Press, 2004) and 'What Human Rights Mean', *Daedalus*, 132 (2003), 36. I discuss Raz's argument in *On Human Rights* (above, n. 2), ch. 2.9 and many of Beitz's points also in *On Human Rights* ch. 2 *passim*.

But, as we have seen, the functional accounts that many looked to (I would also include Feinberg and Nozick as functionalists) are short on explanatory power.

III. A Political Account

Joseph Raz has recently adopted a functional account—what he calls a 'political conception' of human rights. The job of a theory of rights is, he says, first, 'to establish the essential features which contemporary human rights practice attributes to the rights it acknowledges to be human rights' and, second, 'to identify the moral standards which qualify anything to be so acknowledged'.[14]

What *is* 'contemporary human rights practice'? 'The dominant trend in human rights practice', Raz answers, 'is to take the fact that a right is a human right as a defeasibly sufficient ground for taking action against violators in the international arena'.[15] Since Raz himself adopts the political conception, he restricts human rights, without qualification, to the role of limiting national sovereignty; indeed, serious enough violations of such rights constitute the necessary and sufficient conditions for such limits.[16] Perhaps the best characterization of his position comes in his conclusion, where he says that, if one focuses on the real world of 'legal and political practice and advocacy', one finds that the term 'human rights' either relies on their legal recognition 'as limiting state sovereignty' or constitutes a claim 'that they should be so recognized'.[17]

Raz's claim that the function, even merely the predominant function, of human rights in current practice is to limit sovereignty is a factual claim and, I should think, surely false. These days human rights discourse is commonly used in our national life: for example, in the European Union's fairly recent bill of rights and its much more recent incorporation in the legal systems of several member states, in current campaigns against violations of liberty (for example, in Guantánamo), in similar campaigns against torture, and in all the other cases I mentioned earlier in discussing Rawls.

So let us drop the question of whether current human rights practice *is* concerned with the justification of intervention and ask instead whether it *should* be. This question takes us back to Rawls's similar restriction on the role of human rights, and my doubts about Rawls apply to Raz too. What does Raz offer in support of

---

[14] Raz, J. this volume, 327.

[15] Ibid. 328: Raz seems uncertain how strong he wants to make this claim. He says in this passage merely that the 'dominant trend' in human rights practice is to regard them as justifying intervention, which leaves space for many other trends. In the same vein, he writes that justifying intervention is merely 'the predominant mark of human rights in human rights practice', which of course leaves space for several other marks. Ibid. 334.

[16] Ibid. 324: 'all and only such [i.e. human] rights should be recognized as setting limits to sovereignty'.

[17] Ibid. 337.

the restriction? Nothing. He merely argues against one alternative: 'the traditional conception'. So let us now look at that.

IV. Traditional Accounts

Traditional accounts, Raz tells us, are 'roughly characterized by four, logically independent features'. First, they aim to derive human rights 'from *basic features* of human beings which are both *valuable* and in some way essential to all which is valuable in human life'. Second, 'human rights are basic, perhaps the most basic and the most important *moral rights*'. Third, traditional accounts pay 'scant attention to the difference between something being valuable and having a right to it'. Fourth, the rights they promote 'tend to be individualistic ... what each person can enjoy on his or her own'.[18] Raz mentions only two modern 'traditionalists': Alan Gewirth and me. But I do not recognize my beliefs in Raz's description of traditional accounts.

Let me explain my view; it shows how unsuccessful Raz's distinction between traditional and political accounts is. I start with ethical judgments as applied to the assessment of our societies—the actual judgments not just of philosophers but also of political theorists, legislators, international lawyers, officials of NGOs, and civil servants. That is, I start with the continuous, developing notion of human rights running through the history I sketched earlier—call it the 'historical notion'. How may we remedy the indeterminateness of the historical notion? Although the theological content of the term 'human rights' was abandoned, the ethical content was not. From time to time in the course of history one encounters the idea that human rights are protections of our human status and that the human status in question is our rational or, more specifically, normative agency. It is in my attempt to make the sense of the term 'human rights' more determinate that I suggest that we adopt this part of the tradition, that we see human rights as protections of our normative agency, of what I call our 'personhood'.

But personhood cannot be the only ground for human rights. It leaves many rights too indeterminate. For example, we have a right to security of person. But what does that exclude? Would it exclude forcefully taking a few drops of blood from my finger to save the lives of many others? Perhaps not. To up the stakes, would it also not exclude forcefully taking one of my kidneys? After all, the two weeks it would take me to recover from a kidney extraction would not deprive me of my personhood. Where is the line to be drawn? The personhood consideration on its own will not make the line determinate enough for practice. To fix a sufficiently determinate line we should have to introduce considerations such as

---

[18] Ibid. 323, author's italics.

these: given human nature, have we left a big enough safety margin? Is the right too complicated to do the job we want it to? Is the right too demanding? And so on. We must consider how human beings and societies actually work. So, to make the right to security of person determinate enough we need another ground, call it 'practicalities'.

I propose, therefore, two grounds for human rights: personhood and practicalities. The existence conditions for a human right would, then, be these. One establishes the existence of such a right by showing, first, that it protects an essential feature of personhood, and, second, that its determinate content often results from the sorts of practical considerations that I have roughly sketched.

My statement here of the personhood account is too abbreviated to persuade doubters, but I have discussed it more fully elsewhere.[19] I propose, as I have said, that we see human rights as protections of our normative agency. That is not a *derivation* of human rights from normative agency; it is a *proposal* based on a hunch that this way of remedying the indeterminateness of the term will best suit its role in ethics. The requirement that it suit ethics holds out prospects—realized, I should say—of supplying standards for determining whether an account of human rights is 'right' or 'wrong'. What I do is distant from what Alan Gewirth did recently, in seeking to establish human rights by appeal to certain logical necessities. That he too makes human agency central to his project does not make his project close to mine. His first step is to derive rights from agency in the prudential case: every agent, even the purely self-interested, must accept, on pain of contradiction, that 'I have rights to the proximate necessary conditions of my action'. His next step is from the prudential case to the universal: the agent must accept, because of the logical principle of universalizability, and again on pain of contradiction, that 'all other agents equally have these rights', thus establishing them as *human* rights. In contrast, I claim no logical necessity for my proposal that we see human rights as protections of normative agency. Indeed, some of my colleagues not only reject it but also make plausible, contradiction-free counter-proposals that must in some way be seriously assessed.

How would one go about assessing my proposal? Ultimately, by deciding whether it gives us human rights that fit into the best ethics overall. More immediately, by working out its consequences, especially its consequences for supposed human rights that we find contentious or unclear. And by assessing my proposal against counter-proposals: for example, the counter-proposal that the ground of human rights is not solely normative agency but certain other values as well, or that the ground is not normative agency but basic human needs, and so on. And even by answering largely empirical questions such as how determinate we must make the sense of the term 'human right' to avoid creating serious practical problems for ourselves.

---

[19] Griffin, J., *On Human Rights* (above, n. 2), esp. ch. 2.

It may look as though, in *proposing* a sense for the term 'human rights', I am just stipulating its sense. If so, then it is in the way that the writers in the late Middle Ages who first introduced our modern notion of a 'human right' stipulated its sense. They by no means stipulated arbitrarily. They were trying to get at something that, if not morally foundational, was morally important.

Let us return now to Raz's two categories. Is my account 'traditional' or 'political'? Recall that a 'political' account, first, focuses on the rights acknowledged by 'contemporary human rights practice' and, second, identifies 'the moral standards which qualify anything to be so acknowledged'. That definition fits my account perfectly—vastly better, indeed, than does Raz's description of 'traditional' accounts. One feature that Raz uses to characterize traditional accounts is that they derive human rights from a basic property of human beings (such as normative agency). But, as we have seen, my account contains no such derivation. It contains, rather, a suggested interpretation of human rights as protections of normative agency, an interpretation that has to be tested extensively and as a whole, with no inferential priority going to the idea of normative agency in the course of the test. Another feature, according to Raz, is that traditionalists regard human rights as the most important of moral rights. I do say something about the importance of human rights, namely the contradictory of what Raz attributes to traditionalists: 'it is not', I wrote, 'that what human rights protect is . . . the most important aspect of our life'.[20] I speak of the conditions of personhood—namely, autonomy and liberty—as having a 'special' value to us, which Raz takes to mean 'most important', while I meant 'of a particular sort'. My idea is that we single out the particular value of our personhood—a great but by no means always the greatest value to us—because it is peculiarly vulnerable to threat from those in authority: governments usually, but also institutions such as churches, hospitals, and schools, and—closer to home—parents.

Raz's most interesting objection, to my mind, is that traditionalists (at any rate, I) need a threshold at which the values at stake can support a human right, and they (at least, I) lack the theoretical resources to supply one. The threshold, Raz rightly observes, must be higher than, say, the meagre material conditions needed simply for intentional action. For personhood, I should say, we also need basic education, some leisure, certain freedom to exchange ideas, freedom from certain interferences, and so on. Raz's point is that traditionalists, once they become more generous, have no way to stop becoming still more so. He says that the higher level that traditionalists (at least, I) have in mind is the level at which an agent has 'a good chance . . . of achieving one's goals'. The more education, the more resources, the more freedoms that one has, the better one's chances, it would seem, of achieving one's goals.

---

[20] Griffin, J., 'Discrepancies between the Best Philosophical Account of Human Rights and the International Law of Human Rights', *Proceedings of the Aristotelian Society*, 101 (2001), 4.

But this misses my point. Human rights, I propose, are rights to what allows one to act merely as a normative agent, not as a normative agent with a good chance of getting what one aims at. 'Normative agent' is, I say, a threshold term: once above the threshold, remaining differences in practical rationality or in executive ability or in material resources—all of which there undoubtedly are—do not matter to one's possession of that status. None of these continuing differences in degree above the threshold prevent there being a valuable status that itself does not come in degrees.

What is more, being a normative agent involves not just having certain capacities (autonomous judgment, executive action) but also exercising them. One can violate a good many of a person's human rights without in the least taking away these *capacities*. In general, what a person needs to bear human rights is these capacities, but what the rights protect is their exercise as well. Take the human right to basic education. Cannot an illiterate peasant with no education still be an agent in the sense I mean? Surely. What the peasant would need is a sense of some major possibilities in life, enough leisure to think about and to assess them, and liberty and leisure to pursue the preferred life. One does not have to be literate to be able to do that, though general literacy might well greatly increase the number of persons who could manage it. And more and more education—a bachelor's degree, or doctorate—has very little correlation with a good nose for what matters in life. The same is true of higher and higher IQ. A more sensitive nose for what matters in life and a shrewder sense of how to go about realizing it, on the other hand, would indeed make one a more successful agent. But the great value that we attach to normative agency does not require being so fortunate.

So we can identify states below normative agency (a life entirely consumed by the struggle to keep body and soul together) and states above it (especially well endowed with practical wisdom and material resources). In drawing the dividing line, we should consider the general run of people. And we should focus on the conditions necessary to ensure that this general run of people will be at or above the threshold. Therefore, we should want there to be at least general literacy. In some parts of the world, literacy is the most effective way of reducing infant mortality. And not all people—not many people, I believe—naturally have a good nose for what matters in life. Not all are imaginative enough to sense, unprompted, the broad range of options in life. The higher levels of education—bachelor's degree, doctorate—might (but only might) add yet more practical wisdom or executive skills, but at a lower level one already has a sense of what is or is not worth pursuing and the ability to build a worthwhile life.

Is the dividing line between states below and states above the threshold sharp? Of course not. Will a society have to do considerable work to make it sharper?

Yes. Will contingent matters such as the wealth of a society influence the placing of the line? Inevitably, yes. Will the placing of the line be to some extent arbitrary? Inevitably. Have societies dealt with comparable thresholds before? Often. Think of *mens rea*, the age of consent, the point at which international intervention is justified.

Getting clearer about the threshold is the main way of establishing limits to the demands of human rights. But there are others: for example, clarifying the content of the right to liberty. It is commonly—and to my mind correctly—thought that liberty is not a right to the realization of one's ends but merely to their pursuit. But the notion of 'pursuit' needs no small amount of adumbration. One can be denied one's right of pursuit in various ways, compulsion and constraint being the best known. A less known way is deliberate impoverishment of options. When the Taliban took power in Afghanistan they left Afghan women still able autonomously to choose among available options and freely to pursue the option chosen. The Taliban simply left available only the options that accorded with their own narrow conception of an Islamic woman's life. The Taliban were, of course, gross violators of liberty; what they did was indirect coercion.

So liberty requires a properly rich array of options. But how rich? And how are we to decide? There is a formal constraint on the liberty relevant to the right to liberty: one has a right only to liberty compatible with equal liberty for all. One may not claim from society by right an expensive option in life that would shrink the options of others to the point that would reduce their liberty. There are also material constraints on liberty. One may not claim from society the right to pursue a university post in philosophy when the society is not rich enough to have universities. Even if a society were rich enough to establish new universities when current jobs for philosophers had run out, an aspiring university philosopher would have no good claim that it do so, for various reasons. It would be an extraordinarily inefficient use of the society's resources. And there is no human right to it. If one cannot become a university philosopher, there are other careers in the fairly well-off society we are now imagining in which one can have a thoroughly valuable life. That is, there are alternative worthwhile lives that society may reasonably leave one to get on with.

It is not that a well-off society with an already rich array of options never has an obligation to create yet more. If same-sex couples want to form some sort of civilly recognized union and to raise children within it and, because of our ethical traditions, such ways of life are forbidden, then we should change our laws and our attitudes. This is a matter of liberty. One thing at issue here is whether there are alternatives for same-sex couples that would also constitute thoroughly valuable lives. May we, as with the aspiring philosopher when university jobs run out, reasonably ask same-sex couples to look elsewhere? But the two cases are crucially different. Having children and raising them well is a widespread human aim, a characteristic (though not universal) human conception of a worthwhile life. Indeed, doing so is for the large majority of people their best, and often their only, chance of accomplishing something of great value with their lives.

I propose that we see liberty as a right to the all-purpose means to the pursuit of any plausible conception of a worthwhile life: to education and health, to material provision, to help to overcome the lack of key capacities, to no arbitrary limitations to the array of options that our social conditions provide us with, and so on. The idea of liberty as pursuit thereby helps to fix the level of all-purpose means.

Many of the reasons for the limits it fixes are contingent: what options can a particular society, given the stage of its cultural and material development, provide? Other of the reasons are a mixture of contingent and ethical: given the options that a particular society provides, are there among them alternatives to a particular conception of a worthwhile life that would also allow a worthwhile life? And so on.

Raz thinks that, unlike the 'traditional' conception of human rights, the 'political' conception is able to provide 'good reasons for setting various limits' to what the rights guarantee, but that they are mostly contingent, relative to particular times and places, and so inexplicable on the 'traditional' conception, according to which human rights are universal. But on the best understanding of their universality, only human rights formulated at a high level of abstraction (for example, freedom of expression) are universal; when these rights are formulated relevantly to particular circumstances (for example, freedom of the press), they are clearly not universal (some societies do not have presses, and some, perhaps still today, lack even the concept of a 'press'). To determine the limits of human rights we need both ethical and empirical considerations, for reasons that I touched on in the first two sections and to which I shall now return.

V. The Autonomy of the International Law of Human Rights

Must the international law of human rights at points rest on ethical foundations? In one sense, of course not. It is possible resolutely to exclude all ethical thought in constructing norms of international law—say, by considering instead only the promotion of the national interest.[21] But much the more interesting question is: can the international law of human rights exclude all ethical thought without sacrificing

---

[21] See Goldsmith, J. and Posner, E., *The Limits of International Law* (Oxford: Oxford University Press, 2005).

important forms of rationality—forms needed, for instance, plausibly to spell out the content of the rights and to resolve conflicts between two rights or between a right and other values such as the general good?

The functional accounts of human rights prominent during the second half of the twentieth century, as we saw, lack sufficient explanatory power. As far as I can see, the only satisfactory way of putting this right is by adding evaluative content. Indeed, this is, as far as I can see, the most satisfactory way of doing so. What is more, the authors of these functional accounts do not themselves think that their accounts are fully stated without some contribution from ethics. In Dworkin's version, the discourse of rights rests ultimately on a principle of equality. In Rawls's version, it is seen as embedded in liberal democratic values. In Raz's version, moral standards enter to explain why certain rights may be regarded as having the authority of human rights. (And something similar can be said about the accounts of Feinberg and Nozick.)

Still, might not legal positivists come up with a rule of recognition for the international law of human rights? Yes, they might. But, then, by applying the rule of recognition, might they not conclusively establish that such-and-such is a legal human right? Yes. Then why did I imply earlier that the assertion of a legal human right can, even though satisfying the rule of recognition, be mistaken? Suppose, for instance, that the widely doubted right to periodic holidays with pay meets the rule of recognition. Then there is such a legal human right, and the mistake I spoke of earlier must be on a different level. The level I have in mind is assessment of the discourse of human rights itself. The discourse, I say, suffers from unacceptably great indeterminateness of sense. We must reduce the indeterminateness. How, as a practical matter, we might do so is a large question, which I shall broach (though only broach) shortly. If an evaluative account of human rights—my personhood account or some other—becomes widely enough accepted, the evaluative criteria it introduces will join the institutional-procedural criteria of the rule of recognition eventually to form a more complex standard for the existence of a legal human right. This development—and it would be a development; we are not there yet—would mark a return to the original concept of a right that emerged in the late Middle Ages, a concept without any sharp separation of law and morals, and a concept that has endured up to recent times—indeed, many of our contemporaries still maintain that legal human rights incorporate some of the criteria and authority of moral human rights, though without explicit agreement on what the criteria are. If an evaluative account becomes widely enough accepted, it will work alongside the institutions and procedures of the law of human rights. The influence of law and morals will run both ways: the evaluative account will help determine the content of some human rights in both morality and law, but so will legislation and judicial decision. And not all moral human rights should, for good reasons, become legal human rights and *vice versa*.

VI. The Purpose of the International Law of Human Rights

What purposes do we expect the international law of human rights to serve? The preambles of various United Nations instruments suggest that the ultimate purpose of codifying human rights is to promote peace between nations. This has led some writers to ask: Why not also peace *within* nations? Why not also the promotion, more generally, of *justice*?[22]

I find it odd to suggest that the purpose of human rights is to promote peace. Do not human rights have their own intrinsically valuable purpose: the protection of human dignity? What more point do human rights need than that? They might also promote peace, but, if so, that would be a welcome side-effect. But do they in fact promote peace? The human rights system, originally promoted by the United Nations as productive of peace, is now increasingly recommended as justifying wars of intervention and regulating wars in general. It is true that sometimes forceful intervention aims at separating already warring parties and that such intervention might therefore be seen as promoting peace, all things considered. This may be true of the interventions in Yugoslavia and Rwanda. But it is not true of those in Afghanistan and Iraq. The intervention in Afghanistan had something of the nature of a police action—capturing or neutralizing criminal elements. The intervention in Iraq was justified, after the failure of the first quasi-fictitious justification, as the removal of a regime that seriously violated human rights. One can see, therefore, why the United Nations, at its inception, stressed a strict form of national sovereignty; strict sovereignty would promote peace between nations precisely by prohibiting such intervention. Once human rights became reasons for abandoning strict sovereignty, which they are now considered to be (to my mind rightly), they also become less plausible as promoters of peace.

Wars of intervention could well become a familiar feature of our future. If there continue to be national governments that seriously violate human rights, and if international power-relations do not make intervention dangerous for the intervener, then an effect of the human rights system might turn out to be not perpetual peace but, at least for the time being, frequent war. International forces of intervention may turn out to be rather like policemen: needed until well into a remote future in which there is a substantial improvement in human behaviour. If, as I think, there is a human right to democratic participation in government, and if democracies tend not to wage aggressive warfare on one another, then human

---

[22] Griffin, J., 'Discrepancies between the Best Philosophical Account of Human Rights and the International Law of Human Rights' (above, n. 20), 4.

rights may, in this quite limited way, promote peace. But this would not lessen the problem of violator states.

Might we, at least, say that the purpose of a human rights system is to promote *justice*? I think not. That would be too broad a claim. I appeal again to the non-congruence of the domains of human rights and of justice. There are departments of justice that fall outside the concerns of human rights: for instance, parts of distributive justice, especially the parts that lie above the minimum acceptable level of welfare; parts of retributive justice, and many forms of fairness. What, then, are the functions of international law in general? I would suggest: (1) to make international relations go better than they otherwise would, and (2) to promote human rights. The first function is truly *inter*national, the second largely *intra*national. But both functions have reasonable claims to international scope: the first collectively, the second distributively.

There has been a noteworthy tendency lately to restrict the purpose of human rights to the regulation of a government's behaviour to its citizens. For reasons I gave earlier, this seems to me too limited. What, instead, seems correct is that their purpose is to regulate the behaviour of those in positions of power to those subject to their power—governments, of course, but also, for example, hospitals and parents. One can see why, of all the threats that life brings, those emanating from the powerful in a society should have been singled out for such special measures.

VII. WHICH MORAL HUMAN RIGHTS SHOULD BE MADE LEGAL RIGHTS?

My proposal that we see human rights as protections of personhood is primarily a proposal in ethics, but secondarily with implications for law. However, law has business of its own. There are several possible ways to see human rights. Is not my talk of future days when we converge on just one of them foolishly utopian? Is not moral disagreement an inevitable fact of life in a liberal society? Do we not have to be realistic and face up to it? The law offers society a way of facing up to it, a way of moving beyond disagreement to an agreed solution. When a society develops reasonably fair legal institutions and procedures, do not its legal decisions generally demand respect? If, as I think, we must draw on ethics in deciding the law of human rights, we must also value the law's important function of providing a proper response to value pluralism.

So now when we ask, which moral human rights should be made legal human rights, we will face further questions. On whose list of human rights? And, more seriously, on whose ideas of what they are rights to? And how are we to cope with the considerable uncertainties mentioned earlier about how to resolve conflicts involving rights? These are questions about which we have to hope, utopian or not, that rational persuasion will carry us to some measure of agreement, and that we shall manage to reach a decision that is more than merely procedurally fair, as important as procedural fairness is.

But we should not need a very widely agreed list of moral human rights, or a very full understanding of their contents, for there to be some point in asking which moral human rights should be made legal. I can offer only a few tentative observations.

First, in some cases it would be premature to move from a moral to a legal human right. We have, for example, a long established right to life. We are far from sure, however, what it is a right to. Clearly it includes a right not to have one's life taken without due process. Does it also include a right to rescue? Many of us think so — at least if the benefit of the rescue is great and the cost small. But that thought is only the smallest of first steps. The benefit can be less than life itself, and the cost more than trivial, for the rescue to be obligatory. What exactly are the obligations correlative to this right? There is little understanding of, let alone agreement on, how to go about answering that question. Many philosophers seem to think that at a deep level the only ultimately acceptable decision will be impartial between persons. Many others think that there are major areas of permitted partiality. But nearly all of us are uncertain about the correlative obligations; more thought about all of this is needed. This is not a case of different considered beliefs, with which the law is accustomed to dealing, but a case of lack of beliefs, of plain ignorance. A law is something enacted, interpreted, applied to life; it can of course be vague, but it must have a certain degree of determinateness. The makers and interpreters of a law must be prepared to take a stand. On some matters, though, none are yet prepared to take a stand. Philosophers can contribute to the work needed to be done. So can the law: by step-by-step judicial decision, by legislatures' being prepared to act when they see how further to specify the correlative obligations. But until they are ready, the law is wise to stay silent.

Second, in the case of all human rights there will be competing claims on public funds. The more that a society makes into a matter of law, the more financially burdensome its legal system becomes. Even if violation of a law does not carry penalties, so does not require costly organs of enforcement and adjudication, law requires at least publication and some degree of monitoring, and they cost money that might be better spent on other worthy social goals.

Third, in some cases the legalization of a moral human right can result in intrusive or heavy-handed or destructive behaviour by the law. So the law wisely holds back. Parents should respect, at least in some aspects of life, the autonomy and liberty of their mature children. Even if the law were confined to publicizing the rights of mature children and monitoring their observance, the effects on family relations might be damaging. Even the process of monitoring itself, without publication of the results, could be destructively intrusive. And if the results were publicized, the penalty of shaming could do more harm than good.

Fourthly, in some cases the law quite rightly takes a back seat. We have a moral and legal right to fair procedures in certain decisions that importantly affect us. But sometimes the law allows non-legal institutions to enforce them: schools and universities to expel students; employers to sack workers. It is beneficial to have such decision-making distributed within civil society, with the law serving only as an appeal of last resort. Here the moral human right is already, and necessarily, a legal human right, but the law, as it often does, chooses to restrict its own activity in its service.

CHAPTER 17

....

HUMAN RIGHTS

....

JOHN SKORUPSKI*

I. INTRODUCTION

....

What rights exist is not for us to decide. In contrast, which rights to call human rights does seem to be. How then should we choose to use this notion?

Institutions emerge from many choices. This is happening with the institution or practice of 'human rights': its language, charters, precedents are in development. But the direction of development clearly remains controversial. Whether and why we need a notion of human rights at all, either philosophically or politically and practically, can still be cogently asked. It is not a matter of simply describing an established practice whose actuality is no longer in question.

My conclusion will be that human rights are not distinguished from rights by any *philosophical* criterion. Whereas the question of what rights exist is not a political question, the usefulness of introducing a special category of human rights is; it is a question about what moral aims we ('the international community') should collectively endorse, and how to get there. As one expects with political questions, there are differing views about what we should aim at, in this case about the goal of human rights practice—and obviously ways and means depend on goals. I share the view that declarations of human rights should be levers that help to eliminate serious violations of moral rights in all states, and I shall spell out some of its implications.

* My discussion has been much improved by comments from the audience at the Philosophy of International Law Workshop, and by the editors of this volume. I am especially grateful to Thomas Christiano for his careful and detailed commentary.

II. Rights and Human Rights

Let me put these remarks as guidelines that will structure the discussion.

(1) Human rights should be seen as a sub-class of rights. We should avoid inventing a category of 'human-rights' whose relation to rights proper is unclear. Whereas a toy gun is not a gun, a human right *is* a right. Therefore the philosophy of human rights should anchor them within a general conception of right—that is, of rights and duties of justice proper, as against moral obligations, however weighty, of other kinds.

(2) Human rights are moral rights. That is, they are rights that exist irrespective of whether they are underwritten, or apparently overridden, by positive law, and indeed whether or not we decide to declare them 'human', or to codify them in positive law. It follows that the formulations which codes or charters seek to provide are always in principle open to philosophical critique.

(3) Not all moral rights are human rights. Else what would 'human' add to 'right'? I have said that the point of distinguishing certain rights as human rights is a political point. I should stress that I am using the word 'political' in a favourable, not a dismissive, sense. A political question is a question, as I said, about what we can and should agree (perhaps implicitly) to aim at and how to get there, taking into account the practical realities of world politics. The answer can only emerge from discussions and where necessary compromises among reasonable people with very different views.

These guidelines structure the rest of this paper. In sections III and IV, I set out a definition and outline a normative account of moral rights. The normative account is certainly not in its broad outline novel. It would be disconcerting if it was, since the theory of Right—of rights and corresponding duties of justice—has a long and illustrious history. The main thing I add (section V) is an outline of how moral rights can ramify through collective decisions: an important issue that becomes relevant when we consider in what way human rights can be said to be universal.

I do not in this paper discuss the very big question of whether the doctrine of rights should be grounded in some deeper level of ethics, such as a theory of interests, the good, or autonomy—or whether on the contrary, it needs no such grounding but constitutes in itself a moral domain that is by and large self-standing (though assuredly not completely independent). This is a basic question of moral philosophy. If it turned out that the correct answer had important revisionary implications for our ordinary moral conception of the content of rights, so that that ordinary conception turned out to be importantly flawed in salient ways, then we could not set the issue aside. We would have to consider what basic revisions in our views of moral rights were needed before we could discuss what is particularly distinctive about *human* rights. Some think (for a variety of reasons) that that is the situation, but I am not one of them.

It seems to me that the ordinary moral conception of rights is by and large both self-standing and reasonably clear in its content and limits. Although not insulated from other parts of ethics, it is a relatively autonomous domain. Furthermore, it exerts great moral authority, whether or not people are explicitly aware of it. The implication, if we accept point (2) above, is that a doctrine of human rights can and must build on the ordinary moral conception. The question thus becomes, what rights from within the range of moral rights should be characterized as *human* rights—with what force and why?

In section VI I turn to the political question of 'with what force and why?' As noted, I agree with those who hold that the goal of human rights practice should be to spread protection globally against seriously right-violating abuses of power. For that reason I also agree that the recognition of a right as a human right should have important significance in determining limits of state sovereignty (section VII).

III. Defining Rights

We owe an influential definition of rights to Mill. In his well-known words:

When we call anything a person's right, we mean that he has a valid claim on society to protect him in the possession of it, either by the force of law, or by that of education and opinion. If he has what we consider a sufficient claim, on whatever account, to have something guaranteed to him by society, we say that he has a right to it . . . To have a right, then, is, I conceive, to have something which society ought to defend me in the possession of.[1]

According to this definition, a person has a moral right to something if and only if there is a moral obligation on society to defend them in their possession of that thing, or to guarantee it to them. Mill gives this definition as the middle link in a chain: he defines justice in terms of rights, rights in terms of moral obligations, and moral obligation in terms of the appropriateness of certain sanctions. Duties of justice are distinguished from moral obligations in general by the existence of corresponding rights:

Justice implies something which it is not only right to do, and wrong not to do, but which some individual person can claim from us as his moral right . . . Whenever there is a right, the case is one of justice . . . [2]

---

[1] Mill, J. S., *The Collected Works of John Stuart Mill*, X. *Essays on Ethics, Religion and Society*, ed. Robson, J. M. (Toronto: University of Toronto Press, 1969), 250.
[2] Ibid. 247.

I believe it is correct to define justice in terms of rights (allowing that collectives, corporations, nations, etc. can have rights as well as individual persons). However Mill's definition of 'right' is unconvincing. H. L. A. Hart objected that an obligation on society to protect a person in the possession of something, or guarantee it to them, cannot define 'right' since the relevant obligation on society exists *in virtue* of the existence of the right. Mill's definition, he says, 'puts the cart before the horse'.[3] The objection is sound: we can explain why society has an obligation by appealing to the existence of a pre-existing right, but there may also be other explanations. It is not logically contradictory, as Mill's definition would imply, to say that society should guarantee X to Y even if X has no right to Y. The fact that X has a *right* to it is only one possible reason for guaranteeing it to him. Another possible reason is that he will blow up the world if we don't. There may be good reasons, even a moral obligation, to guarantee something to people with a threat advantage, but that does not show they have a right, a *valid claim*, to it.

I suggest another approach. The point we should focus on is that rights give rise to morally permissible *demands*.[4] If you have not given me permission to use your computer I have a moral obligation not to use it without asking you. (Absent special circumstances: I shall take this constant qualification for granted, so as to not to keep sprinkling it in the text.) More strongly, it is morally permissible for you to *demand* that I do not use it without asking you. When I have promised to meet you at a given time, you are permitted to demand that I do. Suppose, in contrast, that you would like me to meet you even though I have not agreed to do so (and I am not your employee, etc.). You are permitted to request but not permitted to demand that I do. Or suppose that your computer has broken down and I happen to know how to mend it. In some circumstances, where your need is great and the distraction from my own projects small, I may even have a moral obligation (of assistance) to come over and mend it. But most of us would say that you are not permitted to *demand*, as against request, that I do.

A demand is something more than a mere request. Demand is conceptually linked to the permissibility of compulsion: a permissible demand is a request that it is morally permissible to enforce. I do not mean that it is actually possible to enforce it: we may intelligibly demand the return of hostages even if we have no power to enforce this. And of course enforcement doesn't necessarily take the form of physical coercion. Even to say that you demand something is already to exercise a certain degree of exaction; demand is a form of command. To demand something is to imply that enforcement would, if necessary, be permissible; that the very fact that it's been requested gives the other person no moral option but to do it.

---

[3] Hart, H. L. A., 'Natural Rights: Bentham and John Stuart Mill', in his *Essays on Bentham* (Oxford: Oxford University Press, 1982), 103.

[4] 'It is morally permissible to X' means that it is not morally obligatory not to X.

Permissible enforcement must be proportionate to the seriousness of a right-infringement. Just because demanding is already a form of enforcement, when a right is sufficiently trivial it may be disproportionate even to make demands. Suppose, to take an example, that we have previously agreed to have lunch together (and you have not pressured me unacceptably into that agreement). Then you have a right to expect me to be there, a right to be told in advance if possible that I can't come, and a right to remonstrate if I fail to turn up without bothering to tell you and without any excusing reasons—but it might be foolish or petty-minded to do so.

Moreover, where harm or damage is caused to the right-holder by an infringement it is permissible for the right-holder to demand or enforce compensation. The sense of compensation that I have in mind is the broad sense of 'making up for loss' not the narrow, responsibility-accepting, 'making amends for loss because you have caused it'. I can be said to compensate you in the broad sense if I make up in some way for a setback, injury, or interference you have suffered. The act of compensation in this broad sense implies no fault on my part. I might compensate you out of the goodness of my heart for the flood damage to your house even if the flooding is not my fault and I have no obligation to do so. I might do so while disclaiming all responsibility. Furthermore, I may have a moral obligation to compensate even where there is no fault, and in particular no rights-infringement, on my part. We can for example have a communal obligation to compensate very hard-pressed people for the flood damage to their house, although we had no part in causing it. Where there has been a damaging infringement of a right, however, there is not just a moral obligation to compensate on the part of the infringer (if that is called for by the right-holder); it is, further, morally permissible for the right-holder to *demand* compensation from the infringer for the damage caused. Here too, of course, the damage may be so small as to make any demand for damages disproportionate.

A right-holder may empower an agent (another person, an institution) to issue, on his behalf, the demands he is permitted to make. Where the right-holder is not capable of doing so (an orphan infant, say), 'society' in Mill's word can empower an agent to act on his, her, or its behalf. Moreover, for traditional reasons arising from the overall desirability of an impersonal rule of law, society or the state may under certain circumstances impose rules of enforcement; indeed it may take over and exercise the right-holder's permission to enforce, in so far as enforcement goes beyond mere demand. Yet to override is not to cancel. We should not simply say, without qualification, that the right-holder has permission to demand but no permission to enforce. The permission remains latent, as can be seen from the fact that if society is unable to act as the right-holder's agent (for example in situations requiring immediate self-defence), moral permission to enforce reverts to the individual or an agent other than the state. The state can legitimately forbid me from exercising that permission only so long as it exercises it effectively on my behalf.

With these points taken into account we define rights as follows:

> X has a right to Y against Z if and only if it is morally permissible for X or X's agent to demand that Z does not take Y from X, or does not prevent X from doing Y, or delivers Y to X (as appropriate), and to demand compensation for X from Z in the event of damage resulting from Z's non-compliance.[5]

We can also define a *duty of right* (a right-based duty):

> Z has a duty of right to X in regard to Y if and only if X has a right to Y against Z.

Thus Z's duty of right is a duty not to take Y from X, or not to prevent X from doing Y, or to deliver Y to X, as appropriate.

This covers the 'explanatory' aspect of rights noted by Hart. Z's obligation to provide, or not to encroach, is *explained* in terms of X's right: that is, in terms of the existence of a right-generating relation between X, Y, and Z which does not just generate that obligation but also, and more narrowly, generates a permission to make appropriate demands of compliance and compensation from Z.

Suppose Z is a blackmailer who credibly threatens some enormous damage to innocent parties unless we give him a lifelong pension. We may have an obligation to provide it, even though he does not have a right to it. Even if we promise it to him he does not have a right to it, since the promise is given under duress. It is *not* morally permissible for the blackmailer to demand delivery of what we promised, or compensation in the event of non-delivery. Thus it is not the blackmailer's right to a pension that explains our obligation to provide it; this particular obligation corresponds to no duty of right to him.

Permissible demand is what is special about rights. We may have a very strong moral obligation, an obligation of solidarity, or an obligation of assistance, to compensate to some degree people who have fallen into dire need, for example through flooding. But if the flooding is caused by us, there is a duty to compensate arising from a *right* on the part of those flooded against us. They can legitimately *demand* compensation.

IV. Duties of Right and Justice

If this is the meaning of rights, what is their content? Consider this outline of duties of right:

---

[5] I have been helped in formulating this definition by critical comments from Antony Duff.

(i) not to seize others, their possessions, resources, or services, illegitimately, or acquire them through fraud or threat.

(ii) not to cause damage, harm, or injury to others, or to their possessions, resources, or reputation, without legitimate grounds.

(iii) not to withdraw unilaterally from obligations one has freely (without force, fraud, or threat) undertaken.

(iv) to play a fair role in implementing legitimately arrived at collective decisions, including legitimately arrived at decisions as to fair distribution of jointly owned resources.

(v) to play a fair part in supporting legitimate institutions which enforce observance of (i) to (iv) (and (v) itself!) and rectify violations thereof.

If an injustice is a violation of a duty of right then this model becomes a complete theory of justice in *one* sense. Any action that does not violate (i)–(v) violates no duty of right and cannot permissibly be prevented by force or threat. In a more important sense, of course, the model is quite obviously incomplete: it gives no account of what is legitimate or illegitimate where reference to that notion is made, it gives no account of what is fair where reference to fairness occurs, and it says nothing about what constitutes a proportionate enforcement or rectification. Thus for example it says nothing about what a just punishment or a fair burden is. It would be quite right to demand those further accounts in a complete theory of justice, but it is not necessary here. For our purposes, the significance of the model lies in the claim that each of these clauses corresponds to rights, and that there are no rights that do not correspond to these clauses. ((iv) and (v) correspond to rights on the part of the relevant collective against all its members.)

In most ways this is and is meant to be a familiar, though not uncontroversial, account of justice, which makes justice a matter of rights and takes rights to centre on liberty and ownership. 'Ownership' however should be understood in a way that goes beyond the concept of private property vested in an individual; in a broader way, that is, than in some modern understandings of this account. Ownership may be neither individual nor private. A community, clan, tribe, nation, etc. may own or have legitimate access to a territory or a resource—the territory or resource is *its* territory or resource—in such a way that restriction of access or damage to the resource constitutes a violation of that collective's rights.

Suppose there is flooding in village A, caused by our negligence, and also flooding in village B, which produces greater need in B than A, but is not caused by us in any way. Since negligent damage is illegitimate, it is permissible for the victims in village A to enforce compensation on us, and for others to help them enforce it if they lack the power to do so themselves. Compensation proportionate to our share in damaging them is their just due. The villagers in B have no comparable right, assuming we have made them no promises. Moreover it seems to me, as a moral matter, that we ought duly to compensate the villagers in A as a priority over assisting those in B. To bring this point home, suppose the villagers in A are unfortunately powerless to enforce compensation from us. If we know that, is it morally acceptable for us to distribute aid purely in proportion to *need* as between A and B, even though our resources will not then enable us to compensate village A in proportion to our fault and the damage caused by us in A? I believe that village A would have a just grievance if we did that. Village B, in contrast, would have no reasonable grievance if we duly compensated A before working out how much we could help B.

To take another example, if some group or tribe A loses their food sources as a result of a pollution of their territory that is caused by us, we have a duty of justice to them to compensate them. If another group or tribe B loses theirs through some natural disaster in no way caused by us, or through over-hunting (that does not result from a need for food that is itself caused by us), we do not have a duty of right to compensate them, though we may well have a moral obligation to do so. In this example again it seems to me that the duty to compensate A must take precedence over obligations we have to help B.

Also plausible, nonetheless, is that there are cases of need in which a sufferer can permissibly *demand* assistance. In those cases, on my definition, the sufferer has a need-based *right* of assistance. In either of the examples above, if B's need is dire and A's is not, then B may have a need-based right of assistance against both us *and* A. A similarly plausible condition on territorial claims states that they must not leave others with insufficient resources through no fault of their own. Here too those others can permissibly demand a share. In terms of the model of rights I outlined, these are circumstances in which seizure of a resource or territory by, or on behalf of those in need (or by their rescuers), becomes legitimate under (i). How to spell out the circumstances—when they arise, to what extent they involve questions of desert or no-fault on the part of those who claim the right of need, from whom they can be demanded and how—is a major question in the theory of rights. It is not one to be pursued here; but given the scale of unmet need in our world, it is plainly possible that need-based rights have significant practical importance in global justice, even if they are narrowly circumscribed—as rights of compensation certainly do, for example for damage done to others' environment.

V. JUSTICE AND COLLECTIVE DECISION

There is one aspect of my model that is less familiar and requires notice for our discussion of human rights. It arises from clause (iv). The principle underlying (iv) is that *a legitimate collective decision made within a group to pursue some common aim binds its members, by a duty of right to each other, to play a fair part in that pursuit.*

The principle so stated contains the two obvious normative notions already noted, fairness and legitimacy, as well as a less obvious one, namely, membership of a group. How one understands them makes a big difference to one's substantive conception of justice. Specifically, what account is given of a legitimate collective decision and membership makes a very big difference. The model provided by (i)–(v) is not in itself a libertarian view of rights. It becomes libertarian only if one further understands 'legitimate' to mean unanimous, and holds that any group membership can exist only by agreement. (It would then be possible to drop (iv), as all the work could now be done by (iii).)

I am *not* assuming that membership of a group, with its consequent obligations, must always be fundamentally voluntary, nor that the legitimacy of a collective decision always requires unanimity. Modern democratic states are obvious counter-examples to the latter thesis, and at least apparent—in my view real—counter-examples to the former. Families are another. For example the children in a family may collectively decide to support ailing parents in a particular way; if that decision is itself made legitimately, and the distribution of burdens is fair, the children are bound to each other by duties of justice. In an appropriate moral setting the decision may be legitimate even if a particular child was not consulted, or does not agree; either way it may be binding on that child.

In this example we are dealing with what may be thought a *pre-existing* collective obligation (to look after the parents). But a collective decision to pursue a common aim which did not have the character of a pre-existing obligation—for example to fund a national park or a national monument of remembrance—can be binding on those who disagreed with it, in that they can legitimately be required to make a fair contribution in taxes despite their disagreement. Such decisions must observe pre-existing duties of justice; but requiring a contribution from those who disagreed is not itself, already, a violation of justice. Their tax contribution need not be an illegitimate seizure of what they own—or so most of us think. If we are right, then non-unanimous collective decisions about communal aims that do not in themselves concern justice, and which may not even be obligatory, can, in accordance with the basic principle I have stated, generate duties of right. This generation of duties of right happens all the time, and as a result, particular duties of right vary across communities even as the basic principles of justice remain the same. Across communities that operate legitimate methods of securing agreement, what justice concretely requires can vary.

In saying this I do not mean to distinguish between cosmopolitan and political justice. My argument is for a political conception of what makes a right a *human* right, not for a political conception of rights and justice. The principles of justice, expressed in (i)–(v), are universal. There is, it is true, a sense in which justice is not purely cosmopolitan: principle (iv) recognizes the significance, for justice itself, of units other than the individual and the cosmopolis. But that is not to say that the principles of justice are in any respect political.[6]

Many rights, in particular welfare or economic rights, are generated by this process of collective decision. I assume that members of various groups from family to nation have mutual obligations of assistance that go well beyond universal rights of need. It is important to recognize that many of these mutual obligations are based on community or solidarity rather than justice. For examples the citizens of a nation, or members of some other collectivity, may consider that they have mutual obligations to provide free health care or education (or even merely that it would be *good* for their community or polity to do so). By a legitimate collective decision they may decide to provide these things in some manner. Now they all have an individual right against themselves collectively to receive free health care and education, and a duty of right to each other to take a fair part in providing it. Some may argue that all human beings have an obligation to come together in underwriting such rights for all. But that is not the way most people see it. The claims and aims of solidarity are communitarian: they centre on whatever community one feels oneself to belong to, and derive much of their motivating force from the psychological importance and felt claim of communal solidarity.

VI. THE POLITICAL CONCEPTION (1) MORAL LEVERAGE

If human rights are a sub-class of moral rights, the proper sequence a theory of human rights should follow is from a theory of right to the more political question of what rights should be recognized or established as *human* rights. We now have before us, in outline at least, a definition and normative theory of rights, so it is this political question that remains. Philosophers, I should say, have no special expertise in answering it; they speak as citizens not as specialists. The remaining two sections of this paper are offered in that spirit.

What then should we be trying to do with our talk of human rights? I agreed with those who hold that the point is to get moral leverage in eliminating grave rights-violations—specifically, through the force of international law. It is not to change human behaviour for the better in broader and more comprehensive ways. By no means do I think the latter objective pointless; it greatly matters that it should

---

[6] I disagree here with Thomas Nagel's position in his 'The Problem of Global Justice', *Philosophy and Public Affairs* (2005), 33, though I sympathize with the overall thrust of his discussion. Principles (i)–(v) do, it is true, allow for some relativity; political rights of participation, for example, are a function of what constitutes a legitimate collective decision, and the answer to that may be different in different times and conditions. But that does not make the question of what political rights exist itself political.

be continuously pursued in many different ways by many different people. In this process, moreover, morally progressive vanguards have very important roles to play. However human rights declarations are not the right place for moral vanguardism. They should not be asked to shoulder the weight of broad and comprehensive moral improvement. If they are, they risk losing their chance of prompting real delivery, as against lip service. A well-grounded accusation of human-rights violation should have recognized, weighty moral authority.

Not everyone sees it in this way. Many think the task of human rights discourse is to formulate broad values or interests that it is desirable for states to pursue.[7] This seems to me far *too* broad. Such value-grounded rights must be for citizens to collectively decide on and institute with respect to their own state. We might think it desirable to delegate to our state some of our communal obligations or aims, such as providing medical care or pensions to fellow citizens to the levels we think good. Such collective agreement, legitimately done, would, via clause (iv) in my model of duties of right, generate duties of right within our state, and would become part of the moral tradition and system of right in our polity. Equally, an agreement to provide or guarantee certain goods, just because they are goods, not because of pre-existing moral rights, may be arrived at in a wider setting, for example through an agreed social charter among a group of states. But if we judge that the objective of human rights practice is to eliminate grave rights-violations then the rights we designate as 'human' should be important existing moral rights, not merely desirable ethical objectives.

A further, important, point is that human rights have in practice come to be thought of as rights which it is permissible for all, including all states, to demand that all states should positively protect and promote. Call this cross-state demandability. What rights have this feature?

Suppose some rich philanthropists, or some states, get together, and by a legitimate process come to a collective decision to promise everyone in the world free eye treatment, or a basic income. They stipulate that anyone can take advantage of this promise just by signing a form stating that he or she is accepting the offer. Everyone in the world now has a right to free eye treatment or a basic income, just by signing the form. In that sense the right is universal. But it is not *essentially* so. Although everyone now has the right, they have it only against those philanthropists or states who have promised it. It does not exist irrespective of promises made, in this case, promises based on a collective decision which binds its members. Now I think a necessary condition of cross-state demandability is that a right that has this feature is *essentially universal*. Because this right to eye treatment or a basic income arises from a collective decision, that is, is not essentially universal, it is not

---

[7] For example, James Nickel, in his 'Poverty and Rights', *Philosophical Quarterly*, (2005), 55, says that human rights are 'concerned with *ensuring* the conditions, negative and positive, of a minimally good life' (386, my emphasis)—such as basic health care and education.

cross-state demandable either: other states, not involved in the decision, have no standing to demand that the philanthropists or states that engaged in the agreement should deliver on it. That demand can be made only be those who have signed the form, or their appointed agents, or philanthropists or citizens of states involved in the decision.

The rights not to be tortured or enslaved, which I take to be human rights if anything is, are essentially universal. Both are special cases of clause (i) in our model of justice. I have a right that you do not torture me because like everyone else I have a right not to be tortured by anyone. Similarly, a right not to be enslaved is not a right against some particular people who have promised not to enslave. Suppose someone says: 'In this polity there has been no collective decision to outlaw slavery. I can appreciate that there are practical and humanitarian reasons for abolishing it, but at the moment children have no right not to be sold by their parents as slaves.' That would be a false conclusion: children have a right not to be sold into slavery, *whatever* the polity may have decided.

A first condition on human rights, then, is that they are essentially universal moral rights. Since I am not saying that essential universality entails cross-state demandability, we can add that as a second condition. The rights not to be tortured or enslaved satisfy this second condition: anyone, including all states, can legitimately demand that all states observe them.

But given our political aim, we should narrow this down still further. Take the right not to have your property illegitimately seized. This is essentially universal: everyone has that right against everyone. One might perhaps argue that it is cross-state demandable. But, irrespective of whether that is so, if the political point of the notion of a human right is to exert leverage through law on specific serious rights violations, this right is too abstract and unspecific to be a candidate human right, since instances can range from the very important to the very trivial. Whereas philosophical theories of rights as in section IV seek abstract system, human rights documents should be specific and concrete lists, so formulated as to be easily intelligible and acceptable as rights to as many people throughout the world as possible. Their usefulness considerably depends on their widespread intuitiveness and acceptability.[8]

In a lecture on human rights Bernard Williams remarked: 'The charge that a practice violates human rights is ultimate, the most serious of political accusations'.[9] I hope this is widely believed to be true (although I'm not sure it is). If it is, that is a very valuable political asset which we should try our best to preserve. Williams continued:

It is a mark of philosophical good sense that the accusation should not be distributed too inconsiderately, and in particular that theory should not lead us to treat like manifest crimes

---

[8] The human rights documents we actually have strike me as open to serious criticism in this regard. However it would take another paper to pursue this.

[9] Williams, B., *In the Beginning Was the Deed* (Princeton: Princeton University Press, 2005), 27.

every practice that we reject on liberal principle, even if in its locality it can be decently supposed to be legitimate.[10]

I agree that this criterion, of what 'in its locality can be decently supposed to be legitimate', formulates one aspect of the circumstances in which it is sensible to declare a right a human right. Another aspect is that the right in question, while widely recognizable as a right, is in practice often violated, and a third is that violation of the right is a very serious wrong. It is plausible, for example, that today throughout the world slavery cannot be decently supposed to be legitimate, even if it could be decently supposed to be legitimate in the ancient world, say. Yet slavery exists and is in practice, in many places, tolerated; furthermore it is a grave violation of rights. Similar points apply to torture. This is what makes these examples such paradigm candidates for the status of human rights: the gravity of the rights-violation, the impossibility of sincere and reasonable denial that that is what it is, combined with significant toleration and even complicity in practice.

The point of international human rights declarations is to get states to implement and actively protect rights which they may professedly recognize as such, at least could not 'decently' reject, but fail to act on in practice. The right to have non-corrupt government, for example, fits that bill. As does the right not to be arbitrarily incarcerated without due process. By contrast, to declare all forms of theft or illegitimate seizure to be human rights violations would be pointlessly broad and unfocused, even though they all are violations of essentially universal rights, and widely recognized as such. By the same criterion, as Williams notes,[11] a strongly unrestricted right to free speech of the kind whose acceptance most liberals favour (including me) is problematic as a candidate *human* right. Liberal theories of free speech characteristically favour protection even where there is probability of offence and indeed harm to others—that is, more widely than many non-liberal societies favour—by appeal to considerations of social good that are to many of us persuasive, but are notoriously not considerations that no one could *decently*, 'in their locality', reject.

Overall then I propose that the conditions to be met for classification of a right as a human right are: that it is

(a) an essentially universal right ('universality')
(b) whose active enforcement and promotion it is permissible for anyone, including all states, to demand of any state ('cross-state demandability')
(c) and which it is efficacious to distinguish and recognize in international law as demandable of any state ('efficacy').[12]

---

[10] Ibid.   [11] Ibid. 73–4.

[12] I formulate (b) and (c) in terms of what is demandable of *states* to take into account the international law doctrine that human rights documents do not have 'horizontal' effect, i.e. do not directly formulate legal rights against individuals other than states. I do not mean that human rights hold morally *only* against states.

VII. THE POLITICAL CONCEPTION: (II) STATE SOVEREIGNTY

According to (b), human rights are rights whose violation can in principle ground a rectificatory intervention by anyone at all, not just by someone authorized by those whose rights are violated, or by some member of the relevant polity or collective.[13] This idea entails a connection with state sovereignty. Joseph Raz, in his paper in this volume, makes the same connection. The political conception of human rights which he endorses, following Rawls,[14] takes it that human rights are rights which set limits to the sovereignty of states.

For reasons that I do not understand, however, he argues that such rights need not be universal:

Disabling the defence 'none of your business', is definitive of the political conception of human rights. They are rights which are morally valid against states in the international arena, and there is no reason to think that such rights must be universal.[15]

Like me, Raz thinks that 'International law is at fault when it recognizes as a human right something which, morally speaking, is not a right'.[16] We also agree that which moral rights should be placed on a list of *human* rights depends, in part, on what rights-violations can permit intervention in the affairs of a state. But if a violated right is not universal, why is it cross-state demandable? What explains why other states have standing to demand that such violations of non-universal rights be rectified? As I noted, it is not true of all rights that anyone at all has standing to demand that they be respected by others against others. Precisely *because* 'disabling the defence "none of your business," is definitive of the political conception of human rights', it seems to me that human rights must be essentially universal.

Another aspect of the matter, as Raz notes, is that universality implies 'timelessness'—and various writers hold that human rights cannot be 'timelessly' universal. But I think objections to timelessness rest on confusion.

Take the right not to be enslaved. Did slaves in the ancient world have it? Certainly they did. Suppose, science-fictionally, that some powerful group from Elsewhere had come along and enforced the emancipation of slaves on the ancient world. There might be many and various good objections to this intervention. It might do

---

[13] Intervention may take a variety of forms, from simply demanding—and thus claiming the status to demand—that human rights abuses should be rectified, to litigation in international law, sanctions, and military action. The usual difficult questions of proportionality arise; and in the way noted in section II, states may monopolize the permission to enforce.

[14] See Rawls, J., *The Law of Peoples* (Cambridge, Mass.: Harvard University Press, 1999), para. 10.

[15] Raz, J., Chapter 15 in this volume, 332.

[16] Ibid. 329. He doesn't think human rights need be 'basic or very important' moral rights, however (ibid. 337).

more harm than good, would not be understood, might actually set back historical progress towards freedom, etc. But the claim that these slaves had *no right* to be free would not be one of the good objections.

Still, should we say that this right has always been a *human* right? Clause (c) refers to present circumstances, but as it stands it entails that a right which satisfies it is timelessly a human right. We might want to avoid this. If so we could write a temporal reference into the notion of a human right, and amend (c) so that a right is a human right at a time only if (c) is true at that time. I have no particular objection to doing so, and it may avoid misunderstanding; but the fact is that there is no real need: for while (c) as it stands does imply that there was then, in the ancient world, a human right not to be enslaved, it does *not* imply that it would *then* have been sensible and useful to have the right recognized. The question of what rights should *now* be explicitly and internationally recognized, as rights that all states should *now* actively enforce and promote, is a political question addressed to the social and political conditions that prevail today. These conditions do not prevail at all times, and so even if we should now declare a right to be binding on states it does not follow that it either could or should always and everywhere have been so declared.

The point holds for all human rights. Take the right to a fair trial, for example. Is it so shocking to affirm that hunters and gathers in an isolated stone-age tribe had it? It may have been impossible to deliver it—but then the same applies in various situations today. As before, if we say that these hunters and gatherers had a human right to a fair trial we are not implying that it would *then* have been efficacious to declare it binding on 'all states'—or that states and international law then existed. However neither of these points entails that they did not have that human right.

To return to Raz's discussion: he is rightly concerned that we should be realistic about the conditions prevailing in international affairs today. He thinks that these conditions require safeguards against bullying or otherwise unjustified interventions by powerful states, safeguards which may place restrictions of content or procedure on legitimate grounds for intervention. But if we link the idea of what makes a right a human right to the notion of sovereignty-limitation, while also making the doctrine of sovereignty depend on these pragmatic questions about the state of international relations, may we not end up with an *excessively* political conception of human rights? Suppose State A is rather strong and bullying, all too eager to encroach on the affairs of other states, while State B is a state exceeding its legitimate authority, for example by torturing people on a regular basis. Suppose we defend a strong doctrine of the sovereignty of B in the hope of clipping the wings of bullying A. Do we want to say that people in State B (or anywhere else, come to that) don't have a human right against torture?

That would be an undesirable connection. On the view defended here, to establish the right not to be tortured as a human right is to argue two things. We must first show that the right not to be tortured follows from the ordinary substantive conception of rights. We can do that by arguing from clauses (i) and (ii): on any sound account of what can make a seizure or injury legitimate, the seizure and injury involved in torture will entail that it is forbidden absolutely, or at most permitted only in extreme cases and subject to duties of compensation.[17] Secondly, we must argue that it satisfies the criteria for placing it on a list of human rights and thus making its violation a basis of possible intervention. Torture as such is not explicitly mentioned in the general theory of rights. The grounds for distinguishing it as a human right are political, not philosophical. They involve the moral outrageousness of this abuse, certainly, but also the (connected) possibility of getting viable international consensus about having it outlawed. Since both these conditions obtain, it should feature in a list of human rights, even though it requires no explicit mention in a well-formulated general theory of rights.

If the right not to be tortured is a human right then preventive intervention by any other party is in principle permissible. In practice, worries about intervention-abuse arise—whether they concern bullying, self-interest, or sheer counter-productiveness. But they should be dealt with separately. In the sequence of justification, human rights are those rights whose violation permits intervention in principle, *before* safeguards against intervention-abuse have come into consideration. True, I agreed in (c) that in determining what counts as a human right the question of effectiveness is involved. But it is sensible and useful to separate the question of what human rights it is efficacious to declare from that of how to control abusive or misguided interventions. Nor is this the only separate question. There is the question of what contribution to international intervention it might be legitimate to require, by clause (iv) in section IV. Though separate, these questions are connected: if we want to have an internationally agreed enforcement authority, for example, what duties of contribution towards its enforcement activities must that authority be able to impose?

VIII. Conclusion

On the basis of a political judgement, I argued that human rights should satisfy three conditions: universality, cross-state demandability, and efficacy. The political judgment is that human rights declarations and consequent legal procedures should focus on strengthening leverage against grave rights-violations. They should do so by specifying, in transparent terms, what violations are grounds for permissible international intervention. The first condition then follows: human rights must be

---

[17] A right may be permissibly infringed but still leave a residual right of compensation. (See Thomson, J. J., *The Realm of Rights* (Cambridge, Mass.: Harvard University Press, 1990). Thus, if one thinks that torture may be legitimate, though right-infringing, in certain extreme 'ticking bomb' cases (a question I am not considering here) there may still be a duty of compensation.

essentially universal moral rights. I suggested that the ordinary conception of moral rights is sufficiently settled and stable to underpin this condition, without broaching deeper philosophical questions about the foundation of rights as such.

The other two conditions are motivated by the same political judgment. Human rights are rights whose active enforcement and promotion by all states anyone can legitimately demand, and which it is efficacious to recognize in international law as having that standing.

SECTION IX

SELF-DETERMINATION AND MINORITY RIGHTS

CHAPTER 18

MINORITY RIGHTS IN POLITICAL PHILOSOPHY AND INTERNATIONAL LAW

WILL KYMLICKA

I. INTRODUCTION

In the last two decades, minority rights have emerged as an important issue for both international law and political philosophy. Within international law, there has been an explosion of efforts to develop international norms on minority rights, a notion that was explicitly rejected at the end of World War II, and which lay largely dormant for the next forty years. But starting in 1989, minority rights quickly moved to the top of the agenda of several international intergovernmental organizations (IOs). Globally, the United Nations (UN) adopted a Declaration on the Rights of Persons Belonging to National or Ethnic, Religious and Linguistic Minorities in 1992, and a Declaration on the Rights of Indigenous Peoples in 2007. Instruments have also been drafted at the regional level, such as the Council of Europe's 1995 Framework Convention on the Protection of National Minorities, or the 1997 Draft Declaration on Indigenous Rights of the Organization of American States.

Political philosophy has witnessed a similar burst of interest in developing normative theories of minority rights. A number of philosophers have attempted to show how the claims of various minority groups, such as immigrants, indigenous peoples, or sub-state national groups, can be defended within broader theories of justice and democracy. This has generated a plethora of new theories of 'multiculturalism', 'differentiated citizenship', 'the politics of recognition', 'group rights', 'liberal culturalism', and 'pluralistic integration'. For lack of a better term, I will use 'liberal multiculturalism' as a label for these theories, since they all argue that recognizing and accommodating ethnocultural minorities is consistent with, and perhaps even required by, basic principles of liberal-democratic theory. Here again, the first detailed book-length treatments of these issues date from roughly 1989.

The aim of this chapter is to explore how these two developments are related, and to examine whether debates over international norms on minority rights can shed light on political theories of liberal multiculturalism, and vice versa.

II. THE ORIGINS OF LIBERAL MULTICULTURALISM AND INTERNATIONAL MINORITY RIGHTS

The simultaneous emergence of multiculturalist theories and international minority rights norms was accidental, since they have different intellectual and political roots. Liberal multiculturalism emerged out of the liberal-communitarian debate that dominated Anglo-American political philosophy in the 1980s. Communitarians had criticized liberalism for being too individualistic and atomistic, and for being incapable of recognizing the importance of communal and cultural attachments. Liberals responded that communitarian claims about the 'embeddedness' of individuals within communities or cultures were exaggerated, and risked imprisoning people in identities and practices they no longer endorsed.

Much of this debate was pitched at an abstract level, focusing on theories of the self and the good life. But it was quickly applied to a number of policy issues, including questions about the rights of ethnic minorities. Communitarians argued that traditional liberal theories of individual rights were unable to protect such minorities from assimilationist pressures; liberals responded that communitarian demands for 'group rights' were a threat to individual liberty.

It was in this context that theories of liberal multiculturalism first emerged, as a way of transcending the liberal-communitarian divide. Liberal multiculturalists agree with the communitarians that there are legitimate interests in culture and community that deserve protection through various group-specific rights, such as language rights or self-government rights. However, they insist that these interests can be respected while upholding the firm protection of individual rights within groups. Liberal multiculturalism endorses certain 'protective' rights that groups can claim against the larger society, while rejecting 'restrictive' group rights that can be invoked against individual members of the group. For example, self-government rights can help ensure that minorities are not outvoted on key issues, but these self-government regimes should be subject to the same constitutional limitations of respect for individual rights as the central government. This approach offers a distinctly liberal way of accommodating diversity: it protects vulnerable minorities against the majority, but also protects vulnerable individuals within the minority, thereby avoiding the dangers of subordinating individual rights to group rights.

The emergence of minority rights in international law had different origins. It was largely stimulated by the experiences of post-communist Eastern Europe. After the end of the Cold War, there was initially great optimism that liberal democracy would emerge around the world. Instead, what occurred in many post-communist countries was violent ethnic conflict. Overly-optimistic predictions about the replacement of communism with liberal-democracy were supplanted with pessimistic predictions about the replacement of communism with ethnic war. Subsequent events in Rwanda and Somalia suggested that this was a global problem, and that ethnic conflicts were derailing the prospects for peaceful democratization around the world. There was a strong feeling that the international community needed to 'do something' about the threat of ethnic conflict. This was the initial impetus for many of the Declarations and Conventions adopted by IOs in the early 1990s.

So the two movements had different origins. At another level, however, both developments can be seen as seeking alternatives to earlier models of the unitary, homogenous 'nation-state'. Both liberal political philosophy and international relations have traditionally operated with a model of the nation-state which assumes that citizens share a common national identity, national language, and a unified legal and political system. This model of the state was diffused to the post-colonial world, and underpinned the 'nation-building' policies of newly-independent states in the post-communist world. But this model has increasingly been questioned, as people become more aware of the harms, injustices, and violence involved in attempts to implement it. Constructing unitary and homogenous nation-states often requires coercive measures to either assimilate or exclude minorities, such as suppressing minority languages, abolishing traditional forms of minority self-government, enacting discriminatory laws and citizenship policies, even displacing minorities from their traditional homelands. For liberal multiculturalists, the historic adoption of such measures within the West has left a stain of injustice that requires acknowledgement and remedy. For IOs, the ongoing adoption of such measures in post-communist Europe or post-colonial Africa and Asia has generated ethnic violence and instability. In both contexts, there was a growing consensus that some alternative to the traditional nation-state was required.

Both liberal multiculturalism and international minority rights norms can be understood as articulating new models of 'citizenization'. Historically, ethnocultural and religious diversity has been characterized by a range of illiberal and undemocratic relations—relations of conqueror and conquered; colonizer and colonized; settler and indigenous; racialized and unmarked; normalized and deviant; civilized and backward; ally and enemy; master and slave. The task for all democracies has been to turn this catalogue of uncivil relations into relationships of liberal-democratic citizenship, both in terms of the vertical relationship between the members of minorities and the state, and the horizontal relationships amongst the members of different groups. In the past, it was often assumed that the only or best way to engage in this process of citizenization was to impose a single undifferentiated model of national citizenship on all individuals. But proponents of liberal multiculturalism and international minority rights norms start from the assumption that this complex history inevitably and appropriately generates group-differentiated ethnopolitical claims. Moreover, the effort to impose a homogenous national identity often exacerbates rather than diminishes these uncivil relations. The key to citizenization, therefore, is not to suppress these differential claims, but to filter them through the language of human rights, civil liberties, and democratic accountability. This is what liberal multiculturalism and international minority rights norms both attempt to do.

In this respect, both the multiculturalist theories and international norms that emerged in the 1990s can be seen as catching up to the actual practices of Western democracies, which have embarked on an array of experiments in minority rights since the 1960s. And the evidence from these forty years of experiments strongly suggests that minority rights can be an effective vehicle for consolidating relations of democratic citizenship in multiethnic states, at least in some times and places. A wide range of minority rights adopted since the 1960s, including land claims for indigenous peoples, language rights for national minorities, and multicultural accommodations for immigrant groups, have helped to reduce historic hierarchies, equalize opportunities, enhance democratic participation, and consolidate a culture of human rights.[1]

The apparent success of these real-world practices of liberal-democratic multi-culturalism has spurred efforts to formulate political theories of liberal multicul-turalism, which in turn have helped to inform and justify emerging regimes of international minority rights. While the latter were initially developed primarily for short-term conflict prevention, they are increasingly linked to a broader normative vision of how liberal multiculturalism can promote justice and deepen democratic citizenship.

III. Comparing the Two Movements

While recent international minority rights norms emerged alongside normative theories of liberal multiculturalism, and were influenced by them, the two are

---

[1] For the evidence, see Kymlicka, W., *Multicultural Odysseys* (Oxford: Oxford University Press 2007), ch. 5.

not identical. There are some aspects of the theory and practice of liberal multiculturalism that have proven impossible to codify in the form of international norms.

Both movements can be seen as responding to the inadequacy of a purely 'generic' approach to minority rights that seeks to apply the same set of rights to all ethnocultural minorities. An example of this generic approach can be found in article 27 of the UN's International Covenant on Civil and Political Rights, which states that:

In those states in which ethnic, religious or linguistic minorities exist, persons belonging to such minorities shall not be denied the right, in community with the other members of their group, to enjoy their own culture, to profess and practise their own religion, or to use their own language.

This article has been interpreted to apply to the members of all minority groups, no matter how large or small, new or old, concentrated or dispersed, even to visitors within a country. But just for that reason, it cannot address many of the key issues involved in ethnic relations, which are tied to contingencies of historic settlement or territorial concentration. Since article 27 articulates a universal and portable cultural right that applies to all individuals, even migrants and visitors, it does not articulate rights that are tied to the fact that a group is living on (what it views as) its historic homeland. Yet it is precisely claims relating to residence on a historic homeland that are at stake in most violent ethnic conflicts around the world, whether in post-communist Europe (Bosnia, Kosovo, Chechnya), or the West (Basque Country, Cyprus, Northern Ireland), or Asia, Africa, and the Middle East (for example, Pakistan, Sri Lanka, Indonesia, Turkey, Iraq, Israel, Sudan, Ethiopia). In all of these cases, minorities claim the right to govern themselves in what they view as their historic homeland, including the right to use their language in public institutions within their traditional territory, and to have their language, history, and culture celebrated in the public sphere (for example, in the naming of streets, the choice of holidays and state symbols). None of these claims can reasonably be seen as universal or portable—they only apply to particular sorts of minorities with a particular sort of history and territory.

Any plausible approach to these conflicts, whether in international law or political philosophy, needs to address the distinct types of claims raised by these different groups. And this requires supplementing a purely generic approach with a scheme of *targeted* or group-differentiated minority rights. Both international law and multiculturalist theories have accepted this need for a group-differentiated approach. In particular, both recognize the need to distinguish between 'old' minorities, such as indigenous peoples and sub-state national minorities living on their historic territory, and 'new' minorities formed through immigration.

However, multiculturalist theories and international law have approached this issue in divergent ways. I will examine the two main examples of targeted minority rights regimes in international law—targeted rights for 'national minorities' in

Europe, and targeted rights for 'indigenous peoples' at the UN—to see how they compare with theories of liberal multiculturalism.

IV. National Minority Rights in Europe

The most elaborate scheme of targeted rights has developed in Europe, spearheaded by the Council of Europe (CE). Confronted with spiralling ethnic conflict in the Balkans and Caucasus in the early 1990s, the CE adopted norms tailored to the specific types of groups that were involved in these conflicts, which they labelled 'national minorities'. Whereas article 27 lumps together 'national, ethnic, religious and linguistic minorities', and accords them all the same generic minority rights, the CE's norms refer exclusively to 'national minorities'.

What are national minorities? While there is no universally agreed-upon definition, the term has a long history in European diplomacy, where it has referred to historically-settled minorities, living on or near what they view as their national homeland. It was these sorts of 'homeland' groups that were involved in the violent and destabilizing ethnic conflicts that generated the call for European norms, and it was appropriate therefore to focus on them when formulating targeted norms. Most European countries have explicitly stated that immigrant groups are not national minorities, and some have also excluded the Roma from the category of national minority, on the grounds that they are a non-territorial minority. These exclusions are increasingly contested, with the result that the traditional understanding of national minority co-exists alongside newer definitions of the term that are less tied to history and territory. But originally at least, European organizations were primarily targeting their efforts at historically-settled sub-state national minorities living on their traditional territory.

The challenge facing European organizations was to formulate targeted norms for national minorities that would provide effective guidance for dealing with the immediate risks of destabilizing ethnic conflict, but would also promote a distinctively liberal-democratic conception of multicultural 'citizenization' in the long term.

What does liberal multiculturalism suggest regarding the treatment of such groups? If we examine the main cases of sub-state national groups in the West—the Scots and Welsh in the United Kingdom, the Catalans and Basques in Spain, the Flemish in Belgium, the Québecois in Canada, the Puerto Ricans in the United States, the Corsicans in France, the German minority in South Tyrol in Italy, the Swedes in Finland, and the French and Italian minorities in Switzerland—a clear pattern emerges. In each case, sub-state national groups have been offered territorial autonomy (TA), usually through some form of federal or quasi-federal devolution of power, as well as some form of official language status.

These reforms involved a substantial restructuring of the state and redistribution of political power, and so were initially controversial. And yet, today, the basic idea of TA for national minorities is widely accepted. It is inconceivable that Spain or Belgium, for example, could revert to a unitary and monolingual state. Indeed, no Western democracy that has adopted TA has reversed this decision. Moreover, this model is widely seen as successful. It has enabled countries to deal with a potentially explosive issue—the existence of a sub-state group that perceives itself as a distinct nation with the right to govern its historic territory—in a way that is consistent with peace and democracy, respect for individual rights, and economic prosperity. Indeed, several theorists of liberal multiculturalism have presented this model as a central test case of how minority rights and liberal democracy can co-exist, and have explored how the exercise of autonomy by sub-state national groups respects liberal values and promotes democratic citizenization.[2]

Not surprisingly, the initial impulse of European organizations was to promote this model in post-communist Europe. In 1993, for example, the CE's Parliamentary Assembly recommended that any future European minority rights convention should include the following provision:

> In the regions where they are a majority, the persons belonging to a national minority shall have the right to have at their disposal appropriate local or autonomous authorities or to have a special status, matching this specific historical and territorial situation and in accordance with the domestic legislation of the state.[3]

As we will see, this proposal was eventually rejected. But for a time in the early 1990s, it appeared that European legal norms and liberal multiculturalist theories would converge in endorsing a right to TA for national minorities.

The proposed European norm differed in one respect from that endorsed in multiculturalist theories—namely, in the relationship between TA and the principle of self-determination. According to several theorists of liberal multiculturalism, the autonomy of national minorities should be seen, not as a delegation of power from the central state, but as a manifestation of an inherent right of self-determination of nations or peoples. According to these theorists, the interest that people have in their cultural identities and collective life is sufficiently strong to ground an inherent right to govern themselves. Moreover, extending a right of self-determination to national minorities is seen as a matter of moral consistency. International law recognizes the right of all peoples to self-determination, but has restricted this in practice to overseas colonies. For liberal multiculturalists, this restriction is morally arbitrary: internal national groups stripped of their self-government and incorporated into a larger state are just as deserving of self-determination as overseas national groups

---

[2] For an overview, see Gagnon, A. and Tully, J. (eds.), *Multinational Democracies* (Cambridge: Cambridge University Press, 2001).

[3] Council of Europe Parliamentary Assembly, *On an additional protocol on the rights of national minorities to the European Convention on Human Rights*, Recommendation 1201 (1993), article 11.

that have been colonized. Internal colonialism and overseas colonialism are both unjust, and both call for self-determination as a remedy. TA for national minorities, therefore, is seen as part of a more consistent approach to the self-determination of peoples generally.

The proposed European norm, by contrast, explicitly avoided the term 'self-determination'. It affirmed a norm of self-government, but denied that this implied or entailed a principle of self-determination, largely because self-determination in international law has traditionally been interpreted as a right to form an independent state.

This is partly a semantic disagreement, since multiculturalist theorists emphasize that the principle of self-determination should not be interpreted as a right to secede. They recognize that it is impossible to give every nation or people a right to its own state, and that self-determination must be understood therefore as something that is exercised primarily through autonomy within larger multi-nation states—that is, through 'internal' self-determination, such as TA.

In this sense, both multicultural theorists and the CE's proposed norm agree on the substantive issue: they both envision a world of multi-nation states that accord TA to their national minorities, as against traditional unitary nation-states or secession. However, they disagree about how to describe this outcome. International lawyers have been reluctant to describe TA as a form of (internal) self-determination because this challenges the traditional assumption in international law that each state possesses a unified sovereignty. To be sure, this unitary sovereignty must be divided, delegated, and constrained according to domestic constitutional provisions and international norms. But this is different from accepting the claim, advanced by liberal multiculturalists, that sub-state national groups have their own original sovereignty which must be recognized by international law, even if only in the form of TA within larger states. From the perspective of international law, telling sovereign states to delegate rights of self-government to national minorities is less threatening, conceptually and politically, than telling states that they do not in fact possess full and original sovereignty over those groups.

This perhaps reflects a difference in perspective between international lawyers and normative political theorists. For international lawyers, tying TA to self-determination is needlessly provocative, and risks undermining a core premise of international law itself—namely, the existence of sovereign states that are the main agents responsible for fulfilling international law. For normative political theorists, by contrast, the provocation contains an important moral lesson: states need reminding that they did not always possess sovereignty over all the peoples and territories they currently claim, and that addressing the original sovereignty of sub-state national groups is unfinished moral business. Tying TA to self-determination is a way of reminding states that they cannot take their (often ill-gotten) sovereignty over sub-state nations or peoples for granted.

In any event, this momentary convergence between liberal multiculturalism and European norms regarding a right of TA for national minorities did not last. The CE's 1995 Framework Convention for the Protection of National Minorities (FCNM) rejected the Parliamentary Assembly's advice to include a provision on TA. Nor does TA appear in any subsequent declaration of European organizations. Indeed, ideas of autonomy have essentially disappeared from the debate about European standards on national minority rights.

There are several reasons for this, but to oversimplify, the long-term goal of promoting liberal multiculturalism ran into conflict with short-term fears of destabilizing ethnic conflict. While TA was seen as a successful model in the consolidated Western democracies, and a potential long-term goal in Eastern Europe, it was seen as dangerous in the immediate circumstances of post-communist transition.

In particular, two key factors enabling the adoption of TA in the West did not exist in post-communist countries: geopolitical security and human rights protections. First, most post-communist states have one or more enemies on their borders who would like to destabilize the state. One familiar tactic for doing so is to recruit minorities within the state, and to encourage them to engage in destabilizing protest, even armed insurrection. In such a context of regional insecurity, national minorities are perceived as potential fifth-columnists for neighbouring enemies, and autonomy for such minorities is perceived as a threat to national security. This perception is particularly strong when the national minority is related by language or ethnicity to the neighbouring country, and hence is presumed to be more loyal to its 'kin-state' across the border than to its own government. For example, ethnic Serbs living in Bosnia are assumed to be more loyal to Serbia than to Bosnia, ethnic Hungarians living in Slovakia are presumed to be more loyal to Hungary than to Slovakia, etc. Under conditions of regional insecurity, granting autonomy to such potentially disloyal and irredentist minorities is seen as weakening the state in relation to its neighbouring enemies, and indeed as endangering the very existence of the state.

Western countries, by contrast, are surrounded by allies not enemies, and are integrated into broader regional security alliances. As a result, no Western state today has an incentive to use discontented national minorities as a vehicle for destabilizing its neighbours. To be sure, there are historic examples of this. In the past, Germany has incited ethnic German minorities in neighbouring countries as a way to weaken its rival states. But since World War II and the emergence of the North Atlantic Treaty Organization (NATO), the perception of homeland minorities as potential collaborators with neighbouring enemies has disappeared from the West.[4] Relations between states and national minorities are seen as issues of domestic policy, with no repercussions for foreign policy or regional security.

---

[4] This perception still exists in relation to some immigrant groups, particularly Muslim groups after 9/11. But it no longer applies to historic national minorities.

In the post-communist world, by contrast, state-minority relations are heavily 'securitized', perceived in the first instance as issues of national security rather than domestic policy, leaving little space for liberal multiculturalism.

A second factor distinguishing the West from post-communist Europe concerns human rights protection, or more generally the sequencing of minority rights in relation to broader processes of state consolidation and democratization. In the West, Spain excepted, the restructuring of states to accommodate national minorities occurred after democratic consolidation, with well-established traditions of the rule of law, an independent judiciary, a professional bureaucracy, and a democratic political culture. The existence of such well-rooted traditions of liberal constitutionalism was crucial to the emergence of multiculturalism in the West, since it provided a sense of security to all citizens that multiculturalism would operate within well-defined parameters of democracy and human rights.

For example, in so far as national minorities have acquired autonomous governments, these governments have typically been subject to the same constitutional requirements to respect human rights as the central government. In many cases, they are also subject to regional and international human rights monitoring. This reassures everyone that no matter how debates over autonomy are resolved, their basic human rights will be protected. This in turn generates confidence in multiculturalism's potential to replace earlier hierarchical relations with relations of democratic citizenship.

In the post-communist world, however, claims for self-government by homeland minorities were occurring prior to democratic consolidation. As a result, there are fewer guarantees that minorities who receive autonomy will exercise their powers in a way that respects human rights, rather than creating islands of local tyranny that are intolerant of 'outsiders' residing on the territory. In the absence of an effective human rights framework, such outsiders may be dispossessed of their property, fired from their jobs, even expelled or killed. Indeed, this is what has happened in several cases where minorities have established their own autonomous governments: ethnic Georgians were pushed out of the Abkhazia region of Georgia when it declared autonomy, ethnic Croats were pushed out of the Serb-dominated regions of Croatia when they declared autonomy, and so on. Neither side could rely on effective legal institutions and an impartial police to ensure that human rights were respected. Under such conditions, the operation of TA can literally be a matter of life and death.

These two factors help explain the resistance to TA in post-communist Europe. In conditions of regional insecurity, TA can be a threat to the security of the state. In the absence of democratic consolidation, TA can be a threat to the life and liberty of individual citizens who belong to the 'wrong' group. Under these circumstances, the intended goal of liberal multiculturalism—replacing uncivil relations of enmity and exclusion with relations of liberal-democratic citizenship—may be subverted. Institutions designed to promote citizenization in multiethnic states may be captured by actors seeking to perpetuate and exacerbate relations of enmity and exclusion.

Given these obstacles, it is not surprising that proposals to codify a right to autonomy for national minorities failed. To be sure, these proposals always included the proviso that autonomous governments must respect human rights. The basic principle that minority rights are subordinate to human rights is found in every international document on minority and indigenous rights, and is an important commonality with theories of liberal multiculturalism.[5] However, in the context of post-communist Europe, there was a widespread fear that IOs could not enforce this 'paper guarantee'.

Having abandoned a right to autonomy, the minority rights norms ultimately adopted by the CE are weak. Indeed, the FCNM essentially duplicates the generic minority right to enjoy one's culture enshrined in article 27. And having retreated to generic rights, the CE immediately faced pressure to expand its coverage beyond traditional national minorities. After all, why should generic minority rights to enjoy one's culture only be guaranteed to one particular type of minority group? Shouldn't generic minority rights be protected generically? And indeed we see a movement within the CE to redefine the term 'national minority' so that it no longer refers to one type of group amongst others, but rather becomes an umbrella term that encompasses all minorities living on the territory of the state, including indigenous peoples, homeland minorities, the Roma, and immigrant groups.[6] In short, both in its content and coverage, the FCNM has shifted from its original goal of defining targeted rights for ethno-national homeland groups to defining generic minority rights for all groups.

The decision to convert the FCNM from a targeted to a generic minority rights document is understandable—the goal of formulating principles to deal with the claims of ethno-national groups was too ambitious in light of regional insecurity and democratic transition. This is an important and sobering lesson in the difficulties of using international law to articulate the logic of liberal multiculturalism. In the end, the CE was unable to reconcile the short-term goal of conflict prevention in unstable conditions with the long-term goal of promoting robust forms of liberal multiculturalism. And this in turn provides a sobering lesson in the limits of liberal multiculturalism itself: its ability to promote citizenization depends on a number of preconditions that are far from universal.

V. Indigenous Rights at the UN

The second experiment in formulating targeted rights is the UN's efforts to codify rights specifically tailored to indigenous peoples. This is a more successful story,

---

[5] Kymlicka, W., *Multicultural Odysseys* (above, n. 1).
[6] Wheatley, S., *Democracy, Minorities and International Law* (Cambridge: Cambridge University Press, 2005).

and provides an interesting contrast with the European experience with national minorities.

What are indigenous peoples, and how do they differ from national minorities? The term 'indigenous people' has traditionally been used in the context of New World settler states, and refers to the descendants of the original non-European inhabitants of lands colonized and settled by European powers. 'National minorities', by contrast, was a term invented in Europe to refer to groups that lost out in the rough and tumble process of European state formation, and whose homelands ended up being incorporated in whole or in part into larger states dominated by a neighbouring European people. National minorities were active players in the process by which the early modern welter of empires, kingdoms, and principalities in Europe was turned into the modern system of nation-states, but they either ended up without a state of their own ('stateless nations' such as the Catalans and Scots), or ended up on the wrong side of the border, cut off from their co-ethnics in a neighbouring state ('kin-state minorities' such as the Germans in Denmark or Hungarians in Slovakia).

A preliminary way of distinguishing the two is to say that national minorities have been incorporated into a larger state dominated by a neighbouring European people, whereas indigenous peoples have been colonized and settled by a distant colonial European power. But there are other markers that supervene on this basic historical difference. For example, the subjugation of indigenous peoples by European colonizers was a more brutal and disruptive process than the incorporation of national minorities by neighbouring societies, leaving indigenous peoples weaker and more vulnerable. There is also a perceived 'civilizational' difference between indigenous peoples and national minorities. Whereas national minorities typically share the same modern (urban, industrialized, consumerist) economic and socio-political structures as their neighbouring European peoples, some indigenous peoples retain pre-modern modes of economic production, engaged primarily in subsistence agriculture or a hunting/gathering lifestyle. And, as a result of large-scale colonizing settlement, indigenous peoples are more likely to be relegated to remote areas.

So both terms have their origins in Western historical processes. National minorities are contenders but losers in the process of state formation within continental Europe itself; indigenous peoples are the victims of the construction of European settler states in the New World. As such, it's not clear whether either term can usefully be applied outside Europe and the New World. And indeed, as we will see, various African and Asian countries have insisted that neither category applies to them.

However we can find analogous groups in other contexts. For example, several groups in Asia or Africa share the cultural vulnerability, pre-modern economies, and geographical remoteness of some indigenous peoples in the New World, including various 'hill tribes', 'forest peoples', 'nomadic tribes', and 'pastoralists'.

Similarly, there are groups in many post-colonial states that are similar to European national minorities in being active players, but eventual losers, in the process of decolonization and post-colonial state formation. These would include groups like the Tamils in Sri Lanka, Tibetans in China, Kurds in Iraq, Acehnese in Indonesia, Oromos in Ethiopia, or the Palestinians in Israel. Like national minorities in Europe, they may have hoped to form their own state in the process of decolonization, or at least to have secured autonomy. Yet they ended up being subordinated to a more powerful neighbouring group within a larger state, or divided between two or more post-colonial states.

Why did the UN decide to target indigenous peoples, whereas European organizations targeted national minorities? The European motivation was fear of the destabilizing impact of conflicts involving national minorities on international peace and security. The UN's motivation was different—namely, a humanitarian desire to protect a type of group that was seen as distinctly vulnerable, even if this very weakness meant that indigenous peoples are unlikely to threaten international stability.

The task confronting the UN, then, was to develop targeted norms for indigenous peoples that alleviate their urgent vulnerability, while promoting the long-term goals of liberal multiculturalism. What does liberal multiculturalism imply for indigenous peoples? If we consider the status of indigenous peoples in the Western democracies—the Indians and Inuit/Eskimos of Canada and the United States, Maori in New Zealand, Aboriginals in Australia, Greenlanders in Denmark and Sami in Scandinavia—there has been a shift since the 1970s towards recognizing some form of indigenous self-government over (what remains of) their traditional territory. This is reflected in a wide range of land claims settlements, self-government agreements, and recognition of indigenous customary law.

This shift towards autonomy for indigenous peoples was initially controversial, but is now broadly seen as an (overdue) acknowledgement that the colonization of indigenous peoples was unjust, and that some form of decolonization is required, enabling indigenous peoples to re-establish autonomous legal and political institutions, and to regain control over some of their traditional lands. This trend has been endorsed by several theorists of liberal multiculturalism.[7] Like the shift towards TA for national minorities, it is seen as a test case for the compatibility of group-differentiated rights with liberal constitutionalism and democratic citizenization.

Not surprisingly, therefore, the UN's initial impulse was to endorse this model of indigenous self-government. In 1993, the Draft Declaration on the Rights of Indigenous Peoples included the right to control traditional lands and territories, the right to self-government in internal affairs, and the right to maintain distinctive

---

[7] See Ivison, D. et al. (eds.), *Political Theory and the Rights of Indigenous Peoples* (Cambridge: Cambridge University Press, 2000).

juridical customs. As we've just seen, a comparable proposal to enshrine a right to autonomy for national minorities in Europe, also drafted in 1993, was eventually rejected. In the case of indigenous peoples, however, the proposed Declaration was accepted by the UN General Assembly, after many years of negotiations, in 2007. Moreover, the UN Declaration accepts that indigenous autonomy must be understood as a manifestation of a right to (internal) self-determination, as liberal multiculturalists argue.

In this way, the UN's efforts at formulating targeted norms for indigenous peoples have been more successful than European efforts at formulating targeted norms for national minorities, and better reflect the logic of liberal multiculturalism. As a result, many commentators identify the Declarations as a rare example of international law serving as a vehicle of 'counter-hegemonic globalization', promoting justice for the disadvantaged.[8]

The UN's humanitarian focus on indigenous peoples, however, leaves a serious legal vacuum with respect to the security issues raised by national minorities. Conflicts involving ethno-national groups such as the Kurds, Kashmiris, and Palestinians pose a much greater threat to regional peace and security than the struggles of pastoralists or forest dwellers. By deciding to target indigenous peoples rather than national minorities, the UN has no guidelines for addressing these pressing conflicts.

One response would be to supplement UN norms on indigenous peoples with another set of UN norms targeted at national minorities. As I noted earlier, this sort of 'multi-targeting' would reflect the logic of liberal multiculturalism, which involves a range of group-differentiated legal tracks, including distinctive tracks for national minorities and indigenous peoples.

Unfortunately, the prospects for developing global norms on national minorities are non-existent in the foreseeable future. The one attempt to formulate such norms at the global level—the Draft Convention on Self-Determination through Self-Administration submitted by Liechtenstein to the UN in 1994—was never seriously considered. And this shouldn't surprise us. The same factors that inhibited the development of national minority norms for post-communist Europe—namely, fears about geopolitical security and human rights protection—apply to most countries in Africa, Asia, or the Middle East. If European organizations were unable to overcome these fears, despite their formidable economic, legal, and military capacities, it is unrealistic to expect the UN to succeed in this task. And indeed it has never tried.

So, the current UN framework which adopts targeted norms for indigenous peoples but not for national minorities is unlikely to change. Unfortunately, this asymmetry is generating instabilities. In order to understand the problem, we need to recall the broader logic of liberal multiculturalism. As I noted earlier,

---

[8] Anaya, J., *Indigenous Peoples in International Law* (Oxford: Oxford University Press, 2004).

both indigenous peoples and national minorities are treated as 'old' or 'homeland' minorities in most Western democracies. There are important differences between the two types of homeland minorities, but both are acknowledged to have legitimate interests with respect to the governance of their traditional territory, and the expression of their language and culture within the public institutions of that territory. In this respect, they are distinguished from new minorities composed of immigrants, guest-workers, and refugees.

In international law, however, the commonalities between indigenous peoples and national minorities have been obscured. There was, at first, an understandable justification for this trend. As we've seen, the subjugation of indigenous peoples by European colonizers was a more brutal process than the subjugation of national minorities by neighbouring European societies, leaving indigenous peoples more vulnerable, and hence in more urgent need of international protection. As a result, there was a plausible moral argument for giving priority to indigenous peoples over national minorities in the codification of self-government rights in international law.

However, what began as a difference in relative urgency between the claims of indigenous peoples and national minorities has developed into a total rupture at the level of international law. Across a wide range of international documents, indigenous peoples have been distinguished from other homeland minorities, and claims to TA have been restricted to the former. National minorities are lumped together with new minorities and accorded only generic minority rights, ignoring their distinctive needs and aspirations relating to historic settlement and territorial concentration. The distinction between indigenous peoples and other homeland minorities has thereby assumed a significance within international law that is absent in the theory and practice of liberal multiculturalism.

From the perspective of liberal multiculturalism, this attempt to create a firewall between the rights of indigenous peoples and national minorities is problematic. The sharp distinction in rights seems morally inconsistent, because whatever arguments exist for recognizing rights of self-government for indigenous peoples also apply to other homeland groups. This is clear from the UN's own explanations for the targeted indigenous track. In a document, Asbjorn Eide, Chair of the UN's Working Group on Minorities, and Erica-Irene Daes, Chair of the UN Working Group on Indigenous Populations, were asked to explain their understanding of the distinction between 'indigenous peoples' on the one hand, and 'national, ethnic, religious and linguistic minorities' on the other.[9] In explaining why indigenous peoples are entitled to targeted rights beyond those available to all minorities under the generic article 27, the two Chairs identified three key differences: (a) whereas

---

[9] Eide, A. and Daes, E.-I., *Working Paper on the Relationship and Distinction between the rights of persons belonging to minorities and those of indigenous peoples*, prepared for the UN Sub-Commission on Promotion and Protection of Human Rights, UN Doc. E/CN.4/Sub.2/2000/10, 2000.

minorities seek institutional integration, indigenous peoples seek to preserve a degree of institutional separateness; (b) whereas minorities seek individual rights, indigenous peoples seek collectively-exercised rights; (c) whereas minorities seek non-discrimination, indigenous peoples seek self-government. These are indeed relevant differences that liberal multiculturalism attends to. But none of them distinguishes indigenous peoples from national minorities. On all three points national minorities fall on the same side of the ledger as indigenous peoples.

In an earlier document, Daes offered a somewhat different account. She stated that the distinguishing feature of indigenous peoples, compared to minorities in general, is that they have a strong attachment to a traditional territory. As she puts it;

attachment to a homeland is nonetheless definitive of the identity and integrity of the [indigenous] group, socially and culturally. This may suggest a very narrow but precise definition of 'indigenous', sufficient to be applied to any situation where the problem is one of distinguishing an indigenous people [from] the larger class of minorities.[10]

But this criterion—'attachment to a homeland'—picks out homeland minorities in general, not indigenous peoples in particular.

Since the principles advanced within the UN for targeted indigenous rights also apply to national minorities, the sharp gulf in legal status between the two groups lacks any clear moral justification. It may be politically impossible to extend norms of self-government to national minorities, for reasons explored earlier, but we shouldn't ignore the moral inconsistencies this generates.

The sharp distinction between national minorities and indigenous peoples is unstable in another way, as the very distinction is difficult to draw outside the core cases of Europe and European settler states. In the West, as we've seen, there is a relatively clear distinction to be drawn between European national minorities and New World indigenous peoples. Both are homeland groups, but the former have been incorporated into a larger state dominated by a neighbouring people, whereas the latter have been colonized and settled by a distant colonial power. It is less clear how we can draw this distinction in Africa, Asia, or the Middle East.

In one sense, no groups in Africa, Asia, or the Middle East fit the traditional profile of indigenous peoples. All homeland minorities in these regions have been incorporated into larger states dominated by neighbouring groups, rather than being incorporated into settler states. In that sense, they are all closer to the profile of European national minorities than to New World indigenous peoples. And for this reason, several Asian and African countries insist that none of their minorities should be designated as indigenous peoples. However, if we restrict the category of 'indigenous people' to New World States, this would leave homeland minorities in much of the world without any meaningful form of international protection. If

---

[10] Daes, E.-I., *Working Paper on the Concept of 'Indigenous people'*, prepared for the UN Working Group on Indigenous Populations, UN Doc. E/CN.4/Sub.2/AC.4/1996/2, 1996, para. 39.

targeted indigenous norms do not apply in Asia or Africa, then minorities are left with only the weak generic minority rights under article 27, and these provide no protection for homeland-related interests.

In order to extend the protections of international law, therefore, the UN has attempted to reconceptualize the category of indigenous peoples to cover at least some homeland minorities in post-colonial states. On this view, we shouldn't focus on whether homeland minorities are dominated by settlers from a distant colonial power or by neighbouring peoples. What matters is simply the facts of domination and vulnerability, and finding appropriate means to remedy them. And so various IOs have encouraged groups in Africa and Asia to identify themselves as indigenous peoples in order to gain greater international protection.

This push to extend the category of indigenous peoples beyond its original New World setting is a logical result of the humanitarian motivation that led to the targeting of indigenous peoples in the first place. In so far as the motivation for targeted rights was the distinctive vulnerability of indigenous peoples in New World settler states, it was natural to expand the category to include groups elsewhere in the world that share similar vulnerabilities, even if they were not subject to settler colonialism.

The difficult question however is how to identify *which* homeland groups in Africa, Asia, or the Middle East should be designated as indigenous peoples under international law. Once we start down the road of applying the category of indigenous peoples beyond the core case of New World settler states, there is no obvious stopping point. Indeed, there are significant disagreements within IOs about how widely to apply the category of indigenous peoples in post-colonial states.[11] Some would limit it to isolated peoples, such as hill tribes or forest peoples in South East Asia, or pastoralists in Africa. Others, however, would extend the category much more widely to encompass all historically-subordinated homeland minorities that suffer from some combination of political exclusion or cultural vulnerability.

Under these circumstances, attempts to draw a sharp distinction between national minorities and indigenous peoples will seem arbitrary. Moreover, any such line will be politically unsustainable. The problem here is not simply that the category of indigenous peoples has grey areas and fuzzy boundaries. The problem, rather, is that too much depends on which side of the line groups fall on, and as a result, there is intense political pressure to change where the line is drawn, in ways that are politically unsustainable.

As should be clear by now, the current UN framework provides no incentive for any homeland minority to identify itself as a national minority, since national minorities can claim only generic minority rights. Instead, all homeland minorities

---

[11] Kingsbury, B., 'Indigenous Peoples in International Law: A Constructivist Approach to the Controversy', *American Journal of International Law*, 92/3 (1998), 414.

have an incentive to (re)-define themselves as 'indigenous peoples'. If they come to the UN under the heading of 'national minority', they get nothing other than generic article 27 rights; if they come as 'indigenous peoples', they have the promise of land rights, control over natural resources, political autonomy, language rights, and legal pluralism.

Not surprisingly, an increasing number of homeland groups in Africa, Asia, and the Middle East are adopting the indigenous label. Consider the Arab-speaking minority in the Ahwaz region of Iran, whose homeland has been subject to state policies of Persianization, including the suppression of Arab language rights, re-naming of towns and villages to erase evidence of their Arab history, and settlement policies that swamp the Ahwaz with Persian settlers. In the past, Ahwaz leaders have gone to the UN Working Group on Minorities to complain that their rights as a national minority in relation to their traditional territory are not respected. But since the UN does not recognize national minorities as having any distinctive rights in relation to their areas of historic settlement, the Ahwaz have relabelled themselves as an indigenous people, and have attended the UN Working Group on Indigenous Populations instead. Similarly, various homeland minorities in Africa that once attended the Working Group on Minorities have rebranded them-selves as indigenous peoples, primarily to gain protection for their land rights.[12] Leaders amongst the Crimean Tatars, Roma, Afro-Latinos, Palestinians, Chechens, and Tibetans are now debating whether to self-identify as indigenous. Even the Kurds—the textbook example of a stateless national minority—are debating this option.

In all of these cases, national minorities are responding to the fact that the UN's generic minority rights are 'regarded as fatally weak',[13] since they do not protect any claims based on historic settlement or territorial attachments. Given international law as it stands, recognition as an indigenous people is the only route to secure protection for these interests.

The availability of this back-door route for national minorities to gain targeted self-government rights may seem like a good thing. After all, from the perspective of liberal multiculturalism, the underlying moral logic should be to acknowledge the legitimate interests relating to historic settlement and territory shared by all homeland minorities, and expanding the category of indigenous people to cover all homeland minorities is one possible way to do this.

Unfortunately, this is not a sustainable approach. The tendency of national minorities to adopt the label of indigenous peoples is likely to lead to the collapse of the international system of indigenous rights. As we've seen, the UN and other IOs have repeatedly rejected attempts to codify rights of self-government for powerful

---

[12] Lennox, C., 'The Changing International Protection Regimes for Minorities and Indigenous Peoples' (paper presented to the International Studies Association, San Diego, March 2006).

[13] Barsch, R. L., 'Indigenous Peoples in the 1990s: From Object to Subject of International Law?', *Harvard Human Rights Journal*, 7 (1994), 33.

sub-state national groups, in part because of their geopolitical security implications. They are not going to allow such groups to gain rights of self-government through the back-door by redefining themselves as indigenous peoples. If more and more homeland groups adopt the indigenous label, the likely result is that IOs will retreat from the targeted indigenous rights track.

This suggests that the long-term future of the UN's indigenous track is unclear. It is often cited as the clearest success story in developing international minority rights, but its success rests on shaky foundations. The UN has attempted to create a legal firewall between the rights of indigenous peoples and national minorities. This firewall was needed to get the indigenous track off the ground, but it is at odds with the logic of liberal multiculturalism, and politically unsustainable. A durable international framework will require a more coherent account of the relationship between indigenous peoples and national minorities, and a more consistent approach to self-government rights.

VI. Conclusion

New standards of minority rights have emerged within international law at the same time as new theories of liberal multiculturalism have emerged within political philosophy. The two developments are mutually supporting in many ways: the ideals of liberal multiculturalism have helped to shape international law, and international law has helped to promote liberal multiculturalism.

However, there are limits to the extent that international law can serve as a vehicle for promoting liberal multiculturalism. If we compare existing international minority rights standards with the conclusions of liberal multiculturalist theories, there are several gaps. The two converge most closely in the area of indigenous rights, where UN standards closely parallel liberal theories of indigenous rights, particularly in their commitment to self-government, treaty rights, and land claims. There is greater divergence in the area of national minorities. In this context, liberal multiculturalism has generally endorsed some norm of territorial autonomy and official language status, but attempts to formulate such ideas in international law have been decisively rejected. And the divergence is perhaps greatest in the case of immigrants, where there has been no attempt to formulate international standards based on the theories of liberal multiculturalism.

These gaps partly reflect the relationships of power that underpin international law. After all, international organizations are clubs of states, and hence are not neutral arbiters in addressing conflicts between states and minorities. It would be surprising indeed if clubs of states endorsed strong minority rights, particularly where those minorities are seen as posing a powerful challenge to state sovereignty.

But *raison d'état* isn't the whole story. IOs have in fact shown considerable sympathy for ideals of liberal multiculturalism. If current international standards of minority rights provide only a pale reflection of those ideals, this is partly due to genuine difficulties in translating liberal multiculturalism into international law. The preconditions that enabled liberal multiculturalism to take root (unevenly) in the Western democracies do not exist in many countries, and promoting liberal multiculturalism without attention to these underlying conditions can exacerbate rather than mitigate ethnic conflict. Moreover, the basic categories that are used in theories of liberal multiculturalism—such as the categories of 'indigenous peoples' and 'national minorities'—are rooted in the experience of particular regions, and may not work well at a global scale.

These difficulties should not surprise us. The exercise of formulating international standards of minority rights is a relatively recent one, as is the attempt to formulate normative theories of liberal multiculturalism. We are still at the earliest stages of thinking through how the two can and should inform each other.

CHAPTER 19

TWO CONCEPTIONS OF SELF-DETERMINATION

JEREMY WALDRON

I. INTRODUCTION

Article 1 of the International Covenant of Civil and Political Rights (ICCPR) tells us that '[a]ll peoples have the right of self-determination'. It continues: 'By virtue of that right they freely determine their political status'. Stated in this way, the principle of self-determination seems to be a fixed point in our political thinking. Who would deny that the people of a country have a right to determine their own destiny and govern themselves without interference from the outside? I do not mean that self-determination is a platitude. Even in its most widely accepted form, it was the main principle embodied in the decolonization movement and its application in that context had to be fought for, with radical and transformative results.

As a principle, self-determination becomes more controversial when the term 'peoples' in the ICCPR formulation is given a determinate meaning. In its moderate and widely accepted form, self-determination simply means that the people of a country have the right to work out their own constitutional and political arrangements without interference from the outside. There is no particular meaning for 'people' here; it includes anyone who lives permanently within the country in question, and it is compatible with either the homogeneity or the diversity of that population in terms of ethnic or cultural composition. I shall call this the *territorial* conception of self-determination. But sometimes we use 'peoples' to refer to communities of humans who regard themselves as ethnically or culturally distinct.

On this account, the claim that all peoples have the right of self-determination seems to imply that the political world should be organized so that each ethnically or culturally distinct group has charge of its own constitutional and political arrangements. I shall call this the *identity-based* conception of self-determination. It no longer correlates tidily with existing territorial boundaries. A people may exist as a minority in a given country, and the persons who compose that people may think of themselves as having an identity that distinguishes them from other inhabitants of the country where they live. Will Kymlicka's essay clearly envisages something along these lines when he talks, for example, of self-determination for indigenous peoples or for national minorities.[1]

Demands for identity-based self-determination are often radical demands, seeking to reorder the political world. Because many existing societies comprise several peoples who regard themselves as distinct in this way, identity-based conceptions challenge established boundaries and existing political entities. Consider Belgium, with its distinct populations of Flemish and French-speaking peoples; if these groups were to achieve self-determination in the strong sense of separate governments answerable in each case to separate communities, Belgium would be torn apart. Some of the distinct peoples of the world find themselves distributed among a number of adjacent states; the Kurds, for example, are found in Turkey, Iraq, Iran, and Syria. Self-determination in this context might lead to the formation of a new Kurdish state, embodying regions that exist presently in the west of Turkey, the north-east of Syria, the north of Iraq, and the eastern part of Iran.

As I said, everyone pays lip service to the principle laid down in the ICCPR. But a number of the countries just mentioned would go to war to prevent the redrawing of boundaries to accommodate self-determination for the Kurds. And most politicians in Europe would regard it as a catastrophe if the Flemish and French-speaking regions of Belgium were given any greater degree of self-determination than they have already.

Why is this? It is partly because self-determination often involves much more than just the redrawing of boundaries. In countries comprising several distinct peoples, communities often intermingle historically and geographically. So redrawing boundaries for the sake of self-determination imposes heart-breaking choices on those who by intermarriage, for example, have a foot in both camps; and it might well involve humanitarian disaster as populations are uprooted in the process of the disentanglement, either through voluntary migration or, more ominously, as a result of forcible 'ethnic cleansing'.

These are serious concerns and the first part of my argument in this chapter will be devoted to a critique of the identity-based conception as inapposite to a world of mingling and migration, a world of fluid and compromised identities. In the second

---

[1] Kymlicka, W., this volume, 381.

part, I will argue that self-determination is defensible as a political principle only in the more moderate territorial form that I have mentioned.

Some will read this as overkill. Surely, it is only extreme versions of the identity-based conception that need to be criticized—because they are the ones that take us in the direction of geopolitical disruption and ethnic cleansing. Those evils, they will say, should not be used to discredit moderate versions of the identity-based approach. It is surely a relief to hear that proponents of the identity-based approach are not in favour of ethnic cleansing. And maybe there can be liberal versions of identity-based self-determination, accompanied by strong legal restraints against forced population movements, confiscation of land and businesses in a newly-constituted self-determining state and their redistribution to members of the favoured 'nation' or 'people', and other forms of discrimination against those who do not 'belong'. After all, self-determination is not the only principle in the constellation of political values recognized in international law; it must take its place alongside other principles such as human rights, democracy, and the rule of law.

Kymlicka also points out that defenders of self-determination rights for minority groups characteristically look for territorial autonomy rather than outright independence.[2] This is a second dimension of moderation. To use our earlier examples: Belgium already devolves a considerable amount of political and legal decision making to the Flemish and French-speaking regions precisely in order to accommodate moderate aspirations to self-government; Iraq, to the extent that it has a working constitution, recognizes the Kurdish area in the north as a highly autonomous, yet not fully independent region. Kymlicka is surely right that those who are worried by demands for independent statehood made on behalf of minority groups should not be *as* worried by demands for regional autonomy. He is also right to notice, however, that even territorial autonomy may be too disruptive a demand to be countenanced in certain areas of national and international instability.[3]

Also, there may still be versions of the abuses and difficulties that we see most vividly when identity-based self-determination is pushed to an extreme. Even if there are restraints on ethnic cleansing, expropriation, and discrimination, concerns about equal citizenship will remain a worry. If a state is newly constituted as a vehicle for the self-determination of one people, it will be hard to resist the impression that in some sense members of another people coexisting with them in the same society are second-class citizens, not full members of the polity which exists to vindicate the

---

[2] See Kymlicka, W., this volume, 384. There may be even weaker forms of cultural identity rights, requiring not much more than support, recognition and accommodation of distinct cultures within a multicultural society: see ibid. 381 citing ICCPR, article 27. For a discussion of this, see Waldron, J., 'One Law for All: The Logic of Cultural Accommodation', *Washington and Lee Law Review*, 59 (2002), 3 and Waldron, J., 'Minority Cultures and the Cosmopolitan Alternative', *University of Michigan Journal of Law Reform*, 25 (1992), 751.

[3] See Kymlicka, W., this volume, 385–7.

nationhood of this particular people. The situation of Israeli Arabs is a case in point: though Israel does not speak of second-class citizenship, Arab citizens of Israel are subject to a number of legal disabilities and they have to make a life for themselves in society in which an identity which is not theirs is strongly affirmed as the *raison d'être* of the state, and affirmed against an 'other' with whom they—the Israeli Arabs—are always in danger of being identified. Proponents of moderate versions of identity-based self-determination may condemn this as an abuse. But actually it is perfectly consistent with the overall logic of the identity-based approach. If the state is conceived—in however humane a spirit—as the possession of a particular people, its status *vis-à-vis* other peoples coexisting in the same territory is bound to be problematic.

Of course the impact will be lessened in cases where a people have sought only territorial autonomy, not full statehood. Outsiders living in their midst may feel vaguely like second-class citizens *in that region*, but they will not necessarily feel that way with regard to their country as a whole. Still they will know that this region has been demarcated, and separated to a certain extent from the rest of the state in a way that pays primary attention to the political and cultural needs of others, not them. No doubt federalism and decentralization are good things in general; but some may wish that their country had been divided into autonomous regions on some neutral basis other than identity.

In fairness I should add that of course it is something like this feeling—probably a much less benign version of it—that motivates minorities to seek regional autonomy in the first place. *They* have had the experience of not really belonging; *they* have been treated like second-class citizens; and now the boot is on the other foot with regard to members of the overall national majority who happened to have remained in the minority's autonomous region. The Québecois felt like outsiders in Anglo-dominated Canada; but now the measure of autonomy they have secured for Quebec makes English-speaking Canadians living in Montreal feel as though *they* don't belong. And no doubt if a measure of civic autonomy were granted to certain English–speaking suburbs of Montréal, giving them relief (say) from language restrictions, Francophones living in those areas would feel like second-class members of the neighbourhood. The iterations have a sort of fractal quality, whose regress reflects the point I mentioned before: peoples and communities are inevitably intermingled. We should acknowledge that the first step down this road is usually an insensitive assertion of national identity on the part of a country's overall majority group. That is what starts the rot, and of course it is a little unfair to wait until *minorities* invoke identity-based self-determination rights before criticizing the idea. This is why I think it is worth developing the critique at a very general level, taking on not just the extreme forms of identity-based self-determination, but all its forms: extreme and moderate, national and ethnic, majoritarian or minority.

II. Identity-Based Self-Determination

The demand for self-determination is backed up by all sorts of reasons, some of them having to do with historical memories of self-government, some with the indignity of being governed by people who would not dream of allowing themselves to be governed by you, some with the atrocious record of existing states in the way they repress and exploit minorities. As Kymlicka puts it:

Historically, ethnocultural and religious diversity has been characterized by a range of illiberal and undemocratic relations—including relations of conqueror and conquered; colonizer and colonized; settler and indigenous; racialized and unmarked; normalized and deviant; civilized and backward; ally and enemy; master and slave.[4]

That we might say is the negative case in favour of self-determination: it is simply that the experience of the domination of one people by another has been so bad.

Affirmatively, as Kymlicka says, '[t]he task for all liberal democracies has been to turn this catalogue of uncivil relations into relationships of liberal-democratic citizenship'.[5] But he immediately goes on to criticize any attempt to do this through the imposition of a single undifferentiated model of citizenship on all individuals. Why, we may ask, would that be a bad thing? What is lost if we establish and secure a genuinely liberal model of citizenship and human and constitutional rights in a state comprising a variety of ethnic and cultural groups, without any legal or political differentiation in terms of group membership?

The answer, I think—an answer which is assumed rather than argued for by Kymlicka in this essay (though he and others have argued for it elsewhere[6])—is that one of the functions of political community is supposed to be the preservation and nourishing of a particular culture or way of life, and this function will not adequately be performed if the law of a society or its conception of citizenship does not accord significance to individuals' membership of ethnic or cultural groups. I do not accept this argument, and I shall criticize it in what follows. I will respond to two steps of the argument: to the claim that (a) the particularity of a given culture or way of life is of great importance to individuals, even conceived as liberal individualists conceive them, i.e. as persons making and pursuing lives of their own; and to the claim that (b) those for whom a given culture or way of life has this importance need to have a significant degree of political control over its development and over the environment in which it exists. Claim (b) is obviously the most important one for international law; but (a) is its indispensable backdrop.

---

[4] Kymlicka, W., this volume, 379.   [5] Ibid. 380.

[6] See Kymlicka, W., *Liberalism, Community, and Culture* (Oxford: Clarendon Press, 1989); Kymlicka, W., *Multicultural Citizenship* (Oxford: Clarendon Press, 1995), and Margalit, A. and Raz, J., 'National Self-Determination', *Journal of Philosophy*, 87 (1990), 439.

(a) The importance of culture and culturally defined goods and options for individuals is incontestable. When individuals make choices about the way they want to live their lives, the options and the values they consider do not come out of nowhere. They exist as 'definite ideals and forms of life that have been developed and tested by innumerable individuals, sometimes for generations'.[7] As Kymlicka puts it:

Different ways of life are not simply different patterns of physical movements. The physical movements only have meaning to us because they are identified as having significance by our *culture*, because they fit into some pattern of activities which is culturally recognized as a way of leading one's life.[8]

It follows from this, says Kymlicka, that we ought to be 'concerned with the fate of cultural structures . . . because it's only through having a rich and secure cultural structure that people can become aware, in a vivid way, of the options available to them, and intelligently examine their value'.[9]

A similar argument has been made by Joseph Raz. Raz too says that individual flourishing depends on the availability of an array of socially defined options for individuals to pursue in their lives.[10] He draws attention to the importance for individuals of what he calls 'encompassing groups'—groups whose cultures define a menu of choices extending more or less across every aspect of individual and communal life. Membership in such groups, he says, is 'of vital importance to individuals', because it is only through being socialized in a culture that one can 'tap the options which give life a meaning'.[11]

As I have said, the basic thesis here is incontestable. But it does not follow that the flourishing of any particular way of life has the importance that step (a) of the argument requires (and step (b) presupposes). A given individual needs an array of culturally defined options in which to express and consummate his autonomy. But is it necessary for all the options she considers to be located in one and the same encompassing culture? As I have said elsewhere: 'We need cultural meanings; but we don't need homogenous cultural frameworks. . . . We need culture, but we don't need cultural integrity'.[12] Life in a modern multicultural society includes elements of many different cultures, but their boundaries tend to blur, they are each permeable to influence from the others and their purity and independence are inevitably compromised.[13] As a result it is harder to see each culture as separate

[7] This phrase is from Rawls, J., *A Theory of Justice*, (Cambridge, Mass.: Harvard University Press, 1971), 563–4.

[8] Kymlicka, W., *Liberalism, Community, and Culture* (above, n. 6), 65.   [9] Ibid.

[10] Raz, J., *The Morality of Freedom* (Oxford: Clarendon Press, 1986), 203–7.

[11] Raz, J., 'Multiculturalism', in Raz, J., *Ethics in the Public Domain: Essays in the Morality of Law and Politics* (Oxford: Clarendon Press), 177.

[12] Waldron, J., 'Minority Cultures and the Cosmopolitan Alternative' (above, n. 2), 786.

[13] That this *is* the case I think undeniable. Is it something to be deplored or lamented? I don't think so. The juxtaposition, confrontation, intermingling, and *mélange* of cultures that characterizes modern multicultural societies is a good thing: its raggedness, its infiltrations, and the indistinctness of cultural boundaries to which it

from the others or to trace the trajectory of its distinct growth. There are still an immense number of culturally-defined options to choose from; but the options present themselves kaleidoscopically as a variegated array, rather than as a coherent menu of choices provided as parts of a coherent way of life.

Even to the extent that we *can* identify distinct cultures in a multicultural society, and even if a given person thinks of herself as 'belonging' to one culture rather than another, it is not obvious that the integrity of *that* culture is indispensable for the individual's flourishing. People pick and choose among options furnished by a variety of cultures, including cultures that are not 'their own'. They may locate their religious practice and their family ties, their food and recreation in the culture to which they take themselves to 'belong', while looking elsewhere for their politics, their career, and their recreation. I am not even sure that any particular option is always associated with a single culture: a given option may be a hybrid, a product of the overlap between two cultures, or it may reflect the necessity of living with one foot in both camps. Certainly, some people may *prefer* to make all their choices from an array of options defined by a single culture, but that is insufficient to establish that the flourishing of particular cultures is indispensable for meaningful choice or autonomy. (It is certainly insufficient for the purposes of international law.)

How do the defenders of the identity-based conception respond to this point? Raz, who maintains that all the options over which an individual's autonomy ranges need to be structured by a single encompassing culture, says this in part because he thinks that the social practices which constitute options do not 'come one by one'.[14] We should not think of culturally-defined options as independent of one another; we should think, he says, in terms of nets of interlocking practices, integrated with one another in a densely connected array. But I am still not convinced. Suppose Raz is right about interlocking options. Then an individual choosing what to do with her life would have to recognize that a choice of option A from culture C_1 brings a lot of other C_1-baggage with it, whereas a choice of option B from culture C_2 brings with it a lot of C_2-baggage. But still she might choose from a set comprising A and B. Moreover it need not be the case that A brings with it the whole of C_1 and B the whole of C_2. A and B might be cultural fragments, albeit each avulsively trailing a ragged cluster of other cultural materials. I believe that the 'menus' from which people make their autonomous choices have exactly this disorderly character. Of course there may be tensions: my choice of career may make my religious practice difficult in a way that would not have been true had I chosen a career/religion package from the same culture. But people often tolerate or relish a certain tension between different aspects of their lives.

gives rise are all healthy. This is how cultures change and grow, when ragged elements of one culture are brought into relation with ragged elements of another in the real lives of complicated flesh-and-blood individuals in multicultural societies. See ibid. 761–3 and 777–81 and see also the chapter on 'Cultural Contamination', in Appiah, A., *Cosmopolitanism: Ethics in a World of Strangers* (New York: Norton, 2006).

[14] Raz, J., 'Multiculturalism' (above, n. 11), 177.

Raz pursues a version of the same argument when he considers the coordination of one person's choice with those of others around him. When the menu of options for children, for example, differs substantially from the menu from which their parents made life-choices, then we get interpersonal incoherence and the aspiration of every parent 'to understand their children, share their world, and remain close to them' can be frustrated.[15] This concern makes sense if we imagine a multicultural society shaped in the following way: one encompassing group with a traditional culture, C_1, largely intact, lives in the countryside and there are distant cities in which another more modern culture, C_2, is aggressively flourishing. Migrating from the one *milieu* to the other may well be painful and a family in the countryside, some of whose members have moved to the city, may indeed face the difficulties that Raz mentions. But that picture is increasingly unrealistic. What we see in the countries in which these claims are actually put forward are the multicultural *remnants* of various cultures, interacting *everywhere* with one another and with the more aggressive culture of modernity. Everywhere there are more or less modern versions of the traditional culture, and more or less compromised versions of the modernist culture. *Everyone* has a foot in both camps, and the gap between parents and children is at most a difference of degree. Their boundaries of the cultures are indistinct, there is already considerable mutual infiltration; yet people succeed in finding their footing in a *mélange* of traditional and modern elements.

Kymlicka's response is slightly different. He plays down the imperative of purity for the cultures whose flourishing he thinks is important. In his view, what I described above in my characterization of a multicultural *mélange* is just a new culture (C_{1+2}), which exists for a new encompassing group—a group which happens to be a multicultural society. A societal culture, he says, can be 'an open and pluralistic one, which borrows whatever it finds worthwhile in other cultures, integrates it into its own practices, and passes it on to the subsequent generations'.[16] Nevertheless Kymlicka claims that if it exists as *a* culture, the case for preserving it is exactly the same.[17]

But now the distinction between the importance of culturally-defined options and the importance of a single culture to particular individuals has just collapsed. If we insist that the options in a given array are all part of the same culture *simply on the ground that they are available to people in a given society*, then we trivialize the individuation of cultures beyond any theoretical interest, certainly beyond the interest of an identity-based conception of self-determination for the purposes of international law. What becomes now of the rest of Kymlicka's argument about the importance to individuals of *their cultures* being maintained? 'Their culture' is now simply the multicultural *milieu* in which they find themselves; its prosperity is more or less given.

---

[15] Raz, J., 'Multiculturalism' (above n. 11, 178). See also Margalit, A. and Raz, J., 'National Self-Determination' (above, n. 6), 133–4.

[16] Kymlicka, W., *Multicultural Citizenship* (above, n. 6), 211.   [17] Ibid. 85.

It may seem odd to have devoted so much space to this question about the individuation of separate cultures in an essay on self-determination in international law. There are, as I said, conceptions of self-determination which do not require us to go down this road or steer into these controversies and difficulties at all. I will consider what I referred to earlier as the territorial approach in section III. And there are identity-based approaches to self-determination which just take it for granted that the preservation of a people's distinct culture or way of life is a good thing. Fortunately, in the modern debate initiated by Kymlicka, this tends to be argued for rather than simply asserted. So I have taken the opportunity to scrutinize and respond to articulate and well-argued versions of the identity-based approach.

The discussion so far has been about step (a) of the argument. But it is relevant to international law because of what is asserted in step (b): that the valuable existence of a distinct culture can be safeguarded only if the people whose culture it is are in charge—legally and politically—of its growth and development and the environment in which it does its work.[18] Or, if full self-determination is for some reason impracticable or impolitic, then something like regional autonomy seems to be demanded. The idea is that the valuable existence of a distinct culture can be safeguarded only if the people whose culture it is have a degree of legal and political control over it which is greater than the control they would have simply as citizens participating as equals along with all others in an undifferentiated political system. The point of such control need not be the literal preservation of the culture as it happens to be at any given time. But it can involve decisions which shield the culture from certain forms of shock—for example the shock of a sudden wave of immigration. Or it can involve decisions to control or limit outside influences on a culture—filtering access to the Internet, for example, or limiting proselytization by foreign religions, or placing restrictions on foreign ownership of land. Or it can involve decisions to control cultural life itself—through subsidies, education policy, language laws, and so on. There is probably no way of ensuring that cultural change is utterly autarchic; but it is possible for a people to exercise a degree of conscious control on the impact of exogenous influences.

That, as I understand it, is what step (b) of the argument involves. Of course, if step (a) fails, then step (b) fails with it. If humans do not need secure cultural frameworks (but only a variegated array of culturally defined options), then we need not adjust our sense of the appropriate basis for organizing political communities and political boundaries to ensure that each distinct cultural framework is taken care of by its own people. The case for self-determination is predicated on the assumption that the members of an identity-group have an essential investment in the integrity of their culture and that they need empowerment to protect it from

---

[18] Margalit, A. and Raz, J., 'National Self-Determination' (above, n. 6), 440–1, defend a slightly weaker version than this: the right to self-determination is a right to determine whether the culture of the group would be better safeguarded by the political independence of the group or by continued involvement in a large political entity.

being overwhelmed or unduly influenced by other cultures. But once we question how essential that investment is, then its being properly protected comes to seem more like a preference than a necessity. This is clear both for the Raz version and the Kymlicka version of the claim we have been discussing. As we saw, Kymlicka retreats to the view that a societal culture may be open and pluralistic, with none of the unity that is usually associated with the idea of a distinct particular culture. If this is the case, then why should any attention be paid to whether a given change in that 'culture' is appropriate or desirable? No guardianship seems to be needed for the culture as a whole, because 'it' is nothing much more than the sum of its parts at any given time. Raz's account looks potentially more robust; but as we have seen, Raz cannot make the case that the members of a given group need to safeguard their own culture in the way that step (b) envisages: what needs to be safeguarded is the existence of particular options or clumps of options. Since the totality of the options that need to be safeguarded is not associated with any group in particular, it is not clear why the members of any group have any particular claim to guardianship.

A somewhat different version of (b) may look at the political aspect of the culture itself. Margalit and Raz consider the possibility that participation in the distinct political culture of an encompassing group may be an important expressive aspect of one's membership of that group.[19] If the group is not self-determining or does not enjoy a degree of autonomy, then participation in what was once the political side of the culture will become a mere ceremony or charade. How impressed one is by this argument will depend to a large extent on what one thinks in general about the expressive theory of political participation, and whether one thinks societies should be organized and individuated in order to make a particular kind of expressive politics possible.

III. TERRITORIAL SELF-DETERMINATION

If we abandon identity-based conceptions, must we give up self-determination altogether? In this section I want to defend an alternative approach—the one I outlined in the second paragraph of this chapter. It rests on a very different view of what politics and political community are for.

I call my approach 'territorial', because it begins by postulating that the world is already divided up into separate bounded territories, with a population in each. Of course the postulate is question-begging, because we use the principle of self-determination in part to figure out where boundaries should be drawn and what the distinct national territories of the world should be. But it is also worth noting, even at this early stage, that only the most fanatical adherent of the principle of

---

[19] Margalit, A. and Raz, J., 'National Self-Determination' (above, n. 6), 451–3.

self-determination would say that the operation of the principle is the *only* basis on which political boundaries should be set. Many people believe that existing boundaries should be respected and maintained, no matter what the requirements of self-determination, simply because the costs of messing with them are so high. Others believe that there is a strong *presumption* in favour of existing boundaries, though perhaps not a conclusive presumption. People in both categories think that even though existing boundaries are the result of historical accident or the upshot of processes we deplore, still the cost to peace and the disruption involved in altering them would be far greater than any benefits secured in terms of their rationalization under the self-determination principle.

In fact that is not all there is to my position. I will say something shortly to mitigate the question-begging character of my territorial postulate; my conception is predicated on an independent understanding of how the territorial character of political community might in principle be determined. But it is easier to set out the conception initially with this postulate in place.

So assume, initially, a world of well-defined territories. The territorial version of the self-determination principle holds that the people of each territory have a right to work out their own constitutional, political, and legal arrangements without interference from the outside. They should not be ruled or dominated or have constitutional, political, or legal arrangements dictated to them by the inhabitants of some other territory. They should not be colonized, for example, at least not if the colonization involves ruling them from the outside, in the way that (say) Mozambique was ruled by the government of Portugal until 1975, for example, or in the way Ireland was ruled by the Government of the United Kingdom until 1922, or in the way the Ottoman Empire ruled Palestine until the end of the First World War.

According to the territorial conception, the phrase 'the people of a territory' simply refers to all the individual men and women who happen to inhabit the territory in question. It is not assumed that they have any relation to the land much stronger than habitation: they live there, they are making a life there, maybe they were born there and are raising a family there. Of course individual societies will have different rules about citizenship and immigration. (How these rules are set up may well reflect the influence of the one or the other conception of self-determination.) But so far as the broad principle of self-determination is concerned, a people's right to determine what happens in a given territory is not predicated on their having an immemorial or ancestral relation to the land nor on its being an integral part of their shared culture or way of life. Of course, inasmuch as they live *here*, the land will be part of the subject-matter of their self-determination. As inhabitants they claim the right to determine, for example, the basis on which property rights in land are established or the basis on which disputes about resource use or distributive justice are resolved. But the territorial conception does not predicate that right on any relation of people to land that is deeper than ordinary habitation. It will not for example privilege the situation of aboriginal or indigenous inhabitants. In his essay in this volume, Will Kymlicka regards the special claims of indigenous peoples as prime examples of self-determination claims.[20] This is partly because of the distinctiveness of their culture. But I suspect it also has to do with their special ancestral relation to the land they inhabited prior to European settlement. The territorial conception of self-determination, by contrast, does not regard such relations as special. The descendants of indigenous peoples are no less but no more inhabitants of the lands that their ancestors dominated than are the descendants of European settlers. The territorial conception does not privilege anyone's political relation to the land simply on account of its being 'first' or 'prior' to anyone else's. And it certainly does not welcome the deadly conflict that would be occasioned in a country like India, for example, by asking which among a myriad of non-European inhabitants should count as the indigenous people of the land.[21]

Because it does not assume that the entitlement to self-determination is vested in a 'people' with a distinctive identity of its own, the territorial approach will see it more in the light of an individual right, albeit an individual right necessarily exercised in common with the similar rights of millions of other persons. It is like the right to democracy in this regard. It is not the right of a group; instead it comprises the rights of millions of individuals participating in a common exercise of collective decision, under conditions of equality and fairness.

It is important, however, not to identify self-determination and democracy. The right of self-determination is prior to democracy, for it includes the right to decide whether to have a democracy around here, and if so, what sort of democracy to have. Self-determination is violated when we forcibly impose democracy on a country from the outside. Those who favour what is sometimes called 'humanitarian intervention' need to take care, not just that they do not violate sovereignty (for which they usually care very little), but also that they do not violate the principle of self-determination (for which, in this form, they ought to care a lot).[22]

If the territorial approach to self-determination is not based on any particular ethnic or cultural conception of 'the people', and if it does not accrue on the basis of any *special* relation to the land except the contingent fact of habitation—then what principle is it based on? Is it simply a pragmatic doctrine of keeping the peace and avoiding ethnic cleansing? Or is it based on a political philosophy that is as foundational as the philosophy of identity politics that it opposes?

---

[20] Kymlicka, W., this volume, 387.

[21] See also Waldron, J., 'Indigeneity? First Peoples and Last Occupancy', *New Zealand Journal of Public and International Law*, 1 (2003), 55; and Kingsbury, B., 'Indigenous Peoples in International Law', *American Journal of International Law*, 92 (1998), 414.

[22] See also the discussion by Walzer, M., in Miller, D., (ed.), *Thinking Politically: Essays in Political Theory* (New Haven: Yale University Press, 2007), 237 ff.

I believe there is a real foundational difference at stake here. The identity-based conception assumes that states should be formed among people who are already well disposed to one another, on the basis of what they share in their ethnic or cultural identity.[23] The territorial approach rejects that assumption. Foundationally, it assumes that the point of setting up a political community is to preclude or resolve conflict,[24] by providing a legal framework in which interests can be pursued, disputes resolved, justice done, actions coordinated, and public goods secured. If anything, this conception of political community rests upon an assumption of mutual antipathy or least diffidence; it is more like a Hobbesian conception. The idea is that we form political community with those with whom are likely to fight, rather than with those whom we already like and who are, in their identity, already like us. Law's function, on this conflict-and-process oriented model is to keep the peace and provide for cooperation among people who are not well disposed to one another already. Like a market economy it facilitates cooperation among strangers and its formalities are supposed to provide security and a framework for fair dealing when other bases of social lubrication may be lacking.[25] Who needs to join together in this way? If we loosen the grip of identity, if all we have is a potential Hobbesian war of all against all, can we say of any *particular* group of people that they ought to come together and set up a political system? Or must we look for a political community on a cosmopolitan scale? Thomas Hobbes never answered this question and subsequent liberal thinkers followed him in that. There is a dearth of theorizing about the boundaries of political communities in the liberal tradition: writers in the social contract tradition proceed as though the group whose members contract together to solve the problem of conflict were predetermined; but they do not say what the basis of that predetermination is. This has made it very difficult to map liberal contractarian concerns onto determinate principles of territory and self-determination. The best that the social contract theorists have come up with is the principle of individual consent. Locke, for example, simply assumes that there are a number of people in the state of nature who desire to form a political community with one another. This, he says, 'any number of men may do, because

[23] Mill, J. S., *Considerations on Representative Government* (Buffalo: Prometheus Books, 1991), 308, defines a notion of nationality which is based on a more abstract idea of affinity than this: 'A portion of mankind may be said to constitute a Nationality if they are united among themselves by common sympathies which do not exist between them and any others—which make them co-operate with each other more willingly than with other people, desire to be under the same government, and desire that it should be government by themselves or a portion of themselves exclusively'.

[24] Hobbes, T., *On the Citizen*, Tuck, R. and Silverthorne, M. (ed.) (Cambridge: Cambridge University Press, 1998), 74. What interested Hobbes in the foundations of a political system was 'how and by what stages, in the passion for self-preservation, a number of natural persons *from fear of each other* have coalesced into one civil person to which we have given the name of commonwealth' (my emphasis).

[25] Cf. the suggestion in Smith, A., *An Inquiry into the Nature and Causes of the Wealth of Nations*, Cannan, E. (ed.), (London: Methuen, 1904), 18, about the impersonal basis of market economy.

it injures not the freedom of the rest'.[26] That sounds all very well, but it has the unwelcome and unrealistic consequence that in principle *any* group of people who want self-determination are entitled to it simply on the basis of their shared desire.

We do not get a more helpful account in the liberal tradition until the political philosophy of Immanuel Kant, and even then a lot of work has to be done to fill out the position he propounds. Kant's view is that people who find themselves quarrelling over the just use of resources are required, morally, to enter into political community with one another, so that their disputes can be resolved consistently within a single coherent framework of laws. People who live in one another's vicinity—in Kant's phrase 'unavoidably side by side'—are likely to want to take possession of material resources (land or water, for example) as their individual property.[27] But none of us can do that without coming into conflict with others who may want the very patch of land or the very source of water that we are appropriating, and who might have their own theory about how such things are appropriately distributed. Our proximity to each other will therefore generate conflict and we need to establish a basis on which such issues can be resolved in the name of us all.[28]

Why is proximity so important in this account? Disputes can flare up even among people who are distant from one another. Is there something about the nature or intensity of the disputes that flare up locally that explains the need for territorially distinct legal systems? A number of points are relevant here. First, we know that the earth has not been settled homogenously. Some regions are more favourable to habitation than others. The very resources that attract people unevenly to particular locations will also represent occasions for dispute. Secondly, as well as issues of resource use, we tend to have our most frequent dealings, interactions, and exchanges with those close to us. There may be occasional interactions with others elsewhere, but those close to us will be repeat players. Thirdly, there are simple problems of mutual abutment and obstruction, ranging from our physically running into each other to the externalities imposed by the various activities that we perform.

It is true that the sporadic disputes I may have with people all over the world also need to be regulated by law. But showing that a dispute needs to be regulated by law is not the same as showing that its regulation requires *a state*. A state involves a particular kind of law; it is, in Hans Kelsen's words, 'a relatively centralized legal order'.[29] The state presents itself as an interlocking array of all-purpose norms, given

[26] Locke, J., *Two Treatises of Government*, Laslett, P. (ed.) (Cambridge: Cambridge University Press, 1998), sect. 95.

[27] Kant, I., *The Metaphysics of Morals*, Gregor, M. (trans.), (Cambridge: Cambridge University Press, 1991), 124.

[28] See also Waldron, J., 'Kant's Legal Positivism', *Harvard Law Review*, 109 (1996), 1535; and Waldron, J., 'Kant's Theory of the State', in Kleingeld, P. (ed.), *Immanuel Kant: Toward Perpetual Peace and Other Writings on Politics, Peace and History* (New Haven: Yale University Press, 2006), for discussions of the Kantian doctrine.

[29] Kelsen, H., *The Pure Theory of Law* (Berkeley and Los Angeles: University of California Press, 1967), 290.

coherence by a constitution, and associated with a degree of centralization that enables us to personify the legal order and envisage someone's taking responsibility for the overall system of norms. Whatever law exists on a cosmopolitan or transnational basis is not centralized or personified in that way.

I think there is a strong case for saying that the frequency, density, and mutual entanglement of the disputes that arise endemically in a given location or territory makes the legal arrangement we call a *state* particularly appropriate for this context. Among those who live unavoidably side-by-side in a particular territory, the potential for conflict is dense and entangled because of frequent and multi-faceted dealings among the same class of persons. In this setting, what is needed are standing arrangements to deal with endemic conflict, providing a basis on which the resolution of one conflict might help people arrange their dealings in future to avoid other conflicts.[30] We should remember too that people in a given location will not just repeat conflicts of the same kinds with one another but many different kinds of conflict. I buy apples from a neighbouring orchardist, but I also conflict with him over water-rights, and he objects to the chemicals I use in my garden, and I send my children to work part-time as fruit pickers, and one of them may marry one of his children and subsequently divorce, and so on. The resolution of any one of these conflicts may well have a bearing on the resolution of others. Some entity must take responsibility for the big picture, for what Rawlsians would call 'the basic structure' that unites in a coherent whole many different aspects of justice-relations among persons.[31]

Why is it important that all this be sorted out by the very people among whom this thicket of potential disputes arises? Why wouldn't the imposition of a legal framework by an imperial power solve this problem? It would, but not in a respectful way, not in a way that respected the fact that the people themselves among whom these disputes may arise have a perspective on their solution. This is why the contractarian side of Kant's approach remains important. He does not share the Lockean view that we have discretion to pick and choose whom we might enter into political relations with. And the Kantian position certainly denies that people are entitled to do pick and choose on the basis of identity. Political and legal arrangements are set up to deal with conflict that arises from our proximity to one another in a given territory, not to house identity; and since conflict is at its most intense in particular localities, political and legal arrangements have, in the first instance, on this model, a necessary territorial dimension. When you cannot avoid living side-by-side with others, Kant says, 'you ought to leave the state of nature and proceed with them into a rightful condition, that is, a condition of [positive

---

[30] See the discussion of the relation between reasoned elaboration of norms and their self-application by potential disputants in Hart, H. M. and Sacks, A. M., *The Legal Process: Basic Problems in the Making and Application of Law*, Eskridge, W. and Frickey, P. (ed.), (New York: Foundation Press, 1994).

[31] Rawls, J., *A Theory of Justice* (above, n. 7), 7–11.

law]'.[32] Still, it is for the people themselves to do this, that is, to respond to the moral imperative to establish a civil constitution and a system of law. The task is a morally necessary one, but that does not mean that it does not matter who performs it. The task arises because each of the persons involved has a sense of justice—albeit one that may be at variance with another's. The challenge is to find a way that respects that fact, while solving the problem it gives rise to. The Kantian conception does this by maintaining that the problem of disagreement must be solved, while at the same time insisting that it must be solved by those among whom it arises.[33]

I find this model very attractive. Of course one might quibble with the territorial foundation: that certain groups of people focus their aspirations competitively on the same set of resources located in the same space may be thought to be a product of political organization, not a precondition of it. I believe it is both: I believe that the territorial organization of states and legal systems is best understood *in the first instance* as a response to territorially local contestation, though I acknowledge that this is certainly reinforced by political organization. What I have been trying to do in this section is set out the foundational model that underlies the territorial approach. But of course, as we have already noted, its main application in the modern world will be pragmatic in relation to existing boundaries rather than foundational in setting them *de novo*.

The account I have given is not a tidy one, and its direct application in the modern world would be problematic. In the modern world, it makes most sense to adopt a pragmatic and generally respectful stance towards existing territorial demarcations. In much the same way, modern versions of identity-based self-determination are not pure: they too must confront the fact the real world is never as tidy as their culturalist models suggest. Nevertheless, in both cases, it is useful to articulate some foundational ideas and to consider how they differ from one another.

It is probably also true that the differences between the two approaches to self-determination are more ideal-typic than real. Each may approach the other in various regards, inasmuch as culture and identity may grow out of proximity. Still, I hope this consideration of the foundational differences between the two conceptions has been helpful in explaining why they continue to adopt different approaches to the untidiness of the real-world. One view wishes that each people with a culture were in charge of its own affairs, and looks for an acceptable moderate version of that; the other wishes that the inhabitants of each territory could be left alone to fulfill their common duty of making provision for the resolution of disputes and it

---

[32] Kant, I., *The Metaphysics of Morals* (above, n. 27), 121–2. At 77, Kant writes: one must 'be permitted to constrain everyone else with whom he comes into conflict about whether an external object is his or another's to enter along with him into a civil constitution'.

[33] Kant's authoritarianism is not incompatible with this. See Waldron, J., 'Kant's Theory of the State' (above, n. 28), 194–7. As we have seen, self-determination does not commit us to democracy, but it does require that the choice between democracy and authoritarianism be made in some sense by all the inhabitants of the vicinity.

looks for a pragmatic version of that. But still there is a difference, and in the end it is normative and ethical. The comparative advantage of the territorial approach is that, in its pragmatic version, it does not feel any pull towards outcomes that might only be achieved by unacceptable methods, whereas the identity-based approach has to constantly battle this tendency.

SECTION X

INTERNATIONAL ECONOMIC LAW

THE ROLE OF INTERNATIONAL LAW IN REPRODUCING MASSIVE POVERTY

T H O M A S   P O G G E

I. INTRODUCTION

Each day, some 50,000 human beings—mostly children, mostly female and mostly people of colour—die from starvation, diarrhoea, pneumonia, tuberculosis, malaria, measles, perinatal conditions, and other poverty-related causes. Most of this death toll and the much larger poverty problem it epitomizes are avoidable through minor modifications in the global order that would entail only slight reductions in the incomes of the affluent. Such reforms have been blocked by the governments of the affluent countries which, advancing their own interests and those of their corporations and citizens, are designing and imposing a global institutional order that, continually and foreseeably, produces vast excesses of severe poverty and premature poverty-related deaths.

There are three main strategies for denying this charge. One can deny that variations in the design of the global order have any significant impact on the evolution of severe poverty worldwide. Failing this, one can claim that the present global order is close to optimal in terms of poverty avoidance. Should this strategy fail as well, one can still contend that the present global order is not *causing* severe poverty but merely failing to alleviate such poverty as much as it could. I discuss these three strategies in order.

II. THE PURELY DOMESTIC POVERTY THESIS

Those who wish to deny that variations in the design of the global institutional order have a significant impact on the evolution of severe poverty explain such poverty by reference to national or local factors alone. John Rawls is a prominent example. He claims that when societies fail to thrive, 'the problem is commonly the nature of the public political culture and the religious and philosophical traditions that underlie its institutions. The great social evils in poorer societies are likely to be oppressive government and corrupt elites'.[1] He adds that:

the causes of the wealth of a people and the forms it takes lie in their political culture and in the religious, philosophical and moral traditions that support the basic structure of their political and social institutions, as well as in the industriousness and cooperative talents of its members, all supported by their political virtues . . . the political culture of a burdened society is all-important . . . Crucial also is the country's population policy.[2]

Accordingly, Rawls holds that our moral responsibility with regard to severe poverty abroad can be fully described as a 'duty of assistance'.[3]

In response, one might detail the continuing legacies of colonialism, slavery, and genocide which have shaped the political culture of many presently poor societies. Leaving these aside, let me focus on the empirical view that, in the post-colonial era, the causes of the *persistence* of severe poverty, and hence the key to its eradication, lie within the poor countries themselves. Many find this view compelling in light of the great variation in how the former colonies have evolved over the last fifty years. Some of them have achieved solid growth and poverty reduction while others exhibit worsening poverty and declining *per capita* incomes. Is it not obvious that such strongly divergent national trajectories must be due to differing *domestic* causal factors in the countries concerned? And is it not clear, then, that the persistence of severe poverty is due to local causes?

However oft-repeated and well received, this reasoning is fallacious. When national economic trajectories diverge, then there must indeed be local (country-specific) factors at work that explain the divergence. But it does not follow that global factors play no role. We can see this by considering a parallel case. There may be great variations in the performance of students in one class. These must be due to student-specific factors. Still, it does not follow that these 'local' factors fully explain the performance of a class. Teacher and classroom quality, teaching times, reading

---

[1] Rawls, J., 'The Law of Peoples', in Shute, S. and Hurley, S. (eds.), *On Human Rights, The Amnesty Lectures of 1993* (New York: Basic Books 1993), 77.

[2] Rawls, J., *The Law of Peoples, With 'The Idea of Public Reason Revisited'* (Cambridge, Mass.: Harvard University Press, 1999), 108.

[3] Ibid. 37–8, 106–20.

materials, libraries, and other 'global' factors may also play an important role. Dramatic contrasts of success and failure, among students or among less developed countries, do not then show global factors to be causally inert. In the former case, such global factors can greatly influence the overall progress of a class; they can influence the distribution of this progress by being differentially appropriate to the needs and interests of different students; and they can affect the student-specific factors, as when a sexist teacher causes or aggravates motivational deficits in his female students. Analogous to these three possibilities, global institutional factors may greatly influence the evolution of severe poverty worldwide.

Exposure of this popular fallacy does not, however, settle the issue. Dramatic divergences in national poverty trajectories do not prove that decisions about the design of global institutional arrangements do not exert a powerful influence on the evolution of severe poverty worldwide. But is there such an influence?

It is hard to doubt that there is. In the modern world, the traffic of international and even intra-national economic transactions is profoundly shaped by an elaborate system of treaties and conventions about trade, investments, loans, patents, copyrights, trademarks, double taxation, labour standards, environmental protection, use of seabed resources, and much else. These different parts of the present global institutional order realize highly specific design decisions within a vast space of alternative design possibilities. It is incredible on its face that all these alternative ways of structuring the world economy would have produced the same evolution in the overall incidence and geographical distribution of severe poverty.

III. THE PANGLOSSIAN VIEW OF THE PRESENT GLOBAL ORDER

If the design of the global institutional order makes a difference, then what has been the impact of the actual design of this order on the evolution of severe poverty worldwide? Here it is often claimed that we live, in this regard, in the best of all possible worlds: that the present global order is nearly optimal in terms of poverty avoidance.

A commonsense way of questioning this claim might develop a counterhypothesis in four steps. First, the interest in avoiding severe poverty is not the only interest to which those who negotiate the design of particular aspects of the global institutional order are sensitive. Such negotiators are likely to care also about their home government's political success and their compatriots' economic prosperity. Second, these nationalist interests are often in tension with the interest in global poverty avoidance. Third, when faced with such conflicts, negotiators for the affluent states generally give precedence to the interests of their own country's government, corporations, and citizens over the interests of the global poor. Fourth, with 75% of the world's social product,[4] the high-income countries enjoy great advantages in bargaining power and expertise, which enable their negotiators to deflect the design of the global order from what would be best for poverty avoidance. Given these four steps, we should expect the design of the global institutional order to reflect the shared interests of the governments, corporations, and citizens of the affluent countries more than the interest in global poverty avoidance, in so far as these interests conflict.

There is much evidence that this counter-hypothesis is true. The present rules favour the affluent countries by allowing them to continue protecting their markets through quotas, tariffs, anti-dumping duties, export credits and subsidies to domestic producers in ways that poor countries are not permitted, or cannot afford, to match.[5] Other important examples include the World Trade Organization (WTO) regulations on cross-border investment and intellectual property rights, such as the Trade-Related Aspects of Intellectual Property Rights (TRIPs) Treaty of 1995.[6]

Such asymmetrical rules increase the share of global economic growth going to the affluent and decrease the share going to the poor relative to what these shares would be under symmetrical rules of free and open competition. The asymmetries in the rules thus reinforce the very inequality that enables the governments of affluent countries to impose these asymmetries in the first place. Branko Milanovic[7] reports that real incomes of the poorest 5% of world population declined 20% in the 1988–93 period and another 23% during 1993–8, while real global *per capita* income increased by 5.2% and 4.8% respectively. In 1998, income inequality between the top and bottom 10% of humanity was 71:1 at purchasing power parities (PPPs) and 320:1 at market exchange rates.[8]

We can confirm and update his findings with later data. The World Bank reports that, in the high-income Organization for Economic Co-operation and Development (OECD) countries, household final consumption expenditure *per*

---

[4] World Bank, *World Development Report 2009* (New York: Oxford University Press, 2009), 353.

[5] The monstrosity of these subsidies is frequently lamented by establishment economists such as former World Bank chief economist Nick Stern (<siteresources.worldbank.org/INTRES/Resources/stern_speech_makingtr-workforpoor_nov2002.pdf>).

[6] See Pogge, T., *World Poverty and Human Rights, Cosmopolitan Responsibilities and Reforms* (2nd edn., Cambridge: Polity Press, 2008), ch. 9, and <www.cptech.org/ip>. All websites were most recently checked in Sept. 2008.

[7] Milanovic, B., *Worlds Apart, Measuring International and Global Inequality* (Princeton: Princeton University Press, 2005), 108.

[8] Ibid. 107–8. Many economists prefer to make such comparisons at PPPs. But market exchange rates are the more appropriate measure for estimating the influence (bargaining power and expertise) parties can bring to bear. Market exchange rates are also the appropriate measure for assessing the *avoidability* of poverty. For comparing standards of living, market exchange rates are indeed inappropriate. But PPPs are also problematic for assessing very low incomes because the poor must concentrate their consumption on basic necessities, which are cheaper in poor countries but not as affordable as PPPs would suggest. Reddy, S., and Pogge, T., 'How *Not* to Count the Poor', in Anand, S., Segal, P., and Stiglitz, J. (eds.), *Debates in the Measurement of Global Poverty* (Oxford: Oxford University Press, 2009). Also at www.socialanalysis.org.

capita (constant 2000 US Dollars) rose 56.3% in real terms during the period 1984–2004. Consumption expenditure reportedly rose a respectable 48.6% at the median, 36.2% at the 20th percentile, 32.6% at the 10th percentile, and a mere 9.6% over the entire 20-year period at the 1st percentile.[9] There is a clear pattern: global inequality is increasing, and the global poor are not participating proportionately in global economic growth. This pattern is further confirmed by trend data about malnutrition and poverty. The number of malnourished, reported annually by the United Nations Development Programme (UNDP), has in 2009 climbed to over 1 billion[10]—even while the ranks of the hungry are thinned by millions of deaths each year from poverty-related causes. For 1987–2005, Chen and Ravallion[11] report a 24% drop in the population living below $1.25 per day but a 8% *rise* in the population below $2.50 per day (2005 PPP).

Falling further and further behind, the global poor become ever more marginalized, with their interests ignored in both national and international decision-making. Annual spending power under $200 per person does not command much attention from international negotiators when *per capita* incomes in the affluent countries are some 200 times higher. And the interests of poor African countries do not carry much weight when the combined gross national incomes of 26 of them, representing over 400 million people, fall short of the annual sales volumes of the world's largest corporations.

Increasing income inequalities accumulate into even larger inequalities of wealth. A World Institute for Development Economics Research (WIDER) study[12] estimates that in 2000 the bottom 50% of the world's adults together had 1.1% of global wealth while the top 10% had 85.1% and the top 1% had 39.9%. The authors stress that their study may understate global wealth inequality because the super-rich are typically not captured in household surveys.[13]

These data should suffice to refute the Panglossian view: the present design of the global order is not optimal in terms of poverty avoidance. It is clear how this value could be better served: the poorest countries should receive financial support toward hiring experts to advise them how to articulate their interests in WTO negotiations, toward maintaining missions at WTO headquarters in Geneva, toward bringing cases before the WTO, and toward coping with all the regulations they are required

---

[9] See <iresearch.worldbank.org/PovcalNet/jsp/index.jsp> (16 June 2007). Full calculations are on file with the author.

[10] Food and Agriculture Organization of the United Nations, '1.02 Billion People Hungry,' News Release, June 19, 2009. At <www.fao.org/news/story/en/item/20568/icode/>. Compare also annual *Human Development Reports*, e.g. UNDP, *Human Development Report 2007/2008* (Houndsmills: Palgrave Macmillan, 2007), 90. Also at <http://hdr.undp.org/en/reports/global/hdr2007>.

[11] Chen, S., and Ravallion, M., 'The Developing World is Poorer than We Thought, but no Less Successful in the Fight against Poverty', table 7, *World Bank Policy Research Working Paper* WPS 4703 (Aug. 2008), available at econ.worldbank.org.

[12] Davies, J. B., Sandstrom, S., Shorrocks, A., and Wolff, E. N., *The World Distribution of Household Wealth*, WIDER, 5 Dec. 2006, app. 1, table 10a. At <www.wider.unu.edu>.

[13] Ibid. 31.

to implement. Poor countries should face reduced barriers to their exports and should not have to pay for market access by collecting billions in economic rents for 'intellectual property'. The WTO Treaty should include a global minimum wage and minimal global constraints on working hours and working conditions in order to halt the current 'race to the bottom' where poor countries competing for foreign investment must outbid one another by offering ever more exploitable workforces. The affluent countries should be required to pay for the negative externalities we impose on the poor: for the pollution we have produced over many decades and the resulting effects on their environment and climate, for the rapid depletion of natural resources, and for the violence caused by our demand for drugs and our war on drugs.

Examples could be multiplied. There clearly are feasible variations to the present global order that would dramatically reduce severe poverty worldwide, far below the current, staggering figures. This order is *not* optimal in terms of poverty avoidance.

IV. Is the Present Global Order Merely Less Beneficial Than It Might Be?

Can one say that the global institutional order, though clearly and greatly sub-optimal in terms of poverty avoidance, is nonetheless not harming the global poor, not violating their human rights?

This third defence strategy appeals to something like the distinction between acts and omissions. It seeks to diminish the moral significance of the rich states' decision to impose the present design of the global order rather than a foreseeably more poverty-avoiding alternative by assigning this decision the status of a mere omission. Now the rich countries are clearly active in formulating the global economic rules they want, in pressing for their acceptance, and in pursuing their enforcement. The defence strategy must then apply the act/omission distinction at another place: not to how the relevant governments are related to the global rules, but to how these global rules are related to excessive poverty. The idea must be that the rules governing the world economy are not actively causing excessive poverty, thus harming and killing people, but merely passively failing to prevent severe poverty, failing to protect people from harm.

The distinction between acts and omissions is difficult enough when applied to individual and collective agents. Its application to social institutions and rules is at first baffling. When more premature deaths occur under a system of rules than would occur under a feasible alternative, we might say that there are excessive deaths under the existing regime. But how can we distinguish between those excessive deaths that the existing rules *bring about* and those that these rules merely *fail to prevent*? Let us examine three ideas for how this defence strategy can be made to work.

1. First Idea: Invoking Baseline Comparisons

There is much debate about the apparently empirical question of whether 'globalization' is harming or benefiting the global poor. Harm and benefit are comparative notions, involving the idea of people being worse or better off. But what is the implied baseline here—the alternative fate in comparison to which the global poor are either worse off (and therefore harmed) or better off (and therefore benefited by globalization)?

In most cases, it turns out, the popular debate is about whether poverty worldwide has been rising or falling since the latest globalization push began in the 1980s. Yet, this debate is morally irrelevant. The charge is that governments, by imposing a global institutional order under which great excesses of severe poverty and poverty deaths persist, are violating the human rights of many poor people. The plausibility of this charge is unaffected by whether severe poverty is rising or falling. To see this, consider the parallel charges that slaveholding societies harmed and violated the human rights of those they enslaved, or that the Nazis violated the human rights of those they confined and killed in their concentration camps. These charges can certainly not be defeated by showing that the rate of victimization declined. Of course, the words 'harm' and 'benefit' are sometimes appropriately used with implicit reference to an earlier state of affairs. But such a historical baseline is irrelevant here. For even if there were less severe poverty today than there was 15 years ago, we could not infer that the present global order is (in a morally significant sense) *benefiting* the global poor. This inference would beg the whole question by simply assuming the incidence of severe poverty 15 years ago as the appropriate no-harm baseline. Just as the claim that the United States (US) violated the human rights of black slaves in the 1850s cannot be refuted by showing that such slaves were better off than in earlier decades, so the claim that the imposition of the present global order violates the human rights of the poor cannot be refuted by showing that their numbers are falling.[14]

No less inconclusive than such *diachronic* comparisons are *subjunctive* comparisons with a historical baseline. Even if severe poverty were below what it now would be if the preceding regime had continued, we cannot infer that the present regime is benefiting the poor. This inference would again beg the question by assuming the incidence of severe poverty as it would have evolved under continued GATT rules as the appropriate no-harm baseline. By the same reasoning, the military *junta*

[14] See Pogge, T., 'Severe Poverty as a Violation of Negative Duties', *Ethics and International Affairs*, 19/1 (2005), 55, 55–8.

under Than Shwe could be said to be benefiting the Burmese people provided that they are better off than they would now be if the earlier *junta* under Ne Win were still in power.

Sometimes subjunctive comparisons are presented with a historical baseline defined by reference to a much earlier time. Thus, it is said that Africans today are no worse off than they would now be if there had never been significant contacts with outsiders. In response, we should question whether there are knowable facts about such a remote alternate history. We should also, once again, question the moral relevance of this hypothetical baseline involving continued mutual isolation: if world history had transpired without colonization and enslavement, then there would—*perhaps*—now be affluent people in Europe and very poor ones in Africa. But these would be persons and populations entirely different from those now actually living there, who in fact are very deeply shaped and scarred by their continent's involuntary encounter with European invaders. So, we cannot tell starving Africans that *they* would be starving and *we* would be affluent even if the crimes of colonialism had never occurred. Without these crimes there would not be the actually existing radical inequality which consists in *these* persons being affluent and *those* being extremely poor.

Similar considerations refute the moral relevance of subjunctive comparison with a *hypothetical* baseline—the claim, for instance, that greater numbers of people would live and die even more miserably in some fictional state of nature. Many such states have been described, and it is unclear how one can be singled out as the uniquely appropriate specification. Moreover, it is doubtful that *any* coherently describable state of nature on this planet would be able to match our globalized civilization's record of sustaining a stable death toll of 18 million premature deaths per year from poverty-related causes.[15] If no such state of nature can be described, then the present global order cannot be said to benefit the global poor by reducing severe poverty below a state-of-nature baseline. Finally, how can the claim that some people are being harmed now be undermined by pointing out that people in a state of nature would be even worse off? If such an argument succeeded, would it not show that *anything* done to another counts as harm only if it reduces the latter below the state-of-nature baseline? If we are not harming the 3.08 billion we are keeping in severe poverty, then enslavement did not harm the slaves either, if only they were no worse off than people would be in the relevant state of nature.

I conclude that baseline comparisons of the three kinds we have considered are unsuitable for defending any institutional scheme from the charge that it harms or violates human rights. Severe burdens and disadvantages people suffer under some institutional scheme cannot be justified by any diachronic comparison with how such people had fared before or by any subjunctive comparison with how such

---

[15] See Pogge, T., *World Poverty and Human Rights* (above, n. 6), 136–9.

people would have been faring under some preceding regime or in a state of nature. What matters is whether the institutional order in question foreseeably leads to severe burdens that are reasonably avoidable.[16]

2. Second Idea: Invoking the Consent of the Global Poor

Another common way of denying that the present global order is harming the poor invokes the venerable precept *volenti not fit iniuria*—no injustice is done to the consenting. Global institutional arrangements cannot be harming the poor when participation, for example, in the WTO, is voluntary.

This line of argument is refuted by four mutually independent considerations. First, appeal to consent cannot defeat a charge of human rights violation given that, on the usual understanding of moral and legal human rights, they are inalienable and thus cannot be waived by consent. Second, an appeal to consent cannot justify the severe impoverishment of children who are greatly over-represented among those suffering severe poverty and its effects. Third, most of the severely impoverished live in countries that lack meaningful democracy. Thus Nigeria's accession to the WTO was effected by its military dictator Sani Abacha, Myanmar's by the notorious SLORC *junta*, Indonesia's by Suharto, Zimbabwe's by Robert Mugabe, and the Congo's by dictator Mobutu Sese Seko. These rulers' success in subjecting people to their rule does not give them the moral authority to consent on behalf of those whom they are oppressing. Fourth, in so far as very poor people do consent, through a meaningfully democratic process, to some global institutional arrangements, the justificatory force of such consent is weakened by their having no other tolerable option, and weakened even further by the fact that their calamitous circumstances are partly due to those whose conduct this consent is meant to justify. Poor countries need trade for development. They do not get fair trading opportunities under the WTO regime; but one that failed to sign up would find its trading opportunities even more severely curtailed. Any poor country must decide about whether to accept the WTO rules against the background of other rules that it cannot escape and that make it extremely costly to decline.

It is worth mentioning in this context another popular fallacy often adduced in defence of the *status quo*. As empirical research shows, poor countries embracing the new global rules perform better, economically, than countries that do not. This is taken to prove that the new global rules benefit the poor countries. This inference depends on conflating two claims: (A) *Given* the dominance of the rich countries and their rules and organizations, it is better for a poor country to cooperate. (B) The dominance of these rich-country rules and organizations is better for the poor countries than alternative institutional arrangements. Once

---

[16] See Pogge, T., 'Severe Poverty as a Violation of Negative Duties' (above, n. 14), 61.

these claims are properly distinguished, it is obvious that (B) does not follow from (A).

3. Third Idea: Invoking the Flaws of the Poor Countries' Social Institutions and Rulers

A further, popular way of denying that the present global institutional order is harming the poor invokes the success stories—the Asian tigers and China—to show that any poor country can defeat severe poverty under the existing global order.

This reasoning involves a some-all fallacy. The fact that *some* individuals born into poverty become millionaires does not show that *all* such persons can do likewise.[17] The reason is that the pathways to riches are sparse. They are not rigidly limited, but it is clearly impossible to achieve the kind of economic growth rates needed for everyone to become a millionaire. The same holds for formerly poor countries. The Asian tigers achieved impressive rates of economic growth and poverty reduction through a state-sponsored build-up of industries that mass produce low-tech consumer products. These industries were globally successful by using their considerable labour-cost advantage to beat competitors in the developed countries and by drawing on greater state support and/or a better-educated workforce to beat competitors in other poor countries. Building such industries was hugely profitable for the Asian tigers. But if many more poor countries had adopted this same developmental strategy, competition among them would have rendered it much less profitable.

Over the last two decades, China has been the great success story, achieving phenomenal growth in exports and *per capita* income. So China's example is now often used to argue that the rules of the world economy are favourable to the poor countries and conducive to poverty eradication. These arguments commit the same some-all fallacy. Exporters in the poorer countries compete over the same heavily protected rich-country markets. Thanks to its extraordinary ability to deliver quality products cheaply in large quantities, China has done extremely well. But this great success has greatly reduced market share and export prices for firms in many poorer countries. To be sure, the world economy as presently structured is not a constant-sum game, where any one player's gain must be another's loss. Yet, outcomes are strongly interdependent. We cannot conclude, therefore, that the present global institutional order, though less favourable to the poor countries than it might be, is still favourable enough for all of them to do as well as the Asian tigers and then China have done in fact.

This is not to deny that most severe poverty could be avoided, despite the current unfair global order, if the national Governments and elites of the poor countries

---

[17] See Cohen, G. A., *History, Labour, and Freedom* (Oxford: Clarendon Press, 1988), 262–3.

were genuinely committed to 'good governance' and poverty eradication. But this claim provides no moral defence of the rich countries and their present globalization project if it is also true that most severe poverty could be avoided, despite the corrupt and oppressive regimes holding sway in so many less-developed countries, if the global institutional order were designed to achieve this purpose. If we acquit causal factor A because of the necessary contribution made by B, we must acquit B as well because of the necessary contribution by A. But since we cannot acquit both for harm they knowingly produce together, we must conclude that each is responsible for much of the harm.[18]

Still, by assuming symmetry between the two sets of causal factors, this response is too simple, failing to fully expose the responsibility of the rich countries and of their globalization project. There is an important asymmetry. While national institutional arrangements and policies in the poor countries have very little influence on the design of the global order, the latter has a great deal of influence on the former. The global institutional order exerts its pernicious influence on the evolution of world poverty not only directly, in the ways already discussed, but also indirectly through its influence on the national institutions and policies of the poorer countries. Oppression and corruption, so prevalent in many poor countries today, are themselves very substantially produced and sustained by central features of the present global order.

It was only in 1999, for example, that the developed countries finally agreed to curb their firms' bribery of foreign officials by adopting the OECD *Convention on Combating Bribery of Foreign Public Officials in International Business Transactions*.[19] Until then, most developed states did not merely legally authorize their firms to bribe foreign officials, but even allowed them to deduct such bribes from their taxable revenues, thereby providing financial incentives and moral support for the practice of bribing politicians and officials in the poor countries. This practice diverts the loyalties of officials in these countries and also makes a great difference to which persons are motivated to stand for public office in the first place. Poor countries have suffered staggering losses as a result, most clearly in the awarding of public contracts. Preliminary evidence suggests that the new Convention is ineffective in curbing bribery by multinational corporations. And banks in the rich countries continue to invite corrupt rulers and officials in the poorer countries to move and invest their earnings from bribery and embezzlement abroad. Raymond Baker[20] estimates such illicit transfers from poor to rich countries to total at least $500 billion annually. Such practices have created a pervasive culture of corruption now deeply entrenched in many poor countries.

Bribery and embezzlement are part of a larger problem. The political and economic elites of poor countries interact with their domestic inferiors, on the one

---

[18] See Pogge, T., 'Severe Poverty as a Violation of Negative Duties' (above, n. 14), 62–4.
[19] The convention came into effect in Feb. 1999 and has been widely ratified, see <www.oecd.org/home>.
[20] Baker, R., *Capitalism's Achilles Heel* (New York: John Wiley and Sons, 2005).

hand, and with foreign governments and corporations, on the other. These two constituencies differ enormously in wealth and power. The former are mostly poorly-educated and heavily preoccupied with the daily struggle to survive. The latter have vastly greater rewards and penalties at their disposal. Politicians with a normal interest in their own political and economic success thus cater to the interests of foreign governments and corporations rather than to competing interests of their much poorer compatriots. There are plenty of poor-country governments that have come to power or remained in office solely as a result of foreign support. And there are many poor-country politicians and bureaucrats who, induced or even bribed by foreigners, work against the interests of their people: *for* the development of a tourist-friendly sex industry with forced exploitation of children and women, *for* the importation of unnecessary, obsolete, or overpriced products at public expense, *for* the permission to import hazardous products, wastes, or factories, *against* laws protecting employees or the environment, and so on.

In most poor countries, these incentive asymmetries are aggravated by the lack of genuine democracy. This democratice deficit also has global roots. It is a central feature of our global institutional order that any group controlling a preponderance of the means of coercion within a country is internationally recognized as the legitimate government of the country's territory and people—regardless of how this group came to power, of how it exercises power, and of how much popular support it has. International recognition means not merely that we engage such a group in negotiations, but also that we accept its right to act for the people it rules and thereby authorize it to sell the country's resources and to dispose of the proceeds of such sales, to borrow in the country's name and thereby to impose debt service obligations upon it, to sign treaties on the country's behalf and thus to bind its present and future population, and to use state revenues to buy the means of internal repression. This global practice goes a long way toward explaining why so many countries are so badly governed.

The *resource privilege* we confer upon *de facto* rulers includes the power to effect legally valid transfers of ownership rights over resources. A corporation that has purchased resources from a tyrant thereby becomes entitled to be—and actually *is*—recognized anywhere as their legitimate owner. This is a remarkable feature of our global order. A group that overpowers the guards and takes control of a warehouse may be able to give some of the merchandise to others, accepting money in exchange. But the fence who pays them becomes merely the possessor, not the owner, of the loot. Contrast this with a group that overpowers an elected government and takes control of a country. Such a group, too, can give away some of the country's natural resources, accepting money in exchange. In this case, however, the purchaser acquires not merely possession, but all the rights and liberties of ownership, which are supposed to be—and actually *are*—protected and enforced by all other states' courts and police forces.

This international resource privilege has disastrous impact in poor countries whose resource sector constitutes a large segment of the national economy. Whoever can take power in such a country by whatever means can maintain his rule, even against broad popular opposition, by buying the arms and soldiers he needs with revenues from the export of natural resources and with funds borrowed against future resource sales. The resource privilege thus gives insiders strong incentives toward the violent acquisition and exercise of political power, thereby causing *coup* attempts and civil wars. And it gives outsiders strong incentives to corrupt the officials of such countries who, no matter how badly they rule, continue to have resources to sell and money to spend.

The incentives arising from the international resource privilege help explain the significant *negative* correlation between resource wealth (relative to Gross Domestic Product (GDP)) and economic performance. This 'resource curse' is exemplified by many less developed countries which, despite great natural wealth, have achieved little economic growth or poverty reduction.[21] This explanation has been confirmed by two economists from Yale who, using a regression analysis, demonstrate that the causal link from resource wealth to poor economic performance is mediated through reduced chances for democracy:

All petrostates or resource-dependent countries in Africa fail to initiate meaningful political reforms ... besides South Africa, transition to democracy has been successful only in resource-poor countries ... Our cross-country regression confirms our theoretical insights. We find that a one percentage increase in the size of the natural resource sector [relative to GDP] generates a decrease by half a percentage point in the probability of survival of democratic regimes.[22]

Holding the global order fixed as a given background, the authors do not consider how the causal link they analyse itself depends on global rules that grant the resource privilege to any ruling group regardless of its domestic illegitimacy.

The *borrowing privilege* we confer upon de-facto rulers includes the power to impose internationally valid legal obligations upon the whole country. A later government that refuses to honour debts incurred by a corrupt, brutal, undemocratic, unconstitutional, repressive, unpopular predecessor will be severely punished by the banks and governments of other countries. At a minimum, it will lose its own borrowing privilege by being excluded from the international financial markets. Such refusals are therefore very rare, as governments, even when newly-elected

---

[21] UNDP, *Human Development Report 2007/2008* (above, n. 10), 278–80.

[22] Lam, R. and Wantchekon, L., 'Dictatorships as a Political Dutch Disease', Working Paper 795 (Yale University, 1999), 31, 35.

after a dramatic break with the past, are compelled to pay the debts of their awful predecessors.

The international borrowing privilege makes three important contributions to the high incidence of oppressive and corrupt rulers in less developed countries. First, it facilitates borrowing by destructive rulers, who can borrow more money and can do so more cheaply than they could do if they alone were obliged to repay, and thereby helps such rulers maintain themselves in power even against near-universal popular opposition. Second, the international borrowing privilege imposes the often huge debts of their corrupt predecessors upon democratic successor regimes. It thereby saps the capacity of democratic governments to implement structural reforms and other political programmes, thus rendering such governments less successful and less stable than they would otherwise be. (It is small consolation that *putschists* are sometimes weakened by being held liable for the debts of their democratic predecessors.) Third, the international borrowing privilege strengthens incentives toward *coup* attempts: whoever succeeds in bringing a preponderance of the means of coercion under his control gets the borrowing privilege as an additional reward.

Like the formerly tax-deductible bribery of poor-country officials and the complicity by banks in the embezzlement of public funds, the four privileges just discussed are significant features of our global order, greatly benefiting the governments, corporations, and citizens of rich countries and the political-military elites of poor countries at the expense of the vast majority of ordinary people in poor countries. Thus, while the present global order indeed does not make it strictly impossible for poor countries to achieve genuine democracy and sustained economic growth, central features of this order greatly contribute to poor countries' failing on both counts. These features are crucial for explaining the inability and particularly the unwillingness of these countries' leaders to eradicate poverty more effectively. And they are crucial, therefore, to explaining why global inequality is increasing so rapidly that substantial global economic growth since the end of the Cold War has not reduced income poverty and malnutrition—*despite* substantial technological progress and global economic growth, *despite* huge reported poverty reduction in China,[23] *despite* the post-Cold-War 'peace dividend',[24] *despite* substantial declines

[23] The number of Chinese living below $1.25 per day (2005 PPP) is reported to have declined by 65%, or 378 million, and the number of Chinese living below $2.50 per day (2005 PPP) by 36%, or 356 million, between 1987 and 2005 (Chen, S., and Ravallion, M., 'The Developing World is Poorer than We Thought, but no Less Successful in the Fight against Poverty' (above, n. 11), table 7.

[24] Thanks to the end of the Cold War, military expenditures worldwide have declined from 4.7% of aggregate GDP in 1985 to 2.9% in 1996 (UNDP, *Human Development Report 1998* (New York: Oxford University Press, 1998), 197) and to about 2.6% or $1035 billion in 2004 (<yearbook2005.sipri.org/ch8/ch8>). Today, this global peace dividend is worth nearly $1,000 billion annually.

in real food prices,[25] despite official development assistance, and despite the efforts of international humanitarian and development organizations.

V. The Present Global Order Massively Violates Human Rights

In just 20 years since the end of the Cold War, well over 360 million human beings have died prematurely from poverty-related causes, with some 18 million more added each year. Much larger numbers must live in conditions of life-threatening poverty that make it very difficult for them to articulate their interests and effectively to fend for themselves and their families. This catastrophe was and is happening, foreseeably, under a global institutional order designed for the benefit of the affluent countries' governments, corporations, and citizens and of the poor countries' political and military elites. There are feasible alternative designs of the global institutional order, feasible alternative paths of globalization, under which this catastrophe would have been largely avoided. Even now severe poverty could be rapidly reduced through feasible reforms that would modify the more harmful features of this global order or mitigate their impact.

This conclusion is quite distinct from the usual calls for more aid to the poor. There is still so much severe poverty, and so much need for aid, only because the poor are systematically impoverished by present institutional arrangements and have been so impoverished for a long time during which our advantage and their disadvantage have been compounded. It is true, eradicating severe poverty at a morally acceptable speed would impose substantial costs and opportunity costs on the affluent countries. But acceptance of such costs is not generous charity, but required compensation for the harms produced by unjust global institutional arrangements whose past and present imposition by the affluent countries brings great benefits to their citizens.

Given that the present global institutional order is foreseeably associated with such massive incidence of avoidable severe poverty, its (uncompensated) imposition manifests an ongoing human rights violation—arguably the largest such violation ever committed in human history. It is not the *gravest* human rights violation, in my view, because those who commit it do not intend the death and suffering they

---

25   The FAO's Food Price Index (in constant 2002 dollars) fell from 107.9 in 1990 to 90.2 in 2002 without any decrease in the number of malnourished. The Index spiked sharply in the 2006–08 period, reaching a peak of 191.3. It has since fallen back to 172.4. See <www.fao.org/worldfoodsituation/FoodPricesIndex/en>.

inflict either as an end or as a means. They merely act with willful indifference to the enormous harms they cause in the course of advancing their own ends while going to great lengths to deceive the world (and sometimes themselves) about the impact of their conduct—but it is still the *largest* such human rights violation.

VI. The Promise of Global Institutional Reform

Human rights impose on us a negative duty not to contribute to the imposition of an institutional order that foreseeably gives rise to an avoidable human rights deficit without making compensatory protection and reform efforts for its victims. Analogous to the negative duties not to break a promise or contract and not to make emergency use of another's property without compensation, this negative institutional duty may impose positive obligations on advantaged participants: obligations to compensate for their contribution to the harm. Such compensation can take the form of individual efforts (donations to efficient non-governmental organizations) or of bilateral or multilateral government aid programmes. Or it can focus on institutional reform. I close with some comments on this latter option.

In the modern world, the rules governing economic transactions—both nationally and internationally—are the most important causal determinants of the incidence and scope of human rights deficits. They are most important because of their great impact on the economic distribution within the jurisdiction to which they apply. Thus, even relatively minor variations in a country's laws about tax rates, labour relations, social security, and access to health care and education can have a much greater impact on poverty than large changes in consumer habits or in the policies of a major corporation. This point applies to the global institutional order as well. Even small changes in the rules governing international trade, lending, investment, resource use, or intellectual property can have a huge impact on the global incidence of life-threatening poverty.

Rules governing economic transactions are important also for their greater visibility. To be sure, rule changes, too, can have unintended and even unforeseeable effects. But with rules it is much easier to diagnose such effects and to make corrections. Assessing adjustments of the rules within some particular jurisdiction is relatively straightforward: one can try to estimate how a rise in the minimum wage, say, has affected the unemployment rate and *per capita* income in the bottom quintile. (Other things are happening in the economy besides the change in the minimum wage, so the exercise is complex and imprecise. Still, exercises of this sort can be done, and *are* done, sufficiently well in many countries.) It is more difficult, by contrast, to assess the relative impact of variations in the conduct of individual or collective agents. Such an assessment can be confined to the persons immediately affected—for example, to the employees of a corporation or to the inhabitants of a town in which an aid agency is running a project. But such a confined assessment is always vulnerable to the charge of ignoring indirect effects upon outsiders or future persons.

A further point is that morally successful rules are much easier to sustain than morally successful conduct. This is so, because individual and collective agents are under continuous counter-moral pressures not merely from their ordinary self-interested concerns, but also from their competitive situation as well as from considerations of fairness. These phenomena are illustrated by the case of competing corporations, each of which may judge that it cannot afford to pass up immoral opportunities to take advantage of its employees and customers because such unilateral self-restraint would place it at an unfair competitive disadvantage *vis-à-vis* its less scrupulous competitors. Domestically, this sort of problem can be solved through changes in the legal rules that require all corporations, on pain of substantial penalties, to observe common standards in their treatment of customers and employees. Corporations are often willing to support such legislation even while they are unwilling to risk their competitive position through unilateral good conduct.

Similar considerations apply in the international arena, where corporations and governments compete economically. Given their concern not to fall behind in this competition and not to be unfairly handicapped through unilateral moral efforts and restraints, it is perhaps not surprising that individuals, corporations, and governments have been so reluctant to make meaningful efforts toward eradicating global poverty.[26] Again, it is possible that affluent governments and corporations could be brought to do much more by accepting and complying with legal rules that apply to them all and thereby relieve each of the fear that its own good conduct will unfairly disadvantage it and cause it to lose ground against its competitors. Successful efforts to reduce poverty within states exemplify this model of structural reform rather than individual moral effort.

---

[26] Their current effort amounts to approximately $20 billion annually—0.05% of the gross national incomes of the affluent countries—consisting of $7 billion annually from individuals and corporations (UNDP, *Human Development Report 2003* (New York: Oxford University Press, 2003), 290), and another $12 billion (2007) annually from governments in official development assistance (ODA) for basic social services (<mdgs.un.org/unsd/mdg/SeriesDetail.aspx?srid=593&crid=>). Aggregate official development assistance is some 9 times higher, but most of it is spent for the benefit of agents more capable of reciprocation, as is well expressed in this statement recently removed from the USAID's main website: 'The principal beneficiary of America's foreign assistance programmes has always been the United States. Close to 80 percent of the U.S. Agency for International Development's (USAID's) contracts and grants go directly to American firms. Foreign assistance programmes have helped create major markets for agricultural goods, created new markets for American industrial exports and meant hundreds of thousands of jobs for Americans'.

To be sure, this thought is not new, and governments have been very reluctant to commit themselves, even jointly, to serious global anti-poverty measures. Their solemn promise to halve global poverty by 2015 has been reiterated—in cleverly weakened formulations—but has yet to result in serious implementation efforts.[27] Official development assistance (ODA) from the rich countries, once supposed to reach 1%, then 0.7% of their combined GNPs, has actually shrunk throughout the 1990s, from 0.33% in 1990 to 0.22% in 2000.[28] With the 'war on terror', ODA is reported to have grown back in 2007 to 0.27% of the rich countries' combined GNIs due to dramatic growth in spending on Musharraf's Pakistan and post-occupation Afghanistan and Iraq.[29] Yet, even this new $104 billion level is only a third of what is needed to eradicate severe poverty—and only a tiny fraction of this assistance is actually spent for this purpose.

This discouraging evidence suggests that improvements in the global institutional order are difficult to achieve and difficult to sustain. However, this fact does not undermine my hypothesis that such structural improvements are *easier* to achieve and much *easier* to sustain than equally significant unilateral improvements in the conduct of individual and collective agents. We know how much money individuals, corporations, and the governments of affluent countries are now willing to spend on global poverty eradication: about $20 billion annually.[30] This amount is very small in comparison to the harms inflicted on the global poor by clear injustices in the present global order. It is also very small in comparison to what would be required to achieve substantial progress: the amount needed in the first few years of a serious offensive against poverty is closer to $300 billion annually.[31] It is not realistic to hope that we can achieve such a 15-fold increase in available funds through appeals to the morality of the relevant agents: affluent individuals, corporations, and the governments of rich countries. It is *more* realistic—though admittedly still rather unrealistic—to achieve substantial progress on the poverty front through institutional reforms that make the global order less burdensome on the global poor. Accepting such reforms, affluent countries would bear some opportunity costs of making the international trade, lending, investment, and intellectual-property regimes fairer to the global poor as well as some costs of compensating for harms done—for example by helping to fund basic health facilities, vaccination programmes, basic schooling, school lunches, safe water and sewage systems, basic housing, power plants and networks, banks and micro-lending, road, rail, and communication links where these do not yet exist. If such a reform programme is to gain and maintain

[27] Pogge, T., 'The First UN Millennium Development Goal, A Cause for Celebration?', *Journal of Human Development*, 5/3 (2004), 377–97.

[28] UNDP, *Human Development Report 2002* (New York: Oxford University Press, 2002), 202. Also at <hdr.undp.org/reports/global/2002/en>.

[29] <mdgs.un.org/unsd/mdg/SeriesDetail.aspx?srid=568&crid=>.   [30] See n. 26, above.

[31] See Pogge, T., *World Poverty and Human Rights* (above, n. 6), ch. 8. Amazingly, $300 billion is only 0.6% of the global product or 0.8% of the combined gross national incomes of the affluent countries, World Bank, *World Development Report 2008* (above, n. 4), 335.

support from citizens and governments of affluent countries, it must distribute such costs and opportunity costs fairly among them. Transparency will be required in order to assure each of these actors that their competitive position will not be eroded by the non-compliance of others.

The path of global institutional reform is far more realistic and sustainable for three obvious reasons. First, the costs and opportunity costs each affluent citizen imposes on herself by supporting structural reform is extremely small relative to the contribution this reform makes to avoiding severe poverty. The reform lowers an average family's standard of living by $900 annually, say, while improving the standard of living by $300 annually for hundreds of millions of poor families. By contrast, a unilateral donation in the same amount would lower your family's standard of living by $900 annually while improving by $300 annually the standard of living of only three poor families. Given such pay-offs, rational agents with some moral concern for the avoidance of severe poverty will be far more willing to support structural reform than to sustain donations. Second, structural reform assures citizens that costs and opportunity costs are fairly shared among the more affluent, as discussed. And third, structural reform, once in place, need not be repeated, year after year, through painful personal decisions. Continual alleviation of poverty leads to fatigue, aversion, even contempt. It requires affluent citizens to rally to the cause again and again while knowing that most others similarly situated contribute nothing or very little, that their own contributions are legally optional, and that, no matter how much they give, they could for just a little more always save yet further children from sickness or starvation. Today, such fatigue, aversion, and contempt are widespread attitudes among citizens and officials of affluent countries toward the 'aid' they dispense and its recipients.

For these reasons, I believe that today's vast human rights deficit, especially among the global poor, is best addressed through efforts at global (and national) institutional reform. Relatively small reforms of little consequence for the world's affluent would suffice to eliminate most of this human rights deficit, whose magnitude makes such reforms our most important moral task.

CHAPTER 21

GLOBAL JUSTICE, POVERTY, AND THE INTERNATIONAL ECONOMIC ORDER

ROBERT HOWSE AND RUTI TEITEL

What principles of justice ought to guide the evolution of international economic law? In his essay for this volume, Thomas Pogge argues that there is a moral duty on the part of affluent countries not to contribute to the design of a 'global economic order that, continually and forseeably, produces vast excesses of severe poverty and premature poverty-related deaths'.[1] According to Pogge, the existing international economic order represents a violation of this duty, and this violation, which is a human rights violation, leads to an obligation to compensate the world's poor through, *inter alia*, foreign aid. Pogge suggests:

In the modern world, the traffic of international and even intra-national economic transactions is profoundly shaped by an elaborate system of treaties and conventions about trade, investments, loans, patents, copyrights, trademarks, double taxation, labour standards, environmental protection, use of seabed resources and much else. These different parts of the present global institutional order realize highly specific design decisions within a vast space of alternative design possibilities. It is incredible on its face that all these alternative ways of structuring the world economy would have produced the same evolution in the overall incidence and geographical distribution of severe poverty.[2]

---

[1] Pogge, T., Chapter 21 in this volume, 417.   [2] Ibid. 419.

While building on a widely shared moral intuition that the existence of extreme poverty is inhuman and wrongful, Pogge's argument has, in fact, complex and contestable normative and empirical foundations.

When Pogge claims that existing international economic law has contributed to or *caused* in part the existence of extreme poverty, what he is really saying is that had a different set of rules and institutions been devised for the international economic order, the worst forms of poverty could have been eliminated in great measure. He thus judges the existing order against an imaginary[3] counter-vision of the international economic order. The affluent countries violated their duty not to contribute to extreme poverty globally through choosing a set of rules and institutions different from some imagined alternatives, which could have eliminated the most extreme forms of poverty.

At first, Pogge seems to be asserting that evidence of enormous and increasing income and wealth inequalities *alone* proves that the existing rules and institutions are sub-optimal: 'These data should *suffice* to refute the Panglossian view: the present design of the global order is not optimal in terms of poverty avoidance'.[4] This seems to be question-begging if not an outright logical error: however lamentable the realities evoked by the data, they cannot in and of themselves ever establish that alternative rules and institutions *are or were actually available* that could have or could now avoid or lessen these outcomes. A further difficulty here is that increased income inequalities over a given time period might, on some theories of economic development, be necessary to produce in the long term increases in wealth that can ultimately lead to the elimination of extreme poverty. This possibility is suggested by some of the data Pogge cites: the number of the *very* poorest of the poor dropped during much of the period in question (those living below $1 a day), even if income inequalities increased more sharply.

In earlier work, Pogge tended to favour Rawls's difference principle as a basis for global justice: under this principle even quite extreme inequalities of outcome are acceptable if such inequalities maximize the primary social goods of the least advantaged of all. Rawls derived the difference principle from a particular method for establishing the rules of justice for social cooperation, the veil of ignorance, asking what rules reasonable persons would choose without knowing what endowments they might have, i.e. how disadvantaged or advantaged in society they would be due to morally arbitrary factors.

But the approach to inequality that Pogge takes in the present essay seems to have a different foundation: it is not a matter of determining under what conditions or circumstances it is or is not just to allow for morally arbitrary endowments to

---

[3] By 'imaginary' we do not wish to suggest that Pogge's proposals are inherently lacking in feasibility or that they cannot be actualized in the real world. Instead, we mean to indicate that he evaluates the justice of past choices against a conception that does not represent any actual set of proposals that was considered and rejected at a particular historical juncture where the existing order was created or formed.

[4] Pogge, T., this volume, 421 (emphasis added).

affect persons' social and economic chances, but rather of correcting the crimes of colonialism, and related historical injustices, without which according to him 'the actually existing radical inequality' would not exist.[5] Yet by the end of the essay it is not so clear how important these historical injustices are to Pogge's conception of global justice. By suggesting that the right not to live in extreme poverty is a *human right*, Pogge would seem to be saying that there is a demand of justice to eliminate such poverty, whether or not its causes can be traced to the past crimes of imperialism. This duty could plausibly fall on affluent countries due to their capacity to deal with the problem, regardless of whether they acquired such a capacity unjustly, through the crimes of imperialism, and regardless of whether their affluence was, more generally, acquired at the expense of the very poor. Thus, Pogge in many places in the essay is at pains to stress that the measures that would meet the demands of justice as he understands them would come at little cost to the citizens of the affluent countries. If what mattered was the criminality of the affluent countries in the past, rather than their capacity to alleviate poverty today, then it is questionable why the responsibility to eliminate extreme poverty would be strictly limited to measures that come at a low cost to the citizens of the affluent countries. Certainly, on international law principles, reparation for past *wrongful* acts is not limited by the capacity to pay of the wrongdoing state(s). It is a different matter with positive, aspirational duties, such as the realization of social, economic, and cultural rights.

Indeed the ultimate standard for global justice proposed by Pogge turns out not to be premised on egalitarian redistribution. It is an absolute standard (the entitlement of everyone to a minimum level of well-being, in effect to 'human security') not a relative, or equalizing, one (the entitlement to the reduction of *inequality*).[6] The demand for redistribution comes from the failure of the affluent countries to choose rules and institutions that could foreseeably eliminate extreme poverty (understood as a shortfall from the absolute minimum of well-being that is a human right), and not from an imperative to reduce inequality as such.

This brings us back to the difficulty of inferring the existence of a feasible alternative design for international economic order from the fact of increasing inequalities apparently generated from the present order. Pogge himself seems to anticipate the objection that this fact cannot really generate an imaginary or alternative counter-vision of the international economic order, by going on to assert specific alternative rules or strategies that are feasible and that would significantly reduce or contribute to the elimination of the most extreme forms of poverty.

Thus the comparison of the actual rules and institutions of the international economic order to these imaginary alternatives becomes crucial to the persuasive

---

[5] Ibid. 424.
[6] Ibid. 423. Thus, Pogge claims: 'the claim that the imposition of the present global order violates the human rights of the poor cannot be refuted by showing that their numbers are falling'.

force of Pogge's claim; he must make a plausible case that the choice of the existing rules and institutions over these alternatives foreseeably yielded or at least failed to eliminate outcomes of extreme poverty, which would have been avoided had the alternatives been chosen. Pogge is aware that these outcomes may have multiple causes including domestic policies in poor countries. How then to know that the poverty-reducing impacts of these imaginary alternatives would not be significantly or entirely undermined by domestic policies? The moral responsibility if not culpability of the rich countries depends on the proposition that 'most severe poverty could be avoided, despite the corrupt and oppressive regimes holding sway in so many less-developed countries, if the global institutional order were designed to achieve this purpose'.[7] This is a very demanding test for Pogge's imagined alternative international economic order to meet: it must be capable of (foreseeably) eliminating 'most severe poverty' based on what would seem to be worst case scenario concerning the domestic regime.

Let us now turn to such specifics as Pogge provides us concerning this imaginary alternative international economic order, and its effects relative to the existing one. According to Pogge, 'The present rules favour the affluent countries by allowing them to continue protecting their markets through quotas, tariffs, anti-dumping duties, export credits and subsidies to domestic producers in ways that poor countries are not permitted, or cannot afford, to match. Other important examples include the World Trade Organization (WTO) regulations on cross-border investment and intellectual property rights (TRIPs) treaty of 1995'.[8]

By contrast the imagined alternative international economic order would have the following features:

The poorest countries should receive financial support toward hiring experts to advise them how to articulate their interests in WTO negotiations, toward maintaining missions at WTO headquarters in Geneva, toward bringing cases before the WTO, and toward coping with all the regulations they are required to implement. Poor countries should face reduced barriers to their exports and should not have to pay for market access by collecting billions in economic rents for 'intellectual property'. The WTO Treaty should include a global minimum wage and minimal global constraints on working hours and working conditions in order to halt the current 'race to the bottom' where poor countries competing for foreign investment must outbid one another by offering ever more exploitable workforces.[9]

In placing a considerable emphasis on greater market access, Pogge's imaginary alternative international economic order oddly (given what are at times his apparently harsh criticisms of neo-liberalism and global capitalism) depends on one of the main premises of the Washington Consensus: export-led growth can take poor countries out of poverty. While the existing order has reduced barriers to developing country exports considerably, especially when we take account of the preferences that many developed countries provide in respect of a wide variety of developing

---

[7] Pogge, T., this volume, 427.   [8] Ibid. 420.   [9] Ibid. 422.

country imports, Pogge's point is that if the remaining barriers were removed it is foreseeable that much poverty would be eliminated, even on worst-case scenarios concerning domestic policies. Barriers remain significant in some agricultural products, textiles, and clothing, while very many industrial products from developing countries enter developed country markets without facing significant or any tariff barriers, or being subject to quotas, or significant harrassment from anti-dumping or other contingent protection actions. A test of Pogge's hypothesis would be to examine what has happened where developing countries have been able to succeed in product lines for export where barriers are *already* low or even (as is often the case) non-existent. This is arguably the case for the experience of the Asian tigers. Yet, as Pogge notes, 'The Asian tigers achieved impressive rates of economic growth and poverty reduction through a state-sponsored build-up of industries that mass produce low-tech consumer products'.[10] This analysis, which is Pogge's own, suggests that even if an imaginary alternative international economic order reduced barriers to market access in those limited areas where they remain high, positive effects on poverty would still depend on a particular, desirable set of domestic policies for their realization. This in turn undermines the plausibility of Pogge's claim that an alternative international economic order could be designed that would eliminate most severe poverty even on worst-case scenarios concerning domestic policies.[11] Even more than his proposals with respect to reducing market access barriers such as tariffs and quotas, this difficulty plagues his suggestions with respect to strengthening the capacity of developing country governments to participate in the WTO system. These proposals would only likely lead to more optimal outcomes if we assume that the developing country governments are publicly interested, i.e. pursuing a plausible conception of the best interests of their citizens, and not corrupt or despotic.

To return to the issue of market access and competitive conditions for developing countries in global markets, Pogge places particular emphasis on developed countries' subsidies, which, citing various economists, he calls a 'monstrosity'.[12] Here one must distinguish between industrial and agricultural subsidies. On the one hand, there are some industrial subsidies that certainly worsen competitive conditions for some developing countries that would otherwise be competitive in

[10] Ibid. 426.

[11] It is however not entirely clear to us why Pogge needs to make such a strong claim to sustain his argument. Certainly, he is very concerned to show why the effects of bad domestic policies do not excuse the duty to design the international economic order so as to not contribute to or maintain unnecessarily extreme poverty. This is further complicated by the question of whether Pogge intends the proposals to eliminate the resource and the borrowing privileges are regarded as a necessary part of the package. At some points he seems to suggest that the other proposals would work to reduce poverty significantly even without the elimination of the resource and the borrowing privileges. Perhaps this is because the latter reforms depend in the last analysis on regime change for their full positive impact, which may not be so clearly foreseeable from the elimination of these privileges, taken on their own, without assumptions about other political, social, economic, and cultural developments and events. See our detailed discussion of these aspects of Pogge's vision below.

[12] Pogge, T. this volume, 420, n. 5.

the products in the question. What makes the aggregate effects tricky to foresee is that not all subsidy competition in the case of industrial products (e.g. civil aircraft) is largely between developed countries themselves; this 'race to the bottom' can actually benefit poor countries as it reduces the price of imports from developed countries that are necessary for the development of their own economies.

The harmful if not devastating effects of agricultural support measures on developing country agriculture are, on the other hand, well known. But here also there are complexities that detract from the plausibility of Pogge's claim that the imaginary alternatives are easily foreseeable, and obviously feasible. Had there been a massive reduction in agricultural support, it is indeed quite likely that a number of developing countries would have experienced rapid dynamic growth in their agricultural sectors. But one does not even have to suppose worst-case scenarios about domestic policies in developing countries to wonder whether such intensive development of agricultural production would have been sustainable. It would likely, given geographical conditions, have involved heavy deployment of fertilizers, other chemicals and biotechnology, with significant environmental, conservation, health and safety consequences. The introduction of modern large scale agriculture would have not been easily possible without displacement of people, and the land use implications would have arguably been significantly negative from the perspective of mitigating climate change. While we share with Pogge elements of a human rights perspective, we view the problem of poverty in light of the broader concept of human security. Thus, in taking into account the effects of the imaginary alternative international economic order from the perspective of global justice, we are concerned not just with poverty as an economic phenomenon but with the health, environmental, and other human effects (such as cultural effects of displacement of populations) of alternative rules and institutions, short and long term. If all these other effects were to be balanced, the feasibility and foreseeability of poverty reduction would be considerably more questionable, we would argue.

This leads to a larger, more comprehensive point. The limits of existing technologies for industrial and agricultural production, and of alternative energy technologies to this very day, would almost certainly result or have resulted in catastrophic environmental and health impacts, had Pogge's alternative strategy been adopted and *worked*. If barriers to developed country markets had been massively disassembled and this resulted in a huge increase in export-led growth for developing countries, reducing poverty, the increases in production and the increases in consumption in developing countries would have generated unmanageable levels of pollution and toxic waste. Unmanageable, even if developed countries had provided free of charge the best existing 'clean' technologies and pollution abatement methods to the developing countries. This, to us is a central difficulty in Pogge's argument: to accuse the affluent countries of a clear injustice he needs to demonstrate that feasible and minor changes,[13] of only modest costs to the affluent countries or their citizens, would have made a morally decisive difference in terms of poverty reduction. But these kinds of consequences of Pogge's 'minor' changes (assuming they did produce rapidly accelerated export-led growth, which they would need to in order to reduce poverty considerably) suggest that only a radical re-imagination of the social, economic, and technological instruments of development and growth under conditions of globalization could successfully address what might be called the dilemma of human security. We have yet to witness such a radical re-imagination, although alternative globalization theories such as that of Vandana Shiva,[14] are a promising start. But to revert to the underlying structure of Pogge's argument about justice, the changes are very far from obvious or foreseeable.

This is not to say that some of the individual policy prescriptions that Pogge proposes are without merit, or that trying at the margins to find better rules to address poverty is futile. The problem is that Pogge wants not just to advocate the desirability of such policies but to moralize their non-adoption as an injustice for which affluent countries must be held to account. Thus, he rightly says he has to hold the imaginary alternative order to fairly stringent criteria of foreseeability, feasibility, and so on. Spectacular poverty-reducing results from feasible, and as Pogge states it, 'minor' changes have to be foreseeable, in order for the non-adoption of the alternative international economic order to constitute an *injustice*.[15]

In terms of the structure of moral argument, this reflects an uneasy tension between the elements of deontology and consequentialism (which is not to say that, as a general matter, human rights weds one to a deontological moral syntax, nor concern with social consequences to consequentialism). Consider his proposal for a global minimum wage. There is a strong human rights argument for such a measure. Yet on standard economic assumptions (for example elasticity of demand) such a wage might well make some goods and services from developing countries more costly and in so doing result in fewer of those goods and services being consumed, and thus fewer workers in developing countries being employed. Unless domestic strategies are adopted to raise the productivity of labour, find new areas of comparative advantage and so on, the result may well be increased unemployment and poverty.

---

[13] We ourselves doubt whether all of Pogge's proposals in fact represent minor changes: for example, as we argue below, eliminating the borrowing and resource privileges would entail some major structural alterations in the international legal order. But this raises the question of why Pogge thinks it is important to stress, as he does, that minor changes could produce significant poverty-reducing effects. One reason may be the work that feasibility and foreseeability do in establishing a breach of a negative duty in the creation or adoption of key features of the existing international economic order. The larger and the more complex the changes, the more that reasonable people, acting in good faith, could disagree on the feasibility of the changes and the foreseeability of their effects on poverty.

[14] Shiva, V., *Earth Democracy: Justice, Sustainability and Peace* (London: South End Books, 2005).

[15] Pogge, T., this volume, 432: 'Even small changes in the rules governing international trade, lending, investment, resource use, or intellectual property can have a huge impact on the global incidence of life-threatening poverty'; 'small reforms of little consequence for the world's affluent would suffice to eliminate most of this human rights deficit, whose magnitude makes such reforms our most important moral task'.

Do such foreseeable effects (that arguably also have human rights implications) undermine the strong human rights case that it is unjust, i.e. exploitative and dehumanizing, to compensate labour below a certain minimum level? This is a difficult question and Pogge does not answer it. It would clearly be desirable to work both for a global minimum wage and for the domestic policies that ensure that the global minimum wage does not cause new poverty.

The minimum wage proposal leads us to explore a different difficulty with Pogge's argument, i.e. that opposition to such universal labour standards as conditions of global economic order has often come from developing country governments themselves. Pogge's essay contains an extensive and in many ways persuasive response to the argument that the consent of developing countries to the existing rules of international economic order mitigates or eliminates the responsibility of developed countries for their injustice. As he says, in many cases, developing countries were brought to accept these rules because it was suggested that they had no alternative if they wanted to participate in the international economy in an effective manner. The rules were shaped in processes where developing country governments in many cases had marginal influence on the outcomes, or the knowledge even to properly evaluate the effects of the rules on their economies and societies.

But just because developing country consent fails to eliminate the injustice of the existing rules and institutions, this does not mean that a *just* order could feasibly be instituted *without* the consent of developing countries. It is not just oppressive and corrupt developing country governments that object to trade-related labour standards, but democratic ones such as that of India. Pogge often refers to the imposition of the international economic order on developing countries, as if the fact of imposition were itself objectionable, not the effects of the rules themselves. Yet it is certainly true of the labour proposal and perhaps of other elements of Pogge's imaginary counter-vision of the international economic order that developing country governments would not easily consent to the measure in question and thus for the order to be feasible it would have to perpetuate an element of effective coercion by the affluent countries. We would then have the difficulty of accusing affluent countries of injustice through their failing to impose on developing countries against their will the policies dictated by Pogge's principles of justice.

In our own work on global justice, we take a different approach from Pogge: we consider the rules of the international economic order in the context of international law as a whole, including concepts such as sovereignty and self-determination of peoples, and the full range of human rights, not only those that directly seem to bear on poverty and its elimination.[16] By taking international economic law

---

[16] Teitel, R., *Humanity's Law* (Oxford: Oxford University Press, forthcoming 2010), ch. 6; Howse, R. and Teitel, R., *Beyond the Divide: The Covenant on Economic Social and Cultural Rights and the World Trade Organization* (Geneva: Friedrich Eberts Stiftung, 2007). See esp. our discussion of human security.

(largely) in isolation from international law as a whole, Pogge arguably unduly narrows the question of global justice; he sees the crucial or morally significant failure as the non-adoption of discrete 'minor' changes[17] to one specialized set of international rules and institutions, those most closely or directly associated with the international economic order. This comes into particularly sharp relief, when we consider Pogge's proposals to address the role of oppressive and corrupt regimes in causing and perpetuating poverty. Pogge proposes that the affluent countries curtail the borrowing and resource privileges of such regimes. Thus, they would not be able to make enforceable loan contracts with developed country lenders or to engage in international economic transactions (investments, infrastructure projects) that allow them to exploit control over natural resources, presumably to the disadvantage of their own people. Here, clearly, rather than minor or marginal changes to international economic law we are dealing with significant alterations to conventional or mainstream understandings of foundational ideas of the international system as a whole, such as *pacta sunt servanda* (agreements between sovereigns must be kept) and sovereign control over natural resources (something that developing countries insisted on themselves as a fundamental principle of the international order, in the wake of decolonization). This raises real questions about feasibility as well as the foreseeability of effects. In particular, the required weakening of the sovereignty norm would probably entail overcoming considerable resistance from developing countries themselves, not just those that are despotic regimes, but democracies such as India and Brazil, which insist on sovereign self-determination, in fierce opposition, for example, to tying labour rights to trade.

One of us, Teitel, has argued in a forthcoming book, *Humanity's Law*,[18] that changes to the deep structure of international law are indeed implicit in and a necessary tendency of the shift in international law towards the protection of persons and peoples, not just of the interests of sovereign states. In legal terms, this shift has been driven by the evolution of and connections between international human rights law, humanitarian law, and the law of war.[19] Indeed, a consideration of these changes may help illuminate what appear to be tensions or ambiguities in Pogge's theory; he oscillates between a human rights or humanity-based discourse that seems ultimately founded on what citizens and peoples owe to one another, and a sovereignty-based discourse that operates at the level of inter-*state* justice. What may be required is a more precise delineation of rights and responsibilities as between different agents—citizens, states, peoples, corporations—in explicit recognition of the challenge to inter-state approaches to global justice from more intransigently cosmopolitan and humanity-based approaches to international legal order.

---

[17] Again 'minor' is Pogge's characterization. As explained, we ourselves have doubts as to whether in particular the elimination of the resource and borrowing privileges could be characterized as 'minor'.
[18] Teitel, R., *Humanity's Law* (above, n. 16).   [19] Ibid.

Yet such changes, especially to Westphalian notions of state sovereignty, give rise to an important set of dilemmas for global justice. Weakening or suspending the claims to 'sovereignty' or self-determination when asserted by despotic or corrupt regimes, actually confers on other countries, and arguably many of the most powerful ones, new entitlements to 'intervene' elsewhere in the world, imposing their own political and economic judgments. Experience with the UN Security Council in its response to situations in places such as Burma and Sudan suggest that international institutions, in their existing form, are unlikely to judge that regimes are no longer entitled to the full protection of the sovereignty norm in a manner determined by principle rather than power interests. If we think about feasibility, it is unclear what kind of international institution could make the required judgments based on Pogge's principles. In such circumstances, one has to foresee the possibility that the weakening of the sovereignty norm will encourage unilateral judgments particularly by the most powerful countries.

Thus, when we think of real-world feasibility, we need to ask the question of to what extent does such intervention, premised upon the intervening countries' (possibly self-serving) definitions of what is or isn't a corrupt and/or despotic regime, seem fated to reflect their interests, to the extent these are distinct from humanity-based principles of rights and justice? Just as we do not endorse the pre-eminence of the sovereignty norm in the classical Westphalian international statist order, we do not believe either that its suspension in the name of human rights and democracy, while a powerful moral temptation, can be simply and unambiguously understood as just without further analysis.[20] This being said, it is interesting that being in the first instance concerned with what rich *countries* owe, and with the choices states make in constructing international economic rules, Pogge himself still operates within a statist institutional framework, and thus it is difficult to gauge sometimes to what extent the ultimate international order he seeks is grounded in a conception of *inter-state* justice rather than one ultimately grounded in *human rights*.

Here we note a further difference that sets apart our own work on global justice from Pogge's despite our sharing with him at some general level a set of similar normative commitments. We are sceptical about looking at the challenge of building a new, more just international economic order in terms of assigning moral blame and responsibility for the past. In his essay, Pogge understands justice or injustice in terms of the effects of adopting or not adopting a particular set of *rules*: here at least he does not pay sustained attention to the ways in which rules are interpreted and enforced, or more broadly shape meanings and outcomes in complex, sometimes perverse or unpredictable ways. Yet the effects of rules are not really *foreseeable*

---

[20] Indeed the more cautious approach of Rawls to claims of global justice in his *Law of Peoples* seems related in part to a concern to draw some fairly narrow limits to intervention, preserving to a considerable degree the sovereignty norm. Still, even Rawls himself concedes that the sovereign norm is not absolute.

without considering how they are interpreted and applied and by whom, and so this is an issue that is crucial to the very argument that Pogge makes in his essay. Take the rules on intellectual property rights to which Pogge alludes. Interpreted in a balanced way, and as we have argued, in light of human rights including the right to health, the TRIPs agreement, which contains significant limitations or balancing clauses, need not have negative effects on the well-being of people in poor countries. However, certain narrow developed country interests managed to largely capture the interpretative space with respect to TRIPs. Even if, for the sake of argument, we were to suspend our concerns about the formal or explicit content of the rules in Pogge's alternative imaginary international economic order, it is far from clear that more poverty would be eliminated through these new rules, given existing interpretive practices, than would be eliminated through changing the interpretative practices and culture surrounding the existing rules, and especially integrating existing positive international human rights law into the interpretation of the economic rules.[21]

This brings us to the question of collective responsibility for the failure to adopt the imaginary counter-vision of international economic order that Pogge claims would foreseeably eliminate most severe poverty, even on worst-case scenarios about the domestic regime. Pogge says that the failure in question is an injustice of a kind that demands collective responsibility by the citizens of the affluent countries for the payment of reparations or compensation to developing countries. Many of the rules in question were negotiated by particular governmental and business elites, and citizens of affluent countries had as little knowledge and understanding concerning the nature of the rules and their effects, or real world ability to shape them, as did citizens of developing countries. Some of the rules have arguably considerably disadvantaged many citizens/consumers in developed countries themselves, leading to significantly higher prices for basic foodstuffs and medications. And, to return to the problem of interpretation, citizens/consumers/taxpayers of affluent countries have had little day to day ability to shape the interpretative culture surrounding international economic law, which may have a decisive impact on the effects of the *existing* rules. To our minds, these considerations raise important issues regarding the justice of collective responsibility, and its extent. Additionally, they raise issues as to whom the compensation is to be paid. If part of the compensation for instance is for failure to adopt rules that would limit the resource or borrowing privileges of corrupt and/or despotic governments, it would certainly be normatively

---

[21] Indeed, that such an approach would be consistent with the underlying normative commitment to eliminate the most extreme forms of poverty, is illustrated by the work of Margo Salomon, who—greatly influenced by Pogge's earlier work—explores the implications of the positive international law of human rights, particularly the right to development and related social, economic, and cultural rights, for interpretation and application of international economic law, not just its reform at the level of formal rules. See Salomon, M., *Global Responsibility for Human Rights* (Oxford: Oxford University Press, 2008). See also Howse, R. and Teitel, R., *Beyond the Divide* (above, n. 16).

incoherent to offer compensation to those very regimes. Would such compensation have to await regime change, or could it somehow be provided to the people directly?

At times, Pogge appears to boster the moral case by referring to a more distant background of crimes of colonialism that in his view produced the problem of extreme poverty in the first place, or at least the extreme inequality that makes it possible. But if this is the ultimate presupposed normative consideration that makes the duty to compensate coherent, then it really raises with full force transitional justice-related questions of the responsibility of today's citizen taxpayers for injustice committed in an often remote past.[22] This is further complicated by the fact that very many citizens of affluent countries today are the offspring of, or are even directly, victims themselves of colonialism and its heritage. Oddly, and here perhaps we see again the influence of his choice to look at the international economic system in isolation, Pogge (at least in this essay) seems indifferent to issues of global justice posed by immigration; arguably a larger cause of global poverty than the failure to adopt any of his imaginary alternative economic rules, is the failure to alter immigration laws so that citizens in poor countries can freely sell—and develop—their skills anywhere in the world where they are in demand.[23] Since Pogge discusses these issues in other work, it is unclear why he selectively avoids them in the present essay.[24]

Finally, and this goes to the question of foreseeability, in order to moralize the failure of the affluent countries to adopt his imaginary alternative international economic order, Pogge has to introduce a notion of fault, albeit one that stops short of bad faith and has the character of a negligence standard. The negligence standard implies that foreseeability is not a matter of 20/20 hindsight, what we know today on the basis of experience of the rules and how they are interpreted, but what affluent countries ought to have known at the time was likely or foreseeable. At the time those rules were negotiated, there were many responsible economists and policy experts (from both the North and the South), completely independent of affluent country commercial interests, who made arguments that the set of rules in question, in some cases this even included the intellectual property rules, would ultimately pave the way out of poverty for developing countries. Was it really negligence to act upon such opinions, rather than contrary views of economic reality, even if the contrary views seem to us more persuasive today?

---

[22] See Teitel, R., *Transitional Justice* (Oxford: Oxford University Press, 2000), chapter on reparatory justice.

[23] See by contrast, Mangabeira Unger, R., *Free Trade Reimagined: The World Division of Labor and the Method of Economics* (Princeton: Princeton University Press, 2007); and *Democracy Realized: The Progressive Alternative* (New York: Verso, 1998).

[24] Pogge discusses immigration in 'Migration and Poverty' in Bader, V. M. (ed.), *Citizenship and Exclusion* (Houndmills: Macmillan, 1997), 12–27; reprinted in Goodin, R. and Pettit, P. (eds.), *Contemporary Political Philosophy: An Anthology* (Oxford: Blackwell, 2005), 710–20; revised German translation 'Migration und Armut' in Märker, A. and Schlothfeldt, S. (eds.), *Was schulden wir Flüchtlingen und Migranten?* (Westdeutscher Verlag, 2002), 110–26.

The appealing element of Pogge's approach is that it is at its best, a human rights-based approach focused on what is most obvious and compelling and indisputably universal in the common humanity on which human rights are premised—the requirements for survival as a human being. We are sympathetic to this approach even if, as explained above, we think that to be comprehensive and coherent the focus on poverty needs to be extended to human security generally. This being said, we see building a more just global economic order—by which we mean one that aligns with the values of humanity—as a process that requires a new spirit of solidarity between North and South, an orientation towards experimentalism, and to the demands of the future, as shaped by phenomena such as new forms of conflict and other emerging threats to human security such as climate change. Our best shot may be the adoption of policy changes that are not obvious or foreseeable but novel, experimental, and debatable. Moralizing past mistakes and failures and allocating and measuring the blame for them, may be at best a distraction, and at worst an obstacle, to the spirit of solidarity and global common good that we need to face today's and tomorrow's challenges to human security.

SECTION XI

INTERNATIONAL ENVIRONMENTAL LAW

CHAPTER 22

PHILOSOPHICAL ISSUES IN INTERNATIONAL ENVIRONMENTAL LAW

JAMES NICKEL AND DANIEL MAGRAW*

I. INTRODUCTION

The philosophy of environmental law overlaps considerably with philosophical work in environmental ethics. For example, whether species and ecosystems have intrinsic value (in addition to instrumental value) is an issue in both environmental ethics and the philosophy of environmental law. Still, the philosophy of environmental law is not *just* environmental ethics. There are distinctive questions raised by using *law* of any kind to establish and protect environmental norms. Additional questions are raised when the law in question is *international* law. For example, how can international environmental law (IEL), which primarily addresses the actions of governments, regulate environmental problems that are mainly caused by private conduct?

This essay addresses philosophical issues about IEL in the three sections which follow. Section II reflects on the demand of IEL that the world's governments and other actors seriously take into account the interests of future generations when they decide issues involving resources and pollution. Section III considers philosophical

* We are grateful for helpful suggestions made by many people including Daniel Bodansky, Roger Crisp, Stephen Gardener, Dale Jamieson, Steve Vanderheiden, Jeremy Watkins, and the editors of this volume: Samantha Besson and John Tasioulas.

issues about value raised by the requirements of IEL that species and ecosystems be protected. Do these requirements commit IEL to defending the intrinsic value of non-human things—and can we make sense of that commitment? Section IV addresses IEL's attempt to promote measures that mitigate climate change. Our goal throughout will be to show that the philosophical questions raised by IEL are interesting, connected to practice, and worth thinking about. Our discussion also shows how difficult these questions are to resolve.

Treaties creating IEL often begin with broad statements of principle to guide environmental decision-making and the formulation of more specific legal norms. These principles include the following:

Duties to Future Generations. The 1972 Declaration of the United Nations Conference on the Human Environment held in Stockholm asserts in Principle 2 that '[t]he natural resources of the earth . . . must be safeguarded for the benefit of present and future generations . . .'. Principle 5 of the Stockholm Declaration elaborates: 'The nonrenewable resources of the earth must be employed in such a way as to guard against the danger of their future exhaustion . . .'.[1] The 1992 Convention on Biological Diversity, which has been ratified by most of the world's countries, requires its parties to '[i]ntegrate consideration of the conservation and sustainable use of biological resources into national decision-making . . .' (Article 10).

Duties to Avoid Transboundary Environmental Harm and the Polluter Pays Principle. According to Stockholm Principle 21, countries have 'the responsibility to ensure that activities within their jurisdiction or control do not cause damage to the environment of other states or of areas beyond the limits of national jurisdiction'. When such damage has occurred, compensation may be required. The Rio Declaration on Environment and Development (1992) declares the principle that polluters should 'bear the cost of pollution' (Principle 16).

The Precautionary Principle. The 1992 United Nations Framework Convention on Climate Change (FCCC) urges caution in dealing with environmental risks under conditions of partial knowledge: 'The Parties should take precautionary measures to anticipate, prevent or minimize the causes of climate change and mitigate its adverse effects. Where there are threats of serious or irreversible damage, lack of full scientific certainty should not be used as a reason for postponing such measures . . .'.

Cooperation among Sovereign States to Protect Earth's Environment. Stockholm Principle 24 addresses how countries should deal with transboundary environmental issues. It says that 'the protection and improvement of the environment should be handled in a cooperative spirit by all countries, big and small, on an equal

---

[1] We omit citations to IEL documents and treaties since these are easily found using a web search.

footing'. Similarly, Rio Principle 7 begins: 'States shall cooperate in a spirit of global partnership to conserve, protect and restore the health and integrity of the Earth's ecosystem'.

Common but Differentiated Responsibilities. Countries differ enormously in how much environmental damage is caused by their populations, industries, governmental, and military activities, as well as how capable they are of regulating effectively the sources of such damage and to cope with environmental harm. The Rio Declaration says that because of 'different contributions to global environmental degradation' countries have different levels of responsibility for remedying environmental problems. This is the idea of common but differentiated responsibilities ('CBDR'). This idea is made more specific by the Rio Declaration's and FCCC's respective statements that developed countries should 'acknowledge the responsibility that they bear . . . in view of the pressures their societies place on the global environment and of the technologies and financial resources they command' (Principle 7) and 'take the lead in combating climate change and the adverse effects thereof' (Article 3, Principle 1).

The IEL principles listed above assume the current international system of separate, sovereign states, and take national governments to be the main duty-bearers under these principles. To succeed, IEL needs to persuade and pressure the nearly 200 national governments that have front-line responsibility for managing our planet, to create laws and policies that will reduce pollution to tolerable levels, use resources sustainably, and stabilize the climate. In doing this it must deal with countries that have vastly different levels of economic development, scientific and regulatory capacities, and environmental problems. Moreover, because the causes of environmental harm include the ordinary activities of virtually all humans and human organizations (for example, consumption, reproduction, use of buildings, transport, and agricultural and industrial production), IEL's attempt to prevent severe environmental damage must influence nearly everyone's behaviour, directly or indirectly. These are daunting tasks.

As a new and rapidly developing area of law, IEL requires a focus on the *making* and *implementation* of law, not just the interpretation and adjudication of existing legal norms. It also gives us good reason to recognize and accommodate the sources and limits of knowledge needed for effective environmental regulation. Environmental law is science-intensive in ways that many other areas of law are not. Accordingly, IEL must be crafted so as to accommodate changes in scientific knowledge. Attempts to do this have resulted in the use of novel techniques such as inter-governmental scientific institutions to develop scientific consensus on causes and possible remedies of environmental problems, broad framework conventions supplemented with changeable protocols and targets, non-consensus decision-making and easily-modified annexes.

II. TAKING A LONGER VIEW: FAIRNESS TO FUTURE GENERATIONS

As we just saw, the principles of IEL commit governments to taking a long-term perspective in environmental decision-making. An attractive, although not unproblematic, normative approach to doing so proceeds in terms of a duty to avoid serious unfairness to present and future persons. This section explores and develops this approach.[2]

1. Which Goods Require Intergenerational Fairness?

Intergenerational equity is not just about the environment. Ruining the environment or climate and using up many of earth's non-renewable resources are not the only ways in which people living now can make things bad for people living later. The generic question raised by intergenerational equity is how to preserve and transmit over long periods humanity's main assets including human capital, infrastructure, social and political institutions, cultural assets including scientific and technical knowledge, important non-renewable natural resources, and earth's wildness and beauty.

2. Problems in Getting Needed Factual Knowledge about the Future

Taking a long-term perspective in decision-making is risky. Humans do not have much reliable information about the future beyond a decade or two, so we are almost certain to make many mistakes in planning for what will be needed much later. Taking a long-term perspective may do more harm than good given our inadequate knowledge. Costly measures taken now to protect future generations may turn out to have been unnecessary. For example, conserving coal as a resource for future generations may be a wasted and costly effort if future generations have better ways of getting energy than digging up and burning coal. In a period of rapid technological change, it is difficult to predict the circumstances and technologies of

---

[2] Some commentators have suggested that the common-law concept of a trust is helpful in thinking about intergenerational responsibilities. On this view, the present generation holds the earth in trust for future generations and has a duty to those generations to preserve the earth and pass it on to them in good condition. See e.g. Brown, E. W., *In Fairness to Future Generations* (New York: Transnational Publishers, 1989), and Passmore, J., *Man's Responsibility for Nature* (London: Gerald Duckworth & Co Ltd, 1974).

the people who will live even fifty years from now. What changes, for example, will actually result from the use of biofuels, genetic engineering, and nanotechnology? In regard to distant generations, knowing their circumstances, technologies, needs, and preferences is mostly impossible. Since we do not know what technologies distant generations will have, we cannot know much about which (and what quantities of) resources will be needed. Another problem is that we do not know the size of the world's population in future times. Large reductions in population sizes might occur because of epidemics, war, natural and human-caused disasters, or deliberate policy choices.

Although it is hard to predict which resources future generations will need, we can be confident that they will need a liveable earthly home. Fairness requires that we do not pass on to them a planet that has been ruined or gutted. A helpful approach along these lines focuses on ensuring that in the future the biosphere is capable of providing an adequate level of 'ecosystem services'. These services are the benefits that people obtain from the environment, such as food, fibre, fuel, pollination of plants by bees, purification of air and water, protection from UV rays, absorption of wastes, and prevention by vegetation of flooding and erosion.[3] A focus on preserving an earthly environment that can support human life on a large scale shifts the normative requirement from enabling each future generation to be at least as well off as the present generation to enabling future generations to enjoy adequate levels of ecosystem services.

We might hope to outflank problems of inadequate factual knowledge about future people by restricting the temporal horizon. One way to do this is to require that each generation be fair to its successor. This may be the best that we can do, but it does not ensure intergenerational fairness over time. If generation 1 (G1) is fair to generation 2 (G2), and if G2 is fair to generation 3 (G3), and if this relation holds until generation 5 (G5), this does not ensure that G5 got a fair deal from G1. To see this, suppose that G1, G2, and G3 all need a certain non-renewable resource or ecosystem service in order to have decent lives. If G1 uses or destroys half of the entire supply of the resource but passes the other half on to G2 then it is fair to G2, but the result may be that G2 cannot be fair to G3—particularly if the share received by G3 is an insufficient amount to allow G3 to maintain a decent standard of living.[4] A better policy would be to require G1 to be fair to G2 in a way that allows G2 to be fair to G3. This principle is much harder to apply, however, given the limits of our knowledge. And it still cannot ensure that G1 is fair to G4.

---

[3] See Millennium Ecosystem Assessment, *Ecosystems and Human Well-Being: Synthesis* (Washington, DC: Island Press, 2005), 40. See also *Ecosystem Services: A Primer*, <http://www.actionbioscience.org/environment/esa.html>. All websites were most recently checked in Dec. 2008.

[4] Dale Jamieson has noted (e-mail correspondence) that environmental injustices can skip generations. If toxic material buried by G1 creates a huge explosion during the time of the G5s, then G1 may have been fair to G2–G4 but not to G5.

3. The 'Non-Identity Problem' and Intergenerational Fairness

Does it make sense to think that we have duties of fairness to persons in the distant future who do not yet exist and perhaps never will? When those people exist will they have moral complaints against us even though by then we will be long dead?

It is easy to imagine someone acting on a perceived duty to be fair to persons who do not yet exist. A rich grandmother who is planning the disposition of her estate may decide that it would be wrong to give an inheritance exclusively to the two grandchildren she already has since others may still be born. Because she wants to be fair to grandchildren who are not yet born she prescribes that some part of her estate be divided equally among all of her grandchildren who are alive at a certain time after her death—whether or not they are already alive at the time she makes her will. She wants to avoid a situation in which her future grandchildren lodge complaints of unfairness against her because they got no inheritances from her while their already-born siblings or cousins got large sums.

What if the current choices of policies (or estate plans) caused different people (or grandchildren) to be born? Suppose the rich grandmother's will specified that only grandchildren born in leap years would receive bequests, and this caused the parents to bear children at different times than they would otherwise have chosen. Would we still think that the grandmother's actions could be unfair to her future grandchildren? After all, they would owe their existence as the specific persons they are to their grandmother's will. This question is raised by Derek Parfit's 'non-identity problem'.

Parfit asks us to imagine a 14-year-old girl who chooses to have a child and who, because she is so young, gives her child a bad start in life.[5] Can we criticize this girl by saying that the decision she made was 'worse for her child'? If we are referring to her actual child, Parfit thinks not. Her choice was not worse for him since without that decision he would never have existed as the particular person he is: 'If she had waited, this particular child would never have existed. And, despite its bad start, his life is worth living'. Parfit goes on to argue that whether or not we believe that causing someone to exist can benefit them, we must reach the conclusion that, all things considered, the teenage mother did not make things worse for her son as the particular person he is. And if her choice did not make him worse off, perhaps the much better health and opportunities enjoyed by his sister, born later when his mother was better positioned to raise a child, are not unfair to him.

Still, Parfit allows that there is a sense in which the girl's decision was worse for, or against the interests of, her child. When we say this, however, we cannot be speaking of the particular person to whom she gave birth. 'If we claim that this

---

[5] Parfit, D., *Reasons and Persons* (Oxford: Oxford University Press, 1984), 358–61.

girl's decision was worse for her child, we cannot be claiming that it was worse for a particular person. We cannot claim, of the girl's child, that her decision was worse for him. We must admit that [in this statement] the words "her child" do not refer to her child'.

Parfit generalizes this point to future generations. When we make major policy choices pertaining, say, to energy policy or nuclear waste disposal we affect which particular people will be born in the future. Different policies will influence which people reproduce with whom and at what times. In many cases the future people who seem to be disadvantaged or treated unfairly would not have existed if some other policy had been chosen. Just as in the case of the teenage mother, we cannot say that, all things considered, our choices were worse for those particular people. If our choices were bad, the problem cannot be that our choices made those particular people worse off. If we acted wrongly, *they* cannot be the victims or people who have standing to complain.

The non-identity problem seems to stand in the way of applying the idea of intergenerational fairness to people in the distant future since it prevents us from using notions such as 'harmed' and 'made worse off' in application to particular future persons. The fairness principle sketched above concerns avoiding *severe* unfairness. The imposition of serious harm or substantial risk of it is a factor in making unfairness severe. Many forms of unfairness are harmless (for example, cheating in no- or low-stakes games). Their 'victims' can complain, but not very loudly. Engaging in harmless unfairness can reveal bad character and bad intentions. But seriously harmful forms of unfairness are the ones we really care about, that we speak of as injustices. When an innocent person goes to jail, or racial discrimination costs a person a good job, we take the unfairness involved very seriously. These considerations provide one reason for thinking that a workable notion of intergenerational fairness cannot do without the concept of harm.

Can we avoid this problem by using a different normative vocabulary or approach? For purposes of discussion let's use the example of people in our era greedily and thoughtlessly using up non-renewable resources that future generations are likely to need. One possibility is to focus entirely on the character (virtue or vice) rather than the consequences of our generation's actions. This approach does not consider the consequences of our actions for particular future people. It allows us to say that our actions displayed greed, short-sightedness, and lack of concern for the needs of future people. It makes no claim, however, that the actual people who will live in the future will be made worse off by our actions.[6]

---

[6] Alan Holland advocates this sort of approach. He thinks that because 'there is simply no way of telling . . . what process should be put in place to secure the desired outcome' we should ignore outcomes 'and settle instead for a "procedural" understanding of our responsibilities regarding future generations'. See 'Sustainability: Should We Start from Here?', in Dobson, A. (ed.), *Fairness and Futurity* (Oxford: Oxford University Press, 1999), 46–68 at 67.

If evils are generated by our short-sighted actions, perhaps they are what Feinberg classified as 'non-grievance evils'.[7] Such evils can either be 'welfare-connected' or 'free-floating'.

Another possibility is to limit our claims about fairness to living people. This approach focuses entirely on people who are currently alive, but emphasizes that some babies just born are likely to live for a century or more. If some of the babies born today will live for 100 years, we can consider the harm to them caused by our greedy and short-sighted use of non-renewable resources. Here the non-identity problem is avoided entirely. When these babies become adults, or senior citizens, they will be in a position to complain about having been harmed by and treated unfairly by our policy choices. Beyond this, our attempting to fairly consider the needs of people a century from now can establish a cultural practice of thinking about impacts on people who live in the future that extends its time horizon forward with each day's new births.[8] This approach does not allow us to speak of harm to particular people in the *distant* future, but it does allow us to consider harm and unfairness to real people that occurs many decades from now. Perhaps this time frame is long enough since our ignorance about the future (discussed above) often prevents our seeing even a few decades ahead. A problem with this view, however, is that being fair to people who will live a century from now is consistent with being unfair to people who will live later still (also discussed above).

A third possibility is suggested by Parfit himself. He says that as long as we are talking about populations of the same size we can compare the outcomes of different policies by appeal to a principle that he calls 'Q'. That principle says that one policy is worse than another if under the first policy people have a lower quality of life than the (different) people who would have lived had we chosen the second policy. This allows us to say of the teenage mother that 'the child she has now will probably be worse off than a child she could have had later would have been' and thus that 'it would have been better if this girl had waited'. But we must say this without reference to the girl's actual child. The general idea seems to be that if we hold population size constant and abstract from the particular identities of the future persons involved, we can evaluate policies by reference to their effects on people in the distant future. This approach works fine for us now, thinking about people in the distant future that we will never know or meet, since their particular identities and populations sizes cannot be known now and do not matter to us in our decision-making. It does not, however, work so well for them since their particular identities do matter to them. If they wish to complain about our bad resource policies 200 years from now they must do so by abstracting from their own

---

[7] Feinberg, J., *Harmless Wrongdoing: The Moral Limits of the Criminal Law*, vol. iv (Oxford: Oxford University Press, 1988).

[8] This approach can be found in Vanderheiden, S., 'Conservation, Foresight, and the Future Generations Problem', *Inquiry*, 49 (2006), 337. See also Barry, B., 'Sustainability and Intergenerational Justice', in Dobson, A. (ed.), *Fairness and Futurity* (Oxford: Oxford University Press, 1999), 93.

particular identities, by setting aside the fact that they are happy to be alive as the particular persons they are.

A related approach, which we might associate with the Rawlsian tradition, deliberates about impacts on future generations within the constraints of 'public reason' and from behind a veil of ignorance.[9] In choosing moral principles this approach considers representative persons rather than particular individuals, uses an 'objective' conception of value that abstracts from particular preferences (including the value of being alive as the particular person one is), and selects principles for allocating resources between present and future persons on the basis of which principles it would be rational to choose if one did not know when one would live. When we try to be fair to people who will live in the distant future these abstractions will not seem odd to us since in any case we know little about their preferences and identities. But this approach may imply that the 'wrongs' done by current people are not wrongs to actual future people. Once we have chosen principles to govern decisions that might have impacts on representative persons in the distant future, failure to follow those principles might yield non-grievance evils (of one or the other type) rather than harms or wrongs to particular persons.

Parfit's non-identity problem makes it hard to apply a principle of fairness to people in the distant future. Difficult is not impossible, however, since there seem to be some ways of navigating around the fact that different policies cause different people to be born. The price of this detour, however, may be accepting the idea that bad current policies create non-grievance evils—that is, accepting that no particular person in the distant future will have standing to complain about the unfairness of the choices we made. This commits us to the awkward idea that there can be cases of unfairness that no particular person is in position to complain about, but we can probably live with this idea.

4. Legal Approaches to Intergenerational Equity

Two kinds of indeterminacy hinder the successful application of the idea of intergenerational equity. One is normative, pertaining to how we should understand in this context the vague normative idea of avoiding severely unfair policies. Another kind of indeterminacy is factual, pertaining, for example, to the technologies future generations will have and how large their populations will be. An important approach to resolving these indeterminacies emphasizes extended discussion and argument among citizens, intellectuals, scientific experts, and politicians. This approach hopes that a more determinate conception of what intergenerational fairness requires can

---

[9] See Rawls, J., *Political Liberalism* (New York: Columbia University Press, 1993) and 'The Idea of Public Reason Revisited', in *The Law of Peoples* (Cambridge, Mass.: Harvard University Press, 1999). See also Reiman, J., 'Being Fair to Future People: The Non-Identity Problem in the Original Position', *Philosophy and Public Affairs*, 35 (2007), 69.

be found, prove persuasive, and find both widespread acceptance and appropriate implementation around the world.

IEL attempts to speed up and institutionalize this deliberative process though use of legal norms and processes. It uses international lawmaking to produce determinate standards—ones that are, in the words of John Locke, 'known and settled'.[10] Law is often used to give more determinate content to vague moral and political standards. For example, people know that the deliberate killing of human beings is generally morally wrong, but the law of homicide and manslaughter provides a more determinate idea of exactly which actions and intentions are impermissible, which justifications and excuses are valid, and what penalties are appropriate. Law at the national and international levels can be used to specify precise content for the idea of intergenerational equity. Lawmakers learn from moralists, activists, philosophers, and politicians, but then do what those figures cannot do—namely establish known and settled national and international legal standards that can be adjudicated and enforced.

Law cannot remedy factual uncertainty about future technologies and population sizes, but it can specify carefully-established working assumptions about these matters (e.g., that humans will need land for agriculture into the distant future and that successful human reproduction will require protection from certain pollutants such as mercury) provided that those assumptions are regularly evaluated and revised in light of the best scientific knowledge. This approach suggests a demanding programme of legal work that IEL has already begun. But this legal programme is far from completion—and it will be particularly difficult in the area of climate change. The temptation to do too little will be ever present,[11] as will the possibility of doing things that turn out not to work.

III. Expanding the Circle of Protection Beyond Humanity

Many will react to the previous section's focus on intergenerational equity by suggesting that it is too human-oriented to provide by itself an adequate basis for environmental attitudes and decision-making. Indeed, they may go so far as to say that what is distinctive about environmental ethics is that it takes seriously the idea

---

[10] Locke, J., *Second Treatise of Civil Government* (1689), ch. IX, sec. 126. See also the excellent development of this idea by Honore, T., 'The Dependence of Morality on Law', *Oxford Journal of Legal Studies*, 13 (1993), 1.

[11] See Gardener, S., 'A Perfect Moral Storm: Climate Change, Intergenerational Ethics and the Problem of Moral Corruption', *Environmental Values*, 15 (2006), 397.

of caring about nature on grounds that do not derive from concern for human wellbeing. Perhaps our motivation not to kill gorillas should mainly flow from concern for gorillas or for the entire circle of life, not exclusively from concern for future humans.

IEL often emphasizes human interests as the grounds for protecting and preserving nature. As we saw above, the Stockholm Declaration speaks of safeguarding natural resources 'for the benefit of present and future generations'. The Rio Declaration, with its emphasis on sustainability, says that '[h]uman beings are at the centre of concerns for sustainable development. They are entitled to a healthy and productive life in harmony with nature'. IEL, however, prescribes protections not just for humans but also for plant and animal species and for ecosystems.[12] Is this concern merely instrumental? Is it based on the fact that humans find useful the flourishing of these species and systems?

Environmental activists and theorists have often battled against views—including cost-benefit analysis as practiced by most economists—that treat the non-human natural world as a mere resource for humans. They have sometimes gone on to argue that nature has *intrinsic* value, or at least that it would be good for humans to love nature for its own sake. When something is *instrumentally* valuable its value is derivative from something else, the final end the instrument serves. Intrinsic value is not derivative in this way; it is valuable for its own sake. Intrinsic values provide final or non-derivative reasons for action.

Lawyers may be tempted to duck questions about the intrinsic value of nature by suggesting that whether or not nature has intrinsic value does not matter much to IEL since natural objects and systems can have whatever protected status lawmakers choose to give them, and since fully developed legal norms, unlike moral norms, come with their own motivational machinery in the form of sanctions or incentives. Accordingly, whether people take a legal norm seriously does not depend entirely on whether they think it has a strong underlying rationale. On this approach, one might conclude that the philosophy of IEL, unlike environmental ethics, does not need to address the question of whether the protection of nature is supported by the intrinsic value of nature.

This response is unwarranted; however, since IEL norms typically lack strong enforcement machinery and like other parts of law rely heavily on voluntary compliance. Whether countries are willing to ratify treaties containing these norms, and act in accordance with them once they are part of international law, depends on whether their leaders and voters find compelling the reasons for having the norms.

---

[12] On whether IEL is committed to a non-anthropocentric approach see Gillespie, A., *International Environmental Law, Policy and Ethics* (Oxford: Oxford University Press, 1997), 15–18 and 127–36. See also the account of IEL's recent ecocentric tendencies in Bodansky, D., Brunnee, J., and Hey, E. (eds.), *Oxford Handbook of International Environmental Law* (Oxford: Oxford University Press, 2007), 15–16.

If these people find intelligible and persuasive the idea that nature has intrinsic value and is worthy of respect for its own sake, that will provide another reason—in addition to all the human-oriented ones—for taking seriously the norms of IEL. Moreover, governments often need to be prodded by the initiation of litigation to enforce environmental laws. The intrinsic value of natural places, organisms, and systems can help establish standing for individuals or groups trying to do this—even though they themselves have suffered no harm.[13]

One fully intelligible way for something to have intrinsic value to someone is for that person to value or love it for its own sake. Eugene Hargrove claims that for a natural object to have intrinsic value it is sufficient that some human individual or group admires, prizes, or appreciates the natural object *for what it is in itself*. Hargrove calls this 'the intrinsically valued', putting the emphasis on active valuation by humans.[14] It is very common for people to prize animals and natural places in ways that are little connected with the pursuit of their own happiness or that of other humans. Actively valuing nature for its own sake may reflect a person's moral and religious commitments. As part of one's personal moral or religious stance, one might decide to adopt an ecocentric philosophy that views nature as having value of its own. To live in accordance with this philosophy one would attempt to treat nature with respect in one's daily life. This kind of approach allows environmental ethics to use the vocabulary of intrinsic value and to advocate valuing nature for its own sake without taking any position on the metaphysical status of intrinsic value.[15]

Still, valuing something for its own sake—however sincerely and admirably—is insufficient to make it intrinsically valuable. To be intrinsically valuable in a strong sense a thing needs to be *worthy* of being valued for its own sake, and we cannot establish that worthiness by an act of will alone. Being esteemed for its own sake makes something intrinsically *valued*, but it does not show that it is *valuable*. And even if we do not doubt that something is worthy of being valued for its own sake, we may still worry about whether it is worthy of being assigned *enough* intrinsic value to generate environmental duties and rights.

A second approach to understanding the intrinsic value of natural systems and objects suggests that those systems and objects can be *constitutive* rather than instrumental parts of experiences that have intrinsic value. The fact that environmental values are rooted in human valuation and experience does not imply that their objects are simply experiences. The role of birds in the activities of birdwatchers is constitutive, not merely instrumental.[16] More generally, the experience of beauty,

---

[13] Stone, C. D., 'Should Trees Have Standing?—Toward Legal Rights for Natural Objects', *Southern California Law Review*, 45 (1972), 450.

[14] Hargrove, E., 'Weak Anthropocentric Intrinsic Value', *Monist*, 75 (1992), 182.

[15] See McShane, K., 'Why Environmental Ethics Shouldn't Give Up on Intrinsic Value', *Environmental Ethics*, 29 (2007), 59.

[16] Frankena, W., 'Ethics and the Environment', in Goodpaster, K. E., and Sayre, K. M. (eds.), *Ethics and Problems of the 21st Century* (Indiana: University of Notre Dame Press, 1979), 13.

which has widely been thought to be intrinsically valuable, includes experiencing the beauty of natural systems and objects. When one experiences the beauty of Half Dome (a rock formation in Yosemite National Park), Half Dome is a constituent part of that experience. We cannot identify the experience without reference to the rock formation.[17] Thus Half Dome itself could have a type of intrinsic value—which Raz calls 'constitutive' intrinsic value. Still, whether this sort of intrinsic value can support the demanding duties and rights that environmentalists would like to justify is unclear. Are these intrinsically good experiences of sufficient value to confer such great value on their constituents as to justify protective rights for them?

The two kinds of intrinsic value in nature just explained make human life and choice necessary conditions for the value of nature. Some theorists have proposed a stronger type of intrinsic value that can somehow inhere in nature independently of human experience, recognition, or choice.[18] These views may hold that such goodness is as much part of the natural world as a thing's shape or size. It is mainly something about nature, not about human or sentient life, that makes nature worthy of esteem for its own sake. On this view humans just have to recognize the great intrinsic value that is already present in nature—and have the cognitive capacities to do so. While this approach deserves further exploration and development, it relies on such strong and speculative assumptions that it is unlikely to persuade many doubters.

In any case, appealing to the intrinsic value of natural objects and systems is unlikely to provide the powerful argumentative tool that environmental theorists have sought. First, intrinsic value is harder to defend with arguments than instrumental value. The basis for something's intrinsic value often has to be learned or experienced for a person to recognize the value in the thing or activity. Sometimes a thing's intrinsic worth can be explained and shown, but it is generally hard to argue the intrinsic value of something to a person who 'doesn't get it', who cannot see the value in that thing or activity. If a person does not see intrinsic value in preserving a small fish like the snail darter it is going to be hard to argue the point—and even harder if what we need to establish in order to justify moral or legal duties to the snail darter is that its preservation has *great* intrinsic value.

Second, intrinsic values do not always have higher priority than instrumental values. Many of us would, in exchange for a million instrumentally valuable dollars, happily forgo an afternoon in a museum during which we would enjoy experiences with intrinsic value. When an intrinsic value competes with instrumental values, the intrinsic value does not automatically win since intrinsic value comes in different quantities.

---

[17] Raz, J., *The Morality of Freedom* (Oxford: Oxford University Press, 1987), 200.

[18] See e.g. Rolston, H., *Environmental Ethics: Duties to and Values in Nature* (Philadelphia: Temple University Press, 1988), and *Philosophy Gone Wild* (New York: Prometheus Books, 1989). For an environmental ethics developed along Kantian lines see Taylor, P. W., *Respect for Nature* (Princeton: Princeton University Press, 1986).

Third, if things of different kinds have intrinsic value claims on behalf of these things can compete with each other. If both human life and natural systems have intrinsic value, conflicts between these values may not generally favour the natural systems. Philosophers who attempt to avoid 'speciesism' by postulating the equal intrinsic value of humans, animals, and natural systems usually find ways of avoiding the conclusion that the life of a mouse or tree is as valuable as the life of a person.

Fourth, intrinsic value does not automatically connect with duties, respect, or rights. The path from something's having value to people's having duties to it is generally not a simple one. The fact that a person is finding intrinsically valuable pleasure in watching a soaring hawk does not give others a duty not to interrupt the experience by asking the person a question. We are suspicious of the claim made by Brennan and Lo that 'something's possession of intrinsic value generates a prima facie direct moral duty on the part of moral agents to protect it or at least refrain from damaging it'.[19] Perhaps things with great intrinsic value generate such duties of respect. For example, Ronald Dworkin takes the great intrinsic value of human life to explain why people have duties to respect and refrain from capriciously destroying human life.[20] When something has great intrinsic value it is a very bad thing, perhaps even a cosmic shame, if it is destroyed or its enjoyment forever frustrated. From great intrinsic value we may be able to infer rights and duties. In order to reach environmental rights and duties, however, it is not enough for the environmentalist to persuade people that nature has some intrinsic value. What needs to be demonstrated is that nature has such great intrinsic value that it generates duties of respect and preservation.

Finally, if we try to provide each thing of intrinsic value with duties of preservation and respect, we will generate an unmanageably large number of duties. Consider how many things are intrinsically valuable. There are all the particular experiences of sincere love, all the particular experiences of beauty, all the particular instances of personal accomplishment, and so on. If we attach to each such thing high priority duties of preservation and respect, the result will be ethical gridlock. Fill the world with too many serious duties and we will have to spend so much time on these duties that we will have no time for the intrinsically valuable activities. We'll have to find all of our joy in doing our duties. Perhaps all intrinsically valuable things are morally considerable, but we doubt that each and every one of them is a source of a significant duty.

---

[19] Brennan, A., and Lo, Y., 'Environmental Ethics', in Zalta, E. N. (ed.), *The Stanford Encyclopedia of Philosophy* (Stanford University: The Metaphysics Research Lab, Summer 2002), available at <http://plato.stanford.edu/archives/sum2002/entries/ethics-environmental>.

[20] Dworkin, R., *Life's Dominion* (New York: Alfred A. Knopf, 1993), 68–101.

IV. NORMATIVE ISSUES IN ADDRESSING CLIMATE CHANGE

Climate change (CC) poses both a difficult test for IEL and a major opportunity for its further development.[21] The philosophical issues about IEL discussed in the previous sections are important here. Intergenerational equity is relevant because people now and in coming decades will face a strong temptation to pass on to future generations the burdens of mitigating and adapting to CC.[22] Whether nature has intrinsic value also matters in dealing with CC because even if humans can adapt to CC many types of flora and fauna will not be able to do so. Large climate changes will decimate many species of plants and animals.

Average air temperatures on earth rose about one degree Fahrenheit during the 20th century, and larger increases are projected for the 21st. This is 'global warming', a continuing and possibly accelerating process. In recent decades, atmospheric scientists have reached widespread consensus that a substantial part of this warming is caused by the increased presence in earth's atmosphere, caused by human activities, of greenhouse gases (GHGs) such as carbon dioxide, methane, nitrous oxide, ozone, and water vapour. GHGs in the atmosphere tend to absorb infrared radiation from the sun after it strikes the earth. This 'greenhouse effect' traps heat in earth's atmosphere. The 'enhanced greenhouse effect' (resulting from the higher levels of GHGs caused by human activities) is causing higher average temperatures on the earth's surface. The use of fossil fuels in transportation, electricity production, and the heating and cooling of buildings is a major source of increased carbon dioxide in the atmosphere. A warmer earth is likely to have shrinking glaciers and Arctic ice, decreased snow pack in mountain ranges, rising sea levels, and more frequent and intense hurricanes, heat waves, and droughts. Global warming is not a uniform process; it is very difficult to predict which localities will be wetter, drier, warmer, or cooler. This is one reason for speaking of 'climate change' rather than 'global warming'.

Attempts to slow or stop global warming proceed on the belief that if humans reduce the emission of GHGs then the concentration of those gases in the atmosphere will be reduced with consequent reductions in rates or levels of global warming. GHGs stay in the atmosphere and oceans for a long time, however, so the results

---

[21] For a good survey of ethical issues in climate change, see Gardener, S., 'Ethics and Global Climate Change', *Ethics*, 114 (2004), 555.

[22] See Page, E., *Climate Change, Justice and Future Generations* (Cheltenham: Edward Elgar Publishing, 2006).

in terms of lower air temperatures of reducing GHG emissions—even when combined with the use of sinks to sequester GHGs—may be slow in coming. The accumulation of GHGs in the atmosphere has momentum—it will continue to affect earth's climate for hundreds of years even if atmospheric levels of GHGs stop rising. This fact has important epistemological and political consequences. It means that potentially successful but expensive efforts to reduce CC could fail to show clear results in terms of reduced temperatures for many decades. This fact also suggests that the scope of CC law and policy must include not just reduction of GHG emissions but also ways of adapting to a changed climate and responding to sudden natural disasters related to it.

Nearly all of the world's countries have ratified the 1992 United Nations Framework Convention on Climate Change (FCCC). It requires its parties to create national strategies for reducing GHG emissions and to cooperate in learning about and adapting to CC. The 1997 Kyoto Protocol attempted to strengthen the FCCC by moving from broad legal principles to more specific rules and targets. The Kyoto Protocol required separate ratification; it came into force in 2005 and about 165 countries have ratified the protocol as of 2007. Its modification or replacement will be required after 2012. The protocol required developed—but not developing—countries to reduce GHG emissions by specified amounts during the period 2008–12. As we saw earlier, the FCCC endorses a principle of 'common but differentiated responsibilities' that assigns to developed countries more demanding duties than it does to developing countries. The Kyoto Protocol followed this principle by exempting developing countries from emissions targets.

Several factors contribute to the difficulty of finding agreement on measures to mitigate and adapt to CC. First, the measures chosen should be ones that *work*—that actually bring about sufficient mitigation, adaptation, and preparedness. Second, these measures must be *affordable* in the sense that countries can meet their costs while meeting their other responsibilities of equal or higher priority. Third, the measures must be *acceptable* to the countries that are making, or soon will be making, major contributions to GHGs in the atmosphere. Finally, the measures chosen should be *fair*.[23]

In thinking about the moral and political principles that should guide measures to mitigate and adapt to CC we should recognize that IEL itself offers considerable guidance. The FCCC does a good job of setting out plausible principles to govern international responses to climate change. It recognizes 'equity' and 'differentiated responsibilities' based upon differences among countries in contributions to the problem and in capacities to deal with it. It asserts international duties to help countries that are 'particularly vulnerable to the adverse effects of climate change'.

---

[23] On barriers to success in international climate change negotiations see Roberts, J. T., and Parks, B. C., *A Climate of Injustice: Global Inequality, North-South Politics, and Climate Policy* (Cambridge, Mass.: MIT Press, 2007).

It clearly invokes the Polluter Pays Principle (PPP) when it asserts that 'the largest share of historical and current global emissions of greenhouse gases has originated in developed countries', sets out the concept of CBDR, and calls upon developed countries to 'take the lead in combating climate change and the adverse effects thereof'. The FCCC takes account of subsistence as a human right and the goal of sustainable economic development when it sets out the goals of ensuring that 'food production is not threatened' and enabling 'economic development to proceed in a sustainable manner' with consequent growth in 'energy consumption' in developing countries. And the FCCC at least partially recognizes the value of preserving natural systems and processes when it asserts that climate stabilization 'should be achieved within a time-frame sufficient to allow ecosystems to adapt naturally to climate change'.

Other IEL principles we identified earlier support conclusions such as: (1) States and the international community must take action to avert the dislocation and other damage that CC may cause in the future (intergenerational equity); (2) the lack of full scientific certainty about the causes and extent of CC does not obviate the need for action (Precautionary Principle); (3) States have a legal obligation to act to prevent transboundary harm from CC; and (4) if a country breaches its obligation to prevent transboundary harm, it must cease the violation (that is, stop causing CC) and repair or provide compensation for the damage caused.[24]

International human rights law is another source of principles for dealing with CC. For example, all of the major human rights treaties set out a right to life. Perhaps the duties of Governments that flow from the right to life include ensuring that negligently caused CC does not kill people. The International Covenant on Economic, Social, and Cultural Rights (United Nations 1966) sets forth rights to 'an adequate standard of living . . . including adequate food, clothing and housing' (article 11). This reinforces the importance of ensuring that CC does not render vulnerable countries even less capable of feeding and housing their people. More broadly, if CC puts vulnerable countries under great financial and institutional stress, their abilities to respect and protect *any* human rights will suffer. S. James Anaya has argued that respect for the territories and cultures of indigenous peoples has received sufficient recognition in state practice to have become a norm of customary international law.[25] If CC makes traditional lands uninhabitable and traditional ways of life impossible, the rights of indigenous peoples may be violated by ignoring CC and its effects. Finally, scholars and commentators have advocated recognition in national and international law of a right to a safe environment.[26]

[24] See Crawford, J. (ed.), *United Nations International Law Commission's Articles on State Responsibility* (Cambridge: Cambridge University Press, 2002).

[25] Anaya, S. J., *Indigenous Peoples in International Law* (Oxford: Oxford University Press, 2004). See also Anaya, S. J., and Williams, R., 'The Protection of Indigenous People's Rights Over Lands and Natural Resources Under the Inter-American Human Rights System', *Harvard Human Rights Journal*, 14 (2001), 33.

[26] See Hayward, T., *Constitutional Environmental Rights* (Oxford: Oxford University Press, 2005), and Nickel, J., 'The Right to a Safe Environment', *Yale Journal of International Law*, 18/1 (1993), 281, and *Making Sense of Human Rights* (2nd edn., Malden: Blackwell Publishing, 2006), 97–8.

Let's now take a closer look at the implications of the Polluter Pays Principle (PPP) for distributing the burdens of mitigating and adapting to CC. The PPP holds that each polluter should pay the cost of the pollution it causes. Whether the application to CC is straightforward, however, depends on how the PPP is formulated. Recall that the formulation of the PPP in Principle 16 of the Rio Declaration says that 'national authorities should endeavour to promote the internalization of environmental costs and the use of economic instruments, taking into account the approach that the polluter should, in principle, bear the cost of the pollution'.[27] This formulation does not focus on transboundary pollution or address situations with multiple polluters. Nevertheless, we see no conceptual problem in applying the PPP. In our view, the PPP implies (premise 1) that a country that emits GHGs should take as rapidly as practically possible measures that will enable it to stop causing CC and should pay for repairing the damage it has caused or is continuing to cause ('If you broke it, you pay for it'). Add (premise 2) that the developed countries presently do most of the emitting of GHGs, and we get the conclusion that the developed countries should stop causing climate change and pay for most of the damage caused by GHGs. In this way the PPP supports CBDR. The more a country contributes to CC the more it should pay in damages.

Although the PPP implies that developed countries should pay most of the costs of mitigating and adapting to CC, it does not imply that developing countries should be exempted from liability, particularly since their share of total GHG emission continues to rise (for example, by some accounts, China became the largest total—not per capita—emitter in 2007, and its emissions are growing). Still, differential liability for the costs of mitigating and adapting to CC can follow from the PPP itself in the following way. Suppose that within the same timeframe party A negligently or wrongfully does a lot of some dangerous activity and thereby causes major harm to party B, while B negligently or wrongfully does a little of that same activity and thereby causes minor harm to A.[28] The result may be that they owe each other compensation. If, however, we subtract what B owes in compensation to A from the larger amount A owes to B, B will not have to pay anything to A and will in fact receive compensation from A. Further, inability to pay renders inoperative a country's duty to compensate for harms it has caused, even if it does not extinguish that duty. Inability to pay should be understood as 'unable to pay while meeting higher priority obligations', and a country's keeping its people alive

[27] See the Single European Act, Article 25, which states: 'Action by the Community relating to the environment shall be based on the principles that preventive action should be taken, that environmental damage should as a priority be rectified at source, and that the polluter should pay'. Cmnd. 9758 (1986). See also Principle k5 of the European Community's Principles of a Community Environmental Policy, 16 *O.J. Eur. Comm.* (No. C 112) 6 (1973) ('The cost of preventing and eliminating nuisances must in principle be borne by the polluter').

[28] On ways in which CC may be far more damaging to low income countries than to developed countries see Roberts, J. T., and Parks, B. C., *A Climate of Injustice: Global Inequality, North-South Politics, and Climate Policy* (above, n. 23).

is surely of higher priority than paying compensation for GHG pollution. Thus, we are doubtful of Simon Caney's claim that the PPP 'asks too much of the poor'.[29]

The PPP is vague as to how far it extends back into the past. Global warming experienced today is partly caused by emissions made prior to 1992 (roughly the point at which countries had adequate warning about the possibility of causing CC). Under principles of tort law, actors are not normally liable for damages they caused during times when no one knew that their activity was dangerous (though some environmental law, such as CERCLA,[30] provides for something closer to *ex post facto* strict liability). There is also the interesting question of how long countries have to stop causing harm from GHG pollution. If a country learns in 1992 that it may be causing harm to other countries through its GHG emissions, how long does it have to make the transition to a less polluting economy and to remove (or otherwise compensate for) the ongoing CC its past pollution is causing? Does it have full responsibility as it makes that transition? A more plausible view is that full responsibility begins when it fails to make that transition within a reasonable time. Beyond this, what measures count as contributions to reducing CC? Should China, for example, get CC credit for its efforts to control population size (which has the effect of reducing GHG emissions)?

V. CONCLUSION

IEL raises fascinating questions and faces daunting challenges. A great human drama lies ahead as government leaders, international lawyers, and scientific experts work both in their home countries and within the international system to address issues about intergenerational equity and climate change. Great changes in technologies and ways of living are sure to be required. Improved ways of thinking about the environment and its protection are also likely to be needed, and here moral, political, and environmental philosophers have something to contribute. In this paper we have defended taking the idea of moral and legal duties of fairness to future generations seriously, expressed doubts about whether plausible accounts of the intrinsic value of nature can generate high-priority environmental rights and duties, and defended a polluter pays approach to dealing with the costs of climate change.

---

[29] Caney, S., 'Cosmopolitan Justice, Responsibility, and Global Climate Change', *Leiden Journal of International Law*, 18 (2005), 747. Caney says that 'a purely "polluter pays" approach is incomplete' (767) and 'needs to be supplemented' (747).

[30] The Comprehensive Environmental Response, Compensation, and Liability Act (CERCLA), United States Congress, 11 Dec. 1980.

CHAPTER 23

ETHICS AND INTERNATIONAL ENVIRONMENTAL LAW

ROGER CRISP*

I. INTRODUCTION

International environmental law (IEL) is primarily an instrument for human purposes, and these purposes may be moral ones. As an instrument, it could not plausibly be described as blunt. It is difficult to make, to interpret, and to apply or enforce. Nor are its conceptual boundaries sharp. Not only is it hard to say what constitutes 'the environment' (should cultural heritage be included along with the mountains and oceans, for example?), but exactly what counts as law here is unclear. The term often used—'soft'—is more appropriate. But soft, hard-to-define, hard-to-use things can be valuable, and the ends or goals of IEL include some among the most significant yet adopted by humanity.

Environmentalists, lawyers, politicians, citizens, and others who participate in the processes of establishing and applying IEL are pursuing many different goals. What those goals are is largely a matter for the political scientist, sociologist, or anthropologist. The concern of philosophy is normative: Which goals *should* we pursue with IEL as our instrument?[1]

* For comments on earlier drafts I am grateful to audiences in Fribourg and Oxford, and in particular to Samantha Besson, James Nickel, and John Tasioulas.

[1] Note that, in claiming that IEL is an instrument to be used in pursuit of human goals, I am not restricting justifications of it to what are usually called 'teleological' or goal-based ethical theories as opposed to 'deontological' duty-based accounts. A deontological theorist might insist, for example, that there are duties to

My paper is in part a response to the previous paper in this volume, by Nickel and Magraw. In section II, I suggest that attributing moral obligations only to individual persons is plausible in itself and also enables us to avoid certain problems left unresolved by Nickel and Magraw. In section III, I argue against their claim that our obligations to future generations can be understood as a duty of fairness. In section VIII, despite being broadly in sympathy with their conclusion, I offer some objections to Nickel and Magraw's critique of the claim that nature has inherent intrinsic value. The paper also proposes two alternatives to Nickel and Magraw's general approach. I do not choose between them, and there are of course many others. The first, a form of environmental virtue ethics, is outlined in section IV. The second, a dualistic view combining a form of consequentialism with a principle allowing an agent to attach extra rational weight to her own well-being, is sketched in section V. In section VI, I address the question whether justice demands equality between the generations, and argue that it requires at most giving priority to the worse off who do or will exist, regardless of our choices. In section VII, I discuss the so-called 'repugnant conclusion' for well-being-maximizing principles when applied to issues of population. I close the paper with some reflections on the implications of deep disagreement for ethical theory and for the making of IEL.

II. Agency and Responsibility

It is common in environmental ethics for moral responsibility to be attributed to entities other than rational individual agents, and this is perhaps particularly likely when international law, which is usually seen as binding states or governments, is under discussion. Consider for example the Polluter Pays Principle (PPP), according to which each polluter should pay the cost of the pollution it causes. One common moral argument in this area is that, since the developed world caused the problem of climate change, it is morally incumbent on the developed world to fix that problem. To put it crudely, the West—and in particular the United States (US)—should pay, not China or India. Nickel and Magraw offer such an argument, seeing the PPP as an example of the common-sense moral principle, 'If you broke it, you pay for it'.[2]

Such attributions of responsibility, as Nickel and Magraw recognize, raise all sorts of difficult questions.[3] If, for example, some country learns that it is harming other countries through its pollution, how long should it be permitted to have to make a transition to a more environmentally friendly economy? Or, if we accept that some country has a duty to compensate other countries for its past pollution, is it fair for

respect the rights of future generations, duties which impose moral constraints on the pursuit of certain goals. There is no reason why we should not see IEL as an instrument here—as a way of respecting such rights and fulfilling such duties.

  [2] Nickel, J. and Magraw, D., Chapter 22 in this volume, 470.   [3] Ibid., 471.

the government of that country to levy a tax on all its citizens to cover the cost of that compensation, or should it seek to tax according to past levels of pollution? And what if past pollution was carried out by companies which have ceased trading, or individuals who have now died?

Such questions can be made philosophically more tractable if we distinguish between moral and legal responsibility, and limit the former—when speaking strictly—to individual agents. Thus, in preference to a sentence such as 'The Athenians were wrong to put Socrates to death' we might say something like 'Meletus was wrong to charge Socrates, and those who voted for his execution also acted wrongly'. Making this move allows us to avoid questions about allocating responsibility between agents in different categories (as in the case of countries and individual polluters), as well as more foundational questions about whether non-individual entities can 'act' in the way that a human being can. It is also more parsimonious. Once all moral judgments about individual action have been made, what has been left out? Once we have blamed Hitler, his supporters, his generals, his soldiers, and other relevant individuals for their part in the Holocaust, does it make sense to blame, say, the Nazi party or Germany *as well*?

Note that this individualist position at the *moral* level does not prevent us from allowing states, governments, corporations, or other such entities to be *legal* persons, held to account within legal institutions and subject to legal sanctions. As far as IEL is concerned, then, states, governments, and other collective entities can be subject to IEL and held to account for breaches of it. But exactly when and how this is to be done is fundamentally a matter of individualistic morality. Nor does this individualistic moral metaphysics require us to attempt radical reform of moral language. We can still blame some developed country for not doing enough to curb its greenhouse gas (GHG) emissions. But in doing so, we should be aware that, strictly speaking, we are blaming certain individuals within that country for their own individual failures to act.

III. FAIRNESS TO FUTURE GENERATIONS

Are we bound by some duty of fairness to future generations to develop and apply certain norms of IEL? For, a natural line of thought goes, if we continue to deplete resources, we are guilty of serious unfairness to those who live in the future through using resources to a share of which they could claim entitlement.

We might call this position the 'buffet line' view of fairness. On this view, if we continue to deplete resources as we are, we are behaving like the following kind of people in a buffet line. Quite a few people have gone before them and not done all that well, as the buffet was still in the process of being stocked while they selected their options. Now the buffet contains a large selection of choice items. But the stocking process has now finished, and it is clear to those at the table that if they take a larger number of the choice items than their share, those behind them will do worse when they arrive at the buffet. This seems patently unfair, and the late-comers can complain that they have been harmed by their greedy predecessors.

The problem here, as Nickel and Magraw note,[4] is that there is a crucial disanalogy between the buffet line and resource-depletion. The identity of those who exist after us depends on the resource-policy we choose, so that any potential complaint by future generations would fail to take into account that they exist, as the individuals they are, only because we made the choices we did. Imagine a bizarre twist on the buffet line case. The evil and powerful host of the buffet has made it clear that if those at the front do not load up their plates with an excess of the best items, he will kill those who come later. How plausible would the claim of these latecomers be that the plate-pilers have harmed them? If the plates hadn't been piled, then they would no longer exist. So, it might be suggested by contemporary resource-depleters, not only will future generations have no complaint of unfairness or injustice against us, but they should be grateful to us for *benefiting* them.

A good deal of philosophical ink has been spilt over the question of whether we benefit someone we bring into existence, if that person goes on to have a life that is better than nothing—that is, better than a life of no value (a life, perhaps, lived in a permanent coma).[5] Ordinarily, if I say that P benefited Q, then I mean that P did something that was good for Q in some way. Philosophical reflection enables us quickly to see that this good could be instrumental or non-instrumental, and that it could be something *pro tanto* good or good overall. So if I serve you a pleasant dessert, but one that results in terrible indigestion, I can be said to have benefited you to some degree, but to have harmed you overall (you'd have been better off without it). Further reflection will supply us with a tolerably clear definition of the kind of benefit and harm that usually matters in ethics: overall and non-instrumental. On this conception of benefit and harm, P benefits Q when Q's overall well-being is higher than it would have been without P's intervention, and harms Q when Q's overall well-being is lower than it would have been without P's intervention.[6]

It is easy to see why it might be thought that one can benefit (or of course harm) someone by bringing them into existence. Someone might say of their child, for example, that they have benefited her by bringing her into existence because by doing so they have made her life better than it would otherwise have been. But

---

[4] Nickel, J. and Magraw, D., Chapter 22 in this volume, sect. II.3.

[5] See e.g. Bykvist, K., 'The Benefits of Coming into Existence', in Rabinowicz, W. and Rønnow-Rasmussen, T. (eds.), *Patterns of Value, Essays on Formal Axiology and Value Analysis*, 2 (Lund: Lund Philosophy Reports, 2004), 95 and references therein.

[6] This counterfactual definition will need to be tweaked to cover cases of causal over-determination. On this see e.g. Hart, H. L. A. and Honoré, A. M., *Causation in the Law* (2nd edn., Oxford: Oxford University Press, 1985), ch. 8.

it is not as if, had that child not been born, the child's life would have been at some lower level of well-being. There would have been no such life, so nothing to instantiate any well-being at any level. For that reason, it is confusing to speak of benefiting and harming people by bringing them into existence. What one does by bringing someone into existence, who subsequently leads a life that is overall better than a life of zero or neutral value, is create a person whose life is good for them. Any benefits to that person will occur *within* the life, not in creating the necessary conditions for that life itself.

Most of us think that we have duties to, or at least regarding, future generations. But the considerations above suggest that, because we cannot use the notions of benefit and harm in their usual sense, we cannot plausibly see these as duties of fairness as ordinarily understood.

Nickel and Magraw suggest various strategies intended to allow us to continue to speak of intergenerational fairness without having to introduce the problematic notion of harm. One is to limit claims about fairness to those who are now alive. In a sense, of course, this does allow us to speak of 'intergenerational' fairness and unfairness, between older and younger generations. But, as they note, the force of such a 'person-affecting' principle fails to capture what many people take to be the unfairness of present generations, using resources which they ought to be preserving for those who have not yet been born. There is anyway a problem internal to this approach. Even if we assume that our present policy of resource-depletion is likely to make the lives of some of those now alive worse in the future than they might have been, that policy can be seen to be benefiting those very same people now. Further, because of the cumulative nature of environmental damage, and the delay in the emergence of large-scale effects, it could quite plausibly be claimed that the effects on human well-being of our current policy will be felt largely by those who have not yet been born (and who also would not be born were we now to change our policy).

Another option proposed by Nickel and Magraw is to focus on the character of the present generation rather than the consequences of its actions. We might describe the present generation as greedy, short-sighted, or lacking in concern for the needs of future people. The concern mentioned here is for the consequences of actions on future people, so reintroduces the non-identity problem. It may be that the present generation has thought carefully about the needs of future people, and has recognized that members of future generations will not be able to complain that *their* needs have not been taken into account. Likewise, because they are capable of such consideration, they need not be short-sighted. If the accusation were to be repeated against those who do engage in such consideration, it would amount to little more than saying that the present generation has failed to see its duty to reign in its consumption, which is essentially the conclusion we are trying to reach. What about greed? Greed can involve unfairness, when it consists in someone's taking more than their share. But to use the notion in this way to ground a charge of unfairness would again be viciously circular. For the non-identity problem throws doubt on the very idea that future generations have any *entitlement* to some array of goods of which they are deprived through present resource-depletion.

Similar problems beset Nickel and Magraw's other suggestions here: the Parfitian view that one policy is worse than another if under the first policy people have a lower quality of life than the (different) people who would have lived had we chosen the second; and the Rawlsian position, according to which decisions should be taken as if from behind a veil of ignorance. These principles can indeed explain so-called 'non-grievance' evils—things which are morally bad but which no one can complain about. Non-grievance evils can ground complaints in the ordinary sense; anyone can complain about those who bring them about. But they cannot ground the 'personal' complaints of a future generation or individual against a past generation or individual, and it is these complaints, based as they are on the notion of harm, that are required for an account of our obligations to future generations in terms of fairness.

IV. ENVIRONMENTAL VIRTUE

Let me return to Nickel and Magraw's suggestion that we focus on the character of present individuals or the present generation. I have suggested that their attempt to ground a duty of fairness in this way is unsuccessful. But the general approach seems to me well worth considering in its own right.

In recent years, there has been a revival of philosophical interest in the notion of virtue, and a movement known as *virtue ethics* has emerged. It is difficult to distinguish virtue ethics from other theories.[7] In one common form, it advocates approaching ethical issues by asking what a virtuous person would do (or advise) in that situation. And one attains a conception of such a person from reflection upon the materials available to one in the morality one has been brought up to accept (so-called 'common-sense morality').

Modern virtue ethicists tend to see themselves as in various ways 'neo-Aristotelian', and Aristotle does indeed provide a helpful framework for understanding virtue. Aristotle noticed that, to live a human life well, a person has to feel or act correctly in certain significant spheres, spheres central to any human life. All human beings feel anger and fear for example, and the virtuous person will experience those emotions correctly. Nearly all human beings have control of some financial resource, and again the virtuous person will act correctly within the financial sphere. But what does 'correctness' amount to? Here Aristotle states his famous 'doctrine of the mean':

---

[7] See Crisp, R., 'Virtue Ethics and Virtue Epistemology', *Metaphilosophy*, 41 (2010).

To have [these feelings] at the right time, about the right things, towards the right people, for the right end, and in the right way, is the mean and best; and this is the business of virtue. Similarly, there is an excess, a deficiency and a mean in actions. Virtue is concerned with feelings and actions, in which excess and deficiency constitute misses of the mark, while the mean is praised and on target, both of which are characteristics of virtue.[8]

The virtuous person, then, will feel anger or give away money at the right time, in relation to the right things and the right people, and so on. What about the vices? Take anger. There are essentially two directions in which one can go wrong. The first is to feel anger at the wrong time, or about the wrong things, and so on, while the second is to *fail* to feel anger at the *right* time, about the *right* things, and so on. Aristotle calls the former the vices of excess, the latter the vices of deficiency. And because there are many ways to go wrong, there are pluralities of vices.

So let us now consider the sphere which has become so central to modern life: the environment, including both the natural environment and those human and other sentient beings inhabiting it.[9] It is interesting to ask exactly which feelings and actions characterize virtue in this sphere. As far as feelings are concerned, I suggest that two will be central: respect for the environment, and a sense of moderation. And the right actions in the environmental sphere will be those that accord with these feelings.

In the case of respect, there are many clear examples available of the deficient vice. Consider those very rich individuals who purchase large private jets for their own leisure use. But it is not implausible that the deficient vice is in fact exemplified by most of us, in smaller ways, when we choose, for example, to take a long-haul flight for a slightly better holiday than we could have had at home. We might even want to speak of modern culture itself as deficient in these ways.

Note that, in the case of the sense of moderation, we need not become mired in non-identity problems, through thinking that there are identifiable individuals to whom we are being unfair if we deplete resources. The general idea is to take Aristotle's largely self-regarding virtue of moderation and place it in a context where the interests of others (in general, rather than particular others) are what place the limits on what counts as appropriate use of some resource. Here the common vice is one of excess (and this must be close to what Nickel and Magraw have in mind when they speak of greed).

There is conceptual room in this account for excessive respect for the environment and for deficient use of natural resources. Both can perhaps be found in those extreme environmentalists who are prepared to inflict disproportionate costs on human beings so as to protect the environment.

---

[8] Aristotle, *Nicomachean Ethics*, ed. and trans. Crisp, R. (Cambridge: Cambridge University Press, 2000), 2.6, 1106b21–7.

[9] See also Sandler, R. L., *Character and Environment: A Virtue-Oriented Approach to Environmental Ethics* (New York: Columbia University Press, 2007).

V. CONSEQUENTIALISM, RIGHTS, AND THE DUALISM OF PRACTICAL REASON

So far, then, we have seen that, because we cannot plausibly speak of harming or benefiting future generations, any attempt to ground the apparent moral obligation we have towards future generations on these notions, or on any duty which involves them, such as a duty of fairness, will not succeed. Further, because any view postulating 'person-affecting' duties[10] towards future generations will fail, the arguments above also rule out positions which ascribe rights to future generations, since any right must correlate with a duty. One alternative position, discussed in the previous section, is a form of virtue ethics rooted in reflection upon common-sense morality.

Another alternative is consequentialism, the view according to which all that matters are certain consequences of our actions. One common version of consequentialism is the 'act utilitarian' view, according to which each of us is required to bring about that history of the world which instantiates the greatest overall well-being. My guess is that, when informed of the non-identity problem and confronted with this option, many environmentalists and international lawyers would say that it is in fact something like this goal that motivates them, not a desire to avoid harming future generations or being unfair to them.

One of the major objections to consequentialist moral theory over recent decades has been that it is excessively demanding. Imagine that there is very strong evidence that, if we are to produce the greatest amount of well-being over time, we shall have to make very large sacrifices of our own well-being now for the sake of benefiting future generations. How should we weigh our well-being against that of others?

One old and still very common response is rational egoism, according to which all our reasons for action depend on the advancement of our own well-being. Some philosophers, in the so-called contractualist tradition which found its canonical statement in the work of Hobbes, have claimed that morality itself should be seen as a system in which rational egoists place constraints on one another for their mutual benefit. Since future generations, on most theories of well-being, cannot affect us, it is hard for contractualists to argue for duties to preserve the environment for future generations. But this is not the only problem with contractualism. Most people, on reflection, will reject egoism, thinking that, for example, if we can advance the well-being of others to some huge degree at very small cost to ourselves, then it would be irrational or unreasonable not to do so.

Nevertheless, to return to act utilitarianism, many will think that a theory which requires us to act so as to increase the overall level of well-being by some very small

---

[10] See Parfit, D., *Reasons and Persons* (Oxford: Clarendon Press, 1984), ch. 18.

amount at huge cost to ourselves is indeed too demanding. What I suggest, then, is a form of what Henry Sidgwick called the *dualism of practical reason*, according to which reasons are grounded in both our own well-being and that of others, but our own well-being is given some additional rational weight.[11] So we may be required to make some sacrifice for the sake of well-being overall, but there are limits to how much may be demanded of us. Where those limits are is a matter of judgment. But it is clear that they are very far from being breached by our current levels of sacrifice. It is heartening that in recent years the issue of climate change has risen higher up the political agenda. But far greater sacrifices are required from individuals and groups of individuals if we are to fulfil our environmental duties.

One significant point here is that the sacrifices concerned are largely of resources. One of the tragedies of modernity is that it has resulted in the despoliation of much of the earth with little benefit to present generations. Once the wealth of an individual human being is above a certain quite low threshold, increases in that wealth tend to do little or nothing to advance that person's well-being (unless the wealth concerned is huge).[12] So, since the good to be promoted by our sacrifice is so great, and because the sacrifice is primarily not of what ultimately matters to us, the case for environmentalism, in international law and other spheres, is strong.

VI. EQUALITY

Another serious objection to act utilitarianism, according to which all that matters is the total amount of well-being and not how it is shared around, is that it can make no room for the value of equality. Consider another, yet more bizarre, version of the buffet line case. Imagine a possible world in which a powerful god creates buffet lines. Those who come into existence queue up at the buffet, eat their food, and then go out of existence. The god has decided that the identities of those who will come into existence later will depend on how much food is selected by those now existing. Let us call those now in the line *Group 1* and those who will come into existence *Group 2*. Now consider the following pair of outcomes, called *Equality* and *Inequality*:[13]

---

[11] See Crisp, R., *Reasons and the Good* (Oxford: Clarendon Press, 2006), ch. 5.

[12] See e.g. Layard, R., *Happiness: Lessons from a New Science* (London: Allen Lane, 2005). Positive psychology takes well-being to consist primarily in mental states of contentment. But the argument here carries across to plausible preference accounts of well-being and 'objective list' accounts, according to which what matters are goods such as knowledge, friendship, and personal relationships (all of which come relatively cheap).

[13] Adapted from Crisp, R., 'Equality, Priority, and Compassion', *Ethics*, 113 (2003), 745.

	Group 1	Group 2
Equality	50	50
Inequality	90	10

The numbers here represent the amount of well-being the diners can expect from their food. If existing diners pile their plates, they will do very well, and those who come after them far less well. But remember that the identities of those in Group 2 depend on the decisions taken by Group 1, so they cannot plausibly complain that any duty *to them* has been violated by the earlier choice. The value of each outcome in terms of well-being is equal. But is there not something to be said for *Equality*? And, it may be claimed, we are in an exactly analogous situation regarding future generations.

But exactly *what* is to be said in favour of *Equality*? One obvious answer is that equality is valuable in itself—or perhaps rather that inequality is bad in itself. But this view seems implausible once one reflects upon cases in which egalitarianism favours 'levelling down'—that is, for example, favouring *Equality* over another outcome in which Group 1 is at 80 and Group 2 at 90.[14]

A common response to this problem with egalitarianism is to advocate so-called 'prioritarianism', in which no value is attributed to equality in itself, but priority is given to the worse off. Imagine, then, that the scenario above concerned outcomes for existing people. Then we could favour *Equality* as giving appropriate priority to the well-being of the worse off. The problem is that prioritarianism is best understood as a person-affecting principle. In the case of existing individuals, we can say that justice requires that the worse off be given priority because they could have been better off and there is no good reason why they should not have been. But in the case of future generations, because of non-identity, the worse off could not have been better off. What could have happened is that some other individuals would have occupied their 'space', and lived a life of higher quality.

So, one might seek to combine prioritarian concern for people who do exist or will exist independently of our choices, with a well-being-maximizing principle covering our obligations to future generations whose identities will be affected by our choice (and hence are in this sense 'contingent'). Nils Holtug outlines one such view:

Prioritarianism should be applied only to necessary individuals and a complementary principle—e.g. total utilitarianism— . . . only to contingent ones. An individual is necessary relative to the comparison of two outcomes if and only if she exists in both. And an individual

---

[14] See Parfit, D., 'Equality and Priority', in Mason, A. (ed.), *Ideals of Equality* (Oxford: Blackwell, 1998), 1, 9–11.

is contingent relative to the comparison of two outcomes if and only if she exists in one but not the other. Call this principle 'pluralist prioritarianism'.[15]

Holtug goes on to reject the view on the ground that it violates transitivity. Compare the three outcomes in Fig. 23.1, in which each shading represents a single group of people (so group p features in every outcome, q in A and B, and r only in C), the vertical axis represents quality of life, and the dotted line the level below which priority is to be given to the worse off:

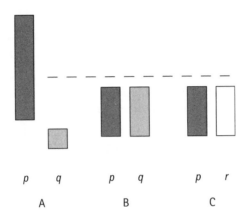

Fig 23.1.

According to pluralist prioritarianism, Holtug suggests, though B contains less overall well-being than A, it is at least as good as A, as long as the worse off (q) are given appropriate priority. And C is at least as good as B, because both B and C are equally good for both necessary (p) and contingent persons (q and r). But A might well be better than C, since in this comparison q and r are contingent.

Holtug has not identified here a genuinely worrying case of intransitivity. In the case depicted in Fig. 23.1, the three outcomes A, B, and C are all available to us. Now it is true that were C not available, then the pluralist prioritarian would judge B to be at least as good as A. But the availability of C makes q contingent in the pluralist prioritarian's comparison of A, B, and C. So A is superior to both B and C, each of which is equally valuable.

The upshot of this is that the impartial principle we should adopt regarding future generations is a purely maximizing one, which allows some extra weight to be given to our own well-being. This has the—*prima facie* odd—implication that, if we do think that the worse off should be given priority, we may be required to bring about an outcome in which 'units' of well-being are evaluated entirely impartially, in the

[15] Holtug, N., 'On Giving Priority to Possible Future People', in Rønnow-Rasmussen, T., Petersson, B., Josefsson, J. and Egonsson, D. (eds.), *Hommage à Wlodek: Philosophical Papers dedicated to Wlodek Rabinowicz*, <http://www.fil.lu.se/hommageawlodek/site/papper/HoltugNils.pdf>, 10–12. (All websites most recently checked in Nov. 2009.)

knowledge that those who come to exist in that outcome will be required to give priority to the worse off and so weight the well-being of the worse off more heavily than that of the better off.[16] But once one reflects upon what person-affectingness means in this context, that implication should come to seem less strange.

VII. The Repugnant Conclusion

Derek Parfit has identified another worrying apparent implication of an act utilitarian principle when applied to the problem of population size:

For any possible population of at least ten billion people, all with a very high quality of life, there must be some much larger imaginable population whose existence, if other things are equal, would be better even though its members have lives that are barely worth living.[17]

The repugnant conclusion appears to follow because, when we are considering various population outcomes, a loss in quality can be compensated for by a gain in quantity. There are several ways of trying to deal with it.[18] An obvious one is to deny its repugnance, drawing attention in particular to the fact that in the more populated world billions more people have lives worth living than in other populations. Intuitions differ on this matter, however, and I am inclined to think that, though a loss in quality of life can sometimes be made up for by a gain in quantity, the world with the very large population described by Parfit is worse than the first world, with a population of at least ten billion. This implies that at some point in the series, a move to a larger population is not justified by a gain in quantity of lives lived. One argument for such a 'discontinuity' of value moves from the intrapersonal to the interpersonal case.[19] Consider the following example:[20]

Haydn and the Oyster. You are a soul in heaven waiting to be allocated a life on Earth. It is late Friday afternoon, and you watch anxiously as the supply of available lives dwindles. When your turn comes, the angel in charge offers you a choice between two lives, that of the composer Joseph Haydn and that of an oyster. Besides composing some wonderful music and influencing the evolution of the symphony, Haydn will meet with success and honour in his own lifetime, be cheerful and popular, travel and gain much enjoyment from field sports. The oyster's life is far less exciting. Though this is rather a sophisticated oyster, its

---

[16] Crisp, R., 'Equality, Priority, and Compassion' (above, n. 13). I have argued that justice requires us to give priority to the worse off only when the worse off do not have 'enough'.

[17] Parfit, D., *Reasons and Persons* (above, n. 10), 388.

[18] For an outline of various responses, see Ryberg, J., Tännsjö, T., and Arrhenius, G., 'The Repugnant Conclusion', in Zalta, E. N. (ed.), *The Stanford Encyclopedia of Philosophy* (Spring 2006 edn.), <http://plato.stanford.edu/archives/spr2006/entries/repugnant-conclusion>.

[19] The term 'discontinuity' and an argument for it can be found in Griffin, J., *Well-Being* (Oxford: Clarendon Press, 1986), 85–9; see also Rashdall, H., *The Theory of Good and Evil* (Oxford: Oxford University Press, 1907), ii. 38–41.

[20] See Crisp, R., *Mill on Utilitarianism* (London: Routledge, 1997), 24.

life will consist only of mild sensual pleasure, rather like that experienced by humans when floating very drunk in a warm bath. When you request the life of Haydn, the angel sighs, 'I'll never get rid of this oyster life. It's been hanging around for ages. Look, I'll offer you a special deal. Haydn will die at the age of seventy-seven. But I'll make the oyster life as long as you like'.

Many people believe that the life of Haydn is more choice-worthy than that of the oyster, however long. And yet they would accept that some loss of quality in the life of Haydn could be more than compensated for by some gain in number of years lived. This again implies discontinuity at some point, and if such discontinuities are found in comparing different options for an individual, there is no obvious problem in extending that analysis to cover choices between whole populations.

VIII. Anthropocentrism and the Value of Nature

Much of my discussion so far has concerned future generations of human beings, and is therefore open to the charge of anthropocentrism. Climate change and other environmental problems, it will be said, are the result of just such an attitude. Rather, we should see the natural environment as having value in its own right, independently of any value it might have for human beings, and indeed independently of human beings themselves.

It is worth noting that the question of anthropocentrism cannot be avoided through the adoption of environmental virtue ethics. The respect of nature characteristic of the virtuous person itself involves certain attitudes to nature *as valuable*, and this raises the question of what kind of value is possessed by nature. For it could be claimed that respect for nature is in essence an extension of, or parasitic on, respect for human beings.

Nickel and Magraw describe two conceptions of intrinsic, or non-instrumental, natural value (where something's having value is taken to be equivalent to its being valuable, not merely its being valued).[21] The first—*constitutive intrinsic value*—essentially involves human experience, attributing value to genuine experiences of natural values such as beauty. Nickel and Magraw note that many environmentalists, seeing such value as still too dependent on human experience, prefer the notion of *inherent intrinsic value*. On this view, nature is valuable in itself, 'independently of human experience, recognition, or choice'.

Nickel and Magraw claim that, given the large and speculative assumptions made by this approach, it is unlikely to persuade many. I am not so sure. Indeed it could be suggested that anyone who is sympathetic to the notion of constitutive value is

---

[21] Nickel, J. and Magraw, D., Chapter 22 in this volume, sect. III.

well on the way to accepting inherent value. For the phenomenology of the kind of experiences Nickel and Magraw have in mind—contemplating Half Dome, for example—is plausibly understood as the *discovery* of value independent of the viewer. One's attitude of awe, wonder, or respect regarding Half Dome is *not* directed at the organic whole made up of one's own experience and Half Dome itself. It appears rather as an attitude to Half Dome itself, as an object of independent value.

Nickel and Magraw have several arguments against the notion of inherent intrinsic value. The first is that intrinsic value is hard to defend with argument: 'If a person does not see intrinsic value in preserving a small fish like the snail darter it is going to be hard to argue the point'. This is an empirical claim, for which Nickel and Magraw provide no evidence. I see no reason to think that people are any less likely to be persuaded that there is inherent intrinsic value in nature than of most other ethical claims. The global environmental movement is huge and growing, and I would hazard that a majority of its participants would be ready to accept that there is inherent intrinsic value in the environment. Anyway, in philosophy, what matter are arguments and plausibility, not persuasiveness or popularity.

Nickel and Magraw's second argument is that intrinsic values do not always have a higher priority than instrumental values. On the face of it, this looks rather unlikely, on the assumption that only an intrinsic value can outweigh an intrinsic value. Nickel and Magraw's example here is my readiness to exchange an afternoon of intrinsically valuable experiences for a million instrumentally valuable dollars. But this example illustrates well that even to speak of 'instrumental value' as value is somewhat misleading. The dollars have no real value to me, except in so far as they are means to something independently valuable. If I were told that one condition of my receiving the dollars would be that I never spent them, I would stick with the museum. It is of course true that conflicts between inherent intrinsic natural value and human well-being could not plausibly always be decided in favour of the natural value. Parts of paradise must be paved, and some parking lots put up. But nothing in the notion of inherent intrinsic natural value suggests that it has to be seen as incommensurably weightier than any other value.

Their third worry is that, if different kinds of thing have intrinsic value, we shall face conflicts between, say, human life and natural systems, and the natural systems may not always win. This is something that any reasonable proponent of inherent natural value will accept. To believe in something as valuable does not require one to believe that it must win in any competition with other values.

Nickel and Magraw are also doubtful of the claim that intrinsic value can always ground significant duties of respect or preservation. If I am looking at a hawk, they claim, you have no duty not to interrupt that experience by asking me a question. But why not? Could you not have waited? True, your duty to refrain is not in this case all that significant; but then neither is the value of looking at the hawk (unless it is a very rare one which I have been seeking for years). Nickel and Magraw argue that, since there are large numbers of intrinsically valuable things, we cannot attach duties to respect and preserve all of them, since this would result in 'ethical gridlock': 'We'll have to find all of our joy in doing our duties'. But this does not follow, unless we assume that all these duties to respect and preserve must be significant even in cases where the value is insignificant. Often, we can just ignore such duties, since many of them will anyway be negative and protective of things which we have no desire anyway to damage. And often it will be defensible to adopt a strategy towards the natural environment which does not require constant consideration of whether duties are being violated by our actions. To walk down to the river I shall have to trample some grass and a few wild flowers. But once I have worked out that such actions are defensible, I can just go ahead and do them without further ethical reflection every time.

Despite my doubts about Nickel and Magraw's arguments, I also find the notion of inherent intrinsic natural value to be of little significance in the grounding of our ethical reasons and hence of international environmental law (though this is not to deny that arguments appealing to, or laws assuming the existence of, such value could be useful).[22] Perhaps the most famous thought experiment in this area is that of G. E. Moore's two worlds, one beautiful, the other ugly, neither of which any individual ever sees.[23] Moore himself appears to believe that we have a reason to bring about the first world: 'Would it not be well, in any case, to do what we could to produce it rather than the other?' I am willing to allow that the beautiful world may be better than the ugly, in so far as it contains more aesthetic value. But I fail to see why an agent should see any reason to bring it about except in so far as some benefit might accrue to some sentient being or other—including the agent, perhaps, if the bringing about is itself enjoyable (this view might be called *welfarism*). If there is some *cost* in well-being, either to the agent or to others, in the bringing about, then there is a reason against it. And if there is neither benefit nor cost, then there is nothing to be said in favour of or against the bringing about. An example of Jonathan Glover's nicely brings out the force of the link between reasons and well-being:

My sympathies are strongly on the side of Sidgwick here, being quite unmoved by any of the excellences of universes eternally empty of conscious life . . . If, travelling in a train through the middle of a ten-mile railway tunnel, I saw a man leaning out of the window into the darkness, I might wonder what he was doing. If it turned out to be G. E. Moore spraying the walls of the tunnel with paint, because painted walls are better than unpainted ones, even if no one ever sees them, I should not be able to prove him irrational. But I should not accept his offer of the use of a second paint spray, except possibly out of politeness.[24]

[22] For the opposite view, see Tasioulas, J., 'International Law and the Limits of Fairness', *European Journal of International Law*, 13 (2004), 993, 1012–14. D. Schlossberg argues that Nussbaum and Sen's 'capabilities' approach can be extended to include non-sentient natural systems; see *Defining Environmental Justice* (Oxford: Oxford University Press, 2007), 148–9.

[23] Moore, G. E., *Principia Ethica* (Cambridge: Cambridge University Press, 1903), 83–5. This section of the paper is adapted from my *Reasons and the Good* (above, n. 11), 62–3.

[24] Glover, J., *What Sort of People Should There Be?* (Harmondsworth: Penguin, 1984), 110.

A version of the Moorean scenario in which there is a cost to at least one individual and no gain to any other illustrates the second kind of case mentioned above (imagine, plausibly enough, that in Glover's case Moore finds spraying the walls of the tunnel rather unpleasant). It is no objection, then, to international environmental law that it is anthropocentric, unless what is meant is that it gives too little weight to the interests of non-human sentient beings.

IX. Disagreement and Resolution

The final topic I want to raise is the relation between ethical theory and IEL. There is limited consensus in environmental ethics and a wide variety of ethical theories compete with one another. Nickel and Magraw suggest a theory based on a duty of fairness to future generations. In this paper, I have suggested two further possibilities: an environmental virtue ethics, or a form of consequentialism which requires promotion of well-being while recognizing the force for each agent of the reason to promote their own well-being. Or consider again the question, discussed by Nickel and Magraw, of whether non-sentient objects can be non-instrumentally valuable in themselves. As they show, it is difficult even to state clearly what such a claim amounts to. But it is quite likely that any reasonable statement of the view will be the subject of serious disagreement, even after a good deal of serious and impartial reflection by both sides. The conclusion I would draw from this example—one of a huge number—is significantly more sceptical than Nickel and Magraw's. Sidgwick seems to me to capture the epistemic position well:

If I find any of my judgments, intuitive or inferential, in direct conflict with a judgment of some other mind, there must be error somewhere: and if I have no more reason to suspect error in the other mind than in my own, reflective comparison between the two judgments necessarily reduces me temporarily to a state of neutrality.[25]

It will be tempting in cases of deep disagreement to believe that your opponent must somehow be making some mistake, perhaps an error in logic or a failure to attend properly to the available evidence. It is hard to deny, of course, that there are variations in the quality of different people's epistemic positions. The views of someone who has been brainwashed, for example, can usually be safely ignored. Further, we now have a good deal of information from experimental psychology about the biases and distortions in thought to which human beings are especially prevalent, and we can and should examine our own and others' views in the light of that information.[26] But often it will turn out that your opponent would be equally

---

[25] Sidgwick, H., *The Methods of Ethics* (7th edn., London: Macmillan, 1907), 342.
[26] See e.g. Kahneman, D., Slovic, P., and Tversky, A. (eds.), *Judgment Under Uncertainty: Heuristics and Biases* (Cambridge: Cambridge University Press, 1982).

entitled to hold the same belief about you, and this only focuses yet further the argument for suspension of judgment.

Does this mean that the philosophical attempt to provide an ethical or normative ground for international environmental law has run into the ground? I cannot see why, since the kind of suspension of judgment of which Sidgwick speaks here does not prevent two parties to a debate continuing to insist that things *appear* to them in a certain way. Philosophical discussion, then, can continue, but in a less dogmatic way than it tends to at present. Since often you have no justification for thinking that you have got it right and others are mistaken, that gives you a good reason for trying to see things from their perspective and engaging in constructive discussion with them in the hope of consensus.

But what about practice, and in particular the practice of making IEL? It is indeed often said that the problem of deep disagreement is especially profound for the making of public international law in general, given the huge differences between states in culture, history, and ideology. Imagine that you, the representative of country A, are advocating the exclusion from some desert area, which overlaps the border of country B, of all human beings, on the ground that the area has intrinsic value which requires protection. I, on the other hand, the representative of country B, cannot accept the notion that non-sentient beings can have intrinsic value, and wish to allow human beings to visit the area in some regulated way. As we argue, it becomes clear that we are in a situation where suspension of judgment is called for. But how, then, are we to resolve our dispute, given that things still appear to us quite differently?

The answer must be by some method of resolution which we can both accept as reasonable, and the natural direction here must be towards some kind of democratic decision procedure. Such procedures are already instantiated within the theory and practice of IEL. At the individual level, for example, Principle 10 of the 1992 Rio Declaration includes the 'Public Participation Principle', according to which 'Environmental issues are best handled with the participation of all concerned citizens'.[27] And of course the discussions leading to international treaties, conventions, and declarations usually rest on some broadly democratic basis. There are problems with voting rules, arising out of voting paradoxes, for example, or issues concerning the weighting of votes. But such problems are often practically surmountable, and are anyway far from specific to the domain of IEL. More worryingly, democracy itself is less valued by some individuals and states than others, and this confounds the already existing problem of the different levels of interest different parties have in participating in the practices of establishing and acting on IEL. Here it is important to provide incentives to come to the table, either explicitly, as in the form of trade advantages, or implicitly, primarily in

---

[27] Bell, S. and McGillivray, D., *Environmental Law* (Oxford: Oxford University Press, 2006), 61.

creating a sense that it is in the interest of no party to be left out of the process of discussion. In general, it is clear that the more open discussion and sharing of ideas and perspectives there is, the more likely it is that individual states, despite often differing greatly from one another, may converge on IEL-based solutions to environmental problems. Once such convergence can be institutionalized in IEL itself, one might reasonably hope that the implications of IEL and any sanctions available to it will become significantly clearer and hence IEL a more powerful and focused tool.

In recent years, in fact, international law-making has become increasingly consensus-based.[28] There is a case to be made for majoritarian democracy, however, especially in the case of high-level decisions about matters of serious and urgent concern such as climate change. Here, where non-trivial sacrifice may be called for, politicians are especially ready to pursue self-interest under the cover of ethical principles such as that of national sovereignty. Of course, the politics here cannot be shifted entirely onto moral ground, but it is important that those sincerely pursuing moral goals, or indeed rational self-interest over the longer term, not be disheartened by fundamental moral disagreement. Not only is there anyway a great deal of consensus on conclusions of arguments, but it is entirely reasonable to continue to advocate to others the premises one finds plausible.

Much IEL is aspirational and it must play its part in one of the great political challenges facing the world at present: to persuade the citizens and hence the politicians of the richer countries—especially the US—that it is their responsibility to support governmental action on climate change and other environmental problems. One major step forward would be the creation of some kind of 'umbrella' convention analogous to the GATT in the area of trade. This could include not only principles governing conflicts between free trade and environmental principles, but also ways of encouraging further development and adherence to principles of sustainable development, precaution, preventative action, and so on, and indeed to principles ascribing a human right to a decent environment which might counterbalance certain liberty-rights such as that to have as many children as one wishes, to live and work wherever one wishes, and so on.[29] There may even be a case for seeking to ascribe such a right to future generations, even though, as we have seen, such rights have little philosophical plausibility. IEL is a tool, as I began by saying, and, to a degree, in the political context so is ethical rhetoric.

---

[28] Boyle, A. and Chinkin, C., *The Making of International Law* (Oxford: Oxford University Press, 2007), p. vii.

[29] See e.g. the 'Ksentini' Report, discussed in Bell, S. and McGillivray, D., *Environmental Law* (above, n. 27), 80. Quite how such an umbrella convention could be arrived at is, to put it mildly, a difficult question. If Boyle and Chinkin are to be believed (ibid. 197–200), it would be beyond the capacity of the International Law Commission.

SECTION XII

LAWS OF WAR

CHAPTER 24

LAWS OF WAR

JEFF McMAHAN[*]

I. INTRODUCTION

Doctrines of the just war predate formulations of the law of war by many centuries. Yet classical accounts of the just war are presented as matters of law—not positive law or law devised by human beings, but natural law, or law that is inherent in the nature of things. War, like other human activities that raise moral issues, was held by the classical just war theorists to be governed by immutable moral laws that were part of the natural order, no less real or objective than the laws of nature. This early presentation of morality as a matter of law prefigured, or perhaps inaugurated, the recurring tendency to blur the distinction between the morality of war and the law of war, a tendency that persists to this day.

In this essay I will offer a brief sketch of the evolution of thought about the morality of war and the law of war, noting the reciprocal influence of each upon the other.[1] I will argue that despite our tendency to conflate them, the laws of war are quite distinct from the moral principles governing war, and that what these laws permit and prohibit must at present diverge in fundamental ways from what is permitted and prohibited by morality. I will also argue, however, that our ultimate aim should be to achieve the greatest possible congruence between law and morality

---

[*] I have benefited in writing this paper from comments by the editors and discussions with Thomas Hurka, David Rodin, and, especially, Henry Shue.

[1] My historical understanding is much indebted to Stephen C. Neff's illuminating and insightful history of moral and legal thought about war, *War and the Law of Nations: A General History* (Cambridge: Cambridge University Press, 2005).

in this area, and that this will require both rigorous moral analysis and innovations in the design of new international legal institutions.

II. A Brief History

Classical accounts of the just war were individualist in character, in that they applied principles that were thought to govern moral relations among individuals outside the context of war to individual action in war. War was seen as continuous with other human activities rather than as an altogether different domain of action governed by altogether different principles. The classical just war theorists assumed that although the individual combatant's relation to the sovereign might mitigate his responsibility for his action in war, individuals and their acts were nevertheless the basic units of evaluation rather than collectives and collective action.

Because much of the classical writing on the just war was the work of philosophically sophisticated theologians, it is unsurprising that it was concerned primarily with the rightness or wrongness of individual action. But as the power of states and their secular political leaders increased, it is natural that the influence of political and juridical thinkers increased as well and that the focus of concern gradually shifted from the acts of individual combatants to the large-scale acts of states and their rulers. War gradually came to be understood as a condition obtaining among states, in which individual combatants had little significance other than as the instruments of states.

Although in general philosophers have had little to say about war, the arguments of Hobbes had a transformative effect on the way that many theorists thought about the normative dimensions of war. While Hobbes retained a belief in natural law, it was not a natural law the classical theorists would have recognized, in that it dictates egoism rather than anything recognizable as morality. Morality arises, according to Hobbes, only when people, acting wholly from self-interest, agree to submit themselves to a sovereign whom they invest with the power to enforce compliance with rules of constraint that it is in their interests to have, provided that the rules are rigidly enforced. On this view, morality is an artefact, a product of agreement. There is little to distinguish it from law. Hobbes thus provided a foundation for the idea that the rules we live by are not given by God or discovered in the nature of things. Morality is something we create; law, therefore, cannot coherently be formulated to conform to an independently-given conception of morality. Law, like morality itself, consists of principles that we devise and enforce to facilitate the pursuit of our interests and the achievement of our purposes.

The idea that law can be a product of agreement and need not be modelled on natural law is one of two Hobbesian views that profoundly influenced the subsequent development of the law of war. The other is that because morality itself derives from the sovereign, there can be no moral limit to the prerogatives of the sovereign. This laid the philosophical foundations for the doctrine of the sovereign equality of states. Each state was conceived as a political community with a sovereign at its head. But in the absence of a super-sovereign to enforce agreements among them, states could not be morally constrained in their relations with each other. The most important implication of this view is that states have a sovereign prerogative to resort to war whenever it is in their interest to do so—an implication that was eventually recognized in law and practice during the 19th century.

The body of doctrine about the regulation of war that gradually supplanted medieval doctrines of the just war was known as the law of nations. The earliest juridical writers on the law of nations were deeply imbued with traditional natural law theory but sought to supplement it with principles that could be understood as the products of agreement between or among states. As legal and, in particular, political theorists became increasingly enchanted with the idea of states as agents in international affairs, the law of nations became correspondingly more collectivist and pragmatic in character. At the same time, the increasingly influential Hobbesian conception of sovereignty restricted what the law of nations might say about the permissibility of the resort to war. Medieval just war doctrines had insisted on various conditions for the permissibility of resorting to war. These conditions, the most important of which was that there must be a just cause for war, constituted the doctrine of *jus ad bellum*. This doctrine gradually declined in importance, however, until by the 19th century, the resort to war came to be regarded as a legally acceptable means of pursuing state policy: 'politics by other means', in the depraved words of Clausewitz.

The decline of *jus ad bellum* began relatively early and was recognized even by Grotius, though he himself advanced an unusually detailed and sophisticated account of the requirement of just cause. He observed that peace treaties tended not to stigmatize the vanquished side as the wrongdoer or to demand that the vanquished compensate the victor for costs incurred during the fighting of the war.[2] These practices suggest that even in the early phases of the development of the law of nations, there was comparatively little concern with the determination of which party was in the right and which was in the wrong. The focus shifted to *jus in bello*, or the principles governing the conduct of war, which ultimately came to be regarded as entirely independent of *jus ad bellum*. Eventually, as I noted earlier, *jus ad bellum* faded into insignificance and by the 19th century, states were recognized as having

---

[2] Grotius, H., *De Jure Belli Ac Pacis Libris Tres*, Kelsey, F. W. (trans.), (Oxford: Clarendon Press, 1925), repr. by William S. Hein & Co. (Buffalo, NY, 1995), 809–10. Also see Neff, S. C., *War and the Law of Nations* (above, n. 1), 118.

a legal permission to resort to war as a matter of national policy.[3] As Amos Hershey wrote in 1906,

International Law ... does not consider the justice or injustice of a war. From a purely legal standpoint, all wars ... are neither just nor unjust. International Law merely takes cognizance of the existence of war as a fact, and prescribes certain rules and regulations which affect the rights and duties of neutrals and belligerents during that continuance.[4]

The idea that war is a sovereign prerogative of states that cannot be subject to legal restriction could hardly survive the First World War unscathed, and by the end of the Second World War it had become clear that the most important goal of the international law of war had become the prevention of war rather than the mere regulation of the way that wars are conducted. This led, however, to an extreme oversimplification in the direction opposite to that in which the law of war had been developing over the preceding three or four centuries. The UN Charter, written in the aftermath of the Second World War, recognized only two conditions in which it could be legally permissible for a state to use military force against another state: first, when the use of force has been authorized by the UN Security Council and, second, in 'individual or collective self-defence if an armed attack occurs'.[5] So even though the law of *jus ad bellum* was radically revised over the course of the 20th century, it remains crude and simplistic, and the focus of the international law of war remains on *jus in bello*. Thus, in her comprehensive survey of the law of war, revised in 2000, Ingrid Detter writes:

Distinguishable from the thus largely obsolete jus ad bellum are the rules on warfare and the humanitarian rules that apply within a war, the jus in bello. It may appear that since the right to war has been abolished there would not be any need for rules in war. However, it is clear that given the number of and intensity of present-day conflicts, both international and internal, there is a great need for the regulation of the humanitarian issues.[6]

Detter describes *jus ad bellum* as 'largely obsolete' because in law it has now been reduced to a single simple rule: in the absence of authorization by the UN, a state may go to war against another state only in individual or collective self-defence against aggression.

Despite the efforts of the classical just war theorists, and of the theorists, such as Grotius, who straddled the transition between the classical theory of the just war and the law of nations, our understanding of the morality of the resort to war has never been very advanced. In part this is because philosophers have never paid serious attention to the morality of war. It is true that during the last quarter of the 20th century, there was a stirring of interest in the morality of war among philosophers that has persisted and even increased. The irony is that, at least until just recently,

---

[3] See Neff, S. C., *War and the Law of Nations* (above, n. 1), 163–4, 189, and 201.

[4] Hershey, A. S., *The International Law and Diplomacy of the Russo-Japanese War* (New York: Macmillan, 1906), 67, cited in Neff, S. C., *War and the Law of Nations* (above, n. 1), 167.

[5] See UN Charter, articles 2(4) and 51.

[6] Detter, I., *The Law of War* (2nd edn., Cambridge: Cambridge University Press, 2000), 157–8.

the understanding of the just war that has dominated the revival of this tradition of thought has been closely modelled, not on the classical theory, but on the law of war as it developed over the 20th century, thus reversing the original direction of derivation, when the law of nations slowly emerged through the gradual revision of the theory of the just war. Thus the work that is widely and correctly recognized as the most substantial contribution to the revival of just war theory—Michael Walzer's *Just and Unjust Wars*—follows international law in claiming that the only general and non-contentious just cause for war is defence against aggression, though he concedes that there are rare exceptions to the principle that 'nothing but aggression can justify war', the most important of which is one that customary international law has also begun to recognize—namely, that a war may permissibly be initiated 'to rescue peoples threatened with massacre'.[7] Walzer also argues that the principles of *jus in bello* are logically independent of *jus ad bellum* and thus that combatants on both sides in a war have the same rights and liabilities, including, in particular, the 'equal right to kill'.[8]

III. Morality, Domestic Law, and International Law

Throughout the history of thought about war that I have traced, morality and law have been repeatedly conflated. As I noted, the classical just war theorists presented an account of the morality of war that was also an account of natural law. During the long transition from natural law accounts of the just war to fully positivist accounts of the law of nations, it was often unclear whether writers on the normative regulation of war understood themselves to be advancing ideas about morality, ideal law, or actual law. These ambiguities have continued to infect discussions of the normative dimensions of war since the revival of just war theory during the Vietnam war, as readers of Walzer's *Just and Unjust Wars*, with its various references to just war, the law of war, and 'the war convention', will recognize.

I believe that the morality of war and the law of war are utterly different, just as morality and law in domestic society are utterly different. This is not to say, of course, that the *content* of morality and law must be utterly different. For the most part, the prohibitions of domestic criminal law track corresponding moral prohibitions. But law is an artefact, consciously designed to serve certain purposes, whereas morality is not. I believe that morality is for the most part discovered, not made: it is what it is, whether it 'works' for us or not. But even if one thinks that morality is ultimately a human creation, it was certainly never consciously

---

[7] Walzer, M., *Just and Unjust Wars* (New York: Basic Books, 1977), 62 and 108.   [8] Ibid. 41.

formulated, agreed on, and enacted in the way that law now is. Its origins, sources, and status are of course the subject of much debate, but almost no one thinks that morality is exactly like law, either in origin, form, or content.

To avoid the confusions that plague much of the moral and legal literature on war, it is important to keep the morality of war and the law of war conceptually distinct. Yet ultimately we should seek to bring the content of the law into congruence with the permissions and prohibitions of morality, just as we have sought to do, with considerable success, in domestic law—especially in criminal law but to a significant degree in civil law as well. There are at present substantial obstacles to reforming the law of war in the image of morality, but we can begin to overcome them once we have a clearer understanding of what we are aiming to achieve. To do this we must investigate the morality of war in abstraction from various pragmatic considerations that require compromises of moral principles in the formulation of the law.

Common-sense morality and domestic law share a common structure of justification for the infliction of harm. While they both recognize that the intentional infliction of harm on a person can sometimes be justified as the lesser evil, or by reference to the informed consent of the victim, the principal form of justification to which they both appeal involves the claim that the victim of the harm has acted in a way that now makes him morally vulnerable to that harm. Because of something the victim has done, he has no right not to be harmed—at least not in a certain way, for a certain reason, and, perhaps, by certain persons (that is, he may still have a right not to be harmed in certain ways, for certain reasons, or by certain people). Another way of making this point is to say that according to common sense morality and domestic law, the most common and least controversial justification for intentionally harming another person is that the person *deserves* to be harmed, or is *liable* to be harmed, because of something he has done—usually an act of wrongdoing, or an act that has inflicted, or may otherwise inflict, a wrongful harm.

In cases of conflict, the moral positions of the protagonists are usually asymmetrical. Both domestic law and morality, for example, recognize that in most cases of justified self-defence, the initial defender is justified in acting in self-defence while the aggressor or wrongdoer is not justified in defending himself against the victim's defensive action. This moral asymmetry between wrongdoer and victim, or potential victim, is often a matter of justice. The morality of self-defence is a matter of *preventive justice*. Justified self-defence—and justified defence of others—normally involves the *ex ante* redistribution of inevitable harm away from those who are innocent and toward those who are responsible for a threat of wrongful harm. If it is inevitable that someone will suffer a harm, those who are morally responsible for that fact are the ones who, as a matter of justice, should suffer it. It would be unjust to allow the harm to befall the innocent instead.

While preventive justice is concerned with the *ex ante* redistribution of harm in accordance with liability, *corrective justice*, which is the goal of the law of torts, is concerned with the *ex post* redistribution of harm, or loss. In corrective justice, losses are transferred from those who have suffered them but were not responsible for them to those who were responsible. In contrast to the law of torts, criminal law is generally understood as aiming at *retributive justice*, though to the extent that preventive defence and deterrence are among the legitimate aims of punishment, it may also be said to be concerned with preventive justice. To the extent that criminal sanctions are a matter of retribution, the justification for punishment must appeal to the claim that the defender *deserves* to be harmed. But if criminal sanctions are intended only to prevent the offender from being able to cause further harm, or to deter him or others from committing similar offences in the future, the justification may appeal only to the claim that the offender is *liable* to be harmed.[9]

The international law of war does not so obviously aim at justice in the way that domestic law does. Some legal theorists, such as George Fletcher, deny that war has anything to do with justice.[10] Others think that while the legal doctrine of *jus ad bellum* does distinguish between just and unjust wars, considerations of justice do not extend into the law of *jus in bello*, since the rules of *jus in bello* are neutral between those who fight in a just war ('just combatants') and those who fight in the absence of a just cause ('unjust combatants'). While the law of *jus ad bellum* gives an asymmetrical account of justification—the defender is justified in fighting but the aggressor is not—the law of *jus in bello* is symmetrical, in that the justification that just combatants have for fighting applies equally to unjust combatants.

It is curious that the law of *jus in bello* should be symmetrical, and thus apparently at variance with considerations of justice, when the morality of individual conflict, the domestic law, and the international law of *jus ad bellum* are all largely asymmetrical. Why are the legal rules governing the conduct of war symmetrical, or neutral between just and unjust combatants? Why, that is, do these rules take no account of the considerations of justice that are recognized in the law of *jus ad bellum*? There are various possible answers, of which I will review five. Each of the first four has many adherents, though I think none of them offers a plausible justification for the neutrality of the laws of *jus in bello*—that is, for

---

[9] The distinction between desert and liability, as I understand it, is this. If a person deserves to be harmed, there is a reason for harming him that is independent of the further consequences of harming him. Giving him what he deserves is an end in itself. But a person is liable to be harmed only if harming him will serve some further purpose—for example, if it will prevent him from unjustly harming someone, or will compensate a victim of his prior wrongdoing. For a person to be liable to be harmed, a condition of instrumental efficacy must be satisfied; but no such condition applies to desert.

[10] Fletcher, G. P., *Romantics at War: Glory and Guilt in the Age of Terrorism* (Princeton: Princeton University Press, 2002), 3–9.

the absence of any relation between the laws of *jus in bello* and the law of *jus ad bellum*.

IV. Consent

According to one view, the same morality that governs relations among individuals outside the context of war also governs the conduct of war, so the symmetry in the law of *jus in bello* does not reflect a corresponding symmetry in some set of moral principles that apply only in war and are different from those that govern relations among individuals in other contexts. Rather, the symmetry is traceable to a way in which war itself is importantly different from other kinds of conflict. In most instances of violent conflict, at least one party is an entirely unwilling participant. And even in cases in which the initial victim of an aggressive attack responds with enthusiasm, clearly relishing the prospect of a fight, there is no suggestion that he thereby grants his adversary permission to attack him. Some people claim, however, that war is different, in that all those who fight as members of a military force in war consent, at least implicitly, to be attacked by their adversaries.[11] Participation in war is, on this view, relevantly like boxing, or duelling. The moral justification that each combatant has for fighting is that his adversaries have consented to fight and therefore to be attacked. The law of *jus in bello* simply reflects this moral reality. So law and morality actually coincide in recognizing that all combatants in war are subject to the same rules and have the same rights and status.

I think, however, that it is a mistake to suppose that all, or even most, combatants consent to be attacked. It seems absurd to suppose, for example, that a young Polish man who learns that the Nazis have invaded his country and rushes to enlist in order to fight them thereby consents to be killed by the Nazis. Yet it can be argued that when he puts on the uniform, he is consciously identifying himself as a legitimate target. Wearing the uniform certainly makes him a conspicuous target and is therefore in an important sense highly imprudent, so he must have an important reason for wearing it. The reason given by convention is that the uniform functions as a marker of a legitimate target of attack. Thus it can be argued that to identify oneself conspicuously as a legitimate target of attack just *is* to consent to be attacked.

This, however, conflates consenting with upholding a convention. The Polish soldier might reason as follows: 'There is a convention that says that combatants should attack only other combatants, who are identified as such by their uniform. It is crucial to uphold this convention because it limits the killing that occurs on

---

[11] The most sophisticated defence of this view of which I am aware is Hurka, T., 'Liability and Just Cause', *Ethics and International Affairs*, 20 (2007), 199.

both sides in war. I therefore wear the uniform to signal that I am someone the convention identifies as a legitimate target. In doing this I am not consenting to be attacked or giving the enemy permission to attack me; rather, I am attempting to draw the enemy's fire toward myself and away from others, in much the way a parent might attempt to draw the attention of a predatory animal toward herself and thus away from her child, whom she hopes thereby to enable to escape—though of course in this case the drawing of attention is mediated by convention.'

One way to see that this is correct is to suppose that wearing the uniform did signify consent. And suppose that the Polish patriot refuses, on principle, to consent to be attacked by the Nazis. The Nazi invasion is unjust and one cannot, he thinks, consent to any of the evil that is done in the course of it. But if wearing the uniform involves consenting to be unjustly attacked and not fighting is tantamount to capitulation, his only honourable option seems to be to fight without joining the army or wearing the uniform. If he and others were to adopt this option, their private defensive action would not violate the moral rights of the Nazis. It would be morally justified. And assuming that their consent is what would justify the Nazis in attacking them, it seems that in this case the Nazis would have no moral right to kill them, even in self-defence.

The law is obviously not modelled on any view of this sort. According to the law, Poles who carried out military operations against the Nazis without distinguishing themselves as combatants would be unlawful combatants whose action would be perfidious and might, indeed, count as murder. Yet it would be odd if the law were to condemn the only morally honourable course open to victims of aggression. Something is wrong with the reasoning we have been following and it is clear that the mistake is to assume that enlisting and wearing the uniform involve consenting to be attacked in the way that stepping into the boxing ring involves consenting to be hit. Acceptance of combatant status does not involve consent but only recognition of the convention that permits attacks on combatants but forbids attacks on non-combatants.

Even if just combatants did consent to be attacked, it would not follow that unjust combatants would not wrong them by attacking them. Consent does not always effectively waive a right. Suppose, for example, that in 1800 a villain who has already wronged a man wants to harm and humiliate him further. He therefore makes a false accusation and challenges the man he has wronged to a duel. The wronged man accepts the challenge from a sense of honour, refuses to fire his weapon, and is killed by the villain. His consenting to the duel may make this killing morally different from murder, but it does not *justify* it or make it permissible.

Finally, even if combatants consent to be attacked and are not wronged by being attacked by enemy combatants, it does not follow that unjust combatants have the same justification for fighting that just combatants have. For the action of unjust combatants supports an unjust cause and therefore injures and wrongs people other than the just combatants who are its immediate victims, including innocent people who are harmed as a side effect of attacks against military targets. It is, therefore, untenable to suppose that consent establishes a special moral symmetry between just and unjust combatants that is absent in most other forms of conflict and that the symmetry in the law of *jus in bello* reflects this underlying moral symmetry.

V. KILLING IN WAR AS INDIVIDUAL DEFENCE

There are three other attempts to justify the symmetry in the law of *jus in bello* that all claim that this legal symmetry corresponds to an underlying moral symmetry, though this moral symmetry is found, not in the familiar morality that governs relations among individuals outside of war, but only in a separate, distinct morality that applies only in and to the state of war. The first such view holds that this distinct morality of war has the same structure as ordinary morality but a different content. It accepts that the strongest and most widely applicable form of justification for harming and killing an individual appeals to the claim that the individual is liable to be harmed or killed, but it offers a criterion of liability to attack in war that is different from the criteria of liability that govern other forms of conflict. On this view, what makes a person morally liable to attack in war is simply that he poses a threat to others. Defenders of this view sometimes note that the original meaning of 'innocent' is 'unthreatening', so that, understood in this way, the innocent in war are non-combatants, while combatants are non-innocent. If, as is customary, we also take 'innocent' to refer to those who are not liable, then combatants, who are threatening, are liable to attack in war, while non-combatants are not.

This view offers a symmetry account of the justification for defensive killing in war. Combatants on each side threaten those on the other and thus are liable to be killed in self-defence. On this view, necessary and proportionate self-defence is always self-justifying—a claim that is radically at odds with the strongly asymmetrical morality of self-defence outside the context of war, which holds that there can be no justified defence against an attack to which one is morally liable.

Among the many problems with this view, which I have criticized at length elsewhere, is that there is no reason why this essentially Hobbesian account of self-defence should be thought to apply in war but not in any other conditions.[12] Indeed, it does not apply consistently even in war, since both morality and law recognize that *jus ad bellum* is governed by an asymmetrical account of self-defence, according to which the victim of aggression has a right of defence while the initial

---

[12] See McMahan, J., 'The Ethics of Killing in War', *Ethics*, 114 (2004), 693, and 'On the Moral Equality of Combatants', *Journal of Political Philosophy*, 14 (2006), 377.

aggressor does not. Why should an asymmetrical account of self-defence apply to states, while a symmetrical account applies to the agents of those states in the same context?

VI. Collectivism

Many moral and political theorists continue to adhere to the collectivist conception of war that I briefly described earlier. They believe that there is a distinct collectivist morality that applies to war. At the level of *jus ad bellum*, this morality parallels the morality that governs relations among individuals, with this difference: the agents to whom it applies are states, not persons. Its principles of self-defence, for example, are asymmetrical; thus only the initial victim state, and not the aggressor, has a right of self-defence, as in the case of individuals. Yet the impermissibility of a state's action in fighting an aggressive war is not transmitted to the action of the unjust combatants who do the actual fighting. They act permissibly provided they obey the moral principles governing the conduct of war, which are, like the laws of *jus in bello* that are modelled on them, neutral in character.

How does the collectivist view explain the neutrality of these principles? One suggestion is that when people act collectively under the aegis of the state, it can be permissible for them to act in ways that would be impermissible if they were acting as private individuals.[13] It has not, however, been satisfactorily explained how, by establishing political relations *among themselves*, people could confer on themselves permissions to treat *others* in ways that would be impermissible in the absence of those relations. And even if this moral alchemy could be explained and justified, it would remain mysterious why the permissions are restricted to *jus in bello*. If the political relations among individuals that make them citizens of the same state create special permissions, those permissions should extend to the political leaders and thus to the acts of the state itself, making *jus ad bellum* permissive in the way that *jus in bello* supposedly is.

Another suggestion is that the collectivist view implies that the moral principles of *jus ad bellum* apply to the acts of states, and therefore to the acts of political leaders that determine what states do, but not to the acts of individual combatants, who are merely the instruments of states. But this itself requires explanation. One explanation is that combatants cannot be responsible for *jus ad bellum* because they lack the knowledge necessary to judge whether a war is just as well as the power either to initiate or to prevent war. But if combatants cannot be responsible for *jus*

---

[13] See Kutz, C., 'The Difference Uniforms Make: Collective Violence in Criminal Law and War', *Philosophy and Public Affairs*, 33 (2005), 148. For a critique of the collectivist view, see McMahan, J., 'Collectivist Defenses of the Moral Equality of Combatants', *Journal of Military Ethics*, 6 (2007), 50.

ad bellum, the principles that govern their action cannot refer to judgments of *jus ad bellum*, but must be neutral.

This cannot be right. By engaging in various acts of unjust aggression, Nazi Germany initiated a war in which many millions of innocent people were killed. Among them were millions of combatants who fought against the Nazis. These were morally wrongful killings even though they may have involved no violation of the laws of *jus in bello*. It is absurd to suppose that sole responsibility for these killings lies either with an abstract collective, the German State, or with a handful of political and military leaders, most of whom only gave orders and never killed a single person. The claim that Nazi combatants cannot have acted wrongly in killing enemy soldiers because they could not be responsible for judging whether their war was just or unjust is false. Morality often requires people to make difficult judgments, and to accept responsibility if they get it wrong—a demand that is particularly exigent when what is at issue is killing.

VII. CONSEQUENTIALISM

The fourth and final possibility I will mention is that while both common sense morality and domestic law are deontological in character, there is a distinct morality of war that is rule-consequentialist. Perhaps because the stakes are so high, the morality of war, both *jus ad bellum* and *jus in bello*, is just a matter of which rules work best in practice. And the rules that work best—and that we would all agree to be guided by if we were rational—are unambiguous and easily applicable rules that prohibit aggression, forbid attacks on civilians, require humane treatment of prisoners, permit all combatants to attack enemy combatants rather than making unjust combatants liable to legal sanctions, and so on. The law and morality of war thus coincide because their aims are the same: to minimize the occasions for war and the harms involved in warfare.

This view invites a number of questions, such as how the consequences of war are to be evaluated in determining what the correct rules are. Ought the rules to permit a certain degree of national partiality? Ought they to aim at the minimization of harm overall or ought they attribute greater weight to harm to the innocent than to harm to the non-innocent? If the latter, how exactly are innocence and non-innocence to be understood? A more fundamental question is why we should abandon the central elements of common sense morality, including ordinary principles of liability, in the context of war. These principles may, of course, become difficult or even, in some instances, impossible to apply in the confused circumstances of war, but that is different from their having no application at all. Principles of liability are important because they tell us when people have forfeited certain rights. If we assume that outside the context of war people have a right not to be unjustly attacked or killed, we have to be able to explain what happens to that right in war, when rule-consequentialism supposedly takes over.

In order for a different morality to apply in conditions of war, war must be different in some fundamental way from other kinds of conflict. But it seems to differ primarily only in scale. There is, of course, a political dimension—states are usually involved—and there is therefore greater coordination among people on all sides to the conflict. But otherwise it is hard to see why an entirely different morality should apply in conditions of war. If, moreover, war really were governed by a quite different set of moral principles, it would be essential to be able to determine precisely when a condition of war obtains and when it does not. In order to determine, for example, whether a killing is permissible or is instead an instance of murder, one may, on this view, need to know whether the perpetrator and victim are combatants in a war. This could make sense as a matter of legal doctrine but as a claim about basic morality it is hard to believe.

These general doubts about whether there is a special morality that is specific to war also apply, of course, to the view that war is governed by symmetrical liability rules, and to the view that it is governed by a special collectivist morality.

VIII. The Divergence between Morality and the Law of War

There is really only one morality. There is no special morality that supplants ordinary morality whenever conditions of war obtain. War is, moreover, continuous with other areas of human activity. It differs from other conflicts, including individual self- and other-defence, only in scale and complexity. The morality of killing in war is therefore asymmetrical, just as killing in individual self-defence is. Since the law of *jus in bello* is fully symmetrical, or neutral between just and unjust combatants, the law diverges from morality.

Perhaps the main reason for this divergence is that the requirements of morality are particularly difficult to discern in conditions of war. The most important of our epistemic disabilities in this area lies in determining whether there is just cause for war. For a variety of reasons, most combatants believe that the war in which they are fighting is just. This is almost as likely to be true of unjust combatants as it is of just combatants. And most unjust combatants who perceive or suspect that their cause is unjust are more likely to *assert* that it is just and fight anyway than to admit that their side is in the wrong and then have to decide whether to fight or to refuse to fight. As long as states that fight unjust wars can continue to declare their war to be just and legal without authoritative correction, whatever rights can be claimed by just combatants will be claimed by unjust combatants as well.

Whatever is legally permitted to the just will be done by the unjust as well; therefore an asymmetrical law of *jus in bello* that followed morality in granting permissions to just combatants that it denied to unjust combatants would be ineffective in constraining the latter.

One possible way to establish symmetrical laws of *jus in bello* would be to grant legal permissions to just and unjust combatants to do whatever it is morally permissible for just combatants to do, and to prohibit in law whatever just combatants are morally forbidden to do. This would exempt unjust combatants from legal liability for many serious moral wrongs, but if we assume that morality forbids just combatants to attack civilians intentionally, or to torture or kill prisoners, then such laws may in practice be restrictive enough. Indeed, it might be thought that the laws we have now could for the most part be explained and defended in just this way.

But this is false. It cannot be ruled out, for example, that justice could permit, or even favour, the killing of certain civilians, if they bore heavy responsibility for an unjust war and killing them could somehow make a more significant contribution to the achievement of their adversaries' just cause than an attack on combatants. It is, in fact, doubtful that the idea of universal civilian immunity has any foundation in basic, non-conventional morality. Rather, this idea has various sources. These include the interest of each belligerent in preserving its society from destruction, the fact that civilians in general pose no threat, so that killing them usually serves no military purpose, and the view that combatants are professionals who, like police and fire-fighters, consent to the risks involved in their work and are restricted by their professional code to fighting only against others like themselves. But even if it can be morally permissible, on occasion, for just combatants to attack civilians who are not innocent in the relevant sense, it would be disastrous to have a legal rule that permitted attacks against civilians, even if only in highly restricted circumstances. For, as I noted, unjust combatants would inevitably claim the right to act on this permission, probably more frequently than just combatants would, and just combatants would be tempted to avail themselves of the permission more often than they would be entitled to. And it is more important to deny this legal permission to the unjust, and to prevent its being abused by the just, than it is to offer it to the just on those rare occasions when they would be morally justified in acting on it. At least at present, therefore, the laws of *jus in bello* must deny to both just and unjust combatants certain options that would on occasion be morally permitted to the just.

The suggestion that the laws of war must diverge from morality raises a number of questions. What, for example, should the aim of the law be? It might be to minimize overall harm, to mitigate the destructiveness of war in general while giving priority to the prevention of harm to the innocent, or to induce people to act in ways that would best protect rights and promote justice. Doubtless there are other possibilities.

Another question is whether it could be acceptable, as a means of achieving one of these ends, for the law to deliberately permit forms of action that are seriously wrong—for example, acts that violate rights. I believe, for example, that just combatants do nothing to lose their moral right not to be attacked, but that the consequences of holding unjust combatants criminally liable for killing just combatants in war would be worse than those of legally permitting these killings and that the law ought therefore to permit them, at least at present. But this seems to involve the intentional creation, as a means of preventing bad consequences, of conditions in which people will predictably violate the rights of others. Suppose for the sake of argument—I do not claim that this is true—that for an unjust combatant to kill a just combatant in war is murder. The challenge here is to explain how a non-consequentialist morality could endorse a law that permits this form of murder, and do so as a means of preventing bad consequences.[14] I think the explanation is that legally permitting a form of murder is morally quite unlike committing a murder as a means of preventing others from committing a greater number of murders. It is simply to create legal conditions in which there will be less wrongdoing of a serious nature—for example, in which people will predictably violate fewer rights rather than more. But doubtless more needs to be said about this.

IX. Narrowing the Gap

Many people think that the laws of war have been designed to reduce both the frequency and the destructiveness of war. Most of these same people also believe that these are the proper goals of the law. But, while the factual claim may be correct, the normative claim is mistaken. The analogous normative claim about the law of self-defence is that it should aim to deter conflicts and to minimize harm to all concerned. But it would be a mistake for the law of self-defence to assume that harm to wrongful aggressors matters in exactly the same way that harm to innocent victims does. The principal aim of the law of self-defence should be justice: the deterrence of wrongful attacks and the prevention of harm to the innocent via the necessary and proportionate harming of those who have made themselves morally liable to be harmed. The aim of the laws of war should ideally be the same. (Sometimes, of course, considerations of justice are outweighed by the necessity of avoiding great harm. Justice is not the whole of the morality of war. But it is the dominant part.)

At present, however, it is simply not feasible for the laws of war—particularly the laws of *jus in bello*—to track considerations of justice closely. The most significant

---

[14] I am indebted to David Rodin for pressing me to address this challenge.

impediment is epistemic. As I noted earlier, it is difficult for people in general, and for active-duty military personnel in particular, to determine whether a war is just. In part because of this, there are good reasons to believe that war would involve more rather than less injustice if the laws of *jus in bello* were at present to become asymmetrical between just and unjust combatants. It may be that the existing symmetrical laws of *jus in bello* work at least as well as any laws could in present conditions to achieve just outcomes in war.

Yet we could do considerably better in bringing the law into conformity with the demands of justice if we could change the conditions in which the laws would operate.[15] We could, for example, begin to overcome the epistemic obstacles by achieving a better understanding of *jus ad bellum*, understood in moral terms. The relevant issues received serious attention only during the classical and transitional phases of the just war tradition. After that, as we have seen, the law gradually abdicated control over the resort to war, then suddenly reversed itself by adopting a crude, highly restrictive doctrine that is clearly at variance with morality. The work of the classical theorists, though suggestive, is deficient in at least two important respects. First, the discussions of such matters as just cause are quite brief and therefore lack the sustained, rigorous analysis and argument necessary to understand these matters well. Second, the classical discussions are contaminated by religious presuppositions. A defensible understanding of *jus ad bellum* will have to be purged of appeals to sacred texts and church dogmas. Although secular moral philosophy is still in its infancy, it has made extraordinary progress over the past forty years and is now poised, with the analytical tools it has developed, to provide an understanding of *jus ad bellum*, and of the morality of war in general, that is deeper, more rigorous, and better grounded than any previous work in the just war tradition.[16]

An enhanced understanding of *jus ad bellum* will not, of course, mitigate the epistemic problems faced by military personnel, political leaders, and others if it remains an arcane doctrine found only in philosophy books. Once the moral dimensions of *jus ad bellum* are better understood, the knowledge must be disseminated. Part of this process will involve education. Because participation in war is not only physically but morally perilous, we owe it to those who fight on our behalf to train them not only for combat but also for the competent exercise of moral judgment in matters concerning war. But even this would leave an unfair burden on soldiers if they were going to be legally liable for matters of *jus ad bellum*. What is ultimately needed is for an enhanced moral understanding of *jus ad bellum* to find expression in a detailed, nuanced law of *jus ad bellum* that could then be interpreted by an impartial, neutral international court charged with the responsibility for

---

[15] See Buchanan, A., 'Institutionalizing the Just War', *Philosophy and Public Affairs* 34 (2006), 2.

[16] The observation that secular moral philosophy is still in its infancy is made by Derek Parfit at the end of his magisterial *Reasons and Persons* (Oxford: Oxford University Press, 1984), itself perhaps the best evidence of the progress that has recently been achieved.

making authoritative judgments about this body of law, preferably while wars are in progress, or even prior to their initiation.[17] If combatants or potential combatants could look to the determinations of such a court for guidance concerning the legal status of a war in which they were fighting, or were about to fight, this could mitigate the epistemic constraints that are at present the greatest obstacle to holding individuals accountable for fighting in unjust wars. It would not, however, enable us to have legal rules of *jus in bello* that would be identical to, or even correspond closely to, the morality of *jus in bello*. This is because unless unjust combatants are acting to prevent just combatants from pursuing their just cause by impermissible means, *any* violent action they take is morally impermissible. Yet because unjust wars will continue to be fought even if they are denounced as unjust by an authoritative and epistemically reliable juridical body, it will remain essential to have laws that have a chance of constraining the action of unjust combatants. These laws will necessarily permit acts of war that are morally impermissible. But they will prohibit some morally impermissible acts of war that unjust combatants might otherwise have no incentive to refrain from doing. The laws governing the action of unjust combatants might not be identical with those governing the action of just combatants, though they might be more effective if they were. What is most important is that laws would exist that applied to the action of those identified by the relevant court as unjust combatants, and those individuals would be held legally accountable as individuals for observing those laws. If unjust combatants could be motivated to obey those laws, that would not only diminish the violation of rights and the destructiveness of war, but also mitigate the unjust combatants' offenses against morality.

[17] I explore this possibility in greater detail in 'Individual Responsibility and the Law of *Jus ad Bellum*', in Yitzhak Benaji and Naomi Sussman, (eds.), Reading *Walzer* (London: Routledge, 2011).

CHAPTER 25

LAWS OF WAR

HENRY SHUE[*]

The laws of war reference the same fundamental moral touchstones as the law and morality of ordinary life, but they focus on stiffening the edges of the violations ripped by war through normal rules, in order that the breaches in the standards are not torn more widely than the persistence of international conflict makes necessary. The moral and legal prohibitions of ordinary, peaceful life are violated by war. Rather than condemning the violations inherent in violent conflict, the laws of war have concentrated on preventing the exceptions from swallowing the rules. This has involved insisting upon limits where ordinary law and morality maintain complete prohibitions: limitation, mostly without endorsement of what is not condemned.

The article entitled 'Basic Rules' at the beginning of the section on 'Methods and Means of Warfare' in the 1977 Geneva Protocol I says: 'In any armed conflict, the right of the Parties to the conflict to choose methods or means of warfare is not unlimited'.[1] This generalizes, and phrases as a negative limit on means rather than a specific positive acceptance of an end, the principle that had famously prefaced

* I have benefited greatly from conversations on these topics with Janina Dill, Per Ilsaas, Seth Lazar, Jeff McMahan, and David Rodin.

[1] 1977 Geneva Protocol I Additional to the Geneva Conventions of 12 August 1949, article 35; a convenient source is Roberts, A., and Guelff, R. (eds.), *Documents on the Laws of War* (3rd edn., Oxford: Oxford University Press, 2000), 442. Also see <http://www.icrc.org/ihl.nsf/FULL/470?OpenDocument>. All websites were most recently checked in Dec. 2007. Roberts and Guelff suggest that 'perhaps the most fundamental customary principle is that the right of belligerents to adopt means of injuring the enemy is not unlimited'—the principle is expressed in art. 35. They view the principles of proportionality and discrimination as specific limits resting on 'the more basic principle that belligerent rights are not unlimited' (9). This more basic formulation appeared in the 1874 Brussels Declaration, art. 12, and in the 1880 Oxford Manual, art. 4. These may be found, respectively, at <http://www.icrc.org/ihl.nsf/INTRO/135?OpenDocument> and <http://www.icrc.org/ihl.nsf/FULL/140?OpenDocument>.

the 1868 St Petersburg Declaration: 'The only legitimate object which states should endeavour to accomplish during war is to weaken the military forces of the enemy'.[2] The conduct of war can have only one legitimate purpose: harming the armed forces of the adversary—St Petersburg Declaration. This is because the means of war are not unlimited—Geneva Protocol I. The laws for the conduct of war, customary and conventional, are about limiting means, irrespective of ultimate ends beyond military victory.

The St Petersburg Declaration was agreed only in 1868 at the beginning of the modern codification of the laws of war at the dawn of the age of the multilateral treaty.[3] The underlying principle of discrimination, however, is an expression of ancient custom, put colourfully in the Laws of Manu as follows:

He should not kill anyone who has climbed on a mound, or an impotent man, or a man who folds his hands in supplication, or whose hair is unbound, or anyone who is seated or who says, 'I am yours'; nor anyone asleep, without armour, naked, without a weapon, not fighting, looking on, or engaged with someone else; nor anyone whose weapons have been broken, or who is in pain, badly wounded, terrified, or fleeing.[4]

A characteristically Christian formulation of the principle of discrimination came in tenth-century France from the Peace of God movement, which proposed 'that the weak who could do no harm should not themselves be harmed'.[5] This thought is the source of the original distinctive, now-archaic usage within the morality of war of the word 'innocent' to mean those not harming. An early Sunni Islamic formulation prohibits the killing of 'those who are not belligerent and do not participate in war, such as women, children, hermits, old men, the blind, the chronically ill and the like'.[6]

---

[2] 1868 St. Petersburg Declaration, Preamble; Roberts, A. and Guelff, R. (eds.), *Documents on the Laws of War* (above, n. 1), 55.

[3] For the historic significance of the move from natural international law to contractual international law and its attendant multilateralism, see Reus-Smit, C., *The Moral Purpose of the State: Culture, Social Identity, and Institutional Rationality in International Relations* (Oxford and Princeton: Princeton University Press, 1999), chs. 1, 2, and 6. The best way to quickly appreciate the variety of the conventions constituting the laws for the conduct of war is to look at a good collection, such as Roberts, A., and Guelff, R., (eds.), *Documents on the Laws of War* (above, n. 1).

[4] Anonymous, *The Laws of Manu*, O'Flaherty, W. D. and Smith, B. K. (trans.) (London: Penguin Books, 1991), 137–8.

[5] Parker, G., 'Early Modern Europe', in Howard, M., Andreopoulos, G. J., and Shulman, M. R. (eds.), *The Laws of War: Constraints on Warfare in the Western World* (London and New Haven: Yale University Press, 1994), 41. Parker draws on Cowdrey, H. E. J., 'The Peace and the Truce of God in the Eleventh Century', *Past and Present*, 46 (1970), 42. For a more theoretically rich discussion, see Hartigan, R. S., *The Forgotten Victim: A History of the Civilian* (South Holland, Ill.: Precedent Publishing, 1982), 65–77.

[6] Ibn Taymiyyah, T., *Ibn Taymiyyah Expounds on Islam: Selected Writings of Shaykh al-Islam Taqi ad-Din Ibn Taymiyyah on Islamic Faith, Life, and Society*, Muhammad Abdul-Haq Ansari (trans.) (Riyadh: General Administration of Culture and Publication, 2000), 544; cited in Brahimi, A., 'Just War and Jihad in the War on Terror: An Examination of the Moral Justifications for War Made by George W. Bush and Osama bin Laden', D.Phil. thesis (Oxford, 2007), 22 n. 52.

The formulation from the Peace of God, the formulation from Ibn Taymiyyah, and the formulation at the heart of the St Petersburg Declaration have the same distinctive focus on resisting the unnecessary enlargement of an uncondemned but usually unendorsed exception, a form and function that I want to suggest are characteristic of, and fundamental to, the laws of war. The Peace of God does not say: 'You should harm the strong who are able to harm you—go ahead, attack them'. Passing over without comment the question of who may be harmed, this Christian movement simply says, in Parker's words, 'the weak who could do no harm should not themselves be harmed'.[7] Indeed, the Truce of God movement, 'which made its appearance a generation or so later', proposed one possible logical extension, that there should be certain periods—truces—when no one at all, weak or strong, could be harmed.[8] Similarly, the St Petersburg Declaration, while it does in fact say that 'states should endeavour . . . to weaken the military forces of the enemy', is clearly not aimed at urging forward attempts at weakening of enemy forces, which is primarily presupposed, although admittedly endorsed as well, but is aimed fundamentally at preventing this necessary concession to the violence of war from 'leaking' into unnecessary excesses. The Declaration immediately goes on after the restriction of attacks to combatants to propose the extremely strict requirement that, whenever possible, combatants should avoid causing the deaths of adversary combatants: 'For this purpose it is sufficient to disable the greatest possible number of men; this object would be exceeded by the employment of arms which uselessly aggravate the sufferings of disabled men, or render their death inevitable'.[9] The objective of the measures proposed in the Declaration is to minimize death and suffering by combatants. Death is not avoidably to be made inevitable for combatants—they are not to be 'wasted', in the term of the era of the war in Vietnam—and their suffering is not to be aggravated uselessly.

The present-day cliché has it that wars are 'about killing people and breaking things', which is still perfectly compatible with killing only certain people, namely, combatants and not non-combatants. The Declaration, indeed, endorsed two kinds of limits: it 'limited harm to combatants' in two distinct senses. It first limited the harm to combatants in the sense that it restricted harming to the harming of combatants only—no one except combatants could be harmed. But, secondly, the harm that could be done to combatants was itself limited—no one who could

---

[7] Parker, G., 'Early Modern Europe' (above, n. 5), 41.

[8] Cowdrey, H. E. J., 'The Peace and the Truce of God in the Eleventh Century' (above, n. 5), 42. 'These Truces depended upon Episcopal sanctions. Their scope was gradually extended, so that the truce of 1115 not only protected certain seasons, but also sought to introduce a continuous peace for three years', 62. This did not work out.

[9] Roberts, A., and Guelff, R. (eds.), *Documents on the Laws of War* (above, n. 1), 55.

only be wounded non-fatally was to be wounded fatally and even that wounding was to be done with the minimum of suffering because its purpose was temporary disablement, not pain or permanent crippling, much less death. The first limit is a limit on scope; it is the principle of discrimination. Today the first, emphatic rule of the customary law for the conduct of war is: 'The parties to the conflict must at all times distinguish between civilians and combatants. Attacks may only be directed against combatants. Attacks must not be directed against civilians'.[10] The principle of discrimination remains deeply entrenched.

Within that limited scope, the second limit is a limit on severity. The Declaration takes for granted that there is a reasonably well-established custom that combat should involve military forces exclusively. Indeed the statement about the only acceptable purpose being the weakening of the adversary's military forces is preambular and is presented as a description of customary practice. The principle of discrimination, then, is endorsed in passing but taken already to be established at that time. The limit actually being advanced by the Declaration is not the already customary limit on the scope of targeting, but a yet-unestablished limit on the permissible severity of harm to the permissible targets, which the Declaration hopes to accomplish specifically through limits on weapons and munitions.[11]

The general purpose of limiting severity of harm was also strongly advocated in the landmark catalogue of custom—virtually contemporary with the Declaration—the Lieber Code of 1863 (same year as the founding of the International Committee of the Red Cross).[12] Article XVI of the Lieber Code, issued by US President Lincoln only five years prior to the St Petersburg Declaration, contains the same fundamental appeal for a limit on the severity of harm to combatants: 'Military necessity does not admit of cruelty—that is, the infliction of suffering for the sake of suffering or for revenge, nor of maiming or wounding except in fight, nor of torture to extort confessions'.[13] One is not to maim outside of the fighting, but it is taken for granted

---

[10] Henckaerts, J. and Doswald-Beck, L., *Customary International Humanitarian Law*, vol. i. *Rules* (Cambridge: Cambridge University Press for the International Committee of the Red Cross, 2005), 3. This is the most authoritative recent statement of the customary law of war.

[11] Given the continued legality today of nuclear weapons of mass destruction, this specific means of limitation—limitation on weapons—has so far had severely limited success. Needless to say, the story of weapons limitation, while important and of course unfinished, is too long to pursue here. Biological and chemical weapons of mass destruction were made illegal, and the widespread and remarkably rapid ratification of the 1997 Ottawa Convention on the Prohibition of Anti-Personnel Mines (in spite of the opposition of the 'sole superpower') has returned proposals to limit weapons to the agenda.

[12] The path-breaking modern survey of customary law, drawn up by Francis Lieber, a German-born professor of history at Columbia University, for US President Abraham Lincoln, was the Lieber Code, promulgated by Lincoln on 24 Apr. 1863 as General Orders No. 100, Instructions for the Government of Armies of the United States in the Field—see Hartigan, R. S., *Lieber's Code and the Law of War* (South Holland, Ill.: Precedent Publishing, 1983), 45; or Friedman, L. (ed.), *The Law of War: A Documentary History*, vol. i (New York: Random House, 1972), 158. Hartigan contains commentary and other useful documents including correspondence with Lieber. See also <http://www.icrc.org/ihl.nsf/FULL/110?OpenDocument>.

[13] Hartigan, R. S., *Lieber's Code* (above, n. 12), 48; Friedman, L. (ed.), *The Law of War* (above, n. 12), 161.

that within the fighting one will of course attempt to maim, according to Lieber in 1863. One is permitted 'to disable the greatest possible number of men' in so far as this is intended 'to weaken the military forces of the enemy', but one is prohibited from 'maiming or wounding except in fight', according to the Declaration in 1868. Versions of this second kind of limit on the severity of harm are also recognized elements of the customary laws of war today. The current Rule 70, for example, says: 'The use of means and methods of warfare which are of a nature to cause superfluous injury or unnecessary suffering is prohibited'.[14]

Accordingly, the form taken by the laws of war, conventional and customary, and the function played by them are clear. First, it is presupposed that the rules of law and morality applicable in peace-time—applicable to ordinary life—will be violated. To this extent, a practice of war is presupposed, and it is not treated as conceivable that an army would participate in a war and not pursue a relatively favourable outcome through the violent infliction of harm. Second, those violations of peace-time prohibitions are not protested and may even be to some degree accepted or endorsed.[15] Often no comment is offered on whether the practice of war is justified or not justified, although it is taken as obvious that war produces great evil in the form of deaths, wounds, and suffering. Nothing in the standards proposed is made to turn on whether any particular war is or could be justified. Third, the purpose of the laws of war is to put a brake on the violations—to hold various lines of limitation, e.g., limits on scope and limits on severity. The purpose of the laws is to minimize the rights violated and the evils committed, given that the practice is present. The goal is to make war a rule-governed practice, with rules that limit its violations and its evils. It is not the

[14] Henckaerts, J.-M., and Doswald-Beck, L., *Customary International Humanitarian Law* (above, n. 10), 237. Arguably limits of this second kind (on severity of harm) are today fairly weak. For example, Rule 85 says merely that 'the anti-personnel use of incendiary weapons is prohibited, unless it is not feasible to use a less harmful weapon to render a person *hors de combat*'—the echo of the St Petersburg Declaration is discernible but weak. Rule 86 restricts lasers only if they are 'specifically designed' to cause permanent blindness. The Laws of Manu had mandated: 'Fighting in a battle, he should not kill his enemies with weapons that are concealed, barbed, or smeared with poison or whose points blaze with fire' (above, n. 4), ch. 7, verse 90. As mentioned earlier, limits on weapons, which might limit the severity of harm to combatants, as distinguished from limits on targets, which limit the scope of harm by excluding non-combatants, have historically not proven especially successful. The most successful recent effort to ban a weapon, the 1997 Ottawa Convention on Anti-Personnel Mines (Roberts, A., and Guelff, R. (eds.), *Documents on the Laws of War* (above, n. 1), 645–66), rested on the observation that mines are inherently indiscriminate in killing more non-combatants than combatants, thus in effect arguing the case against them on the basis of scope, not severity. Limits on targets are now also under great pressure from Air Force bombing practices—see text below.

[15] Professor Lieber himself clearly believed that some wars are justified, saying in article XXX: 'War has come to be acknowledged not to be its own end, but the means to obtain great ends of state, or to consist in defense against wrong'. On the whole, his contention is that restraint is the mark of civilization as embodied in the practices of the 'modern regular wars of the Europeans' (art. XXV). Thus, he appeals, not to the tradition of just war, but to the tradition of regular war—for a clear account of the important differences between just and regular war, see Reichberg, G. M., 'Just War and Regular War: Competing Paradigms', in Rodin, D., and Shue, H. (eds.), *Just and Unjust Warriors: The Moral and Legal Status of Soldiers* (Oxford: Oxford University Press, 2008).

purpose of these rules to end the practice, or to maintain it. The practice is simply presupposed.[16]

The fundamental contention is: whatever exactly are the justifications or excuses for the violations not protested, those reasons do not carry across the line being drawn in the sand by the laws of war. You will in fact be wounding enemy forces—no need and no justification for killing them. You will in fact be attacking combatants—no need and no justification for attacking non-combatants. The laws of war have the form: no rationale for the violations of the ordinary rules carries past this point—stop here. This reasoning itself is compatible both with believing that war is never justified but will nevertheless in fact sometimes occur and with believing that war is sometimes justified. It is presupposed that the prevention of all wars is either not possible or not desirable in the short term; if it were, that might have been the means to the minimization of its violations and evils. In the short term, the goal is to limit the violations and evils caused by the wars that are fought.

I think the fundamental attitude of the laws of war to the violations of the absolute prohibitions against attacks, assaults, wounding, and killings that are part of ordinary law and morality can be well captured with the contemporary pithy phrase 'shit happens'. We are dealing with war. In wars terrible actions are taken: assaults, attacks, wounding, and killings are carried out. That they happen in every war does nothing to make them less terrible, but to prevent them all we must prevent all wars. The prevention of wars is a morally urgent task, but it is not the task of the laws of war. The purpose of the laws of war is to constrain the 'shit' when the 'shit' happens: when armies are assaulting and attacking, the laws of war specify firm limits.[17] This same purpose was stated more elegantly in the Preface to the Oxford Manual of 1880: 'to restrain the destructive force of war, while recognizing its inexorable necessities'.[18]

The result is that, in a phenomenon similar to that of some seeing the glass half empty and some seeing the glass half full, the stand taken by the laws of war at the

---

[16] This is one basis for maintaining the traditional separation between the justification of the resort to war and the justification of the conduct of war, accepted but problematized in Walzer, M., *Just and Unjust Wars: A Moral Argument with Historical Illustrations* (4th edn., New York: Basic Books, 2006), and currently hotly debated by philosophers—see Rodin, D. and Shue, H., *Just and Unjust Warriors* (above, n. 15).

[17] Even if the intended purpose of the laws of war is to constrain various kinds of terrible actions that will in any case be happening, it is a legitimate question whether in fact they function, even if completely inadvertently, to facilitate war. Robert L. Holmes made the argument that, however good the intentions of just-war theorists, they are in fact the handmaidens of war—see his *On War and Morality* (Oxford and Princeton: Princeton University Press, 1989). International relations specialist Nina Tannenwald has analysed the shadow permissive effects of prohibitory norms—see her *The Nuclear Taboo: The United States and the Non-Use of Nuclear Weapons Since 1945* (Cambridge: Cambridge University Press, 2007). Tannenwald observes how, for example, a prohibition on the build-up of nuclear weapons tends to promote the toleration of a build-up of conventional weapons and how the prohibition on the first-use of nuclear weapons seems to permit their possession. She is of course noting empirical, not conceptual, connections.

[18] *The Laws of War on Land* (Oxford, 1880). See <http://www.icrc.org/ihl.nsf/WebPrint/140-FULL?OpenDocument>.

edges of the exceptions can be seen as complicity in the exceptional violations not condemned or as continuing protection of all not included within the exception. In recent years some philosophers—most notably, Jeff McMahan—have been asking, in effect: but what about the violations of the ordinary rules that are not challenged by the laws of war? What about the terrible violence this side of the lines being drawn by the laws of war? How can it be justified to harm or kill combatants, such as defenders against aggression, who in various respects are at least as lacking in moral responsibility for the commission of any wrong as any 'innocent' non-combatant?

I am tempted to say that the McMahan critique of the laws of war is criticizing them for something that they do not do and do not claim to do: they are justifying limits on violations of ordinary prohibitions, and they do not claim to be justifying the violations short of the limits. Even if that were an appropriate observation, it would not reveal anything inherently objectionable in McMahan's project. It is perfectly acceptable, and sometimes quite important, to criticize laws for their omissions. If the laws prohibit only B and C, it can obviously be appropriate to ask: and what about A? Why is A not prohibited as well? And in fact I think a more appropriate characterization of McMahan's project is that he is asking why the limits embraced by the laws of war are where they are: why do they say 'stop here' instead of having said 'stop farther back there'. If our business is protecting the 'innocent', what about the 'innocent' combatants, for example, as well as the 'innocent' non-combatants?

McMahan proposes that we should think in dualistic terms, formulating a 'morality of war' that is 'quite distinct' from the law of war.[19] As I have just indicated, the laws of war attempt to limit war's death and destruction by distinguishing combatants from civilians and military objectives from civilian objects. These general categories—combatants and civilians—operate so that persons are assumed to be civilians (and objects are assumed to be civilian) unless specified necessary conditions are satisfied.[20] Persons are combatants only if they satisfy the criteria. McMahan proposes instead to distinguish among individual persons on the basis of what he calls 'liability to attack' during war, which he maintains is largely the same concept as liability to attack in the circumstances of individual self-defence in peace-time.[21] As he explains in his chapter in this volume, liability to attack has at

---

[19] McMahan, J., in this volume, 493.

[20] The particular conditions for qualifying as a combatant are in some dispute. The United States rejects the shorter list in 1977 Geneva Protocol I, art. 44, as insufficient (above, n. 1).

[21] He does not explicitly discuss objects, which are extremely important for restrictions on air attacks, but it is possible that if his criterion for persons were workable, it could be extended to objects. I have elsewhere criticized specifically the use of argument by analogy here and provided a more general critique of McMahan's approach—see Shue, H., 'Do We Need A "Morality of War"?' in Rodin, D. and Shue, H., *Just and Unjust Warriors* (above, n. 15). For an even more comprehensive critique of McMahan's overall approach, see Lazar, S., 'The Right to Kill? A Critique of Jeff McMahan's Theory of Liability to Defensive Killing, and its Application to War' (on file with author).

least two necessary conditions. The first liability shares with deserving harm: 'the victim of the harm has acted in a way that now makes him morally vulnerable to that harm. Because of something the victim has done, he has no right not to be harmed—at least not in a certain way, for a certain reason, and, perhaps, by certain persons'.[22]

Two features of this first necessary condition leap out. First, it depends upon having adequate and accurate information about the morally relevant past behaviour of individual persons before a decision is made whether to attack them, even though you are under attack by them. The kind of information required by the laws of war, by contrast, is information readily observable in the present, such as whether arms are being carried; normally, in the circumstances of war, if a person is not carrying some weapon, he is not attacking you (although in a 'philosopher's hypothetical' he could be attacking with his bare hands—not, in reality, a large problem). Second, McMahan's first necessary condition requires, not a visual perception or other fairly quick observation (is a weapon visible?), but a discriminating moral judgment based on an appropriate quantity and quality of evidence: has this individual's past behaviour been such as to render her 'morally vulnerable' to attack?[23] The decision whether it is morally permissible to fire on another person in a combat situation is being said to depend on the moral character of that person's earlier actions as well as her current ones.

The second necessary condition for liability to attack distinguishes it from deserving harm:

[I]f a person deserves to be harmed, there is a reason for harming him that is independent of the further consequences of harming him. Giving him what he deserves is an end in itself. But a person is liable to be harmed only if harming him will serve some further purpose—for example, if it will prevent him from unjustly harming someone, or will compensate a victim of his prior wrongdoing. For a person to be liable to be harmed, a condition of instrumental efficacy must be satisfied; but no such condition applies to desert.[24]

If you view yourself as justly defending yourself against unjust harm, you could easily construe an attack on your attacker as the prevention of unjust harm. The second necessary condition will readily be thought to be satisfied and so probably play little role when it is believed that the first necessary condition has been satisfied. It is the first condition, necessary for both being liable to harm and for deserving harm, that will then be my concern.

[22] McMahan, J., in this volume, 498.

[23] I am not suggesting that one can always, easily, and instantly see whether someone is a combatant or a civilian—ask a soldier who has maintained a check-point through which terrorists masquerading as civilians are attempting to pass with concealed weapons (or at which they are planning a suicide attack with a hidden explosive device)! These, however, are problems caused by the attempt by non-civilians to exploit the protection intended for civilians by violating the requirement for combatants to carry weapons openly. The difficulties are not the result of correctable faults in the legal criterion. But McMahan's moral criterion depends on adequate information about each particular person's morally relevant past behaviour.

[24] McMahan, J., this volume, 499 n.9.

First, I believe that McMahan's suggested first necessary condition is utterly impossible to implement in any circumstances remotely resembling war. In what I take to be an attempt to pre-empt the kind of critique I am about to offer, McMahan writes with regard to his proposed standards of liability, which are the core of his 'morality of war': 'These principles may, of course, become difficult or even in some instances impossible to apply in the confused circumstances of war, but that is different from their having no application at all'.[25] I do not know what this distinction means: a principle that is impossible to apply in the circumstances of war has no application at all to those circumstances—no application to war. Ought presupposes can. If it is to be the case that one ought to employ McMahan's conception of individual liability as part of one's guide about how to act during war, it must be possible to do so. But it is impossible.

When, for example, one is facing hundreds to thousands to hundreds of thousands of armed attackers, one cannot accurately acquire and discriminatingly assess adequate evidence about each individual attacker to discriminate those morally liable to attack from those not morally liable to attack before deciding how to respond. Now it may appear that I am about to embrace some conception of collective moral liability: if it is impossible to make judgments of individual liability, one might be tempted to argue, judgments of collective moral liability will have to be made. And McMahan's paper already contains a critique of 'collectivism'.[26] But the mistake that I believe that McMahan is making is not that he has formulated the wrong criteria of moral liability for the circumstances. The mistake is to assume that decisions within war can be based on any criterion of moral liability whatsoever. The mistake is to attempt to operate with a criterion of moral liability at all; the mistake is not to have one set of moral criteria rather than another.

The basic mistake is to over-moralize war. Christopher Kutz has brilliantly characterized McMahan's error as being an attempt at 'attuning the evils of war to the wrongs of the parties'.[27] No one is to die in war except individuals who morally deserve, or rather are morally liable, to die. It is profoundly to be wished that war could become like that. War would actually not be so bad if—as the fulfilment of McMahan's criteria would guarantee —no just defenders would die and only unjust attackers would be wounded or die. A major part of the horror of war is that, in Kutz's terms, the evils bear no relation to the wrongs.

The laws of war do not contain a criterion of moral liability to attack; they recognize that moral liability can play no role. Combatants are legally liable to attack; civilians are legally immune from attack. There is no suggestion, or presupposition, that carrying arms openly and wearing a uniform, for example, makes one morally liable to attack. Judgments of moral liability are not being made. This is indeed McMahan's complaint: he wants the laws of war to be moralized,

---

[25] Ibid. 504.   [26] Ibid. 503–4.
[27] Kutz, C., 'Fearful Symmetry', in Rodin, D. and Shue, H., *Just and Unjust Warriors* (above, n. 15).

specifically to incorporate a requirement of moral liability that he correctly sees is not there. My contention is that it cannot function there and that, since ought presupposes can, it is not the case that it ought to function there.

Since McMahan has pre-emptively conceded that his principles of liability 'become difficult or even in some instances impossible to apply in the confused circumstances of war', I will not belabour the reasons why. Some, however, deserve at least a mention. Nowadays it is popular to emphasize technological change in war and focus especially on 'stand-off weapons', weapons fired miles, if not continents and seas, away from the presumed location of their targets. Ballistic missiles and cruise (air-breathing) missiles are dramatic examples, but actually many centuries-old methods of warfare, such as the naval bombardment of cities, and of course air bombing of cities, involve what are essentially stand-off weapons. Certainly this is far removed from face-to-face combat in which one can literally see whether one's possible target is carrying a rifle. One reason to note the significance of such long-distance killing is to observe, in fairness to McMahan, that this phenomenon is also a problem for the criteria in the laws of war. A fighter pilot cannot possibly see whether many of his intended targets are carrying arms or wearing uniforms, which seems to mean that the literal requirements are increasingly archaic. It is still easier to think generally how to modify the current legal criteria, however, than it is to imagine how the individual moral assessments that McMahan would like to require could be made in the time and place of combat, but it is not unproblematic.

Furthermore, the critique of McMahan's suggestion does not turn on warfare's being high-tech. Tim O'Brien's agonizing chapters, 'The Man I Killed' and 'Ambush', describe the deepening distress of an American soldier in Vietnam as he stares empathetically into the face of a Vietcong soldier he has just killed in an ambush and fantasizes about how the 'slim, dead' young man might have felt about the war: 'He lay face-up in the center of the trail, a slim, dead, almost dainty young man ... His chest was sunken and poorly muscled—a scholar, maybe ... Frail-looking, delicately boned, the young man would not have wanted to be a soldier and in his heart would have feared performing badly in battle'.[28] The US invasion of Vietnam was wrong, and the American soldier ought not to have been in Vietnam killing Vietnamese. But suppose this American soldier believed he ought to be there—O'Brien's character is actually more complicated and more real—and had been ordered to guard a trail and stop any Vietcong troops who came along. How should he apply the individual moral liability test? Should the American stop frail-looking soldiers and interview them before deciding whether to attack? Which language should the interview be conducted in? Many Vietnamese looked small and frail to Americans; this was a Vietcong soldier carrying a deadly weapon. What if the

---

[28] O'Brien, T., *The Things They Carried* (London: Flamingo, 1991), 119–31, 121, and 123; and (New York: Broadway Books, 1998), 124–34, 124, and 127.

Vietcong soldier is the first of a dozen who will emerge from around the bend and then kill the American and several of his comrades before the liability assessment is complete? Should the American soldier, perhaps, refuse completely to conduct ambushes? Can he apply the individual moral liability test more effectively running across an open field firing an automatic weapon toward unseen enemies waiting in the underbrush for him?

Some may respond that I am raising practical problems and making pragmatic objections, but that greatly understates the severity of the difficulty. Ought presupposes can, and one cannot assess the individual moral liability of adversaries during deadly combat. Any decent philosopher can imagine hypothetical alternatives: fight six days a week and on the seventh rest and let trained specialists assess the relative moral liability of all combatants in the area on both sides and assign each combatant one of various differently coloured caps to wear depending on their degree of liability: black caps for those with murder in their hearts. But if one could arrange weekly truces, one could probably arrange a cease-fire. People agreeable to fighting in such a morally responsible manner are likely to be agreeable enough not to fight at all.[29] Hypotheticals of this kind are so little like war that they can only mislead us about war. 'Impractical' here means impossible. 'Impossible' means impossible: can't be done.

I agree with McMahan that 'there is really only one morality'.[30] I even agree that assignments of moral liability to harm on an individual basis must be made whenever they can be made; I am not hinting at some conception of collective moral liability. But individual assessments cannot be made during war. And people cannot have a duty to do what cannot be done. This makes the determination of who lives and who dies among combatants in war brutal, always arbitrary, and often cruel. What Iranian poet Reza Baraheni wrote about life in general is surely true at least of casualties in war: 'No one dies in the right place or in the right hour and everyone dies sooner than his time and before he reaches home'. Or as Bao Ninh's protagonist puts it:

What remained was sorrow, the immense sorrow, the sorrow of having survived. The sorrow of war . . . But for those still living to know that the kindest, most worthy people have all fallen away, or even been tortured, humiliated before being killed, or buried and wiped away by the machinery of war, then this beautiful landscape of calm and peace is an appalling paradox. Justice may have won, but cruelty, death and inhuman violence had also won.[31]

The human rights of combatants cannot be respected during war—this is one of the worst of war's many awful features.[32] Our highest achievable goal, I believe,

---

[29] This is reminiscent of the Truce of God movement's suggestions in the eleventh century for moving beyond the Peace of God movement's stand, mentioned earlier.

[30] McMahan, J., this volume, 505.   [31] Ninh, B., *The Sorrow of War* (London: Vintage, 1998), 179–80.

[32] Some of them can—there is no excuse for torture even in a war in which the fate of a nation actually is at stake, as Professor Lieber and President Lincoln both understood. Also see Kelley, Gen P. X., and

is to try to restore respect for the rights of civilians, especially during air attacks, as suggested below.

In his concluding section, 'Narrowing the Gap', McMahan suggests—completely rightly, I believe—that rather than attempting somehow to adjust the rules for the conduct of war in order to make war more humane or fair for combatants, we should turn our attention, at least for now, to the rules for the resort to war. As Yoram Dinstein has observed,

[S]ubsequent to the virtual demise of the just war doctrine, the predominant conviction in the nineteenth (and early twentieth) century was that every State had a right—namely, an interest protected by international law—to embark upon war whenever it pleased. The discretion of States in this matter was portrayed as unfettered. States could 'resort to war for a good reason, a bad reason or no reason at all' . . . War came to be characterized as 'a right inherent in sovereignty itself'. Moreover, the war-making right was thought of as the paramount attribute of sovereignty.[33]

The coming into force of the United Nations Charter has radically transformed this situation.[34] Arguments on both sides of current disputes about humanitarian intervention show how seriously the Charter must be taken, even by those who advocate not always abiding by it.[35]

McMahan's specific proposal is the following:

What is ultimately needed is for an enhanced moral understanding of *jus ad bellum* to find expression in a detailed, nuanced law of *jus ad bellum* that could then be interpreted by an impartial, neutral international court charged with the responsibility for making authoritative judgments about this body of law, preferably while wars are in progress, or even prior to their initiation. If combatants or potential combatants could look to the determinations of such a court for guidance concerning the legal status of a war in which they were fighting, or were about to fight, this could substantially mitigate the epistemic constraints that are at present the greatest obstacle to rewriting the laws of *jus in bello* in asymmetrical form, thereby bringing them into greater harmony with considerations of justice.[36]

Turner, R. F., 'War Crimes and the White House: The Dishonor in a Tortured New "Interpretation" of the Geneva Conventions', *Washington Post*, 26 July 2007, A21.

[33] Dinstein, Y., *War, Aggression and Self-Defence* (4th edn., Cambridge: Cambridge University Press, 2005), 75–6. I have attacked this conception of sovereignty in 'Limiting Sovereignty', in Welsh, J. M. (ed.), *Humanitarian Intervention and International Relations* (Oxford: Oxford University Press, 2004), 11–28 and 184–6.

[34] I do not agree that the United Nations Charter standard is 'crude and simplistic' (McMahan, J., this volume, 496), but space is not available here to take up issues about resort to war. Compare Dinstein, Y., *War, Aggression and Self-Defence* (above, n. 33), 85–91 and 117–50. My two quite different overviews of conduct, resort, and their relation are in 'War', in LaFollette, H. (ed.), *The Oxford Handbook of Practical Ethics* (Oxford: Oxford University Press, 2003), 734; reproduced in Evangelista, M. (ed.), *Peace Studies: Critical Concepts in Political Science* (London and New York: Routledge, 2005), i. 142; and in Skorupski, J. (ed.), *Routledge Companion to Ethics* (London: Routledge, forthcoming).

[35] Buchanan, A., 'Reforming the International Law of Humanitarian Intervention', in Holzgrefe, J. and Keohane, R. (eds.), *Humanitarian Intervention: Ethical, Legal, and Political Dilemmas* (Cambridge: Cambridge University Press, 2003), 130.

[36] McMahan, J., this volume, 508–9.

Unfortunately for McMahan's proposal for the employment of a standard of individual moral liability, this suggested use of authoritative rulings about the resort to war actually rests on a collective standard of moral liability. I will conclude by trying briefly to show this. As I understand it, once the authoritative international court has ruled that side B was unjustified in going to war, at least the combatants on side B would be considered morally liable to attack.[37] This is a collective judgment of moral liability: everyone on side B is morally liable because side B is unjustified.

This does not deal with one of the fundamental underlying problems: individuals who conscientiously and sincerely believe that their side is justified in spite of the fact that it is objectively unjustified—good people who are mistaken about this war. Suppose we grant that because of the excellence of its procedures—or for some other reason—the determinations of the international court are objectively justified. So, when the court rules that side B is not justified, the ruling is objectively correct and ought to be accepted by everyone, including all potential combatants on side B. However, further suppose that a substantial majority of side B's citizens, all of whom are decent, reasonable people, after conscientious consideration, conclude that this time the court is mistaken—perhaps its being so completely mistaken in this case, which after all is the case they believe they know best (their own case), genuinely undermines its authority in their minds. In any case, they volunteer to fight for side B. If everyone who fights for an objectively unjustified side is morally liable to attack, they are. But this is a collective criterion of responsibility, namely being on the side that is objectively unjustified, no matter your reasons for being there, no matter your other beliefs, no matter your own behaviour throughout the rest of your life.

On my understanding of the realities of war, many of those killed on both sides are probably 'conscientious persons courageously doing what they believe is right'. But then I do not believe, any more than its historical originators did, that the laws of war can be fine-tuned to be sensitive to the moral liability of individual combatants. McMahan does, but his proposal does not achieve his goal.

The most pressing concerns about the laws of war today, I believe, are entirely different from McMahan's, namely how seriously the capacity of those laws to actually limit modern warfare, especially the use of the most advanced airpower, which has arguably transformed warfare over the last century, is being eroded. One might well look at the laws concerning the resort to force and ask about their capacity to restrain a hegemon like the contemporary United States from attacking whomever it wishes to attack, currently in the guise of the 'pre-emption' of terrorism.[38] However, I will consider the laws for the conduct of war and focus on

---

[37] Perhaps non-combatants as well, since McMahan attaches little weight specifically to the principle of discrimination.

[38] I have done this elsewhere. See 'What Would A Justified Preventive Military Attack Look Like?' and 'Introduction' (with David Rodin) in Shue, H. and Rodin, D. (eds.), Preemption: Military Action and Moral Justification (Oxford: Oxford University Press, 2007), 222–46 and 1–22.

the crucial laws regarding targeting, which determine, among other matters, what may legally be attacked from the air. Three factors converge to undermine effective restraint and to magnify the danger that the exceptions will now swallow the rules after all.

The first is the flexibility and vagueness of the crucial term 'military objective', and the simple deception of the public and self-deception by leaders—not always separable from each other—made possible by this looseness of the term. Notoriously, US President Harry Truman presented the city destroyed by the first atomic bomb, Hiroshima, to the American people as 'an important Japanese Army base', adding, with a strong suggestion of just retribution: 'The Japanese began the war from the air at Pearl Harbor. They have been repaid many fold'.[39] Various influential Air Force officers had concluded that the entire population of Japan was 'a proper military target', with Colonel Harry F. Cunningham writing in the Weekly Intelligence Review of the US Fifth Air Force, 'For us, THERE ARE NO CIVILIANS IN JAPAN'.[40] Nina Tannenwald notes that President 'Truman wrote in his journal at the Potsdam conference that he had told the Secretary of War to use the bomb "so that military objectives and soldiers and sailors are the target, not women and children". He added, "He and I are in accord. The target will be a purely military one ... " '.[41] Yet Truman wrote this entry *after* he had approved the target list including Hiroshima and Nagasaki.[42] Did he actually believe these were the names of military objectives? Ronald Schaffer concluded that the criteria for targets adopted by the target selection committee for the atomic bombs

guaranteed that the bombs would be dropped on cities. Targets were to be important militarily and were to include troop concentrations or centers of military production. Any small or strictly military objective had to lie within a much larger area susceptible to destruction by bombing. Yet the city that contained it must be relatively free from conventional bombing damage and susceptible to destruction by an A-bomb. This would assure that the new weapon's effects could be measured.[43]

Thus, whether Truman was deceiving himself about his own awful responsibility, was being deceived by subordinates who never seriously considered not using for maximum shock the weapon invented at such enormous trouble, or was knowingly misleading the public is a complex historical issue not essential to pursue here. What the decision in favour of the atomic bombings of two Japanese cities in 1945 powerfully suggests is that at best the concept of a military objective is highly plastic and susceptible to both deception and self-deception.

[39] United States, White House, 'Statement by the President', 6 Aug. 1945, <http://www.trumanlibrary.org/publicpapers/index.php?pid=100&st=Hiroshima&st1=>.
[40] See Schaffer, R., *Wings of Judgment: American Bombing in World War II* (Oxford: Oxford University Press, 1985), 142 (capitalization in the original).
[41] See Tannenwald, N., *Nuclear Taboo* (above, n. 17), ch. 3, n. 47.
[42] Bundy, M., *Danger and Survival: Choices about the Bomb in the First Fifty Years* (New York: Random House, 1988), 79.
[43] Schaffer, R., *Wings of Judgment* (above, n. 40), 143.

The extreme malleability of 'military objective' was made all the more clear by the bombing conducted by the United Nations forces in Korea, led by the United States, in the next major conflict after World War II. Robert Pape found:

Despite public claims that only military targets would be attacked, in fact target selection focused on undermining civilian morale. To hide the true nature of the attacks from public scrutiny, FEAF [Far East Air Force]'s Deputy for Operations, General Jacob E. Smart, planned that 'whenever possible attacks will be scheduled against targets of military significance so situated that their destruction will have a deleterious effect upon the morale of the civilian population'.[44]

Similarly, Sahr Conway-Lanz concludes from a careful historical study:

Early November [1950], when U.N. soldiers first fought with Chinese units, marked the end of American restraint on the destruction of enemy cities . . . The U.N. Command adopted a policy of the purposeful destruction of cities in enemy hands after the intervention of the Chinese. The FEAF began incendiary raids against urban areas reminiscent of World War II, and [commanding General] MacArthur spoke of making the remaining territory held by the North Koreans a 'desert'. The perception of the war from the United States, though, changed little. Military officers and the press continued to discuss the violence in Korea as if its application continued to be discriminate and as if risks to noncombatants had not increased. The objects of attack were still 'military targets,' but the implicit definition of the term 'military target' had grown to include virtually every human-made structure in enemy-occupied territory.[45]

1977 Geneva Protocol I made an effort to tighten the specification of a military objective. The pivotal provisions are in Article 52:

1. Civilian objects shall not be the object of attack or of reprisals. Civilian objects are all objects which are not military objectives as defined in paragraph 2.

2. Attacks shall be limited strictly to military objectives. In so far as objects are concerned, military objectives are limited to those objects which by their nature, location, purpose or use make an effective contribution to military action and whose total or partial destruction, capture or neutralization, in the circumstances ruling at the time, offers a definite military advantage.

3. In case of doubt whether an object which is normally dedicated to civilian purposes . . . is being used to make an effective contribution to military action, it shall be presumed not to be so used.[46]

Has Protocol I succeeded in making the category of 'military objective' less susceptible to abuse? The chief reasons why not are the second and third factors now eroding the barriers protecting non-combatants.

---

[44] Pape, R. A., *Bombing To Win: Air Power and Coercion in War* (Ithaca, NY: Cornell University Press, 1996), 160. Paper argues compellingly that all such attempts to break the will by bombing civilians have been failures.

[45] Conway-Lanz, S., *Collateral Damage: Americans, Noncombatant Immunity, and Atrocity after World War II* (London: Routledge, 2006), 103. This is a subtle study arguing that the general public in the US never abandoned its commitment to noncombatant immunity as it understood it.

[46] 1977 Geneva Protocol I, art. 52 (above, n. 1).

The second factor is the refusal by the nation with by far the most powerful air force, the United States, to ratify 1977 Geneva Protocol I, leaving the US unbound by it as treaty law. Complementarily, the US insists that it is, in the technical sense, a 'specially affected nation', with the implication that US State practice should strongly influence which elements of the content of the Protocol (and many other treaties) may be construed as expressive of customary law.[47]

The third compounding factor is recent progressively aggressive efforts by the US to make the definition of military objective more permissive than it is in 1977 Geneva Protocol I, article 52(2) by systematically replacing 'effective contribution to military action' with more inclusive categories:

While the US Army's Field Manual 27–10 contains the same language as Article 52(2) First Additional Protocol, recent official proclamations feature a change to the wording of the definition of a military objective. While in the 1997 Field Manual 90–36 on the joint targeting process the attribute 'war-sustaining' is introduced as a criterion for mission assessment, and in the Joint Doctrine for Targeting of 2002 it is used to *explain* the definition of military objectives, it has *entered* this definition in Military Commission Instruction No. 2 of 2003. Military objectives are there defined as 'those potential targets during an armed conflict which, by their nature, location, purpose, or use, effectively contribute to the opposing forces's *war-fighting or war-sustaining capability* . . .' [italics added]. In the Operational Law Handbook of 2007 the definition of a military objective at first repeats the language of Article 52(2), while the attribute 'war-sustaining' is then utilised to define the use of an object in the meaning of that same provision and thus serves to *interpret* the definition of a military objective. These changes appear to broaden the definition of military objective to include more targets.[48]

These progressively more permissive readings of the category of military objective, accompanied by accordingly more permissive practice and the doctrine that 'specially affected states generate practice that *must* be examined in order to reach an informed conclusion regarding the status of a potential rule', would constitute a strategy for softening up the constraints in customary law.[49]

Although Dill understatedly characterizes these changes as 'appear to broaden the definition', replacing 'make an effective contribution to military action' with 'effectively contribute to . . . war-fighting or war-sustaining capability' is a gigantic

---

[47] See 'U.S. Initial Reactions to ICRC Study on Customary International Law', consisting of (a) a letter from John B. Bellinger, III (Legal Adviser, US Department of State) and William J. Haynes, II (General Counsel, US Department of Defense) to Dr Jakob Kellenberger (President, ICRC), accompanied by (b) 'Illustrative Comments on Specific Rules in the Customary International Humanitarian Law Study', both at <http://www.state.gov/s/l/rls/82630.htm>. See specifically letter, note iii, which invokes Meron, T., 'The Continuing Role of Custom in the Formation of International Humanitarian Law', *American Journal of International Law*, 90 (1996), 238 and 249. I am grateful to Janina Dill for pointing to the significance of the debate over the interpretation of 'specially affected nation'.

[48] Dill, J. [University of Oxford], 'U.S. Air Force Targeting Since the End of the Cold War', memo prepared for 'Human Rights at War: A Comparative Study of the Effectiveness of the *Geneva Conventions*', Peace Studies Program, Cornell University, 9 Nov. 2007 (on file with author—citations omitted).

[49] Letter from Bellinger, J. B. and Haynes, W. J., to Kellenberger, J. (above, n. 47), n. iii (emphasis in original).

leap. One has moved from (1) effective contribution to military action to (2) effective contribution to capability for military action, thus including facilities and personnel at an additional layer: capabilities, whether contributing at the time to military action or not.[50] An adversary's 'war-sustaining capability' could be interpreted to include the best part of its entire economy. If everything capable of sustaining military action becomes a military objective, protection for non-combatants will have reached the vanishing point. During the Korean War, military objectives were already interpreted by the US Air Force, in Conway-Lanz's phrase, 'to include virtually every human-made structure in enemy-occupied territory'.[51] What is the purpose of ongoing efforts now to loosen the language still more?

I have, in effect, defended the laws of war against the critique by McMahan by arguing that his goals for them are too ambitious and that their own goals have always been more modest: limitation of violation, not prohibition of violation. I have argued that a modest goal attained may be preferable to an ambitious goal unattained. But then the modest goal must in fact be attained. If the laws of war, and in particular the category of military objectives central to targeting, no longer protect most of civil society and the non-combatants who people it, then they have failed to achieve even the bare minimum. I have not attempted to settle that empirical question here, but I have indicated reasons to believe that it is very much open because the protections are under sustained attack by the US government.[52]

---

[50] The inclusion of capabilities as military objectives could, in addition, serve as a basis for preventive war, which is precisely war to destroy capabilities before they lead to action. See Shue, H., and Rodin, D., *Preemption* (above, n. 38). The crescendo of declarations that military objectives include capabilities has come under the Bush/Cheney Administration that advocates preventive war sugar-coated as 'preemption'.

[51] Conway-Lanz, S., *Collateral Damage* (above, n. 45), 103.

[52] For more of the reasons for concern, see Shue, H., 'Bombing to Rescue?: NATO's 1999 Bombing of Serbia', in Chatterjee, D. K., and Scheid, D. E. (eds.), *Ethics and Foreign Intervention* (Cambridge: Cambridge University Press, 2003), 97; and Shue, H., and Wippman, D., 'Limiting Attacks on Dual-Use Facilities Performing Indispensable Civilian Functions', *Cornell International Law Journal*, 35 (2002), 559. For the argument that in the current war in Iraq, the US is doing better than in the past, although still not as well as it could, see Kahl, C. H., ' "In the Crossfire or the Crosshairs?" Norms, Civilian Casualties, and U.S. Conduct in Iraq', *International Security*, 32 (2007), 7. For drawing this article to my attention, I am grateful to Janina Dill, who has noted that the measures on which the US is doing better are primarily measures of apparent intent, while the measures on which it is not doing better are primarily measures of results—also see Dill, J., 'U.S. Air Force Targeting Since the End of the Cold War' (above, n. 48). Further see Shue, H., 'Target-selection Norms, Torture Norms and Growing U.S. Permissiveness' in Sibylle Scheipers and Hew Strachan (eds.), *The Changing Character of War* (forthcoming).

HUMANITARIAN INTERVENTION

CHAPTER 26

HUMANITARIAN INTERVENTION

THOMAS M. FRANCK

I. INTRODUCTION

Let's face it: 'humanitarian intervention' sounds good. And, if humans were angels, it would *be* really good. Who would not favour an arrangement whereby, whenever bad things were about to happen to people as a result of the venal machinations of their own rulers, or of fellow citizens, angels would fly to their rescue?

[handwritten margin note: showing of motivated by susceptibility to bribery]

But, alas, humans are not angels. If anyone is to rescue persons from their venal governments or fellow citizens, it would have to be other governments and citizens: themselves mere humans, subject to venality.

These harsh realities combine to create a legal and moral dilemma: should international law permit humanitarian intervention, knowing that it may be used by high-minded citizens and governments of one state to save multitudes of persons imperiled in another state, but, also, that it may be used by those less spotless to justify a ruthless invasion of another state for reasons, purely or primarily, of their selfish national interest?

For that matter, should humanitarian intervention be legal whenever interveners honestly conclude that some government's 'gross human rights violations are an affront to civilized standards'? Professor Luban has demonstrated that such an intervener's conclusion—that a government's behaviour is 'uncivilized'—may merely reflect 'a distinction based on social sentiment' of the intervening state 'rather than universal reason'. Thus, applying standards of 'civilized' behaviour to specific instances (even when such standards have been broadly defined in global conventions), to some degree is likely to reflect culturally specific values.[1] 'Fighting for human rights', Luban concludes, 'proves to be far more precarious, both practically and philosophically, than friends of humanitarian intervention would like to believe'.[2]

As to a matter so important to social order, the law must speak. The law, however, perforce speaks in broad, usually binary, categorical generalities. It may *prohibit* assault, yet *permit* persons to act in self-defence. But it does not readily accommodate nuances, which, in a particular situation, may become a problem when, because of law's arbitrary categories, the spirit of the rule is in conflict with its text. If I attack you just before you attack me, am I committing an assault or acting in self-defence? The binary character of law—it must be one thing or the other—can have adverse social consequences: seeming sometimes arbitrarily and inadvertently to prohibit what ought to be allowed, or allowing what ought to be prohibited.

It may be noted, in passing—and we shall be adverting to it, again, later in this essay—that the law, in almost all countries, tries to mitigate such incongruities between the law and justice by allowing the judges, or the jury, some latitude in sentencing, or in the rendering of verdicts. In this way, the law mitigates the consequences of the illegal conduct. Acts that may be technically illegal will nevertheless be regarded as necessary and justified by the institutions that apply the law.

One need not search far to find examples either of the problem or of the law's attempts to resolve it through some version of a doctrine of mitigation or exculpation.

First as to the problem: when, as is now the case, international law's 'black letter' text seems to prohibit all humanitarian intervention in matters 'essentially within the domestic jurisdiction of a state'[3] (except with the prior permission of the veto-prone UN Security Council), then the strict letter of the law may appear actually to require the silent acquiescence of all states in dreadful events. Consider, for example, the genocidal murder of hundreds of thousands of Tutsis by their Hutu compatriots. The Security Council, as these events unfolded, was deadlocked by threat of recourse to the veto. An intervention unauthorized by the Council, although illegal, might have saved the Tutsis. On the other hand, were the law to allow states to intervene whenever they saw what seemed to be the egregious

---

[1] For example, what is one to make of an African government that sets about methodically to deprive previously privileged white farmers of their property without compensation? Is this an egregiously racist violation of persons' right to their property, or the redressing of an old wrong by which those property rights were earlier concentrated in the hands of the settler population?

[2] Luban, D., 'Intervention and Civilization: Some Unhappy Lessons of the Kosovo War', in DeGrieff, P. and Cronin, C. (eds.), *Global Justice and Transnational Politics: Essays on the Moral and Political Challenges of Globalization,* (Cambridge, Mass.: MIT Press, 2002), 79–80.

[3] United Nations Charter, art. 2 (7).

oppression of another state's population, that might encourage profligate recourse to force in unwarranted circumstances and in violation of state sovereignty.

As this example makes evident, everything depends upon who interprets the extent of the 'necessity' that exists in specific circumstances. In his 1921 essay on humanitarian intervention, E. C. Stowell defined his subject as the 'reliance upon force for the justifiable purpose of protecting the inhabitants of another state from treatment which is so arbitrary and persistently abusive as to exceed the limits of that authority within which the sovereign is presumed to act with reason and justice'.[4]

That definition still, today, seems as serviceable as any subsequently devised by legal scholars. As with other attempts at definition, however, it leaves much undefined. Who decides when a government's treatment of those within its territorial jurisdiction is so 'arbitrary and persistently abusive' as to deny it the benefit of the normal right of non-intervention? For that matter, what do the terms 'arbitrary and persistently abusive' mean? How 'clean' must be the 'hands' of an intervening power and how pure must be its motives? And, most important: is humanitarian intervention a right, a fact of life, or just an aspiration?

Stowell, in his essay, refers to a 1910 study of the same topic by A. Rougier, which observes that 'humanitarian considerations will never be the *sole* motive' of the intervener. 'The intervening powers will, as soon as the opportunity for intervention arises, assess its advisability subjectively in terms of their immediate interests . . . Barbarous acts are committed by the thousands every day in some corner of the globe which no state dreams of stopping because no state has an interest in stopping them'.[5] Is it legally or morally acceptable that there should be a *right* to intervene that is exercised not when it serves the interests of those being arbitrarily and persistently abused, but, rather, those of the intervening power?

Equally daunting is the problem of humanitarian intervention's modalities and duration. Again, Stowell anticipates the modern legal and moral concern with this aspect of the practice.

Whenever one power intervenes in the name of humanity in the domain of another power, it cannot but impose its concept of justice and public policy on the other State, by force if necessary. Its intervention tends definitely to draw the [other] State into its moral and social sphere of influence, and ultimately into its political sphere of influence. It will *control* the other State while preparing to dominate it. Humanitarian intervention consequently looks like an ingenious juridical technique to encroach little by little upon the independence of a State in order to reduce it progressively to the status of semi-sovereignty.[6]

---

[4] Stowell, E. C., *Intervention in International Law*, repr. in Sohn, L. B. and Buergenthal, T. (eds.), *International Protection of Human Rights* (Indianapolis: Bobbs Merrill, 1973).

[5] Rougier, A., 'La Théorie de l'intervention d'humanité', *Revue générale de droit international public*, 17 (1910), 468, 525–6, reproduced in Sohn, L. B. and Buergenthal, T., *International Protection of Human Rights* (above, n. 4), 140.

[6] Ibid. 141.

Is it desirable that there should be a *right* to save others by imposing on them the political and social values of the intervening power?

In recent times, there has been an effort to reshape the discussion that swirls awkwardly around state action in implementing an asserted *right* to humanitarian intervention whenever it occurs: as in the military action authorized by the United Nations Security Council in 1994 to oust a brutal Haitian *junta* and restore the democratically-elected government of President Jean-Bertrand Aristede, or in the North Atlantic Treaty Organization (NATO) action in 1999 that claimed to have prevented an imminent genocide in Kosovo. In 2001, in the wake of these interventions and the concern they precipitated, several governments, led by Canada, sought to circumnavigate these concerns by changing the focus of discussion from a *right of humanitarian intervention* to a new *responsibility to protect*.[7] It remains to be examined whether this change in the discourse's terms of reference has improved the chances of reaching a global consensus about the legality and morality of using force to protect imperiled populations from the egregious actions of their own governments.

II. Humanitarian Intervention in Historical Context

Professor Ryan Goodman has written an essay that seeks to demonstrate that the formal recognition of a *right* of humanitarian intervention would not open the door to its exploitation by aggressive states bent on exploiting any humanitarian exception to the non-intervention rule.[8] 'Drawing on recent empirical studies', he contends 'that legalizing [humanitarian intervention] should in important respects *discourage* wars with ulterior motives . . .'.[9]

The historical record does not seem to uphold this contention. Writing a quarter of a century ago (with Sir Nigel Rodley) I came to the opposite conclusion. Citing Rougier's definition of 1910,[10] we concluded from the historical record of such interventions that they were rarely used for genuine humanitarian purposes.

There are few more reactionary ideas ever to have sought the imprimatur of 'international law' . . . The principle 'permitted' outside powers to invade sovereign states for all sorts of

---

[7] Evans, G. and Sahnoun, M. (co-chairs), *The Responsibility to Protect*, Report of the International Commission on Intervention and State Sovereignty (Ottawa: International Development Research Centre, 2001).

[8] Goodman, R., 'Humanitarian Intervention and Pretexts for War', *American Journal of International Law*, 100 (2006), 107.

[9] Ibid.

[10] Ibid. 'The theory of intervention on the ground of humanity is properly that which recognizes the right of one state to exercise an international control by military force over the acts of another in regard to its internal sovereignty when contrary to the laws of humanity'.

spurious reasons, but primarily to prevent the indigenous populace changing religions, or, especially, the socio-economic systems imposed by their governments. On balance, very little good has been wrought in its name.[11]

On the basis of evidence of state conduct in the three decades since we wrote, I have developed what may be a more nuanced view of humanitarian intervention, but have not much changed my bottom line. The practice of the past thirty years has rather confirmed my belief that it would not advance humanitarian values to legalize humanitarian intervention *except* (as the law already provides) upon the authorization of the Security Council. Before turning to the evidence of recent state practice, however, it is useful to recapitulate the earlier record of such interventions in the past two centuries.

The first organized system of systematic intervention was organized by the European Holy Alliance after the French Revolution of 1789. The new rules approved by the Congress of Aix-la-Chapelle in 1818 were designed as a 'perpetual system of intervention' by the Powers, 'adapted to prevent any such change in the internal forms of their respective governments as might endanger the existence of their monarchial institutions'.[12] In 1827, Great Britain, France, and Russia intervened 'to prevent the complete subjugation of the Greek people',[13] and to advance the Greek claim to self-determination against the Ottoman Empire. According to Wheaton, however, the

moving causes of intervention in the affairs of the Ottoman Empire were the apprehension that Russia would gain a formidable preponderance in Europe, if she became, substantially if not in form, the mistress of the Black Sea and the Dardanelles, and the great interest of England to preserve the existence of a neutralized and guaranteed power in Egypt and the Levant with reference to her Indian Empire.[14]

That humanitarian concerns were not necessarily salient in Western policy towards the Turks was made clear in 1853–54 when Russia tried to assert a unilateral right to protect persecuted Christian subjects of the Sultan and found itself embroiled in the Crimean War, with Britain and France on the side of the Ottomans.[15] Evidently, the dedication of the West to Greek rights of self-determination and to the protection of Christians in the Turkish domains was not entirely immune to more mundane countervailing interests. In this respect, it is also notable that the Concert of Europe, in 1815, entirely failed to support the ambitions of the Polish people for self-determination when the issue arose at the Congress of Vienna.[16] In other words, the cause of humanitarian intervention and support for

[11] Franck, T. M. and Rodley, N. S., 'After Bangladesh: the Law of Humanitarian Intervention by Military Force', *American Journal of International Law*, 67 (1973) 275, 277–8.

[12] Wheaton, H., *Elements of International Law* (1866), reprod. in Brown Scott, J. (ed.), *The Classics of International Law* (Oxford: Oxford University Press, 1936), 79.

[13] Stowell, E. C., *Intervention in International Law* (above, n. 4), 127.

[14] Wheaton, H., *Elements of International Law* (above, n. 12), 99 n.   [15] Ibid.

[16] Nicolson, H., *The Congress of Vienna, a Study in Allied Unity: 1812–1822* (New York: Harcourt Brace and Company, 1946), 179–80.

self-determination were pursued, no doubt to much popular self-congratulatory rhetoric about sustaining people's 'rights', when—and only when—it coincided with other, less lofty but more important strategic and economic interests of the period's dominant powers.

These examples illustrate two problems, both practical and also philosophical, with humanitarian intervention as a 'right' of states. The first is that it may be misused as a cover for the pursuit of meaner objectives by an unprincipled intervener. The second is that the recognition of a 'right' to intervene for humanitarian reasons is not tantamount to ensuring that such intervention would actually occur in instances where mercantile and military interests do not coincide with humanitarian needs.

Another, related problem is that, in a decentralized international system, it may be difficult to distinguish between true humanitarian crises and others cleverly misrepresented as such in order to bring about an intervention. In 1860, the five European Powers intervened with the Ottoman Porte to secure protection and local self-government for the Maronite Christians of Mount Lebanon, after 5,500 of them had been reported killed by Druse forces. Yet, according to Lord Dufferin, the British High Commissioner to Syria, 'the original provocation proceeded from the Christians, who had been for months beforehand preparing an onslaught on the Druses, which their leaders confidently expected would terminate, if not in the extermination, at all events in the expulsion, of that race'. Dufferin further reported that the Christians were told by their clergy 'that their endeavour to attain undisputed possession of the Lebanon would be warmly countenanced by the Powers of Christendom'.[17]

Whatever the merits of these disputations, it is surely true that the international system does not yet mandate state recourse to the sort of legitimate and effective machinery for finding facts and assessing responsibility that would ensure, in each instance, that interventions are undertaken only in legitimate situations of genuine necessity. Such machinery has been brought into operation on an *ad hoc* basis in some recent instances at the request of the Security Council, as in determining the facts regarding the situation in Sudan's Dafur province after 2005. But, while recourse to such legitimate fact-finding may, nowadays, potentially provide an assured basis for humanitarian intervention, it is still a process that is rarely employed. Without such assurance, however, interventions, were they to be legalized, might well be undertaken against an innocent party at the instigation of those who stood to benefit most. In the case of the Mount Lebanon intervention, for example, it ultimately proved impossible to establish, convincingly, either the facts

---

[17] Minutes of the British Commissioner on the Judgments proposed to be passed on the Turkish Officials and Druse Chiefs by the Extraordinary Tribunal of Beyrout. Correspondence relating to the Affairs of Syria: 1860–1 (Part I). Cd. No. 2800, in Great Britain, 68 *Parl. Papers* 17, Item No. 351, Inclosure 2 (1861). These and related documents are reproduced in Sohn, L. B. and Buergenthal, T., *International Protection of Human Rights* (above, n. 4), 167–8.

or the ultimate responsibility for the alleged atrocities against which the powers claimed to be intervening.

Much the same can be said of the interventions of 1877–8 in which Russia, with the support of Austria, Prussia, France, and Italy, stripped the Turks of their Balkan provinces. Although humanitarian motives were touted, the British government was highly sceptical. Professor Fenwick wrote that 'alleged humanitarian motives were in most cases influenced or affected by the political interests of the intervening state or states'.[18] Similarly suspect was President's McKinley's 1898 intervention in Cuba which, in his message to Congress, he characterized as undertaken 'in the cause of humanity and to put an end to barbarities, bloodshed, starvation and horrible miseries'.[19] Others noted 'the powerful influence of endangered investments and trade'.[20]

More recently, some of the same fact-scepticism was expressed by critics of the NATO campaign against Belgrade, who argued that the concerns about Serb atrocities against the Muslim population of Kosovo were unproven or exaggerated and, moreover, that Serb reprisals were deliberately provoked by the Kosovars themselves in order to create the justification for an intervention in their favour.

Thus, it appears that there are instances of uncertainty about the key facts and there are other instances of flat-out fact misrepresentation. History is full of examples of egregious distortion of the facts by states claiming to be implementing a 'right' of humanitarian intervention. In 1931, Japan claimed to have invaded Manchuria for humanitarian reasons.[21] Just before launching his takeover of the Sudetenland, Adolf Hitler wrote to British Prime Minister Chamberlain, about the ethnic Germans in Czechoslovakia who 'have been maltreated in the unworthiest manner, tortured, economically destroyed and, above all, prevented from realizing for themselves also the right of nations to self-determination'.[22] The message asserted that Czech 'madness' had caused 120,000 refugees to flee and that the security of more than 3 million ethnic Germans was at stake.

Evidently, humanitarian intervention is not only fraught with problems of factual uncertainty, but also with abuse by those who find convenient cover in the 'right' to intervene for bogus 'humanitarian' purposes. It is true that a legal principle cannot be faulted for being abused by the unprincipled. However, a legal principle that lends itself to frequent abuse—as humanitarian intervention has done—may not state a desirable rule, or may state it badly.

---

[18] Fenwick, C., 'Intervention: Individual and Collective', *American Journal of International Law*, 39 (1945), 650.

[19] Fitzgibbon, R. H., *Cuba and the United States 1900–1935* (New York: Russell & Russell, 1935), 22.

[20] Ibid. 25.

[21] Excerpts from the remarks of the Japanese representative to the League of Nations Council are to be found in Brown, P. M., 'Japanese Interpretation of the Kellogg Pact', *American Journal of International Law*, 27 (1933), 100.

[22] Letter from Reich Chancellor Hitler to Prime Minister Chamberlain, 'The Crisis in Czechoslovakia, 24 April–13 October, 1938', *International Conciliation*, 44 (1938), 433.

These are instances of interventions based on dubious recitations of fact occurring before the Second World War. Many more examples took place in the period after the War, despite the strictures of the new United Nations Charter, which, in its Article 2 (4), appears definitively to ban military intervention by states, except with the prior authorization of the Security Council. In 1956, Soviet tanks crushed the popular uprising in Hungary, claiming 'to put an end to the counter-revolutionary intervention and riots'[23] and reactionary efforts 'to stab the Hungarian people in the back'.[24] Twelve years later, Moscow defended its intervention in Czechoslovakia as a mission 'to clean up the atmosphere . . . and to allow the Czechoslovak people to put order in their home'[25] in the face of 'enemies . . . shaking the foundations of law and order and trampling laws underfoot'.[26] In intervening in the Dominican Republic in 1965, Washington proclaimed its object to be to prevent bloodshed and to assist 'the people of that country . . . to freely choose the path of political democracy, social justice, and economic progress'.[27] Bringing democracy to the people of Iraq also became one of the justifications for the invasion of that country in 2003, especially after the failure to find weapons of mass destruction.[28] Interventions on the unsupportable pretext of humanitarian necessity remain an incessant phenomenon today, despite its explicit probibition in Article 2 (4) of the Charter. It does not seem likely that such bogus interventions will diminish if the law is changed to permit each powerful state to determine for itself when to engage in humanitarian interventions.

This is not to say that every military initiative taken under the rubric of 'humanitarian intervention' is based on false evidence and motivated primarily by the self-interest of the intervener, although Professor Brownlie, for one, has concluded, that 'the state practice justifies the conclusion that no genuine case of humanitarian intervention has occurred, with the possible exception of the occupation of Syria in 1860 and 1861'.[29] At least as to some events occurring since this opinion was expressed, a more complex picture has emerged. It may be argued that India's intervention in Bangladesh in 1971, the introduction of troops (ECOMOG) of the Economic Community of West African States (ECOWAS) in Liberia and Sierra Leone (1989–99), as well as NATO's action against the Federal Republic of Yugoslavia to compel its army's withdrawal from Kosovo (1999), are instances, whether or not precipitated by mixed motives, in which interventions had an incontrovertibly humanitarian effect. Without them, it is likely that many more persons would have died.

---

[23] Ambassador Sobolev, 11 UN SCOR 754th Meeting (1956), 10.
[24] Ibid., 11 UN SCOR 756th Meeting, (1956), 27.
[25] Ambassador Tarabanov, UN Doc. S/PV, 1443, 23 Aug. 1968, 146.
[26] Ambassador Malik, UN Doc. S/PV, 1445, 24 Aug. 1968, 118–20.
[27] President Johnson, Statement of 1 May 1965, *Department of State Bulletin*, 52 (1965), 743.
[28] *Weekly Compilation of Presidential Documents*, 41 (2005), 1856.
[29] Brownlie, I., *International Law and the Use of Force by States* (Oxford: Clarendon Press, 1963), 340.

III. Problems Lawyers Have With Humanitarian Intervention

There are two orders of problems lawyers are likely to encounter when thinking about humanitarian intervention. The first is of a *primary order* and encompasses the interface between humanitarian intervention and sovereignty. In his address to the General Assembly on 20 September 1999—after it had become apparent that some 800,000 Tutsis had been murdered in the Rwandan genocide while nations stood by and the Security Council could not agree to authorize a rescue—Secretary General Kofi Annan asked whether, had there been a regional coalition of the willing able to intervene, they should have refrained from doing so because one permanent member of the Council had withheld its consent.[30] If the Charter were construed strictly, the lawyer's answer would have to be 'yes'.[31] But, Annan summoned states to reconceptualize the law's black-letter text, urging them to embrace a new legal 'principle that massive and systematic violations of human rights—wherever they may take place—should not be allowed to stand' because, he said, the 'sovereign state, in its most basic sense, is being redefined by the forces of globalization and international cooperation'.[32]

As the Secretary General discovered during the ensuing general UN debate, states expressed a neutral or negative reaction to these admonitions. Governments were reluctant to embrace his views on the need to limit sovereignty, even in instances of egregious violations of human rights. This reluctance, however, cannot be attributed to a general preference for strict compliance with the law of non-intervention, even at the cost of 800,000 dead Tutsi. Rather, the resistance to reconsideration of the interface between sovereignty and the protection of persons' most fundamental humanitarian rights must be understood in the context of a widely-shared concern with *second-order* considerations.

These second-order issues are less salient, perhaps, than the first-order issue of sovereignty, but the uncertainty surrounding them is determinative of many states' reluctance even to consider a change in the law that would diminish sovereignty and potentially increase the legal ambit of humanitarian intervention. It thus behooves lawyers who share the Secretary General's humanitarian instincts to address these second-order concerns *first*, as a necessary prelude to obtaining agreement to any acceptance of the general principle of humanitarian intervention. States, by

---

[30] Report of the UN Secretary General, GAOR, 54th Sess., 4th Plenary Meeting, 20 Sept. 1999, A/54/PV.4, 2.

[31] See General Assembly Declaration on the Inadmissibility of Intervention, G.A. Res. 2131 (XX), 21 Dec. 1965, 20 GAOR Supp. 14, 11–12, U.N. Doc. A/6014. The resolution condemns armed intervention 'for any reason whatsoever' and brooks no exceptions, not even for the protection of human rights.

[32] Report of the UN Secretary General (above, n. 30).

joining the UN and many other sovereignty-limiting regimes, have indicated a willingness to accept some limitations on their autonomy—but, first, they want to see the fine print. These second-order concerns arise from the historical practice of humanitarian intervention assayed in the preceding section.

An example may demonstrate that these concerns are not of purely historical origins, but have contemporary resonance. In 1971, the government of Pakistan, controlled by military officers from West Pakistan, imposed a severely repressive regime on East Pakistan, causing much suffering, including the deaths of 1 to 2 million persons and the flight of an estimated 8 million refugees across the border into India. On 3 December, the Indian army entered East Pakistan in a campaign that led to the province's declaration of independence as the new nation of Bangladesh. India defended its intervention by claiming that Karachi had embarked on a 'campaign of genocide'[33] and, perhaps more accurately, that it was committing egregious atrocities against its own population. It is instructive to note the response of Ghana's Ambassador Akwei, senior spokesman for the newly-independent nations of Africa:

> It is not for us to dictate to Pakistan what it should or should not do. We can offer advice; we can offer friendly intimations and hints, but we have to respect the sovereignty and territorial integrity of every State Member of this Organization . . . once intervention in the affairs of a Member State is permitted, once one permits oneself the higher wisdom of telling another Member State what it should do with regard to arranging its own political affairs, one opens a Pandora's box.[34]

It is that fear of opening a wide hole in the wall protecting states against unilateral intervention by more powerful peers which causes most governments to refuse to enter into a discussion about legitimating humanitarian intervention, even in situations where everyone knows that it ought to occur. In their minds, the subject conjures up a panoply of 'horribles' that rather than being merely fanciful, is actually closely based on real past malpractice.

On the other hand, it is probably not true that states categorically reject the primary order principle proposed by the Secretary General, that 'massive and systematic violations of human rights—wherever they may take place—should not be allowed to stand'.[35] They would probably agree that, had there been a regional force capable of intervening to save the Tutsis, it should have been deployed, with or without the authorization of the Security Council. Indeed, article 4 (h) of the Constitutive Act of the African Union stipulates 'the right of the Union to intervene in a Member State pursuant to a decision of the [Union's] Assembly in respect of grave circumstances, namely: war crimes, genocide and crimes against

---

[33] SCOR (XXVI), 1606th Meeting, 4 Dec. 1971, 16, para. 167.
[34] Ambassador Akwei (Ghana), U.N. Doc. A/PV.2002, 7 Dec. 1971, 31.
[35] Report of the UN Secretary General (above, n. 30).

humanity' when such intervention is authorized by two-thirds of its members.[36] Since African states have been among the most vociferous in opposing a general *right* of humanitarian intervention, it is possible to infer that these states' objections are not to humanitarian intervention as such, but to the circumstances under which any such general right is likely to be exercised.

These objections are well enough founded to oblige any reputable lawyer advising states (other than the most powerful) to point out that humanitarian intervention has been, in practice, a 'right' claimed primarily by strong states acting against the weak; that it has been used largely to advance the national interest of intervening states under pretext of promoting purely humanitarian objectives; that it has been employed in circumstances in which the facts do not support the intervener's assertion of a humanitarian crisis; and that in many instances of real humanitarian crisis, no humanitarian intervention was undertaken by any of those capable of it, because of the lack of a national interest or a sense of moral obligation.

A lawyer advising all but the most powerful states would also point out the inadequacies in defining the procedural aspects of a proposed 'right' of humanitarian intervention. A law, to be legitimate, requires a serious effort at formulating clear definitions of what is allowed and what is prohibited, and at constituting a credible process for determining, in specific contested instances, *which is which*. Stowell's definition of humanitarian intervention ('reliance upon force for the justifiable purpose of protecting the inhabitants of another state from treatment which is so arbitrary and persistently abusive as to exceed the limits of that authority within which the sovereign is presumed to act with reason and justice') illustrates this inadequacy, for it seems to assume that governments of sovereign states might agree to a law-reform that gives others a right to intervene against them whenever they are seen to be acting 'unreasonably and unjustly', and that they would do so *before* defining what those terms mean, or what institution, in each instance, would actually decide whether they were acting in such a way as to make them eligible for intervention. Such a cart-before-the-horse presumption defies reason and, thus, dooms to failure any effort to bring about a needed, but difficult, legal reform.

States' insistence on addressing the second-order issues first is not a pretext to avoid revisiting the primary-order question. In a few specific contexts, after the secondary 'who decides?' questions had been addressed, states actually accepted a 'right' of humanitarian intervention. A 2004 report of the Secretary General's High Level Panel, made up of senior officials of leading governments and international institutions, managed to agree that the UN Charter should be read, in the light of state practice, to have determined that 'the principle of non-intervention in internal

---

[36] Constitutive Act of the African Union, 11 July 2002, art. 4(h), <http://www.africa-union.org>. All websites were most recently checked in Nov. 2007.

affairs cannot be used to protect genocidal acts or other atrocities, such as large-scale violations of international humanitarian law or large-scale ethnic cleansing, *which can properly be considered a threat to international peace and security and as such provoke action by the Security Council*.[37] In other words, when the Security Council determines that events within a state constitute 'genocidal acts or other atrocities', an intervention may be taken to have been authorized. Similarly, as noted, the states of the African Union appear also to have accepted that there is a right to intervene regionally, in situations where a government is found to be engaged in war crimes, genocide, or crimes against humanity, when such an intervention has been authorized by a two-thirds majority of the member states.

Evidently, there is a degree of willingness on the part of governments, despite their sovereignty concerns, to accommodate a legal right of humanitarian intervention, *but only if:*

1. That right is limited to circumstances such as war crimes and genocide, offences that are relatively well defined by the law of nations, and
2. The decision as to whether those circumstances have actually arisen, in any particular instance, is vested in a trusted institution that does not merely reflect the self-interest of a powerful state.

When these preconditions are met, resistance to the exercise of a right of humanitarian intervention seems largely to dissipate. Thus, there was no serious objection, in 1994, when the Security Council authorized a coalition of the willing to intervene against the oppressive military *junta* which had seized power in Haiti.[38] In 1998–9, when collective measures were taken against the Serb-Yugoslav regime's repression of its Kosovar population,[39] the facts on the ground had been established by UN observers and the opposition of Russia and China to NATO's humanitarian intervention found no resonance among the other members of the Council who, overwhelmingly, rejected an invitation to censure the initiative.

If this analysis is correct, the *right* of humanitarian intervention already exists, at least contingently, but it is exercisable, legally, only after the intervention has been authorized by a legitimate institution.

This procedural approach has its weaknesses; but, when it works, it seems to adjust two countervailing concerns: that populations be protected from the excesses of their own governments, *and* that such protection not be used as pretext for the powerful to assert their self-interest against the weak.

---

[37] UN Secretary General, *A More Secure World: Our Shared Responsibility*, Report of the Secretary General's High Level Panel on Threats, Challenges and Change, UN Doc. A/59/565, 2 Dec. 2004, 65, para. 200. Italics added.

[38] UN Security Council, S/RES/940 (1994), 31 July 1994.

[39] UN Security Council, S/RES/1160 (1998), 31 Mar. 1998; S/RES/1199 (1998), 23 Sept. 1998; S/RES/1203 (1998), 24 Oct. 1998; S/RES/1244 (1999), 10 June 1999.

The lawyerly approach to the problematic of humanitarian intervention, there-fore, would seem to be to urge a shift of focus from the primary issue—will, or should, the law recognize such a right?—to the secondary issue—how is such a right to be defined and implemented? Even so, that tactical rearrangement of the agenda does little to resolve a further issue made salient by the current emphasis on 'the Responsibility to Protect'.[40] That issue is: what to do when, faced with a humanitarian crisis, no state is interested in responding, or when, in seeking to respond, the Security Council is blocked by a permanent member's arbitrary exercise of, or threat of, a veto.

These are related but separate issues.

As to the situation where states evince no interest in intervening to protect an endangered population, the problem is not one of law but of political will. The 2005 World Summit Outcome sought to address this deficit. The leaders of UN members, meeting on the Organization's 60th anniversary, declared: 'we are prepared to take collective action, in a timely and decisive manner, through the Security Council, in accordance with the Charter, including Chapter VII [authorizing the use of force], on a case-by-case basis and in cooperation with relevant regional organizations as appropriate, should peaceful means be inadequate and national authorities manifestly fail to protect their populations from genocide, war crimes, ethnic cleansing and crimes against humanity'.[41]

It remains to be seen whether this decision actually does strengthen the political will of the states that have the responsibility for authorizing humanitarian interven-tions. What if the exhortation fails? Here the distinction must be made between an actual and a technical failure to authorize a demonstrably necessary intervention. An actual failure to authorize a humanitarian intervention occurs when a voting majority of the members of the Security Council—nine or more of its fifteen members—remain unconvinced that it should be undertaken. There are various reasons why they might be reluctant. The extent of the humanitarian crisis might not have been demonstrated. Or its imminence might be doubted. Both may, in part, be addressed by better international forecasting and monitoring. Or, the costs of intervention might be thought excessive, or to exceed the potential benefits.

The matter is rather different when the failure to authorize is purely procedural: the result of opposition by just one or two permanent members of the Council wielding the power of the veto to frustrate the large majority's readiness to intervene in what they see as a catastrophic humanitarian crisis.[42] Both the Liberian and Kosovo cases are instances of such institutional failure, due not to a failure of political will on the part of the large majority of its members, but to the threat of a veto by one (or two) permanent members who see it in their interest to protect a client state. The failure, in 2005–6, to take forceful measures with respect to

---

[40] Evans, G. and Sahnoun, M., *The Responsibility to Protect* (above, n. 7).
[41] UN General Assembly, World Summit Outcome, GAOR RES/A/60 (2005), para. 139.
[42] UN Charter, article 27 (3).

the humanitarian crisis in Dafur is similarly attributable not to lack of will or of evidence, but to the veto's power to frustrate that will and circumvent the evidence.

In these instances, the argument for strict compliance with the letter of the law is much weaker. The law, of course, remains the law and no violation of it is ever completely cost free, if only because violations undermine respect for the law, emboldening others, in less salubrious circumstances, to turn scofflaw. Yet, not all violations of the law are of equal gravity, and, in some circumstances, the mitigating effect of the circumstances may come close to—but are not quite—exoneration. In the instances of Liberia, Kosovo, and Dafur, the Security Council was not being called upon to act in circumstances of insufficient, or seriously contested, information. In respect of the crises in Liberia, Kosovo, and Dafur, the Organization had sent observers to report on the dimensions of the crisis and had received reports largely without ambiguity. They had been made fully aware of the urgency and gravity of the humanitarian crisis. The impetus to act was, simply, stymied, by the procedure that permits one or two permanent members to prevent action.

In such circumstances, when a coalition of the willing takes it upon itself to act without the necessary authorization, they still violate the law, and take their chances on mitigation of the consquences. In both the instances of intervention in Liberia and Kosovo, the relevant regional organizations intervened in the absence of the requisite Security Council authorization, which was unobtainable due to the reluctance of a permanent member. Subsequently, when it became incontrovertible that the intervention had been both humanitarian in effect and essential in the circumstances—that nothing less would have saved large numbers of persons from carnage—the Council, *ex post facto*, implicitly approved the unauthorized actions.[43] The states which acted without authorization were able to demonstrate the overwhelming necessity of their action—including their good faith in having exhausted the alternatives and in using no more force, and for no longer, than absolutely necessary. Accepting that rationale, the Security Council, by joining in the operation—'partaking of the fruit of the poisoned tree', sceptics might say—deliberately waived the imposition of consequences on those who acted without authorization and, instead, endorsed and co-opted the humanitarian mission.

Mitigation, even when it amounts to the waiver of any consequences for a breach of the law, does not transform the unlawful act into a lawful one. In that sense, mitigation is not tantamount to exculpation. The killing of a person in reasonable self-defence is not murder even though it be intentional killing. On the other hand, shooting a survivor trying to clamber into a lifeboat already filled to utmost capacity *is* murder. While it is not exculpable, yet the circumstances are likely to be cause for mitigation.

---

[43] Both interventions and their subsequent ratification are examined in Franck, T. M., *Recourse to Force: State Action Against Threats and Armed Attacks* (Cambridge: Cambridge University Press, 2002), 174.

To this important distinction it needs be added, however, that international law, while no different in having distinct concepts of mitigation and exculpation, has a somewhat softer dividing line between them than do most domestic legal systems. International law is formed by both the consent of states (usually in treaties) but also by state behaviour (custom). In domestic legal systems, on the contrary, state laws against jay-walking do not repeal themselves merely because the practice is endemic among urban pedestrians. International law, no doubt because of its weaker powers of compulsion, is more responsive to violations which, if repeated and little resisted, may become the new law. That, for example, is how, in day-to-day practice, an abstention in Security Council voting came to be treated as not constituting a veto.[44] If, in the practice of the Security Council, *bona fide* humanitarian crises addressed by action through NATO, the Inter-American system, or the African Union increasingly came to be treated as normal and adopted *ex post facto* by the Council, then the law of the Charter may be said to have adapted in practice.

Such adaption is most likely to occur if the Security Council acts *post hoc* to legitimate humanitarian operations not authorized by it. Such legitimation may be explicit or, as in the cases of Liberia and Kosovo, inescapably implicit in the Council's participation in the aftermath of the interventions. It should be recalled that it was decided at San Francisco that, in 'the course of the operations from day to day of the various organs of the Organization, it is inevitable that each organ will interpret such parts of the Charter as are applicable to its particular functions. The process is inherent in the functioning of any body which operates under an instrument defining its functions and powers'.[45] The law of the Charter, to a large extent, is what the principal organs do in fact. If the Council repeatedly were to engage in the retroactive legitimation of what its majority consider *bona fide* humanitarian interventions by 'decent' coalitions of the willing in undeniable circumstances of extreme necessity, then the law will have moved, slowly and imperceptibly as is its wont, from a practice of selective mitigation towards a redefinition of the relevant legal norm.

One of the least acknowledged duties of the lawyer is to counsel a client when a law may be disobeyed: as when a driver ignores traffic laws in speeding a seriously injured passenger to the hospital. Although this is not always understood by the laity, law is not scripture. Its rules caution those to whom they are addressed, but subject, always, to the superior rule of reason. Law is perfectly capable of mitigating

---

[44] This evolution, although entirely inconsistent with the literal wording of UN Charter art. 27 (3), was endorsed by the International Court of Justice, *Legal Consequences for States of the Continuing Presence of South Africa in Namibia (South West Africa) notwithstanding Security Council Resolution 276 1970*, Advisory Opinion [1971], 16 I.C.J. Reports, 22, para. 22.

[45] Statement of Committee IV/2 of the San Francisco Conference, Report of Committee IV/2 of the United Nations Conference on International Organization, San Francisco, 12 June 1945, UNCIO Doc. 933, 13 UNCIO Docs. 703, 709–10.

the consequences of a violation, providing the violator can demonstrate that the violation avoided a significantly greater wrong.

In practical terms, this means that a lawyer, advising governments able and willing to intervene in a humanitarian crisis even when formal authorization has been blocked by a veto, would be discharging his or her professional responsibility in counselling that such unauthorized intervention would only incur a serious risk of international disapproval if it turned out to have been unnecessary, or unnecessarily costly in execution. If, on the other hand, the operation turns out to have saved many lives that would otherwise have been lost, the international system, in time, will almost certainly adopt it as its own and share in the costs and obligations of bringing it to a successful conclusion. That, at least, was the case both in Liberia and Kosovo.

In tendering such advice the lawyer is not relativizing the law. He or she is pointing to the well-known fact that law encompasses an element of what philosophers know as 'situational ethics'. When a law is broken to prevent some greater harm than that from which the law seeks to provide protection—when, for example, it can be demonstrated to a court that a breach of the law has prevented the occurrence of some far greater wrong—then the law will still insist that it has been violated, but will mitigate the consequences of the unlawful act.[46] Lawyers know that a legal strategy encompassing mitigation, far from undermining the law, saves normativity from being pushed over the cliff into *reductio ad absurdum* by those who insist on its uniform application without due regard to the circumstances in which the rule is operating.

Note, however, that mitigation always depends upon the proof of special circumstances, and upon such proof being both presented to, and accepted by, a credible forum. This is quite different from, and far more restrictive than, Professor Fernando Tesón's 'liberal cosmopolitan' exception, by which the law would *permit* (as distinct from *mitigate*) humanitarian intervention, and do so in any situation of tyranny or anarchy (without stipulating *in whose opinion*).[47] As I have indicated earlier in this essay, while such a sweeping transformation of the law, from prohibiting unauthorized interventions to permitting them, may someday be the way the international system adapts to its failure collectively to carry out its self-defined obligation to protect victims of humanitarian crimes, we are not at that point, yet. Moreover, we are unlikely ever to reach that point unless there is in place a credible procedure for validating the extent of an alleged humanitarian crisis and the *bona fides* of the motives and means of the responders.

---

[46] See Franck, T. M., 'What, Eat the Cabin Boy?' in Franck, *Recourse to Force* (above, n. 43), ch. 10, 174 ff.

[47] Fernando Tesón, 'The Liberal Case for Humanitarian Intervention', in Holzgrefe, J. L. and Keohane, R. O., *Humanitarian Intervention: Ethical, Legal and Political Dilemmas* (Cambridge: Cambridge University Press, 2003), 93.

IV. Conclusion

Dr Taylor Seybolt has captured the problem with aphoristic directness: 'military intervention for human protection purposes can *only* be justified in humanitarian terms if the intervention does more good than harm'.[48] Unfortunately, this involves an acute analysis of each specific instance, as well as a prediction about the likely costs and benefits of intervening, set against those of not intervening. The evident difficulty of making such predictive assessments, case by case, suggests that any rule is likely to be useless unless accompanied by a rule about how the rule is to be applied. *Who, or which institution, is to make the call.* Until that issue is addressed, a norm will not help much.

But norms may do serious harm. When they seem to command that which is widely regarded as immoral or absurd, harm ensues not only to those the law should protect, but to the institution of law, itself. Above all, law must make sense to those to whom it is addressed. If states willing to sacrifice their own personnel and resources in an effort to rescue large numbers of critically endangered citizens of another state are required by law to desist, then the law will be widely regarded as stupid, even evil, and it will (and should) be ignored.[49]

On the other hand, if the law stipulates that, whenever citizens of a state are endangered by their own governments, other governments may come to their rescue, *and provides no machinery for determining when the threshold for such legitimate intervention has been crossed in specific instances*, then the law will be regarded, rightly, as a license for aggression.

In the light of actual experience with claims of a right to humanitarian intervention, the law cannot accommodate such a general right to intervene. It has shown itself far too open to abuse.

On the other hand, the law can, and has, made provision for collective measures in extreme cases of humanitarian abuse, measures determined by the Security Council in exercise of its authority under chapter VII of the UN Charter. This right of collective intervention is resistant to abuse, as it requires the approval of the many diverse interests in the Council.

---

[48] Seybolt, T. B., *Humanitarian Military Intervention: the Conditions for Success and Failure* (Oxford: Oxford University Press, 2007), 3.

[49] A good example: under the Charter of the African Union, the members, by two-thirds majority, may decide to intervene in a member state when convinced that genocide or egregious violations of humanitarian law are unfolding there. This is not strictly permitted by art. 53 of the UN Charter, but does reflect the general perception that, in extreme circumstances, it is important that the fates of peoples should not be sealed by a legal requirement of inaction by those willing to rescue them.

The trouble is that collective action by the Council can too easily be stopped by a single veto, even in situations evidently warranting action.[50]

There is no need—and, indeed, no possibility—to address such abuses by law. The problem lies with the political practice of the permanent members of the Council: a problem law is unlikely to resolve. But law and lawyers must take care not to make the problem worse. Thus, if collective action is stymied by threat of a veto, but a coalition of the willing has clear proof that the alternative to collective action is the imminent death of large numbers of persons and that timely intervention can save far more persons than will be lost by it, then the coalition should act, aware that its nominally illegal action will not incur significantly adverse consequences because those judging the action, in the circumstances, will reject such consequences.

Law can provide useful yardsticks. For example, humanitarian intervention is justifiable only to save human lives, not to alter political or social systems. Or, humanitarian intervention is justifiable if, demonstrably, it saves substantially more lives than it sacrifices.

But, law is useless, and may even be harmful, if its yardsticks are not wielded by a credible interlocutor. Lawyers can devise institutional settings for the legitimate application of law's rules, but, pending their adoption, should avoid extravagant claims on the law's behalf.

---

[50] Efforts to limit the veto in such instances were tried in recent years, but have all failed. See Wheeler, N. J., 'A Victory for Common Humanity? The Responsibility to Protect after the 2005 World Summit', *Journal of International Law and International Relations*, 2 (2005), 95, 102–3.

CHAPTER 27

HUMANITARIAN MILITARISM?

DANILO ZOLO*

I. 'ANGELIC' INTERVENTIONS

At the start of his essay, Thomas Franck informs the reader that humans are not angels. If they were, it would be enough to think that 'humanitarian interventions', even those carried out using armed force and involving the loss of innocent lives, would be like 'angelic interventions' and therefore for the greater good. If we were angels, we could be certain that any 'humanitarian' military intervention by one state against another would have the protection of the rights of the citizens of the other state as its ultimate goal. The defeat of a state whose political authorities are tarnished by serious human rights violations would therefore coincide with the triumph of the universal values of the international community and not with the particular interests of the state involved in the military action. This optimistic hypothesis supports the view of Michael Glennon who argues that in such a case the use of force may be considered as an instrument to achieve the goal of the 'great ideal of justice',[1] which must override the formalism of the mummified canon of international law that opposes any use of force that has not been formally legitimized by international institutions. If force of arms is used to do justice 'the law will follow', thereby legitimizing the *fait accompli* in positive law or via custom. The respect for state sovereignty, as Michael Ignatieff and others have suggested, becomes a secondary problem when confronted with the duty to protect human rights that reflect universal values. The universality of human rights must

* Translated from Italian by Joanna Bourke-Martignoni.
[1] Glennon, M. J., 'The New Interventionism', *Foreign Affairs*, 78 (1999), 3, 7.

thereby correspond to the universality of the armed interventions necessary for their protection.[2]

Thomas Franck admits, however, that this attitude does not and cannot reflect reality for those who do not believe in human angels. He does not hide his distrust towards an indiscriminate apologia *à la* Fernando Tesón[3] for the use of force for humanitarian ends. Franck wisely—and it must also be said, rather obviously—thinks that it is necessary to distinguish 'genuine' humanitarian interventions from those that are insincere and opportunistic. It may be that the humanitarian emergency is a mere invention by one power seeking to interfere in the domestic jurisdiction of another state for political and/or economic reasons. Or, it could be the case that a civil war of comparatively minor dimensions is turned into something much bigger by a large power to justify aggression against a militarily weak state that it has decided to occupy for strategic purposes.

One cannot but agree with Franck concerning the requirement of a rigorous verification of the motives and aims of those that declare that they are using force in pursuit of a generous 'humanitarian' vocation. How can one forget the radical scepticism expressed by Carl Schmitt, in his famous maxim: *wer Menschheit sagt, will betrügen*? Those who seek to clothe a military attack in humanitarian clothing are in fact imposters: looking to consecrate their own war as a 'just war' and to morally denigrate their adversaries by isolating them as enemies of humanity and being hostile to them to the extent of extreme inhumanity.[4] Franck appears to be aware of this very serious risk. Nevertheless, it seems to me, he does not provide normative criteria that enable us to clearly distinguish between the (probably few) 'genuine' humanitarian interventions and the (probably many more) 'false' humanitarian interventions.

Franck's historical review of cases of violent 'humanitarian intervention' is both ample and sketchy and does not constitute a reasonable basis for the identification of general rules to oppose genuine and false military humanitarianism. He takes us back to the Holy Alliance, to the 'question of the Orient' and the incident involving Maronite Christians on Mount Lebanon, resurfacing in the mid-eighteenth century when the very notion of 'humanitarian intervention' was unknown, and then refers, without any historiographical differentiation, to contemporary events such as the invasion of Haiti in 1994 or the war over Kosovo in 1999. A correlation is thus being made between historical contexts that are difficult to compare in legal and even less in ethical terms. The contemporary notion of 'humanitarian intervention' appears to me to be indissociable from the emergence of the doctrine of human rights and in particular the internationalization of these rights with the Universal Declaration of Human Rights (1948) and the International Covenants on Economic, Social

---

[2] Ignatieff, M., *Human Rights as Politics and Idolatry* (Princeton: Princeton University Press, 2001), 37.
[3] Tesón, F. R., 'The Liberal Case for Humanitarian Intervention', in Holzgrefe, J. L. and Keohane, R. O. (eds.), *Humanitarian Intervention* (Cambridge: Cambridge University Press, 2003), 93.
[4] Schmitt, C., *Begriff des Politischen* (Berlin: Duncker & Humblot, 1963).

and Cultural Rights and on Civil and Political Rights that were both adopted in 1966.

Aside from the above, it seems incorrect in historico-political terms not to take into consideration the radical novelty of the 'humanitarian interventions' that occurred in the second half of the last century, notably following the fall of the Soviet empire and the end of the bipolar system of international relations. Ever since the 1970s, different international institutions have supported the principle of 'humanitarian intervention' as a right of intervention by the international community within the borders of one state to control possible violations of human rights and to provide aid to the affected populations. In the United States, during the Carter presidency, arguments grounded in the international protection of human rights were officially presented as a legitimate motive for interference in the internal affairs of a state.[5]

In the 1990s, however, the perspective of humanitarian intervention became a key element in the United States' strategy and a growing number of ethical and legal claims were made to legitimate it. The subject of humanitarian intervention came to the fore as a result of a series of documents, issued by political authorities in the United States, justifying the unilateral use of force as humanitarian intervention. As early as August 1990, President George Bush outlined a project for global peace which he baptized the 'new world order'. The United States, according to Bush, had won the last world war—the Cold War—and must therefore take on the role of planning the future international order and developing its principles and rules.[6] The following year, George Bush's project was refined in the *National Security Strategy of the United States*.[7] At the beginning of 1992, the strategic plans laid out by the President were further developed in the *Defence Planning Guidance*.[8]

In the meantime, a sizeable specialist literature elaborated the military-strategic implications of the concept of 'global security' that lay at the heart of these documents.[9] The United States, it was argued, thus had at its fingertips the 'extraordinary opportunity' to build a peaceful and just international system inspired by the values of freedom, the rule of law, democracy, and the market economy. The organization of a system of global security involved two crucial strategic innovations. It was necessary to redefine the defensive strategy of the North Atlantic Treaty Organization (NATO) which was no longer bound to respect the Warsaw Pact following its dissolution. The traditional geographic coverage

---

[5] Albala, N., 'Limites du droit d'ingérence', *Manière de voir*, 45 (1999), 82–3.

[6] Zolo, D., *Cosmopolis* (Cambridge: Polity Press, 1997), 35–8.

[7] President of the United States, *National Security Strategy of the United States* (Washington: The White House, 1991).

[8] The document drafted by a Department of State staff member was published in the New York Times on 18 Mar. 1992 and subsequently elaborated upon.

[9] See among others, Wolfowitz, P., 'An American Perspective', in Grove, E. (ed.), *Global Security* (London: Brassey 1991), 19; Art, R., 'A Defensible Defense: America's Grand Strategy after the Cold War', *International Security*, 15 (1991), 1, 5–53; Gaddis, J. L., 'Toward the Post-Cold War World', *Foreign Affairs*, 70 (1991), 2, 102.

of the Atlantic Alliance had to be expanded to respond to the increased risk of international disorder emanating from a plurality of regional areas.[10] In a world that was no longer bipolar, the transatlantic association that had previously guaranteed the military presence of the United States in Europe had to be rebuilt on new foundations. It was felt that the new association should be based on a strategy that was proactive and not defensive, expansive and not only reactive, dynamic and flexible rather than static and rigid.

Second, and decisively, the global security strategy required the great powers responsible for world order to give up the old Westphalian principle of non-intervention in the domestic jurisdiction of nation states. This in order that they could implement and legitimate a right-duty of 'humanitarian intervention' in the event that they were required to forcibly intervene to resolve internal crises in a state as a means of preventing or halting serious human rights violations.

This strategy was confirmed in theory and carried out in practice following the Gulf War in 1991, due to the activism of the United States and British governments who without any explicit authorization from the United Nations engaged in the humanitarian operation *Provide Comfort* in Northern and Southern Iraq. Following this, during the period 1992–4, the policy of humanitarian intervention was affirmed despite falling outside any normative reference, including the UN Charter. The intervention by the United States and several other powers in Somalia, which was motivated by the need to guarantee access to food and health supplies, rapidly became transformed into a bloody military conflict whose objectives, while increasingly removed from the institutional goals of the United Nations, coincided with the interests of certain powerful oil companies. The perspectives for an analogous 'humanitarian' intervention in the territory of the former Yugoslavia remained both uncertain and tragically controversial for a lengthy period. In the end, NATO forces assumed the role of intervener as though the organization, born out of the Cold War, had transformed itself into an emanation of the United Nations rather than a politico-military structure aligned with the defence of Western interests and dominated by the United States. The military activity of NATO in the former Yugoslav territories during the Bosnian war (1992–5) and above all in the war over Kosovo (1999) became officialized with the tacit consent of the United Nations.

It is only within these particular strategic and normative contexts over the past 15 years that the problem of 'humanitarian interventions', and especially those that have been decided by NATO, may be understood. Further, it is only within this context that an eventual criterion for distinguishing 'genuine' from 'false' humanitarian interventions may be established. The distinguishing criterion, as it will be seen, must refer in the first instance to positive international law in force,

---

[10] Wörner, M., 'Global Security: The Challenge for NATO', in Grove, E. (ed.), *Global Security* (above, n. 9), 100–5.

and in particular to the United Nations Charter and the multilateral Covenants concerning human rights, as well as to customary international law. It is therefore necessary to exclude historical events prior to the Second World War along with any generic references to normative principles or criteria of 'international ethics' that it is argued should prevail over international law.

The reference to universal and deontological 'international ethics' is, in the vast majority of cases, instrumental—Michael Walzer's ethics of war being a case in point—and is conditioned by political evaluations, religious beliefs, and symbolic universes that are very different from one another. Moreover, these are normative choices that may be manipulated on the basis of disparate and divergent meta-ethical doctrines, beginning with the Weberian opposition between ethics of intention and ethics of responsibility. Edward Carr has concisely stated that it is not international politics that can be conceived of as a function of ethics, but rather it is international ethics that lends itself to use as a function of national politics. According to Carr—whose thesis appears to be of renewed currency following the fall of the Soviet empire—this inversion of the functions of ethics and politics was particularly striking in the Anglo-Saxon world in the first half of the twentieth century. The effect of this inversion has been that, unconsciously yet systematically, the specific interests of the British and North American world have been mistaken for the general interests of humanity.[11]

That which in the West (and in particular within the Anglo-Saxon culture) is called 'international ethics' is in reality a legacy of Judaeo-Christian traditions assumed to be 'ordinary morality' or the 'common sense of moral justice'.[12] It is asserted—by Charles Beitz, Stanley Hoffmann, Joseph Nye, and Michael Walzer among others—that no philosophical or epistemological justification is required for this kind of ethics as it is taken for granted that they are imbued with a universally-recognized form of rationality and a normatively superior authority than that of any other moral tradition.[13] In reality, such ethics are lacking in authorized and authoritative normative sources and are not supported by any international consensus. In this way, 'international ethics' are profoundly different from modern international law which despite its weak operational efficiency, presents itself as a positive and consolidated legal system, endowed with the authoritative normative source of state sovereignty, articulated through international institutions and supported by widespread international recognition.

However—and this is a critical point—according to Franck and also to Glennon and Allen Buchanan, it is necessary to refer to ethics due to the fact that the

[11] Carr, E. H., *The Twenty Years' Crisis 1919–1939* (London: Macmillan, 1956).

[12] Franck, T. M., 'Interpretation and Change in the Law of Humanitarian Intervention', in Holzgrefe, J. L. and Keohane, R. O. (eds.), *Humanitarian Intervention* (above, n. 3), 216.

[13] Beitz, C. R., *Political Theory and International Relations* (Princeton: Princeton University Press, 1979); Hoffmann, S., *Duties Beyond Borders*, (Syracuse: Syracuse University Press, 1981); Nye, J. S. Jr., *Nuclear Ethics* (New York: Free Press, 1986); Walzer, M., *Just and Unjust Wars* (New York: Basic Books, 1992).

international law on humanitarian intervention does not provide prescriptions that are morally and rationally acceptable.[14] The United Nations, argues Franck, does not possess the decision-making procedures or the adequate practical instruments: in many cases military humanitarian intervention is inevitably illegal due to the fact that this illegality is conditional upon its timeliness or its effectiveness. This was demonstrated *a contrario* by the genocide in Rwanda and, Franck maintains, it has been shown in a positive way during the war launched by NATO in 1999 against the Federal Republic of Yugoslavia. According to Franck, in cases such as these the violation of international law is a moral imperative and this was especially true of the decision taken by the United States—and thus by NATO—to intervene in the Balkans to prevent 'an imminent genocide in Kosovo'.

In such a situation, Franck considers that the violation of international law was faultless and even laudable, due to the fact that it concerned a use of force that the majority of the United Nations' Security Council viewed as a good faith intervention by a 'decent coalition of the willing'. To maintain that an international norm prohibits an intervention of this type, argues Franck, is to give credit to an international law that must be 'widely regarded as stupid, even evil', and that therefore may be justifiably disobeyed. This appears to be a central point, because it was the war over Kosovo that, according to many commentators, was the most important and meaningful event in terms of 'humanitarian intervention' during the last decade of the 1990s.[15] It was presented as the most moral and just of the 'new wars': an intervention to stop the genocide being perpetrated by an oppressive regime led by a bloodthirsty tyrant. The following responds to Franck's evaluation of the war over Kosovo in greater detail.

II. NATO's 'Humanitarian War' Against the Federal Republic of Yugoslavia

With regard to the intervention by NATO against the Federal Republic of Yugoslavia, Franck maintains that it was a case in which 'the intervention had an incontro-vertibly humanitarian effect'. He adds that the 'overwhelming necessity' of the war was demonstrated by the NATO authorities who in 'good faith' had exhausted all alternatives to the use of force which was deployed in the measure and for the time that were strictly necessary. Had it not been for the intervention by Western armies, many more people would have lost their lives due to the ruthless repression by the

---

[14] Buchanan, A., 'Reforming the International Law of Humanitarian Intervention', in Holzgrefe, J. L. and Keohane, R. O (eds.), *Humanitarian Intervention* (above, n. 3), 130.

[15] See Keohane, R. O., 'Introduction', in Holzgrefe, J. L. and Keohane, R. O (eds.), *Humanitarian Intervention* (above, n. 3), 1.

Serb militia of the Kosovar-Albanian minority. According to Franck, this is a decisive criterion for distinguishing a 'genuine' humanitarian intervention from an intervention that is 'false' or otherwise wrong. The use of force for humanitarian purposes 'is justifiable if, demonstrably, it saves substantially more lives than it sacrifices'. Second, Franck argues that even prior to the armed intervention by NATO, the Security Council had been completely apprised of the gravity of the humanitarian crisis that was unfolding in Kosovo and that the opposition from China and Russia did not meet with a consensus amongst the other members of the Council which had refused the proposal to prohibit the intervention. In brief, it is asserted that the majority of the international community was in favour of NATO's decision to use force.

Theoretically, and this argument will be elaborated below, the criterion proposed by Franck for the identification of the authenticity and legitimacy of an armed humanitarian intervention—the *a posteriori* calculation of the number of human lives saved—is both impractical as well as legally unsustainable. Regarding Kosovo, it is clear that neither was there a genocide against the Kosovar-Albanian minority underway nor was there a risk that this would occur: the political and military authorities within NATO never advanced a thesis of this kind. In reality it was a civil war that opposed the Serb militia against the Kosovo Liberation Army (*Ushtria Çlirimtare ë Kosovës*, UÇK), an organization with an ultra-nationalist bent that relied on the systematic use of terrorism. The ruthless repression carried out by the government in Belgrade against the independence movement was matched by a guerrilla army of no less than 10,000 armed soldiers, in large measure supplied with material from Kosovar communities abroad: in Switzerland, Germany, and above all the United States where a substantial pro-Kosovar lobby led by Senator Robert Dole made itself heard in the Congress.[16] In addition, the United States administration had declared on several occasions that it considered Kosovo, to an even greater extent than Bosnia-Herzegovina, to be a geopolitical space of fundamental strategic interest for American national security.[17]

In Kosovo then, a civil war was underway that was not particularly violent, above all when compared to other conflicts within the same Mediterranean area such as the tragedy of the Palestinian people or the civil war in Algeria where, during the same period, approximately 90,000 civilians were massacred to the absolute indifference of the Western powers. In Kosovo, the number of victims of the civil war in the year preceding the attack by NATO did not exceed 2,000,[18]

---

[16] Vickers, M. and Pettifer, J., *Albania* (London: Hurst and Company, 1997); Mastrolilli, P., 'La lobby albanese in America', *Limes* (1998), 3, 287–90.

[17] In 1994 President Clinton told the new Secretary of State, Lawrence Eagleburger, to send a short telegram to the United States Ambassador in Belgrade with instructions to read it personally to Milosevic. The telegram read: 'In case of a conflict in Kosovo caused by a Serb action, the United States will be ready to use military force against the Serbs in Kosovo and against Serbia itself'. See Calvo-Platero, M., 'Le tentazioni di una superpotenza', in Berselli, E. et. al. (eds.), *La pace e la guerra* (Milan: Il Sole 24 Ore, 1999), 126–7.

[18] This data, corroborated by the Council for the Defence of Human Rights and Liberty in Prishtina, is generally accepted. It is sufficient to point to the statements by United States Minister of Defence William Cohen,

while there were approximately 3,000 deaths during the two and a half months that NATO's intervention lasted. The horrors of 'ethnic cleansing' that have been attributed to the Serb militia and imputed to the exclusive political (and criminal) responsibility of the government in Belgrade, must be viewed with caution, in particular with respect to Kosovo. The massacre at Raçak on 15 January 1999, which was adopted as an emblem of Serbian barbarity and was used as the decisive pretext for the military attack by NATO against the Federal Republic of Yugoslavia is highly controversial and certainly not well documented.[19] Further, the conduct of the Serbian government which appeared to be aimed at diffusing the situation through an application of the Holbrooke-Milosevic Agreement of October 1998, did not assist it in avoiding the NATO military intervention. In signing the agreement, Milosevic had accepted the internationalization of the Kosovo crisis and additionally agreed to considerable limitations upon Yugoslav sovereignty.[20]

To all this, it must be added that the military intervention by the United States and European forces led to the deaths of thousands of innocent people along with the denial of basic human rights for tens of thousands of others. During the course of the more than 10,000 bombing missions by approximately 1,000 Allied fighter planes and the use of more than 23,000 explosive weapons, including missiles, bombs, and various other projectiles, NATO also destroyed the civilian and productive infrastructure of an entire country. Serbia and Vojvodina were subjected to 78 days of uninterrupted bombing by planes flying at such a high altitude that they were out of range of anti-aircraft defences and inevitably going to inflict devastating 'collateral damage'. Human Rights Watch gathered evidence of at least 500 Yugoslav civilian deaths in approximately 90 mortal incidents caused by weapons that missed their intended targets. In this way, writes David Luban, NATO's humanitarian intervention

sent a message that could hardly be lost on the world: that Americans considered one American life to be worth thousands of Yugoslav lives—hardly a resounding endorsement of the doctrine of universal human rights.[21]

NATO authorities have officially admitted, or at least have not denied, the deaths, mutilation, or serious injuries of Serbian, Kosovar-Albanian, and Roma civilians due to the erroneous bombing of chemical plants, automobile factories, passenger trains, refugee convoys, public markets, hospitals, and prisons (23 deaths occurred in the Istok Kosovo prison). In an attack pre-ordered by NATO command during

who on 16 May 1999 denounced the killing of 100,000 Kosovar Albanians, and to NATO's official estimate of 10,000 victims; See Lodovisi, A., 'La grande dissipazione', *Guerre e pace*, 7 (1999), 60, 14.

[19] The Finnish investigative committee has been unable to reach conclusions on the issues of responsibility, the actual sequence of events, and the identity of many of the victims; See Morozzo della Rocca, R., 'La via verso la guerra', *Limes*, supplemento al n.1/99, 24–5.

[20] Ibid. 20–1.

[21] Luban, D., 'Intervention and Civilization: Some Unhappy Lessons of the Kosovo War', in De Greiff, P. and Cronin, C. (eds.), *Global Justice and Transnational Politics*, (Cambridge, Mass.: MIT Press, 2002), 82.

the night of 23 and 24 April 1999, a missile bombardment destroyed the Belgrade television building where 150 journalists and employees were working, killing 16 and injuring an equal number. In addition to the above, the United States and British bombers used cluster bombs which release devices similar to anti-personnel mines and have the greatest impact upon children. The unexploded remnants of these bombs continue to cause casualties in Kosovo and in Serbia today. Further, NATO's Secretary-General at the time, George Robertson, admitted that the A10 tank-buster bombers supplied by the United States, conducted 100 missions during the course of which 31,000 depleted uranium projectiles were dropped.[22]

As to the *a posteriori* calculation of victims—given that we must in a certain sense add and subtract the total number of bodies from a sort of enormous 'humanitarian' morgue—it is important to remember that the war that NATO wanted did not halt the violence or the bloodshed in Kosovo. As in any other war, the war for Kosovo has left a long train of hatred, fear, corruption, prostitution, misery, and death in its wake. Ethnic discrimination, repression, and systematic human rights violations—denounced by Amnesty International on numerous occasions[23]—have continued undiminished but in the opposite direction: against the defeated Serbs, through terrorist actions by the UÇK, the Presevo, Medvedja and Bujanovac Liberation Army (UÇPMB), and the Kosovo Security Corps (TMK).

More than 300,000 Serbian and Roma people became refugees, while 2,000 people, the majority of Serbian ethnicity, were killed or disappeared. Approximately 150 Orthodox monasteries and churches were destroyed, a fact which has recently been deplored by UNESCO. These violations occurred despite a large NATO military presence in Kosovo and in spite of the fact that the United States, using a logic that it is difficult to define as 'humanitarian', illegally constructed an imposing military base in the heart of Kosovo—the largest base built since the Vietnam war—after levelling three entire hills previously used for wheat cultivation. The base is Camp Bondsteel, located close to Urosevać, which can house up to 5,000 soldiers and it has also been secretly used to hold detainees from Afghanistan and Iraq.

If what has been laid out above is correct, it becomes difficult to accept Franck's contention that 'the "clean hands" of participants in NATO's action was unassailable, in the sense that its members evidently had no territorial designs on Kosovo and appeared to be fighting a war for purely humanitarian objectives and mostly with means calibrated to avoid excessive and collateral damage'.[24]

As for the information sources available to the United States, Franck should have recalled that in April 1999, a month after the aerial attacks by NATO against

---

[22] From the statement made by the Italian Under-Secretary of Defense, Paolo Guerrini; See Nese, M., 'Allarme insensato', *Corriere della Sera*, 11 Mar. 2000, 10.

[23] Amnesty International, *Serbia*, Index EUR 70/001/2006; Amnesty International Report, *Kosovo (Serbia). The United Nations in Kosovo. A Legacy of Impunity*, 8 Nov. 2006, Index EUR 70/015/2006.

[24] Franck, T. M., 'Interpretation and Change in the Law of Humanitarian Intervention', in Holzgrefe, J. L., and Keohane, R. O (eds.), *Humanitarian Intervention* (above, n. 3), 226.

the Yugoslav Federation had started, the United Nations High Commissioner for Human Rights, Mary Robinson, severely criticized the NATO bombardment. According to Robinson, the Security Council had a duty to decide whether NATO's military campaign was in conformity with the legal principles in the UN Charter and to give an urgent decision on the subject. Robinson stated that civilians subjected to the NATO bombing campaign were suffering serious violations of their human rights. She added that the International Tribunal for the Former Yugoslavia in the Hague had the role of assessing the behaviour of the members of the UÇK and of the members of NATO, and not only the Serbian militia. NATO could not be considered to be the sole judge competent to decide upon the modalities of a war involving civilian persons and targets.[25] Several weeks later Brazilian diplomat Sergio Vieira de Mello denounced the 'humanitarian disaster' caused by the NATO bombings and declared both the UÇK militia and the Serbians responsible for serious violations and abuses in Kosovo.

If the above is true, the idea advanced by Franck that NATO remedied an 'institutional failure' by cancelling out the effect of the paralysis imposed upon the Security Council by Russia and China, in order 'to protect a client state', also falls by the wayside. In fact, the opposition of Russia and China (and of India) to the unilateral use of force by NATO, not only corresponded to the expectations of their constituents who represent the vast majority of the world's population, but was also perfectly in accordance with the UN Charter and with general international law. Moreover, the numerous condemnations and official protests against the illegal actions of NATO, coming from all of the different geopolitical areas of the world, including the 12 Latin American countries within the Rio Group and the 114 states in the Non-Aligned Movement, should not be underestimated.[26]

III. An Unsustainable Criterion

The lengthy discussion of the war over Kosovo serves to demonstrate that the reconstruction proposed by Franck does not provide plausible support for the criterion that he uses to identify the authenticity and the legitimacy of an armed humanitarian intervention. The mere calculation of the human lives saved is not sustainable.

This is above all an *a posteriori* criterion, which fails to offer any guidance concerning the decisions to be taken about the existence of a serious humanitarian emergency or about the necessity to undertake an armed unilateral intervention in

---

[25] Robinson, M., *Report on the Human Rights Situation Involving Kosovo*, 30 Apr. 1999, <http://www.unhchr.ch/html/menu2/5/kosovo/kosovo_main.htm>.

[26] Zappalà, S., 'Nuovi sviluppi in tema di uso della forza armata in relazione alle vicende del Kosovo', *Rivista di diritto internazionale* (1999), 975.

lieu of hypothetical alternatives such as peace-keeping or peace-building missions focusing on monitoring and civilian assistance with the consent of the belligerents. On one hand, the number of victims that a civil war could have is unforeseeable, even in the near future, particularly if the adversaries—or one of them—use weapons of mass destruction or terrorist tactics. On the other hand, balancing the preventive and final numbers of victims in a large-scale military intervention is always controversial, and often impossible to define in empirical terms, as was the case with the Gulf War of 1991.

The decisive argument must, however, be of a normative character grounded in the international legal system and not in a presumed international ethic to be used at will to deform the law for its own ends. The first point is that a war based on a unilateral decision by one state, or an alliance of states, against a sovereign state is, in light of the UN Charter and general international law, an aggressive war and constitutes an international crime of such gravity that the Nuremburg Tribunal defined it as a 'supreme international crime'. It is hardly necessary to underline that the prohibition on the unilateral and preventive use of military force in article 2 (4) of the Charter is the pillar that holds up the entire structure of the United Nations.[27]

A second point concerns the ban on the use of violence against the civilian population, prohibited in the fourth Geneva Convention. Nobody has the right to take the lives of (thousands of) innocent people during military operations that, as a result of the use of weapons of mass destruction, inevitably lead to massacres of the civilian population. In the case of Kosovo, this occurred systematically and was rationalized by the NATO military authorities through a cynical recourse of the formula of 'collateral damage'. In reality, these operations should be considered as war crimes and as crimes against humanity and the Prosecutor for the International Criminal Tribunal for the Former Yugoslavia (ICTY), had her decisions not been dependent upon the NATO authorities, should have conducted an inquiry and indicted those responsible. In the event, the Prosecutor did not conduct any inquiry and all of the accusations formally levelled at NATO were dismissed.[28]

There is a third argument that is of great legal importance. The question of whether the political authorities in a state, or in a military alliance between states, have the right to indiscriminately take the lives of people who are unquestionably innocent—women, children, elderly, sick, detainees, nomads—trading them off against those of others purportedly in danger of being killed and presumed to be innocent. Who has the power to deny the right to life of innocent people using instruments of mass destruction 'to do justice'? If it is true that the right to life is a fundamental personal right, the doctrine of human rights cannot be conceived of as a utilitarian theory that values the life and death of people in an aggregate way,

[27] Gaja, G., 'The Long Journey towards Repressing Aggression', in Cassese, A., Gaeta, P. and Jones, J. R. W. D. (eds.), *The Rome Statute of the International Criminal Court: A Commentary* (Oxford: Oxford University Press, 2002), 427–8.

[28] Zolo, D., *Invoking Humanity* (London: Continuum International, 2002), 5, 106–20.

adding and subtracting the good of life and the evil of death as though they were fungible or interchangeable. In my opinion, the authorities in a military alliance such as NATO cannot exert the power of life and death over innocent people as though they were the reincarnation of Roman popes who in the name of God gave their blessing to Catholic armies going off to massacre the infidels.

Ultimately, it must be asked in general whether modern warfare, with its means of mass destruction, can be 'contracted out' by the United Nations to the great powers, or to military alliances such as NATO, while attributing to them the role of protecting values deemed to be universal such as human rights. We thus find ourselves confronted with an antinomy. If we sustain the view that all individuals are subjects of the international legal system, since they are holders of inviolable and inalienable rights, this means that they are above all entitled to the right to life, reaffirmed in article 3 of the Universal Declaration of Human Rights of 1948. Second, the recognition of individuals as rights holders also involves recognizing the right to *habeas corpus*, another fundamental right contained in the Universal Declaration, which provides that nobody can be subjected to treatment that interferes with his/her physical integrity, liberty, relationships, or goods unless his/her behaviour has been examined and found to be in violation of criminal law. And this implies that everyone is entitled to 'a full and public hearing, by an independent and impartial tribunal'. Finally, in article 7, the Universal Declaration recognizes the right of everyone to equality before the law.

The legitimization of 'humanitarian war' would be a contradiction negating all of the principles discussed above. In the case of the war over Kosovo, for example, a collective death sentence was applied to thousands of Yugoslav citizens without any inquiry being conducted into their personal responsibility. The principle of equal legal treatment was also violated. It should not be forgotten that in the territory of the former Yugoslavia the alleged humanitarian protection of human rights was simultaneously pursued according to incompatible approaches. The International Criminal Tribunal for former Yugoslavia (ICTY) used its repressive power in application of the principle according to which nobody may be subjected to penal sanctions in the absence of a judgment holding them personally and intentionally responsible for the crimes committed. In addition, the Statute of the ICTY excludes the death penalty from its list of sanctions. This treatment, which at least formally respects certain important principles of the rule of law, was reserved for a tiny minority of citizens of the former Yugoslavia, most of whom held high-level positions within the political or military hierarchies and were accused of international crimes. On the other hand, thousands of ordinary citizens were subjected to a very different treatment—deadly bombardments which not only destroyed human lives but also caused serious damage to the civilian and productive infrastructures of an entire country.

The prohibition on aggressive war in the UN Charter cannot be considered in any case, to borrow another of Franck's expressions, to be a 'stupid, even evil' norm. In a manner not dissimilar from that of Ignatieff, a great apologist for liberty rights, Franck appears to forget that modern warfare constitutes the most radical negation of subjective rights. Modern wars conducted with increasingly sophisticated and deadly weapons are designed to destroy—disproportionately, indiscriminately, and without any limits—lives, goods, and rights. Only those who underestimate its destructive and deadly impact could exalt modern warfare as an appropriate instrument for the protection of rights and the achievement of justice. *Dulce bellum inexpertis*, warned Erasmus from Rotterdam many centuries ago.

IV. Humanitarian Intervention and International Law

The war over Kosovo appeared to have concretized the practice of humanitarian intervention, since the humanitarian motivation was explicitly assumed as a *justa causa* of a unilateral and asymmetric war. Nevertheless, the theory according to which the finality of human rights protection should prevail over respect for the integrity of a state's domestic jurisdiction, thereby justifying the use of force, is by no means compelling and may be countered with valid legal arguments. This is the case both for situations in which the use of force has been authorized by international institutions and even more so in those, such as in Kosovo, where it has not.

It can first of all be asserted, along with Bruno Simma, that there is no customary norm that, departing from the principles contained in the UN Charter, confers the Security Council with the power to authorize the use of force in humanitarian emergencies.[29] A customary rule of this type would have to emerge out of the uniform practice of states and a general conviction that their behaviour was legal. On the contrary, in this case the practice is anything but uniform with regard to the consistency of sanctioning violations. In several cases, for example in Somalia in 1992, it was considered necessary to have recourse to armed intervention, whereas in others, such as Chechnya, diplomatic measures in the form of a (mild) censure of the authorities in Moscow was all that was deemed necessary. In other cases again—the bloody repression of the Kurdish minority by Turkey—there was no reaction at all from the international community.

Other equally valid arguments may be used to counter the theories of many authors who, particularly in the United States and Great Britain, have lent their

---

[29] Simma, B., 'NATO, the UN and the Use of Force: Legal Aspects', *European Journal of International Law*, 10 (1999), 1, 3. According to Simma, 'In contemporary international law, as codified in the 1969 Vienna Convention on the Law of Treaties (articles 53 and 64), the prohibition enunciated in Article 2(4) of the Charter is part of *jus cogens*, i.e. it is accepted and recognized by the international community of states as a whole as a norm from which no derogation is permitted.'

support to the legitimacy of the use of force for humanitarian reasons even in the absence of an authorization from the Security Council. The strategies used to argue this case fall into three rough categories:

1. Under the most radical position, which is taken by authors such as Michael Ignatieff, Fernando Tesón, and Robert Keohane,[30] the international protection of human rights is legitimate and morally compulsory independent of international law. The norms in the UN Charter regulating the use of force are becoming more and more obsolete as an expression of the archaic Westphalian conception of international relations. The dogma of national state sovereignty should be abandoned and respect for domestic jurisdiction must be conceived as an instrumental value that should not obstruct the international community from intervening to prevent or halt atrocities such as the Rwandan genocide. In these cases, the failure of the international community to provide assistance is a behaviour that is viewed as being much more worthy of censure than a military intervention in violation of the positive norms of international law.

2. A second group of authors—among these are Michael Glennon[31] and Antonio Cassese—underline the requirement to update international law through the introduction of new norms that permit and regulate armed interventions for humanitarian reasons. The pronouncements made by Kofi Annan and the 16 members of the High Level Panel that he created in December 2004 supported this view. According to the Secretary General and his advisers, it was necessary to amend the provisions on the use of force by the Security Council, contained in chapter VII of the UN Charter, in order to include 'the collective international responsibility to protect'.[32] This would require a new hypothesis of intervention by the Security Council: an armed intervention against a state responsible for serious violations of the fundamental rights of its own citizens, even in the absence of a threat to international peace and security. The same proposal had already been made by the International Commission on Intervention and State Sovereignty (ICISS), created following an initiative by the Canadian government, in its report entitled *The Responsibility to Protect*, which was published in December 2001 and placed at the disposal of the United Nations.[33] Finally, on 28 April 2006, the Security Council adopted resolution 1674 which in its articles 4 and 26 confirmed the doctrine of the 'Responsibility to protect' and provided the Council with the

---

[30] Ignatieff, M., *Human Rights as Politics and Idolatry* (above, n. 2); Ignatieff, M., 'State Failure and Nation-Building,' in Holzgrefe, J. L. and Keohane, R. O. (eds.), *Humanitarian Intervention* (above, n. 3), 299; Tesón, F. R., 'The Liberal Case for Humanitarian Intervention', in Holzgrefe, J. L. and Keohane, R. O. (eds.), *Humanitarian Intervention* (above, n. 3); Keohane, R. O., 'Political Authority after Intervention: Gradation in Sovereignty', in J. L. Holzgrefe and R. O. Keohane (eds.), *Humanitarian Intervention* (above, n. 3), 272.

[31] Glennon, M. J., 'The New Interventionism' (above, n. 1).

[32] *A More Secure World: Our Shared Responsibility*, underline http://www.astrid-online.it/Cartella-p/ONU/index.htm.

[33] <http://www.iciss-ciise.gc.ca>.

possibility, when faced with a serious violation of human rights and international humanitarian law, to declare a threat to international peace and security and to adopt appropriate measures.[34] Antonio Cassese went much further by advocating the recognition of new international legal norms that would regulate armed humanitarian interventions in the absence of an authorization by the Security Council.[35]

3. Finally, other authors, in particular Jane Stromseth,[36] whose views are not far removed from those of Franck, have argued that it is futile and even erroneous to attempt to codify a new international humanitarian law that would, under certain conditions, justify the use of force in situations of 'humanitarian catastrophe'. This was, according to Stromseth, the situation in Kosovo in 1999, which rendered necessary the NATO military intervention, an intervention that was exemplary in its respect for the laws of war.[37] It is asserted by these authors that what is required is a flexible and evolutionary interpretation of international legal norms in such a way as to encourage the formation of new customary rules and to overcome the dogma of state sovereignty. What it is necessary is not the creation of new international legal norms coupled with a demand that these be rigorously interpreted and applied, as suggested by Cassese. On the contrary, the ambiguous legal status of humanitarian intervention should be maintained, this normative uncertainty providing fertile ground for the gradual emergence, case by case, of a consensus amongst the international community concerning the humanitarian use of force.

V. HUMANITARIAN MILITARISM

In my opinion, this sort of humanitarian militarism deserves, in each of its three varieties, to be subjected to theoretical critique and to be opposed in the political arena.[38] It is absolutely not about setting a superior, imaginary 'international

---

[34] United Nations Security Council, Resolution 1674, 28/4/2006, S/RES/1674 (2006). The Security Council Resolution does not have a general normative value and does not introduce a new hypothesis regarding the use of force in respect of that provided for in art. 39 of the UN Charter. For a critical analysis of the document and of the whole doctrine of the 'responsibility to protect' see Alvarez, J. E., *The Schizophrenias of R2P*, Panel Presentation at the 2007 Hague Joint Conference on Contemporary Issues of International Law, The Hague, the Netherlands, 30 June 2007.

[35] See Cassese, A., 'Ex iniuria ius oritur', *European Journal of International Law*, 10 (1999) 1, 23–5; Cassese, A., 'Zolo sbaglia, il diritto va aggiornato', in Bobbio, N., et al., *L'ultima crociata?* (Rome: I libri di Reset, 1999), 34. *Contra* Simma, B., 'NATO, the UN and the Use of Force: Legal Aspects' (above, n. 29), 1–6; Chinkin, C. M., 'Kosovo: A "Good" or "Bad" War?', *American Journal of International Law*, 93 (1999) 4, 841.

[36] Stromseth, J., 'Rethinking Humanitarian Intervention: The Case for Incremental Change', in Holzgrefe, J. L. and Keohane, R. O. (eds.), *Humanitarian Intervention* (above, n. 3), 232.

[37] Ibid. 249.

[38] Simma, B., 'NATO, the UN and the Use of Force: Legal Aspects' (above, n. 29); Luban, D., 'Intervention and Civilization: Some Unhappy Lessons of the Kosovo War' (above, n. 21), 79; Miller, R. W., 'Respectable Oppressors,

ethic' off against the 'international ethics' supported by the proponents of armed humanitarian intervention. It is more a question of demanding in political and legal terms the respect for and the application of the principles and rules of international law in force, in particular those norms for the defence of international security, peace, and the protection of human rights. The risk of humanitarian militarism is that it will lead to the legitimization of the unilateral and asymmetric use of military force by those that claim to be great powers. The multiplication of arguments for the legal or moral legitimacy of recourse to violence may cause a weakening of the already limited normative and regulatory capacities of international law. The end result will be that the institutional and normative mechanisms that currently control the use of international force will vanish and the entire apparatus of the United Nations will be reduced to legitimating the *status quo* imposed by a few states through the use, or the threat of the use, of their overwhelming military power. The 'humanitarian' proposals for an open violation of international law in the name of superior ethical principles, and the hypothesis of a militaristic 'update' of international law in either codified or customary form, would both equally erode the prospect of less ruthless and more pacific international relations.

The Western ideology of humanitarian intervention, which claims to promote Western values throughout the world—such as the Western values underlying the doctrines of human rights and of democracy—in reality coincides with a generalized strategy of promotion of the 'vital interests' of individual 'humanitarian' states, or alliances of these, presented as the interests of the international community which must prevail over national sovereignty. The weakening of the multilateral system of collective security through the waging of unilateral and asymmetrical wars entails a return to the 'anarchic' situation that preceded the creation of the international institutions in the last century such as the League of Nations and the United Nations. In a context tending towards anarchy, the increasing claims to the legitimacy of the use of force by the great powers is one of the possible causes of the parallel rise of so-called 'global terrorism'.

The war by NATO over Kosovo proved the technological, informational, and military supremacy of the Western armies. It also showed the willingness of the United States to make use of its own military supremacy without taking international law into consideration, attributing to itself an absolute *jus ad bellum* that would find its extreme expression several years later in the aggressive war against Iraq. Terrorism, particularly that which is purportedly based in Islam, could be considered as the anarchic and nihilistic reply to the nihilism of those states attempting to dominate the world through the systematic use of force. Terrorist fundamentalism

Hypocritical Liberators: Morality, Intervention, and Reality', in Chatterjee, D. K., and Scheid, D. E. (eds.), *Ethics and Foreign Intervention* (Cambridge: Cambridge University Press, 2003); Byers, M., and Chesterman, S., 'Changing the Rules about Rules? Unilateral Humanitarian Intervention and the Future of International Law', in Holzgrefe, J. L., and Keohane, R. O. (eds.), *Humanitarian Intervention* (above, n. 3), 177.

is a response to the fundamentalism of a power that has the tendency to assume hegemonic and despotic characteristics on a global scale.

There is no doubt that it is necessary today to ensure the international, and not only national, protection of human rights. It would, however, be illusory to think that it is possible to construct a sort of global state based on a cosmopolitan rule of law that transcends national state structures. If the objectives of international law are peace and security, then the problem is to ensure that transnational interventions for the protection of human rights are compatible with cultural diversity, including the identity and dignity of peoples and the integrity of the legal-political structures that they have freely established. The use of military force by the great powers cannot obliterate the underlying causes that throughout the world—the Palestinian, Iraqi, and Chechen situations are cases in point—lead to the explosion of civil wars, of bloody ethnic conflicts, and to ethnic cleansing and genocide. Civil wars have deep motivations that cannot be suffocated by military force but it is necessary to try to stem them by getting the people involved as central protagonists in the peace process. Military intervention by a great power—which inevitably occurs too late—not only fails to resolve conflicts but very often leads to their aggravation, adding atrocity to atrocity, suffering to suffering, hatred to hatred, as has been seen in Kosovo but also in Somalia, Afghanistan, and, most strikingly, in Iraq. Given this situation, the ambitions of single powers, or military alliances such as NATO, to set themselves up as the universal custodians of human rights and democratic institutions must be rejected. The respect for rights and the subordination of power to democratic rules are delicate goods that only the development of civil institutions, the acquisition of a minimum level of economic well-being, and above all a commitment to cultural debate and to political struggle can produce locally. This will occur only within the timeframe and according to the customs of cultures that are often far removed from the Western traditions of the rule of law and the doctrine of human rights. Any other approach—including the rhetoric of the 'Responsibility to protect'—runs the risk of being little more than cultural imperialism and, in more serious cases, imperialism *tout court*.

SECTION XIV

INTERNATIONAL CRIMINAL LAW

FAIRNESS TO RIGHTNESS: JURISDICTION, LEGALITY, AND THE LEGITIMACY OF INTERNATIONAL CRIMINAL LAW

DAVID LUBAN*

I. WHAT IS INTERNATIONAL CRIMINAL LAW?

As the name suggests, 'international criminal law' (ICL) refers to applications of criminal law across borders. ICL encompasses three overlapping bodies of law:

(1) *Domestic criminal law applied transnationally.* The oldest and least controversial is the application of a state's domestic criminal law to conduct outside the state's borders. Criminal law represents governments' efforts to protect important societal interests, and obviously assaults on those interests can come from outside the state as well as inside. A hacker in Russia steals identities in Argentina; drug smugglers in Malaysia conspire to sell heroin in the United States; a sniper in Serbia assassinates

* I would like to thank Antony Duff, Paul Kahn, Jenny Martinez, Steve Ratner, and John Tasioulas for comments on an earlier version of this paper, as well as participants in the workshops related to this volume and workshops at Wake Forest University, Temple Law School, and Yale Law School.

a pedestrian in Bosnia. There is nothing conceptually problematic about Argentina, Bosnia, or the United States recognizing these as domestic-law crimes and punishing the perpetrators if the states can catch them. Difficulties arise only because conduct outside one state's territory almost always occurs within the territory of another state with its own sovereign interests. That raises questions of which state interests justify transgressing borders to legislate conduct in another state's territory, and how states should resolve conflicts over criminal jurisdiction. These are profound questions, because seemingly-arcane issues of jurisdiction mirror philosophical issues about state sovereignty and its limits.

Traditional legal theory offers well-defined answers to the first question. The theory begins with the recognition that a state consists of a territory, the people who live in it, and a government. These are, of course, merely the material constituents of the state—its Aristotelian 'material cause'—and a complete theory of the state would also need to specify the structural relationships among these constituents and the aims of state organization: the state's formal and final causes. But the traditional legal theory derives state interests from the constituent elements alone, generating four jurisdictional principles:

(a) The *territorial principle*, which gives states jurisdiction over crimes committed in their territories, as well as crimes committed elsewhere with effects in their territories.

(b) The *nationality principle*, which gives states jurisdiction over crimes committed by their own nationals.

(c) The *passive personality principle*, which gives states jurisdiction over crimes committed against their nationals.

(d) The *protective principle*, which gives states jurisdiction over crimes committed against vital governmental interests—crimes like espionage, for example, or counterfeiting the state's currency, or smuggling immigrants or contraband across its borders.

These familiar principles are staples of every international law textbook. That does not mean they lack challenges or perplexities; some states push the principles further than others are willing to accept. The fact remains, however, that all states accept the core of the four principles.

Most states also accept—in theory, at least—so-called *universal criminal jurisdiction* (UCJ), which allows any state to prosecute certain crimes committed anywhere in the world. Grotius asserted that every state has jurisdiction over 'gross violations of the law of nature and of nations, done to other states and subjects'.[1] However, for many years, piracy was the only recognized UCJ crime, not because of its moral

---

[1] Grotius, H., *The Rights of War and Peace, Including the Law of Nature and of Nations [De Jure Belli ac Pacis]*, Campbell, A. C. (trans.) (Washington and London: M. Walter Dunne, 1901) (Elibron Classics reprint), II.20.XL, 247.

awfulness but because it is committed outside the territorial jurisdiction of all states. More recently, legislators as well as theorists have returned to Grotius's 'moralized' rationale, and proposed UCJ over the narrow set of crimes that are subject to international tribunals: genocide, crimes against humanity, war crimes, and torture. But this proposal has met with mixed responses among states as well as theorists, and in recent years has encountered significant political opposition. The opposition arises from the fear that UCJ would lead to politicized prosecutions. During a short and ill-fated experiment with universal jurisdiction, Belgium launched investigations, many based on complaints by advocacy groups, of numerous world leaders—until threats by the United States forced Belgium to repeal its UCJ statute.[2] Critics charged that Belgium's courts had become the tool of political interests. But supporters of UCJ can respond (rightly, in my view) that the real politicized abuses in such cases are the crimes politicians commit under colour of their office, nonchalantly assuming that their power should grant them impunity.

The theoretical question arises of what state interests UCJ serves. Universal jurisdiction does not assume any tangible connection between the crime and the state. It seems, therefore, that UCJ can be justified only if states have distinctively moral interests in repressing crimes (or at least certain crimes) wherever they occur. That assumption is hard to reconcile with liberal or minimalist accounts of the legitimacy of state power: liberals generally suppose that states have no self-standing moral interests, and minimalists argue that legitimate state power includes only the smallest set of powers necessary to protect the security and well-being of the state's citizens. In my view, the real basis for UCJ lies in the idea that perpetrators of infamies offend not against state interests but human interests—the perpetrators are indeed 'enemies of all mankind'—and that states prosecuting infamies under UCJ act merely as surrogates. This assumption that major international crimes are, quite literally, crimes against humanity (regardless of their legal label), is debatable.[3] But the assumption underlies not only UCJ, but also international tribunals to

---

[2] Belgian procedure permits crime victims to initiate criminal prosecutions; and none of the high-profile prosecutions originated with state prosecutors. For the most thorough English-language study of UCJ, see Reydams, L., *Universal Jurisdiction* (Oxford: Oxford University Press, 2003). Reydams is highly critical of ambitious use of UCJ. On the political crisis created by Belgium's prosecutions, see Frankel, G., 'Belgian War Crimes Law Undone by Its Global Reach, Cases Against Political Figures Sparked Crises', *Washington Post*, 30 Sept. 2003. The legitimacy under international law of universal jurisdiction was debated in the *Arrest Warrant Case* (Democratic Republic of Congo v. Belgium), International Court of Justice, General List No. 121, 14 Feb. 2002. The case concerned Belgian efforts to arrest Congo's foreign minister for international crimes. Although the ICJ decided the case in Congo's favour without reaching the question of whether international law permits UCJ, several judges wrote separate opinions on that question, of which the opinions of Judges Guillaume and Bula-Bula against UCJ, and Judges van den Wyngaert, Buergenthal, Higgins, and Kooijmans (the latter three in a joint opinion), favouring UCJ, are particularly interesting. Judge Bula-Bula emphasizes the neo-colonialist implications of Belgium prosecuting an official of its former colony; and, in this connection, it is significant that other famous UCJ cases involved Spanish efforts to prosecute officials of Argentina, Mexico, Guatemala and Chile.

[3] I defend the claim in Luban, D., 'A Theory of Crimes Against Humanity', *Yale Journal of International Law*, 29 (2004), 124.

try these crimes. Without it we shall have a hard time justifying any distinctively international criminal law.

(2) *Treaty-based or 'hybrid' transnational criminal law.* Beginning in the early twentieth century, states began to recognize that crimes committed by multinational criminal gangs can be repressed only through international cooperation. The result has been multilateral treaties on subjects ranging from counterfeiting and drug trafficking to war crimes and *apartheid*. The treaties share a common structure: they require parties to enact domestic criminal laws against the conduct; they require parties with custody of an accused offender either to extradite the suspect to a state with jurisdiction over the crime or to prosecute the crime themselves; and they require parties to establish a kind of UCJ that will enable them to prosecute the crime if extradition fails. Treaty-based international crimes are a hybrid of domestic criminal law applied transnationally and what I shall later call 'pure' international criminal law. On the domestic-law side, the point of the treaty is to get states to use their municipal legal systems to repress crimes like aerial hijacking or narco-trafficking. On the international side, however, these treaties create a distinctive kind of domestic criminal law: a body of criminal laws governing deeds of international rather than merely domestic concern—laws, moreover, that would not exist without international efforts to establish them.

(3) *'Pure' ICL.* Finally, there is a distinctive body of law that originated in the post-World War II international tribunals, designed to punish a handful of the most evil crimes: crimes against humanity, genocide, serious war crimes, and aggressive war. Most people who speak of ICL have these crimes and these tribunals in mind. There is no accepted name for this category of crimes. One might call them 'the great crimes', because they represent the very worst atrocities that people commit against each other. Typically, they are mass atrocities; indeed some scholars (not including me) argue they must meet some threshold level of awfulness, involving hundreds or thousands of victims, before they become the legitimate business of the international community rather than domestic criminal justice systems. One might also call them 'tribunal crimes', because they are the subject-matter of the Nuremberg and Tokyo tribunals, the International Criminal Tribunal for the Former Yugoslavia (ICTY) and the International Criminal Tribunal for Rwanda (ICTR), the Special Courts for Sierra Leone, Cambodia, and East Timor, and the International Criminal Court (ICC). But 'tribunal crimes' is not entirely accurate: States can enact domestic laws to punish them—Canada, for example, has a statute on crimes against humanity, and many states have anti-genocide statutes. Iraq executed Saddam Hussein for crimes against humanity under Iraq's own criminal code. Furthermore, as we have seen, proponents of UCJ believe that the great crimes can be tried by any state that gains custody of the perpetrator. I shall usually refer to them as 'pure international crimes'—pure, in that their criminal character originated in international rather than domestic law, and international rather than domestic legal institutions.

These three bodies of ICL overlap, and not only because treaty-based international crimes and pure international crimes can be prosecuted within domestic legal systems. They also overlap because, as pure international criminal law developed, it has added some treaty-based crimes to its list of offences. Notwithstanding the overlap among these three bodies of ICL, the remainder of this paper focuses on pure international crimes, because these raise distinctive problems and, now that the ICC is up and running, they are especially compelling.

II. The Roots of Pure ICL

Although there were intimations of ICL prior to World War II, ICL in its modern form originated at Nuremberg, and was fortified by the United Nations' resolution recognizing genocide as a crime. The Nuremberg Charter defined three categories of crimes: *crimes against peace* (the planning or launching of aggressive war), *war crimes*, and *crimes against humanity* (gross violence and persecution against civilian populations, including within one's own state). The Nuremberg framers, particularly chief US prosecutor Robert Jackson, focused principally on the crime of aggressive war, which, self-evidently, can be launched only by a group. Furthermore, at Nuremberg the definitions of crimes against peace and crimes against humanity both emphasized the organized, group-based nature of their perpetration. This emphasis on group perpetrators persists to the present day. Under the Rome Statute of the ICC, war crimes must either be widespread or else the result of a plan or policy; and crimes against humanity require a 'widespread or systematic attack against a civilian population', where 'attack against a civilian population' is defined as an attack resulting from or furthering a state or organizational policy.

The crime of genocide has a different emphasis. To be sure, genocide appears in Nuremberg law as the crime against humanity of extermination; but in current law the two crimes are defined differently, and therein hangs a tale. The word 'genocide' was coined by the remarkable Polish-Jewish lawyer Raphael Lemkin, in his 1944 book *Axis Rule in Europe*. Lemkin's word did not catch on immediately. It appears in the earliest draft of the Nuremberg Charter, but disappears (I don't know why) from subsequent drafts. After the war, Lemkin launched a tireless one-man lobbying campaign to recognize the uniqueness of the crime of genocide. It was all the more remarkable because Lemkin was a refugee with no family, no job, no money, and no connections—the 'totally unofficial man', in the words of an admiring 1957 newspaper editorial.[4] Miraculously, his campaign succeeded a few years later, when the United Nations opened the Convention on the Prevention and Punishment

---

[4] Quoted in Power, S., *'A Problem from Hell', America and the Age of Genocide* (New York: Basic Books, 2002), 76. Power's narrative of Lemkin's career is riveting.

of the Crime of Genocide for state adoption. (After the vote, reporters found the exhausted Lemkin alone in a side room, weeping.) Parting company with the framers of the Nuremberg Charter, Lemkin focused not on the group character of the perpetrators but the group character of the victims. Lemkin believed that groups as such possess value over and above the value of all the individuals in them.[5] Thus, to qualify as genocide, an attack must be directed against national, ethnic, religious, or racial groups 'as such', and intended to destroy the group in whole or in part.

The curious result of Jackson's and Lemkin's emphasis on group perpetrators and group victims was that at its origin, modern ICL had little to do with individual human rights. Jackson was principally interested in criminalizing aggressive war; crimes against humanity focus on 'civilian populations', not individual rights; and Lemkin cared about national minorities as groups, rather than as collections of individuals.

Only after the human rights revolution that began with the 1948 Universal Declaration of Human Rights have we come to think of ICL as the use of criminal law to enforce basic human rights. This is a retrospective reinterpretation of the original impetus for ICL, and both Jackson and Lemkin would have thought it a misinterpretation. Misinterpretation or not, however, it has become the dominant conception of ICL, and today we take it for granted that ICL aims to mobilize international institutions against gross human rights violations, just as domestic criminal law mobilizes governmental institutions against domestic rights violations.

III. The Aims of International Criminal Trials

From its inception at Nuremberg, there has always been something extraordinary about pure ICL and the tribunals that adjudicate it. Dealing as it does with acts of extraordinary violence, systematically perpetrated, and typically on a large scale, pure ICL comes into play only in times of cataclysm: wars and civil wars, bloody ethnic or religious struggles, political upheavals, revolutions or other changes of basic political systems. Instead of being normal parts of the daily functioning of government, international criminal trials occur after governments have fallen or been radically altered.

The trials then form part of *transitional justice*—the legal regimes that arise when one form of government replaces another.[6] Where ordinary criminal law

---

[5] Lemkin, R., *Axis Rule in Occupied Europe* (New York: Carnegie Foundation, 1944), 91. For criticism of this idea, see Kukathas, C., 'Genocide and Group Rights' (unpublished).

[6] The important observation that ICL emerges from the confluence of domestic criminal law, human rights law, and transitional justice comes from Danner, A. M. and Martinez, J. S., 'Guilty Associations, Joint Criminal

is a product of continuity, pure ICL is a product of discontinuity, of upheaval and political rupture. Inevitably, then, the trials take on political overtones; and sometimes the requirements of politics and those of criminal justice are in tension with each other. Politics is broad, partial, and forward-looking; criminal justice is supposed to be narrow and impartial.

The foundational question about criminal law is what justifies punishment, which is, after all, a form of state violence. Standard justifications (retribution, general and special deterrence, incapacitation, rehabilitation) all raise familiar and difficult justificatory problems, which are no less acute in ICL than they are in domestic legal systems. To be sure, they may take on different configurations in ICL than those familiar from domestic criminal justice. For example, special deterrence will seldom be necessary, because the defendant in the dock of an international tribunal is unlikely ever again to be in the circumstances in which he committed his crime. For related reasons, there is scant need to incapacitate or rehabilitate many low-level perpetrators, who (under the familiar dynamics of the 'banality of evil') may be ordinary, law-abiding citizens, good men and good neighbours, in peacetime.[7] On the other hand, incapacitating toxic political leaders—a Goering, a Milosevic, a Charles Taylor—can be absolutely crucial.

But, in addition to the familiar quartet of retribution-deterrence-incapacitation-rehabilitation, ICL recognizes other purposes, and these raise problems of their own. The curious feature about ICL is that in it the emphasis shifts from punishments to trials. Thus, it is often said that the goal of ICL lies in promoting social reconciliation, giving victims a voice, or making a historical record of mass atrocities to help secure the past against deniers and revisionists. The legitimacy of these goals can be questioned, because they seem extrinsic to purely legal values. But what is often overlooked is that, legitimate or not, they are goals of trials, not punishments. Indeed, the punishment of the guilty seems almost an afterthought (not to them, of course). Perhaps that is because, as one often says, no punishment can fit crimes of such enormity; or because compared with their trial, their punishment lacks didactic and dramatic force. Whatever the reason, it is remarkable that the centre of gravity so often lies in the proceedings rather than in their aftermath. That is not an objection to the trials, if they are conducted fairly. But the use of the trial as political theatre puts pressure on its fairness; furthermore, international trials have at best a spotty track-record of promoting social reconciliation, giving victims a voice, and making a record.[8] Under some circumstances, truth and reconciliation commissions may

Enterprise, Command Responsibility, and the Development of International Criminal Law', *California Law Review*, 93 (2005), 78.

[7] This is a key point in Drumbl, M. A., *Atrocity Punishment and International Law* (New York: Cambridge University Press, 2007).

[8] Martti Koskenniemi advances these criticisms with great force in 'Between Impunity and Show Trials', *Max Planck Yearbook of International Law*, 6 (2002), 1. One problem is that the forensic setting can backfire, and license all-out assaults on witnesses and history. In Canada's *Zundel* and *Finta* trials, Douglas Christie,

do a better job, without the need for punishment; if so, the question of what justifies punishments in international criminal trials becomes even more compelling.

In my view, the most promising justification for international tribunals is their role in *norm projection*: trials are expressive acts broadcasting the news that mass atrocities are, in fact, heinous crimes and not merely politics by other means. In recent years, philosophers have studied expressive theories of punishment; the norm-projection rationale adds an expressive theory of trials.[9] As the Allies recognized at Nuremberg, the alternatives to trying murderous generals and politicians are summary punishment or impunity, each of which, in its own way, is a backhanded admission that *raison d'état* and *Kriegsraison* are a legitimate part of public morality. Only trials can communicate the inherent criminality of political violence against the innocent. The decision not to stage criminal trials is no less an expressive act than the creation of tribunals; and the expressive contents associated with impunity or summary punishment are unacceptable: both are assertions that political crime lies outside the law. The point of trials backed by punishment is to assert the realm of law against the claims of politics.[10]

Although the centre of gravity in international tribunals lies in the trial, not the punishment, punishment following conviction remains an essential part of any criminal process that aims to project a no-impunity norm. Truth and reconciliation commissions have important virtues, but they have a hard time escaping the unwelcome expressive contents that go with impunity: these crimes, they seem to say, are not for the law to handle. Sometimes, no doubt, the short-term need for political reconciliation in a war-shattered society will outweigh the longer-term importance of asserting the realm of law. But all forms of impunity, including politically indispensable impunity, carry the cost of perpetuating a world in which political violence is presumed to transcend law.

Of the traditional aims of punishment, norm projection most closely resembles retribution, at least when retribution is understood, as Jean Hampton proposes, as

a well-prepared, strategically adept defence lawyer, badgered, humiliated, and confused Holocaust survivor witnesses, accused expert-witness historians of relying on hearsay (as if historians ever rely on anything else!), boldly denied that the Nazis had ever gassed Jews, and, in Finta's case, won an acquittal for crimes against humanity. See the disturbing accounts of the *Zundel* case in Douglas, L., *The Memory of Judgment: Making Law and History in the Trials of the Holocaust* (New Haven: Yale University Press, 2001), and *Finta* in Landsman, S., *Crimes of the Holocaust: The Law Confronts Hard Cases* (Philadelphia: University of Pennsylvania Press, 2005).

[9] I am sympathetic with the view of expressivism in Anderson, E. S. and Pildes, R. H., 'Expressive Theories of Law, A General Restatement', *University of Pennsylvania Law Review*, 148 (2000), 1503, and the expressive accounts of punishment in Duff, R. A., *Trials and Punishments* (Cambridge: Cambridge University Press, 1986), 235, and Jean Hampton's contributions to her and Jeffrie G. Murphy's *Forgiveness and Mercy* (Cambridge: Cambridge University Press, 1988). Robert Sloane and Mark Drumble have also argued that the expressive function of punishment and Mark Drumbl have is the one most suitable for international criminal law. Sloane, R. D., 'The Expressive Capacity of International Punishment', *Stanford International Law Journal*, 43 (2007), 39 and Drumble, M. A. *Atrocity and International Law* (above n. 7, 11–12, 173–9).

[10] In Duff's words, 'to remain silent in the face of crime would be to betray the values which the law expresses, and to which we are committed'. Duff, R. A., *Trials and Punishments* (above, n. 9), 236.

an *expressive defeat* that reasserts moral truth against the wrongdoer's devaluation of the victim.[11] But ICL uses the ceremonial of the trial, rather than the infliction of punishment, as its primary vehicle for expressing moral truth; and the moral truth it expresses is not the moral equality of perpetrator and victim, as Hampton suggests is the aim of retributive punishment. Rather, ICL's moral truth is the criminality of political violence against the innocent, even when your side hates the innocent as an enemy. Carl Schmitt famously defined 'the concept of the political' as the friend/enemy relation, with the strong implication that political violence against the enemy defines the human condition and lies beyond good and evil. The moral truth that international tribunals express is, quite simply, the negation of this familiar political amoralism. International criminal law stands for the proposition that crime is crime regardless of its political trappings.

IV. National Sovereignty and the Legitimacy of International Tribunals

The major obstacle to establishing ICL lies in the international character of its tribunals, which subjects acts of sovereign states to criminal scrutiny by the 'international community', something of a gaseous invertebrate under the classical Westphalian theory of equal sovereign states.

As I suggested in the preceding section, characterizing sovereign acts as crimes is a momentous, even utopian, decision. As Paul Kahn has argued, in the Western political imagination, states are gods, and this is no less true of contemporary secular states.[12] Like gods, states do not admit their own mortality, and they demand devotion and obedience. Every state, liberal constitutional states no less than absolute monarchies, claims the ultimate authority over its citizens: to make them die and kill on the sovereign's behalf. That a state has no military draft at the moment is irrelevant: all states claim the authority to conscript, and all states cloak the profoundly illiberal project of sacrificing lives for the supposed salvation of others in the language of religion. The American soldier killed in the line of duty in Iraq has made 'the ultimate sacrifice' for his country, politicians' language nearly identical to Islamists' talk of 'martyrdom'.

Viewed from outside a religion, human sacrifice looks like murder or suicide. Viewed from within, it is a non-criminal and in fact supremely meaningful form of violence. Kierkegaard described Abraham's sacrifice of Isaac as a 'teleological

---

[11] Hampton, J., 'The Retributive Idea', in Hampton, J. and Murphy, J. G., *Forgiveness and Mercy*, (above, n. 8), 124.

[12] Kahn, P. W., *Putting Liberalism in Its Place* (Princeton: Princeton University Press, 2005), 228.

suspension of the ethical', meaning not that it was a justified killing but that the language of justification simply does not apply to it. The kinds of mass violence that ICL addresses take place within what participants regard as struggles to the death between groups, in which killing and humiliating the enemy likewise seems like a supremely meaningful form of violence. When ICL redescribes it as crime—mere crime, nothing more—the effect is not much different than redescribing the sacrifice of Isaac as an attempted murder. In one sense, the description is straightforward and uncontroversial. But it is only straightforward once we stand outside the religion of state, race, ethnicity, and nation, and dismiss them as gods that failed. Within the religion, crime-talk is blasphemy.

For that reason, establishing a pure international criminal law of universal application is a momentous and radical project, equivalent in its way to the early secularists' deflationary view of state authority as manifestation of human rather than divine will. We are not there yet. Not even the so-called 'likeminded' states that promote the ICL project are heretical enough to reject the religion of sovereignty. For states to call other states 'gods that failed' is a Damoclean sword, for they themselves are nothing more than gods that have not yet failed.

In legal terms, the gulf between the transcendent claims of sovereignty and its deflation in ICL raises the jurisdictional question of what right international tribunals have to try nationals of states that do not wish them to be tried. For each of the principal tribunals, the jurisdictional question received an answer that was only partly satisfactory on classical Westphalian terms:

(1) At Nuremberg, the four major powers conducted the trial, but none of the traditional principles of transnational criminal jurisdiction except universality can explain why Great Britain (for example) could try Germans for the persecution of Jews in Germany or the murder of Gypsies in Poland. Allied lawyers argued that Germany's unconditional surrender and the collapse of the Nazi regime made them Germany's new government, but under pre-existing treaty law an occupying power must maintain the laws of the occupied country—a constraint that obviously reflects classical ideas about the sacredness of state sovereignty.[13] The Nuremberg Tribunal, criminalizing conduct even if it was legal under Nazi law, violated this sovereignty-based principle of treaty law.

(2) The United Nations Security Council (UNSC) established both the Yugoslav and Rwanda tribunals under its peacekeeping powers, but the Security Council's powers are themselves limited by states jealous of their sovereignty. The UNSC can act only to 'maintain or restore international peace and security' (the condition given in article 39 of the UN Charter); and the argument that post-conflict trials would help

---

[13] For discussion of the jurisdiction problem at Nuremberg, see Woetzel, R. K., *The Nuremberg Trials in International Law* (New York: Praeger, 1960), 54, esp. 82. The treaty law is article 43 of the 1907 Hague Convention.

maintain or restore international peace and security was speculative and perhaps even far-fetched. The more hostile critics thought—not without reason—that the true aim of the tribunals was to deflect attention from the politically embarrassing fact that neither the Security Council nor any of the major powers did much to stop the atrocities while they were happening.

(3) The ICC operates on a theory of delegated jurisdiction—that is, states parties transfer to the ICC their own territorial and nationality jurisdiction over pure international crimes. But it is far from obvious that criminal jurisdiction is something a state *can* legitimately delegate to whomever it chooses. If it can delegate criminal jurisdiction to the ICC, then why not to the Kansas City dog-catcher, the World Chess Federation, or the Rolling Stones?

Even with the added premise that sovereignty never includes the right to commit the great crimes, we need an additional step to reach the proposition that outsiders can try and punish them. As we saw in the earlier discussion of UCJ, that step will require us to recognize a kind of universal moral interest in condemning the great crimes. This moral interest has precious little institutional embodiment, however. Obviously, there is no political community called 'humanity' that authorizes the tribunals; nor are they products of anything like a world government.

V. Legitimacy Through Fairness

My own view is that the legitimacy of international tribunals comes not from the shaky political authority that creates them, but from the manifested fairness of their procedures and punishments. Tribunals bootstrap themselves into legitimacy by the quality of justice they deliver; their rightness depends on their fairness. During the first Nuremberg trials, prosecutors fretted that acquittals would delegitimize the tribunal; in hindsight, it quickly became apparent that the three acquittals were the best thing that could have happened, because they proved that Nuremberg was no show trial.

In the same way, it is essential that the ICTY, ICTR, and ICC deliver champagne-quality due process and fair, humane punishments—which, in most respects, they do.[14] Lacking world government to authorize international tribunals like the ICC, their authority must be largely self-generated by strict adherence to natural justice. Only in that way can they project a normative vision that might compete with the Westphalian orthodoxy.

---

[14] The only real criticism of the ICC so far is that its statute does not establish an office of defence counsel along with the highly professionalized prosecutor's office. Some observers criticize ICTY and ICTR for tolerating low quality defence counsel.

The term 'natural justice' is perhaps a misnomer, because the basic procedural rights recognized world-wide today are products of centuries of tinkering, not pure reason alone. As embodied in international treaties, they include the right to a speedy, public trial before an impartial tribunal that bases its decision solely on the evidence, under rules designed to reach accurate verdicts; the right to offer a defence; the right to be informed of the charges, in a language that the accused understands, through a written indictment that specifies the charges and the conduct charged; the right of the accused to confront the witnesses against him; the right of the accused to have compulsory process for obtaining witnesses in his favour; the right to counsel and the privilege against self-incrimination; and the ban on double jeopardy (*ne bis in idem*).[15] Natural justice also includes the right to appeal; and it includes familiar duties of prosecutors: to pursue cases only when there is probable cause, to disclose exculpatory evidence to the accused, and more generally, to seek justice rather than victory. Finally, it includes humane conditions of confinement and reasonable punishments.

One important fact about these requirements is that only tribunals that have some kind of internationally recognized state authorization—paradigmatically, authorization by a multilateral group such as the UN—are likely to be able to satisfy them. Evidence must be gathered from foreign war zones by trustworthy and impartial investigators, evidentiary chains of custody must be maintained, defence counsel and judges recruited and paid, defence witnesses subpoenaed across borders, appellate panels created and staffed, rules written, safe, humane prisons found, and long-term confinements monitored. Realistically, only states can carry out these tasks. Thus, even though I believe the legitimacy of international tribunals arises from their fairness rather than their political pedigree (their state authorization), in actual fact state authorization will be contingently indispensable to achieve procedural fairness. That, ultimately, is why it will not do to grant criminal jurisdiction to the Rolling Stones or the World Chess Federation. Once we look carefully at what it actually takes to achieve fair procedures and punishments, the natural-justice account turns out not to be vulnerable to imaginary counter-examples in which vigilantes abduct defendants, try them 'fairly', and punish them. No such vigilantes could hope to meet the stringent requirements of natural justice.

Not every civilized legal system satisfies all the requirements of natural justice. (In my view, the United States, with its savagely harsh prison sentences and brutal super-maximum security units, violates the last two conditions.) It may not be essential that international tribunals be tops along every dimension of natural justice; but, because tribunals must earn their legitimacy rather than inheriting it, they cannot be far from the top on any of them.

---

[15] All these rights can be found in articles 14 and 15 of the International Covenant on Civil and Political Rights, as well as the Rome Statute of the ICC.

VI. The Principle of Legality

In criminal law, the most fundamental requirement of natural justice is the Principle of Legality. Traditionally, the principle received expression in the Roman maxims *nullum crimen sine lege* (no crime without law) and *nulla poena sine lege* (no punishment without law). The first means that conduct may be criminalized only if publicly-accessible law spells out all the elements of the crime; the second means that the law must, in addition, sentence only according to a legally-specified scheme of punishments. Combining these, the Principle of Legality asserts that conduct may be criminalized and punished only if the crimes and punishments are explicitly established by publicly-accessible law. The Principle seems close to the core of the rule of law, in two distinct ways: first, by tying crime and punishment to law rather than the ruler's arbitrary will; and second, by insisting that law must be publicly accessible, therefore integrated into the daily life of the people it governs.

The Principle of Legality generates corollaries, as important as the principle itself: the prohibition on vaguely-defined crimes, requirements of fair notice and non-retroactivity, and the principle of lenity, which asserts that if a criminal statute is ambiguous, the version most favourable to the defendant is the correct version. Each of these helps ensure that people are not punished for conduct that they had no definitive way to know had been criminalized. In the remainder of this paper, I examine, and attempt to resolve, some significant tensions between pure international criminal law and the Principle of Legality.

The most obvious such tension, which figured prominently at Nuremberg, is simply that the tribunal applied novel law retroactively. Although war crimes are a traditional category of criminal law, crimes against peace and crimes against humanity were novel. The problem of retroactivity dogged the *ad hoc* tribunals as well, because they were established after the crimes. True, their statutes were modelled on pre-existing ICL, so the substantive criminal law was not retroactive.[16] But the ICTY broke legal ground on important issues, most dramatically in its holding that the war crimes law governing international armed conflict applied in the Bosnian civil war as well.[17]

---

[16] The substantive criminal law of the ICTY statute combines the war crimes provisions of the Hague and Geneva Conventions, the Genocide Convention, and the definition of crimes against humanity drawn from Allied Control Council Law No. 10, which slightly modified the Nuremberg Charter and was used in the second round of Nuremberg trials. The ICTR statute also uses familiar definitions of crimes drawn from pre-existing law.

[17] International Criminal Tribunal for the Former Yugoslavia, *Prosecutor v. Dusko Tadic* (Case IT-94-1-A), Judgement of 15 July 1999, paras. 68–171, available at <http://www.un.org/icty/tadic/appeal/judgement/tad-aj990715e.pdf>. All websites were most recently checked in Nov. 2007.

Larry May, in his book *Crimes Against Humanity*, argues that the Principle of Legality requires defendants to receive fair notice of all elements of the crime, including the jurisdictional element. In May's words, 'defendants should have been able to see, at the time they acted, that what they were doing was a violation of international law'. The ICTY violates the fair notice principle because the tribunal post-dated the crimes. May objects to the 'plight'—his word—'of some of the Bosnian Serb "small fry" now in jail at The Hague who had no hint that their acts, as unspeakable as they may be, were even remotely likely to land them in jail and awaiting trial before an international tribunal'.[18]

Finally, as Allison Danner and Jenny Martinez have argued, the contemporary connection between ICL and international human rights law creates a standing tension between ICL and the Principle of Legality.[19] Human rights law adopts the standpoint of protecting victims, and therefore requires laws to be read broadly in cases of ambiguity.[20] But criminal law adopts the standpoint of protecting defendants, and the principle of lenity requires ambiguous statutes to be read narrowly.

To illustrate the conflict: common article 3 of the Geneva Conventions offers a list of basic human rights that must be guaranteed to all captives in armed conflicts not of an international character, for example protection against 'outrages upon personal dignity', including humiliating or degrading treatment. In so far as article 3 is a human rights instrument, the vague notion of 'outrages upon personal dignity' must be read expansively. But in so far as article 3 is also a criminal prohibition—as it was, for example, in US law, where until 2006 all violations of article 3 were war crimes—it must be read as narrowly as possible. The Principle of Legality gave a pretext to US President George W. Bush to pressure Congress to retroactively decriminalize humiliation tactics after the Supreme Court declared that article 3 applies to Al Qaeda captives.[21]

The result seems deeply embarrassing for ICL. If these examples truly demonstrate that international tribunals violate the Principle of Legality, and the Principle is truly central to natural justice, and—finally—natural justice is necessary to bootstrap ICL into legitimacy, the result seems to be that ICL has no legitimacy.

In response, I will argue that the Principle of Legality has less importance in ICL than in domestic criminal law systems, and therefore that legality-based objections to the ICL enterprise are not fatal. Even if the Principle of Legality lies at the core

---

[18] May, L., *Crimes Against Humanity: A Normative Account* (Cambridge: Cambridge University Press, 2005), 109.

[19] Danner, A. M., and Martinez, J. S., 'Guilty Associations' (above, n. 6), 89–90.

[20] Two textbook statements of this principle appear in European Court of Human Rights, *Soering v. United Kingdom*, [1989] ECHR 14 (7 July 1989), para. 87, reprinted in 28 I.L.M. 1066, 1091–1092 (1989); *Prosecutor v. Dusko Tadic* (above, n. 16), para. 96.

[21] I refer to Bush's legality-based argument as a 'pretext' because he also stated that his objective in changing the law was to permit his programme of harsh interrogation to continue. The Principle of Legality does not require decriminalizing outrages on personal dignity; it requires only that standards be specified more concretely.

of domestic rule of law, its role in ICL is far more peripheral. To see why, we must begin by asking a fundamental question: what justifies the Principle of Legality?

There are two main arguments for the Principle, one based in the action-guiding character of law and the other in the need to curb abuses of state power. The first is that to punish people without fair notice of the elements of crimes and the scheme of punishments violates their reasonable expectations that their behaviour is legally innocent. This familiar argument is inherent in the notion that law is meant to be action-guiding. Inadequately specified law cannot guide actions, and it is unfair to punish failures to be guided by laws incapable of guiding. The second is that, historically, rulers have used vague, discretionary, underspecified criminal law to target and repress opponents—perhaps the most notorious example being the provision of the Nazi criminal code prohibiting any conduct that affronts 'healthy folk-sentiment'.[22] Call these the *fair notice argument* and *government abuse argument* respectively.

VII. THE GOVERNMENT ABUSE ARGUMENT

I begin with the government abuse argument, which insists on the Principle of Legality as a safeguard against arbitrary punishment by governments under cover of vague, underspecified law. The response in the case of pure ICL is straightforward: there is simply much less danger of government abuse in ICL than in domestic legal systems, because ICL arises from weak, decentralized institutions rather than strong, concentrated ones. Sceptics point to the free-floating, cosmopolitan character of the tribunals in order to attack their legitimacy. But exactly the same facts demonstrate that the worry about abuses of the legal process by holders of state power is not a powerful one. The Principle of Legality still matters in tribunal prosecutions, but not as a safeguard against despotism.

Arguably, the government abuse argument has more force applied to domestic prosecutions of international crimes under universal jurisdiction. Even here, however, the danger seems slight. UCJ prosecutions depend on the infrequent, difficult, and almost random processes of gaining custody over perpetrators, and it is unlikely that significant state interests can be advanced by abusively prosecuting nationals of other states for pure international crimes. It is possible, of course. For that reason, the legitimacy of UCJ prosecutions will depend on common-sense safeguards against abuse: procedural fairness, of course, but also prosecutorial independence from the political branches of the government, and absence of prior political

---

[22] Gesetz zur Änderung des Strafgesetzbuchs vom 28. Juni 1935, 1 Reichsgesetzblatt 839. See Müller, I., *Hitler's Justice: The Courts of the Third Reich*, Deborah Lucas Schneider (trans.) (Cambridge, Mass.: Harvard University Press, 1991), 74.

strife between the state conducting the trials and the defendants. Without these safeguards, the Principle of Legality will indeed kick in as an essential protection against government abuse. But, when a state with no political axe to grind against the defendant and whose jurists aren't under the thumb of politicians prosecutes great crimes under a UCJ statute, the Principle of Legality loses its central place in the pantheon of legal values.

VIII. THE FAIR NOTICE ARGUMENT

Even if the lack of world government weakens the government-abuse rationale for the Principle of Legality, the fair-notice rationale remains central to the idea that law exists to guide human action. Isn't it a mere travesty to try people under retroactive law, before tribunals that didn't exist when they committed their crimes, or under vague legal standards that expand to disfavour the defendants?

My basic response to the fair-notice argument is that when the deed is morally outrageous—*malum in se*, as criminal lawyers say—then no reasonable expectations of the defendants are violated when they are tried for it. The Nazi leadership, with the blood of 50 million people on their hands, fully expected summary execution if they were defeated. Their own ideology rejected the *Rechtsstaat* (and with it the Principle of Legality) in favour of the law of tooth and claw. If anything, the Nuremberg trial treated them better, not worse, than they had reason to expect. That is why Jackson described the Nuremberg defendants as 'hard pressed but ... not ill used', because they are 'given a chance to plead for their lives in the name of the law. Realistically, the charter of this tribunal, which gives them a hearing, is also the source of their only hope'.[23] Though there is no getting around the fact that the Nuremberg Tribunal applied law retroactively, it did not treat the defendants worse than they had reason to expect, which is the moral basis for the ban on retroactivity. Thus, even if pure international criminal law was born in sin at Nuremberg, the sin was a venial one. What mattered was that the defendants got a fair trial; that, plus the fact that the law of the Nuremberg Charter criminalized only actions that are morally outrageous, confers a legitimacy on the trial that outweighs its formal violation of the Principle of Legality.

By the time of the Balkan Wars, the Nuremberg principles and the Geneva Conventions had been part of international law for forty years. Were Yugoslav soldiers and militiamen 'on notice' of this law? To answer this question, it is important to recognize that fair notice in criminal law always involves the legal

---

[23] Justice Jackson's Opening Statement, Nuremberg Trial Proceedings, Volume 2: Preliminary Hearings to the Ninth Day, 2 International Military Tribunal, *Trial of the Major War Criminals before the International Military Tribunal: Proceedings Volumes*, 101–2 (1946). Here I am summarizing my argument from Luban, D., 'The Legacies of Nuremberg', in *Legal Modernism* (Ann Arbor: University of Michigan Press, 1994), 355–6.

fiction that publishing the law in some officially sanctioned manner places people on notice of it. This is a fiction, of course, because most people most of the time have no idea when or where to look for changes in the criminal law. Fair notice, in other words, inevitably means *constructive* notice, even in domestic legal systems. In this constructive sense, the Yugoslav perpetrators were on notice that Nuremberg law, Geneva and Hague law, and the Genocide Convention applied to them. Ignorance of the law is no excuse.

Sometimes, however, ignorance of the law *is* an excuse. In domestic legal systems, when law imposes unusual, surprising, or counterintuitive requirements, fairness demands that accused persons actually (not just constructively) know that the law prohibits their conduct. Thus, for purely regulatory, *mala prohibita*, offences prosecutors will have to prove not only that the accused knew what he was doing, but also that he knew that what he was doing was illegal. For such offences, knowledge of the legal as well as behavioural element of the offence is required for guilt, on pain of violating the requirement of fair notice.[24]

May seems to have some argument like this in mind when he argues that it is unfair to 'Bosnian small fry' to try them before an international tribunal unless they knew at the time of their crime that it fell within the jurisdiction of pure ICL. However, the argument fails, because the war crimes and crimes against humanity charged against prison guards who tortured and raped camp inmates are hardly the kind of regulatory, *mala prohibita* defences that demand actual, rather than constructive, notice of their legal prohibition. The more egregiously awful the conduct is intrinsically, the more it signals its own probable legal prohibition, and the less reasonable the defendant's expectation of innocence or impunity—doubly so because murder, rape, torture, and beatings are central domestic-law crimes in every legal system in the world. The Bosnian guards who gang-raped and tortured their captives may have expected to get away with it—but that is different from a reasonable expectation of impunity.

I want to turn, finally, to the worry raised by Danner and Martinez that the human rights rationale behind ICL runs afoul of the principle of lenity, and therefore of the Principle of Legality. This, it seems to me, is a deeper and more significant worry than concerns about retroactivity, because it concerns a fundamental clash between the world-views of human rights and criminal law. Here too, however, I shall argue that the Principle of Legality represents the less important principle.

Recall that the principle of lenity says that if a criminal statute is ambiguous, it must be read in the way most favourable to the accused. Why is that? The reason, according to the fair notice argument, is that the defendant needs to be told unambiguously whether his conduct is criminal under the statute. Let's use the

---

[24] In US doctrine see, e.g., *Lambert v. California*, 355 U.S. 225 (1957) and *Liparota v. United States*, 471 U.S. 419 (1985). For more detailed discussion of these ideas about *mens rea*, see Luban, D., 'The Publicity of Law and the Regulatory State', *Journal of Political Philosophy*, 10 (2002), 296.

term 'grey zone' to describe the zone of ambiguity in the statute—the conduct that is forbidden under one reading but not under the other. Then it appears that the accused doesn't have adequate notice about whether grey-zone conduct is permitted or forbidden.

It follows that the only way he can be certain his conduct is legal is to steer clear of the grey zone. Even if grey-zone conduct is legal, he engages in it at his peril. That seems to violate one of the basic tenets of liberal legality, namely that the law permits anything that it doesn't expressly forbid.[25] We are entitled to walk to the very boundary of the law, so long as we don't step over it.

Yet this doctrine carries undeniable costs. It encourages envelope-pushing, loopholing, and pettifoggery. Perhaps that is an acceptable cost when the issue is tax 'evasion'; and perhaps it is downright desirable when the issue is political speech that angers the government. But when the legal issue concerns basic human rights and their violation, envelope-pushing is the last thing we should want. The outrageous memos written by US government lawyers to loophole the law against torture offer a vivid illustration of what happens when ruthless men and women, bent on evading human rights protections, probe and twist the law for ambiguities.[26] In cases like these, it should count as a plus, not a minus, if ambiguity or vagueness in the law discourages actors from the grey zone. The human rights law mode of reading pure ICL statutes—filling gaps and resolving ambiguities in favour of victims of human rights violations—simply has far more to recommend it than the principle of lenity. These statutes, after all, deal with the great crimes, and the grey zone at their margins is bad enough that we should welcome any inhibition the criminal law creates on people choosing to inhabit them.

There is one important exception to this conclusion, and that is the case of certain war crimes. Under the ICC's statute, it is a war crime to take actions that cause disproportionate civilian deaths or environmental damage (article 8 (2) (b) (iv)). But no formula exists for calculating proportionality. Soldiers in combat always try to inflict the maximum lawful amount of force when they have to—that is

---

[25] Contrast this with Aristotle's deeply illiberal view that the law forbids whatever it does not expressly permit. *Nicomachean Ethics*, 5.11, 1138a, 5–7.

[26] Luban, D., 'The Torture Lawyers of Washington', in *Legal Ethics and Human Dignity* (Cambridge: Cambridge University Press, 2007), 162; Waldron, J., 'Torture and the Common Law, Jurisprudence for the White House', *Columbia Law Review*, 105 (2005), 1681, esp. 1701–3. Envelope-pushing was an official policy of the Bush Administration; in the unapologetic words of the head of the National Security Agency, 'We're going to live on the edge . . . My spikes will have chalk on them . . . We're pretty aggressive within the law. As a professional, I'm troubled if I'm not using the full authority allowed by law' (Priest, D., 'Covert CIA Program Withstands New Furor, Anti-Terror Effort Continues to Grow', *Washington Post*, 30 Dec. 2005, p. A1). He was talking about electronic surveillance, not torture, but many Americans were deeply troubled even by the surveillance issue.

On the more general point that mistake-of-law defences should not be available to sharpies who use them as an excuse for exploring the grey zone, see Kahan, D. M., 'Ignorance of the Law *Is* an Excuse—But Only for the Virtuous', *Michigan Law Review*, 96 (1997), 127. Kahan argues that existing criminal law recognizes this point.

both how they safeguard themselves and how they accomplish their missions. To tell them that not only must they obey the law of war, they must also steer clear of the grey zone seems unfair and wildly unrealistic. These are, after all, men and women fighting for their lives in conditions close to hell. Other laws of war are also fuzzy or contestable: for example, opinions differ over whether targeted killings of enemy militants violate the prohibition on intentionally targeting civilians (article 8 (2) (b) (i)). In these examples, the special conditions of war suggest that the principle of lenity should govern criminal prosecutions, because it is unreasonable to expect actors not only to abide by the law but also to steer clear of the grey zone. I hasten to add, however, that this will not be true of all war crimes. In some cases, the argument that soldiers should be deterred from the grey zone applies full force—for example, in the prohibitions on cruel and degrading treatment of captives.

IX. Conclusion: Legitimacy From the Bottom Up

The institutions of ICL are fragile, weak, and—to be perfectly honest—less important than the attention they receive warrants. Realistically, the current ICC may reach very little of the world's most awful conduct. Nevertheless, opponents of the ICC, particularly in the United States, view it in exaggerated, paranoid terms; supporters, churning out reams of commentary on legal minutiae before the first case has been tried, can fairly be accused of living in a fantasy-world of their own, where the court has already been fully normalized into a global rule of law.[27]

The reason for the attention, the fantasies, and the conspiracy-theories woven around the ICL enterprise is not hard to see: as I have argued, even if the institutions are weak, their project is a fundamental challenge to statism and nationalism, which (unlike ICL) are fighting faiths. That the project gets any backing at all from states is remarkable; it testifies to a world-wide cosmopolitan yearning coming from below—and not only on the part of liberal elites, as conservative opponents of ICL invariably believe. It is the yearning to escape the eternal cycle of crimes that the fighting faiths commit in the name of states, nationalities, and religions. Against the bloodshed of mass political violence, the ICL project has little to offer except the dramatic force of legal trials that attach

---

[27] For relevant examples of criticisms of the ICC, see e.g. Bolton, J. R., 'The Risks and Weaknesses of the International Criminal Court from America's Perspective', *Law and Contemporary Problems*, 64 (2001), 167–80; Goldsmith, J. L., 'The Self-Defeating International Criminal Court', *University of Chicago Law Review*, 70 (2003), 89–104; Goldsmith, J. L. and Krasner, S. D., 'The Limits of Idealism', *Daedalus*, 132 (2003), 47.

labels like 'war crimes', 'genocide', and 'crimes against humanity'. Lacking the authority of world government, these norms build their legitimacy from the bottom up, by the fairness of their proceedings and the moral power they project. The success of the project is improbable; its failure, if it happens, is the failure of law itself.[28]

---

28 After this paper was written and revised, two significant publications appeared focusing on the Principle of Legality in international criminal law: Gallant, K. S., *The Principle of Legality in International and Comparative Criminal Law* (Cambridge: Cambridge University Press, 2009) and Van Schaack, B., 'Crimen Sine Lege: Judicial Lawmaking at the Intersection of Law and Morals', *Georgetown Law Journal*, 97 (2009): 119–92. Gallant's treatise provides a thorough analysis of the jurisprudence of the Principle of Legality from Nuremberg through the international tribunals; Van Schaack's instructive article provides a more compressed analysis of this jurisprudence. Her view is, I believe, more or less consistent with the arguments I have offered here. She agrees that the practice of ICL has involved significant judicial lawmaking that, at least on its face, calls into question the legitimacy of international tribunals. However, Van Schaack argues that under an approach to the Principle of Legality developed by the European Court of Human Rights, the jurisprudence of the tribunals by and large pass muster. On inspection, this approach includes 'reference to non-positive law', including 'changes in society that might render an old rule offensive, anachronistic, or presently unworkable . . . , even when the defendant could not have known precisely when the critical societal changes took effect'. Ibid., 178–9. Given the breadth of this procedure, Van Schaack's conclusion—that the European Court's approach respects the Principle of Legality—and my conclusion that when it comes to trying the great crimes in international tribunals the strict positivist requirement of fair notice loses importance are not as different as they might seem. Gallant argues that 'legality is . . . necessary today to the prevention of tyranny. . . . As the international criminal law system becomes more effective, the need for strict enforcement of legality increases rather than decreases'. Gallant, *The Principle of Legality*, 405. Readers will perceive that my argument above regarding the Government Abuse Argument leads me to doubt Gallant's conclusion here.

CHAPTER 29

AUTHORITY AND RESPONSIBILITY IN INTERNATIONAL CRIMINAL LAW

ANTONY DUFF[*]

I. INTRODUCTION

Theft committed in Poland by one Polish citizen against another is not a crime under English criminal law, nor is it triable in an English court. The same is true of most crimes under most domestic criminal codes: the criminal law claims authority only over wrongs committed within the state's territory (the Territoriality Principle) or impinging on its interests (the Protective Principle), or sometimes over wrongs committed abroad by, or against, its own citizens (the Nationality Principle and the Passive Personality Principle).[1] A nation state's criminal law generally takes no interest in wrongs committed abroad by and against foreigners: they are not its business. Sometimes, however, it claims a universal authority over wrongs committed anywhere in the world, by and against citizens of any state: an official anywhere in the world who uses torture 'in the performance or purported performance of his official duties' commits a crime under English law, and can be

* Thanks to participants in the Oxford workshop, and especially to John Tasioulas, for helpful comments on a previous draft of this paper.

[1] See generally Hirst, M., *Jurisdiction and the Ambit of the Criminal Law* (Oxford: Oxford University Press, 2003), chs. 1, 5. For examples of the Nationality and Passive Personality Principles, see e.g. French Penal Code art. 113.6–7, German Criminal Code s. 7.1–2, UK Sex Offenders Act 1997 s. 7.

tried for it in an English court.[2] But by what moral right can English law claim authority over a Chilean torturer; by what right can English courts try and convict him?

A similar question is raised by international criminal tribunals, and the International Criminal Court (ICC)—I'll focus here on the ICC.[3] The ICC's jurisdiction over a case often depends on the agreement of the state within whose territory the crime was committed, or of which the alleged perpetrator is a citizen—an agreement given either by becoming a party to the Rome Statute, or by accepting the Court's jurisdiction in the particular case;[4] but it also claims an independent universal jurisdiction when alleged crimes are referred to it by the Security Council.[5] In so far as the ICC's jurisdiction depends on the agreement of the state that could claim jurisdiction on the basis of territoriality or nationality, it could be portrayed as a delegated jurisdiction grounded both legally and morally in the undisputed jurisdictional authority of the state: but on what moral ground could its claims to universal jurisdiction be founded?

In Section II of this chapter, I discuss and criticize David Luban's answer to this question. In Section III, I lay the foundations for a somewhat different answer, which I then develop in Section IV.

II. Fairness to Rightness

If a criminal court is to be morally justified in convicting a defendant, it must be able to sustain three claims: that the conduct constituting the alleged crime was criminal under a system of law binding on the defendant; that the court has authority to try him; and that his guilt has been proved through a fair process which respected the demands of natural justice. In domestic courts, these claims are related but separable: a court might lack jurisdiction over some crimes; or its procedures might not be fair. But for international criminal courts, Luban argues, the second claim must be grounded in the third.

The legitimacy of international tribunals comes not from the shaky political authority that creates them, but from the manifested fairness of their procedures

---

[2] UK Criminal Justice Act 1988 s 134, giving effect to UN Convention against Torture and other Cruel, Inhuman or Degrading Treatment or Punishment (1984): see *R v Bow Street Metropolitan Stipendiary Magistrate ex parte Pinochet Ugarte* [2000] 1 AC 147. See generally Reydams, L., *Universal Jurisdiction: International and Municipal Legal Perspectives* (Oxford: Oxford University Press, 2003); Luban, D., 'A Theory of Crimes Against Humanity', *Yale Journal of International Law*, 29 (2004) 85, 146–56 on Belgium's universal jurisdiction statute.

[3] See Cassese, A., *International Criminal Law* (Oxford: Oxford University Press, 2003), 340.

[4] See Rome Statute of the International Criminal Court 1998, UN doc. A/CONF.183/9, arts. 12–15.

[5] Rome Statute, art. 13 (b). I deal later with the further point that the ICC operates under a principle of complementarity given which cases are admissible only if they have not been duly investigated or prosecuted by a state with jurisdiction.

and punishments. Tribunals bootstrap themselves into legitimacy by the quality of the justice they deliver.[6]

Some version of the first claim is of course also crucial: however fair the courts' procedures, they must be applied to alleged crimes that are their business. Luban suggests that the kinds of wrong that properly concern international criminal courts are those that offend against 'human interests', which human beings therefore have a shared interest in condemning and repressing.[7] It might be tempting then to argue that, just as domestic courts act in the name and on behalf of the political community whose law they administer, and gain their authority from that source, international courts have authority in so far as they act in the name and on behalf of the community of 'humanity'. Luban rejects that argument: humanity does not constitute a political community that could authorize such courts; our interest in the repression of such wrongs is one that we have not as members of a community, but as 'a set of human individuals'.[8] That is why the courts' claim to legitimacy must rest on the fairness of their procedures rather than on their authorization by any appropriate political community.

But legitimacy cannot, I will argue, be bootstrapped in this way. A court's procedures might be impeccable; the defendant might be guilty of wrongdoing that merits condemnation and punishment: but unless this court can claim jurisdiction over him, it cannot legitimately try him. Even if English courts delivered 'champagne-quality due process',[9] and Polish courts did not, this would not give an English court the right to try the Polish thief for a theft committed in Poland; nor can such claims to procedural propriety give international courts an authority they would otherwise lack. A defendant's challenge 'By what right do you try me?' must be answered if the trial is to be legitimate; the answer 'our procedures respect the demands of natural justice' is not an answer to that challenge.

This is an aspect of any practice of calling people to account for alleged wrongdoings: those who would do the calling must have the standing to do so. Suppose that a group of my neighbours, worried about the decline in marital fidelity, take it upon themselves to bring local adulterers to book, and turn their attention to me, as an alleged adulterer. I might not deny that adultery is wrong, or that I am an adulterer who must answer for his adultery to those whose business it is—to my wife and family, to our mutual friends. But I might reasonably insist that it is not my neighbours' business: they have no right to call me to answer for my adultery; nor can the fairness of their procedure give them that right. Now a criminal trial, I will argue, should be understood as a process which calls alleged

---

[6] Luban, D., in this volume, 579.
[7] Ibid. 571; for a developed argument about the idea of 'crimes against humanity', see Luban, 'Crimes Against Humanity' (above, n. 2).
[8] Luban, D., 'Crimes Against Humanity' (above, n. 2), 137 (see 124–41 generally).
[9] Luban, D., this volume, 579.

wrongdoers to answer charges of wrongdoing, and to answer for such wrongdoing if it is proved against them. The legitimacy of that process depends both on its procedural fairness, and on the court's authority to call the defendant to answer; a deficiency in one of these dimensions cannot be compensated by adequacy, or even by perfection, in the other.

The significance of this point is concealed by some accounts of the proper aims of the criminal law, and of criminal trials. Consider, for instance, Michael Moore's account of the purpose of criminal law as a 'functional kind': 'to attain retributive justice' by 'punish[ing] all and only those who are morally culpable in the doing of some morally wrongful act'.[10] To put the matter in this way is to begin with an impersonal demand of justice, that the guilty be punished, and then to identify a human practice whose purpose is to meet that demand. The Preamble to the Rome Statute can be read in a similar way: the parties affirm 'that the most serious crimes of concern to the international community as a whole must not go unpunished and that their effective prosecution must be ensured', and declare their determination 'to put an end to impunity for the perpetrators of these crimes'.[11] They recognize, we could say, the force of the impersonal demand that such crimes must be punished, and accept a shared responsibility to ensure that that demand is satisfied. What concerns me here is not the content of such demands, but their form: we start with a demand that X be done, and then as a separate inquiry ask who can properly be charged with the responsibility of ensuring that X is done.

If we take this approach either to crime in general, as Moore does, or to 'the most serious crimes' that concern the ICC, we will see good reason to give national courts priority, and to accept the ICC's 'principle of complementarity'—that it can try only cases that have not been properly investigated by a state with jurisdiction.[12] National courts are usually better placed to prosecute those who commit such wrongs within their territories; and a respect for state sovereignty requires that they normally be left to do so.[13] However, there are serious crimes which the states within whose national jurisdiction they fall might well not prosecute, notably those committed systematically by or with the tacit support of officials of the state: their seriousness strengthens the demand that their perpetrators be punished, but they will probably not be punished by the state that has primary jurisdiction. In such cases, other states might intervene by claiming universal jurisdiction over such crimes:[14] but justice is more likely to be done by a system of international criminal justice to fill the gap

---

[10] Moore, M. S., *Placing Blame: A General Theory of the Criminal Law* (Oxford: Oxford University Press, 1997), 33–5.

[11] Rome Statute, Preamble.   [12] Rome Statute, art. 17.

[13] See Hirst, M., *Jurisdiction* (above, n. 1), 10–11; May, L., *Crimes Against Humanity* (Cambridge: Cambridge University Press, 2005), 8–14.

[14] See n. 2, above; the line of argument sketched here would explain why s. 134 of the UK Criminal Justice Act 1988 covers torture only when it is committed by, or with the consent or acquiescence of, an official.

left by nation states, and that is the proper role of the international criminal court.[15] Given the pragmatic and principled priority that should be accorded to national jurisdiction, however, an international court should have the right to act only when the nation state that has initial jurisdiction fails to take action: hence the principle of complementarity.

If we add to this line of thought about the role of international criminal courts the thought that the 'foundational question about criminal law is what justifies punishment',[16] we might see international criminal trials in primarily instrumental terms: their function is to identify accurately (by procedures which respect the human rights of those involved) the perpetrators who are to be punished. To explain why in international criminal law 'the emphasis shifts', as Luban notes, 'from punishments to trials', we might appeal to other extra-legal purposes: 'promoting social reconciliation, giving victims a voice, or making a historical record of mass atrocities'. Or we might appeal, as he appeals, to the 'expressive' role of trials 'in *norm projection*: trials are expressive acts broadcasting the news that mass atrocities are, in fact, heinous crimes and not merely politics by other means'.[17] Now he is surely right to identify a distinctive role for criminal trials, continuous with but not reducible to the purposes of criminal punishment: their role is not simply to identify those who are to be punished; they have an independent, non-instrumental significance. But that distinctive role is not best captured by talking of 'expressive' acts, partly because that makes the defendant's role in the trial an essentially passive one: he is the object of judgment (whose fate is to be determined), part of the vehicle through which the relevant norms are projected, and perhaps part of the audience to whom they are projected; but he has no essential active role in the proceedings. We should, I will argue, talk of communication rather than expression, since whereas expression is an essentially one-way activity that requires only an audience or object, communication is (at least in intention) a two-way process that seeks actively to engage the other. Criminal trials, I will suggest, should be seen as attempts not simply to identify the guilty, or to express norms, but to engage the defendant in a communicative enterprise.

This will suggest a different way of understanding international criminal law, which begins not with the impersonal thought 'they ought to be punished', but with the (collectively) personal thought 'we ought to call them to account': this will show why trials are so important; it will also, when we ask who 'we' are,

---

[15] Compare Altman, A., and Wellman, C., 'A Defense of International Criminal Law', *Ethics*, 155 (2004), 35. This line of argument applies particularly to intra-national 'crimes against humanity' (see Rome Statute, art. 7). Other crimes falling under the ICC's jurisdiction, such as war crimes and the crime of aggression (arts. 5, 8; the crime of aggression awaits definition), are clearly international in their direct impact, and thus obviously invite the attention of an international court; the questions that concern me here about the ICC's authority are raised most sharply by crimes whose material character is intra- rather than inter-national.

[16] Luban, D., this volume, 575.   [17] Ibid. 575–6.

highlight the issue of what gives international courts the authority that they claim.

III. The Criminal Trial as a Calling to Account

To begin to develop this suggestion, I will sketch an account of domestic criminal trials. We should see them not merely in instrumental terms, as identifying those who, being guilty, are to be punished, but rather as the forum in which alleged wrongdoers are called to account by the polity whose laws they have allegedly flouted.[18]

A trial summons a defendant to answer a charge of criminal wrongdoing: though the prosecution must prove that she committed the offence, she is called to make an initial answer to the charge, by a plea of 'guilty' or 'not guilty'; in giving that answer, she accepts the court's authority to summon her, and to judge her. If the prosecution then proves (or she admits) that she committed the offence, she must answer not just *to* the charge, but *for* her commission of the offence. It has been proved that she is criminally responsible for that offence: whilst she can still avoid conviction (criminal liability), by offering a defence, the onus shifts to her to offer one. The trial does not simply treat the defendant as someone on whom judgment must be passed: it addresses her as a responsible agent, who should be called to answer in this way; it gives her a central, active role in the process. That process is in several ways communicative. The initial stage of charge and plea is communicative: that is why it matters that the defendant be fit to plead—able to understand and respond to the charge. The prosecution's case is addressed not just to the fact-finder, but to the defendant, as a case that—the prosecutor claims—she must answer; the verdict is addressed both to a wider public and to the defendant. If she is convicted, the significance of the verdict is not merely that she is liable to punishment: the verdict condemns her wrongdoing, as a formal, public message of censure that she is expected to understand and accept.

Why should trials take this form? The simple answer is that this is what we owe both to victims and to alleged perpetrators of crimes. What is salient about crimes is their wrongful character: what matters is not just (if at all) that harm was done and must be repaired (as 'restorative justice' theorists urge), but that wrong was done.

---

[18] I draw here on Duff, R. A., Farmer, L., Marshall, S. E., and Tadros, V., *The Trial on Trial III: Towards a Normative Theory of the Criminal Trial* (Oxford: Hart Publishing, 2007), and Duff, R. A., *Answering for Crime* (Oxford: Hart Publishing, 2007). This account of the trial is based on the 'adversarial' trials that are characteristic of common law systems; I cannot here discuss its relation to more 'inquisitorial' systems—although I would argue that they too should be ways of calling alleged wrongdoers to account.

We owe it to victims to show that we take their wrongs seriously, by seeking to call the perpetrators to account. We owe it to perpetrators to respond in this way, by calling them to answer for the wrongs they committed, because that is to treat them as responsible agents—as agents who can and should be called to answer for their actions.[19]

If it is plausible to see criminal trials in this light, an obvious question arises: by and to whom is the defendant called to answer—and by what right? The labelling of English criminal cases, 'R v. D', might suggest an Austinian answer: defendants are called to account by the sovereign whose orders they have allegedly disobeyed, in virtue of the sovereign's authority (or power) over them. A better answer for what purports to be a liberal democracy, self-governed by a genuinely common law, is that defendants are answerable to their fellow citizens (in whose name the courts act) for public wrongs that they commit, in virtue of their shared membership of the political community. Crimes are 'public' wrongs,[20] not in the sense that they harm 'the public' as distinct from any individual victims, but in the sense that they are wrongs that concern the 'public', i.e. all members of the polity, in virtue of their shared membership; the criminal trial is the forum in which we formally call each other to account, as citizens, for such wrongs.[21]

That is why the theft committed by a Polish citizen against a fellow Pole in Poland is not morally, as it is not legally, within the jurisdiction of English courts. On Moore's view, the English legislature and courts have reason to claim jurisdiction over such crimes, since they are wrongdoings that merit punishment, and it is the criminal law's function to ensure that they receive it; the reasons against claiming jurisdiction (to do with respect for national sovereignty and with the efficient division of punitive labour) appear later in deliberation, as reasons not to pursue that in principle claim. But that is implausible. The point is rather that the Polish theft is not the business of the English legislature or courts: the thief is not answerable to them, or to members of that polity, for what he has done.

That is also why the trial's legitimacy, as a matter of the court's standing to call this defendant to account, is separate from the substantive issue of the defendant's guilt, and from procedural issues of natural justice. One question concerns guilt: did the defendant commit the offence charged; if so, has he a defence? Another question concerns proof and procedure: can the defendant's guilt be proved by a process that respects the presumption of innocence and the demands of natural justice? But a

---

[19] This is a normative, not a descriptive, account: although it appeals to features of our existing criminal process, I do not suggest that the trials that actually take place in our courts are, or are so conducted that they could readily be, processes through which alleged wrongdoers are called to account.

[20] See, classically, Blackstone, W., *Commentaries on the Laws of England* (Oxford: Clarendon Press, 1765–9), iv. 1, 5—although Blackstone tended to talk as if crime must involve some harm or injury to 'the whole community'.

[21] Temporary residents or visitors are also both protected and bound, as guests, by the polity's laws, and must answer in its courts for wrongs that they commit within its territory: but an account of the authority of the criminal law must begin with citizens, since it is they who constitute the polity whose law it is.

third and independent question concerns the court's authority: does this court have the standing to call this person to answer this charge? Suppose that a defendant has been convicted by an impeccable process (perhaps he admits that he committed the crime), but shows on appeal that the court had no right to try him: he had been promised immunity by the prosecutor; or he had diplomatic immunity; or the crime was committed outside the court's jurisdiction. He is entitled then to have his conviction overturned: not because he is entitled to an acquittal (that would imply that the court had the right to try him, but should have found him not guilty), but because he should not have been tried for that crime by that court; the court lacked legitimate authority to call him to answer.

It is always open to defendants in domestic courts to ask: 'By what right do you try me?' The court must be able to answer that question, and I have suggested that an adequate answer cannot just appeal to the justice of the court's procedures, or to the wrongfulness of the alleged crime. It must show how that crime, as allegedly committed by this defendant, is the proper business of this court; and I have suggested this involves showing that it is the proper business of the political community to which the defendant belongs, and to whose members he must answer for his violations of their shared, public values.

It might be objected that such grounding in community is not a necessary condition of criminal jurisdiction. Some wrongs are of course private matters, not eligible for public trial or punishment: but once a wrong is a public wrong, justice demands that the perpetrator be brought to book. It might be desirable that criminal wrongdoers should be called to account in the courts of a political community to which they belong: for a wide range of crimes, we might therefore appropriately recognize that domestic law and domestic courts should have exclusive jurisdiction. Those courts still ultimately act, however, in the name not (only) of their local political community but of justice, whose demands are neither grounded in any such community nor addressed only to its members: especially in the case of serious and wide-reaching wrongs of the kind over which the ICC claims jurisdiction, we should see those demands of justice as being addressed to anyone who can fulfil them, and therefore recognize that another state's courts, or an international court, can claim the standing to call the perpetrators to account in the name of justice, despite the absence of any nexus of community between perpetrators, victims, and the court, so long as the courts' procedures can be shown to respect the demands of both retributive and natural justice.[22]

This objection can succeed only if we can plausibly explain the distinction between 'private' and 'public' wrongs without appealing to ideas of community: but I do not think that we can do so. What is 'private' in this context is what I can claim to be my, or our, business but not yours; what is 'public' is what I must admit to be your

---

[22] John Tasioulas and Jeff McMahan pressed versions of this objection on me; I hope that I have not distorted their arguments too drastically.

business as well as mine or ours. Now the identity of the 'we' and the 'you', and the determinations of what is whose business, are context-dependent.[23] My adultery is a private matter in relation to the criminal law, but not in relation to my marriage, or to my church: that is, I must admit that it is my wife's business, and the business of fellow members of my church (if that is the kind of church I belong to), that they have the right to call me to account for it; but I can deny that it is the business of the criminal law. A husband's violence against his wife, by contrast, though it might take place 'in the privacy of the home', is a public wrong, in the sense that it properly concerns not just him and his wife, but 'the public'—all of us; it is the business of the criminal law. A 'public' wrong is a wrong that is the proper business of some 'public'; but we must therefore be able to specify the public whose business it is. In the case of adultery, it might be fellow members of my church—of my religious community; in the case of my misconduct as a teacher, the relevant public is my students and colleagues—the fellow members of the academic community to which we all belong; in the case of criminal wrongdoing it is . . . what? The answer suggested here, for domestic crimes, is that it is my fellow citizens—the fellow members of the polity to which I belong.[24] But the key point is that if we are to identify a wrong as a public wrong, we must be able to identify the relevant public to whom the wrongdoer is answerable: we cannot simply appeal to some impersonal demand of justice that the wrongdoer be punished.

IV. Answering to Humanity?

If the criminal trial is seen as a process through which alleged wrongdoers are called to account by those to whom they are answerable, we can both see more clearly why, as Luban notes, the trial should be so central to international criminal law, and highlight the importance of the question of who can call such perpetrators to account.

The parties to the ICC statute were determined 'to put an end to impunity for the perpetrators' of these 'most serious crimes of concern to the international community as a whole'.[25] Now the most obvious way to put an end to impunity is to punish, but calling to account can also end impunity: our recognition of such crimes is manifest in our efforts not (merely) to punish their perpetrators, but to hold their perpetrators to proper account.[26] Of course we also demand that they

---

[23] See further Duff, R. A., *Answering for Crime* (above, n. 18), 50–1.

[24] See further Marshall, S. E., and Duff, R. A., 'Criminalization and Sharing Wrongs', *Canadian Journal of Law and Jurisprudence*, 11 (1998), 7.

[25] Rome Statute, Preamble (above, n. 11).

[26] That is why truth and reconciliation Commissions can, even if they promise immunity from punishment, be appropriate ways of addressing the crimes of the past, by calling their perpetrators to account.

be punished, and see it as a failure of justice if they walk free after conviction: but the value of trying them in a criminal court is not just that this is the appropriate way to get them punished, or that this also projects the relevant norms; it is that in being tried they are held to account for their crimes. Suppose that a defendant dies shortly after conviction, or for some other reason cannot be punished: justice has still been done by his trial, since he has been held to account.

There are two important aspects to such processes of holding to account. The first has been noted: a calling to account must be not merely *of* someone who is accountable, but *by* some person or body to whom he is accountable. The second I will return to later: it concerns the status of the defendant as someone who is called to answer—that he is thereby treated as a responsible member of the normative community to which he must answer. For the moment, however, we must focus on the first aspect.

When an ICC defendant asks 'By what right do you try me?', what kind of answer could be given? An answer must show that the court acts in the name of some group to whom the defendant is answerable for his alleged crimes. It is not enough to argue that the wrongs he allegedly committed are terrible wrongs whose perpetrators ought to be punished: the trial's legitimacy depends upon the acceptability of the court's claim to act in the name of those who have the right to call the defendant to account. In whose name, then, can the ICC claim to act? To whom are the perpetrators of such crimes answerable? There are two obvious possible answers to these questions: each is problematic.

The first answer is that they are answerable to the particular political communities within and against which they committed their crimes: Augusto Pinochet was answerable to the Chilean people for the crimes he committed against them (individually and collectively), and should properly have been called to account in a Chilean court,[27] Saddam Hussein was rightly tried in an Iraqi court for his crimes against the Iraqi people.[28] Such a view still leaves two roles for an international criminal court. First, it can deal with crimes whose impact is genuinely international, especially when committed by states rather than individuals: only an international court could really try 'the crime of aggression'.[29] Second, however, it can fill some of the gaps that national courts might leave—acting on behalf of the political communities which those courts fail to represent as they should. An official who uses torture in the service of an oppressive regime should ideally answer for that wrongdoing to the polity whose citizens he helps to oppress. But this might not be likely, or practicable: a regime is unlikely to put its own officials on trial; even when it falls, its successor might be reluctant to prosecute such crimes. In such cases, if

---

[27] As the Chilean courts had started to do before his death: part of the story was told in *The Guardian* on 30 Oct. 2006; <http://www.guardian.co.uk/chile/story/0,1935376,00.html>. All websites were most recently checked in Nov. 2007.

[28] Which is not of course to say that his trial was appropriately conducted.

[29] See Rome Statute, art. 5; and above, n. 15.

the crimes are serious enough to warrant the costs involved, it might be appropriate for an international court to claim jurisdiction or, absent such a court, for courts of other states to claim jurisdiction on behalf of the citizens whose own courts have let them down.

This view can readily explain why the ICC should respect the principle of complementarity:[30] if its role is to discharge responsibilities that national courts are unable or unwilling to discharge, it can claim the right to act only when the national courts have failed to discharge their responsibilities. But it faces two problems.

The first is that just when the arguments for international jurisdiction seem strongest, there might be doubt about whether there exists a political community to which the perpetrator could answer, on whose behalf the international court could claim to act: if, for instance, the 'widespread or systematic attack[s]' on 'civilian population[s]' that constitute 'crimes against humanity'[31] are successful enough, there might be no surviving political community to which perpetrators and victims all belong. One answer to this problem is that the existence of a political community is as much a matter of normative aspiration as of empirical fact: we can say, for instance, that state officials' crimes against members of the black majority in *apartheid* South Africa were committed against their fellow citizens, not because such fellow citizenship was given substantial reality, but because it should have been. Another answer is that calling such wrongdoers to account is one of the ways in which political community can begin to be (re)built—although national courts are better placed than international courts to do this. I am not sure that such answers are adequate: 'crimes against humanity' could surely involve such systematic, successful attacks that there really is no basis left on which to identify a political community to which their perpetrators ought to answer; but such perpetrators should not escape being called to account.

The second problem concerns the ICC's authority to act on behalf of the political community in which the crimes were committed: by what right can it claim to act in their name? In so far as it deals with crimes over which parties to its statute have jurisdiction, or which are referred to it by a state with jurisdiction,[32] it can claim authority, as a matter of delegated jurisdiction: but what of cases in which it claims a universal jurisdiction independent of any such authorisation?[33] If such claims are to be sustained, they must appeal to some normative relationship between the court and those for whom it claims to act: but what can that relationship be? The obvious answer to this question leads us to a second account of the ICC's authority—that it acts in the name of 'humanity': what gives it the right to intervene on behalf of members of more local polities whose national courts have let them down is our shared humanity; but that is not far from saying that the perpetrators should have

[30] See Rome Statute, art. 17; and above, n. 12.   [31] Rome Statute, art. 7(1).

[32] See Rome Statute, arts. 12–13.

[33] Or cases in which national courts claim universal jurisdiction: see Rome Statute, art. 13 (b); and above, nn. 2 and 5.

to answer not merely to their polity, but to humanity. It is to that account that we must therefore turn.

There is no doubting the rhetorical resonance of the idea of answering to humanity. The Preamble to the Rome Statute declares the signatories' '[c]onscious[ness] that all peoples are united by common bonds, their cultures pieced together in a shared heritage', and the need to punish 'the most serious crimes of concern to the international community as a whole'; and must we not see 'crimes against humanity' as crimes for which the perpetrators must answer to humanity? But can we make any substantive sense of this idea, in particular of 'humanity' as a community to which wrongdoers could answer, or in whose name a court could act?

We need not try, implausibly,[34] to portray humanity as a *political* community: the most we need is the idea of humanity as a moral community. Nor need we portray humanity as the victim of 'crimes against humanity', as if what gives humanity the standing to call their perpetrators to account is that the crimes somehow harm humanity as a whole. Some theorists make such claims: the Preamble to the Rome Statute talks about 'grave crimes' which 'threaten the peace, security and well-being of the world'; Hannah Arendt argued that 'mankind in its entirety [can be] grievously hurt and endangered' by the attempt to exterminate a particular ethnic or religious group;[35] and Larry May articulates the 'international harm principle'.[36] Such claims resemble those by which theorists sometimes explain the idea of crimes as public wrongs, by identifying harms that crimes do to 'the public' as distinct from individual victims—by creating 'social volatility', for instance, or by undermining the conditions of trust, or by taking unfair advantage of the law-abiding.[37] Such accounts distort our understanding of the criminal wrong that should be punished: a rapist should be condemned and punished not for the social volatility or loss of trust that he caused, nor for the unfair advantage that he supposedly took over those who restrain their criminal impulses, but for the wrong that he did to the person whom he raped. Crimes are 'public' wrongs in the sense not that they harm 'the public', but that they properly concern 'the public'—all members of the relevant community; they are wrongs that we share in virtue of our membership of that community.[38] A crime against humanity should be one that properly concerns us all, in virtue simply of our shared humanity.

---

[34] As Luban points out: see 'Crimes Against Humanity' (above, n. 2), 124–41.

[35] Arendt, H., *Eichmann in Jerusalem* (rev. edn.; London: Penguin Books, 1994), 269; see Altman, A. and Wellman, C., 'A Defense' (above, n. 15), 41–2.

[36] May, L., *Crimes Against Humanity* (above, n. 13), ch. 5 (see Altman, A. and Wellman, C., 'A Defense' (above, n. 15), 40); compare Luban, D., 'Crimes Against Humanity' (above, n. 2), 138–9.

[37] See Becker, L., 'Criminal Attempts and the Theory of the Law of Crimes', *Philosophy and Public Affairs*, 3 (1974), 262; Dimock, S., 'Retributivism and Trust', *Law and Philosophy*, 16 (1997), 37; Murphy, J., 'Marxism and Retribution', *Philosophy and Public Affairs*, 2 (1973), 217.

[38] See further Marshall, S. E. and Duff, R. A., 'Sharing Wrongs' (above, n. 24).

The Rome Statute's Preamble talks about 'the most serious crimes of concern to the international community as a whole', and 'unimaginable atrocities that deeply shock the conscience of humanity'. Many kinds of wrongdoing, committed in communities far from ours, are not our business: we can be moved by them, and wish that they were not committed, but lack the standing to call their perpetrators to answer for them. We often lack that standing as individuals; nor do we have it collectively, through our states or whatever international institutions we create. But some kinds of wrong should concern us, are properly our business, in virtue of our shared humanity with their victims (and perpetrators): for such wrongs the perpetrators must answer not just to their local communities, but to humanity.

But is there such a 'we': a 'we' not of some local community, but of humanity as such? Is it not overblown rhetoric to say that all human beings are 'united by common bonds, their cultures pieced together in a shared heritage'? Once we recognize that a community, in the sense relevant here, need not involve close ties or deep structures of richly shared interests, we will see that we can talk of the human community without espousing any radical, and controversial, form of cosmopolitanism. We recognize others (or, sometimes, recognize that we should recognize others) as fellow human beings—which is to recognize that they have a claim on our respect and concern simply by virtue of our shared humanity:[39] that recognition is displayed, for instance, in responses to disasters and desperate need in distant parts of the world, as well as to the kinds of atrocity that motivate calls for universal criminal jurisdiction. We can also talk, cautiously, of a shared life:[40] of lives structured, albeit in profoundly different ways, by such central human concerns as birth, life, and death; of the needs that flow from our social or political nature;[41] of sharing the earth as a natural (and fragile) environment. We can also see the creation of the ICC as one of the ways in which the moral ideal of a human community might be given more determinate and effective institutional form: the existence of a community is often a matter more of aspiration than of achieved fact, and a recognition of human community could be a recognition of what we should aspire to create.

Much more clearly needs to be said about answering to humanity, and about the kinds of wrong whose perpetrators should have to answer to humanity; but I want

[39] Those of a Kantian disposition might talk of recognition of our fellow membership, as rational beings, of the Kingdom of Ends, but I think it more helpful to talk, less rationalistically, of shared humanity: see Gaita, R., *Good and Evil: An Absolute Conception* (London: Macmillan, 1991), esp. ch. 3; and *A Common Humanity* (London: Routledge, 2002).

[40] Compare Aristotle, *Nicomachean Ethics*, VIII. 5 on friendship as requiring not merely mutual good will, but 'living in each other's company' (see Marshall, S. E., 'The Community of Friends', in Christodoulidis, E. (ed.), *Communitarianism and Citizenship* (Aldershot: Ashgate, 1998), 208).

[41] Something that Luban makes central to the idea of a crime against humanity: 'Crimes Against Humanity' (above, n. 2). He also insists that we share such concerns not as members of a community, but as 'a set of human individuals' (ibid. 137; see above, n. 8); my claim has been that we need to see ourselves as at least an embryonic moral community.

to turn to the second aspect of the conception of international trials as callings to account, concerning the defendant's standing.

V. Hostis Humani Generis?

The idea that crimes against humanity are those whose perpetrators should answer to humanity expresses a sense of solidarity with the victims of such crimes: we share, or should share, collectively in the wrongs that they have suffered, and share a collective responsibility to respond to those wrongs by calling the perpetrators to account. But we must also note the status that this conception accords to the perpetrators themselves.

Luban insists that his account of crimes against humanity should not lead us to 'demonize the perpetrators, to brand them as less than human, and hence to expel them from the circle of those who deserve human regard': but he also insists that they are *hostes humani generis*, enemies of humanity; he talks of a 'vigilante jurisdiction in which the criminal becomes anyone's and everyone's legitimate enemy', and quotes with apparent approval Arendt's imagined explanation to Adolf Eichmann that 'no one, that is, no member of the human race, can be expected to want to share the earth with you'.[42] The idea of *hostis humani generis*, however, implies something like the kind of 'demonization' that Luban is anxious to avoid: if we are to see international criminal trials as a way of calling those who commit such wrongs to account, we must be able still to see the perpetrators as full members, rather than as enemies, *humani generis*.

Consider Blackstone's account of a pirate as *hostis humani generis*; 'As he has renounced all the benefits of society and government, and has reduced himself afresh to the savage state of nature, by declaring war against all mankind, all mankind must declare war against him'.[43] Blackstone went on to say that 'every community hath a right, by the rule of self-defence, to inflict that punishment upon him, which every individual would in a state of nature have been otherwise entitled to do'.[44] But what 'an enemy of mankind' implies is not punishment, but one of two other, quite different ideas. The first is that of an outlaw—someone who has put himself, by his atrocious wrongdoing, outside the reach or protection of the law; the second is that of an enemy in war: in neither case is punishment appropriate. Outlaws are, if we take the idea literally, fair game for anyone (as far as the law is concerned): one commits no offence in killing them; one need not justify it, as one must justify

---

[42] Luban, 'Crimes Against Humanity' (above n. 2). 120–3, 140; quoting Arendt, H., *Eichmann in Jerusalem* (above, n. 35), 279.

[43] Blackstone, *Commentaries* (above, n. 20), iv. 5, 71.   [44] Ibid.

killing a human being 'under the King's peace';[45] if we kill them or lock them up, this is a matter of defence against a threat, not of punishment. Enemy soldiers are not fair game in that way—they are protected by the laws of warfare: but their killing in the course of the war, or their imprisonment as prisoners of war, is again not a matter of punishment, but of wartime defence.

Taken literally, *hostis humani generis* describes an outlaw rather than an enemy soldier, since soldiers are still protected, as members *humani generis*, by the rules of war. But to put someone on trial, and to punish him for his wrongdoing, is to treat him as a member of the normative community under whose laws he is tried and punished. He is called to answer to the charge and, if the charge is proved, to answer for his crime: but thus to call someone to answer is to address him as a fellow member of a normative community whose values he can be expected to understand and accept; it is also to commit ourselves to listening to, and to taking seriously, any answer that he chooses to offer.[46] To put those who perpetrate crimes against humanity on trial is thus to treat them with the respect that is still, on this account, due to them as responsible members of the normative community of humanity.

Part of the value of this conception of criminal trials is that it emphasizes the defendant's status, not as an enemy or a dangerous threat who must be destroyed or rendered impotent, but as a fellow member of a normative community who is called to answer to his fellows for what he has done—and whose fellows must be ready to answer to him for their treatment of him. But this also highlights a challenge facing any attempt to build a system of international criminal justice: that of showing how we should, and can, recognize that status even in those who have committed the most terrible crimes. It is (relatively) easy to say, in the context of domestic criminal law, that however tempting it might be to portray offenders as outsiders, as a threatening 'they' against whom 'we' must protect ourselves, we must recognize them as fellow citizens—and to mean it; it is much harder to say that (other than as a piece of shallow rhetoric) of those whose crimes properly count as 'crimes against humanity', or to urge that on their victims. Gaita's attempt to show what this perspective entails helps us to see what it involves, and to see why it is so hard to accept:

[Some] may say that even such people are owed unconditional respect, meaning not that they are deserving of esteem, but that they are owed a kind of respect which is not conditional

---

[45] Part of the classical definition of murder in English law (aimed primarily at exempting those who kill 'in the heat of war': see Coke, E., *Institutes of the Laws of England* (London: Society of Stationers, 1628), iii. 47). Philosophers have sometimes talked in worryingly similar terms of the status of offenders: see e.g. Morris, C. W., 'Punishment and Loss of Moral Standing', *Canadian Journal of Philosophy*, 21 (1991) 53, 61, 72.

[46] I would also argue that criminal punishment, understood as a communicative enterprise of censure, must treat the offender as a fellow member of the normative community (see my *Punishment, Communication and Community* (New York: Oxford University Press, 2001)).

upon what they have done and which cannot be forfeited. Some will say that even the most terrible evil-doers are owed this respect as human beings and that we owe it to them because we are human beings. That amounts to saying that they remain our fellow human beings whatever they do.[47]

Gaita's concern is with the way in which recognizing another as a fellow human being involves recognizing him as 'a certain kind of limit [an 'absolute' limit] on our will'; 'no human being may be acted against as though we were ridding the world of vermin'.[48] But such recognition of fellow humanity brings positive as well as negative demands: a demand, for instance, that we help the other if he is in desperate need; but also, I have suggested, that we respond to his wrongdoing, however terrible and 'inhuman' it was, not by simply destroying him, but by trying to bring him to answer for it.

International criminal trials, if understood as I have argued we should understand them, thus express an aspiration to do justice not only to the victims of the crimes with which they are to deal, but also to the perpetrators of those crimes; when we think about just what that aspiration involves, we must realize how morally demanding it is.

[47] Gaita, R., *Good and Evil* (above, n. 39), 2.
[48] Gaita, R., *Good and Evil* 3, 9; see also 6, on Eichmann's trial.

INDEX